REAL AND PER CAPITA *GNP*		PRODUCTION, CONSTRUCTION ACTIVITY, AND PROFITS						
Gross national product		Index of industrial production	New construction activity	Profits after federal income taxes to stockholders' equity for all manufacturing corporations	Population	Unemployment as percent of civilian labor force	
Current prices	1958 prices		Value put in place				
Per capita dollars	Billions of dollars	1967 = 100	Billions of dollars	Ratio	Millions of persons	Percent	Year
846	204	21.6	10.8	——	121.9	3.2	1929
734	184	18.0	8.7	——	123.2	8.7	1930
610	169	14.9	6.4	——	124.1	15.9	1931
464	144	11.6	3.5	——	124.9	23.6	1932
442	142	13.7	2.9	——	125.7	24.9	1933
514	154	15.0	3.7	——	126.5	21.7	1934
566	170	17.3	4.2	——	127.4	20.1	1935
644	193	20.4	6.5	——	128.2	16.9	1936
700	203	22.3	7.0	——	129.0	14.3	1937
652	192	17.6	6.9	——	130.0	19.0	1938
691	209	21.7	8.2	——	131.0	17.2	1939
755	227	25.0	8.7	——	132.1	14.6	1940
933	264	31.6	12.0	——	133.4	9.9	1941
1,171	298	36.3	14.1	——	134.9	4.7	1942
1,402	337	44.0	8.3	——	136.7	1.9	1943
1,518	361	47.4	5.3	——	138.4	1.2	1944
1,515	355	40.6	5.8	——	140.0	1.9	1945
1,475	313	35.0	14.3	——	141.4	3.9	1946
1,605	310	39.4	20.0	15.6	144.1	3.9	1947
1,757	324	41.0	26.1	16.0	146.6	3.8	1948
1,719	324	38.8	26.7	11.6	149.2	5.9	1949
1,877	355	44.9	33.6	15.4	151.7	5.3	1950
2,128	383	48.7	35.4	12.1	154.3	3.3	1951
2,201	395	50.6	36.8	10.3	157.0	3.0	1952
2,285	413	54.8	39.1	10.5	159.6	2.9	1953
2,246	407	51.9	41.4	9.9	162.4	5.5	1954
2,408	438	58.5	46.5	12.6	165.3	4.4	1955
2,492	446	61.1	47.6	12.3	168.2	4.1	1956
2,575	453	61.9	49.1	10.9	171.3	4.3	1957
2,569	447	57.9	50.0	8.6	174.1	6.8	1958
2,731	476	64.8	55.4	10.4	177.1	5.5	1959
2,788	488	66.2	54.7	9.2	180.7	5.5	1960
2,831	497	66.7	56.4	8.9	183.7	6.7	1961
3,004	530	72.2	60.2	9.8	186.5	5.5	1962
3,121	551	76.5	64.8	10.3	189.2	5.7	1963
3,296	581	81.7	67.7	11.6	191.9	5.2	1964
3,525	618	89.2	73.7	13.0	194.3	4.5	1965
3,814	658	97.9	76.4	13.4	196.6	3.8	1966
3,996	675	100.0	78.1	11.7	198.7	3.8	1967
4,306	707	105.7	87.1	12.1	200.7	3.6	1968
4,590	726	110.7	93.9	11.5	202.7	3.5	1969
4,769	723	106.6	94.9	9.3	204.9	4.9	1970
5,096	746	106.8	110.0	9.7	207.0	5.9	1971
5,546	793	115.2	124.1	10.6	208.8	5.6	1972
6,155	839	125.6	135.5	12.8	210.4	4.9	1973
6,592	821	124.8	134.8	15.5^P	211.9	5.6	1974

*Details may not add to totals due to rounding and to minor statistical discrepancies.
^{P}Includes first three quarters only.

Money & Banking

SIXTH EDITION

DAVID R. KAMERSCHEN
Professor and Head
Department of Economics
University of Georgia
Athens, Georgia

EUGENE S. KLISE
Late Professor Emeritus
Miami University
Oxford, Ohio

Published by

H24   **SOUTH-WESTERN PUBLISHING CO.**

CINCINNATI   WEST CHICAGO, ILL.   DALLAS   PELHAM MANOR, N.Y.
PALO ALTO, CALIF.   BRIGHTON, ENGLAND

Copyright ©1976
by SOUTH-WESTERN PUBLISHING CO.
Cincinnati, Ohio

*Library of Congress Catalog
Card Number: 75-26451*

ISBN: 0-538-08240-2

2 3 4 5 6 K 1 0 9 8 7 6

Printed in the United States of America

Preface

Money and banking is the subset of economics which is concerned with the nature, history, and functioning of money-creating institutions, including techniques developed for their control and the interrelations between monetary, price, and employment theories.[1] The combination of the two words money and banking emphasizes that commercial bankers are not merely *retailers* of money but are *manufacturers* of money. Commercial banks create deposits which serve as money. It is therefore logical that the theory of money and the institutional organization of the monetary and banking system should be dovetailed.

The study of money and banking can be both a stimulating and a trying experience. It is stimulating because it touches directly the most challenging problems facing our economy — inflation, unemployment, balance of payments fluctuations, and economic growth and welfare. The primary concern of this book is to analyze the impact and significance of monetary policy, as well as fiscal and incomes policies, to our economy.

The study of money and banking is trying because there are no absolute answers or "eternal truths." There are many differences of opinion among experts. These controversies stem from the evolutionary character of money and banking. Monetary institutions and regulations are constantly changing to meet new problems or better cope with old ones. Moreover, the theory of money (demand and supply) also changes both as the institutions evolve and as human behavior within society evolves. This is in specific contrast to other fields of study, such as the grammatical structure of a dead language or the known theorems of geometry. In a world of change, it is certainly comforting to reflect that a straight line is the shortest distance between two points, and that it always has been and always will be, within a Euclidean framework.

Any differences of opinion concerning money and banking should certainly not lead us to wonder, in discouragement, whether there can be any real purpose in studying a subject in which the experts themselves do not always agree.[2] Rather, such differences emphasize the importance of the controversy

---

[1]See the excellent precis by William L. Miller, "Money and Banking," *A Dictionary of the Social Sciences*, edited by Julius Gould and William L. Kolb (New York: Free Press, 1964), p. 439.

[2]Two leading students of money put it this way: "Economists have long recognized that variations in the stock of money influence the economy. There has been less universal agreement on precisely what in the economy money affects, how the effects are transmitted, the strength of the effects, the length of time before the effects are observed, and the stability of the relationship." William E. Gibson and George G. Kaufman, "Money, Monetary Policy, and Economic Activity," printed as a preface to their *Monetary Economics: Readings on Current Issues* (New York: McGraw-Hill Book Co., 1971), pp. 1–4. The quote is from page 1.

within the field. If there were universal agreement on all questions relating to the theory and practice of money and banking and fiscal policy, everything could be efficiently handled by a few computers. We know, however, that there is no substitute for human compassion and judgment. We know, too, that different people may interpret the same facts differently. Sometimes disagreement results mainly from the different assumptions or suppositions from which people start their reasoning. Often, too, differences are the natural consequence of the disparate priorities people attach to various goals, such as full employment, stable prices, balanced foreign trade, or reduced income inequality. Moreover, since money is evolutionary, it adapts to the needs of society. No one "invented" money. It arose out of social, not individual, needs. As we have learned to meet our needs more effectively through better organization and as needs have changed, organizations have grown from many small sole proprietorships to great corporations; from absolute self-sufficiency to cooperative specialization and trade. Gold or silver, once an adequate money form, was first supplemented, but finally replaced, by credit money. Monetary changes over the last 40 years have been many and great. They will likely continue. The implications for trade, employment, production, income, and even the nature of our economic organization are profound.

In general, the core of this book continues to be those sections relating to monetary theory and monetary and fiscal policies. These sections have been updated and expanded to include greater discussion of such topics as the new monetarism, the Phillips Curve, and the term structure of interest rates. Considerable additional economic and financial data has been added as endsheets to the book for the student's convenience. Two short new chapters have been added, one reviewing the basic concepts of economic supply and demand and the other analyzing monetary events since 1971.

Those familiar with the previous edition will find that this revision has been, in many respects, substantial. Detail has been pruned and discussion of matters of primarily historical interest has been greatly condensed to permit a more deliberate theoretical analysis. An introductory text in money and banking which dwells on descriptive aspects is as unbalanced as the purely theoretical volume. The latter describes only the forest. The former details the trees, branches, twigs, and leaves. Neither is complete unto itself.

Some historical, institutional, and descriptive material is both needed and desired. Before plunging into a sea of theory we should establish some landmarks and learn something about the vessel itself. A brief review of past history provides a proper perspective and warning against complacent assumptions that we have now solved all the basic problems. Moreover, knowledge consists, in part, of the identification of errors and limitations to current study. We are not likely to move forward toward truth if we extinguish the lamp of experience.

While the number of chapters has been reduced from 32 to 28 and many pages have been rewritten, changes have not been made merely for the sake of change. This edition, like its subject, is hopefully only an evolutionary stage.

With this edition a study guide is also now available to accompany the text. It is hoped that students will benefit greatly from its use. It contains several hundred true-false, multiple-choice, and "completion" questions as well as numerous problems and projects. The instructor's manual also contains additional objective questions (and answers!), as well as answers to the discussion questions at the end of each text chapter.

While previous users of this book will recognize the indelible influence of Professor Eugene S. Klise within the text, I completed this revision after Professor Klise's untimely death in 1973. Several years ago I was one of the many students on the Miami (Ohio) campus fortunate enough to have an interest stimulated in money and banking by the wit, charm, and urbane manner of Professor Klise's provocative classes. His virtues were greatly appreciated by his students and colleagues and are sorely missed.

I am also heavily indebted to the economics faculty at Miami (Ohio) for making me aware that economics is both exciting and challenging. While Miami may be known in football circles as the "cradle of coaches," to its students it more accurately should be labeled the "font of fine teaching." I would also be remiss if I did not take this opportunity to express my great appreciation and gratitude to Ms. Judy Griffin for her considerable editing and typing skills. Finally, this acknowledgement would be incomplete without a word of appreciation for the increasing encouragement from and patient forebearance of my family. Now we can get back to Little League, "Colts" football, and Stone Mountain.

David R. Kamerschen

Athens, Georgia

Contents

Introduction   Supply and Demand: A Review

This text examines the sometimes confusing but always important human invention called money. Since the economist's familiar supply and demand apparatus is used often in this investigation, this chapter will review these basic tools. But before doing so, it is worth investigating why the topic of money, credit, and banking should require a whole book if it is merely a routine application of supply and demand analysis.[1]

UNIQUE FACTORS IN MONETARY ANALYSIS

Money is a difficult and sometimes diffuse topic which requires rather sophisticated demand and supply analyses. Three major factors account for this complexity.

Micro and Macro

One reason for the complexity of money is that its analysis represents a fusion of both microeconomics and macroeconomics, where the former looks at small, individual units—the household, the firm, the resource owner—and the latter looks at large, aggregate units—all households, all firms, all resource owners. Both the Marshallian firm supply analysis and consumer demand analysis emphasized in microeconomics and the Keynesian aggregate supply analysis and aggregate demand analysis emphasized in macroeconomics are indispensable.

Institutional, Descriptive, and Historical Factors

There are a myriad of institutional, descriptive, and historical factors which must be coalesced into a comprehensive study of money. What is the Federal Reserve? What are its purposes, powers, and functions? When did it start? What is the gold standard? Are we on it, off it, or in it? Is most of our money legal tender? Lawful money? Fiat money? Representative money? Is there branch or unit banking in the state? And so on.

---

[1]In this chapter, for convenience, we assume that the interest rate is determined by the demand and supply of money, credit, or loanable funds. Credit and loanable funds differ from the money supply in that they are flow variables with a time dimension, whereas the money supply is a stock variable at a given moment in time. This distinction, however, is not important for the major purposes of this chapter.

Government's Role

If we assume that wheat is produced under conditions approximating pure competition, the money market is quite different from the wheat market. In contrast to Adam Smith's invisible hand of competition, there is the quite visible hand of government in monetary matters on both the supply and the demand side. On the supply side, it is sometimes assumed that the quantity of money is a rigidly and precisely policy-determined variable of the non-profit-motivated monetary authorities—the U.S. Treasury and the Federal Reserve (Fed)—and that the quantity of money does not respond to short-run fluctuations in demand. If this were so, the full brunt of equilibrating the demand and supply of money would fall, by default, entirely on the demand for money. But this isn't realistic. The government is not, at this stage, able to control precisely the money supply in any manner it chooses. Moreover, at times the Fed has been more interested in controlling economic variables other than the stock or flow of money, such as the interest rate.

Perhaps the most important reason why the Fed cannot singlehandedly control the money supply is that the dominant component of the money stock is demand deposits in profit-motivated commercial banks, and these deposits are an increasing function of the interest rate available from loans to private borrowers and of available reserves. Commercial banks are like other profit-maximizing enterprises in that they have an incentive to expand their output when the price goes up. (The willingness to borrow these demand deposits from commercial banks is a negative function of the interest rate that borrowers must pay on these debts to the banks.)

The interest rate is also an administered rather than purely competitive price because the government is an important demander or borrower of money. To finance countercyclical policy and to refinance existing obligations, the government must be active in the money market. In wartime, the government becomes the economy's major borrower of money.

Banking is also less subject to the rigors of competition than is wheat because the 16 largest banks, representing about one tenth of one percent of all the banks in the United States, hold about one third of all the banking system's deposits. However, most banks in the United States are relatively small, single unit banks. Of the 14,384 commercial banks in the United States, almost 11,000—over 75 percent—are too small for efficient operation given prevailing economies of scale. Yet many maintain that the performance in the banking industry, while far from perfect, has been rather good on the whole.

Pure competition in the banking industry would be suicidal.[2] Competition pushes the production rate of any commodity to the point at which its price is exactly equal to its costs of production. Pure competition would make money very inefficient as a medium of exchange since the costs of producing money are quite low, and subsequently vast sums of money would be required to carry out even modest transactions. In general, a commodity with a zero price

[2]Boris Pesek and Thomas R. Saving, *Money, Wealth, and Economic Theory* (New York: Macmillan Co., 1967).

cannot serve as a medium of exchange (who wants it?), and one with a low price can serve only inefficiently.

Other Factors

There are additional minor factors that make the money market unique. One factor is that the pricing system does not function in the money market as completely as it does in some other markets. Typically, competitive prices serve both a *rationing* function and an *incentive* function. High prices serve to ration presently available supplies among demanders. This rationing is necessary because people's wants are in totality greater than the society's means for satisfying these wants. One means of allocating the available output is with a price system in which sufficiently high prices are placed on scarce goods until the market clears and the decisions of demanders and suppliers are mutually consistent. This is called *equilibrium;* and if once attained, equilibrium tends to be maintained. Other possible methods of distributing society's scarce output are by custom, fiat and decree, and first-come-first-served.

Prices also usually function as an incentive for increasing or decreasing future supplies depending on whether prices are high or low relative to production costs. Stated differently, high prices *inhibit demand* and *elicit supply* in a free market. But in money markets, the forces of supply and demand do not always operate unbridled. Banks do not, for various reasons, like to change the interest rate to match every change in the demand and supply of money. If, for instance, money is tight, banks do not always let the interest rate climb to the market-clearing point. This means that the scarce funds are allocated on the basis of additional factors—preference given to, say, large or favored customers, local or community enterprises, relatives, and so on.

There are other institutional restraints on interest rates. The Fed, through Regulation Q, has set a maximum on the interest that can be paid on time and savings deposits. Congress in the Great Depression of the 1930s, through the Banking Act of 1935, made it illegal for banks to pay interest on checking accounts. (In the 1920s the rate rose as high as 5 percent.) Individual states have usury laws which set maximum interest rates. It is important to note that the two legal regulations that make commercial banks most different from profit-maximizing, nonbank financial institutions are that no interest can be paid on demand deposits and that required reserves held to satisfy legal requirements are non-interest-bearing.

It is also claimed that money is different from other commodities because it is not desired for its own sake but rather for what it will buy. This is misleading, if not incorrect. Money is useful in and of itself because it permits people to economize on the costs of exchange and provides a completely liquid asset which can be resold at a net price close to its original purchase price. Even if the desire for money were indirect, it would not make money unique. Factors of production such as capital, labor, and land are not desired for direct satisfaction, but indirectly for the services they provide in producing final goods and services. In fact, money can be usefully thought of as a factor of production which, like most factors, yields a flow of output and which generally is subject to diminishing (and perhaps even negative) returns on this flow of output.

WHY MONEY IS AMENABLE TO DEMAND AND SUPPLY ANALYSIS

Despite the peculiarities previously discussed, the demand and supply of money can, with tolerable accuracy, be analyzed through Marshallian supply and demand analysis. Let's see why and how.

Money and the Interest Rate

Basically, the demand curve for money is downward sloping and the supply curve for money is upward sloping, as with most commodities. As the price of money (i.e., the interest rate) increases, people try to economize and get by with smaller cash balances to accommodate their day-to-day transaction needs and to satisfy their speculative and precautionary asset desires. Clearly both their transaction and asset demands for money are a function of the interest rate. Similarly, the supply of money is positively related to its price (i.e., the interest rate). Many students are perplexed in their study of money and banking because they fail to realize that money, like most other goods, lends itself to supply and demand analysis.

Substitution and Income Effect

It is useful to think of money, like other commodities, as being subject to a substitution and an income effect. The substitution effect reflects the greater *willingness* of people to buy, say, steak as its *relative price* falls, while the income effect reflects the greater *ability* of people with given money incomes to buy more steak as its *absolute price* falls. Because people tend to buy more of most commodities as their (real) incomes go up, goods with positive income effects are called "normal" or "superior" goods. Commodities such as horsemeat, powdered milk, and hominy grits, which many people buy less of as their incomes go up, are called "inferior" goods. Most people wish to hold more money for its greater liquidity to satisfy their speculative and precautionary desires as their incomes go up. Thus, money is a "normal" or "superior" good.

DEMAND AND SUPPLY APPARATUS

We will now quickly review the basic Marshallian concepts of supply, demand, and equilibrium, and the fundamentals of elasticity. This brief review will illustrate how monetary economics can be analyzed within a supply and demand framework.

Equilibrium

A competitive market establishes price at the point of intersection of the buyers' demand and the sellers' supply, such as point E in Figure I-1. Prices cannot be maintained above the equilibrium price because an excess supply or surplus will develop, causing suppliers to lower their selling prices. Similarly, prices cannot be maintained below the equilibrium price because an excess demand or shortage will occur, causing demanders to raise the offered buying price. Thus, a state of equilibrium tends to be self-perpetuating.

PRICE PER UNIT

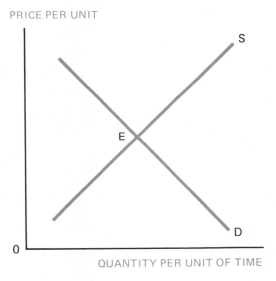

QUANTITY PER UNIT OF TIME

Figure I-1   Supply and Demand Equilibrium

Demand Analysis

In economics, *demand* is a schedule showing the various quantities of a commodity that buyers are willing and able to purchase per unit of time at various prices. The law of demand states that ordinarily price and quantity demanded are inversely related. The lower the price of steak, the more will be bought per unit of time—day, month, year, or whatever. The higher the price of money—i.e., the higher the interest rate— the less money will be demanded. The two reasons for the negative slope of a demand curve are the substitution and income effects discussed earlier.

Of course, the demand for a commodity such as steak depends on factors other than its price. Consumers' tastes and preferences for steak as compared with those for other commodities are important. Other important determinants of demand are: prices of related goods, such as pork chops and chicken; number of consumers in the market; level and distribution of consumers' incomes; and consumers' expectations as to the future prices of commodities.

Since a demand curve represents the functional relationship between the amount demanded of a good per unit of time and its price, all these other determinants are assumed given or constant. If any of these factors—income, tastes and preferences, expectations, prices of related goods, or the number of consumers—change, the entire demand curve shifts. This shift is called a *change in demand*. In contrast, a *change in quantity demanded* refers to a movement along a given demand curve caused by a change in the price of the good itself. This change is illustrated in Figure I-2 by the movement along demand curve D_1 from point a to point b.

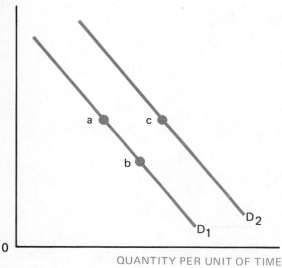

PRICE PER UNIT

QUANTITY PER UNIT OF TIME

Figure I-2   Changes in Demand and
Quantity Demanded

A clear distinction must be made between these two quite different changes. If we analyze the demand for steak, an increase (decrease) in the price of steak leads to a decrease (increase) in the *quantity demanded* of steak. Since none of the determinants or parameters that determine the level and shape of the demand curve have shifted, this price change causes a movement along a given demand curve. In contrast, if, say, consumers' incomes go up (down), the entire demand curve shifts to the right (left). This shift is a *change in demand*, for, at every price, the amount demanded has changed. For example, Figure I-2 illustrates an increase in demand in the shift from D_1 to D_2 or the movement from point a to point c.

Supply Analysis

Supply is a schedule showing the various quantities of a commodity that sellers are willing and able to sell per unit of time at various prices. The law of supply states that ordinarily price and quantity supplied are positively related, as in Figure I-3. Higher prices promise greater opportunities for profits and encourage sellers to expand their output.

As in the case of demand, there are other determinants influencing supply, which again are assumed to be given or constant parameters for a particular supply curve. The most important forces held constant in drawing a supply curve are the level of technology, the prices of factor inputs, and the time period allowed for adjustment. Again, the distinction should be maintained between a *change in quantity supplied*—which is a movement along a given supply curve caused by a change in the price of the good itself, such as the movement from point f to point g along supply curve S_1 in Figure I-3—and a *change in supply*—which is a shift in the entire supply curve caused by a change in one or more of the supply determinants, such as the shift from S_1 to S_2 or the movement from point f to point h in Figure I-3. An improved technology or a lower price for labor inputs would cause an increase or rightward movement of the entire supply curve, for example.

PRICE PER UNIT

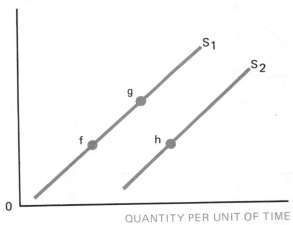

QUANTITY PER UNIT OF TIME

Figure I-3   Changes in Supply and
Quantity Supplied

Elasticity Concept

An important property of a demand or supply curve is the degree of responsiveness of quantity demanded or supplied to a change in price. Does a change in price bring about a large or small change in quantity demanded or supplied? The numerical coefficient showing the comparative magnitudes of the price and quantity changes is called *elasticity (E)*. More precisely, the coefficient of elasticity of demand (supply) is measured by dividing the percentage change in quantity demanded (supplied) by the percentage change in price; that is $E = \%\triangle Qx/\%\triangle Px$, where $\triangle$ means a change, Qx is the quantity demanded (or supplied) of commodity x, and Px is the price of commodity x. When the quantity change is proportionally larger (smaller) than the price change, E is said to be *elastic (inelastic)*. When the relative magnitudes are the same, E is unit or *unitary elastic*. Thus, a function is elastic, inelastic, or unitary elastic depending on whether $E > 1$, $E < 1$, or $E = 1$, respectively.

The two extreme values of E are zero and infinity. In Figure I-4, supply function S_2 indicates that quantity is completely unresponsive to price changes, so $E = 0$. If there is a change in demand, the price will change, but not the quantity supplied. Supply function S_1 represents the other extreme in which quantity is completely responsive to price changes, so that $E = \infty$. Practically all changes in demand will shift quantity, but not price. Generally, the E value is $0 < E < \infty$, as exemplified by S_3—both price and quantity change as demand shifts.[3]

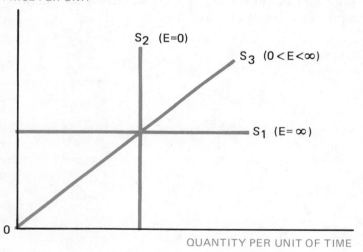

PRICE PER UNIT

S_2 (E=0)

S_3 $(0 < E < \infty)$

S_1 $(E = \infty)$

0

QUANTITY PER UNIT OF TIME

Figure I-4   Measures of Price Elasticity

The measure of price elasticity of demand is also related to the total amount of expenditures (total revenue from the point of view of the sellers) that buyers expend for the commodity at different price levels. When demand is elastic (inelastic), the total amount expended on the good is inversely (directly) related to the change in price. If demand is unitary, the total revenue is invariant to price changes. For instance, if demand is elastic, the total outlays increase (decrease) in response to a decrease (increase) in price. Businesspeople contemplating a sale, for example, would prefer demand to be elastic so total expenditures would increase as they cut their prices.

---

[3]While our comments in this section relate specifically to supply, the same basic analysis would hold with respect to demand.

SUMMARY AND CONCLUSION

Commercial banks are a unique form of private financial institution in that they have the power to create money within the guidelines set forth by the U.S. Treasury and the Federal Reserve. The first part of this text will be devoted to understanding the process of generating and maintaining a money supply. The latter half of the text merges monetary economics with macroeconomic theory to explain the demand for money by households, businesses, and government.

The equating of supply and demand determines equilibrium in the money market. A general equilibrium approach, using *IS-LM* analysis, will be developed later to show how simultaneous equilibrium is achieved in both the financial market for money and the product market for goods and services. Always bear in mind that it is as dangerous to overestimate as it is to underestimate the importance of money in our economy.

The study of monetary economics fuses microeconomic and macroeconomic theory with a host of institutional and historical factors. The supply and demand apparatus dealing with money and financial markets is further complicated by the significant role played by government.

Normally the demand (supply) for any good or service or any factor of production is inversely (directly) related to its price. Money, with some exceptions due to various institutional constraints, is also subject to the same laws of supply and demand.

A change in demand (supply) shifts the entire function and is caused by the changing of one or more of the determinants of demand (supply) other than the price of the good itself. On the other hand, a change in quantity demanded (supplied) refers to a movement along a given function and is due entirely to a change in the price of the good itself.

An elasticity coefficient (E) measures the proportionate degree of responsiveness of a change in quantity to a change in price. If $E > 1$, $E < 1$, or $E = 1$, the function is said to be elastic, inelastic, or unitary, respectively. If $E > 1$, $E < 1$, or $E = 1$, total expenditures move in the opposite direction, in the same direction, or remain unchanged, respectively, as price changes.

Discussion Questions

1. What factors might cause the demand and supply for money to be more complex or less amenable to a more ordinary supply and demand analysis?
2. "Price has nothing to do with scarcity, otherwise stale beer should be expensive." Evaluate and comment.
3. An increase in the demand for hamburgers could be caused by which of the following: (a) a decrease in the price of a complimentary good, such as catsup; (b) a decrease in the price of beef; (c) a decline in the price of factors employed in beef production; (d) a technological innovation which sharply decreases the cost of beef production.

4. Consider each of the following five statements as a separate piece of information about a demand schedule and determine if demand is elastic, inelastic, or unitary, or whether there is insufficient information in the statement to determine the elasticity.
   a. If price decreases, quantity demanded increases.
   b. If price increases by 10 percent, quantity demanded decreases by 5 percent.
   c. If the price increases by 10 cents, quantity demanded declines by 5 units.
   d. If a 10 percent larger quantity is placed on the market, the total expenditure on the commodity remains the same.
   e. If the price decreases by 10 percent, total expenditures on the commodity increase by 5 percent.
5. A demand curve that falls from left to right on the conventional demand diagram shows that the lower the price, the greater the total expenditure for the commodity. True or false? Why?

PART 1
Money: Currency

Chapter 1   The Nature and Significance of Money

How important is money? Ask the thousands of workers, striking for months to get a clause protecting their wages from a decline in the value of money. Ask the thousands who have lost their jobs because their employers were unable to borrow money. Ask the businesspeople whose companies have failed because the value of money was changing or the cost of borrowing money was prohibitive. Ask the stockholders, contemplating a substantial loss in their portfolios as a result of tight money policies. Ask the retired workers, struggling to stretch their fixed pensions or Social Security benefits to meet living costs, steadily rising because the value of money is falling. Ask the citizens whose government has been overthrown, partly because it debauched the nation's money.

Money and the consequences of monetary policies affect everyone—old and young, rich and poor, white and black, college graduate and grade school dropout. These policies may promote prosperity and a rising standard of living, or they may lead to unemployment, bankruptcies, and even dictatorships. They become constantly more important as the complexity and interdependencies of civilization increase. The better we understand them, the better we can control them to serve the needs of society.

Hardly a week goes by without news articles concerning money, monetary policy, and banking. The value of the dollar has been falling almost continuously for a generation. The relationship between national currencies and gold has changed, as have the interrelationships between the leading currencies themselves. The silver coinage of the United States, unchanged for more than a century, was replaced by a copper alloy. To most people, the "thin red line" probably suggests today not a few outnumbered soldiers but the edges of the "sandwich" coins (first issued in 1965) in their pockets. The cost of money (that is, interest rates) has risen to the highest level in more than a hundred years.[1] Billions of dollars have been trimmed from the value of the

---

[1]The terms of Treasury borrowing operations were continually hitting new highs in 1974.

nation's stocks and bonds. Some profits have fallen and unemployment has risen as the government has tried to check the erosion of the dollar. Press releases by banks, the Treasury, and the Federal Reserve System make headlines with increasing frequency. Monetary policy, in eclipse for nearly forty years, has suddenly re-emerged as an important control over prices, production, and employment. Banking authorities have introduced new regulations to control the banking system.

Certainly there have been many changes. We should add, however, "as usual." At no time in the last two centuries have money and banking stood still. During the first hundred years, governments were busily changing their coinages. In commercially sophisticated countries, the foundations of modern banking were being laid. Over the second hundred years, coins became an insignificant component of the total money stock, supplemented and largely replaced by money in the form of bank credit—bank notes and demand deposits. Central banks, such as the twelve Federal Reserve Banks in the United States, were developed to help stabilize banking.

There were great changes a generation ago, when for the first time it was no longer possible in most countries for citizens to demand that their money be redeemed in gold. For the first time, the United States government insured bank deposits. Interest rates were brought down to record lows, where many expected them to remain forever. Most economists at that time underestimated the effectiveness of monetary policies as a control mechanism, arguing that by its taxing and spending policies the government could much more effectively regulate business activity. There was little demand for bank loans, so banks invested heavily in Treasury securities. During the first years after World War II the banks quickly sold many of these securities and once again were lending billions of dollars to the public. Interest rates began to rise.

Is this record of ceaseless change really an indication that money and banking are makeshift institutions that people have never understood and probably never will? Or is it, rather, evidence of the evolutionary character of these institutions? They have developed and will continue to develop to meet the changing requirements of a dynamic society. Here is the heart of the matter, and herein lies their importance. If, as was true a thousand years ago, our institutions, our agricultural techniques, and our whole apparatus of production and exchange remained unchanged from one century to the next, we could reasonably expect little change in money and banking. Conversely, monetary institutions of the horse and buggy era can hardly be expected to meet the requirements of the space age.

Monetary institutions and regulations are constantly changing to meet new problems or better cope with old ones. A mere record of the changes that have been made in the past is in itself of little value. The important thing is to understand *why* the changes were made and *how* they were expected to improve the usefulness of financial institutions. Then we are in a better position to realize how the usefulness of money may continue to be increased in the future as the needs of society continue to change. Certainly we should know better than to suppose that money is something which can never be changed.

At the same time we should also be able to avoid repeating past errors and to work out sound answers to our new monetary problems.

This brings us to the next question. Why does money matter? To put it differently, why is a properly functioning money supply important, not merely to bankers, financiers, and politicians, but to everyone? How does it affect investments, business, income, and employment?

Money is indispensable to our system of production and exchange. All economic activity is measured, guided, and facilitated by money. More than $10 trillion changes hands annually in the United States today—approximately $20 million a minute, 24 hours a day. This incomprehensibly huge sum results from our production, distribution, and exchange of goods. (The total value of final goods and services currently produced is only about an eighth of the figure above. Many things are paid for several times in the course of production. There are also transfer payments, such as the purchase of a used car or of securities on the stock exchange, that have nothing to do with current production.) In an incredibly intricate process, people receive money from society in exchange for their services, for raw materials that they make available, or for the use of productive equipment that they supply directly or indirectly. By circuitous routes people return the money to society as they spend it for the things they want. In an unceasing process the money goes from producers to consumers and back to producers.

This circular flow of income is a concept of the greatest importance to which we shall return again. It is introduced here to bring out a simple but basic point that is sometimes overlooked. Money never belongs to itself, nor is it ever without an owner. As someone well phrased it, "The money is always there. Only the pockets change." Every dollar in the country belongs, at all times and without exception, to somebody—perhaps to an individual, perhaps to an organization. The process of the income flow also helps to explain the nature of money. *Money* may be defined in a functional sense as anything generally used in the purchase of goods and services and in the discharge of debts.

All sorts of things have been used as money—various metals, salt, stones, clam shells, even woodpecker scalps. Cigarettes took on the functions of money for a brief period in parts of Europe at the close of the Second World War. By far our most important money today is in the form of bank accounts on which checks are drawn. But whether payment is made by giving up gold coins, dollar bills, cartons of cigarettes, or bank deposits, if these items are regularly used and generally accepted as a means of payment, money is being used. The only common factor in all these payments is general acceptability, based on limitation of supply relative to demand. Such payments are in contrast to barter; a student may "pay" a classmate for a book by giving another book in exchange, but books are not generally used as a means of payment and hence are not money.

Money may also be defined as an evidence of debt owed by society. People with $100 in their pockets are entitled to call on society to provide them with the things they want up to the amount of $100. Money is seldom wealth, but it is a claim on wealth and on other things.[2] As a result of the elaborate process referred to previously, society has agreed to owe these individuals, and it gives them money as evidence. As long as they hold the money, society is in their debt. When they spend the money, society discharges its obligation to these particular individuals by providing them with the things they demand. But note that society still owes as much as before, for someone else now holds the money that constitutes the claim on society.

At first glance this second definition may appear confusing. It seems paradoxical to think of money as evidence of a continuous debt. Remember, however, that each time money changes hands, there is also an economic good surrendered or a service performed.[3] Anyone who holds money but prefers to hold goods may easily secure the goods and let someone else hold the money. Unless the money becomes worthless, as has occasionally happened in severe inflation, it will at all times constitute an effective claim on goods (or an effective means of discharging a debt owed by the holder of the money).

The two definitions of money—(1) anything generally used in the purchase of goods and services and the discharge of debts, and (2) an evidence of debt owed by society—are supplementary rather than alternative. The second definition is useful in understanding the basic nature of money. It is less precise than the first, however, for it includes in addition to money many other evidences of debt such as bonds, debentures, promissory notes, mortgages, and savings passbooks. The first definition helps determine the line between money and near-money. When one is studying, for instance, the effects of changes in the money supply, one must know what is to be counted as money.

FUNCTIONS OF MONEY

Society needs money for several purposes. No matter what types of money a country uses, the money must perform certain functions.

Standard of Value

Most importantly, money must serve as the *standard of value*. It is the common denominator. We express the value of all economic goods in terms of money and call these money values *prices*.

As a standard, money is unique in that it is an inconstant standard. Other standards of measurement, such as the minute, the pound, or the foot, are as nearly constant as science can construct. A deviation of as much as one tenth of 1 percent would be considered intolerable. The length of the yardstick with which the salesperson measures draperies varies only microscopically from

---

[2]Wealth consists of scarce material goods. Boris P. Pesek and Thomas R. Saving in *Money, Wealth, and Economic Theory* (New York: Macmillan Co., 1967) make a sophisticated argument that money is *net* wealth. However, their interesting approach is not generally accepted by economists.

[3]Exception: Money ordinarily changes hands also when someone obtains a loan or repays it. One evidence of debt is exchanged for another, as will later be described.

one year to the next. The value of money, the yardstick with which we measure all economic values, may vary by any amount because the value of money is its purchasing power. The higher the prices, the lower is the value of each piece of money. So when prices double, the value of money is half what it was before. The general and continuous rising of prices of goods and factors of production without any concomittant increase in quality is called *inflation*. The continuous falling of most costs and prices is called *deflation*. Inflation decreases and deflation increases the value of any savings held as monetary wealth. (All savings need not be held in this form.)

In spite of its variability, money as a standard of value is indispensable. We are so accustomed to this convenience that we take it for granted. Yet without it modern civilization could not have developed nor could it be maintained. Specialization requires exchange, and exchange, while not impossible without the use of money, is made incomparably easier by its use as a common denominator.

Even a communist state must use money, unless it can force its citizens to surrender *all* freedom of choice. Visionary reformers sometimes dream of a society in which everything is free and money obsolete. Their imagination is greater than their understanding. An ant society or even a very primitive human society has no need for money, but human society today cannot do without it. Money permits individuals to obtain the goods and services *that they prefer*. Without money, the state could no doubt still arrange the mass production of workers' clothes, all of the same material and style. Some government bureau would draft the necessary workers into the garment industry and supply one uniform a year free to every citizen. Everyone would also receive the prescribed ration of flour, milk, and so on. All goods would be free. In this utopia no money would be needed—*if everyone were satisfied with the goods distributed*. But if you happened to prefer rice to potatoes or would rather have a pair of skis than a new uniform, your only hope would be that perhaps you could arrange a trade or, more likely, a long series of trades to get what you wanted—if, indeed, it were available at all. Also, and even more important, you would have little freedom to choose your occupation. You might want to become a lawyer, but the state might decide you should be rolling steel. Decisions as to what will be produced and how, how much, by whom, and for whom to produce have to be made somehow. While money is especially important as a tool in motivating people in a free enterprise capitalistic economy, it permits some freedom of choice even in a communistic dictatorship.

Long before the development of paper money or even of coins, people had begun to use money. As early as 3000 B.C. the Egyptians were using gold, silver, and copper as money. More than two thousand years were to elapse before the invention of coinage, but gold, silver, and copper were nevertheless money in the sense that they were used as standards of value. One hundred bushels of wheat, 50 yards of cloth, 10 pounds of meat or fish— each was considered to be worth some amount of gold (or silver or copper).

Standard of Value and Price System. The development of a common standard of value was a tremendous economic advance. The only way values can be estimated otherwise is to decide for each good how much it is worth in terms of all other goods available. If 21 commodities are being produced and exchanged, each of these is worth some amount of each of the other 20. Of the 420 sets of values, half are duplicates, of course; for when we have decided the value of wheat in terms of cloth, we have also decided the value of cloth in terms of wheat. There are 210 separate valuations involved with these 21 commodities.[4] If, however, one of them is adopted as the common measure of value and all other goods are valued in terms of this single commodity, there are only 20 values or *prices*.

Standard of Value and Specialization. Clearly the complexity of valuations would increase greatly as the number of commodities increased. With 20,001 commodities, one of which is adopted as the standard of value, there are 20,000 prices. But if no common standard were used, there would be more than 200 million sets of values. Under such a handicap, the process of exchange would operate creakingly at best. It would be too difficult for all concerned to be sure a trade was to their best advantage. Without a well-developed system of exchange, specialization would be discouraged. As in primitive times, production would be very low as people tried to produce all the goods they needed for their own consumption rather than to specialize and trade their output for the goods they wanted.

Standard of Value and Accounting Records. Since everything bought and sold is measured in terms of money, it is possible to maintain accounting records and to make up financial statements. It would be very difficult for businesspeople to know whether they were operating at a profit or a loss if the only records they kept were in terms of physical inventory. Even the corner grocer could have little knowledge of the success of operations if he knew only that the store contained more cans of corn but fewer cans of beans, more pounds of coffee but fewer pounds of butter, than it did a year ago. This use of money as a *unit of account* is closely related to its use as a standard of value.

Medium of Exchange

The other major function commonly attributed to money is that it serves as the medium of exchange.[5] This use of money is emphasized by the definition that states that money is anything generally used for making payments or

---

[4]Allowing for duplications, the general formula for the number of different exchange ratios required for a number of commodities (n) is $n\ (n-1)/2$.

[5]Some writers state that money should rightly be considered a pure abstraction serving *only* as a standard value. With considerable logic they argue that we should not identify a unit of measurement that is abstract with the physical instrument that we use in our measurements. A yard is a certain distance. A yardstick is a convenient means of counting yards. The yardstick we can pick up and handle; the yard itself we cannot. Similarly, they say, if we call money the standard of value, we should remember that it is entirely abstract. The pieces of paper or metal

discharging debts. From trade that was originally on a barter basis, society has progressed to the use of money. Rather than exchange goods for goods, people prefer to exchange goods for money and then exchange the money for other goods. The tremendous advance provided by this intermediate step lies in the fact that, so long as money is acceptable to all, the buyer need not trouble to find a seller who needs the particular goods or services that the buyer is capable of producing. There is a separation between transactions that is of benefit to both parties.

A barter system operates under what has been called the "double coincidence of wants." It is not enough that the person with something to exchange find someone who wants this product and has *something* to offer in exchange. There would be little point to the exchange if the goods offered by either party were not desired by the other party. Anyone wishing to exchange goods by barter must find someone who not only wishes the goods offered by the first, but who can, in exchange, supply goods that are desired by the first. Or the individual can make a whole series of trades until finally obtaining something he or she wants. This, too, is inefficient and time-consuming. Barter is also inefficient in that without a standard of value and medium of exchange it is more difficult and/or more costly to negotiate contracts for future activities and to store future claims on output.

Only when wants are simple and more or less standardized can barter work with any success. In colonial days beads, gunpowder, and whisky might successfully be traded for furs. As long as the Indians continued to desire the commodities offered by the traders and the traders continued to desire the furs, there was no problem. But in the immeasurably more complex framework of modern society, it is much easier for the farmer to sell wheat to whoever wants it than to find someone who happens to have some product that the farmer desires. Likewise, when the farmer wants clothes, gasoline, or tools, it is much easier to buy these goods with the money previously received than to find stores and service stations that would have use for wheat or to make twenty or thirty trades before the wheat is converted into gasoline.

Standard of Value Often Not Medium of Exchange

The two functions, standard of value and medium of exchange, are the most important ways money serves society, and all other functions are derived from them. Before other functions of money are taken up, it should be noted that there are various types of money, and a particular type need not

---

that we use as a medium of exchange may be called credit or currency, but should not be confused with the invisible, intangible unit of value.

The reasoning is persuasive. The principal difficulty is that this definition of money is in violent contradiction to our everyday usage. We must remember always that a dollar bill or a handful of silver is not "money" but currency. We cannot correctly speak of the quantity of money, nor its velocity of circulation, for these concepts should be reserved for currency and credit. *Money* in the abstract sense would have no dimension other than that of value. Most writers feel that the gain in logic offered by such a definition is outweighed by its inconvenience. There seems little likelihood that it will ever be generally accepted by either the public or economists and financial writers. Rather than substitute the terms *currency* and *credit* in most places where we might otherwise use the word *money*, it appears preferable to follow general usage.

serve in both these roles. In earlier times when the only money was in the form of coins, the standard of value was more likely to be also the medium of exchange. In the United States today our standard of value, the dollar, is defined in terms of gold. However, the gold dollar is not the medium of exchange. There never have been any dollars coined according to the present definition of the gold dollar.[6] Also, from 1933 to 1974 it was illegal for Americans to hold gold. (This law was changed as of December, 1974.) We could not lawfully use even our old gold coins as a domestic medium of exchange. Moreover, on August 15, 1971, President Nixon terminated the convertibility of the dollar into gold and other reserve assets even for foreign central banks and governments.

Before 1933 gold dollars were allowed to circulate freely. But even in that period they were seldom used as a medium of exchange. People occasionally stored gold in their safe deposit boxes, but they did not often carry it around to make their daily purchases. The gold was mostly held by the banking system as a backing for other types of money more generally used. These other types of money which then as now were fulfilling the role of medium of exchange were not, however, the standard of value. Rather their value was kept equal to the standard of value, the gold dollar. The monetary systems of most other civilized nations were operated in the same way, with one type of money constituting the standard of value and other types constituting the medium of exchange.

Other Functions of Money—Store of Value and Standard of Deferred Payments

Thirdly, money constitutes a store of value. This characteristic of money permits producers to sell their product and then delay as long as they wish before taking the goods of others. It gives them a *time option*. So long as they hold the money, they can at any moment exercise their claim, but they need not take other goods as soon as they have sold their own. There are many ways in which this function of money is helpful to society. People who are paid once a month or farmers who receive most of their income at one time during the year are able to spread their expenditures out evenly from day to day, spending their store of money as their needs require. People are able to put money aside for a later time—for retirement, for the education of their children, for the purchase of a business. They can defer their consumption as they choose, and they can accumulate funds for investment.

In the absence of money one could accomplish the same thing by storing commodities. It would be much less convenient and quite expensive, however, to build up a store of meat, vegetables, clothing, gasoline, and other goods for later use. Perishable articles would require costly processing; some, such as electricity, could hardly be stored at all in any quantity. Other goods would be out of style or inferior to the current product by the time they were finally

---

[6]The gold dollars formerly coined, about two thirds the weight of a dime, are nearly twice the weight of the official gold dollar as now defined but not coined.

used. A person who in 1925 bought a phonograph and stored it away to be used in 1975 would hardly have as much as a person who in 1925 put aside money and bought a quadrophonic system in 1975.

Although other commodities besides money are stored, money has the advantage over most other commodities of not deteriorating in storage. There may be a shrinkage in the purchasing power of money or there may be, as in the thirties, an increase in the purchasing power of money. But the number of dollars that are stored away will be the same as the number of dollars later available.[7] Nonmonetary commodities set aside for storage also suffer the disadvantage of illiquidity, where *liquidity* is a commodity's capability of being resold quickly at close to its purchase price.

The store-of-value function of money is not an unmixed blessing. The fact that spending may be indefinitely postponed ordinarily presents no difficulties since some people are currently spending their income, some are postponing spending, and others are spending past income. But if the public generally decides to postpone spending—if nearly everyone is trying to use money as a store of value and to increase monetary holdings—prices fall, markets disappear, and depression ensues. It is for this reason that it is so important today to learn more about money and how to control and direct its effects.

Fourthly, money functions as a standard of deferred payments. Often individuals find it inconvenient to pay cash. They may prefer to purchase on credit such items as groceries, fuel, and gasoline, settling accounts at the end of the month. The importance of money as a standard of deferred payments is even greater in contracts covering a longer period of time. In such cases it may be all but impossible to pay cash. The majority of automobiles are paid for over a period of a year or more. And the average person in buying a home enters into a contract to pay specified monthly amounts over a period of from ten or fifteen to as long as thirty years.

PRIMORDIA—A SIMPLE MODEL

The nature of money can be illustrated with a simple model to which we shall occasionally refer. Imagine you are living in Primordia, a community that has never used money. You have no contact with other groups, so all trading is within the community. Over the course of the years only three industries have developed—fishing, hunting, and farming. On a typical day Primordia has available for consumption 2,000 pounds of fish, 1,000 pounds of meat, and 3,000 bushels of wheat. Production can easily be shifted from one industry to another,[8] but the public is satisfied with the present composition

---

[7]There are still the dangers of fire, theft, and so forth, to be sure, but it remains true that money is more easily stored than most other things. Loss through defaulted bonds, unsuccessful investments, business failures, and the like is irrelevant to this discussion, for in such instances the individuals are not holding money. They have given up money in return for a claim on or a share in some undertaking. Part of the income they receive from such holdings is a compensation for the risk of loss, and part is compensation for the very fact that they have given up money, at least temporarily.

[8]It is also assumed that constant returns to scale exist so that output always changes by the same proportion as each of the inputs.

of total output. There is, therefore, no incentive to expand one industry at the expense of another.

Since the productive structure is in accord with the public's pattern of wants, the composition of output must reflect the public's relative preferences for fish, meat, and wheat; that is, the community as a whole values 1 pound of meat as the equivalent of 2 pounds of fish or 3 bushels of grain. Alternatively, 1 pound of fish is worth ½ pound of meat or 1½ bushels of grain, and 1 bushel of grain is worth ⅓ of a pound of meat or ⅔ of a pound of fish. With the three commodities, each has two ratios of exchange for the other commodities.

These ratios are, however, only approximate. They apply to Primordia as a group, not to all individuals at all times. Even if an individual wheat farmer never eats fish, he may sometimes find he can get more meat if he trades his wheat for fish, then trades the fish for meat. The important thing for the farmer is to find someone who wants his product, then trade again if necessary to get what he himself wants.

Introduction of Money

Suppose Primordia now turns to "money" simply by agreeing, formally or informally, that wheat shall be the medium of exchange and standard of value. Instead of two exchange ratios for fish and two for meat, there is now only one exchange ratio for each. Wheat is now the common standard of value.

Also, producers will accept wheat in payment for their own product, knowing that they can always exchange the wheat for other products. Wheat is therefore acceptable as a medium of exchange, even if the sellers of meat or fish already have on hand far more wheat than they can possibly use for their own consumption. Less time is required for exchanges, since, regardless of their occupations, buyers will pay for purchases with wheat to be held or spent whenever and for whatever the recipients of the wheat may want.

Effect of an Increase in Money

Next, consider this question. Since wheat is now money, will fishermen and hunters be better off if they change occupations and begin growing wheat? They will have more money; everyone will have more money. In fact, if everyone turns to farming, Primordia will have nothing except wheat. Rather than being better off, however, people will obviously be much worse off. We know they prefer a combination of wheat, fish, and meat, rather than wheat alone.

Observe also that if wheat production increases and the output of fish and meat declines, then for two reasons it will take more wheat to buy a pound of fish or meat. In the first place, because fish and meat have become more scarce they will be worth more in terms of wheat even if wheat production is the same as before. In the second place, because wheat has become more plentiful it will be worth less in terms of fish and meat even if their production is the same as before.[9] For both reasons prices, in terms of wheat, will rise.

Although our model is an enormous simplification, it is far from being completely unrealistic. All around the globe societies did independently develop money of this general nature. Especially since they were producing more than three commodities, it was much more convenient to use one commodity (or possibly two or three) as a common measure of value and as a medium of exchange than to depend on barter. Only the most primitive tribes failed to develop money of some type.

ATTRIBUTES OF MONEY

There are certain qualities that satisfactory money must possess. The development of credit money has changed the relative importance of these attributes, with some attributes considered to be of great importance at some time in the past being given little consideration today.

Attributes Formerly Significant

In earlier centuries credit money was seldom used. Most money then had the same value as a commodity that it had as money. It was for this reason that metals, particularly gold and silver, were so widely used as money. They deteriorated little; they were fireproof, waterproof, and vermin resistant. They were easily recognizable. They could be divided into units of convenient size, and they could be melted and rejoined into larger units.

As compared with other money metals, gold possessed the special advantage of an extremely high intrinsic worth. The $20 gold piece formerly coined in the United States was a little heavier than the silver dollar. A thousand dollars in gold could be carried in a large pocket.[10] If the 50 coins were melted, the gold would still be worth $1,000.[11] Silver possessed the same characteristic of portability but to a lesser extent. At the other extreme, as far as metal moneys were concerned, was the iron money of ancient Sparta. It must have been very awkward to carry around much purchasing power in the form of iron, but presumably that was the intention of the Spartans, who were notably opposed to any form of luxurious living and had little desire to develop trade or encourage business. In more recent times Sweden had an 8-daler copper coin weighing 31 pounds. In contrast, India once used a gold coin about the size of a pinhead.

---

[9]We "inflated the money supply." Later we shall see that in a more complex economy an increase in the quantity of money will not necessarily cause a rise in prices, but it almost certainly would in the simple model presented here. In general, inflation results from an increase in the supply of money *relative* to the demand for it, where the demand for money depends on people's wealth, income, and the interest rate. An absolute change in monetary supply or demand is not necessarily a relative change.

[10]It would weigh less than 4 pounds, as compared with the 59 pounds weight of 1,000 silver dollars.

[11]Assuming that the coins were full weight, unworn, and undamaged.

The qualities of portability, divisibility, and recognizability were at one time stressed as important attributes of money. The development of credit money makes them of much less importance today. One-hundred-dollar bills are easier to carry than $20 gold pieces, and when checks can be written for a million dollars or more, it is not too important to find money material that is of great intrinsic worth and hence easily portable. Since checks can be written for uneven amounts, the attribute of divisibility of money loses much of its significance. So far as recognizability is concerned, it is probably no easier to counterfeit paper money than metal money.

Acceptability

Whether or not money possesses any of the attributes mentioned previously, if it is to do its work satisfactorily it must be acceptable. One reason that gold was so widely used as money was that gold as a metal was in universal demand, that is, was generally acceptable. Yet money need not necessarily be based upon a precious metal. For money to have value and therefore be acceptable, it must be limited in supply relative to demand and the productive capacity of the country. The fear that private parties would not restrict the issuance of money has caused the federal government to usurp the constitutional power to control monetary institutions.

As long as money is acceptable, that is, as long as it is universally desired and one can always find others who will give up goods or services to receive money, it makes little difference—at least at the time—what kind of money it is. It need not even be called money. A communist state might declare that it was doing away with money and setting up a currency to be called "labor credits." Such currency might be entirely paper, with no relation to gold or silver. Yet so long as people who received it knew that they could pass it on to someone else, receiving goods in return, the currency would, in fact, be money no matter what the state might choose to call it.

This acceptability is the basis of what is called *liquidity*. People can, if need arises, dispose of all their assets, but on less-liquid assets they are likely to take a loss or be obliged to wait indefinitely until they can find someone who wants those assets. They may be able to sell their homes for only half of what they paid for them; their stocks and bonds may have to be sold at a loss; for their furniture and personal effects they may receive only a small fraction of the purchase price. But for $1,000 they need never take less than $1,000 or less than $1,000 worth of other things. Money represents the ultimate in liquidity. Other things are only relatively liquid, with some things more liquid than others, but none as liquid as money.

Stability

Stability in the value of money is also essential if money is to do its work satisfactorily. Particularly when money is being used as a store of value or as a standard of deferred payments, it is important that its value should not be gyrating wildly. Skyrocketing inflations, as in Germany in 1923 and Hungary in 1946, completely destroy the value of money and wipe out the savings of millions. At the height of the hyperinflation in Germany, prices were doubling every two weeks, and in Hungary they were doubling every two or three days! Similar runaway inflations occurred in Russia in 1921–1923, Poland and Hungary in 1923, Greece in 1944, and Austria and China after World War II. In such instances, one may as well forget about having $50,000 in the bank when butter is selling at $1 million a pound. Nor are great increases in the value of money much better. If prices drop steeply and rapidly, one may easily find that the house bought for $20,000 and on which he or she still owes $12,000 is worth only $10,000 on the current market. Corporations that have borrowed money may find it impossible to repay the loans later if the value of money has greatly risen, as in the thirties. Even if they are operating at capacity, they find that their dollar receipts are insufficient to pay for assets acquired at a time when prices were much higher.

Unstable money causes difficulties also with the use of money as a medium of exchange. If people lose confidence in their money, they try to dispose of it as fast as possible; and the increase in the rate of turnover of money causes the value of money to drop even faster. Similarly, the attempt to hold on to money in a period of falling prices encourages further price declines and a breakdown of the medium of exchange function of money.

Stability is not quite the same thing as unvarying constancy. A plausible argument can be presented in favor of a gently falling value of money, that is, for gradually rising prices. Various writers have also shown that an upward-drifting value of money can be beneficial. And of course arguments have been given for a constant value of money. All can agree, however, that sudden and drastic changes in the value of money are undesirable.

Legal Attributes of Money

Besides the inherent attributes of money, there are two attributes that certain money receives by law. These are *legal tender* and *standard money*.

Legal Tender. Certain types of money are declared by law to be legal tender. The purpose of declaring money legal tender is to increase its acceptability. If debtors offer such money in payment of a money debt, the creditors will probably accept it, even if they would prefer some other form of money. If they refuse the payment, they still have the right to collect the debt, but can collect no interest from the time they refused the offer of legal tender to the time they finally are paid.[12]

At one time the rules and laws concerning legal tender were somewhat complex, but the matter is simple today. All United States currency, either coin or paper, is legal tender in any amount.[13] Demand deposits, although our most important money, are not legal tender; nor are checks, even if they are certified.

---

[12]If the original contract called for the delivery not of money but of real estate or stock or other nonmonetary assets, the debtor cannot at his or her option substitute legal tender to fulfill the contract.

[13]Excluding gold coin and gold certificates, which the public may no longer use as money.

Standard Money. The money of ultimate redemption is called *standard money*. (We shall have more to say about this in the next chapter.) Early in our history, money other than standard money was redeemed in silver. From 1833 to 1933, redemption was in gold, except for a few years during and after the Civil War when United States notes were standard money. At the present time our standard money within the country is paper.

SIGNIFICANCE OF MONEY

We have already noted that material civilization is based upon specialization and exchange, and that for the efficacious operation of a modern society, money is indispensable as a standard of value and medium of exchange. But the importance of money goes far beyond these functions. Money is not merely a passive mechanism to facilitate a comparison of values and an exchange of goods. It is much more than a simple lubricant for the economic machine. It has enormous and complex importance as a regulator of economic activity. Later we shall analyze some of these complicated relationships. At this point we will take a necessarily superficial look at the significance of money to our economy.

Money and Efficiency

In our world of scarcity, there is not enough of any of the factors of production to meet all possible uses to which they might be put. They must somehow be rationed among many competing uses. During a war they are likely to be doled out by government bureaus on the basis of their relative importance to national defense in one application as compared with another. The rest of the time the rationing under free enterprise is less obvious but nonetheless real. There are no forms to fill out and official priorities to secure. The factors go to whoever has the money to pay for them. Through the operation of the price system in a free economy, the quantity of productive factors that are supplied to the market place corresponds to the quantity demanded. The price system serves not only a rationing function but also an incentive function. High (low) prices induce increases (decreases) in future supplies in accordance with consumer wishes. Money facilitates both the rationing and the incentive functions.

Money facilitates efficiency not only by making possible a price system, but also by enabling firms, through loans of money, to gain command over productive factors. Banks lend a lot of money to businesspeople. Since they want to be repaid, the bankers lend to businesspeople who appear reliable and successful. They study carefully the financial records of firms applying for loans. The person who has been particularly successful can usually expand operations with the aid of money supplied by the bank. This benefits not only the producer personally but society as well. It is in the interest of the general public that production be directed by the most efficient producers who can get the maximum product from a given amount of scarce productive resources.

Changes in the Value of Money

We have already noted that money is an inconstant standard. When the general level of prices moves up or down, we have a change in the value of money. During the depression of the thirties, money was worth more than it had been a few years earlier. Since World War II, the value of money has fallen. These processes of deflation and inflation respectively have caused changes in the distribution of wealth and income among economic classes and in the level of total output.

Redistribution of Wealth and Income. A change in the value of money makes some people richer, some poorer. When, as recently, the value of money falls, people on fixed money incomes find their real incomes shrinking. The person living on a pension of $400 a month, or the person whose income is $400 a month from the insurance company or from corporate or government bonds is certainly living less well today than was possible on the same sum ten or twenty years ago. Anyone who is repaid when prices are high gets back less purchasing power than was lent. However, once the inflation is anticipated, it gradually becomes built into market prices. An unforeseen rise in the value of money, on the other hand, naturally benefits those on fixed money incomes and also creditors, but it erodes the financial position of debtors. If the debtors are successful in repaying their debts, they give up more purchasing power than they originally borrowed. If unsuccessful, they may lose whatever property they have when their creditors sue for payment.

Effect on Production. Changes in the value of money are important also because they may affect the level of production. When prices are rising, profits tend to be high and business is stimulated. Often the stimulus is excessive, leading to the overexpansion of industry followed by recession and perhaps a general breakdown of the economic system, such as the breakdown that occurred about forty-five years ago. Prices then are likely to fall, and a falling price level will probably intensify a recession or depression. As prices begin to fall, the public is led to expect further price declines. Instead of buying more goods when prices are lower, people tend to buy less than ever in the hope that prices will fall still further.

If changes in the value of money are so disrupting, arbitrarily redistributing wealth and income and disturbing the balance of the economic system, why should we not stabilize the value of money? Clearly this question concerns us all. Unfortunately it is not easily answered. Before we can attempt to answer it, we need to find out how our money system works, to understand what causes the value of money to change, and to recognize other issues which are interwoven with the issue of price stability.

Cause of Changes in Money's Value

Why does the value of money change? Three important theories have been advanced. Each contains some truth. Each has had important implications for monetary policy.

Commodity Theory. Until less than two hundred years ago, most of the civilized world's money was in the form of gold and silver coins. Any pieces of these metals had the same monetary significance. Coins were used only because they were convenient to handle. A person might be willing to sell a piece of land for a hundred ounces of gold. Whether the metal was in the form of a gold brick or coins was not of fundamental importance. Nor was it significant whether the person received 5 coins or 10 or 100—as long as their total weight was 100 ounces. In short, the heavier the coin (assuming all coins were made of the same alloy), the more it would buy.

As the world progressed from commodity money to credit money, the amount of metal represented by the monetary unit no longer had the simple and direct relationship that it once had. Some theorists, however, continued to stress the commodity aspect of money. They maintained that if a nation was on the gold standard and reduced the gold content of its standard coins, the money would necessarily and immediately be worth less than before. This type of analysis underlay the devaluation of the dollar in 1934.[14]

Quantity Theory. Other theorists concentrated upon the relationship between the quantity of money and its value. The total quantity of money might change for various reasons. These theorists believed that if the quantity of money was increased when the nation was at full employment, prices would rise. If the economy was not at full employment, an increase in the quantity of money would cause an expansion of output and eventually, after full employment was reached, a rise in prices.

The quantity theory did not so much deny the commodity theory as modify it to emphasize what appeared more important to quantity theorists. In the 19th and early 20th centuries, nations seldom redefined their coins to contain less (or more) metal. Hence, the *approximate* value of the money did not greatly change. On the other hand, the quantity of credit money could be changed by the banking system and by the monetary authorities. Also, a nation's stock of metal money might rise because of great mining strikes, war indemnities received, or trade surpluses. Whatever the cause of the increase, and whether the increase was in credit money or in metal money, the greater quantity of money would lead—according to the quantity theory—to a decrease in its value, eventually to be checked by a gold outflow and contraction of the money supply.

Income Approach. During and after the depression of the thirties, an increasing number of economists took the position that the quantity of money is a permissive rather than a causal factor. As John Maynard Keynes[15] once remarked, "A fat man needs a longer belt, but wearing a longer belt won't make a man fat." An increase in the quantity of money will not necessarily

---

[14]See Chapter 3.
[15]John Maynard Keynes (1883–1946) was the celebrated British economist who fathered the income theory in his *General Theory of Employment, Interest, and Money* (New York: Harcourt, Brace & World, 1936).

cause an increase in either prices or the volume of production and employ-ment. According to the income approach, instead of increasing the quantity of money in depression and expecting money income necessarily to increase, we should concentrate directly on increasing money income. But if money income continues to grow rapidly after the economy has recovered to the full employment level, the value of money falls. This has been the situation much of the time since World War II and especially in the early and mid-1970s.

Complicating Factors. The income approach to the theory of the value of money brings out some of the other problems intertwined with that of main-taining a stable price level. We are no longer so sure that the primary objec-tive should be the stabilization of the value of money. Possibly it is more important to try to stabilize production at the full employment level with a constantly increasing production of goods and services in real terms.

It is highly desirable to stabilize the value of money also, if we can figure out how to do it. A constantly rising price level such as we have had for over a third of a century presents serious problems. But we are becoming more and more unwilling to accept the bankruptcies and mass unemployment by which, in earlier years, a price level that was "too high" was brought back to "nor-mal." Our thinking has greatly changed from the almost universal philosophy of a generation ago that "what goes up must come down," and from the belief that in depression the only proper policy, however painful it may be, is to let the depression run its course so that the economy may eventually be rees-tablished on a lower price level.

If a stable value of money were the only thing that mattered, we could manage that without too much difficulty. Unfortunately there are often con-flicting goals. Beginning in 1965 the monetary authorities enforced, until 1970, an increasingly tight monetary policy to check the increasingly rapid rise in prices which was increasing our losses of gold to other countries and seriously undermining international confidence in the dollar. Interest rates skyrocketed. The prices of not only stocks and corporate bonds but also of long-term Trea-sury securities plummeted. Construction activity was slowed. Employment and business generally declined. Then from 1971 into 1975 the "stagflation" problem of rising prices, stagnant production, and high unemployment contin-ued despite the wage and price controls imposed by the Nixon administration and the continued tight money policy of the Federal Reserve. The fact is, for over twenty years we have found ourselves on the horns of a dilemma. Be-cause of such dilemmas, monetary policy must often compromise.

SUMMARY AND CONCLUSION

The most important functions of money are to serve as a standard of value and a medium of exchange. To serve these functions successfully, money must be generally acceptable. The government has declared all forms of United States currency to be legal tender to increase their acceptability. The acceptability of money is affected also by its stability of value.

A price system requires the use of money. Without a price system the complex interrelationships of modern society would be impossible. Specialization and exchange depend on it, as do also the fundamental processes of a free enterprise society which decide what shall be produced, and how, by whom, and to whom it shall be distributed. Further, the level of output and employment is affected by changes in the value of money, and these changes also redistribute wealth and income.

Money is a field in which we do not know all the answers and probably never will. At the same time it is a challenging and tremendously important subject to us collectively and individually. It holds a key to the survival of democracy and free enterprise. In a world in which private enterprise and government dictatorship are arrayed against each other, a monetary system which will contribute to a sound and progressive economy and a steadily increasing volume of production is not simply a convenience to free enterprise. It is a fundamental necessity.

Discussion Questions

1. "Monetary institutions and regulations are constantly changing to meet new problems or better cope with old ones." Comment.
2. "When individuals spend money, they receive goods or services or repay debt, but they give up the money. When a society spends money, it still has as much money as before." Explain why you agree or disagree.
3. "Inflation refers to high prices and deflation to low prices." Evaluate and comment.
4. Which function of money is most important to modern society? Which function is least effectively fulfilled? Briefly explain.
5. Can you use a particular $10 bill in such a way that it will simultaneously perform all four functions of money? If not, how many functions might it serve in a given transaction?
6. If 25 commodities are being produced and exchanged, how many separate valuations or different exchange ratios would there be if none of them is adopted as the common measure of value?
7. If you turn in three used textbooks to the bookstore for one new one, money is not involved in the transaction. True or False? Explain.
8. Why is it less efficient to trade goods directly for other goods than to use a medium of exchange, which requires two transactions rather than one?
9. Why would Primordia be more likely to begin using wheat rather than meat or fish as money?
10. "In general, inflation results from an increase in the supply of money." Evaluate and comment.
11. "The greater is a government's debt, the more inclined is the government to favor inflation." Explain. How, if at all, is the government different from any other borrower in this respect?
12. Briefly summarize the three theories for changes in the value of money.

Chapter 2   Money: From Commodity to Credit

A dollar isn't what it used to be. Nor is money. Over the centuries, the nature of money has drastically changed.

COMMODITY MONEY

Money began simply enough. A commodity (or in some countries two or three commodities) came into general use as a medium of exchange.

Early Development and Advantages

Any commodity might be adopted as a medium of exchange. Different parts of the world have adopted such commodities as metals, clam shells, stones, and grain. Most generally used were gold and silver. Like other metals, they possessed certain qualities that were desirable in a commodity money: durability, recognizability, divisibility, and uniformity. They had the additional advantage of a high intrinsic worth. A little went a long way. A pound or two of silver or a few ounces of gold would exchange for large amounts of other goods.

Coinage was invented about 660 B.C., a thousand years or so after society began to use metal money. The metal was cut into pieces of uniform weight and quality as certified by the seal of the issuing authority. Money was still a commodity, but in more convenient form. Prices were still reckoned in terms of the amount of gold or silver one should offer or demand for other goods. (In fact, the names of these early coins were usually weights; a thousand years ago the British used a pound of silver as their standard of value.) Buyers and sellers no longer had to weigh and test the metal for every transaction. The convenience of coinage increased the acceptability of metal money.[1]

Eventual Decline of Commodity Money

Two thousand years more went by with no further monetary developments in the Western world. Later it would be discovered that the Chinese

---

[1]Even today in many parts of the world, gold coins are more acceptable than uncoined gold. This premium on coins was so great that it encouraged a fantastic counterfeiting operation some years ago, netting a $2 million profit for the imaginative promoter. The bizarre feature was that the counterfeit coins actually contained (slightly) more gold than the British coins they imitated!

had begun to use paper money, but in Europe the only money was in the form of coins. Goods were still being bought and sold only by transferring these pieces of metal.

Finally, about three hundred years ago a change in money began. Paper money was introduced. Mistakes were made at first. Often this paper money became valueless. Gradually people learned how it could be properly issued and how its value could be maintained. Today paper money has almost entirely replaced coins in all but small transactions. Money, originally a physical commodity, has become largely abstract.

Disadvantages of Commodity Money

There are several disadvantages to a monetary system consisting only of metal (or any other commodity). The invention of coinage helped make commodity money easier to use, but even coin money has serious limitations. Large payments are inconvenient. Furthermore, there is the problem of providing an adequate supply of money. There is only so much gold and silver, and even if it were all minted into coins, there would not be very much money per individual. To some extent this shortcoming would be offset by the fact that a small money supply induces a low price level, so the individual would only need a small quantity of money. However, a distribution of money favorable to growth of industry and trade would be difficult to achieve with a small stock of money. A country in a period of rapid expansion needs a considerable expansion of its money supply for the development of its commerce and industry. It may gradually acquire coins from other countries developing at a slower rate or not at all, but such a process of adjustment is intolerably slow.

Finally, when money derives its value from its component material, the money can have full value only when it is full weight. A fresh, undamaged coin will weigh slightly more than an old, worn coin or a shaved or drilled coin, and will therefore be worth more. Thus, each piece of money must be inspected to ascertain its true value.

Until about a century ago, the value of most coins was generally determined by their metallic content. A fresh coin, unworn and undamaged, had the same value as bullion that it had as money.[2] If the bullion value were at any time greater than the value of the coin as money, people melted the coins and sold the bullion. At such times business suffered from a scarcity of coins, for as fast as the government minted more coins, the public melted them down. To make the problem of supplying adequate coinage more difficult, at such times the Treasury found that bullion was not presented to its mints, for the price offered elsewhere was higher than the Treasury's price. When the Treasury had coined its existing stocks of bullion, it could not continue to replace the coins melted down by the public.

---

[2]Bullion is metal from which coins are struck.

SUBSTITUTES FOR COMMODITY MONEY

Paper money today is of two types, representative money and credit money. These types of money reflect two stages in the evolution of money from a simple commodity to a sophisticated abstraction.

Representative Money

The first step away from commodity money was the introduction of *representative money*. When representative money is used, gold or silver is placed in the vaults of the Treasury or the banks. In the latter case, for every metal dollar they receive, these depositaries issue a dollar of paper money. Every paper dollar is therefore backed 100 percent by metal and can at any time be exchanged for the metal.[3]

By putting the actual gold or silver away in the vaults and issuing paper to represent it dollar for dollar, society gains several advantages. Large payments are easier to make with the certificates, the money supply is more portable and divisible, there are no coining costs, and there is no wear and tear on the gold or silver. The certificates are easily transportable and can be printed in any denomination. A worn $10 bill is worth just as much as a fresh one since, regardless of whether the certificate is new or almost worn out, it is a claim on a fixed amount of gold or silver held in storage.

Representative money is an obvious convenience to commerce and an economy for society, because only paper is being worn out, not precious metals. On the other hand, representative money is more susceptible to fire and theft, is easier to counterfeit, and involves some engraving costs.

Credit Money

Still later, *credit money* was developed. When credit money is used, banks and governments issue promises to pay, usually backed by a partial reserve in coins.[4] Since these promises are payable on demand and to bearer, they are a convenient medium of exchange. Of course, if such promises are to circulate freely, the credit of the issuer must be very high. As long as that credit rating is unquestioned and everyone is sure that payment will be promptly and surely made whenever the notes are presented, the amount of the metal reserve held against them makes little difference to their acceptability. The reserves will be fractional at best—possibly 20 or 30 percent.[5] There may be no reserves at all.[6] Ordinarily, however, law or custom requires some

---

[3]See the discussion of silver certificates, p. 48, and the early note issues of the goldsmiths, p. 117. The silver certificates of varying denominations which circulated from 1878 to 1967 had a silver backing which was worth less as a commodity than as money.

[4]See discussion of notes, pp. 45–47.

[5]If reserves of 100 percent were held, the paper would be representative money, not credit money.

[6]See Federal Reserve Bank notes, p. 293; Federal Reserve notes, p. 47.

minimum reserve in coins or bullion, partly for the purpose of maintaining public confidence in the notes.

Although almost all the paper currency in circulation in this country today is credit money, by far our most important credit money is in the form of demand deposits, briefly discussed at the end of this chapter. Checking accounts typically constitute about three fourths of our money supply, while paper currency and coins constitute about one fourth. Although there are written records of deposits, and checks are used to transfer deposits, the deposit money itself is completely abstract. Emphatically, a bank's deposits are *not* its vault cash.

Credit money quickly became, in modern economies, by far the most important kind of money. It offers the same conveniences as does representative money together with the enormous advantage of permitting the total stock of money to be controlled more easily. The quantity of money may be either increased or decreased through the expansion or contraction of credit. The world's monetary stock is less closely tied to metal, so its growth rate no longer depends so heavily on new discoveries of gold and silver. A rapidly expanding economy can be provided with an increased money supply much more quickly and easily than when only coins and representative money are used.

In addition to the distinction as to whether money is credit or commodity money and whether the monetary value of the physical materials backing commodity money is equal to its market value, it is also important to distinguish between the privately issued money of commercial banks and the publicly issued money of the Fed and the Treasury. Parts 2 and 3 will explore this latter distinction at length.

STANDARD MONEY

When only commodity money is in use, a coin's money worth is its worth as metal. The value of representative money is equal to the value of the metal that it represents. But how much is credit money worth? And if credit money, representative money, and several kinds of commodity money all circulate simultaneously, how can the value of each be kept equal to that of all the others?

The answer is simple. The government and the banks agree to redeem all other forms of money in the money that the government has declared to be the standard. *Standard* money is the money of *ultimate redemption*. Thus, if the government has adopted a gold standard and the banks and the government will upon demand pay out gold in exchange for any other form of money, then a $5 bill or 5 silver dollars or 500 pennies must all have exactly the same value as a new $5 gold piece, regardless of whether the other forms of money are worn and regardless of the market value of copper or silver bullion. Hence, all forms of money tend to circulate at par.

Under certain circumstances, it is possible for substitute moneys to have less value than, or more value than, the official standard. If the public can easily turn in a $10 bill, for example, for immediate redemption in gold, then the bill must have the same purchasing power as the gold. But if the redemption process requires weeks and perhaps also involves collection costs or special fees, then the value of the substitute money may be somewhat less than that of the standard money. If, in addition, there is some uncertainty as to whether the money will actually be redeemed, then it is likely to circulate at a still greater discount. Most of the money used in the United States in the first half of the 19th century consisted of bank notes, sometimes although not always redeemable in standard money when presented to the issuing bank. Since a Boston merchant could not very conveniently go to Ohio to present Cincinnati bank notes for redemption, and since there was no national banking machinery organized for the redemption of bank notes, these notes frequently circulated at a discount when outside the immediate neighborhood of the issuing bank. If the issuing bank was unknown and its credit rating unobtainable, its notes tended to be worth still less in the market, for holders had no way of knowing whether the bank could actually redeem its notes. Hence, during this period of our history we frequently were using notes with values ranging all the way from 100 cents on the dollar to nearly zero. Later, improved banking facilities and improved means of transportation and communication caused discounts of this sort generally to disappear. Today we take for granted that all of our money has the same value.

It may seem paradoxical that standard money may have a lower value than other forms of money. However, redemption takes place upon the demand of the person who holds nonstandard money, not upon the demand of the issuer. Hence, if there is a tendency for nonstandard money to have a lower value than standard money, the tendency is offset by the redemption provision, subject to the limitations listed above. But if, on the other hand, the *standard* money has the lower value, then there will be no redemption. No one is going to demand to be given a money of lower value in exchange for the money already held. During the Civil War both the South and the North were on paper standards. Both governments, in other words, refused to redeem in gold or silver and paid out paper only. These paper dollars were the official standard of value. As they were issued in ever-increasing quantities to help pay the costs of the war, their value fell. Prices in terms of the paper standards rose, but anyone who could pay with gold or silver coins could buy at lower prices than if that person were to pay with the currencies that temporarily were standard money. Of course, the respective governments would have been happy to "redeem" any gold or silver with paper money, but since no one was foolish enough to demand redemption of that kind, none took place. Under such conditions nothing could make the value of the standard money equal to that of other moneys, and the standard money might for years have a lower value than the temporarily nonstandard gold and silver.

Although there are various modifications, in the final analysis there are just two basic types of monetary standards—*commodity standards* and *paper standards*. A nation using a commodity standard defines its currency in terms of some commodity or commodities. More importantly, the government keeps the value of the currency equal to the value of a given quantity of some commodity or commodities by freely redeeming the currency, directly or indirectly. Paper standards are not so maintained no matter how they may be defined.

Primordia—the Wheat Standard and Credit Money

Returning to the three-industry economy of the preceding chapter, let us suppose that Primordia progresses to the use of credit money. Although it has not learned the technology of paper manufacture, it has discovered the convenience of clay tablets as an exchange medium.

If these tablets were backed by a 100 percent reserve in wheat, they would be representative rather than credit money. But we shall assume that only a partial reserve is maintained. There are 10,000 bushels of wheat held as monetary reserves, but 50,000 tablets have been placed in circulation, each tablet a legal claim for one bushel of wheat. Primordia is using wheat as a standard of value, as before, but because the public finds the tablets more convenient as a means of payment, the tablets have become the principal medium of exchange.

Everything runs smoothly as long as everyone is confident that should they ever want to redeem the tablets for wheat, it can easily be done. Credit expansion has made it unnecessary to reduce consumption to increase the supply of money, so living standards have not been lowered to permit the greater quantity of money.

There is admittedly always the possibility that pessimism or panic may occasionally cause the breakdown of this system. If a widespread lack of confidence impels everyone at the same time to demand wheat, obviously the stock of wheat will be exhausted when only one fifth of the tablets have been redeemed. As most of the community's money is credit money redeemable upon demand, this risk is inescapable. However, the Primordians would rather take the risk than return to a money that can be increased only by reducing the production of consumption goods to allow the creation of more commodity money.

Automatic Commodity Standards

During the 19th and early 20th centuries it was widely believed that commodity standards automatically provided the proper regulation of interest rates, the price level, and the quantity of money. Little if any discretionary monetary management was required, and indeed, would probably be an undesirable interference with the proper responses brought about by the standard itself. Money would take care of itself.

The most familiar commodity standard is the gold standard. Many nations still link their currencies to gold, directly or indirectly. However, the relationship was much tighter during the main era of the international gold standard, from the middle to latter 1800s through 1913, or even up to 1934.

The term "gold standard" must be employed with caution as it has been used to refer to a number of different monetary arrangements, including the gold-coin, gold-exchange, and gold-bullion standards. Since President Nixon formally terminated gold convertibility in August, 1971, the United States has been in limbo. The dollar was devalued in 1971 and 1973. The official price of gold went from the $35 an ounce price established in 1934 to $38 an ounce in 1971 and to $42.22 an ounce in 1973. In the free tier of the two-tier gold system set up in the late 1960s, the price of gold went to over $195 an ounce in 1974.

The Gold-Coin Standard. The automatic *gold-coin* standard in widespread use during the half century preceding World War I was based upon the following requirements:

1. The currency must be defined in terms of gold. The value of the standard unit (dollar, franc, mark, etc.,) is declared equal to the value of a certain *weight* of gold of specified purity. This definition simultaneously establishes the price of gold. For instance, from 1934 to 1971 when the dollar was defined as one thirty-fifth of an ounce of gold, the price of gold was established as $35 an ounce.
2. Gold must be freely coined. In other words, the Treasury must buy without limit all gold it is offered. (The first of these requirements is met by our present type of standard, as was also the second until some years ago. Since 1968, however, the Treasury has not bought gold freely.[7] None of this gold is actually minted at the Treasury.)
3. There must be no restrictions on the circulation or use of gold coins, which are unlimited legal tender. If the public wishes to use them as money, export them, melt them, or hoard them, it is free to do so. (It may not, however, shave, drill, or otherwise deface coins.)
4. All other forms of money are redeemed in gold coin whenever the public so demands. In other words, the Treasury freely sells gold. (Neither the third nor fourth requirement is met by our present standard.)
5. The price of gold (that is, definition of the monetary unit) is fixed. The Treasury continues, year after year, to buy and sell gold at an unvarying price. (We raised the price of gold in 1934 when we abandoned the gold-coin standard.[8] In December, 1971, we raised the official price to $38, and in February, 1973, we raised it again to $42.22.)

In adopting a gold-coin standard, a government could define its standard money to contain whatever amount of gold it wished. Common sense, however, would suggest that if a peso were defined as one one-thousandth of an ounce of gold, the gold peso would not be coined at all. The smallest practical gold coin would be, perhaps, the 100-peso coin. Conversely, a peso containing an ounce of gold would have so great a purchasing power that it would be unsuitable as a basic unit; most prices would be expressed in terms of fractions of pesos rather than in pesos, and fractional coins (not made of gold) as

[7]See also pp. 68–69.

[8]Since the gold value of the dollar was decreased from 23.22 to 13.71 grains of pure (fine) gold—there are 480 grains of gold to the ounce—the official price of gold was raised from $20.67 to $35.00 an ounce.

small as one one-thousandth or one five-thousandth of a peso would probably be necessary. Thus, practical considerations would suggest that the government adopt a gold content somewhere in the general range of perhaps one tenth to one one-hundredth of an ounce for its monetary unit.

As noted in requirement 1, the gold content of the coin simultaneously determines the price the nation pays for gold. Suppose that the United States dollar was defined as .0286 of an ounce of gold, the German deutsche mark as .01 of an ounce, and the British pound as .1 of an ounce. Thirty-five dollars would then equal one ounce of gold, as would 100 deutsche marks and 10 pounds. Obviously the price of $35 an ounce would be neither higher nor lower than the price of 100 deutsche marks in Berlin or £ 10 in London.

A great advantage of the automatic gold standard was that it set a limit to the possible fluctuations in foreign exchange rates. In the hypothetical example above, since $35 buys one ounce of gold and 100 deutsche marks buys one ounce of gold, then $35 should buy 100 deutsche marks and vice versa. Thus, the *mint ratio* between the dollar and the deutsche mark would be 35/100 or .35; between the deutsche mark and the pound, 100/10 or 10; and between the dollar and the pound, 35/10 or 3.5. The *mint par* price of deutsche marks in New York would therefore be $0.35; of pounds in Berlin, DM10, and of pounds in New York, $3.50. As long as anyone could ship $350 in gold to London where, as 10 ounces of gold, it would be worth £100, no one would be willing to pay much more than $3.50 to buy £ 1; nor would an Englishman be willing to receive much less than $3.50 for £ 1. True, shipping gold involved some costs, but they were seldom significant enough to affect the price of foreign exchange rates by more than 1 percent. In our example, the foreign exchange rates might have varied from about $3.48 to $3.52, but gold shipments would have promptly begun had the dollar price of the pound moved outside this range. Many bankers and financiers were aware that if the pound were selling in New York at, for example, $3.55, they could pick up a completely riskless profit by selling £ 1 million at that price, taking $3.5 million of their receipts and buying gold, paying about $20,000 of shipping costs, and pocketing the balance of $30,000. Even at $3.53 they would make a quick and certain profit of about $10,000, as they would also at $3.47. This stability facilitated international trade and capital movements since everyone always knew almost exactly how much they would receive for, or have to pay for, the currency of another country with which they wished to do business.

The Gold-Bullion Standard. An early and slight variant of the gold-coin standard was the automatic *gold-bullion* standard.[9] A nation could define its money in terms of gold and its Treasury could buy and sell gold freely, yet that nation need not ever actually coin the gold. As gold began to recede more and more into the background as hand-to-hand money, leaving paper money to function as the medium of exchange, some countries saw no advantage to

---

[9]As indicated in footnote 2, bullion is metal from which coins are struck. Pure gold would be much too soft to coin, so gold bullion contains some alloy, usually 10 percent, to harden the coins.

coining gold. As long as the government continued to sell gold freely, there was no reason to prefer gold coins to other types of money, any of which could be exchanged for gold. If someone did demand gold, usually the person did not want coin specifically, but gold itself, to be hoarded or exported or perhaps used in the arts. Often it would be melted, perhaps to be recoined by some foreign country. Later it might return to the first Treasury to be recoined and stored again until someone demanded it and perhaps again melted it. The coinage expense appeared to be unnecessary since gold coins, as coins, were so little in demand.

If a nation declared its currency, the peso, to be worth one tenth of an ounce of gold, anyone presenting 10,000 pesos for redemption would be entitled to 1,000 ounces of gold. However, that gold need not be in the form of coins. It could just as well be a single bar or brick of gold. The only effective difference to the public between the gold-coin and the gold-bullion standard would be that individuals could obtain smaller amounts of gold by the former. With the gold-bullion standard, people had to take a fairly large gold bar, worth probably several thousand dollars. They could not redeem currency in small amounts. The gold-bullion standard was sometimes called the gold standard of the rich.

Both the above varieties of gold standard were called *automatic* because people believed that these standards needed no supervision or control. All forms of money—paper, copper, silver, and gold—would have the same purchasing power since all the nonstandard money could be exchanged for gold at any time. The value of money, it was argued, would necessarily be stable when it was defined in and redeemed in a fixed quantity of gold.

If inflation did temporarily set in, gold mining would become less profitable. Labor and other costs of production would rise, but the price of gold, fixed by law, would remain unchanged. As gold production declined, the nation's supply of gold would grow more slowly than before.

Of greater and more immediate importance, the inflation would cause gold to drain to other countries. The high prices would lead to a drop in exports as foreigners reduced their purchases. Automatically imports would rise as lower priced goods from other countries began to outsell the high priced domestic products. The result of this decrease in exports and increase in imports would be an outflow of gold to settle the unfavorable balance of trade (that is, the surplus of imports over exports). Finally the gold outflow would, it was believed, induce a fall in the general price level. Gold would be more scarce, so an ounce of gold would be worth more in terms of other goods. With the price of gold constant, the prices of other goods would have to fall if an ounce of gold was to have a greater buying power. The fall in the domestic price level would lead eventually to a favorable balance of trade and a gold inflow.

Some felt that the fall in the price level was due not so much to the decrease in the stock of gold in particular as to the decrease in the stock of money in general, for with the automatic gold standard the total money supply expanded and contracted with changes in the gold stock. Modern analysis throws greater emphasis on the income effects of the changes in exports and imports than on changes in either money or gold. But whatever the line of reasoning, the conclusion is the same. Gold movements under the automatic gold standard tend to be self-corrective. Both outflows and inflows generate forces that encourage a reversal of the gold movement. This corrective action was long regarded as ideal. Not until later was the gold standard to be regarded as a breeding ground for inflations and depressions—due to exactly this same corrective action that was once regarded as its greatest virtue. Today governments pursue a monetary management policy which does not dictate that changes in the gold stock should be the major determinant of changes in the money supply. For instance, while the stock of monetary gold in the U.S. fell by about 50 percent between 1950 and the early 1970s, the monetary authorities increased the money supply by about 100 percent.

The Gold-Exchange Standard. Some nations preferred to link their money to gold indirectly. They held foreign balances instead of domestic gold stocks as reserves against their money. Instead of redeeming in gold, they redeemed in currency (or bank deposits) of a nation that did redeem in gold. Their currencies were as good as gold; at the same time they were able to invest their foreign balances in high-grade short-term investments. A gold hoard of a billion dollars yields no income. A billion dollars of Treasury bills earns several million dollars a year, depending on interest rates.

From 1958 to 1971 the gold-exchange standard acquired its greatest importance.[10] As a result of international defense commitments, foreign aid programs, and various other causes, the United States every year bought more from the rest of the world than it sold.[11] Some of the deficit was offset by gold shipments from the United States. Primarily, foreign countries increased their holdings of short-term claims against the United States. These interest-earning dollar balances, rather than gold bullion, were serving as monetary reserves for many countries.

A gold-exchange standard operates in somewhat the same fashion as the gold standard proper, especially if both are allowed to operate automatically. In the absence of controls, a rising price level leads finally to a fall in exports, a rise in imports, and a decline of money in circulation. Prices cannot rise indefinitely under these circumstances. Eventually they fall, the quantity of money increases, the fall in prices is checked, and sooner or later prices probably rise again.

In practice, since no form of gold standard has been permitted to operate entirely automatically, particularly in the 20th century, the operation of gold-exchange standards has been more erratic than is implied in the preceding paragraph. Short-term capital movements were disastrously unsettling at the outset of the world economic collapse of the 1930s, and they have become troublesome again today.

In November, 1973, the seven major nations owning gold rescinded the "two-tier" system—i.e., "official" and "free" market prices—which since

---

[10]On August 15, 1971, President Nixon suspended the gold-exchange standard by abandoning convertibility of the dollar into gold and other reserve assets. In fact, the popularity of chemical element 79 for monetary purposes has been on the wane for almost 60 years.

[11]See discussion of balance of payments, Chapter 26.

March, 1968, had barred official dealings with the private market, kept the official price low (then at \$35 an ounce), and allowed the free market price to fluctuate. In fact, there had been no official market since the United States stopped convertibility of dollars into gold on August 15, 1971. But the November decision to abandon the two-tier system allowed central banks to sell gold in the free market, but not to buy—under international monetary rules which were not changed—at a price in excess of the official \$42.22 per ounce. The U.S. sold several thousand ounces of gold in early January, 1975. Whether the U.S. or any other country will sell additional gold in the future remains to be seen.

The Silver Standard. Some countries used silver instead of gold for their standard money. Indeed, a century ago the silver standard was in more common use than the gold standard. In all that we have said about gold standards, we might substitute the word "silver" for "gold." The analysis would be the same no matter what metal—or other commodity—we declared standard.

However, for a wealthy nation there is a practical consideration that favors gold rather than silver. Such a nation will likely have a large money supply, and, to maintain either the gold or silver (automatic) standard, the nation will require large monetary reserves of one metal or the other. Since an ounce of gold is worth many times more than an ounce of silver, a much smaller physical quantity of gold is needed.

The Bimetallic Standard. There is one other commodity standard of at least historical importance. Some nations, including the United States, at one time attempted to define their money in terms of both gold and silver simultaneously. Nonstandard money was redeemed in either gold or silver. The Treasury would *not*, however, redeem gold in silver or silver in gold. If one held either silver or gold, he held standard money already.

These standards were unsatisfactory. In practice, what was a bimetallic standard de jure (that is, legally) turned into either a gold or a silver standard de facto (that is, actually). When a government adopted a bimetallic standard, it set the prices at which it would buy or sell both metals. The actual prices it set did not affect other prices. The general price level for other goods would adjust to whatever value the Treasury gave its money when it declared what the gold or silver content of the money would be. What did make a great deal of difference was the relation or *ratio* between the Treasury's price for silver and its price for gold. Unless the Treasury set those prices in the same ratio as the market values of the two metals, the Treasury would overvalue one metal and undervalue the other. It would be able to buy the overvalued metal, but the undervalued metal would all flow to the market. The only standard money in circulation would be the overvalued metal. The nation's standard would be de facto monometallic, even though it was de jure bimetallic.

Even if the mint ratio set by the Treasury did at the outset correspond to the market ratio, the market ratio could change at any time. There might be great new gold discoveries or there might be a substantial increase in the market's demand for silver—perhaps as a result of fashion, perhaps because of important new uses for silver in industry, perhaps because some country decided to adopt a silver standard. Any of these developments would cause an ounce of gold to be worth fewer ounces of silver on the market. Or the change might be in the other direction, and gold on the market would be worth more ounces of silver than before.

The double standard was impractical. The *fixed* mint ratio did not adjust to the *changing* market ratio, and bimetallism was abandoned.

It is not likely to be restored. A century ago there was some justification for the claim that the world's stocks of gold and silver were too small for a nation to acquire large enough reserves of either metal alone, so that treasuries needed to hold both the precious metals. The tremendous increase in the stock of both metals over the last century and, more importantly, the development of modern banking techniques and economies in the use of metal reserves permit adequate reserves to be based on either metal by itself.

"Automatic" Commodity Standard—Conclusion. If the monetary standard will "automatically" make the proper adjustments, any sort of management or control by the banks or government is not only unnecessary, it is undesirable. For this reason the greatest popularity of the automatic gold standard coincided with the greatest acceptance of the concept of laissez-faire. Following Adam Smith's declaration in 1776 that the "invisible hand" of competition would automatically guide production into the channels of greatest value to society and that government should leave business alone, for more than a century Americans were convinced that the role of government should be minimized. The gold standard (or any of the other commodity standards above) seemed to offer in the area of money the same sort of automatic and optimum control that competition was supposed to guarantee in the field of production. Natural forces, unfettered and unthwarted by people and their often bungling decisions, would direct all for the best.[12]

Yet even in its heyday the gold standard in the United States was never a completely automatic standard. Interferences were created. Tariffs were imposed, obstructing the free flow of trade which the gold standard required for its automatic responses. Also, the development of banking and the expansion of credit changed the ratio between gold reserves and other money. Further, changes in interest rates were used to prevent the consequences dictated by the automatic gold standard. Especially after the development of the Federal Reserve System, the monetary authorities gave much thought to the question of how they could best offset inflows and outflows of gold. But through it all they took for granted that the so-called automatic gold standard should be maintained. The United States, England, and most of Europe were on gold. Some countries, especially if they produced large amounts of silver, were on silver, but the principle was the same. The standard was automatic in form.

---

[12]This reaction against the 18th century philosophy of government regulation was at the time called liberalism. Times change. As new philosophies arose reemphasizing the role of government, laissez-faire came to be regarded as conservative.

Then, almost overnight, the so-called automatic gold standard was swept aside. In its place we have today the managed standard. This standard is usually related to gold (or silver), but is largely a paper standard. The role of gold and silver in monetary institutions is almost certain to continue declining in importance in the years to come.

Paper Standards

From time to time in the past, nations were forced to use paper standards, especially in wartime. To pay its bills, the government printed paper money. As more and more of this money was issued, the government found that it could not redeem the currency in gold or silver. Thus, paper came to be, temporarily, the money of ultimate redemption, and the nation was on a paper standard. At such times, specie (coin) disappeared from circulation. Anyone lucky enough to have silver or gold hoarded it and used the paper money to pay bills. For unless different kinds of money are all freely interchangeable, several types of money can seldom circulate simultaneously. Bad money drives out good, according to Gresham's Law.[13]

While such an *involuntary* paper standard was in effect, the public expected the government eventually to return to a specie standard. No one supposed the government had any intention of trying permanently to base its money on paper. The paper standard was required to meet the emergency. A soon as conditions permitted, redemption in gold (or in silver, if the country had been on a silver standard) would resume. This expectation, it was once believed, was the only reason the paper money had any value.

The better we realize the abstract quality that money has assumed in the course of its development, the more we question the necessity of having gold or silver or any other commodity as the standard. At least under ideal conditions it should be possible for money to be issued with no specific reserves of coin, bullion, or other commodities behind it. Even when American citizens had the right to demand gold for their money, few asked for it. As long as they could get gold any time they wanted it, they had confidence in the money. The confidence is what counts, not the means by which the confidence is created. We may decide someday that we can cut entirely free from gold, no longer redeeming our money internationally in gold or even defining

---

[13]In more precise terms, Gresham's Law states that if coins contain metal of different value and each contains equal legal-tender power, then the cheapest ones will be used for payment and the better ones will disappear from circulation. This principle was recognized by others before Thomas Gresham (1519–1579), but he has been associated with it ever since he explained to Queen Elizabeth several hundred years ago why it was that, in spite of all the new coins she had ordered minted and put into circulation, only the worn and defaced coins circulated. Anyone who happened to receive any of the new coins held on to them, since they contained a little more bullion than the worn coins. A novel illustration of Gresham's Law in operation occurred at the end of World War II, when for a while cigarettes were used as currency in much of Europe. The cigarettes that most often "circulated" were the off-brands. More recently, United States silver coins rapidly disappeared into hoards; they were replaced by the new mostly copper coins. For some reason this development came as a surprise to the Treasury and the administration.

the dollar in terms of gold.[14] At present, however, this seems impractical. We can hardly be confident that our affairs would be wisely enough or courageously enough administered for such money to be satisfactory. There would be constant encouragement for monetary expansion. We are in all likelihood not ready for a completely abstract monetary standard.

Primordia Revisited

Suppose we stretch our imaginations a little to see how a pure paper-standard money might have developed. On the basis of one simple, admittedly unrealistic assumption, a society might have moved directly from barter to a paper (or clay-tablet) standard.

Earlier we assumed that wheat was one of three products. One bushel of wheat is the same as the next. It can easily be divided or added to other wheat without affecting its usefulness, and it can easily be stored for considerable periods with no loss. For all these reasons it was a practical choice as money or as a monetary standard in Primordia.

But now we shall assume that the three industries of Primordia are fishing, hunting, and dairy farming. Milk, like wheat, has the desirable money quality of homogeneity. But neither milk nor fish nor meat can possibly be stored for years, nor can they circulate as a trade medium for months or even days. Each must be consumed almost immediately. None is a suitable commodity to use as money.

Suppose, however, that some Primordian philosopher eventually discovers how to facilitate trade by eliminating the necessity for barter. As a result of his recommendations the government places in circulation clay tablets, redeemable in goods.

We need not concern ourselves with the mechanics of issuing this money. Possibly the government would force the public to accept the tablets in exchange for goods and services demanded by the government, but in turn agree to receive them for payment of taxes. In any case we assume that the public realizes the convenience of the tablets and uses them as money.

The government might declare each tablet to be redeemable in stated quantities of fish, meat, or milk, at the holder's option. This would be a multiple commodity standard, not a clay-tablet standard.

We shall suppose, however, that each tablet is simply a claim, with *no quantity of any commodity specified*. If by one means or another the public is led to accept these tablets and to use them as a medium of exchange and standard of value, then a clay-tablet standard has evolved. Even though the people have no direct personal use for the tablets, they will accept them as long as they are sure others will give them meat, fish, or milk in exchange for the tablets.

---

[14]At this time it is not absolutely certain that the August, 1971, decision to terminate the convertibility of the dollar into gold for foreign central banks and governments and the decision to cease buying gold for monetary purposes will continue indefinitely.

If we assume Primordia is best satisfying its wants with a total daily production averaging 2,000 pounds of fish, 1,000 pounds of meat, and 4,000 gallons of milk, we know the relative values of the three commodities. We cannot say what their prices will be, but we do know the price of each if we know the price of any one of them. Clearly, if 1 clay tablet will buy a quart of milk, then 8 tablets will buy a pound of fish, and 16 tablets a pound of meat. If meat sells for 480 tablets a pound, milk must be selling for 30 tablets a quart.

This naturally raises the question of what will decide the value of the tablet. Will it be worth a cup, a quart, or several gallons of milk?

In this simple economy the most important determinant will be the number of tablets placed in circulation, that is, the quantity of money. It seems reasonable to suppose that the value of a tablet will be less, the more of them that are issued. An inflation of the money supply would, exactly as with a commodity-standard money, increase total demand by giving everyone more units of purchasing power. Prices would tend to rise, "other things being equal."

There are two important qualifications to the proposition that an increase in money will lead to a rise in prices:

1. *Total production of goods might also be rising.* Under this circumstance a proportionate increase in money is more likely merely to maintain the existing level of prices than to raise it. If at such a time the quantity of money is not increased, the quantity of money becomes relatively smaller in comparison with the stock of goods it is financing. Each piece of money must do more work; prices would tend to fall.
2. Even if total production does not increase, *the public's desire to hold money as a store of value might increase.* To maintain the same amount of money in daily hand-to-hand use, the authorities might find it necessary to increase the total stock of money. Otherwise, prices would tend to fall.

In short, money would not necessarily become worthless simply because it was neither defined in nor redeemable in a particular commodity such as wheat (or gold or silver). However, we cannot jump to the conclusion that we have proved the practicability of such a standard. One advantage of a money supply tied somehow to gold (or some other commodity) is that, as long as the rules are observed, the gold requirements impose limits upon permissible changes in the quantity of money. With no built-in limits, a paper-standard money would have to be controlled in some other way; for if money is issued without limit, it will definitely become worthless.

We would be evading the question entirely if we were to state that as long as it is properly managed a paper standard can maintain a stable purchasing power. What constitutes proper management of money is a complex question and the subject matter with which much of this book will be concerned.

Managed paper standards are used today in most of the world. They are a compromise between specie standards and paper standards. Like specie standards, a managed standard is usually defined in terms of gold (or silver) or in terms of another currency so defined. Until 1968, the U.S. Treasury was

ready to buy all gold (or silver) offered, and it would sell it to foreign governments, sometimes freely, sometimes under restrictions. But domestically the
country has been operating on a paper standard since 1934. Citizens presenting money for redemption can get nothing but paper from the government. Gold is not coined, since it will not be used domestically, and foreign
governments wanting gold find that gold bars are more convenient than coins
since they are easier to count. However, since 1971 the U.S. government has
recognized no obligation to redeem in gold even to foreign treasuries.

Being a hybrid, therefore, this type of standard is not easy to classify.
Classification depends upon where the emphasis is placed. The United States
was from 1934 to 1971 on the international gold-bullion standard. Now the
international monetary situation is in a state of limbo. Although it is not entirely accurate, perhaps the simplest description of our international monetary
position is that we now have a de jure gold exchange standard and a de facto
dollar standard. But with respect to domestic affairs, we are on a type of
paper standard.

The popularity of these managed paper standards that developed during
the depression of the thirties lies in the fact that they permit more flexibility in
domestic policy than does the gold standard. With the gold standard, a rise in
prices presently requires a fall in prices. The rise is generally popular. People
on fixed incomes suffer, but employment is high, business is booming, and
profits are soaring. The fall is much less pleasant. It is likely to require unemployment and depression. We never find it easy to work the price level
back down. The problem has become especially acute in the 1970s as we face
the double-edged sword of "stagflation," rising prices coupled with high unemployment.

With the managed paper standard, the fall is not necessarily inevitable.
The economy can be stabilized at the higher level of prices. The difficulty is,
as everyone knows, that nations find it easier to let prices continue to rise
than to stabilize them at any level. After prices have been allowed to rise
every year for thirty years or more, halting the rise is nearly impossible without precipitating a crisis. An important problem faced by most countries
today is whether to make a more determined effort to halt the decline in the
value of their money or whether to allow a continuous rise in prices and read-
just business practices to accord with such a money.

MONEY IN CIRCULATION IN THE UNITED STATES

The total amount of money in the U.S. economy is approximately $285
billion. There are three monetary institutions which issued this money: the
Treasury, the Federal Reserve, and commercial banks. While the Treasury is
the sole issuer of coins and issues a modest amount of paper money, "Treasury currency" represents the smallest share of the three, usually less than 3
percent of the money supply. The majority of our paper currency is in the
form of Federal Reserve notes issued by the Federal Reserve Banks. Most of
our money, however, is in the form of demand deposits issued by commercial

banks. The total figure does not count currency and deposits held by Federal Reserve Banks and the Treasury.

In Table 2-1, currency in circulation is determined by subtracting currency *held* by the Treasury and Federal Reserve Banks from total currency they have *issued*. There is no way of knowing exactly how much of this currency defined as *in circulation* is actually held by the public and how much has been destroyed or lost over the years. However, such losses would probably not exceed 2 or 3 percent of currency issued, or a fraction of a percent of total money in circulation. Also, as shown in Table 2-1, if we wish to determine how much money the general public holds, we must deduct vault cash of the banks from total money in circulation.

Table 2-1   Money in Circulation in the United States
January 31, 1975
(In millions of dollars)

Federal Reserve notes			$ 67,451
Treasury currency			
Dollars	795		
Fractional coin	7,489		
		8,284	
United States notes	322		
Other (In process of retirement)*	286		
		608	
Total Treasury currency			8,892
Total currency in circulation			76,343
Total demand deposits, adjusted**			216,100
Total money in circulation			292,443
Total money in circulation	292,443		
Less: Vault cash in banks	7,499		
Total money held by public	$284,944		

Source: Department of the Treasury, Form 1028.
*Includes silver certificates, Treasury notes of 1890, Federal Reserve Bank notes, and national bank notes, all of which the Treasury has been retiring for years.
**"Adjusted" demand deposits do not include interbank deposits nor deposits belonging to the federal government. Also, items in process of collection are subtracted to avoid double counting. While a check is being collected, the amount of the check appears as a deposit in both the collecting bank and the bank from which, in a few days, it will be collected. Finally, this figure has been adjusted for seasonality.

Federal Reserve Notes

By far the most important type of currency in the hands of the public is the Federal Reserve note, issued by and a direct liability of the Federal Reserve Banks. Federal Reserve notes amount to about 75 times as much as all our other circulating paper currency put together, and with no trouble could replace these other issues. They are paid out by the 12 Federal Reserve Banks to any member banks that need currency to meet withdrawal demands of depositors. Thus, the public really determines how many Federal Reserve notes will be in circulation.

Expansion of Note Issue. Federal Reserve notes are printed by the Comptroller of the Currency, who delivers them to the Federal Reserve Agent at each Bank.[15] The Agent is responsible for the notes until the Bank wishes to place them in circulation. The Agent then releases the notes to the Bank, receiving in return the same dollar value of gold certificates and United States government securities or occasionally other collateral.[16] The Agent has the responsibility of holding this collateral as long as the notes are out of custody. In effect, the Agent holds the collateral in trust for the Bank, which receives any income from it. However, it is specifically set aside to provide security for the note issue.

Imagine the Agent as holding the keys to two safe deposit boxes in the vaults of the Bank. One box contains a stock of Federal Reserve notes. The other contains securities pledged by the Bank against the notes the Agent releases to the Bank's circulation department. The total dollar content of the two boxes will be unchanged by note issues, for when a million dollars of notes is paid out from one box, a million dollars of securities is placed in the other. If there is a steady public demand for more notes, the security box will be filling up, but the currency box will be nearly empty. The Agent then requests more notes from the Comptroller of the Currency, which of course increases the total dollar content of the two boxes.[17]

The Federal Reserve Banks can ordinarily supply any amount of notes the public may wish to hold. By turning over to the Agent a million dollars worth of collateral, the Bank can obtain a million dollars worth of Federal Reserve notes. If it wishes, the Bank can take these notes and buy another million dollars worth of securities and turn them over to the Agent for more notes. With the additional notes, still more securities can be bought to serve as backing for still more notes, and so on.

Limitations on Note Expansion. Such a method of currency issue may appear to permit the Federal Reserve to force an unlimited amount of currency into the hands of the public. However, if the Federal Reserve Banks issued more currency than the public wished to hold, the 12 Banks would find the notes piling up in their own vaults. The Banks cannot force the public to hold the additional currency. The thousands of banks in the country would not draw out the new Federal Reserve notes; and even if, as suggested above, Federal Reserve Banks undertook to put the notes in circulation by paying out the notes to buy bonds, the public would return the redundant currency to

[15]See pp. 256, 271.
[16]In fact, Agents hold little of the Fed's gold certificates and discounted paper as collateral. The principal security today is Treasury securities.
[17]The role of the Comptroller is entirely passive. He is merely the job printer.

the banks and the member banks would then return it to the Federal Reserve Banks. The Federal Reserve would have increased its earnings through the purchase of various assets; but since the Federal Reserve does not operate for profit, the procedure would be pointless. In short, the Treasury and the Federal Reserve regulate the *size* (but not the velocity) of the money supply, but the public ultimately determines its *composition* among coins, currency, and demand deposits.

Until 1968, Federal Reserve notes had to be backed at least 25 percent by gold certificates. In other words the total note issue of the Federal Reserve Banks could not be more than four times the amount of gold certificates they held.

This limitation was one that could be changed by law if conditions should require. Until 1945 Federal Reserve notes in circulation had to be secured at least 40 percent by gold certificates. When, in 1945, in accordance with this requirement, the Federal Reserve almost reached the limit of its note issuing power, Congress reduced the gold certificate requirement to 25 percent. In 1968 it was removed entirely.

Treasury Currency

When we distinguish between Treasury currency and Federal Reserve notes (see Table 2-1), we are simply indicating the agency with the primary responsibility for the various issues. The Federal Reserve Banks are directly liable for our most important currency, which they issue; but the Treasury is ultimately liable for that currency as well as for all other currency in circulation, some of which was issued by the Treasury, some by other institutions.

Some years ago most of the Treasury's currency was paper. In 1954 the Treasury's $2.7 billion of circulating paper was 50 percent greater than its coinage in circulation. Since then, largely as a result of the Treasury's silver policy (see Chapter 3), the circulation of coins has approximately tripled, while the circulation of Treasury paper currency has been nearly eliminated. Treasury currency will become even less important in the future since the paper component will probably remain constant. However, the coinage component will likely grow with the overall economy.

Paper. Paper currency issued by the Treasury is partly in the form of certificates, partly in notes. The difference between the two is simple. The certificate is a warehouse receipt, backed 100 percent by coin or bullion. It is representative money. The note, like any promissory note, is a promise to pay.[18] It is not backed by an equal amount of coin or bullion, though against some notes a partial reserve in gold certificates was once required. The note is credit money.

---

[18]Unlike ordinary promissory notes, the notes issued by the Treasury and the Federal Reserve Banks do not bear interest because they are payable on demand, rather than after 30 days or more, and because they involve little or no credit risk.

Of Treasury paper currency actually in circulation, all except one small issue is being retired. None is serving any useful purpose.

There is a small issue of United States notes (once known as "greenbacks") in circulation. These were issued during the Civil War and as a result of political compromises have never been retired. Constituting less than 1 percent of our total paper currency, they are unnecessary and could easily be replaced by Federal Reserve notes. However, they do no harm and will probably not be retired.

Silver certificates were at one time an important Treasury currency, with more than $2 billion of them in circulation as recently as 1961. The Treasury used them for silver purchases in the same way that the Treasury uses gold certificates (described at the end of this chapter) for gold purchases. When the Treasury was buying silver, not to make into coins but principally to support the market price of silver and take silver off the market and into the vaults of the Treasury, the silver "cost" the Treasury only the expense of printing the certificates. In 1967 the Treasury began rapidly retiring them, announcing that any not presented by June 30, 1968, would not thereafter be redeemed in silver, nor would a reserve of silver continue to be held against them after that date. Today silver certificates are no longer listed separately and, like the various note issues, are now credit money unsecured by any physical asset.

All other Treasury paper has for many years been in process of retirement. Some of it will, according to the records, remain in circulation forever, for part of the paper money that the Treasury must still list as in circulation has long since been destroyed or lost and will never find its way into retirement. These various issues, although no longer necessary, were originally created to meet specific needs of the times. In 1890 the Treasury issued notes instead of silver certificates to pay for silver it was buying. The Federal Reserve Bank notes, discussed in a later chapter, were an emergency currency. Although the Federal Reserve Banks originally issued them, the Treasury has assumed responsibility for them. National bank notes, also discussed later, were once our most important paper currency but were long ago superseded by Federal Reserve notes. The Treasury has assumed the responsibility for the National bank notes also.

Coins. All coins are Treasury currency. Although once the principal money in circulation, they are a very small component of modern monetary systems. They are convenient for small transactions and necessary for pay telephones, parking meters, juke boxes, and vending machines. It would be inconvenient to write a check every time we bought a newspaper or a pack of cigarettes, and, if we used paper currency in denominations of less than a dollar, the paper would wear out very quickly from rapid turnover.

For a hundred years gold was coined in the United States, but this practice ended a generation ago. We have for the most part also discontinued the coinage of silver, at least for use as a medium of exchange. Occasionally a few commemorative part-silver coins are struck, but they quickly disappear from hand-to-hand circulation into collectors' hoards.

From 1791 until 1965 we used silver (with 10 percent copper added to harden it) for most of our fractional coins and for the silver dollar which occasionally circulated. In 1965 the Treasury began to issue "sandwich" coins, with a copper and nickel alloy facing on a copper core.[19] The nickel (75 percent copper, 25 percent nickel) and the cent (95 percent copper, 5 percent tin and zinc) were until 1966 listed as *minor* coins to distinguish them from the silver coins with a much higher intrinsic worth.[20] Today, except for silver dollars, all coins in circulation are included under the heading of *fractional coins*. The term *minor coin* loses its significance when all coins in actual use have become token money.

Since today our money is based primarily on credit rather than on the value of the commodity of which the money is made, the metal used for coins is insignificant. Stainless steel or aluminum alloys would serve as well, and some countries use these materials. We don't expect to get $20 worth of paper in a $20 bill; why should we expect to get $.25 worth of metal in a quarter?

Since the introduction of the present fractional coins, silver coins have disappeared from hand-to-hand circulation. People are hoarding them because they are worth more as silver than as money. Thus, total coin "in circulation" is at an all-time high.

In short, of the approximately $8 billion of coins issued by the Treasury, only a part are today in hand-to-hand use. The rest, including all the silver dollars and nearly all of the fractional silver coins, are in private hoards.

Demand Deposits

Demand deposits are by far the most important money in the United States. About 90 percent of the total dollar volume of payments is handled by checks, which transfer the ownership of the invisible, intangible money we call demand deposits.

There are two kinds of deposits: *demand* deposits and *time* (or *savings*) deposits. Both are simple *liabilities of banks*. In the case of demand deposits, the bank agrees to pay money on demand at any time and to whomever the owner of the deposit may wish. The owners of such deposits send written orders to the bank instructing the bank to pay specified sums to designated persons. Usually these instructions are written on high-grade noneraseable paper of convenient size, but checks may be written on anything. On one occasion a check was even written on a metal plate and signed with a blowtorch. And in 1970 industrialist William Lear paid $780,000 of income taxes with a check painted on a small turbine wheel from an engine he was developing.[21] The important point is that the bank agrees to honor a customer's demands up to the amount of deposit credit the customer has with the bank.

---

[19]Specifically, dimes, quarters, and half dollars have a layer of copper between two layers of 75 percent copper, 25 percent nickel—the same alloy long used for the five-cent coin. This so-called cupro-nickel alloy was used 2,000 years ago by the Chinese; over the last 85 years 20 countries have been using it.

[20]The composition of both minor coins was temporarily changed during World War II to free copper for other uses.

[21]Mr. Lear's highly successful business career has never been checked by failure to realize the value of publicity.

These deposits are *liabilities*, not assets, of the bank. They are not piles of coins or packages of $10 bills. They are sums the bank owes to its customers—*only figures in the bank's records*.

Because of their great convenience, particularly in making large payments and in making payments at a distance, demand deposits have become our most important type of money. The householder mails checks the first of the month to pay bills and make the payments on the home and car. The retailer and the manufacturer write much larger checks to pay creditors and workers. We could make all these payments with currency, but the payments would be awkward and expensive. Such shipments would have to be insured or sent by armed messengers. It is much simpler to write checks. Americans write over 30 billion checks a year on their more than 70 million checking accounts.[22]

If the person who receives the check carries an account with the same bank as does the writer of the check, the bank simply changes its records. It owes one person $50 more, the other $50 less. The person who has gained the deposit will presently transfer it to someone else, and so it moves along from one account to another. If more than one bank is involved, the operation is a little more complex but the principle is the same. The banking *system* owes no more and no less as a result of this writing of checks. It merely owes different individuals from day to day as we transfer among ourselves by checks the ownership of deposits owed by the banks.

A word of warning: *It is the deposits, not the checks, which are money.* Checks transfer deposits, but checks are not money.

Time Deposits

Time deposits include savings deposits of individuals as well as funds that business firms have agreed to leave on deposit for a specified minimum period of time. The owner does not have the right to withdraw them on demand, although the bank generally permits the owner that privilege for savings deposits.

Such deposits are ordinarily not counted as money, for their ownership cannot be transferred in the same way. A person with $300 in a savings account may decide to use those savings to buy a television set. But that person cannot directly pay the dealer with the savings account. He must go to the bank with the passbook and secure "money"—currency or a draft (check) on a demand deposit that the savings bank holds with a commercial bank. The individual pays for the television set with the currency or by endorsing the check of the savings bank, but not by transferring the savings account as such.

---

[22]Because demand deposits are so widely used, large-denomination currency is no longer necessary in the United States today. In 1969 the Treasury and the Federal Reserve jointly announced an immediate end to the issuance of $500, $1,000, $5,000, and $10,000 bills. (It is possible that the purpose of withdrawing the large bills may have been, at least in part, to make operations a little more difficult for tax cheaters and criminals, who often prefer to use currency rather than bank deposits which are more easily investigated.)

The savings account is referred to as "near-money." The most important examples of near-money are: (1) time deposits, (2) the cash value of insurance policies, (3) U.S. government short-term securities and bonds, and (4) other easily liquidated assets. To call such assets money, however, would obscure the distinction between money and nonmoney. If time deposits were defined as money because they can easily be turned into money, it might be argued that bonds, mortgages, stocks, and other assets should also be called money. To avoid this all-inclusiveness, money is ordinarily defined narrowly by most economists as M_1 to include coin, currency, and demand deposits, but not time or savings deposits. But some writers do include time deposits on the grounds that the dividing line between time and demand deposits is often so faint that the owner does not distinguish between them.

There are three commonly used definitions of money:

M_1 = currency and coin in circulation plus demand (checkbook) deposits

M_2 = M_1 plus time deposits (other than large certificates of deposit) at commercial banks

M_3 = M_2 plus deposits at non-commercial-bank thrift institutions, such as credit unions, mutual savings banks, and savings and loans

The historical trend from 1947 to 1974 of these definitions of money and of other components of the money stock is shown in Table 2-2. Roughly, in 1974 M_1 was about $284 billion, M_2 was $614 billion, and M_3 was $955 billion. A more recent figure for the money supply can be found in the monthly *Federal Reserve Bulletin* or the annual *Economic Report of the President* (which comes out in February). Updated figures can be estimated by adding about 5 to 6 percent per year to the latest annual figures shown in Table 2-2.

Several other points are worth noting in Table 2-2. Time and savings deposits at commercial banks or deposits at nonbank thrift institutions are each considerably larger than commercial bank demand deposits, which in turn are more than three times as large as the currency component of the money supply. Table 2-2 also points out the dramatic growth in large certificates of deposit (CDs). CDs are merely time deposits with a specified date of maturity, such as one or two years from the date of deposit. Most of these are nonnegotiable and are held by households. Large CDs ($100,000 or more) are negotiable and are held mostly by business firms. Time deposits have grown exuberantly since the 1960s due largely to the introduction of negotiable CDs in 1961.

OTHER MONEY

Since we defined currency in circulation as currency issued by but not currently held by the Federal Reserve Banks or the Treasury, it follows that the total money stock of the United States includes more than just the money in circulation. The noncirculating part of the total money stock is composed mostly of *till* money, gold and silver bullion, and gold certificates.

Table 2-2   Money Stock Measures, 1947–1974
(Averages of daily figures; billions of dollars, seasonally adjusted)

Dec. 19--	Overall measures			Components and related items						
	M_1	M_2	M_3	Currency[1]	Deposits at commercial banks				Deposits at nonbank thrift institutions[5]	U.S. government demand deposits (unadjusted)[6]
					Demand[2]	Time and savings[3]				
						Total	Large CDs[4]	Other		
47	113.1			26.4	86.7	35.4				1.0
48	111.5			25.8	85.8	36.0				1.8
49	111.2			25.1	86.0	36.4				2.8
50	116.2			25.0	91.2	36.7				2.4
51	122.7			26.1	96.5	38.2				2.7
52	127.4			27.3	100.1	41.1				4.9
53	128.8			27.7	101.1	44.5				3.8
54	132.3			27.4	104.9	48.3				5.0
55	135.2			27.8	107.4	50.0				3.4
56	136.9			28.2	108.7	51.9				3.4
57	135.9			28.3	107.6	57.4				3.5
58	141.1			28.6	112.6	65.4				3.9
59	143.4	210.9	299.4	28.9	114.5	67.4		67.4	88.5	4.9
60	144.2	217.1	314.4	29.0	115.2	72.9		72.9	97.3	4.7
61	148.7	228.6	336.5	29.6	119.1	82.7	2.8	79.9	107.9	4.9
62	150.9	242.8	362.9	30.6	120.3	97.6	5.7	92.0	120.1	5.6
63	156.5	258.9	393.2	32.5	124.1	112.0	9.6	102.3	134.4	5.1
64	163.7	277.1	426.3	34.3	129.5	126.2	12.8	113.4	149.2	5.5
65	171.3	301.3	462.6	36.3	134.9	146.3	16.2	130.1	161.3	4.6
66	175.4	317.8	485.2	38.3	137.0	157.9	15.4	142.5	167.4	3.4
67	186.9	349.6	532.6	40.4	146.5	183.1	20.5	162.7	183.0	5.0
68	201.7	382.3	576.8	43.4	158.2	204.1	23.5	180.6	194.5	5.0
69	208.7	392.2	593.5	46.1	162.7	194.5	11.0	183.5	201.3	5.6
70	221.4	425.3	642.8	49.1	172.3	229.3	25.4	203.9	217.5	7.3
71	235.3	473.1	727.9	52.6	182.7	271.2	33.5	237.7	254.9	6.9
72	255.8	525.7	823.2	56.9	198.9	313.8	43.9	269.9	297.5	7.4
73	271.5	572.2	895.3	61.6	209.9	364.5	63.8	300.7	323.1	6.3
74	284.3	614.3	955.0	67.7	216.6	420.3	90.3	330.0	340.7	4.8

Source: *Economic Report of the President* (Washington: U.S. Government Printing Office, 1975), Table C-52, p. 310, and *Federal Reserve Bulletin* (March, 1975), p. A14.

M_1 = Currency plus demand deposits.

M_2 = M_1 plus time deposits other than large CDs at commercial banks.

M_3 = M_2 plus deposits at nonbank thrift institutions.

Note: The figures given in this table may not agree exactly with those given in Table 2-1 because the sampling was taken at a different date.
[1]Currency outside the Treasury, the Federal Reserve Banks, and the vaults of all commercial banks.
[2]Demand deposits other than those due to domestic commercial banks and the U.S. government, less cash items in process of collection and Federal Reserve float, plus foreign demand balances at Federal Reserve Banks.
[3]Time and savings deposits other than those due to domestic commercial banks and the U.S. government. Effective June, 1966, excludes balances accumulated for payment of personal loans (about $1.1 billion).
[4]Negotiable time certificates of deposit issued in denominations of $100,000 or more by large weekly reporting commercial banks.
[5]Average of the beginning- and end-of-month deposits of mutual savings banks and savings capital at savings and loan associations.
[6]Deposits at all commercial banks.

The Treasury and the Federal Reserve Banks need to keep some currency on hand as *till* money to pay out when it is demanded. They ordinarily hold between them $2 or $3 billion of the currencies previously discussed. Most of this, naturally, is in Federal Reserve notes.

The Treasury defines its stock of money to include the value of the gold and silver bullion in its vaults. From time to time the Treasury may sell silver and gold for industrial use, but, when the metals pass from the Treasury to the public, they are no longer defined as money. Obviously, if the Treasury sells metal to either foreign treasuries or central banks, the currency in circulation in this country does not increase no matter what the monetary consequences may be abroad.

The public no longer has the right to hold gold certificates, although since December, 1974, they may hold gold. A few million gold certificates, lost or destroyed over the years, are technically "in circulation" but are no longer officially listed. Of the $11.6 billion of gold certificates outstanding in January, 1975, practically all were in the vaults of the United States Treasury. The Treasury uses these certificates to purchase gold. When the Treasury writes a check on a Federal Reserve Bank to pay for gold, the Treasury may then print the same amount of gold certificates and either deposit them with the Bank or, leaving the certificates in its own vaults, earmark them as belonging to the Bank. Thus, the gold costs the Treasury nothing other than the expense of printing a few bills.[23]

Besides their convenience for gold purchases, the gold certificates were important in the past because they were the legal reserve held against most of our paper currency and also, ultimately, against deposits. Today they have no direct relationship to either currency or deposits.

SUMMARY AND CONCLUSION

Money, in the broadest sense, has been used for more than 3,000 years. Early civilizations discovered independently the convenience of using some widely desired commodity as a medium of exchange and standard of value, rather than depending on barter.

Paper money was eventually introduced, first as representative money, later as credit money. Against every dollar of representative money there is a dollar of reserves. Against every dollar of credit money there are only fractional reserves, or, perhaps, no reserves at all.

In this country credit money, particularly demand deposits, has replaced both commodity money and representative money. Demand deposits are an invisible, intangible, and completely abstract form of money.

Ultimately, public preference determines how the money supply will be apportioned among its three components—coins, currency, and bank deposits—and its rate of turnover, or "velocity," although the Federal Reserve and the Treasury determine its size.

---

[23]Today the Treasury seldom incurs even this minor expense. Since the gold certificates will not circulate anyway, there is no reason for printing them. Instead the Treasury simply credits the gold certificate account of the Federal Reserve. In effect, it is promising the Federal Reserve Banks that, if and when the Treasury does print these certificates, they will belong to the Federal Reserve Banks.

Discussion Questions

1. Is it easier or more difficult today than it was a thousand years ago to increase a nation's stock of money? Explain.
2. What are the advantages of a money supply which can be increased?
3. What, if any, standard money are you likely to hold today?
4. Has standard money ever, in recent years, been worth less than other money? Briefly discuss.
5. Suppose that the U.S. Treasury's price for gold is $35, the German Treasury is paying DM140, and the French Treasury is paying Fr175.
   a. What is the mint par in New York of the deutsche mark and the franc?
   b. Suppose that the U.S. raises its price of gold to $70 an ounce. What direct effect, if any, will this have on gold movements, assuming the German and French prices for gold remain unchanged? (Do not consider possible repercussions from changes in foreign trade, speculations, etc.)
6. When, as in the 19th and early 20th centuries, the mint par of the pound sterling was approximately $4.87, explain the action you could profitably have taken if the price of the pound rose to $4.92 or $4.93.
7. "What goes up must come down." Does the type of monetary standard have any bearing on the validity of this familiar phrase?
8. Explain briefly how gold exchange standards may be helpful in avoiding worldwide depressions.
9. Explain how an increase in a nation's gold reserves may result from:
   a. A lowered standard of living or lowered growth rate.
   b. Neither of the above.
10. An occasional reformer takes the position that we would be better off if we would return to gold and do away with all other types of money. What practical objections would there be to following such a prescription literally?
11. What is Gresham's Law?
12. Suppose that a century or so ago a government found that some of its coins were constantly disappearing from circulation. The government decides to supplement its coins with credit money. What do you think would be the probable result:
    a. On full-weight coins?
    b. On worn, light-weight coins?
13. In the Primordia example, how might clay tablets have been issued on the basis of a milk standard? On the basis of a multiple standard? As purely credit money?
14. Since many people may be hoarding money, how can the authorities possibly know the amount of each kind of currency in circulation?
15. Now that the gold reserve requirement against Federal Reserve notes has been eliminated, what checks are there, if any, to prevent an excessive issue of Federal Reserve notes?
16. Who directly determines the amount of currency to be held by the public? Briefly explain.
17. Is any of our money today not legal tender? Why or why not?
18. Briefly describe the three most commonly used definitions of money.
19. Discuss the relative merits and the relative size of the three most commonly used measures of the money stock.
20. What has accounted for the dramatic growth in time and savings deposits since 1961?

Chapter 3   Currency Evolution and Monetary Legislation

Ordinarily we can take for granted our smoothly functioning currency system. Once in a while, however, some change may be necessary. We discontinued the coinage of gold in 1934 after prohibiting Americans from holding gold for monetary (or nonindustrial) purposes. In the mid-sixties, we discontinued the silver coinage we had been using for more than a hundred years. More recently, in 1971 the Nixon administration ended convertibility of the dollar into gold even for foreign central banks.

Generally our coins have been freely interchangeable for more than a century. More importantly, our paper currency also has become uniform. Five dollars of any kind of coins (other than collectors' items) or paper currency will buy the same amount as will $5 of any other kind. There is an ample supply of currency which can be smoothly expanded or contracted to meet public demands. When more coins or more paper money are required, this money quickly flows out of the Treasury and the banking system.

A satisfactory currency does not just happen. It evolves. For generations we stumbled along with a totally inadequate currency. Little by little we patched it here, trimmed it there, and stretched it someplace else. We made many mistakes as we went along. But as we began to better understand the nature of money and the basic problems involved with money, we did gradually develop a satisfactory currency. Because our currency resulted from an evolutionary process, it does contain some unnecessary components, litter accumulated over the years. Because it has resulted from political as well as economic forces, our currency falls far short of the theoretical ideal. But it does meet our requirements reasonably well. It is a vast improvement over our first fumbling monetary experiments.

A SHORT HISTORY OF OUR CURRENCY BEFORE 1930

A clutter of foreign coins, domestic coins, and paper money, the latter often of little value, constituted our money supply in the period just before the Revolution. Earlier the settlers had relied heavily on barter and had various commodities as money. The continental currency issued to pay for the Revolutionary War resulted in inflation which amounted to an arbitrary and hidden tax. The experience with monetary overissue during the Revolution was not to be the last for this country. The United States continued to experience coinage and currency difficulties from 1791 to 1860.

The bimetallic standard legally in effect in the United States during our early history, in which both gold and silver were freely coined, was actually a silver standard at first. No gold circulated. When the price of gold was raised in 1834, silver disappeared and we were on a de facto gold standard. To provide fractional coins and prevent their being melted for their silver content, Congress made fractional silver subsidiary, rather than standard, coinage. Fractional silver coins were no longer freely coined, and they contained less silver than before. But they held their value because they were redeemable in standard money. Since their money value was greater than their bullion value, they remained in circulation. Finally, for the first time in our history we had a satisfactory coinage system and, after three quarters of a century of national existence, we could at least escape the necessity of declaring foreign coins to be legal tender.

During the War of 1812, the Treasury issued notes that were almost the same as paper money. Later, during the Civil War, the Treasury paid a large part of its bills by issuing United States notes, called greenbacks. A few of them were retired later, but most are still circulating, an unnecessary but harmless vestigial remnant.

Since the market price for silver had long been above the $1.2929 at which the Treasury stood ready to buy silver freely for coinage into dollars, Congress voted in 1873 to discontinue free coinage of the silver dollar. A great decline in the international price of silver occurred soon afterward, and strong political pressure developed for a return to free silver. The result was the economically pointless purchase of a great quantity of silver by the Treasury in the 1890s.

The silver tide was running out, however, at least temporarily. After drawing closer and closer to a de jure gold standard, the United States finally officially adopted the gold standard in 1900. Nothing more was heard of silver for a generation, except for the silver sold by the United States during World War I and later repurchased from domestic mines at an artificially high price. Apparently we had by then solved our currency problem and settled the question of our monetary standard.

MONETARY ADJUSTMENTS

The currency system we developed more than a century ago handled routine requirements quite adequately. With the adoption of the gold standard, de facto, in 1834 and the adoption of subsidiary silver coinage in 1853, the United States was generally assured of a sufficient and uniform coinage. During the Civil War, coins disappeared; but in normal times the supply of coins expanded and contracted to meet the public demand. One might easily have concluded in 1900, when the gold standard was finally written into the statutes, that few changes would be required in the future. By 1934 United States coinage laws had not changed significantly in 80 years.

Then abruptly began a series of changes that were to extend over several decades. The difference between the coinage legislation of the 20th century and that of the 19th was profound and basic.

Changes in our coinage laws in the 19th century were adjustments. They took for granted that the money value of coins should be equal either to their intrinsic value or to the intrinsic value of other coins in which the government would at any time redeem them. These adjustments were refinements to a basically unchanged institution.

Changes of the 19th century might be compared to improvements in carburetors and ignition systems, whereas 20th century revisions compared more to the replacement of the internal combustion engine with a turbine (or, perhaps, something less predictable). Twentieth century changes evidenced a completely different philosophy of the role of coins.

We began to think of coins as being tokens, partly because credit money gained importance so rapidly, partly because by 1900 gold coins seldom circulated, and partly because for many years the silver content of our coins was far below their monetary value. Coins are valuable for much the same reason poker chips are valuable. Every player will accept them. They are more durable and more convenient than fractional denomination paper currency. Their intrinsic value is really no more important than the intrinsic value of paper currency.

In a little over forty years we scrapped our gold coins; scrapped our silver coins; reneged on the government's written promise to pay its obligations in gold; prohibited the holding of gold coins or gold bullion; bought thousands of tons of gold and silver and sold most of it; expanded Treasury paper currency in circulation and retired most of it; held a floor under silver prices; held a ceiling over silver prices; issued $2 billion of fractional silver and placed in circulation nearly half a billion silver dollars, most of which went into hoarding; thrice raised the price of gold; raised the Treasury's selling price for silver; lowered the gold certificate requirement against Federal Reserve notes and deposits in the Federal Reserve Banks, and finally removed it altogether; discontinued buying and selling gold freely except in transactions with foreign treasuries; halted gold sales entirely; allowed gold sales in special circumstances; and finally allowed individual purchasing and holding of gold once again as of December, 1974. Quite a busy 41 years!

Some of these developments would perhaps have occurred eventually in any case. They were encouraged by the dislocations of the depression of the 1930s. Not only in the United States but in most industrialized nations the gold standard of the 19th and early 20th centuries disappeared almost overnight. By 1914 most statesmen, economists, and bankers agreed that the gold standard was the best standard, at least for a nation with a highly developed banking system. Although World War I forced Europe temporarily to abandon gold, there was almost universal agreement that all nations should return to gold as quickly as possible, and most did so in the early 1920s. By contrast, there has been little general enthusiasm for a readoption of the free gold standard since it was set aside in the depression of the 1930s.

Even before the depression of the 1930s the gold standard was failing to operate according to its own logic. Apart from the matter of tariffs and banking controls mentioned on page 40, there was the troublesome question of short-term capital movement. The gold standard theory assumed that as gold moved into a country, the price level rose, an unfavorable balance of trade eventually ensued, and the gold flowed out again. But in the late 1920s, as gold flowed into the United States, business profits increased.[1] This increase in corporate earnings led to higher prices in the stock market. The rising stock prices in turn encouraged foreigners to invest in the hope that the bull market would continue. Their purchases not only drove stock prices still higher, but also added more fuel to the fire by causing still more gold to flow into the country. Thus, as far as the stock market was concerned, the gold standard acted perversely. As prices rose, more gold flowed in rather than out.

Other difficulties may appear with these short-term capital movements. Normally a central bank may expect to attract gold by raising the interest rate level and to encourage gold exports by forcing interest rates below the level prevailing in other countries. This policy had been traditional with the Bank of England, which usually found foreign investors very sensitive to interest rate changes. As one of their spokesmen once put it, "We can almost pull gold out of the ground with the discount rate." Unfortunately, the central bank may find, as did the Federal Reserve in 1929, that low interest rates during a stock market boom result in more funds being borrowed for speculation. These borrowed funds, spent for stocks, drive stock prices higher. More gold comes in as foreign investors become more interested than ever in the roaring bull market. The low interest rate has backfired.

There is a further, more fundamental difficulty. Even if short-term capital movements do respond properly to interest rate changes, domestic requirements will often prevent an interest rate level that would encourage the desirable capital movements. In inflation, a high interest rate level would restrain consumption and investment. Unfortunately the high rate would tend also to attract short-term capital, resulting in an undesired gold inflow. In depression, low interest rates encourage investment and consumption, but they cause gold losses as short-term capital moves abroad to receive a higher return.

The appropriate interest rate policy would be easy to formulate if we could ignore the effect of interest rates on either short-term capital movements or domestic spending. When both issues must be considered, and one frequently requires low rates at the same time the other requires high rates, the decision of the monetary authorities is a difficult one.

In the face of such problems, the corrective influences of gold movements may operate, not gradually, but suddenly, after considerable delay. They might be compared to stopping a car by running it into a telephone pole.

BANKING DIFFICULTIES, 1929–1933

The stock market crash in the fall of 1929 ushered in one of the most prolonged and severe depressions in our history. Prices fell, business failures

---

[1]Although wholesale prices were remarkably constant during the 1920s, leading most observers at the time to conclude that credit was not over expanded, costs were being gradually reduced. There was a profits inflation rather than a price inflation.

greatly increased, and unemployment rose to disastrous levels. (Almost one fourth of the labor force was idle in 1933.)

For two reasons the banking system was under heavy pressure. First, bank losses increased because many borrowers were unable to repay their loans. If the borrower goes broke and the loan must be written off as uncollectible, the bank's assets are reduced. If losses are heavy, the bank's assets may become less than its liabilities, and the bank, like its defaulting customers, is insolvent. In the 1920s, bank failures averaged about 500 a year (5,067 failures from 1921 to 1929), but the average during the years 1930 to 1933 was about 2,000 a year (7,763 failures from 1930 to 1933). In contrast, from 1946 to 1970 only 252 banks failed. The major reason for the outstanding record since 1933 was the establishment in 1933 of a most successful government agency, the Federal Deposit Insurance Corporation.

The second pressure on the banking system occurred when many depositors became frightened that their banks might fail, so they went to the banks to withdraw their deposits in cash. Under our system of fractional reserve banking, the banks never hold enough cash to pay off all their depositors at once. Only a small part of their assets is in the form of cash. Most bank assets are in the form of loans and investments, temporarily unavailable for depositors. At that time the banks did not have adequate means of securing much additional currency. Regardless of what might be true for the banking system as a whole, the banks found, as individual firms, that their survival depended upon their achieving as liquid a position as possible. They made few loans; they extended few loans; and wherever possible they called loans. Their desire to have fewer loans outstanding was naturally sharpened by their fear that, with business rapidly worsening, borrowers would be unable to repay. But even if banks had been confident that they would eventually receive payment, they wanted to cut their loans to the bone.[2] The more liquid their assets, the greater the chance that they might be able to satisfy their depositors' calls for cash. This curtailment of credit resulted in still more failures for businesspeople unable to pay off their debts. The business failures caused still more losses for the banks.

The banking system in the United States staggered along under this load for two years. Even though 800 banks failed in the three months ending in January, 1931, the real crisis was still two years away. During these first years of the Depression there was not the unreasoning panic that appeared later.

The Flight from Gold

The international situation deteriorated rapidly in the summer of 1931. During the preceding year a number of countries had left the gold standard, but they were countries producing raw materials, so their actions had few

---

[2]The interrelationship between loans, deposits, and reserves cannot be spelled out at this point. For the moment we shall have to say generally that the fewer loans (and investments) a bank is holding, the greater the proportion of its money and near-money items to its deposits, hence the more liquid the bank.

repercussions elsewhere. Gold still backed the currencies of the world's leading industrial nations.

In 1931 both Germany and England went off the gold standard. A number of countries immediately followed. Short-term capital withdrawals pressured New York, for investors feared that the United States might be the next to abandon gold. Within six weeks the United States lost $725 million in gold to these foreign depositors. The twofold pressure upon the banks (mentioned above) intensified since money had become tight, and an epidemic of bank failures swept the nation. Between June, 1931, and the following February, 2,241 banks failed in the United States; and as the number of failures climbed, public alarm mounted.

Panic

Some attempts were made in 1932 to rescue the banks. The Reconstruction Finance Corporation was organized to lend to banks and other financial institutions in need of assistance. The Glass-Steagall Act permitted the use of government bonds as collateral against Federal Reserve notes and, under the circumstances prevailing at the time, increased the amount of "free" gold at the disposal of the Federal Reserve. But even though in many parts of the world and in many lines of industry in this country the bottom appeared to have been reached in the summer of 1932, the banking crisis did not come until that winter and the following spring. The fact that it was an election year may have had something to do with it. No one knew what the policies of the new administration would be, and President-elect Roosevelt showed little interest between November and March either in cooperating with President Hoover or in revealing his own plans. Rumors of inflation spread. People exchanged deposits for currency to be hoarded and shifted deposits from weak banks to stronger ones.

Bank Holidays

Finally the bank holidays began. In October, 1932, the governor of Nevada declared a two-week bank holiday. This holiday gave Nevada banks the chance to close their doors temporarily. It protected them from their creditors (depositors) demanding payment, and gave them a breathing space to increase their liquidity.

The first bank holiday attracted little attention. A few desert banks would be closed for a couple of weeks. But the holiday was extended. Elsewhere, a number of cities declared bank holidays. Before long, bank holidays were spreading like wildfire.

In February, 1933, a run developed on two of Detroit's major banks. The governor of Michigan declared a bank holiday, tying up nearly $1,500 million. Many people were caught unprepared, with almost no cash in their pockets. Western Union did a land-office business in money orders as people frantically wired to friends and relatives for currency.

The governors of Louisiana and Maryland also declared bank holidays in February. Alarm became panic. Pressure on banks still open for business intensified. Bank runs became more frequent. The public, which until this point had been content to receive paper currency in exchange for its deposits, now demanded gold. The gold stock of the Federal Reserve Banks fell so low that on the afternoon of March 3 the Board for the first time suspended the requirement that a 40 percent gold reserve be held against their notes.

The knowledge that even the mighty Federal Reserve Banks were vulnerable, unable to maintain their normally required liquidity, hardly restored public confidence in the commercial banks. To prevent the bank runs that would inevitably follow this latest development, the governors of most of the other states fell into line and declared bank holidays. In a few states the banks were allowed to operate, but depositors were not allowed to withdraw more than 5 percent of their accounts. As Franklin D. Roosevelt rode down Pennsylvania Avenue to his inauguration, almost every bank in the nation was closed or operating under restrictions. It was a dramatic beginning for the new administration and a tragic ending for the old.

Banking at a Standstill

Sunday, March 5, officials of the Federal Reserve Banks and leading commercial banks conferred feverishly in Washington to avoid complete collapse of the banking system. Monday morning President Roosevelt proclaimed a four-day national bank holiday, to last until Friday, March 10. It was all too evident that the banking system could not possibly survive the panic at its present height. During a financial panic, when few are bringing currency into banks and almost everyone is attempting to withdraw it, the banks soon run out of cash unless—as was not then the case—the banks have unlimited credit resources at the central bank and the central bank has unlimited power to create more paper money. The four-day national bank holiday provided a breathing period and allowed Roosevelt to call an emergency session of Congress to pass legislation dealing with the crisis. During this period the banks were forbidden to pay out any more gold.

EMERGENCY BANKING ACT

March 9, Congress met and in a few hours passed the *Emergency Banking Act*. For a number of months thereafter—during the so-called "honeymoon"—the President told Congress what he wanted and Congress passed the requisite legislation. At this time the country needed above all strong leadership to restore public confidence, and Congress was glad to give the President any powers and any legislation that he requested. The Emergency Banking Act confirmed the action already taken by the President and gave him sweeping powers to control banking, currency, and foreign exchange.

To prevent the reopening of weak banks and to help restore public confidence in the banks, Roosevelt extended the bank holiday indefinitely but provided that banks might again resume operations after the regulating authorities had inspected them individually and found them to be sound. In this way the public was to be reassured, since a bank would be open only because it had been certified to be sound. The banks were again forbidden to pay out gold.

Preferred Stock

The banks were encouraged to strengthen their financial position by raising additional capital. In view of the appalling record of bank failures during the past year, one could not expect anyone in his right mind to subscribe to bank stocks. Accordingly the federal Reconstruction Finance Corporation was authorized to purchase stock in the national banks. Until this time banks ordinarily issued only common stock. On this occasion they issued preferred stock, for the RFC required greater security than the banks' common stock represented, particularly at that time. The sale of the additional stock gave the banks the opportunity to increase their cushion of capital to better protect depositors.

Federal Reserve Bank Notes Authorized

To make sure that the banks could secure plenty of currency if, when they reopened, the public did continue to withdraw deposits, the Federal Reserve Banks were authorized to issue Federal Reserve Bank notes. Since no gold reserve was required for this currency (unlike the Federal Reserve notes at that time), the Federal Reserve could issue any amount demanded. These notes were secured either by government obligations or by commercial paper at 90 percent of its face value. The Federal Reserve could never "run out" of Federal Reserve Bank notes, for by buying more government securities it would have the necessary collateral for still more Federal Reserve Bank notes. As the situation actually developed, this provision was unnecessary, for the worst of the bank panic was over.

Further Restrictions on Gold

On March 10, the Secretary of the Treasury announced that no gold or gold certificates could be exported without a Treasury license. This announcement, like the preceding actions, was considered to be an emergency measure. Most people felt and most monetary authorities recommended that we should before long return to the automatic gold standard. Hoarding gold certificates and gold coin and bullion was prohibited on April 5, and all holders of gold or gold certificates were required to surrender such money and receive other forms of money in exchange.[3] In spite of this development, the general

---

[3]Exceptions: rare coins; gold earmarked for foreign accounts; and gold licensed for industrial, professional, or artistic use, or for other justifiable purposes.

belief still was that as soon as conditions permitted we should return to our former standard. The President gave no indication that sweeping and permanent changes were in prospect; government spokesmen specifically emphasized that we were not leaving the gold standard.

Toward the end of April, $1.25 billion of currency had been redeposited in the banks and gold reserves were mounting to the highest level since the fall of 1931. As a creditor nation we could normally expect to receive gold from the rest of the world, and the balance of trade was in our favor. The banking crisis had been overcome and confidence in the banks had largely returned. Therefore when, beginning April 20, the Treasury suddenly adopted an extremely restrictive policy regarding licenses for gold export, far-reaching changes in our money for the first time appeared imminent.

DOWNFALL OF THE GOLD-COIN STANDARD

The combination of political and economic pressures of the Depression quickly crumbled the foundations of the gold-coin standard. The monetary standard that, unofficially at least, we had been using for a century was swept away almost overnight by a series of legislation.

Thomas Inflation Act

The passage of the Thomas Amendment to the Agricultural Adjustment Act on May 12, 1933, clearly indicated that a structural change in our monetary system was taking place. This bill made all United States coins and paper currency full legal tender. Until this change, gold and gold certificates had been the principal legal tender.[4] In addition the Thomas Amendment gave the President sweeping discretionary powers. These included the power to restore bimetallism, the power to reduce the gold content of the dollar, and the power to issue up to $3 billion of greenbacks. None of these powers were exercised. (Devaluation was the result of later legislation.) Under the provisions of the Thomas Inflation Act, the Treasury received a little silver in payment on war debts. Otherwise the Act was significant principally as it foreshadowed events to come.

Repeal of the Gold Clause

The next important monetary legislation was the repeal of the gold clause in contracts, June 5, 1933. A great many bonds and other evidences of debt, both public and private, called for payment in gold dollars containing 25.8 grains of gold, 9/10 fine. Such clauses reflected our unsatisfactory experiences with paper money such as the continental currency or the greenbacks of the Civil War period. These clauses were included to protect creditors who might

---

[4]Specifically, until 1933 Federal Reserve notes, national bank notes, and silver certificates were not legal tender in settlement of private debts. Checks have never been legal tender.

be repaid at a time when the country was on a depreciated paper standard and, if paid in paper, would receive less than the value of what they had lent.[5] Note especially that even if paper money were declared legal tender, it could not lawfully be forced upon a creditor whose contract specifically provided that payment be made in gold.

Congress now declared that such contracts were against public policy, and that all such obligations were to be discharged by the same number of dollars of any legal tender. Three weeks earlier all forms of United States currency had been made legal tender. A number of cases challenging the constitutionality of this legislation were carried to the Supreme Court without any notable success.

Devaluation

The rapid succession of legislation in the spring of 1933, including many acts not relating directly to money and banking, caused a strong belief that inflation might be imminent. Prices moved up rapidly as the pace of buying increased. The recovery was short-lived, however, and by midsummer prices were falling. The administration repeatedly had promised to raise prices and restore prosperity, if not by one means then by another. In October, Roosevelt went further, stating that the administration intended, after restoring the price level,[6] to establish a dollar that would maintain a constant value for a generation.[7]

The same month, President Roosevelt directed the Reconstruction Finance Corporation to buy gold at prices determined from day to day by the Secretary of the Treasury. For ten days this policy was restricted to newly mined domestic gold, but on November 3, 1933, the RFC began to purchase gold abroad. Until 1933, our mint price for gold had for a century been $20.67 an ounce. The RFC began buying at $31.36. The Secretary of the Treasury gradually raised the price, and by January 31 the RFC was paying $34.45.

These gold purchases had been strongly urged upon the administration by the expert on agricultural economics, Professor George Warren.[8] Warren based his diagnosis on a rigid commodity theory of the value of money. Other writers also noted the relative scarcity of gold that resulted from the decline in world gold production after 1915 and the increase in the production of most other goods and services. A number of these writers also felt that some increase in the value of gold (that is, fall in prices of other goods) was a likely consequence. No other responsible economist, however, emphasized this particular factor as heavily and as exclusively as did Warren and his coworker, Professor Frank A. Pearson.[9]

---

[5]For example, anyone who lent money several years ago and is repaid today.
[6]There never was any specific announcement as to just what price level was to be restored.
[7]This was considerably less ambitious than Hitler's proposal to establish the Third Reich for a thousand years, but equally unsuccessful.
[8]George F. Warren and Frank A. Pearson, *Prices* (New York: John Wiley & Sons, 1933). See especially pp. 392–393.
[9]George F. Warren and Frank A. Pearson, *Gold and Prices* (New York: John Wiley & Sons, 1935). See especially p. 107.

They asserted that by varying the price of gold—that is, by varying the gold content of the dollar—the government could immediately raise prices to any level it wished and maintain them there. The appeal of such claims was naturally irresistible at a time when, despite all that either the Republicans or the Democrats had been able to do, prices had for four years been falling almost without interruption. Many orthodox advisors, including bankers and most economists, assured Roosevelt that Warren's theories were erroneous; that the price level could not be changed merely by changing the price of gold, and that the policy should not be undertaken. But they could offer no magic formula to raise prices, and Warren insisted that his plan would work.

It is true that if a country devalues its currency, it will find its exports stimulated and its imports reduced by the change in foreign exchange rates resulting from the devaluation.[10] This, said Warren, was only the beginning. He claimed that domestic as well as international prices would all be affected overnight.[11]

His arguments were not supported by the subsequent course of events. As early as December, 1933, the price of newly purchased gold had been raised to more than $34, which amounted to a de facto devaluation of almost 40 percent. The index of wholesale prices compiled by the United States Bureau of Labor over this period was as follows:

1933	September	70.8
	October	71.2
	November	71.1
	December	70.8
1934	January	72.2

Prices of some of our exports tended to strengthen, but mostly the cheaper dollar did not so much increase the dollar price of items sold to foreigners as increase the physical amount of such sales made at the former prices. It was erroneous to suppose that prices even of exports would, without exception, advance proportionately as the dollar was depreciated.[12]

Although gold purchases at rising prices had made the dollar worth less in terms of foreign currency, there had been no formal devaluation. The dollar continued to be defined as 25.8 grains of gold, 9/10 fine, as it had been for a century. If gold were being coined, $20.67 could be minted from an ounce of pure gold (.9 × 25.8 grains = 23.22 grains; 480/23.22 = $20.67). Since the RFC was paying more than $34 an ounce by January, devaluation was in effect even though it had not been formally adopted.

The Gold Reserve Act

The Gold Reserve Act, enacted January 30, 1934, provided the final machinery for devaluation. Previously the Thomas Amendment had given the

---

[10]Assuming that other countries do not devalue also.
[11]George F. Warren and Frank A. Pearson, *Gold and Prices* (New York: John Wiley & Sons, 1935). See especially pp. 194–195.
[12]See also Chapters 14 and 27.

President discretionary power to devalue. The Gold Reserve Act removed the discretionary element and required that the President fix a new weight for the dollar which should be between 50 and 60 percent of the current weight. (That is, the dollar was to be devalued by not more than 50 percent and not less than 40 percent.) The President the next day proclaimed the new weight of the gold dollar to be 15 5/21 grains, 9/10 fine. This was 59.06 percent of its former weight and established a mint price of $35 an ounce.

There were a number of other provisions in the Act:

1. When the gold stock was revalued, a profit would result, since each ounce of gold would now be worth more dollars than before. Congress wanted to be sure that this profit accrued to the credit of the government rather than to the advantage of private individuals and organizations. For almost a year citizens had been forbidden to hold gold, but the Federal Reserve Banks held great quantities as reserves against notes and deposits as required by law at that time. The Act provided that all gold held by the Federal Reserve be transferred to the Treasury and gold certificates be given in exchange. Henceforth, the Federal Reserve would hold gold certificates rather than gold as legal reserves.
2. Since gold certificates could not be paid out into general circulation, Federal Reserve notes, previously redeemable in gold or gold certificates, were henceforth to be redeemable in "lawful money," which now included all money except gold and gold certificates.
3. Gold coinage was prohibited and existing gold coin was to be melted into bars.
4. A stabilization fund of $2 billion was to be set up out of the profits from the devaluation. The Treasury would use this fund to stabilize fluctuations in foreign exchange rates.[13]

We operated under this form of gold standard for a little over 30 years. The Treasury freely bought gold, that is, bought all gold it was offered, at $35 an ounce. It sold gold freely at $35 an ounce to foreign treasuries and central banks. Gold was the ultimate (and fractional) reserve against our deposits and all our paper currency except silver certificates. This provision set an upper limit to the total stock of money. American citizens could not demand that their money be redeemed in gold, as they had been able to do before 1933, for the nation was now on a domestic paper standard. Internationally it was on a gold bullion standard.

Before the dollar was devalued, the Treasury held $4 billion in gold. Devaluation, by simultaneously raising the price of gold and reducing the weight of gold in the dollar, automatically revalued the Treasury's gold at nearly $7 billion, a sum hitherto unprecedented.

Gold Movements since 1934

For a number of years following the adoption of the new standard and the higher price for gold, gold flowed in a torrent to the United States. For seven

---

[13]After World War II, most of the fund was diverted to the International Monetary Fund. See Chapter 27.

years we received gold at an average rate of more than $2 billion a year, to bring our stock to more than $23 billion by 1941. This was about 80 percent of the total known monetary stock of the entire world. (No reliable statistics are available respecting Russian gold holdings.) At the rate gold was coming to this country, with apparently nothing to turn the tide, it appeared possible that in three or four years more we might find ourselves in the curious position of being the sole owners of the world's gold. Some writers were deeply disturbed by the prospect that other nations, after exchanging thousands of tons of their gold for our more useful goods and services, would then declare they had no further use for gold and allow us the doubtful privilege of storing it and guarding it forever—a modern dragon with his Rhine-gold.

These forebodings may not have been entirely groundless, but they were not realized. During World War II we lost about 15 percent of our gold, but regained it by 1947. By 1949 our holdings reached their all time peak, in excess of $24 billion. There were substantial losses in 1950 and again in 1953, but since the losses in other years were small and in some years gold was again flowing into the country, we were still holding nearly $23 billion of gold by 1957. But beginning in 1958 a rapid and sustained decline set in. Our persistent international deficits and foreign bankers' mounting distrust of the dollar led to a loss of $8 billion of gold in seven years. By February, 1965, the Treasury held only $15 billion of gold. Something had to be done at once.

Our gold stock had fallen to the lowest level since 1939. While in 1939 $15 billion of gold was far more than we needed, by 1965 it was dangerously inadequate. Foreign creditors had enormously increased the amount of their short-term claims against us in the form of bank deposits and short-term notes of American corporations and governmental units. They had the right at any time to demand payment in gold. Our gold stock was much too small for us to honor all these claims, even if we paid out every ounce of it. To add to the unease of foreign bankers, almost all our gold was required, indirectly, as reserve against our domestic money supply, which was more than four times as large as in 1939. (The reserves at that time required against deposits and notes of the Federal Reserve Banks were in gold certificates rather than gold itself. Since the certificates are representative money, not credit money, every time the Treasury sold a million dollars of gold, it was compelled to withdraw a million dollars of gold certificates from the Federal Reserve Banks, shrinking their reserves.) With our "free" gold, gold not needed for domestic reserves, we could not possibly pay much more than a twentieth of the short-term debt we had run up.

We cannot here consider the causes and possible eventual cures for our persistent deficits. (See Balance of Payments, Chapter 26.) We shall here note only that the stopgap measure hastily adopted in February, 1965, to deal with the emergency was to take still another step away from the automatic gold standard. Congress quickly ruled that Federal Reserve Bank deposits should henceforth be exempted from the requirement of a 25 percent reserve in gold certificates, thus freeing about $4.5 billion of gold to meet possible foreign demand. The only remaining link between our domestic money and gold was the continuing requirement that Federal Reserve notes be backed 25 percent by gold certificates.

Gold Crises

To this point the Treasury had never refused to sell gold freely to foreign treasuries and central banks. In effect, the United States, with the world's greatest gold stock, was fixing the world price for gold. The purpose of these sales was to make the dollar as good as gold internationally. Foreigners holding claims against us would be willing to continue to hold them, and even to increase their credits to us—but only as long as they were confident that they could exchange them for gold at any time at $35 an ounce. If that confidence were severely shaken, a run on the dollar would be inevitable. Every creditor would try to exchange claims for gold before the United States Treasury:

1. ran out of gold, or more likely
2. refused to sell any more gold, or
3. devalued the dollar, that is, raised the price of gold.

The world's financial centers were close to panic in the spring of 1968. Great Britain, like the United States, troubled with a chronic international deficit, had been forced in November, 1967, to devalue the pound for the third time. In the same year the balance of payments deficit of the United States was over $3.5 billion and showed no indications that it would ever be eliminated. Many financial writers at home and abroad concluded that the dollar, also, would inevitably be devalued again. If the United States were to raise its price for gold, then anyone who had bought it at $35 an ounce could expect to sell it back to the Treasury at the new, higher price, perhaps doubling or tripling their money.

Normally three or four tons of gold a day were sold on the London gold market. In ten days in March, 1968, over 900 tons were sold. Most of it was supplied by the United States Treasury, still trying to maintain confidence in the dollar. The Treasury's gold reserves dropped from about $12.5 billion on January 1, 1968, to less than $11 billion, at which point almost every dollar of gold was tied up as the reserve at that time required against Federal Reserve notes. The Treasury's shelves were almost bare.

For various reasons (see Chapter 27) the United States neither devalued the dollar nor declared a (total) gold embargo. Instead, the requirement that Federal Reserve notes be backed at least 25 percent by gold certificates was abolished, freeing all gold still remaining in the Treasury's vaults. Also, along with several other nations, the Treasury agreed to continue gold transactions at $35 an ounce, but only between *governments*. Treasuries would no longer supply gold to private investors, nor would they be committed to buy it freely. Henceforth, the gold reserves of their respective monetary systems would continue to be international reserves; and if they changed hands, only the ownership, not the total, of international reserves would be affected. From then on, the price of gold in the private sector of the market would be free to seek its own level, presumably above $35 an ounce. This was the so-called *two-tier price system*. For several months the price in the private sector was above the price in the reserve sector. Eventually, in 1970, the United States agreed to make limited purchases of new gold if and when it might be available at or below $35 an ounce. At that time this step was necessary to keep gold as good as the dollar.

In late 1970 and early 1971, short-term funds began to leave the U.S. due to more favorable interest rates abroad and the threat of a U.S. devaluation. This movement, coupled with our weak balance of payments position, led to a massive conversion of Eurodollars into other currencies, especially the stronger ones likely to appreciate.[14] In 1971 the U.S. had its first trade deficit (i.e., the dollar value of its imports was greater than the dollar value of its exports) in this century. Moreover, our gold stock had dwindled from over $24 billion in 1949 to about $10 billion in 1971. While foreign central banks in "strong" currency countries tried, under International Monetary Fund rules, to maintain their fixed par values by purchasing the avalanche of dollars being offered in the market, they also expanded their money supplies.[15] This they did not want to do. Finally, on August 15, 1971, the Nixon administration ended the convertibility of the dollar into gold. To the surprise of some, the resulting floating exchange rates did not destroy international trade relations.

The December, 1971, Smithsonian Agreement, agreed to by the 10 major Western industrial nations, attempted to restore fixed exchange rates within a wider band of possible fluctuation (from 1 percent to 2¼ percent on either side of par). Although the fixed exchange rate was called *central value* rather than par value, the difference was not profound. These new central values produced an average depreciation of the dollar of about 12 percent against the major trading nations to help remedy our balance of payments problem. The Smithsonian Agreement also devalued the dollar about 9 percent, raising the price of gold from $35 to $38 an ounce. Within 14 months (February, 1973), the United States devalued again, raising the gold price an additional 11 percent to $42.22.

The 1968 gold crisis led the central banks of seven leading nations including the U.S. to agree not to buy or sell gold in the private market. The August, 1971, suspension of convertibility of dollars into gold made the 1968 agreement an anachronism. Thus, in November, 1973, we nullified this March, 1968, agreement. Its termination allowed official sales of gold into the private market to dampen fluctuations. But by present IMF rules foreign governments cannot buy gold either from the market or from each other in the foreseeable future, although they may sell gold. The rule is that no member of the IMF shall sell gold below its official price or buy gold at a price above its official price.

---

[14]Eurodollars are deposits in foreign banks, mainly in Europe, that are on the foreign banks' books as payable in U.S. dollars rather than in the currency of the country where the bank is located.
[15]The International Monetary Fund (IMF) is an organization of about 126 non-Communist countries that regulates financial transactions between foreign countries.

In June, 1974, the world financial leaders agreed on an outline of a new world monetary system that would attempt to replace gold with *Special Drawing Rights* (SDRs) as the primary world money. At that time there were about $9.5 billion of SDRs in the world. The SDR was created in 1969. The monetary agreement replaced gold with the SDR as the basic unit of international value. It also contained guidelines under which nations could allow their currencies to fluctuate against one another. It also provided that: (1) the IMF should investigate currency reserves of member nations to determine if they are out of hand, and (2) special help would be available for nations experiencing serious balance of payments problems because of the large increases in oil prices. In particular, it specified that countries may use gold as collateral at prices above the official price of $42.22 an ounce for borrowing purposes.

The United States was the leader in encouraging industrial nations to replace gold with the SDR, which is nothing but a bookkeeping entry on IMF account books. The allocation of SDRs by the IMF to member nations creates value under which nations can buy and sell goods on world markets. The IMF originally distributed about $9.5 billion in SDRs according to a rigid formula based on a nation's contribution to the IMF. Thus, the developing nations received only small amounts of SDRs, whereas the developed nations received the lion's share. Nations disagree on how these SDRs should be shared and used. The developing nations want a bigger share at no extra cost to use for development purposes. This issue is known as the "SDR-link." Developed countries, such as the U.S. and West Germany, would end up exchanging cash for the SDRs of the developing world, a practice which developed nations feel would be an inflationary form of foreign aid over which they would have little direct control.

The value of the SDR previously was based on the U.S. dollar, whose value in turn was based on gold. But when the United States decided in 1971 against paying its international debts in gold, it made the value of the SDR quite unstable, causing its value to rise and fall with the dollar. The 1974 agreement valued the SDR in terms of a "basket" of currencies reflecting the average value of 16 world currencies, of which the U.S. dollar would be the most important (i.e., the dollar would account for about 33 percent of the total value). In June, 1974, the SDR was worth about $1.20, having changed from its original value of $1.00 after two official dollar devaluations. Under the plan, the SDR carries a basic interest rate of 5 percent when loaned between governments, though the actual rate could vary from the 5 percent level, depending on fluctuations in other interest rates.

The roles of the dollar, gold, and SDRs in the world economy continue to evolve. We shall have much more to say about this topic in later chapters.

CONTRAST OF PRESENT GOLD STANDARD WITH AUTOMATIC GOLD STANDARD

Neither the persistent gold inflow before World War II nor the sustained and massive outflow from 1958 to 1971 could have occurred under the conditions of the automatic gold standard. Long before our gold stock had doubled, our prices would have risen and prices would have fallen in countries that had sent us gold. Our exports would have declined, our imports increased, and the gold would have begun to flow out of the U.S. as a result of the change in the balance of trade. Similarly, changes in the price levels here and abroad would have precluded the continuous drain we have experienced since 1950.

We should not jump to the conclusion that our changing from a gold coin to an international gold-bullion standard was the sole reason or even the primary reason that gold movements were no longer self-correcting. The change of standard no doubt contributed, but the more basic reason was that we were not on the automatic gold standard. To be sure, we had never been on a completely automatic standard, since tariffs had always to some extent interfered with its operation. But we had taken our first long step away from the automatic gold standard when we established the Federal Reserve System in 1913. In pre-Federal Reserve days, a change in our gold stock was almost inevitably followed promptly by a similar and proportionate change in our demand deposit total. There was a fairly constant ratio between gold and other money. But the Federal Reserve Banks (and the central banks in other countries) developed techniques to insulate the money supply from gold movements, so that gold movements no longer necessarily resulted in price movements. The change to the international gold-bullion standard was a further step toward a money supply regulated by deliberate policy rather than by automatic forces.

Discretionary monetary policy has important advantages over an automatic standard, as will appear in later chapters. However, it does have the disadvantage that gold movements may be much greater. Few prices rose by more than 10 or 15 percent during the 1930s while our gold stock was trebling. More recently, instead of falling as we lost half of our gold reserves, wholesale prices have risen considerably, and consumer prices have risen even more (nearly double the wholesale price increase). Table 3-1 illustrates the total gold stock held by the United States compared with its total money supply for selected years from 1914 to 1974. The table indicates that there is no significant relationship between the domestic money supply and domestic holdings of gold. It also shows that there is no inexorable association between the wholesale price level and the gold stock level. The price level's lack of responsiveness to gold movements is the fundamental reason that gold flows today can be so great and can continue so long.

Causes of Gold Flows

The basic cause of gold movements is simple enough, even if there is no simple way to control them without creating other pressing problems. A nation's gold stock increases when it is buying less from foreigners than it is selling to them.

A gold flow is a result, not a cause. Foreign nations a generation ago were not shipping us gold and then deciding what to buy with the dollars we paid them for the gold. They had already bought more than they could pay for with goods and services, so they either owed us for the balance or settled it with

Table 3-1   Comparative Values of the Gold Stock,
the Money Supply, and the Wholesale
Price Level in the United States
for Selected Years
(Millions of U.S. Dollars)

Year	Gold	Money Supply	U.S. Gold as Percentage of U.S. Money Supply	Wholesale Price Index
1914	$ 1,526	$ 11,615	13.14	37.3
1915	2,025	11,403	17.76	38.0
1920	2,639	23,721	11.13	44.5
1925	4,112	24,949	16.48	56.6
1930	4,306	25,075	17.17	44.6
1935	10,125	25,216	40.15	41.3
1940	21,995	38,661	56.89	40.5
1945	20,083	94,150	21.33	54.6
1950	22,820	110,225	20.70	81.8
1955	21,753	130,609	16.66	87.8
1960	17,804	138,568	12.85	94.9
1965	13,806	167,200	8.26	96.6
1966	13,235	170,300	7.77	99.8
1967	12,065	183,100	6.59	100.0
1968	10,892	197,400	5.52	102.5
1969	11,859	203,700	5.82	106.5
1970	11,072	221,300	5.00	110.4
1971	10,206	236,000	4.32	113.9
1972	10,487	255,500	4.25	119.1
1973	11,652	266,600	4.37	134.7
1974	11,630	283,800	4.10	160.1

Sources: U.S. Department of Commerce, *Historical Statistics of the United States, Colonial Times to 1957* (Washington: U.S. Government Printing Office, 1960), pp. 646–649. U.S. Department of Commerce, *Historical Statistics of the United States* (Washington: U.S. Government Printing Office, February, 1965). *Federal Reserve Bulletin*(s) (February, 1967), p.258; (November, 1971), p.A17; and (January, 1974), p.A16. Wholesale Price Index based on 1957–1959 = 100 for 1914–1925 and 1967 = 100 for 1930–1973. Adapted from Elmer R. Gooding, "The Gold Standard Revisited," *Arizona Business* (May, 1974), p.7. The authors have added the figures after 1973.

gold. Since 1958 we have been buying from (and giving or lending to) other countries more than we have been selling them, so we have settled the difference either by giving them dollar deposits (or other short-term promises to pay), or, until 1971, by selling them gold.

For several reasons an imbalance of payments may arise, causing gold movements. The most obvious but not the only cause is the same one that the automatic gold standard theory emphasized. If prices in general are rising in one country and elsewhere prices are rising less rapidly (or are unchanged or falling), the country will find it is exporting less, importing more. Through the gold standard the various currencies are related to each other, and their respective abilities to purchase goods other than gold should be related in the same way. If we are paying $42 an ounce for gold and Germany is paying 168 deutsche marks an ounce, then 4 deutsche marks equal $1 in terms of gold. And if a particular grade of steel that sells for $40 a ton in the United States can be bought for much less than 160 deutsche marks in Germany—and if this is characteristic of nearly all commodities in the two countries—then there will be little we can export profitably and a great deal that we can import.

This factor of comparative price levels is part of the explanation for both the gold inflow 40 years ago and the recent outflow. Although the Depression was world-wide, it was especially severe and prolonged in the United States. Other countries found good bargains in American raw materials and manufactured products, and also in real estate and securities. (General Motors at around $4 a share and United States Steel at around $6 were attractive investments for anyone with money and a little faith.) Since World War II many prices have risen more in this country than abroad, so we have found it harder to sell.

When a nation on the gold standard devalues its currency (raises the price it pays for gold), it lowers the price of its currencies to other countries on a gold standard, unless of course the other countries also devalue their currencies at least proportionately.[16] Thus, devaluation by a single country will encourage a gold inflow, because it forces a change in foreign exchange rates that stimulates the exports and reduces the imports of the country that devalues. We must especially emphasize that by raising its price for gold a nation is not paying more for gold than are other countries. For an ounce of gold it is paying more dollars (or pesos, etc.) than before, but they are smaller dollars. If Great Britain defines the pound as one tenth of an ounce of gold and we define the dollar as one forty-second of an ounce, gold is £10 an ounce in London, and $42 an ounce in New York. Neither price is higher; they are identical. And if the United States then decides to raise the price of gold to $100 an ounce, it is still paying no more than is Great Britain, for $100 \times 1/100 = 42 \times 1/42 = 10 \times 1/10$. In other words, all that any gold standard country will pay for an ounce of gold is an ounce of gold coins[17]—the smaller the coins, the more coins to the ounce. Indirectly, however, by stimulating exports and discouraging imports, a unilateral devaluation will encourage a gold flow, unless or until domestic prices rise in the devaluing country. (See Chapter 27.)

Other Factors

Several other factors help determine how gold will flow. Many of these elements were especially evident during the World War II years. These other factors are:

---

[16]If the dollar had eight times the gold content of the peso, then 8 pesos would equal $1. If we then reduced by 50 percent the gold content of the dollar, the new mint par would necessarily be 4 pesos equal $1.

[17]Or the same amount of some other money, most likely demand deposits.

1. interest rate differences among countries,
2. relative investment safety among countries,
3. export volume,
4. availability of goods for export, and
5. defense commitments and foreign aid programs.

A marked difference in interest rates encourages banks to borrow in the country where rates are low and lend in the country where rates are high. This operation tends to cause gold to flow from the low interest area to the high.

For reasons of safety, capital may be transferred from one country to another. Some of the gold we received when war clouds were gathering over Europe resulted from foreigners' purchases of real estate and securities in the United States, where their investments would be less subject to destruction or confiscation.

By far the most important single cause of the gold inflow to the United States was our massive volume of exports during the first years of World War II, before the lend-lease program began. From 1939 to 1940, we received more than $5 billion in gold. From 1930 to 1941 the monetary gold stock of the U.S. increased from $4 billion to almost $23 billion.

For several years after World War II, while Germany, France, England, Japan, and other nations were digging out of the rubble, the United States was the only industrial nation whose productive machinery had not been damaged by the war. Since our goods were about the only ones available, they were in great demand, both for survival and for reconstruction. There was little, other than gold, that foreign nations could send us in return.

Today, we have defense commitments and foreign aid programs to maintain. Our military expenditures overseas and our loans and gifts to foreign nations since World War II have encouraged the gold outflow.

Although the list is not complete, perhaps we have said enough about factors responsible for gold movements to show why they are not easily controlled today. Changes in price levels are not promptly smoothed out, as they would tend to be under the automatic gold standard. To be sure, governments and central banks can exert strong pressures upon price levels through fiscal and monetary policies, but the results cannot possibly be expected to approximate those mechanically effected by an automatic gold standard. That is, of course, exactly why discretionary management has almost universally replaced the automatic control exercised by gold. When the automatic gold standard was taken for granted, however, the depression and unemployment which reduced inflated prices were accepted as inevitable. Governments are reluctant to undertake a deliberate program of deflation and unwilling to place monetary stability before the requirements of international defense and foreign aid. Those who look toward the gold standard as a panacea for the world's current economic ills are recommending the equivalent of a "Model T" for space age travel. Tempting though it may sometimes be to turn our backs on the rest of the world and devote our full attention to enjoying the highest standard of living in history, we simply cannot do it even if we are thinking only of our own best interests. Also, it is socially undesirable and politically suicidal to throw millions of people into bankruptcy, reduce our output of goods and services, and slacken our rate of growth. These circumstances were endured only as long as everyone felt they were the inescapable consequences of and corrections to inflation and were necessary for the maintenance of the indispensable gold standard. Today these effects would certainly be the political ruin of any government that deliberately undertook to create them.

All our money today is pure credit, neither redeemable in nor even limited in amount by our gold stock (or any other tangible restraint). Can the value of the dollar be stabilized in a free market framework, or must we finally choose between continuous inflation and a system of price and wage controls, or in other words, a state-directed economy? This question cannot be answered yet with any assurance. We shall attempt a discussion of the issue involved later.

THE SILVER MERRY-GO-ROUND

From earlier colonial days until a few years ago, silver coins circulated in this country (except briefly in the early 19th century). For 2,000 years silver was widely used as money. Today the only full-bodied silver coins are in coin collections. Why?

Since silver is no longer part of our money supply, we could perhaps ignore the wild gyrations of silver since 1932. However, they admirably illustrate some basic economic principles and fallacies. Also, they help explain the difference between the money of today and that of a generation ago. Besides, they provide an object lesson in the difficulties involved in the frequently recommended programs of both price floors and price ceilings.[18] Incidentally, they also offer a note of caution to those inclined to take too seriously the pronouncements of government officials.

The United States government set a floor under the silver price at a time when all prices were falling. Although the program was pointless and in some respects harmful, at least it was workable. The market price could not possibly fall below the Treasury's price, for the Treasury was willing to buy all silver offered. These purchases "cost" the Treasury nothing, since it paid for the silver by printing silver certificates.

Later, when all prices were rising, the government attempted to put a ceiling on silver prices. Naturally the program failed, and the only question is why it took the government so long to realize that it could not possibly succeed. Keep in mind that both price floors and price ceilings are artificial prices—the first higher, the second lower, than the free market price would otherwise be. As noted above, the Treasury could make its price floor effective by the simple device of buying silver in unlimited quantities. In enforcing a price ceiling, however, it could sell silver only so long as it still had silver in its vaults. In a few years nearly all its silver had been sold at the artificially

---

[18]The problems involved in maintaining nonequilibrium price floors and ceilings are discussed in the Introduction.

low price. Then the Treasury was forced to halt its sales, and the market price jumped abruptly higher. Silver coins quickly disappeared as the public realized that, despite repeated government pronouncements to the contrary, the coins were or would soon be worth more as bullion than as money.

A Bonus for Silver

As we noted briefly at the beginning of this chapter, the issue of free silver apparently died at the end of the 19th century. With the passage of the Pittman Act in 1918, the ardent adherents of silver did succeed in requiring the government to replace the silver that it supplied to England at the end of World War I, but there was no increase in our stock of silver, which was still unnecessarily large. Most of it lay in the Treasury vaults.

But the silver issue came amazingly to life during the Depression of the 1930s. Among the torrent of inflation proposals, none was more persistently advocated than "doing something for silver." That no sound argument was presented was apparently irrelevant. The handsome Treasury profit that eventually resulted was entirely accidental.

Arguments Presented for a Bonus for Silver

Advocates of "a bonus for silver" usually presented the following arguments in its favor:

1. We could stimulate the domestic silver-mining industry.
2. We needed inflation.
3. We could increase our exports to nations on a silver standard.

Technically, silver mining would be stimulated. However, it is a very small industry.[19] There were other less harmful and far more effective ways to stimulate industry than by raising the price of silver. In fact, there may not have been any net increase in employment as a result of putting more miners to work. The high price of silver bullion resulted in a higher price for silverware; and in the silver-fabricating industry, more people lost jobs after (and to some extent because of) the rise in the silver price than gained jobs in the silver-mining industry.

Although inflationary monetary techniques may have been necessary, silver was not needed. Our stocks of gold, even before devaluation, were more than adequate to permit substantial inflation; and devaluation was going to raise the stocks to a still higher figure. If we simply want to inflate the money supply, we can achieve the same results with any issue of money. Every dollar created through silver purchase could, instead, have been created as paper money, either by the Treasury as greenbacks or, preferably, by the Federal Reserve.

---

[19]Although Senator Pittman, of (silver-producing) Nevada, worked tirelessly from 1912 to 1940 for silver legislation, in fact the divorce business was creating more income in Nevada than was silver-mining.

On first thought, such paper money may appear "unsound" and may hence rapidly fall in value. But a fall in the value of money was exactly what the economy needed. If prices did start to rise rapidly, the issue of paper money could have been checked or diminished. Also, a rapid fall in its value due to lack of confidence in such an issue of paper was quite unlikely in view of the large gold stocks we held, shortly to be vastly increased by devaluation. Finally, there is not much difference between paper money backed by the credit of the Federal Reserve and the Treasury and paper money backed by silver when silver is not a standard money. The legal reserves of the Federal Reserve and the basis of the entire bank credit structure were gold. Ten one-dollar silver certificates backed by silver with a market value at that time of $5 or less were not a sounder form of money than a $10 Federal Reserve note backed, at that time, by at least $4 of gold and by government securities and other collateral which brought the total security behind the note to $10.

The argument that if we set a higher price for silver Mexico, China, and other nations on a silver standard could buy more of our goods was superficial, shortsighted, and selfish. What raising the price of silver really accomplished was a change in foreign exchange rates with the silver standard countries, just as raising the price of gold changed them with gold standard countries. Our devaluation of the dollar had not affected the exchange rates between the dollar and silver currencies. Despite Professor Warren's predictions, the prices of everything we bought and sold did not immediately rise in direct proportion to our increase in the price of gold. Since our devaluation would no more increase the silver price than it would the price of cotton or any other product, our higher gold price did not affect the dollar value of the currencies of silver standard countries. We then took care of these currencies. Explaining how anxious we were to improve the world economic situation, we pointed out that if we were to pay twice as much for silver as we had previously been paying, then half as many foreign silver coins would buy a hundred United States dollars. In other words, a given dollar amount of our goods would now cost the silver countries half as much as before in terms of their own money. We would generously extend to them the same advantage we had offered, by devaluation, to the gold standard nations.

The trouble is that in the long run nations pay for their imports with their exports. (Other items not considered here enter into the overall balance. See the discussion of balance of payments, Chapter 26.) By increasing the value of their currency, we were making it almost impossible for them to export to us anything except their currency. The effect was similar to putting a high tariff on their goods and simultaneously subsidizing American producers to dump our products into the silver standard countries at any price.

In two respects our higher silver price differed in its effects from our higher gold price.

1. Nearly all the gold standard areas promptly devalued their own currencies, so that the dollar cost them as much or even more than it had before. Devaluation was relatively easy to accomplish since few coins were actually circulating. Nations could not simply devalue their silver money, their hand-to-hand coinage.

2. When nations are on a gold standard, we can say that the price of gold is the same everywhere, although expressed in different units. But if, on the gold standard, we agree to pay higher prices for wheat or silver or any other commodity except gold, then our price may certainly be higher than the price elsewhere. In terms of gold, our price for silver was well above the prevailing world price. Naturally we received thousands of tons of silver from abroad.

This artificially high silver price drained the reserves of the silver standard nations. China found its reserves being smuggled out and sold to the United States Treasury. The Chinese government attempted to halt the drain at home and appealed to the Treasury to modify its policy. The flow of silver continued and China was forced to a managed standard. Mexico was in a somewhat more favored position, being a large producer of silver. As a result of our higher silver prices, it did benefit just as, for example, Columbia would have benefited if we had agreed to pay a higher price for coffee. However, our price was so high that Mexico, too, was forced off the silver standard, to which it did not return until 1952. Thus, our silver policy undermined the stability of the currency of friendly nations and destroyed their demand for monetary silver by forcing them to paper standards.

In short, although there was not a single sound argument presented for the program, the New Deal silver policies swept through. These policies gave the silver interests almost everything they wanted short of an outright return to bimetallism.

Silver Subsidies, 1933–1963

We need not concern ourselves with details of the now discontinued silver subsidy program. The most important legislation was the Silver Purchase Act of 1934 which required the Treasury to continue buying silver until silver constituted one fourth of our total monetary reserves or until its market price rose above $1.2929 an ounce. Beginning in 1941, the Treasury bought from domestic producers only.

In making its silver purchases, the Treasury imposed a seigniorage charge, so that the price the seller received ranged from $.645 in 1934 to $.905 after 1945. Thus, the Treasury was paying, in 1946, $905 for a thousand ounces of silver and was issuing $905 of silver certificates to cover the purchase cost. Since a silver dollar contains less than an ounce of silver, more than $1,000 could be coined from 1,000 ounces of silver. By issuing only $905 of certificates against silver bullion sufficient for the coinage of nearly 1,300 silver dollars, the Treasury was not fully monetizing the silver it bought. Only $905/$1.2929, or about 700 ounces of silver, at the official valuation of $1.2929, were needed to back up the certificates. The other 300 ounces were so-called "free" silver.[20]

Originally the Treasury was not allowed to sell any of its silver except at $1.29 an ounce, a figure far above the market price. Under wartime pressures

---

[20]Note that this terminology has no connection whatever with "free silver" as applied to unlimited coinage.

the Treasury was finally permitted to sell its "free" silver to industry at a price half a cent above its purchase price. These sales at $.91 an ounce continued after World War II, and paradoxically resulted in the Treasury's holding *down* the market price of silver.

THE DISAPPEARANCE OF SILVER

With the postwar decline in the value of the dollar, nearly all prices and costs were rising. With silver selling for $.91 an ounce, silver mining was becoming unprofitable. Between 1950 and 1960, world silver consumption was consistently above production. Silver producers had been glad to have the Treasury buying silver at a fixed price when that price was above the free market price. They were not happy to have the Treasury then selling silver at the same price when, otherwise, the market price might rise.

The interest of the Treasury and the public was more important than that of the silver mining industry. By June, 1959, the Treasury had acquired the greatest silver stock in the world's history (3.4 billion fine ounces). Part was circulating as fractional silver coins, but most was required collateral against the silver certificates issued when it was purchased. This collateral silver was in the form of silver bars, about seventy thousand tons of which were locked up in the Treasury vaults. There were also 212 million ounces of bullion against which no certificates had been issued. This was the silver that the Treasury was free to sell, without contracting the circulation of silver certificates. With the strong world demand for silver, the Treasury's free silver quickly dropped 90 percent in sixteen months, to about 20 million ounces.

At this point President Kennedy, in November, 1961, instructed the Treasury to stop selling free silver. He also directed that $5 and $10 denominations of silver certificates be withdrawn from circulation. This action freed the silver behind them, so that it could, when necessary, be used for coinage requirements. At the same time he asked Congress:

1. to repeal the legislation requiring the Treasury to purchase silver at $.905, and
2. to authorize the Federal Reserve Banks to issue notes of $1 denomination, so that the $1 silver certificates, like the certificates of higher denomination, could be retired and replaced by Federal Reserve notes. The retirement of all silver certificates would free about two billion ounces of silver, an amount that the Secretary of the Treasury optimistically declared would be adequate to meet our coinage requirements for twenty years or so.

In response to this announcement, the market price of silver jumped the following day from $.91 to $1.0075.[21] By September, 1963, silver was selling

---

[21]Speculators had a field day. It was clear by the middle of 1961 that the Treasury would presently stop selling silver at $.91, either by executive order or because it had run out of free silver. It was clear also that the demand for silver exceeded current production, and that the price of silver would inevitably rise when the Treasury stopped supplying it at $.91. Buying silver on as little as a 5 percent margin, the silver itself serving as collateral for a loan of 95 percent of the amount of the transaction, speculators reaped quick and handsome profits. One man reportedly

at $1.29, the highest price since 1920.[22] The price could not rise higher than this as long as silver certificates were freely available and the Treasury was redeeming $129 of certificates with 129 silver dollars or the same weight (100 ounces) of silver bullion.

Congress eventually completed its deliberations and passed the requested legislation, which was signed by the President on June 4, 1963. The law requiring the Treasury to purchase newly mined domestic silver at $.905 was repealed, and Federal Reserve Banks were authorized to issue Federal Reserve notes in $1 denomination. The road was cleared for retirement of the silver certificates. Treasury spokesmen quickly explained that the retirement of the certificates would be a very gradual affair, since the issuance of more Federal Reserve notes would require a larger portion of our dwindling gold supply to be earmarked as backing for Federal Reserve notes. The course of events showed unmistakably that the Treasury had failed to grasp the real nature of our silver currency problem.

Coins and Vending Machines

Treasury spokesmen repeatedly suggested that the increasing coin shortage, which threatened to become critical, was a consequence of the rapidly expanding use of vending machines and that increasing the coin supply more rapidly would easily solve the problem.[23] They announced in 1964 that their 1965 output would be double that of 1964 and triple that of 1961.[24]

Vending machines may well have had at least something to do with the coin shortage. Certainly the amount of pennies and nickels in circulation also increased. However, this increase was much smaller than the silver coin increase. Also, to some extent the increased demand for coins may have been the result of the scarcity of dimes, quarters, and half-dollars. People had to have something with which to make change. Nickels were at least better than merchants' scrip or paper fractional currency, both of which people considered using. In any event, several circumstances showed that vending machines certainly were not the principal reason for the increased demand for coins.

---

bought 10 tons of silver in late 1961. For this he paid $291,000, of which he borrowed all but $14,500. Less than a year later he sold out for $380,000.

Americans, incidentally, were discouraged from sharing these speculative gains. Although it was lawful for Americans to buy, hold, and sell silver, until 1963 they were effectively excluded from this market by a 50 percent surtax (over and above income tax) on any gains from such transactions. Foreign speculators, however, made out well, and it was rumored that a few Americans had also profited, operating through the comfortable anonymity of numbered accounts in Swiss banks.

[22]The price in 1919 was finally and briefly bid up to the record figure of $1.3285 as a result of the large coinage requirements of the Allies during and after World War I. This price was high enough to threaten the circulation of not only silver dollars, but even fractional silver. However, because a license was required for the exporting of silver bullion, our silver stock was little decreased.

[23]In 1964 some banks were rationing coins. Other agencies, including some churches and some vending firms, were selling coins at a premium. In 1974 pennies were in short supply despite the fact that three times as many pennies were minted in 1974 as in 1967, and some retailers gave change in candy and scrip when pennies were called for.

[24]Other nonmonetary demands for silver—for electronics, photographic film, and silverware—increased also. But the analysis for vending machines would hold for these uses as well.

From 1940 to 1960 fractional silver in circulation increased in the neighborhood of $50 or $60 million a year. By 1963, when the annual increase was double the average yearly increase of 1940–1960, it began to appear doubtful that vending machines were really the principal cause of the coin shortage. When, two years later, new coins were being supplied by nearly seven times the quantity of a few years earlier, the vending machine explanation was even less credible. The machines simply were not increasing that rapidly.

In the second place, vending machines could hardly be held responsible for the sudden increase in the demand for silver dollars, of which the Treasury had 161 million on hand at the end of 1960. For more than a century there had been little demand for silver dollars. As recently as 1940, only 46 million were in circulation. Between 1950 and 1960 the Treasury had been paying out about 14 million a year. But by December, 1962, its stock had dropped by 65 million, and a year later it held only 28 million. At the end of March, 1964, after several days of million-dollar withdrawals, the Treasury had less than 3 million silver dollars remaining in its vaults, at which point it declared it would henceforth deliver silver bullion upon demand, but no silver dollars.

Even more convincing evidence appeared. When the new nonsilver fractional coins were introduced, they circulated—but silver coins still were scarce. An important reason for choosing the particular alloy adopted for the new dimes and quarters had been that vending machines would, without alteration, accept either the old or the new coins. Since the machines were not hoarding the silver coins, who was?

Coins and Coin Collectors

The Treasury then offered a second explanation. Coin collectors were holding silver coins, expecting them to appreciate in value because of their eventual scarcity. This reasoning even persuaded Congress to authorize, in 1964, a $600,000 appropriation for the coinage of 45 million silver dollars, the first to be struck in 30 years.[25] To reduce their possible scarcity value, the mint was also directed to continue dating all silver coins 1964 and to put a 1965 date (later discontinued) on all coins of the new issue.

There was, perhaps, some validity to this explanation. The publicity given to the proposed coinage change may have caused a temporary increase in the number of coin collectors, who were perhaps less interested in building a coin collection than in making a quick profit by selling to genuine collectors. Certainly the activity and the advertising of the coin dealers increased a great deal after 1964. By 1966 they were offering bags of a thousand dollars, supplied at that price by the mint two years before, for $1,500.

---

[25]These dollars were not coined, and it is most unlikely they ever will be. True, in 1971 the Treasury began minting dollars again, but these coins have nothing whatever to do with money. Unlike the dollars authorized in 1964, they contain only 40% silver. More importantly, each dollar was sold for three dollars or for ten dollars if specially minted as a so-called "proof" coin. Naturally no one is going to use ten of these dollars to make a ten dollar purchase. They have been bought only by coin collectors or as souvenirs. As a circulating coin the silver dollar, like the gold dollar and our other silver coins, has disappeared forever.

With hundreds of millions of silver dollars in the hands of the public and with 12 billion fractional silver coins in circulation, it seems almost incredible that enough people would be convinced of the eventual scarcity of these coins to cause the coin shortage.[26]

Coins and Hoarding

The most important cause of the disappearance of silver coins is the one Treasury spokesmen were late to acknowledge, perhaps because they were unaware of it, perhaps for some other reason. It was very simple. The public was hoarding silver.

Look at Table 3-2. Recall that in November, 1961, the Treasury's stock of free silver was nearly exhausted and the Treasury was directed to stop selling silver at $.91. Note the sudden increase in the demand for fractional silver in 1962 and the accelerating pace of silver coinage in the following years. It would require quite a stretch of the imagination to suppose that the connection between the ending of $.91 silver and the great jump in the demand for silver coins was due to chance.

Why should people suddenly begin to hoard silver coins? For the perfectly logical reason that it appeared the coins would soon be worth more as metal than as coins—exactly the same reason that led people to hoard gold until that was made illegal. Recall that fractional silver coins disappeared from circulation more than a century ago for the same reason. They were brought back into circulation in 1854 by a reduction in their silver content that made melting them unprofitable.

By 1900 the market price of silver had declined so much that the money value of our fractional coins was double the value of their silver content. This "cheap" money did not drive out other forms of money, in accordance with Gresham's Law, because it was convertible into other money. At first it could be exchanged for gold. Since 1933 silver coins have been converted only into paper, but because either a paper dollar or two half-dollars would buy more than would the metal content of the coins, they circulated side by side.

Since 1950, however, the world's consumption of silver has outrun production. By 1963 all that kept the price of silver from rising above $1.29 an ounce was that the Treasury was selling at that price from its silver stockpile. It appeared almost certain that within a very few years the Treasury would stop selling silver at $1.29, just as in 1961 it stopped selling it at $.91.[27] The

---

[26]In 1893 there were 2.5 million Columbian Exposition half-dollars minted. Today one of these coins is worth $4 or $5. By contrast, there have been 1.2 billion Kennedy half-dollars minted. While for various reasons there may be more people who would like to have the latter coin, enough were minted to provide six for every man, woman, and child in the United States. Coin collectors will not likely pay a great premium for a coin in such great supply.

If you have ever watched a dog teasing another dog by pretending he is looking for a buried bone, you may have noticed that sometimes he seems to forget that it started as a put-on. He begins to believe a bone must really be there. Did the coin dealers convince even themselves?

[27]This is, of course, the difficulty with trying to maintain a ceiling price. If the price is too low to cause an increase in current output, your stock will probably be exhausted sooner or later and the price will then be free to seek its own level.

price would then again be free to rise. Holders of silver dollars and silver bullion, who had purchased at lower prices, could then take their profit.

Silver Demonetized. Treasury officials suggested in 1963 that the retirement of the silver certificates would be stretched out over a 10-year period. Once more they had underestimated the problem.[28] Three years later three fourths had been retired, and it had become clear that the rest would be quickly retired or no longer redeemable.

After initially halting the sale of free silver in 1961, the Treasury resumed it in 1963, but at $1.29. The justification for the policy was this: even if the Treasury refused to sell its free silver at any price, law required it to sell silver at $1.29 an ounce to anyone who would pay for it with silver certificates; for $129 of silver certificates constituted a claim on 100 ounces of silver in accordance with the price set in 1791. The government, therefore, decided to sell silver at $1.29, whether payment was made in silver certificates or in any

Table 3-2   Fractional Coins in Circulation
June 30, 1940–1974
(In millions of dollars)

Year	Subsidiary Silver		Minor Coin		Total Fractional Coin	
	Amount	Yearly Increase	Amount	Yearly Increase	Amount	Yearly Increase
1940	$ 384		$169		$ 553	
1950	965	$ 58*	361	$19*	1,326	$ 77*
1960	1,484	52	549	19*	2,033	71*
1961†	1,548	64	585	36	2,133	100
1962	1,664	116	629	44	2,293	160
1963	1,790	126	676	47	2,466	173
1964	1,987	197	736	60	2,723	257
1965	2,355	368	825	89	3,180	457
1966					3,782	602
1967					4,160	479
1968					4,827	667
1969					5,308	481
1970					5,646	338
1971					5,990	344
1972					6,383	393
1973					6,793	410
1974††					7,489	696

Source: *Federal Reserve Bulletin*(s).
*Average
†Sale of "free" silver at $.91 halted in November, 1961.
††January 31, 1975, data.

---

[28]Or were trying to discourage the hoarding of silver by the skeptical public.

other kind of money. The all-important consideration was to hold the market price of silver down as long as possible. The mint was grinding out the new, nonsilver coins at top speed; but if, before a sufficient supply of these copper-nickel alloy coins had been issued, the market price of silver were to rise substantially, it was (finally) clear that a drastic coin shortage would surely result. Even if the sales only postponed a rise in the market price, they would give the Treasury additional time to supply the new coins.

When someone bought silver by surrendering certificates, the certificates were retired and the silver held against them could be released to the buyer. When someone bought silver with any other kind of money, only free silver could be released.

Sales of free silver, modest at first, eventually soared abruptly as speculators began buying silver for export, convinced that the removal of the ceiling price was imminent. Within four days, buyers took more than 20 million ounces, or one fifth of the stock remaining in the Treasury. On the fifth day (May 18, 1967) when the Treasury announced that, beginning the following day, there would be no more unrestricted sales of free silver at $1.29, almost 20 million ounces more were taken, leaving the Treasury with less than 60 million ounces. As in 1961, the cupboard was nearly bare when the door was finally locked.

At the same time that it halted its unrestricted sales of free silver, the Treasury also banned the "melting, treatment, and export" of silver coins, effective immediately.[29] Briefly the Treasury continued to sell free silver at $1.29, but only to domestic industrial users. Still the rapid drain continued, reducing the Treasury's stock to less than 45 million ounces by early June.

Beginning in July, the Treasury entirely abandoned its ceiling price on free silver. Until 1970, about 2 million ounces a week were sold, by sealed bid, to the highest bidder. Since these transactions no longer have any close relation to the subject of money, we need not concern ourselves with them.

Although it changed its free silver policy, the Treasury temporarily continued to redeem silver certificates. Only with this currency could buyers still purchase silver from the Treasury at $1.29. With the free market price well above that figure, a premium appeared on silver certificates for which buyers were glad by July to pay $1.25.

---

[29]This ruling was repealed in 1969, so hoarders are now free to melt their coins. However, if they have been holding them since 1963, their investment has not been spectacularly successful; and if they are holding coins bought at a premium a few years later, their investment has probably declined in value. (We are considering only bullion value, not the value of some rare coins as collectors' items.) Although the price of silver did make a then record high of $2.56 in 1968, it then declined and most of the time was well below $2.00 until the early 1970s. In 1974 the price of silver went to over $6.00 an ounce. By early 1975 it was back to $4.50 an ounce.

When they were fresh from the mint, $1,390 of fractional coins contained 1,000 ounces of silver. Today most of them are a little worn from circulation. There might be about 990 ounces of silver in this bag of coins. At $1.60 an ounce the $1,390 of coins would be worth about $1,584 as bullion. However, the holder of a small coin hoard would ordinarily sell it to a dealer, who could arrange to sell coins by the ton to the refiner. Thus, the individual could expect to receive only part of the $194 difference between the coin value and the bullion value. With luck the individual might get a premium of as much as $120 from the dealer. This profit of $120 on an investment of $1,390, held for 8 or 10 years, is hardly exciting—about 9 percent, or 1 percent a year—over a period when interest on Treasury bonds rose to the highest level in a century.

Finally, to avoid the necessity of forever retaining millions of ounces of silver in the Treasury as backing for silver certificates officially still in circulation but for the most part actually lost or destroyed, the government ruled that after June 30, 1968, silver certificates would no longer be redeemable in silver. Any still in the hands of the public at that time would be on the same footing as all our other paper money. All silver still in the Treasury vaults would then be free silver.

Silver Coinage in Great Britain. Compared to our fumbling silver policy and consequent coinage problems, Great Britain handled the silver problem smoothly. For 350 years British coins had a silver content of 92.5 percent. This standard had a tradition going back to Saxon times. Nevertheless, in 1920 Britain reduced the silver content to 50 percent and in 1946 eliminated silver entirely in favor of a copper-nickel alloy.[30] Most of Great Britain's coins were quietly retired, with little of the confusion that surrounded our own currency experiments. Not being silver producers, the British were free to work out a rational silver policy, unfettered by political requirements.

SUMMARY AND CONCLUSION

The history of our currency before 1830 is replete with examples of our failure to understand simple monetary economics. Over the next hundred years, we did gradually develop a satisfactory, although still not perfect, currency.

The changes in our coinage between 1934 and 1975 were profound, far greater than all our earlier coinage changes combined. Where earlier we occasionally made adjustments of 4 or 5 percent, in 1934 we raised the price of gold by more than 70 percent and began to buy silver at a price far exceeding its true market value. During the early years of these three decades, the Treasury accumulated the greatest hoard of gold and silver held by one nation in the history of the world. In recent years the Treasury lost more than half of its gold and practically all of its silver. The relation of our coins, paper currency, and bank deposits to gold and silver has been fundamentally altered. We may well wonder just what all this legislation accomplished.

It is impossible at this point to attempt a clear and detailed evaluation of the changes in our gold policy. We may agree that the devaluation in 1934 was undertaken primarily for unsound reasons, but that it turned out well in the long run. Devaluation necessarily affected the price of the dollar in terms of foreign currencies. Also, it placed a higher dollar value on the gold stocks

---

[30]Dimes and quarters coined in the United States since 1965 have been 75 percent copper and 25 percent nickel, bonded to a pure copper core. Previously they were minted with 90 percent silver and a 10 percent copper alloy. The high price of silver and Gresham's Law quickly drove the estimated $2.5 billion of pre-1965 dimes and quarters out of circulation into private hoards. Nickels and pennies have always been token money in which the market value of the contained metals was always substantially below the face value until 1974, when soaring copper prices made the 95 percent copper penny scarce. (Half of the 60 billion pennies went out of circulation.)

held by the Treasury, permitting a greater volume of currency and deposits. Policies to help the nation recover from the Depression of the 1930s, to convert and expand production immensely during World War II, and to maintain a high level of output and employment after the war were all helped by the tremendous gold reserves held by the Treasury.

By denying individuals the right to hold gold, the government enabled each ounce of gold to be used to its full extent, that is, as a fractional reserve against our money rather than as money itself. This policy also greatly increased the ability of the government and the banking system to implement their policies.

By eliminating the gold reserve requirement against Federal Reserve deposits and notes, the government freed gold for international use. For the first time, our money supply was to be regulated entirely by individuals, with no direct relation to gold. It is simply impossible to know now how this system will work out. At this writing, we have experienced several difficulties. Everything depends on the skill of the monetary authorities and their ability to withstand political pressures and public opinion. Such a system is admirably flexible. At the same time it is far from foolproof, as we are now well aware.

Some monetary conservatives are convinced that we are about to experience a devastating worldwide deflation and depression as nations attempt to work their way back to something like an automatic gold standard. However, monetary evolution seems more likely to proceed along the road it has been traveling in recent years. Possibly by a general devaluation of all currencies, possibly by less dependence on gold and one or two currencies as international reserves, the world may solve its present liquidity problems, and international gold movements will be less disturbing.[31]

The evaluation of our amazing silver policy of the last 40 years presents no problem. The sole basis of the massive silver purchases was politics. In more recent years, as the government moved to cut its silver drain, its policy was a series of uninspired, last moment improvisations.

There is simply no rational economic justification for the silver purchases begun in 1934. There is even less reason for the government to buy and store silver at artificially high prices than for it to buy eggs or butter. Admittedly, storage problems are simpler with silver since there is no deterioration, and it is convenient that the silver "costs" the Treasury nothing. However, our silver purchases merely resulted in a generous subsidy to silver producers. The silver was not required for monetary purposes. The program was the result of a strong silver bloc in Congress. The six silver producing states, although sparsely populated, were represented by twelve Senators who, regardless of party affiliation, could be counted on to back any legislation supporting silver. On a political basis the policy is quite easy to understand.

Our stumbling retreat from silver coinage was hampered by the long postponement of the issue. Probably silver coins could have easily been phased out of circulation if politics had permitted us to begin 40 years ago. Then the

---

[31]See also Chapter 27.

free market price of silver was far below its present level, and there was no indication that the value of the silver content of our coins might someday exceed their monetary value. If we had begun at that time to circulate coins of nickel and copper, the public would have had two coinages, *neither* with an intrinsic value of more than half its monetary value. Certainly the silver coins would have been worth more as metal than the nickel-copper coins, but 40 years ago their money value would have been so far above their metal value that no one would have wanted to hoard them. Gradually the silver coinage could have been retired as it wore out. It would have been returned to the Treasury, melted, and sold to industry.

Instead, Congress waited until the last possible moment, when clearly coinage requirements would soon exhaust the Treasury's silver stock and the market price of silver would have to rise. Then it introduced the new coinage and was surprised to find Gresham's Law still operative and silver coins rapidly disappearing.

Perhaps we should concede a sort of mad consistency to the government's silver policy. Having bought silver when we did not need it, at a price far above its true value, the government followed through by selling it for less than it would bring in a free market. The one encouraging conclusion we may hopefully draw is that silver's political role is finished.

Discussion Questions

1. Why do you imagine that the attempted retirement of "greenbacks" (United States notes) was so unpopular?
2. Although 50 years ago most people felt the so-called automatic gold standard was the most sound basis for a nation's money, few bankers or economists urge that it be restored today. Why?
3. "Neither the persistent gold inflow before World War II nor the sustained and massive outflow from 1958 to 1971 could have occurred under the conditions of the automatic gold standard." Explain.
4. "Rather than pay for the Revolutionary War by taxation, our government primarily issued Continental currency." Evaluate.
5. Our Federal Reserve note today, like the Continental currency, has nothing behind it other than the government's promise to pay. Does this imply that the Federal Reserve note too will someday be "not worth a Continental"?
6. In recession, it may be desirable to attract foreign short-term balances and also to stimulate domestic production. What dilemma does this pose for monetary policy?
7. What was the emergency currency authorized during the bank holiday in 1933? What was its principal advantage, and how does it compare with the Federal Reserve note of today?
8. If one country alone devalues, what would probably be the effect on its employment and standard of living?
   a. Assume the country was already at full employment.
   b. Assume the country was in a depression.

 9. Suppose we reduce the gold content of the dollar to 1/45 of an ounce and therefore raise our price for gold. If other countries continue paying the same price for gold as they were previously paying, would our higher price bring more gold to the U.S.? Explain.

10. What was the "two-tier" price system for gold and how has it been expected to stabilize the world's monetary gold reserves?

11. What has been the relationship between the domestic money supply, the gold stock, and (wholesale) prices in the United States since World War I?

12. Why was the United States forced to devalue the dollar in 1971 and again in 1973?

13. Until very recently, silver certificates were a major component of our currency. If we are getting along without them now, why did we feel they were necessary for nearly a century?

14. In buying or selling metal that it coins, the Treasury can maintain a price floor forever, a price ceiling only temporarily. Explain.

15. In the hundred years following the Civil War there was a great increase in the use of demand deposits. Can you suggest how this might have been related to the many coinage changes of the last three or four decades?

16. By early 1968, many dollar bills were being sold for a dollar and a quarter. Why? Are such bills selling at the same price today? Why?

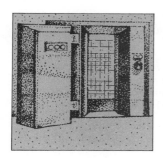

PART 2
The Commercial Banking Process

Chapter 4 Credit, Credit Instruments, and Credit Institutions

People progressed, as we have seen, from barter to a common medium of exchange and standard of value, and from this primitive commodity money was developed the more convenient coined commodity money. There progress halted for 2,000 years until, in about the 17th century, the foundations of banking and credit were laid. Today most of our payments are made by means of bank deposits. More importantly, the development of banking made possible for the first time a discretionary control over money. Monetary policy, although not a panacea, can often be a powerful implement of overall control, useful in restraining inflation and countering recession. Out of fashion for a generation, monetary policy has received a renewed emphasis since 1968.

Until the invention of bank credit creation, there was no way to flexibly expand or contract money or to smoothly adjust interest rates to the credit needs of the moment. To be sure, a king of the Middle Ages—indeed, an emperor of ancient Rome—could call in the currency, recoin it to contain more alloy, and thus increase the nation's stock of money. This practice, however, was simply a revenue device, a substitute for taxation. It provided money with which the ruler could pay soldiers or build palaces and monuments. It could not be done gradually; it could not be easily reversed. It had nothing to do with monetary policy as the term is generally understood today.

Even when, in the 18th century, the foundations for modern commercial banking were being laid, a unified monetary policy could not develop. That development had to wait until the second stage of banking evolved—the central banks (in the United States, the twelve Federal Reserve Banks), which control the many competing individual commercial banks.

Today we take all these changes for granted. Yet the development of our system of credit and banking came slowly and painfully, with little previous experience on which to build and many misconceptions to lead us astray. So intangible a thing as credit cannot be marketed as simply and obviously as can wheat. Yet a bank's business is basically to buy and sell credit. Credit instruments are its stock-in-trade. Also, on the basis of its own credit a bank creates money which is transferred by credit instruments.

Most economic activity is two-sided. If there is to be a deal, there must be both buyer and seller; both landlord and tenant; both employer and employee; both an expenditure and a receipt of money. So it is with credit. For every dollar of credit created, there is a dollar of debt created. For every credit asset, there is a liability. Unless there is a borrower, there can be no lender.

There is a peculiar quirk in most people's thinking about debt and credit. They tend to think of debt as a burden, something that weakens or acts as a drag on the economy. At the same time they think of credit as a benefit, something that stimulates the economy and is the lifeblood of trade. They are happy to read that bank deposits are rising, but worried to read that the government, businesses, or consumers are going into debt. We could just as consistently be happy to see that more people were employed, but disturbed because employers now have larger payrolls to meet.

The confusion arises from the fact that, from the point of view of individuals, it does make a difference whether they are debtors or creditors. As debtors, they are turning over part of their income to pay interest on and repay the principal of loans. As creditors they are on the receiving end. For society as a whole, however, these payments all cancel out.

The most elementary fact about credit is that there must be two parties to the transaction. The borrower is a debtor; the lender is a creditor. One is impossible without the other. Also, whatever constitutes a debt to one person—whether based on an oral contract or evidenced by a written document—constitutes an asset to someone else. When we are considering the economy as a whole, therefore, debt and credit are always two names for, and two ways of looking at, the same thing.

Credit (debt) involves giving (receiving) goods or purchasing power now in return for a promise to receive (repay) the goods or purchasing power later. Sometimes a specific commodity or good will be lent and repaid, as in the case of the speculator who sells General Motors short, that is, sells stock that he or she does not have. He or she borrows the stock to deliver to the buyer and later buys the same stock, at a lower price if the speculation is successful, and turns it over to the lender. The speculator borrowed stock and repaid with stock. However, people generally borrow money and repay the debt with money. The borrower may want to speculate, expand a business, meet a payroll, or perhaps buy some household equipment. For any of these and thousands of other purposes, a money loan, later repaid with money, is by far the most convenient arrangement.

Often the borrower does not actually receive money. A person may sign an installment contract, promising to make monthly repayments over a period of time, and in exchange receive a new car rather than a check or a handful of currency. Basically, however, the bank or other lending agency is, in such a case, lending money; but the lender itself, rather than the borrower, turns the money over to the automobile dealer. In the exposition that follows we shall generally ignore this superficial difference and discuss credit based upon money transfers from the creditor to the debtor and back to the creditor.

Whether or not an individual, a corporation, or a government can obtain credit depends upon whether people are confident that the loan or other credit will be repaid when it is due. One may make a loan to a friend or relative in trouble, knowing that the loan is probably a gift. But for business loans, lenders carefully consider the borrowers' credit ratings before parting with their money. Lenders base their decisions on four characteristics of the borrowers, often said to be the four Cs of credit: character, capacity, capital (i.e., net worth), and collateral. The fundamental basis of credit is trust. Borrowers' credit ratings are established by their character, capacity, and capital. Character is the most important. Their collateral will also be taken into account if they are required to put up security for the loan.

TYPES OF CREDIT

When classifying anything, there are usually a number of different bases of classification, all of which overlap. The students in a classroom can be divided into the tall and the short or the juniors and the seniors or into various other categories. When we classify the various types of credit, we find there are at least four common divisions.

Production v. Consumption

The first division depends upon whether the credit is for production or for consumption. The traditional concern of commercial banks has been with credit for production.[1] Their name, in fact, derives from the commercial loans that were at one time almost the only form of credit that they extended. In the 20th century, consumption loans have grown in importance, largely as a result of the growing importance of, first, automobiles and later many other consumer durable goods. A generation ago bankers tended to look with a jaundiced eye upon consumption credit. If one lacked the money to buy something, one should first save the money and then buy, instead of going into debt. As they saw the rapid growth of other lending institutions and the billions of dollars in loans these firms were making to consumers, the bankers began not only to tolerate consumption credit but actively to solicit this kind of business.

Long, Short, and Intermediate

Credit may be extended for as short a period as a part of a day, or it may run for 50 years or more. Short-term credit includes anything up to a year, intermediate credit runs from one to five years, and long-term credit runs over five years.

---

[1]Commercial banks are those that carry demand deposits and maintain checking accounts for their customers.

There are many areas where credit is needed for only a short period of time. A farmer may need to borrow the money to pay the harvest crew. The crop will be sold a few weeks later. A merchant may borrow the money to buy Christmas toys that will soon be sold. A student may borrow from a roommate until a check arrives from home. A manufacturer may borrow to meet a payroll so an order can be completed and payment received.

Often credit is needed over a longer period of time. A cattle rancher may need to be carried for two or three years before the beef is ready for the market. Air conditioning may be a profitable investment for a restaurant or store, but the credit may need to run for several years.

In some instances, really long-term credit is needed. Unless exceptionally lucky, a farmer who has borrowed most of the money to buy a farm will probably not be able to pay it off in five or six years. Few homeowners can make large enough monthly payments to get out of debt in less than fifteen or twenty years, and many take longer. When a public utility company borrows money to build a dam, string more lines, or buy generators, it repays the loan out of the earnings of future years. So does a college when it borrows the money to build additional dormitories or a stadium.

Public Credit

Credit may be extended to the private sector of the economy, to individuals and business firms. It may also be extended to the public sector, including governmental units on all levels from municipal to national. During wars, national governments have always borrowed heavily. Today they often borrow in peacetime as well, particularly in depression. (Often a government borrows during a depression in a deliberate attempt to increase the flow of national income.) In addition, states and municipalities borrow heavily, especially for building highways and schools.

The credit of the public sector of the economy depends primarily upon its ability to tax, since this ability represents its capacity for repayment. Character is also important to a government's credit standing. A government finds it difficult to borrow if it has repudiated its debts in the past.

Public credit, like private credit, may be long term, short term, or intermediate. Like private credit also, it may be for production or consumption. The definition of consumption credit is not entirely clear in the case of public credit, however, because most government operations are not carried on like a business—to make a profit. We tend to think of a toll road as a productive enterprise; but if the same road is made a freeway, we may decide it is no longer productive and now represents consumption credit. Similarly, funds borrowed for war expenditures are considered as almost entirely consumption credit. Yet the eventual benefits from a victory are far more important than the advantages of having larger movie screens and bigger automobiles, the development of which requires funds we unhesitatingly classify as production credit. (The historical trend of public and private debt in the United States is shown on the endsheet.)

Direct v. Indirect

Originally all credit was direct. Someone lent spare money or goods directly to the borrower. Much credit today is still of this form. Individuals and nonfinancial corporations buy bonds and other evidences of debt, sell goods on credit, make personal loans, and in other ways make credit available directly.

But an important characteristic of modern society is the financial institution, developed for the purpose of indirect credit extension. Funds are left with a savings bank, which takes over the responsibility of finding safe and profitable lending opportunities. Life insurance companies do an enormous volume of lending, as also do savings and loan companies. Investment trusts also receive funds from the public and in some instances lend the funds through bond purchases, although more commonly they purchase stocks. The most important of these financial intermediaries is the commercial bank.

When any of these financial institutions receives funds from the public, it *issues its own obligations in exchange*. The insurance company issues policies that obligate it to pay specified amounts if certain events happen—if you die, or if your property is damaged, and so on. The investment trust issues shares or certificates that give you a certain share in its earnings and assets. The savings bank gives you a deposit, contracting to repay you with interest, but requires you to come to the bank with your passbook when you wish to withdraw any money. It may, in addition, require 30 days' advance notice. The commercial bank also gives you a deposit, but this deposit is payable on demand and transferable by check, and the bank performs various services for you in connection with handling your account.

Creation of Money. The evolution of these intermediaries has increased the total credit and debt in existence. Much of this credit and debt has been duplicated. If the public, instead of buying $1 million of bonds (direct credit), turns $1 million into savings banks that then buy the bonds (indirect credit), we have a total debt (and credit) of $2 million instead of $1 million. One million dollars is owed to the banks by the issuers of the bonds, and another million dollars is owed to the public by the banks. Why has this duplication come about? Because for reasons we will discuss later, the public would to some extent rather hold the bank's obligations than the obligations of the original borrower. In effect the bank has traded its obligations for the direct obligations that the public was holding before the bank was organized. Where once there were only the bonds, now there are both bonds and deposits.

There is a fundamental difference between the indirect credit obligations issued by the commercial bank and the indirect obligations issued by any other financial institution. Whatever the institution, the exchange of its liabilities for the direct liabilities held by the public increases the total debt and credit. But in the case of commercial banks only, the exchange *also increases the money supply*. This increase occurs because the obligations of the commercial banks (demand deposits) are so easily transferred and so acceptable that—unlike insurance policies, investment trust certificates, or savings pass-books—they are *themselves money* and are in fact by far the most important part of our money supply. This development has tremendous implications for the economy. It permits the banking system to create money simply by issuing its own promises to pay. Most of the rest of this book will be devoted to explaining how this process works, how it can be controlled, and what significance it has for the level of income and employment.

Effects of Financial Intermediation. *Financial intermediation* is the public's use of financial institutions as middlemen in the flow of money from investors to borrowers and back. Rather than find investment opportunities themselves, savers deposit their money with the intermediaries which find the borrowers for them. These institutions provide a useful service by reducing the costs to individuals of negotiating transactions, procuring information, achieving diversification, and attaining liquidity. *Disintermediation* occurs when savers reduce their funds in financial institutions to buy securities directly.

The increased importance of financial intermediaries has had the effect of reducing the demand for money, increasing money's velocity (see the end-sheet of this text for the time path of income velocity), and lowering interest rates. The safety and liquidity of intermediary liabilities such as commercial savings or savings and loan deposits have lessened people's desire to hold non-interest-bearing money. These near-monies issued by financial intermediaries are sometimes included in the broad definition of the money supply (M_2 and M_3) by those who feel they are such close substitutes for currency and demand deposits that they are an integral part of the money supply. The financial intermediaries use the funds released from cash holdings to buy bonds and thereby drive down the interest rate. Although interest rates have increased generally in the last 25 years, this increase has happened in spite of and not because of financial intermediation.

This burgeoning growth in financial intermediaries has caused some problems in using monetary policy as an anticyclical device. The Gurley-Shaw hypothesis, named after its originators and major expositors, John G. Gurley and Edward S. Shaw, emphasizes that the growth in these near-monies can be troublesome since financial intermediaries are for the most part outside the jurisdiction of the Federal Reserve.[2] Gurley and Shaw think that intermediation hinders the effectiveness of Fed stabilization policy, especially policies controlling inflation.[3] Any attempt to reduce spending on real and financial assets by cutting the money supply can be foiled. The increase in interest rates caused by such a cut allows intermediaries such as savings and loan associations to raise the rates paid on deposits, coax out idle money balances, and lend borrowers (spenders) the funds they need to purchase assets. Thus,

---

[2] John G. Gurley and Edward S. Shaw, *Money in a Theory of Finance* (Washington: Brookings Institution, 1960).
[3] Their thesis also has some interesting implications for economic growth.

the Fed has difficulty in controlling inflation when it cannot control the creation of near-monies by nonbank financial intermediaries.

In the 1950s and early 1960s the Gurley-Shaw hypothesis seemed to collide with the truth quite often. But in the tight money periods of 1966, 1969, and 1974, financial disintermediation occurred. People shifted funds out of financial intermediaries and directly purchased securities. The intermediaries raised complaints but did not adjust their deposit rates high enough to stay competitive with direct securities because, for one reason, they couldn't by law go above the legal ceilings imposed by the supervisory agencies. For another, they were hesitant about raising rates for all depositors when their portfolios were predominately long term and included many assets with low yields acquired in earlier time periods.

FORMS OF CREDIT

Credit may be classified on the basis of whether or not it is extended on the basis of formal documents called credit instruments.

Informal Credit Arrangements

Some credit is handled informally with little or no actual evidence. Small sums are often lent with only an oral promise to repay. Charge accounts involve no regular credit instruments. Telephone and electric bills are usually paid monthly, and in many other lines credit is commonly extended to customers on a retail, wholesale, or manufacturing level. Unlike the credit instruments discussed in the following section, this kind of credit is not often transferred. Sometimes a firm may sell its slow pay accounts at a discount to a collection agency rather than fight for payments itself. And sometimes a firm applying for a loan may pledge its accounts receivable as security for the loan. Generally, though, a firm handles its own accounts receivable.

Credit Instruments

Credit instruments are formal documents drawn up as evidences of credit. They are of two types: *promises* to pay and *orders* to pay. Most instruments may easily be transferred from one holder to another. Some, such as checks, are so readily transferable that they are regularly used as a means of payment, almost entirely replacing coins for all but the smallest transactions.

Both types have a far older history than most people realize. They came into use even before coinage was invented. Almost 3,000 years ago the Assyrians were using both promises and orders to pay. They wrote the terms of the agreements on clay tablets and baked the tablets to preserve them and prevent alteration. Since coins were not yet used, these instruments ordinarily specified the payment of some weight of gold or silver. The Babylonians also regularly used credit instruments; however, credit instruments were less important in the less commercially oriented Greek and Roman civilizations.

Commercial banks and other financial institutions create credit, sometimes as creditors, sometimes as debtors. Their principal assets are credit instruments, which they buy and sell. By one type of credit instrument (checks) the public continuously changes the ownership of the credit liabilities of the commercial banks (demand deposits).

Promises. There are two kinds of promises to pay, with no clear dividing line between them. In a general way we can say that one (notes) is more likely to be concerned with short-term credit than is the other (bonds). This distinction, however, does not always hold. In either case, though, we simply have an instrument of credit which indicates that the borrower agrees (promises) to repay the sum lent, at a specified annual rate of interest, at a specified time.

Orders. Instead of being in the form of a promise to pay, a credit instrument may be an order to pay. Orders to pay are called *drafts*. The person who signs a draft is the *drawer*, and the person or firm ordered to pay is the *drawee*. A draft may be drawn against a person or persons, a corporation, or a bank.

The most common draft is the *check*. When we write a check we are drawing a draft against our bank, ordering it to pay a certain sum. By previous agreement we know that the bank will honor this draft so long as the check does not exceed our balance at the bank. Because we are all familiar with such drafts and find their use convenient, demand deposits are our most important money. Several other countries rely more on coin and currency.

ATTRIBUTES OF CREDIT INSTRUMENTS

The most important attributes of any financial instrument are its yield, liquidity, and safety. In fact, the major function of financial intermediaries is to provide greater liquidity and safety through trading their own financial claims for the financial claims of others. The cost to users of these services is sometimes a smaller yield than if they assumed the greater risk and less liquidity themselves.

Yield

The *yield* of an asset refers generally to its return over cost. The *current yield* refers to the dollar return per year divided by the current market price of the debt obligation. For instance, most bonds pay a fixed yearly sum as interest and ordinarily are sold in $1,000 denominations. Therefore, if a bond promises to pay $1,000 at the end of 10 years, has a nominal (or coupon) yield of 8 percent or $80 a year in interest, and sells for $900, the current yield is $80 ÷ $900 or 8.89 percent. If the cost (market price) of the bond is $1,100, the current yield is $80 ÷ $1,100 or 7.27 percent. The nominal interest rate is based on the face value of the bond and is unlikely to be exactly the same as the current yield. The (average) yield to maturity takes into account capital gains (or losses) and interest payments.[4] If an 8 percent, 10-year bond is bought at $900, the purchaser receives $80 a year in interest and a capital appreciation of $100 over the 10-year period or an average of $10 a year. Therefore, the average return including both interest and capital appreciation is $90 and the (average) yield to maturity is $90 ÷ $900 or 10 percent. If the purchaser paid $1,100 for the bond, the yield to maturity would be $70 ÷ $1,100 or 6.36 percent.

Liquidity

Liquidity is an asset's capacity to be resold quickly at close to its purchase price. Only money has complete liquidity, but of course it has no yield.

Safety

Safety of principal refers to the degree of risk that the instrument will decline in market value. There are risks both from default and from changes in market values. In the latter case, if interest rates fall (rise), the market value of bonds necessarily rises (falls).

Different assets allow people to select the precise configuration of yield, liquidity, and safety that is best for them. Generally speaking, the greater the liquidity or safety of an asset, the lower the yield. There is usually a trade-off among these three desired attributes.

FUNCTIONS OF CREDIT IN THE ECONOMY

Business, government, and the consumer depend upon credit. Business uses short-term credit to finance inventories and long-term credit to expand its plants and equipment. For the American consumer and the government, credit is indispensable.

Scale Economies

Credit allows mass production economies to develop. If manufacturers could use only profits to expand their production, many companies would never be able to expand. Extension of credit provides manufacturers with capital to expand their production; and the more a company produces, the more profit potential it has because of its increased sales potential. Also, the

---

[4]That is, the yield will depend upon the price *actually paid* for the bond (or alternatively, upon its *current market* price), the yearly payment, and the number of years the bond still has to run. Other things being equal, the closer a bond is to maturity, the closer its market price must be to its face value. Consider two bonds, both paying $35 a year, both selling to yield 7%. One will mature in one year, the other in 10 years. The market price of the former will be $967.29; of the latter, $751.30. Clearly, if the one-year maturity were discounted by nearly $250, the yield (including interest payment) would exceed 35%. But this discount, spread over 10 years, raises the yield from 3½% to only 7%. In our following examples we use, for simplicity, simple rather than compound interest. The books used by most financial institutions which calibrate yield to maturity use compound interest.

larger the production volume, the cheaper the production costs. Thus, larger sales volumes and cheaper production costs mean more profit for manufacturers—funds with which the manufacturers can again expand production and renew the cycle. In this cyclical expansion pattern, credit is almost indispensable. It is the stimulus that starts the cycle by allowing the small producer to produce a little more.

Regulation of the Economy

Like fire, credit is a dangerous servant of humanity. Its results can be disastrous. It must be watched and regulated. Kept within its proper bounds—which can never be exactly defined—it contributes to a rising prosperity, an increasing flow of goods, and jobs for all. Out of control, it can induce roaring inflation followed usually by painful depression.

The commercial banks and more especially the 12 Federal Reserve Banks are largely responsible for credit conditions in our economy. They can encourage credit expansion or force a contraction in credit. When inflationary pressures are strong, the banking system is primarily responsible for containing them by putting the brakes on credit expansion. In the case of recession, the banks can encourage recovery by making credit easier. The regulation of credit together with the allocation of credit are the primary functions of the banks. Herein lies their greatest significance to the economy. Through its dominant role in the credit structure, the banking system carries a formidable responsibility for regulating the economy.

SIZE AND COMPOSITION OF CREDIT INSTITUTION ASSETS

The major financial intermediaries in our country are, as shown in Table 4-1, in order of asset size: commercial banks, savings and loan associations,

Table 4-1   Total Assets of Financial Intermediaries at Year-End
(In billions of dollars)

Financial Intermediary	1945	1955	1960	1965	1970	1973*
Commercial Banks	$160.3	$210.7	$257.6	$377.3	$ 576.2	$ 806.4
Savings and Loan Associations	8.7	37.7	71.5	129.6	176.2	272.4
Life Insurance Companies	44.8	90.4	119.6	158.9	207.3	252.1
Mutual Savings Banks	17.0	31.3	40.6	58.2	79.0	106.6
Finance Companies	4.3	17.1	24.1	41.0	60.4	88.3
Investment Companies	1.3	7.8	17.0	35.2	47.6	46.5
Credit Unions	0.4	2.7	5.7	10.6	17.9	28.6
Private Pension Funds	2.8	18.3	38.2	73.6	110.8	131.5
State and Local Pension Funds	2.7	10.7	19.6	33.1	58.0	80.2
TOTAL	$242.3	$426.7	$593.9	$917.5	$1,333.4	$1,812.6

Source: Adapted from *1974 Savings and Loan Fact Book* (Chicago: United States League of Savings Associations, 1974), p. 53.
*Preliminary

life insurance companies, private noninsured pension funds, mutual savings banks, sales and consumer finance companies, state and local government retirement funds, investment companies (mutual funds), property and casualty insurance companies (not shown, but about $63 billion at the end of 1973), and credit unions. Commercial banks are easily the largest and most diversified in terms of assets and liabilities of the financial intermediaries. About the only major financial asset they do not hold is corporate stocks, which law prohibits them from acquiring. All these financial intermediaries are in competition with each other to acquire assets by issuing claims. The savers look at the relative yield, liquidity, and safety of the claims of the various thrift institutions before deciding where to place their funds.

The asset and liability composition of these financial intermediaries reflects three basic influences: the nature of their liabilities, their legal constraints, and tax considerations. For example, if an intermediary's liabilities are unpredictable, it must have liquid assets. If an interest rate ceiling is set by law, the intermediary cannot raise its rates above that ceiling. And if the intermediary is subject to federal taxation, its portfolio may contain many tax-exempt municipal bonds.

CREDIT INSTITUTIONS OTHER THAN COMMERCIAL BANKS THAT SERVE INDIVIDUALS

Because the commercial banks and the Federal Reserve Banks are the only nongovernmental agencies in this country that have the power to create money, they are the financial institutions with which we are primarily concerned, and will be the subject matter of the next several chapters.[5] However, there are a great many other noncommercial banks, corporations, and individuals that play active parts in the nation's financial affairs. These will be briefly reviewed in the following sections. First, we shall take up the more important institutions that accept public savings and the private concerns other than banks that supply loans to individuals. Next, we shall discuss government credit agencies. The services of trust companies, which do not come under either of these categories, are available to both individuals and businesses and will be discussed at the end of the chapter together with several other financial institutions that serve business.

Depositaries

Institutions that accept public savings are called *depositaries*. The principal depositaries are savings and loan companies, mutual and stock savings banks, and life insurance companies, all of which began operations in this country well over a hundred years ago. Credit unions are much less important because of their much shorter history, but they are growing rapidly. Pension funds are intermediate in both size and rate of growth. Finally, for 56 years

---

[5]The Federal Reserve Banks are quasi-governmental. They are not operated primarily for profit, and they work closely with the government. They are, however, privately owned.

(1910–1966) the government operated the postal savings system, which is now discontinued.

Because of space constraints we cannot discuss in detail all of these institutions, but we do want to examine savings and loan associations more fully because of their size, rapid growth, and unique evolution.

Savings and Loan Companies. Savings and loan, or building and loan, associations are financial intermediaries which accept savings from the public and invest those savings mainly in mortgage loans. Always corporations, they can be classified as mutual (without capital) or capital stock (with capital) institutions, as insured or noninsured, or as state or federally chartered. Presently there are over one and one half times as many state chartered associations as federally chartered ones. Since the establishment of the first building and loan association in Philadelphia in 1831, the nature of these organizations has undergone considerable growth and change, particularly since World War II. By 1973 they had become second, in terms of total assets, only to commercial banks as financial intermediaries.

Today savings and loan associations are very similar to savings banks. Ninety percent are mutual organizations. They have a continuous life; as some loans are paid off, new loans are made. Also, funds are left with them by many who have no intention of building and are interested only in the rate of return.

Until quite recently, funds supplied by savers were technically accounts rather than deposits. The basis for this distinction was that accounts presumably represented purchase of an interest in, rather than money lent to, the organization. The members were considered to be owners receiving dividends rather than creditors receiving interest. However, since 1968 all federally chartered savings and loan associations have been authorized to acquire savings in the form of deposits, certificates, or other accounts, as well as by their traditional passbook accounts. They may now pay interest rather than dividends to their customers.

Traditional distinctions between banks and savings and loan associations are steadily blurring. Savings banks are today, more than ever before, turning to real estate loans. The savings and loan associations, at the same time, are acquiring more liquidity than they formerly had and their system now resembles the banking system in a number of respects. As explained below, they have their own central banks from which they may borrow, and 97 percent of their liabilities are insured by a federal agency. Their liquidity is increased by the secondary market for mortgages approved by the Federal National Mortgage Association, which will purchase mortgages guaranteed by the Veterans Administration or the Federal Housing Administration. Since 1966 their interest rates have been controlled, as bank rates have been for many years. Also, most of the saving and loan associations are now required to maintain liquidity ratios of from 4 to 10 percent (comparable to the reserve requirements of commercial banks).

Today there are about 3,400 savings and loan associations operating under state charters and 2,000 under charters from the federal government as authorized in 1933. Drawing largely upon the experience of the Federal Reserve and the commercial banking system, the government, besides authorizing national charters, set up eleven Home Loan Banks and the Federal Savings and Loan Insurance Corporation. Federal savings and loan associations must belong to these two organizations; state chartered associations may belong. The insurance protects accounts up to $40,000. In the event the association fails, the depositors are given either cash or accounts in another institution, whichever they prefer. Most of the associations, those accounting for 97 percent of the assets, are insured, paying a premium of one twelfth of 1 percent of their total liabilities. The Home Loan Banks, in addition to supervising the member associations, perform central banking functions in lending to the members when they need funds. Almost 5,000 associations as well as a small number of savings banks and one insurance company are members of the Home Loan Bank System.

The rapid postwar growth of the savings and loan associations has been phenomenal. As late as 1941 their accounts totaled less than $5 billion. By 1950 they had shot up to $14 billion, and climbing faster than ever, were about $207 billion by 1973. Besides far outpacing the savings banks, the savings and loan associations have, since World War II, been expanding at a much more rapid rate than have commercial banks.[6] The principal reason for their success is that over most of this period they have been paying dividends at a rate considerably above the interest rate on time and savings deposits. The fast pace of the building industry has also helped them by providing an ample outlet for their funds. They have also benefited from the postwar prosperity that made possible a high level of saving. In 1974 they were authorized to issue negotiable certificates of deposit to compete better with the same financial instruments offered by commercial banks.

Mutual Savings Banks. Mutual savings banks issue claims against themselves in the form of relatively small savings and time deposits, legally payable on short notice. Their assets are predominantly long-term, with real-estate mortgages comprising about two thirds of their assets. They also hold modest amounts of corporate bonds and U.S. government securities.

Life Insurance Companies. Life insurance companies issue claims in the form of life insurance and annuity policies and acquire long-term direct securities such as real estate mortgages and corporate bonds and notes. Although nearly three fourths of their assets are presently held in these instruments, the composition of their portfolios has changed markedly since 1945 when U.S. government securities were quite important.

---

[6] As recently as 1953, deposits of mutual savings banks ($24 billion) exceeded the accounts of the savings and loan companies ($23 billion). But by 1973 the former had grown to about $91 billion, the latter to about $207 billion.

Credit Unions. Credit unions promote thrift among their members and make loans to them, mainly for the purchase of consumer goods such as automobiles. Credit unions issue savings deposit claims against themselves. These institutions first appeared in this country in 1909, but most of their growth has occurred since 1930. In fact since 1945 they have grown faster than any of the older financial institutions.

Pension Funds and Investment Companies (Mutual Funds). Both pension funds and investment companies primarily hold their assets in the form of corporate stocks, although some other long-term claims—real estate, corporate bonds, government obligations, etc.—are held.

Sources of Consumption Loans

Commercial banks are today directly responsible for about a third of all consumption loans. Credit unions are also common sources of consumption loans. Still other possible sources from which consumers may obtain loans include unlicensed lenders, pawnbrokers, consumer finance companies, and sales finance companies.[7]

GOVERNMENT CREDIT AGENCIES

Prior to the Depression, the federal government had set up two agencies in the special field of agricultural credit. However, not until the 1930s did the government, vastly expanding the scope of its operations, undertake the organization of a multitude of often overlapping and frequently reorganized lending agencies. Some of them have passed out of existence, the conditions that required their organization having disappeared. Others have been consolidated or merged with agencies performing similar functions.

The principal federal credit agencies to become established on a permanent basis may be divided into two groups: those that supply credit to and in other ways assist homeowners and renters, and those that assist farmers and small business.

Department of Housing and Urban Development (HUD)

The Department of Housing and Urban Development (HUD) was created in 1965 to take over and expand the operations of the Housing and Home Finance Agency. Its head is a member of the President's Cabinet. HUD is pushing ahead in several directions including city planning and research into new building materials and techniques. Our particular concern, however, is with its financial services. These are provided to meet two basic needs:

---

[7]These institutions are a little different from the others in that they never advance funds to the consumer. Rather, they often finance the dealer when installment sales, especially of automobiles, are made.

1. Adequate housing for low income groups. (This service is supplied by HUD's rental, or public housing, program.)
2. Sound financing for millions of home buyers. (This service is supplied by the Federal Housing Administration, the Federal National Mortgage Association, and the Government National Mortgage Association, all supervised by HUD.)

Subsidized Rental Housing. For many, especially in the cities, homeownership is impossible. They cannot make the payments and maintain the property, and their future plans may be too uncertain to warrant their becoming tied up with real estate. Housing studies seem to indicate that private enterprise cannot profitably supply new homes to rent to those in the lowest income groups. In the past these people have taken over the residences given up by those moving to newer accommodations. By overcrowding and by living in rundown, unsanitary, structurally unsafe homes, they secured shelter of a sort. In short, they lived in the slums.

The desirability of subsidized housing to provide better living conditions for those whom private enterprise cannot adequately supply is generally conceded today, although at one time it was considered rampant socialism. Many people feel that slums are an unnecessary evil for the richest nation in the world. Also, the slums involve high social costs that, if not met one way, must be met another. Better housing is a powerful aid to better citizenship, and it seems more desirable to spend public funds for replacing slums with decent housing than to spend the money for larger police forces and prisons.

Slum renovation is also a desirable area for government expenditures of a countercyclical nature. When such construction programs are undertaken in depression, as many have been, their real cost is very little. Like any building activity at such a time, public or private, these programs do not curtail the production of other goods as might be the case in a period of prosperity. Rather, by increasing income they stimulate additional consumption, helping to raise national income still more and at the same time fulfilling a real social need. Since they do not infringe upon an area in which private capital is actively engaged, they are less likely to cause offsetting declines in private investment than are expenditures for roads, swimming pools, parks, and post offices, and they may be of greater utility. Although their social cost is least in depression, they may be undertaken at other times if the need appears great enough to warrant immediate action.

Provision of low-rent housing requires the cooperation of federal, state, and local authorities. The states have legislation enabling the creation of local housing authorities which must take the initiative in any action involving HUD. The local housing authority first certifies that a need for low-rent housing exists in the community and that the need is not being met by private enterprise. The local housing authority then obtains a written agreement that no property taxes will be imposed by either the state or the municipality upon the project. On the basis of this information, HUD agrees to lend money to cover land and construction costs and also to grant an annual subsidy from funds which Congress appropriates. Without these funds the low rents would be impossible.

HUD obtains its loanable funds from its own capital and by borrowing from the Treasury. As the project gets under way, local authorities borrow the funds necessary to complete the building and usually to repay HUD in full for the money it supplied at the outset. The New Housing Authority bonds issued by the local authorities are secured, both as to interest and as to amortization, by a pledge of the annual contributions that HUD has contracted to pay.[8] When the bonds are finally retired in 30 to 40 years, there is no need for further federal subsidies.

Families are not permitted to live in these projects if their incomes exceed maximum figures. The local authorities set these figures according to the locality and the size of the family. Until 1961 if a family's income rose more than 25 percent above the maximum income permitted, the family was required to move to make space available for others less able to pay for it. Today families, once admitted, are permitted to remain in spite of higher incomes if it appears that they cannot reasonably find decent, safe, sanitary housing. They are, however, required to pay higher rent, and they are expected to locate other quarters within a reasonable period of time.

There have been some HUD projects designed specifically for elderly people of limited means. These projects relieve one aspect of the problems of a rapidly growing sector of older, retired citizens trying to live on inadequate pensions or Social Security payments. Single persons over 62 with low incomes are also admitted to these HUD rental housing projects.

Federal Housing Administration (FHA). The Federal Housing Administration, established in 1934, makes no loans, but has contributed materially to the improvement in home finance in the last forty years. Its primary function is to insure loans made for building, purchasing, or repairing and improving residential property. For this insurance a premium of one half of 1 percent is charged.

The receipts from these premiums, from fees charged, and from investments of the FHA have been sufficient, after the first few years of operation, to pay not only the losses but the entire operating expenses of the FHA so that it no longer receives any funds from the Treasury. To date total income has been about 50 percent greater than the total of operating expenses and losses.

For loans to be insured by the FHA, they must meet certain requirements. Interest rates may not exceed a certain figure set by the FHA in relation to current monetary conditions. Although the loans may run for 20 years and be made for as much as 90 percent of the value of the property, they must be regularly amortized. The amortization payments required must be within the financial ability of the applicant, for it is better to have the loan paid off

---

[8]The unusual combination of a government agency's guarantee and freedom from federal income tax because the bonds are the obligation of a local agency makes these bonds an attractive investment.

than to foreclose, even if the loan is adequately secured. The property must be inspected and approved by a representative of the Federal Housing Administration, a requirement that has restrained unsound construction generally and excessive construction in particular areas.

The great advantage of FHA insurance is that it gives real estate mortgages a national market. Previously home mortgages were difficult to sell outside the immediate local area, making it difficult for the original lender to dispose of a mortgage. Few investors were anxious to lend on the security of houses they had never seen, located in cities they had never visited. Today these investors do not hesitate to acquire mortgages and loans insured by the FHA.

Federal National Mortgage Association (FNMA). Further liquidity for real estate mortgages is created by the Federal National Mortgage Association (FNMA, often referred to as Fannie Mae). The FNMA does not lend money directly to the builder or seller of the property, but provides a *secondary* market for mortgages. When money is tight, it lends against or, if requested, buys acceptable mortgages insured by the FHA or by the Veteran's Administration.[9] At other times when money is easy and lenders are looking for investment outlets, Fannie Mae will sell mortgages from its portfolio. As a result of such operations, interest rates on real estate loans tend to stabilize. Also, of course, mortgages are a more liquid asset.

Whether buying mortgages or lending against them as collateral, the FNMA requires the seller or the borrower to purchase, at the same time, FNMA stock—to the extent of one half of 1 percent of the amount of the loan and from 1 to 2 percent of the amount of mortgages sold.[10] This payment is obviously not designed for the purpose of passing on to customers any losses on the mortgages accepted, since the mortgages are already insured by one or the other of two government agencies. It does, on the other hand, somewhat increase the lending power of the Association. However, FNMA raises most of the funds to finance its secondary market operations by selling its own obligations to private investors. It may, if necessary, also borrow from the Treasury.

In 1968, new government accounting procedures required that all FNMA's mortgage purchases be listed as budget outlays. Accordingly, Fannie Mae was converted into a privately owned corporation, although still under the control of HUD. At the same time a new government agency, "Ginny Mae," was created.

Government National Mortgage Association (GNMA). Like its predecessor, the Government National Mortgage Association (often referred to as Ginnie Mae) may purchase mortgages. It often then sells them, at a loss, to FNMA.

---

[9]Currently, "acceptable" is defined to include mortgages insured since 1954. At one time the FNMA required that mortgages it purchased or against which it lent be insured not more than four months earlier.

[10]As currently determined by the Association.

This may seem to be a strange way to run a business. The point is, of course, that the goal is not to maximize profits but to increase the availability and reduce the cost of credit for homeownership. When credit is tight, the (non-profit) GNMA may provide lower cost loans than the (profit-oriented) FNMA. When GNMA sells the mortgages to FNMA, private funds replace government funds. GNMA's only cash outlay is the difference between the face value of the mortgage (which is what it paid) and the lower price in the market (which it received from FNMA).

In addition GNMA is authorized to guarantee the interest and principal of securities issued by a lending association and backed by FHA and VA mortgages. If a savings and loan association has no more funds to lend, instead of selling some of the mortgages that it holds, it may put them up as collateral behind an issue of its own notes—which will be guaranteed by GNMA.

Home Loan Bank Board

Cooperating with the organizations directed by the Department of Housing and Urban Development are the agencies managed by the Home Loan Bank Board (HLBB). These include the Federal Home Loan Bank System, the Federal Savings and Loan Insurance Corporation, and the federal savings and loan institutions.[11]

The Federal Home Loan Bank System is patterned after the Federal Reserve System except that its members are the savings and loan associations, savings banks, and insurance companies that wish to join. The members buy stock in the Home Loan Banks, keep deposits with them, and borrow from them on the security of their residential mortgages. The Home Loan Banks cannot create money like the Federal Reserve Banks. They lend funds received from the two sources mentioned above and from the sale of bonds to the public. They also set the liquidity ratios that their members must maintain, and they determine the interest rates that members may pay.

The Federal Savings and Loan Insurance Corporation serves the same purpose for the savings and loan companies that the FDIC serves for the commercial banks. By insuring savings deposits, the FSLIC encourages the flow of funds into the savings and loan institutions, increasing the supply of funds available for homeownership.

Evaluation of the Program

As a result of the activities of HUD, the HLBB, and similar organizations, there has been a great improvement in home finance and a marked expansion of homeownership. The growth of building and loan institutions has

---

[11]In the multitude of overlapping agencies we might note also the Federal Home Loan Mortgage Corporation, created in 1970 as a subsidiary of the Home Loan Bank Board. The difference between this organization and the two mortgage associations just discussed is that the first two deal only with VA and FHA mortgages. The new agency creates a secondary market for conventional mortgages, that is, mortgages without the guarantee of the VA or FHA.

been encouraged, increasing the supply of funds available for buying homes. Mortgages have been made more liquid in a number of ways—by government insurance, by their acceptance as collateral for loans by the Home Loan Bank System, by the secondary market created by the FNMA and GNMA, and by the general practice of requiring regular amortization. The added liquidity and safety have resulted in lower interest rates.

Thus, home-buyers pay lower interest rates and make lower down payments than they did a generation ago. Each month they pay something toward retiring the principal of the loan, so they are constantly increasing their equity. With fixed and regular commitments, they find that home purchase is as simple as paying rent. Largely in consequence of these improvements, the increase in homeownership resulted in about 63 percent of the families in the United States owning their own homes by 1970.

Agricultural Credit

Like other businesspeople, farmers frequently need credit. They require long-term loans to purchase their farms, and they need short-term credit to meet current expenses of production. Frequently they need credit also for several years (intermediate term loans) to permit them to buy machinery and equipment.

Due to their importance to the economy (not to mention the importance of their votes to legislators), farmers over the last forty years have benefited from a multitude of special lending agencies organized to meet their needs. As additional credit requirements of farmers appeared, the government usually set up new bureaus rather than increase the authority of existing agencies. Although some agencies have been discontinued, most are still in operation, frequently duplicating the functions of other divisions.

The Farm Credit Administration today supervises and coordinates three separate systems of banks set up to provide credit to farmers. These include:

1. Twelve Federal Land Banks, established in 1916 to provide long-term credit for the purchase of farms and for other purposes.
2. Twelve Banks for Cooperatives and a Central Bank for Cooperatives, organized in 1933, to provide short-term credit to farm cooperatives.
3. Twelve Intermediate Credit Banks, established in 1923 and ordinarily lending for periods of one to three years.

Small Business Credit

The term *small business* is an elastic one. There is no fixed size below which any business may be said to be small. The small business has always been at a disadvantage in securing long-term capital. Without too much difficulty it can secure working capital, both from the banks and from larger corporations that may extend it credit when they sell to it. It usually has to pay a higher interest rate than does big business to offset the greater administrative costs of handling small loans and to compensate for the greater credit risk, however. But, at a price, it can obtain short-term funds. Also, through term loans it can today meet most of its requirements for intermediate credit.

Long-term funds are another matter. Mortgages are a possible answer. If the firm has the necessary assets to pledge, it can borrow from banks or insurance companies. But very often a small business operates in rented quarters with highly specialized equipment, unsuitable security for a loan. It is not practical for small businesspeople to borrow by selling bonds, for their credit rating is not sufficiently high or widely enough known. They may possibly be able to bring in more equity capital, but not usually.

The growth of financial institutions during the last half century, helpful as it has been to business in many ways, has operated to the detriment of small business. A century ago, friends and relatives often lent their savings to the small businessperson. There was little else they could do with their money other than put it in the mattress. Today they can turn it over to the banks, the government, pension funds, savings and loan companies, insurance companies, or other institutions. None of these organizations is set up to supply long-term credit to small business. It appeared that small business might eventually disappear from the American scene unless some way could be found to provide it with long-term funds.

Small Business Investment Act

To meet the need, the Small Business Investment Act of 1958 set up a revolving fund of $250 million to underwrite a new system of lending institutions to be called *small business investment companies*. These companies raise their capital through the sale of stock to individuals and corporations, including commercial banks. They may also sell up to $150,000 of their stock to the Small Business Administration, which supervises the administration of the Act. In addition, the companies may borrow from both private sources and the Small Business Administration. They are authorized to make 20-year loans, with the possibility of 10-year extensions, to small business. They may also lend to homeowners who have suffered losses through disasters. In many instances commercial banks take the initiative in the organization of small business investment companies. Through these companies loans can be made that would be inappropriate for the banks themselves.

The Act also repealed Section 13b of the Federal Reserve Act which had permitted Federal Reserve Banks to make direct loans of working capital to business. The funds that had been appropriated for that purpose were turned over to the Treasury by the Banks. The Act further authorized the Treasury to create a special fund with the released money, out of which it may make grants for research and advice in the field of small business.

Besides helping small business to obtain credit, the Small Business Administration assists in other ways. Small businesspeople may not know the necessary procedures to buy surplus property from the government or to obtain contracts to supply materials to or perform research for the government.

For such activities the SBA provides technical and managerial aid. It also provides financial counseling when such counseling is desired.

CREDIT INSTITUTIONS OTHER THAN COMMERCIAL BANKS THAT SERVE BUSINESS

A wide array of specialized institutions has developed to meet the financial requirements of business. To some extent they compete with the banks; to some extent they provide services not available from banks. They help business obtain funds from the public and they make corporate securities readily marketable. Also, they are qualified to make some loans that banks would normally reject.

Sales Finance Companies

We have already mentioned that sales finance companies loan to consumers, who were the first to benefit from them. Later, wholesalers found them helpful, and today many retailers use the services of sales finance companies. Big business is ordinarily able to get credit, either from banks or by selling securities to the public, on much better terms than are offered by sales finance companies. Small business, however, has always had as much difficulty obtaining credit as have consumers. A bank is about the only agency that will lend to a small business. However, a bank would rather lend working capital, to be repaid within two or three months, than lend longer term credit to a small business. If a small business wishes to buy new fixtures, for example, or to install air conditioning equipment, the bank may be unwilling to lend the necessary funds. Similarly, a garage or small shop might require equipment that would pay for itself in a few years but that its bank might hesitate to finance. The sales finance companies can handle these requirements of business in the same manner as they finance consumers, taking over the installment contract and allowing the firm to purchase the necessary equipment over a period of months or years.

Commercial Finance Companies and Factors

Companies that finance the accounts receivable (not installment contracts) of the borrower are important sources of credit for some businesses. Such lending may take one of two forms.

Commercial finance companies specialize in *nonnotification financing*. They purchase accounts receivable at a discount or lend against them as security, with no notice being given to the customer whose paper is being financed. They assume no risk; if there is any trouble in collecting from the borrower's customer, the borrower, not the finance company, must bear the loss. Several billion dollars of accounts are financed annually by this technique of nonnotification lending with recourse to the borrower. In addition to the commercial finance companies, some commercial banks and sales finance companies also engage in nonnotification lending against accounts receivable.

In the older type of accounts receivable financing, the lender, called a *factor*, purchases at a discount the accounts receivable or lends against them as security, but with two important distinctions from the method described above. The factor assumes the credit risk, so that the seller, once the factor has taken over the accounts, need not be concerned about the credit of the customer. Also, the customer is notified that payments are to be made to the factor.

Investment Banks

In contrast to savings banks and commercial banks, investment banks receive no deposits and their principal function is not so much lending as it is marketing the securities by which corporations and governmental units secure their long-term capital requirements. Until they were forbidden to do so by the Banking Act of 1933, many commercial banks were also in the investment banking field. (The commercial banks may still market government securities—federal, state, and municipal—but may not be associated with the marketing of corporate issues.)

Essentially, an investment bank is a group of individuals, in the form of either a partnership or a corporation, whose business it is to float new issues of stocks and bonds. Less than a century ago even the federal government found their distribution services indispensable, although today the bonds and other obligations of the Treasury are so well established and the support of the Federal Reserve is so great that the Treasury no longer needs to depend upon investment bankers except for certain technical services.[12] For other governmental units, however, and for corporations they are still of great assistance, although the increase in direct placements of stocks and bonds with insurance companies and other large lenders has somewhat reduced the volume of their operations.

Commercial Paper Houses

Similar to investment banks are the commercial paper houses that market *short*-term obligations of business instead of the bonds and stocks handled by the investment banks. Like the investment banks, the commercial paper houses seldom deal with small business for they cannot expect to market successfully the notes of an unknown corporation. Salespeople from these houses sell to their customers the notes of corporations that wish to borrow additional funds for a few months and prefer to borrow in the open market rather than from their banks. Like the investment banks the commercial paper houses are compensated by a small margin between the price at which they buy the issue and the price at which they sell or by a commission if they are acting as brokers rather than dealers.

---

[12]However, in 1963 the Treasury, for the first time in 68 years, turned to investment bankers to float bond issues.

Bill Brokers and Dealers

Some firms specialize in acceptances, either as dealers purchasing them outright or as brokers finding buyers for them. *Acceptances*, especially bank acceptances, are short-term investments of very high grade. Many corporations are glad to invest temporarily excess funds with the practical certainty that the money will be available again when they require it. The increased marketability for acceptances provided by bill brokers and dealers results in low rates on such paper with consequent savings to firms using acceptances as a source of short-term credit. Acceptances are commonly used by firms in the field of foreign trade.

Security Exchanges

In large cities organized markets have been created for trading in publicly held bonds and stocks. Stock exchanges do not distribute new issues, but they facilitate trading in issues already outstanding. These security exchanges may be primarily local concerns, dealing mostly in the stocks of mining and manufacturing companies in the vicinity that are owned mostly by local residents. At the other extreme are the large exchanges (by far the best known of which is the New York Stock Exchange) that deal nationally and internationally in the securities of nearly all the largest corporations. In either case the principle is the same. Stockbrokers and traders, to provide more convenient trading facilities, form an association and arrange a common meeting place. Only members of the association have the right to trade on the floor of the exchange, either for their own account or for the account of others. Companies that wish their securities listed on an exchange apply to the officials of that organization. In general, the exchanges prefer to list the stocks and bonds of well-known established companies, the securities of which are fairly widely held.

Over-the-Counter Market

Securities not traded on the exchanges are transferred in the so-called over-the-counter market. This is not a market at all in the ordinary sense of a central meeting place where all transactions take place. It is a term that loosely includes all the brokers and dealers outside the organized exchanges. If a customer asks a broker to buy an unlisted security, the broker, unless he or she happens at the same time to have another customer who wishes to sell the same amount of the same security, contacts other brokers until one who can supply the desired security is found. Many more issues are traded in the over-the-counter market than are traded on the exchanges, although the majority of such issues are relatively small. The more important securities bought and sold in this manner include those of the United States government, the stocks of many banks and insurance companies, and the tax-exempt securities issued by state and local governments. Despite the lack of centralization there is a continuous market for well-known securities such as these. At the other extreme are the small issues of unestablished companies, the securities of which are often not readily traded due to the limited interest in them and to their narrow distribution. Not only the trading in securities outstanding, but also the primary distribution (that is, original sale) of securities by investment bankers takes place through this network of brokers and dealers that makes up the over-the-counter market.

Trust Institutions

Trust institutions include the trust companies, which do no other business, and the trust departments operated by many banks. The principal function of any trustee is to hold property and administer it for the benefit of others. Like the sales finance companies, these firms serve both business and individuals.

SUMMARY AND CONCLUSION

Credit is one side of a coin, while debt is the other side. Creditors lend goods or services or, more commonly, the funds to buy them. Debtors receive the loans and agree to repay later what they receive today.

The basis of credit is trust. Borrowers' credit ratings are established by their character, capacity, and capital. Their collateral will also be considered if they are required to put up security for the loan.

Credit may be variously classified, according to whether it is for consumption or for production, according to the length of time it is to run, and according to whether it is extended to the private or the public sector of the economy. In modern times a further important distinction has appeared in that credit may be extended either directly or indirectly. Indirect credit duplicates and increases total credit outstanding. Intermediaries, called financial institutions, issue their own credit obligations to the public and take over obligations which the public previously held as direct lenders. So, where once there was a thousand dollar bond held by some person, there now is a thousand dollar bond held by a financial intermediary and a thousand dollar obligation of that intermediary held by the public. The public prefers to hold some of its assets in the form of indirect credit because such obligations are usually safer and more liquid than the direct obligations of the borrower. The commercial banks have become the most important of these intermediaries because their obligations have come to be used as money.

Financial institutions are dealers in credit instruments, which they buy and sell freely if the paper is negotiable. This paper is in the form of either promises to pay or orders to pay. So long as the debtor's credit is good, the claim against that debtor to be paid in the future has a present value placed upon it in the market. The purchaser of the credit instrument gains the difference between the present value and the amount the debtor will eventually pay.

The significance of the banking system to our economy lies not only in its ability to provide credit as a lubricant for the economic machine, but also in its power to exercise a stabilizing force over the whole economic process. As creators of money and as the dominant financial institutions, the banks can largely determine how much or how little credit shall be extended and who shall receive it. Their role is central and their decisions are critical.

In addition to commercial banks and the Federal Reserve Banks, there are a number of other credit institutions in our country. Financial institutions such as savings and loan companies, mutual savings banks, life insurance companies, credit unions, pension funds, investment companies, and various consumer lending companies serve individuals. Some financial institutions, such as sales finance companies, commercial finance companies, factors, investment banks, commercial paper houses, bill brokers and dealers, security exchanges, the over-the-counter market, and trust institutions, serve businesses or both businesses and individuals. Finally, there are a host of federal government credit agencies which benefit both individuals and businesses, such as HUD, FHA, FNMA, GNMA, the Home Loan Bank Board, the Farm Credit Administration, and the Small Business Administration.

Discussion Questions

1. Which of the following would usually be classified as production credit? Briefly explain.
   a. Money borrowed to send a person to the moon.
   b. Money borrowed to build a distillery.
   c. Money borrowed to build a bridge.
   d. Money borrowed to build a home.
   e. Money borrowed to drill an oil well.
2. If all our debt, public and private, were paid off, would we be any richer or poorer? Explain fully the direct consequences, but do not speculate upon possible indirect results.
3. Distinguish between direct and indirect credit and explain the advantage of each to the borrower and to the lender. Give an example of each.
4. Classify the following items as direct credit, indirect credit, or neither. Briefly explain.
   a. General Motors stock
   b. Demand deposits
   c. Federal Reserve notes
   d. Silver certificates
   e. U.S. Treasury bonds
   f. Santa Fe Railroad bonds
   g. Savings and loan accounts
   h. Home mortgages
5. Of all the financial institutions we have discussed, the commercial banks were the most useful in the development of the frontier. Explain.
6. Financial intermediaries have the effect of reducing the demand for money, increasing its velocity, and lowering interest rates. Explain.
7. What possible implication does the rapid growth of the depositaries discussed in this chapter have for monetary policy?
8. What does the Gurley-Shaw hypothesis state? Is it valid?
9. Even though most Americans are not financiers, practically all, rich or poor, are familiar with promises to pay and most with orders to pay. Explain.

10. List and describe briefly the three most important attributes of any financial instrument.
11. Discuss the factors which influence the composition of a financial intermediary's assets and liabilities.
12. What is the most important financial intermediary? Why? What are some others?
13. Today, members of federal savings and loan associations may hold deposits rather than accounts with the association and receive interest rather than dividends. Are these changes in terminology of any real significance?
14. List the reasons for the greater liquidity of the savings and loan associations today than 35 years ago.
15. In what respects are the Home Loan Banks similar to the Federal Reserve Banks? In what important way is their operation different?
16. How do the FHA and the FNMA contribute to real estate financing?
17. Why was it necessary to create the Government National Mortgage Association, and how does this Association supplement the work of FNMA?

Chapter 5   Evolution of the Commercial Bank

There are several types of banks, the most important being commercial banks, savings banks, and firms that handle investment banking. Our primary interest is with commercial banks, for they are the only ones that can expand or contract the money supply. Savings banks, investment banking houses, and other financial institutions were discussed briefly in Chapter 4. In every instance, the term *bank* will refer to a commercial bank unless there is explicit reference to the contrary.

A century ago commercial bankers lent almost exclusively for business and short-run purposes. Governments seldom borrowed except in time of war, and private individuals did not often borrow from the banks to meet their personal needs or desires. Today banks lend billions of dollars to the government and provide billions of dollars of credit for consumers. Moreover, commercial banks perform a host of diverse services besides making loans. However, what is truly unique about commercial banks relative to other financial institutions is not on the asset side, but on the debt side. Only commercial banks among the financial intermediaries have the ability to create and destroy money by issuing and destroying debts which circulate as money. But despite all these factors, for convenience these financial institutions are still referred to as commercial banks.

Although there have been money lenders since ancient times, banks are a relatively recent economic institution. The technique of banking developed in the 17th century, greatly aiding the industrial and territorial expansion that began about the same time.

Three principal reasons explain why banking was not developed earlier:

1. The cornerstone of banking is credit. Banks can operate only as long as they have the public's confidence (as was painfully evident in 1932). In the absence of just and adequate property laws, uniformly enforced, and under the handicap of the poor communications and uncertain transportation of the period, confidence in banking would have been shaky indeed a thousand years ago.
2. Banks were not needed as creators of credit money. Through the long centuries from the fall of Rome to the Renaissance there was little interest in commerce. Nor could finance and trade develop in a morass of ignorance and illiteracy. When no educational facilities were provided for common people, and when even noblemen and kings were often illiterate, the only understandable kind of money was metal. Since the feudal system

relied on self-sufficiency rather than on specialization and exchange, little money was needed anyway. Coins were sufficient.

3. Few loans could have been profitably made. Scholars, rulers, and religious leaders long opposed the taking of interest. From almost the first time money came into use until into the 14th century, interest was prohibited. (Indeed, even today there are fringe groups still arguing that interest should be prohibited.) The Greek philosophers argued that, since money was barren, the lender had no right to receive in repayment any more than was lent. Jewish law forbade Jews to take interest from each other, although it permitted them to lend to others at interest. Roman writers agreed in the condemnation of interest, and the Catholic Church prohibited it. Under such unfavorable circumstances it is not surprising that lending institutions failed to develop. In passing, we may note that nearly all the lending that did take place through this period was for consumption rather than for increasing business profits. Borrowers were likely to be people in distress. To charge them a price for lending them the money they desperately needed appeared to the writers of the day to be taking advantage of their necessity. It should be sufficient if they repaid the loans. Today only the charging of excessively high interest rates—called *usury*—is prohibited by law.

The growth of trade and commerce during the Renaissance led to the opportunity of business expansion on the basis of credit. It became apparent that, if a profit could be made by borrowing money, there was justification in requiring a part of this profit to be surrendered to the lender, without whose cooperation the profit would not have materialized. After this point was conceded, it followed that, regardless of whether the undertaking actually turned out successfully, the lender should have the right to receive interest. In the first place, the lender should be compensated for accepting the risk that he or she may not be repaid the money lent. In the second place, if the lender did not lend the money to the creditor, he or she might employ it profitably in some business venture or lend to someone who would gladly pay for the use of the funds. Money itself was as barren as ever, but people now understood that money could be used in highly productive ways. The climate was more favorable for the evolution of lending institutions.

THE GOLDSMITHS

The first bankers in the modern sense were the goldsmiths, who frequently accepted bullion and coins for storage. Individuals fortunate enough to possess money savings faced the problem of safeguarding them against loss. If they wished to hold them in the form of money, they had only two alternatives—to hide or store the coins themselves, or to turn them over to someone else to store. Since the goldsmiths ordinarily possessed the strongest vaults, they soon became the principal warehousers of other people's gold and silver. Incidentally, during this same period in history, Europe's stock of gold and silver money was being swollen by the tons of bullion being carried from the New World in the Spanish treasure ships. The problem of proper storage became more important than before.

If people store cars or household goods, they expect to get back the identical goods when they take them out of storage. But when they store money, they need not receive back the same coins they surrendered earlier.[1] The goldsmiths had only to agree to return the same number of coins that they received. One result was that the goldsmiths could temporarily lend part of the gold left with them. If few customers would be likely to come in immediately and demand gold, the goldsmiths could take a chance. If they made only short-term, well-secured loans with properly spaced maturities, they could expect to have their loans constantly maturing. Every week, gold would flow back to their vaults, with interest, as loans were repaid. Here was something new! Until now, interest had been receivable, if at all, only on one's own funds. Here was a way to gain interest by using the funds of others.

Note Issue

These loans of their customers' gold were soon replaced by a revolutionary technique. To see how this worked, we look first at the notes the goldsmiths issued.

When people brought in gold, the goldsmiths gave them notes promising to pay that amount of gold on demand. When these notes were first issued, in small amounts, they were handwritten. Later they were printed.

A less obvious but equally important change affecting future credit development was that the notes, first made payable to the order of the individual, were changed later to bearer obligations. In the earlier form, a note payable to the order of Harold Wait would be paid to no one else unless Wait had endorsed the note. This was a desirable feature if, as was normally assumed when goldsmiths first issued their notes, Wait intended to hold the note until he wanted gold. There would be little point in stealing it or in failing to return it to him if someone found it.

But notes were soon being used in an unforeseen way. The noteholders found that, when they wanted to buy something, they could spare themselves the trouble of exchanging their notes for gold. They could use the note itself in payment more conveniently and let the other person go after the gold, which the person rarely did. As the note continued to circulate, perhaps for years after it was issued, the original purpose of the endorsement disappeared. Since it was no longer a desirable requirement, it was discontinued, and notes were issued payable to bearer.

The specie, then, tended to remain in the goldsmiths' vaults. As long as there was no doubt about its security there, the public found that the goldsmiths' notes offered certain advantages over gold or silver just as, in more recent times, most people preferred to carry silver certificates rather than exchange them for the silver dollars in which they were redeemable.

The goldsmiths began to realize that they might profit handsomely by issuing somewhat more notes than the amount of specie they held. These notes

---

[1]Storage of a coin collection may appear to be an exception. However, that would not really involve the storage of money, but of a collection of specific items not considered by their owner as an ordinary means of payment.

issued as loans would be in every respect identical to the notes issued to storers of specie. They would be a promise to pay, on demand, specified sums in gold or silver to the bearer. Once in the hands of the public most of them would likely continue to circulate, and there would be almost as much specie in storage as before. Here was, it appeared, the road to riches. These additional notes would cost the goldsmiths nothing except the negligible cost of printing them, yet the notes provided the goldsmiths with funds to lend at interest. The principle was apparently kept secret for a time, and those who shared the secret reaped large profits from lending at high interest rates the notes which had cost them nothing.

The goldsmiths realized, of course, that if everyone who held their notes were to come in the same day and demand redemption, their stocks of specie would be exhausted and some noteholders would remain unpaid. However, this does not mean that such noteholders would never be paid. Remember that the goldsmiths issued additional notes as loans. With what could borrowers repay the goldsmiths?

1. They might use the goldsmith's own notes. If not reissued, those particular notes could not be presented for redemption since they would already be in the hands of the goldsmith, not the public.
2. Or they might use notes of other goldsmiths, in which case the goldsmith receiving the notes could present them to the other firms, demand gold, and use that gold to retire more notes he himself had issued.
3. Or of course the loans might be repaid in gold or silver, and again the goldsmith would then have the specie to retire some more of his own notes.

Limits on Note Issue

As long as there were no loan losses, or as long as the interest receipts offset the occasional bad loans, there would really be no limit to the amount of notes that might be issued on the basis of the specie held by the goldsmith. All could eventually be repaid.

However, no firm wants to liquidate to pay off a line of noteholders. The important thing was to see that no general demand for redemption took place. Nor was a run likely to begin as long as the public continued to have confidence in the firm. The best way to maintain that confidence was to manage affairs in such a way that the public would never doubt that all notes presented would be promptly redeemed. On that basis the lenders might continue indefinitely lending and relending the money that they printed themselves. And they were to find that the profitability of their lending operations would exceed the profit from their original trade. The goldsmiths became bankers as their interest in manufacture was replaced by their concern with credit policies and lending activities.

They discovered early that, although an unlimited note issue would be unwise, they could issue notes up to several times the amount of specie they held. As long as credit was expanded gradually, the public could be counted upon to absorb the added notes and keep them in circulation.

STARTING A BANK

The easiest way to see the relationships involved in starting a bank is to trace through the organization and early operation of a 17th century bank. Suppose that, after the goldsmiths were replaced by banks organized as such, a group of individuals subscribed $100,000 to establish a bank, the entire amount being paid in specie. The balance sheet of the bank at this stage would appear in a T-account as follows:[2]

Assets (A)		Liabilities & Net Worth (L & NW)	
Vault Cash	$100,000	Capital Stock	$100,000

There is nothing profitable in such a state of affairs, with no income and with the necessity of safeguarding the cash. The bank officers will be anxious to lend their funds and begin earning some interest. Any business organization other than a bank would be able to lend only the $100,000, so that the balance sheet would be changed to read:

A		L & NW	
Loans	$100,000	Capital Stock	$100,000

Since the bank issues notes which the public is willing to accept as money, it would decline to make its loans in the form of gold and silver, and would instead provide the borrower with its notes. By this means the bank might gradually make a considerably larger volume of loans and increase its earnings by several hundred percent. The balance sheet might then read:

A		L & NW	
Vault Cash	$100,000	Notes	$500,000
Loans	500,000	Capital Stock	100,000
	$600,000		$600,000

This illustration has been deliberately oversimplified to bring out the point that a bank's lending power depended primarily on its power to create money. In this quite unrealistic example we have omitted entirely the specie brought in by the public. But from this simple example it should be clear that, as long as the bank can exchange its own promissory notes for those of the borrowers, the bank's loans need not be restricted to the amount of coins it may hold.

Importance of Deposits

In actual operation, coins brought in by the public were important to a bank in three ways. In the first place, the sums of specie left with the bank for

[2]The assets *(A)* of a business are the things of value which it can claim or which it owns; liabilities *(L)* are the claims against it or the amount it owes; and net worth *(NW)* is the differential.

convenience increased the bank's stock of specie. To be sure, every time a customer deposited a dollar of specie, the bank gave the customer a dollar note in exchange. Remember, however, that several dollars of notes could be backed by a single dollar of specie. Every time the bank received a dollar of specie, it was able to place in circulation not only the note it exchanged for the coin but several more notes, issued gradually to borrowers.

In the second place, the greater the total of a bank's assets, the better known the bank became and the greater became public confidence in the bank's notes. The credit rating of a small, unknown bank would be so poor that its notes might tend to be presented rather promptly for redemption. Such a bank could not safely issue many more notes than would be covered by its store of specie. Public confidence was greater in a large bank, and the easiest way to get large amounts of cash was to invite people to deposit surplus funds for safekeeping.

In the third place, the key to the whole operation lay in the public's willingness to leave gold and silver in the banks' vaults and use the banks' notes. If this was not true, then the banks could not possibly issue more notes than the amount of their specie; for every time a note was issued, it would promptly be presented for redemption and the bank would soon have no specie reserves. But as long as the public did prefer the notes to the specie, and as long as the public would regularly bring in to the banks any gold or silver that appeared in circulation, over and above a minimum required for small transactions, then the banks could issue several times as many notes as the amount of their reserves—even if they made all their loans in specie.

Probably, then, before a bank began its lending operations, it would first encourage the public to bring in gold and silver. If this attempt succeeded, the bank might find its assets and liabilities (plus net worth) equal to, perhaps, $500,000.

A		L & NW	
Vault Cash	$500,000	Notes	$400,000
		Capital Stock	100,000
	$500,000		$500,000

As the bank then began to lend, there would be further changes. If the management made its loans by printing more notes and handing these to the borrowers, and if the management felt that notes might be issued to about six times the amount of the vault cash, the books might finally show:

A		L & NW	
Vault Cash	$ 500,000	Notes	$3,000,000
Loans	2,600,000	Capital Stock	100,000
	$3,100,000		$3,100,000

Effect of Lending Specie

Even if the bank made its loans in the form of specie, it might arrive at the same result. If the public preferred to use bank notes rather than specie, the public would return to the bank any excess of specie over the minimum that it wished to hold. If this bank were the only one in the town and it made its loans in specie, then as the borrowers spent the funds, the recipients would gradually return the specie to the banks in exchange for bank notes.[3]

After the first few loans had been made and the specie withdrawn, the books might show:

A		L & NW	
Vault Cash	$200,000	Notes	$400,000
Loans	300,000	Capital Stock	100,000
	$500,000		$500,000

What would be done with this $300,000 of specie withdrawn by the borrowers? We are assuming that the public prefers bank notes to the inconvenience of gold and silver. The specie would be returned to the bank by those who received the borrowed funds. When they exchanged the coins for the bank's notes, the records would show:

A		L & NW	
Vault Cash	$500,000	Notes	$700,000
Loans	300,000	Capital Stock	100,000
	$800,000		$800,000

Again the bank might lend $300,000 of specie, decreasing vault cash to $200,000 and increasing loans to $600,000. After the specie was again returned to the bank's vaults, the bank would hold:

A		L & NW	
Vault Cash	$ 500,000	Notes	$1,000,000
Loans	600,000	Capital Stock	100,000
	$1,100,000		$1,100,000

By repeatedly lending its stock of specie and repeatedly exchanging its notes for the specie as the latter was returned to the bank, the bank might show the same relationships on its balance sheet as it would if it made loans by issuing its own notes. By either method of lending, the bank, with $100,000 of specie provided by sale of capital stock and $400,000 of specie secured from the general public, might finally have earning assets of $2,600,000. If the bank could earn 8 percent on the $2,600,000, it would take in $208,000, out of which, hopefully, it could cover its losses and operational expenses and pay a dividend on its $100,000 of capital stock. Obviously if it were to double its note issue, it would slightly more than double its earnings.[4] It was, however, dangerous to expand a note issue indefinitely because of the ever-present

---

[3]If there were several banks, the general principle would be the same. If all followed this policy of making specie loans, all would benefit by the return flow. If some lent specie and others lent their notes, there would be a tendency for a temporary transfer of funds, with a drain of specie from the banks lending in that form into the other banks. Some of it would later be recovered. Total specie held by all banks together would be little affected.

[4]Assuming it could double its loans without causing a drop in interest rates or an increase in the percentage of losses.

danger that the public might begin to require the notes to be redeemed. The greater the note expansion, the greater was this possibility of embarrassing demands for redemption.

NOTE ISSUE AND MODERN BANKING

Except for the 12 Federal Reserve institutions, banks in the United States no longer issue bank notes. But two fundamental elements of modern banking which evolved are most clearly seen in the practice of note issue: fractional reserves and the monetization of credit.

Fractional Reserves

Today banks are required to maintain reserves against their deposits. But the reserve against deposits, like the reserve originally employed by the banks against the notes, is only partial. As illustrated earlier, because the banks can lend several times as much as their actual store of cash, they are essentially different from other lenders. Thus, individual banks are able to create money, not by expanding their deposits, but by shrinking their reserves.

This unique ability makes their lending far more profitable than it would otherwise be. At the same time it makes a bank unable at any time to redeem all its pledges or liabilities at once. No matter how sound a bank might be, a considerable number of its creditors would be obliged to wait for payment until the bank had converted the bulk of its assets into cash. Banks therefore must be concerned with both profitability and liquidity, where the latter in this context refers to the banks' ability to meet promptly demands to redeem their liabilities. In general, the greater the degree of liquidity and safety of an asset, the lower its yield.

Other business firms operate with fractional reserves also. A railroad, for example, could possibly have a bonded debt of $100 million and less than $1 million of cash on hand, and still be highly successful. The great difference, however, is that in the case of any organization other than a bank, the liabilities are on a time basis. The concern knows that the liabilities must be met the first of the month, or in six months, or in twenty years. It can arrange maturities so that only a limited amount of its obligations will be due at any one time, and can arrange to have the necessary cash on hand on the dates when the cash is required. In contrast, generally the bank's liabilities are payable on demand.[5] Nothing prevents all the holders of demand deposits from coming in the same morning and requiring payment. To be sure that it could meet such an emergency, the bank would need to keep a dollar in reserve, in cash, against every dollar of demand deposits. Then, of course, it would not be a bank at all as we understand the term. It would be little more than a warehouse for money. The only funds it could lend would be those secured by the sale of stock or from reinvested earnings. But a bank knows that, in practice, there is very little likelihood that all its noteholders or its depositors will come

[5]Recently, due to record high interest rates, many demand deposits have been converted to time deposits, to the point that banks' time deposits have exceeded their demand deposits.

in at once.[6] On the contrary, as long as the bank is properly managing its affairs, about as much cash will usually be brought in as will be withdrawn. This is the only reason that the fractional reserve is possible. This discovery, originally utilized in connection with note issues by the goldsmiths, is the basis of our modern banking.

Monetization of Credit

In accepting the notes of its customers and supplying in exchange its own notes, a bank profited because it paid no interest on its notes but charged interest on the notes signed by borrowers. It may appear that it was able to do this because its notes, unlike those of most of its customers, were payable on demand. This was not the fundamental explanation. A part of a bank's loans were call loans. They were quite like the demand notes of the banks themselves. They could be called at any time. Yet borrowers paid interest on call loans.

More importantly, a bank's promises were generally acceptable; hence they could serve as money. The fact that the promises were payable on demand helped to make them acceptable, as did the reputation of the bank.

As we saw in the last chapter, if retailers wished to place large orders of goods with wholesalers but lacked the funds to pay cash, they might ask the wholesalers to let them have five or six months before making payment. This would give them time to dispose of most of the goods and receive from their own customers the money to pay the wholesalers. The latter, however, might find it impossible to extend credit to many retailers, for the wholesalers would have their own costs to meet in the meantime.

There would be a simple solution if the retailers' notes were generally acceptable. In that case the wholesalers could simply endorse such notes from time to time and use them to pay their own bills. Each person who received such a note might endorse it and pass it on when he had some payment to make. When the note finally matured, whoever happened to hold it at that time would present it to the original maker. Of course, if the maker was unable to pay, the holder would turn it back to anyone who endorsed it, who would be required to pay the amount specified and might attempt in turn to recover from any previous endorser. Thirty, forty, or even more collections might be necessary.

The difficulties of such a procedure are obvious. As a minor detail, the retailers' notes are not made out in convenient denominations. This problem could easily be corrected. It would not be so simple to provide satisfactory machinery for collection, especially on distant items. But the principal obstacle is that these notes are not generally acceptable. The wholesalers, we may be sure, would carefully investigate the credit ratings of the retailers before taking their notes. But if they attempted to pass the notes along,

---

[6]In other words, this discovery of fractional reserves is based on the well established "law of large numbers," which very roughly asserts that random movements of a large number of individual items tend to offset one another. The bigger the bank, the less chance that there will be a randomly generated "run" on the bank.

others, knowing nothing of the affairs of the retailers, would have no way of knowing whether the notes would eventually be paid. All later holders would have to depend primarily on the endorsements of the people who surrendered the notes to them. People could not afford to accept such notes unless they had reliable information as to the financial responsibility of the original makers or some endorser. Frequently, the only endorsers known to them would be the people from whom they received the notes and often they would know little of those individuals' credit ratings.

But when banks were organized, the retailers could give their own notes to the banks after they had satisfied the bank officers that they would be able to repay the loan. The banks would then supply their notes which, unlike the retailers', were generally acceptable and required no credit investigation. As long as a bank remained in business, its credit rating was unquestionable.[7] The people whom the retailers paid with these notes had no reason to be concerned with the ability of the retailers to repay their loans. Only the retailers' banks had to be assured of the retailers' abilities to meet the loan obligations. The retailers' creditors received only the banks' promises to pay, and ordinarily they found no difficulty in passing these along to others.

Eventually, to provide a uniform currency, the right of note issue was restricted to the 12 Federal Reserve Banks. But by the time this change was made, note issue was no longer important to the commercial banks since deposit banking had replaced note banking. In the following chapter we shall see that when a bank makes a loan today, it seldom uses either specie or paper currency. By using deposits against which they maintain fractional reserves, the banks monetize credit in a more convenient form than the bank notes formerly used for that purpose.

FUNCTIONS OF BANK CAPITAL

A necessary predicate to understanding commercial bank evolution is an analysis of the functions and sources of bank capital. Bank capital is much like capital provided for any business in that it provides both an incentive and protection. As we have seen, a bank needs capital to continue in operation. In this respect a bank is no different from any other corporation. Funds invested or reinvested by the owners will earn profits if the business is successful. They will be lost in the event of failure. Thus, capital encourages competent management at the same time that it protects creditors.

The most common misconception with respect to capital, whether of banks or of other corporations, is that it represents some sort of special fund or pool of assets out of which losses may be met. It is, of course, not an asset, nor does it correspond to any specific asset such as building or vault cash. It is merely the *difference* between assets and liabilities. The only way in which assets may be increased or decreased without a corresponding change in liabilities is by a change in the capital accounts. The protection provided by

---

[7]If the public distrusted a bank, the bank would probably be forced out of business as its notes were constantly presented for redemption.

capital accounts in liquidation lies in the fact that if the assets have been properly valued and can be liquidated for the amount at which they have been carried on the books, they will sell for an amount that will be more than sufficient to pay off all the creditors. This difference is the total capital, and would be returned to the owners.

Most liabilities of any corporation are definite amounts. Particularly if the concern is in process of liquidation, it is required, so far as it is able, to pay one hundred cents on the dollar on all the claims outstanding against it. However, there is no certainty whatever that it can recover the entire amount at which its assets are carried. Some may necessarily be liquidated at a loss. A bank in receivership may be unable to collect some of its loans. Total receipts from liquidation will be reduced by such losses, as also by any losses incurred through the sale of the bank's investments or other assets. In spite of such losses, creditors may still be paid in full. If the losses are no greater than the total ownership equity as represented by the capital accounts, creditors will be repaid and stockholders will bear all losses.

SOURCES OF BANK CAPITAL

The term *capital* can be confusing because of the variety of meanings we assign to it. In economics we refer to *real capital*, the stock of goods we have accumulated through production. In business and finance we are concerned with *financial capital*. By financial capital, we mean sometimes one thing, sometimes another. We may be referring to a business's total property values when we speak of total capital invested in the business. At another time we may speak of capital in the sense of proprietorship, that is, the funds contributed by the owners of the business.[8] We can use the terms *gross capital* and *net worth* to distinguish between these two entirely different meanings of financial capital. With this terminology, *gross capital* means the total of the assets and *net worth* refers to the funds contributed by the owners. Thus, gross capital equals the total of the net worth plus all liabilities, both long- and short-term. Accounts payable, notes payable, bond issues—any and all of these and other liabilities are included in the total of gross capital.

Since double-entry bookkeeping requires the equality of assets with the sum of liabilities and net worth (capital account), three accounting identities are:

$$\text{Assets} = \text{Liabilities} + \text{Net Worth}$$
$$\text{Liabilities} = \text{Assets} - \text{Net Worth}$$
$$\text{Net Worth} = \text{Assets} - \text{Liabilities}$$

Financial capital has still a third connotation. Financial analysts use the term to refer ordinarily to *long-term* capital. Since they include bonds as well as stocks, they are looking at more than net worth. Since they do not include short-term liabilities, they are looking at less than gross capital. This is the sense in which we shall refer to capital in the following discussion.

---

[8]Contributed directly, by purchase of stock; contributed indirectly, through corporate earnings that are retained rather than paid out as dividends.

In the analysis of banks' balance sheets, directing our study to long-term capital is especially logical. With nonbank corporations, the millions of dollars contributed by bondholders cannot be regarded as increasing the protection of other creditors. More likely the reverse is true, for in the event of liquidation the bondholders are often in a preferred position and must be paid before other creditors. In the case of banks, however, the debenture bonds are subordinated to the liabilities, primarily deposits; that is, depositors must be paid in full before the holders of the debentures are entitled to anything. Thus, debentures provide a cushion of protection for other creditors, just as the other capital accounts do. Debentures, capital stock, undistributed profits, and surplus—these constitute the bank's capital.

Net Worth—Capital Stock, Surplus, Undistributed Profits

The *net worth* of a bank or any other corporation (the equity belonging to the owners) is represented by the capital stock, surplus, and undistributed profits. The *book value* of a share of stock is the total of the aforementioned capital accounts divided by the number of shares of stock. The *par value* is the value at which the stock was brought onto the books at the time it was issued. Consequently, book value will necessarily be above par value as long as the bank is holding any surplus or undistributed profit. If book value were below par value, the bank's capital would be *impaired*, for it would have sustained losses greater than the total of its undivided profits and surplus. *Market value* is the price at which stock is selling in the market and may be either above or below book value since it depends primarily on earnings.

Capital Stock

Although nonbank corporations often include one or more issues of preferred stock and sometimes more than one class of common stock in their capital structures, banks have traditionally been financed by common stock only, of a single class. This is not only the simplest, it is also the most conservative capitalization possible. Dividends on the common stock are likely to be most stable when there are no prior charges against earnings.

Preferred Stock

Until a few years ago, banking authorities placed great emphasis on the desirability of a stable value for bank stocks. They believed the price of a bank stock should rise only gradually, as the bank reinvested its earnings. Drastic changes, especially sharp declines, in the market value of the bank's stock were too likely to weaken confidence in the stability of the bank. Since the bank's credit must be absolutely unquestioned if it is to remain in business, bank management ordinarily (until 1962) refrained from issuing any preferred stocks, capital notes, or debentures. National banks were not permitted to issue such securities. State banks were less restricted; but if they were members of the Federal Reserve System, they were required to obtain the permission of the Board of Governors. The Board did not and still does not approve of this form of financing.

There was one important, emergency exception to this policy. During the depression of the 1930s, banks were encouraged to sell preferred stock. Because of the losses they had suffered, many banks needed more capital. There appeared to be little hope of selling common stock to the public at that time, when public confidence in the banks was badly shaken. The Reconstruction Finance Corporation was willing to provide funds, but since it was rescuing the banks rather than looking for an attractive speculation, it required that its ownership rights be superior to those of existing owners. If the banks were finally to be liquidated, the losses were not to be proportionately shared by the RFC. Its investment was to be repaid in full even though the holders of the common stock received nothing. Only if liabilities still remained after all the capital of the common stockholders had been eliminated could the funds contributed by the preferred stockholders be used to satisfy creditors. The public bought some of this preferred stock, but most of it was taken by the RFC, which at one time held more than a billion dollars of preferred stock, debentures, and capital notes which some banks issued for the same purpose. These securities were later retired.

In 1962 the Comptroller of the Currency again authorized national banks to issue preferred stock and debentures. This time, however, the banks were given permission to diversify their capital structure, not as an emergency measure but as a permanent right. Its purpose was not to rescue banks in distress, but to promote sound banking by facilitating the growth of bank capital. Relatively little preferred stock has been sold, for debentures have proved to be a more attractive alternative.

Common Stock

In contrast to many stocks that are issued with no par value, common stocks of all national banks and many state banks carry a stated par value. Formerly, the holder of stock in any national bank and in many of the state banks was subject to double liability. If the bank failed, the holder might be assessed as much as the par value of the stock to help pay creditors. This provision was supposed to encourage more careful management and to serve as an added safeguard for creditors.

The double-liability feature may at times have been given little thought by investors; but when the banks were trying in 1933 to raise additional capital, the provision was a strong deterrent to the purchase of bank stock. The Emergency Banking Act of 1933 freed new stock sold by national banks from double liability, and the national banking law was later amended to permit the banks to terminate double liability on their stock previously outstanding. State regulations have also been relaxed.

Although it made the sale of bank stock almost impossible after 1932, the additional liability on bank stock might have been desirable if it had ever really accomplished its objectives. It only created a false sense of security. All too often it was impossible to collect from the stockholders, especially when the failure occurred during a period of general depression and liquidation. Between 1863 and 1932 less than a third of such assessments was collected. The newly organized Federal Deposit Insurance Corporation was to provide much greater protection.

Also, national banks are required to continue adding to surplus until it is equal to the par value of the capital stock. This is equivalent to the old double liability but much more efficient. We no longer wait until the bank fails and then order the stockholder to turn over $100 for each $100 (par value) of stock held. Instead we require that, while it is making profits, the bank withhold and reinvest $100 of earnings for every $100 share of stock it has issued. Then if the bank does fail, the extra $100 per share has long since been collected.[9]

Surplus and Undivided Profits

The surplus of a bank results from, first, the premium above par at which the stock is sold when the bank is organized and, second, the reinvested earnings which are gradually transferred to surplus. Part of a bank's surplus is paid in at the time the bank is organized. The practical necessity of such a policy should be apparent. If the bank should at the outset have a few losses, those losses may be absorbed by reducing the surplus figure rather than impairing capital, which would require immediate assessment of stockholders.

In addition to the paid-in surplus, a bank also has an *earned surplus*, resulting from the retention of earnings. Retained earnings are first accumulated in the *undivided profits* account, from which they are transferred, from time to time, to earned surplus. Undivided profits are essentially surplus reported for convenience under another name.

The reason for making this distinction between surplus and undivided profits is that banks do not like to face the necessity of reducing their surplus to offset losses. Even though a surplus reduction does not necessitate a stockholder assessment, it is likely to be considered evidence of poor management or desperate circumstances. Also, Federal Reserve member banks purchase stock in the Federal Reserve Banks on the basis of 3 percent of their own combined capital and surplus, and do not want to be adjusting surplus yearly.

Additions to surplus, or for that matter additions to capital from the sale of more stock, do not directly increase the bank's lending power appreciably. But if the bank by other means increases its reserves, it can more appropriately carry an increased volume of assets and deposits if its capital accounts have also been increased. Obviously a bank with total capital accounts amounting to $1 million could not safely attempt to maintain deposits of $100 million, regardless of the reserves it might hold. If the vigilance of bank examiners did not prevent such a situation from ever happening, the prudence of depositors should.

---

[9]Stockholders are still subject to assessment if the bank's capital is impaired. The distinction between double liability and assessment is that the stockholder has nothing to gain by paying again the value of the stock when the bank fails. The stockholder is paying for a dead horse. Assessment to repair capital losses permits a bank to continue in operation, with the possibility that eventually the losses may be covered.

Debentures (Capital Notes)

Since 1962, when the Comptroller of the Currency authorized national banks to issue debt securities, many banks—national and state, large and small—have sold debentures to increase their capital.[10] Some of the larger banks have sold more than $100 million of such securities, usually of 25-year maturity. Supervisory authorities have indicated that a bank may have as much as 25 percent of its long-term capital in this form. Moreover, the debentures may comprise a permanent part of its capital. Although, unlike the capital stock, they represent debt, not ownership, the debentures are specifically a subordinated debt. In the event of bank liquidation, debentures would be paid off only if and when all depositors had been paid in full.

Like other corporations, banks find debentures attractive for three principal reasons:

1. Interest is a deductible cost. If the bank pays 10 percent on its debentures, its net interest cost, after taxes, is only 5 percent.
2. Debentures permit the bank to increase its capital without diluting the stockholders' equity. Without any additional investment, the stockholders have the same control they had before and continue to receive the entire benefit, directly or indirectly, of all profits.
3. The reason for long-term borrowing by any business firm is the expectation of earning more with the borrowed money than the interest cost by eventually expanding its deposits and assets sufficiently. When a firm earns more with borrowed capital than it costs to borrow it, it is said to be *trading on the equity*.

Debentures—Evaluation

The advantages of borrowing capital have, of course, long been recognized, perhaps most of all by banks' customers. A century ago railroads and, a little later, public utilities issued billions of dollars of bonds and debentures to increase profits on the common stock. Even two hundred years ago when Benjamin Franklin was advising young men to establish good credit so that they might borrow money and let it work for them, he was stating a point of which most businesspeople were already quite aware. The only new development is that banks, too, are now allowed to raise part of their long-term capital by borrowing.

This naturally raises the question, "If the advantages of long-term borrowing were known all along but explicitly denied to banks, why are they now allowed?" Probably our tax structure is part of the answer. After 1941 the advantage of borrowing became much greater when half the interest cost could be passed on to the government. It seems reasonable to assume that this factor at least strengthened the banks' desire for debt financing to supplement equity financing.

There is the disturbing possibility that the authorization of bank debentures may, to some extent, have been based on the generally dangerous

---

[10]Debt securities are usually called debentures, sometimes called capital notes.

premise that since business has been profitable for a number of years, it will always be profitable. Unquestionably one can profit by borrowing when business is good. How about borrowing during recessions?

The disadvantages as well as the advantages of debt financing have been recognized for generations. If a firm is committed to pay 10 percent on borrowed money and its earning rate on total long-term capital drops below 10 percent, holders of common stock must bear the loss. They may even find that nothing at all is left for them by the time interest has been paid.

It may sometime be important again, as it was in 1934, to strengthen public confidence in the banks or, for other reasons, to encourage an increase in bank capital. In recession, banks with large debenture issues will probably find it difficult to sell common stock. At such a time the earnings on common stock will be reduced by the drain of interest payments on the debentures. On the other hand, in recession debt financing is particularly hazardous.

In short, much can still be said for the traditional, conservative approach to bank capitalization. Since business may sometimes slow down, bank stock becomes more speculative when it is accompanied by debentures (or by preferred stock).[11] Apparently on these grounds the Federal Reserve has looked with disfavor on this development in bank financing. The Board of Governors has ruled that "capital notes or debentures do not constitute capital, capital stock, or surplus for the purposes of provisions of the Federal Reserve Act." This statement seems explicit enough.

SIGNIFICANCE OF CAPITAL RATIOS

The total capital structure of a bank is an amount that in itself means little. It must be related to something else. Even if we wish to know only that capital is relatively large or small, we must compare it to that of other banks. However, capital can be more significantly compared to other balance sheet items, in particular to deposits, assets, and particular kinds of assets. If we are considering the status of an individual bank, our study of capital resources has little significance except in relation to the rest of the balance sheet. A total capital of $5 million would be excessive for a bank with total assets of $10 million and insufficient for a bank with total assets of $200 million.

Capital-Deposit Ratio

In comparing capital to deposits, we are recognizing the function of capital as a protection to creditors. If a bank's total capital accounts come to $7

---

[11]We must realize that business may sometimes slow down. Periodically we are told, "Things are different now. They will never be the same." It is usually best to accept such announcements only with large reservations. We were assured in 1928 that we now had tamed the business cycle and would never have another depression. Later we were informed that we would never again see high interest rates, for they were no longer necessary or desirable. We were told that bank loans would never be important again, for banks were buying Treasury securities and corporations were financing themselves out of retained earnings. We have been assured that the monetary and fiscal policies of the Federal Reserve and the government will guarantee us continuous prosperity and continuously expanding employment and output. Time, however, tends to tarnish most pronouncements of this sort.

million and its total deposits are $100 million, the $7/$100 or 7 percent ratio shows that for every $100 owed to depositors, there is $7 of ownership equity or subordinated debt.

Capital-Asset Ratio

Comparing capital to total assets indicates the percentage by which the assets may decline in value before depositors will incur losses. A bank with total assets of $108 million and total capital of $8 million will be able to pay its depositors in full as long as its assets do not decline by more than $8 million, or about 7.5 percent.

Of these two ratios, the second appears more meaningful. The important question is not the abstract and ethical consideration of how much should be supplied by owners and long-term lenders in proportion to funds supplied by depositors, but the practical determination of the amount of protection the cushion of capital affords depositors. Furthermore, protection is provided against the possibility that assets might fall in value. The capital-asset ratio measures this protection directly. In practice, however, it does not really make a great deal of difference which ratio we use, especially since they come to almost the same figure when both are close to 10 percent, as has typically been the case since 1939. Note that for any solvent bank the ratio of capital to deposits will always give a higher percentage result than the ratio of capital to assets—the denominator of the fraction must be larger in the latter case since assets necessarily exceed liabilities by the amount of the capital.

Over the last 150 years the ratio of bank capital to assets has declined dramatically. From values as high as 70 percent in 1800, the ratio has declined rather steadily. By 1945 it was less than 6 percent, an all time low. By 1974 it was approximately 7 percent.

REASONS FOR DECLINE IN CAPITAL-ASSET RATIO

It would be easy to conclude that banks have deliberately encouraged a decline in their capital-asset ratios to increase their profits. It would also be incorrect. To some extent the decline is more apparent than real. Also, the decline is in large part due to developments and policies over which the banking system has no control.

Early Overstatement of Capital

The very high capital ratios of the early 19th century are not strictly comparable with modern figures because, as we have seen, the stated capital of many early banks was largely fictitious. A bank in the pre-national-bank era might, in comparison to assets of $2 million, show a capital of $1 million or more, but much of this capital might be represented by stockholders' notes. The actual protection afforded by such capital might well be less than that provided by $200,000 of capital paid in according to law. Thus, the tightening up of the legislation concerning the payment for capital reduced the amount of capital in proportion to assets without necessarily reducing the degree of protection. If before 1863 banks' capital had been as soundly financed as in the later period, undoubtedly the early ratios would not have been so high.

Special Reserves

Also, capital accounts are smaller today than they were a century or more ago because banks now maintain many special reserve accounts which take over a part of the load formerly carried by the capital accounts. These reserves were formerly uncritically included in surplus and undistributed profits, and thereby helped overstate total capital.

These reserves are not to be confused with the various types of asset reserves to which we have so frequently referred. Their entirely different nature is emphasized by the fact that, instead of appearing as assets, they appear as liabilities or sometimes as deductions from assets. These reserves are of two general classes, *accrual reserves* and *valuation reserves*.

Accrual Reserves. Some reserve accounts are brought on the books to indicate sums for which the bank certainly will be liable at a future date and, more precisely, to show the amount that the bank at present owes on sums that are not yet due. The most common are reserves for taxes and for interest payable on time deposits. As we noted above with respect to surplus accounts, these reserves must not be misunderstood as some sort of asset. Rather, they present a truer picture of the bank's position by recognizing certain liabilities that are not yet payable. Thus, they avoid an overstatement of undivided profits.

Valuation Reserves. No matter how careful their lending policy, bankers know that occasionally losses will be incurred. They do not know which loans or investments will involve losses, nor do they know how great total losses will be.

Logically, any losses incurred should be charged to the period in which the bad loans or investments were made, rather than to a later period when it becomes evident that the loans cannot be collected or that the bonds are in default. Since, in the period in which the loans are made, bankers cannot determine which loans or investments will result in loss, they establish valuation reserve accounts for the amounts of loans and investments that they estimate may not be collected. At the end of a fiscal period they charge the estimated loss during the period to a bad debt account and credit a valuation reserve account. If later they find that some loans actually cannot be collected and that some bonds must be written down in accordance with a lower market value, the losses at that time are charged to the valuation accounts rather than to some expense account of the later period.

There is some similarity between valuation reserves and undivided profits. Either type of account permits assets to be written off without an impairment of the original capital. If clearly excessive reserve accounts are established, they would appear to be an alternative form of undivided profits or surplus, providing an additional cushion of owner equity between the total of assets and the total of liabilities. If, however, they are only sufficient to permit the allocation of losses to the proper period over the business cycle, they cannot be considered equivalent to capital accounts. In any case, the larger the reserves, the less capital accounts are needed for protection.

Retirement of Preferred Stock

A more recent and less important cause tending to reduce bank capital ratios is a consequence of the depression of the 1930s. Capital accounts were necessarily written down when assets were revalued downward during the bank holiday, and preferred stock was issued to create a more adequate capital structure. Since most banks later retired this preferred stock, capital was to this extent reduced.

Rapid Growth of Assets

Over the last century the principal cause of the decline in the capital ratio has been that assets increased much faster than capital. During the entire period, bank capital increased from one year to the next, almost without interruption. But assets increased much more rapidly.

Around the turn of the century, business was expanding vigorously. Giant corporations, mergers, and trusts were formed. Here was the *demand* for the bank credit. At the same time demand deposits were becoming more widely used. The banks found they could expand these liabilities more easily than they had expanded their earlier note liabilities. This represented *supply*. The combination of the great demand for credit and the increased supply caused a substantial increase in loans and investments. During World War I, bank loans and deposits increased faster than ever. And after 1932 there was a drastic drop in the capital ratio. Bank capital increased, but its increase could not begin to keep pace with the enormous increase in assets, which doubled between 1933 and 1941 primarily as a result of a substantial gold inflow.

Between 1941 and 1945, bank assets more than doubled again. This increase too was one over which banks had relatively little control. Almost the entire increase in bank assets during the war years was in their holdings of government obligations. The banks were encouraged by the Treasury, by the Federal Reserve Banks, and by public opinion to support the war effort by lending the Treasury whatever money it needed that it could not get from other sources. Since capital could not be increased at anywhere near so fast a rate, capital ratios inevitably fell.

The percentage of increase in bank assets since 1945 seems modest in comparison with the previous increases. For this rise the government is less directly responsible than for that between 1933 and 1945. However, the banks' activities were not carried on after World War II entirely independent of Treasury policies.

For several years the Treasury continued to insist on the importance of low interest rates to hold down the cost of refunding and servicing the public debt. When the Treasury is borrowing billions at low rates, other borrowers will also be obtaining cheap credit.

The government favored easy money also to stimulate the economy and to promote a high employment level. High interest rates prevent some investment, especially in construction, and to a lesser extent some consumption, especially of automobiles and other consumer durables. Although the Federal Reserve is technically not a branch of the government, it cannot safely ignore the policies and philosophy of the administration. Interest rates until 1965, although somewhat higher than during the thirties, were low by historical standards.

In two ways cheap money policies encourage low capital ratios. In the first place, they encourage borrowing. Some customers who would not pay 10 percent will gladly pay 8 percent. Also, the low interest rates and credit expansion at a time of full employment are likely to cause a rise in prices, making businesspeople more anxious than ever to borrow. In the second place, they encourage lending. To receive $100,000 of interest, a bank must lend twice as much at 4 percent as it would need to lend at 8 percent. Banks, like other businesses, are operated in the hope of making a profit. Other things being equal, the lower the interest rates, the more dollars a bank must lend per dollar of invested capital to make a profit.

Slower Growth of Capital Accounts

In view of the dramatic increase in bank assets, it is remarkable that capital-asset ratios are not lower than they are. Even if bank capital has grown more slowly than assets, it has increased substantially, especially since 1941.

There was little encouragement for the growth of bank capital from 1934 to 1941. After the banking debacle culminating in the closing of all the banks in 1933, the public was not interested in buying new issues of bank stocks. At the same time bank earnings were low as interest rates fell to historically low levels and excess reserves mounted to unprecedented heights. However, since 1941 there has been a rapid increase in bank capital.

By far the greatest part of this increase in bank capital has come from retained earnings. For any corporation with sufficient earnings, it is simpler to increase capital by reinvesting profits than by selling more stock. To bank management, properly concerned with creating an image of stability, reinvestment of earnings has the additional advantage of increasing the book value of the stock. Even more important, the market value of the stock is not decreased, as is almost inevitable if more shares are issued. The sale of more shares of capital stock results in slightly greater total earnings, to be distributed more widely, with less being earned per share. Reinvestment of earnings permits somewhat higher earnings per share, tending to cause a gradually rising market price for the stock.

Although most corporations are likely to find their per share earnings affected adversely by an increase in the number of their shares, banks are not only especially sensitive to this development, they are especially vulnerable to it. There is a special relationship between capital items and the rest of the balance sheet that is largely peculiar to banking. If other corporations increase their capital by selling more stock or bonds, they increase their assets by the same amount. In the case of banks, to the extent that their issues are sold to their own depositors, there is no gain in assets but instead a decline in liabilities. The results on earnings are consequently much less favorable.

Here there are two points to remember. The first is that a bank's earnings are limited by the fact that it can lend only about the amount of its excess reserves.[12] The second is that a bank's capital accounts are not reserves.

It may be argued that an expansion of capital through earnings retention tends also to reduce required reserves rather than to increase legal reserves. This is true. To the extent that the bank's earnings result from interest paid by borrowers who are also depositors, the interest payments have decreased the bank's deposits. The increase in undistributed profits or in surplus is the measure of this drop in deposits, not offset by a decline in assets. Consequently, the increase in the bank's lending power will be much the same whether it sells securities to its own depositors or expands through earnings retention. Either way, the immediate result will be to increase the bank's lending power by only about 10 to 15 percent of the increase in capital. However, the expansion through retained earnings does tend to give at least a slight immediate increase in earnings per share. It is the policy most likely to result in a stable, gradually rising market value of the bank's stock.

ADEQUACY OF CAPITAL

There is, finally, the question of whether today's bank capital ratios have become so low as to threaten the solvency of the banking system. For years the Federal Deposit Insurance Corporation has been calling attention to the low ratio of capital to assets. The concern of the Corporation's directors is natural. They are trying to promote sound banking. More specifically, the FDIC bears much of the losses resulting from bank failures. It is to their interest to see that capital accounts provide a generous margin for the absorption of losses. Their liability in the case of failures may tend to make them overly conservative.

By what standards may we judge the adequacy of bank capital? Capital should be sufficient to permit suitable accommodation of borrowers, adequate return for stockholders, and proper security for depositors.

Accommodation of Borrowers

A bank's capital should be large enough to permit it to serve its customers. Since the amount a member bank may lend to any borrower, other than the Treasury, is by law limited to 10 percent of its capital and surplus, an

---

[12]Chapter 6 discusses reserve concepts in detail. In general, *legal reserves* are the assets that a bank is holding that according to law may be used to meet reserve requirements, such as vault cash and deposit claims against Federal Reserve banks. *Required reserves* are the reserves the bank must hold, as determined by the amount of its deposits and the percentage of reserves specified by regulations. The difference between legal and required reserves is the bank's *excess reserves*.

inadequately capitalized bank cannot make large individual loans that its customers may require. On this score bank capital is probably generally adequate. Bank capital has increased approximately eightfold since 1941. In other words, a typical bank can today make eight times as large a single loan as it could make 35 years ago. Also, to accommodate the occasional borrower whose needs may exceed the bank's capacity, a participating loan may be arranged in which a number of banks take part.

A bank's capital should also be large enough to permit it to assume some degree of risk. This is not to say that a bank should make loans and investments that are "risky" in the ordinary sense of the term. It should be willing to assume a legitimate banker's risk such as would be incurred in lending to businesses with good credit standing. There is the danger, when owner equity becomes very thin, that management may try to make up for the lack of capital protection by restricting its lending to the risk-free area of securities issued or guaranteed by the Treasury. If the banks were to abdicate their role as arbiters of credit and become merely agencies for monetizing the public debt and transferring deposits from one to another, they would fail to meet the requirements of commerce and industry. Other lending agencies would have to be created or developed to replace them. Their function as private institutions would largely disappear, and they would probably be nationalized.

On this score, also, bank capital appears sufficient. True, bank loans were at a low level for a number of years while holdings of government securities were increased more than tenfold. By the end of World War II, when banks held nearly four times the volume of Treasury securities as loans, it may have appeared that they were neglecting other lending and concentrating excessively on the comparatively riskless government loans. This state of affairs was not a result of insufficient capital, nor was it primarily one over which the banks had much control. Business did not want or need to borrow. The government did. Since 1945 the banks have been selling their Treasury securities to increase their loans. By 1974 their loans were more than five times the amount of their Treasury obligations.

Return for Stockholders

Unless an adequate return can be earned, no privately owned business will remain in operation indefinitely. The capital of any business must bear some reasonable relation to its earnings. In this respect the self-interest of stockholders is opposed to the interest of borrowers and creditors. The two latter groups benefit from an increase in the capital ratio. But stockholders do not directly profit from an increase in the capital ratio.

We must, of course, not confuse an increase in capital with an increase in the capital ratio. A bank's earnings, like those of any other business, depend on total assets, not total capital. A bank that is earning, after taxes and all expenses, around 9 percent on total capital accounts is earning less than 1 percent on its total assets, since the average bank today has around $13 million of assets for $1 million in the capital accounts. Total assets might be eventually doubled as a result of a doubling of capital if the bank succeeded in attracting a great many new customers. Then, however, the capital ratio would be as low as before. An increase in the capital ratio requires an increase in capital *without* a proportionate increase in assets. Almost inevitably a capital ratio increase will force a decline in the rate of return on capital.

To justify such a decline, it would be necessary to show that bank earnings are excessively or unnecessarily high, and that sufficient funds to supply needed bank capital would be available even if earnings rates were reduced. Unfortunately the rate of return on bank stock has been modest, taking the period since 1930 as a whole. For a number of years the banks suffered losses; the eventual recovery to an earnings rate of 9 or 10 percent was not very exciting, considering the postwar rise in prices and recognizing also that, unlike the glamor stocks of some other industries, bank stocks seldom offer the promise of spectacular growth.

Security for Depositors

Since only about 60 percent of the total dollar volume of deposits is covered by insurance, the adequacy of a bank's capital is important to depositors, in particular to those with accounts exceeding \$40,000.[13] The FDIC is understandably concerned also to see that capital is adequate, since the greater are the potential losses that the insured banks may absorb themselves through their capital accounts, the less will be the demand upon the FDIC resources. Since its inception, the FDIC has continually urged that banks raise their capital ratios, in particular those banks that are below the national average in this respect.

Now it should be clear that whether a particular institution has a higher or a lower capital ratio than the average is not of much significance in itself. An average is, after all, an average, taking into account all values. If all institutions that are below the present average were to increase their capital ratios to that figure, they would still be below the average since their action would raise it. In other words, no matter how high or low the average, there will always be some below average unless there are none above and every institution has the same ratio. The real question is whether the average itself is too low.

Here we may again refer to the reason that creditors need the protection afforded by a cushion of capital. It protects them against losses, both those due to default and those resulting from the need to convert assets into cash at less than their book value. Clearly the amount of capital required is closely related to the quality of assets and, generally, to the ability of management.

Quality of Bank Assets

When we consider the diversification and liquidity of bank assets today, we find reason to doubt that capital ratios are too low, even though they are

---

[13]Although about 99 percent of the depositors are fully covered, the 1 percent of large depositors not fully covered hold uninsured balances equal to about 40 percent of the dollar value of total deposits.

only two thirds as high as 50 years ago. The composition of bank assets is quite different from what it was half a century ago. Also, the Federal Reserve and the FDIC have strengthened the banking system in many ways. In particular, they have improved banking standards by examination and regulation; and by their ability to support the market they have reduced the likelihood of the disastrous decline in asset values that formerly occurred whenever the banking system was short of reserves.

One asset that certainly cannot decline in market value is the reserve account that a bank keeps with the Federal Reserve. These reserves are today half again as high with respect to deposits as they were before 1933. It hardly seems necessary to require that capital be maintained to prevent a loss in these cash accounts or, for that matter, to prevent a loss in the value of vault cash. A bank will never need to accept less than one hundred cents on the dollar for every dollar of its legal reserves, whether vault cash or deposits with the Federal Reserve. If we were to eliminate these assets from consideration in computing the ratio of assets to capital, our result would be substantially higher.

Moreover, included in the loans and investments of the typical commercial bank are some virtually risk-free assets. About 10 to 15 percent of the total assets of commercial banks today are United States government securities.[14] Most of these securities mature in five years or less, so that even in the absence of Federal Reserve support they could not greatly decline in market value. There could be some decline in the market price of the longer term issues, although the Federal Reserve would certainly support the market in the event of general bank distress. Admittedly the individual bank cannot be sure that the Federal Reserve will be following an easy money policy every time that it may need to liquidate some of its assets. However, even if we ignore the possibility of Federal Reserve support for the long-term issues, we may still feel justified in considering government securities of five years or less as essentially risk free. Another 10 to 15 percent of bank assets are in the form of state and local government securities.

Also virtually riskless is the Federal Reserve stock owned by the member banks and the home mortgages insured by the Federal Housing Administration. Together these items amount to about 2 percent of total bank assets.

ACTUAL COMBINED BALANCE SHEET FOR THE COMMERCIAL BANKING SYSTEM

All the various elements in a commercial bank's capital structure can best be illustrated by Table 5-1, which depicts a simplified balance sheet for all commercial banks combined. It consolidates some minor items and eliminates interbank claims of commercial banks against each other.

---

[14]This ratio has been declining since immediately after World War II when these securities made up 40 percent or more of total commercial bank assets.

Table 5-1   **Consolidated Balance Sheet for All Commercial Banks**
June 30, 1974
(In billions of dollars)

Assets			Liabilities and Capital		
	Amount	Percent of Total		Amount	Percent of Total
Currency and Coin	$ 8.4	0.9	Demand Deposits	$302.8	34.2
Reserves with Federal			Time and Savings		
Reserve Banks	30.1	3.4	Deposits	407.6	46.1
Loans	529.4	59.8	Capital Accounts	61.6	7.0
Securities	189.8	21.5	Other (net)	112.8	12.7
Other (net)	127.1	14.4			
Total	$884.8	100.0	Total	$884.8	100.0

Source: *Federal Reserve Bulletin* (March, 1975), pp. A18–A19. These figures exclude inter-bank claims of commercial banks against each other.

Liabilities and Capital

This balance sheet emphasizes several important facts about commercial banks. As discussed earlier, the capital-asset ratio is just about 7 percent, which means that commercial banks acquired very few of their assets by issuing capital claims. This figure has trended downward at a very slow pace in the post-World War II period. In recent years, time and savings deposit liabilities (46.1 percent) have become larger than demand deposit liabilities (34.2 percent). Most of this bank debt was created and issued when banks acquired securities and made loans.[15]

Assets

Compared with nonfinancial businesses, established banks have very little of their assets in the form of plant, equipment, fixtures, and land. What little common stock they hold are shares in the Federal Reserve Banks which members are required to purchase. Commercial banks have about 4.3 percent of their assets in currency and coin (i.e., vault cash) and deposits at the Federal Reserve, each of which count toward meeting their legal reserve requirements. Since these balances have a zero interest yield, commercial banks attempt to hold them down to the minimal reserve requirement. Over 81 percent of bank assets are in the form of interest-yielding loans and securities. These

---

[15]Deposits created to pay for asset acquisitions, such as loans and securities, and which do not serve as reserves are called *derived* or *derivative deposits*. *Primary deposits* arise when the bank becomes the owner of cash which increases the legal reserves of banks. Most demand deposits are derived deposits. These two concepts are discussed in more detail in the next chapter.

debt claims against others represent the bread and butter of a modern commercial bank. In general, most of the investments are long-term debt instruments of the federal (10 to 15 percent of total assets) and state and local (10 to 15 percent of total assets) governments and of business. While commercial banks are the major source of short-term, highly liquid loans to business, they do loan for a variety of purposes.[16] In fact, the asset portfolio of commercial banks is typically the most diverse of all the financial intermediaries.

Liquidity

By most measures bank liquidity has declined substantially in the post-World War II period. For instance, the widely used measure of the ratio of total loans to total deposits has risen sharply.[17] The banks have cut liquidity to maintain profitability in the face of rising costs. Is this a problem? Not if the assets and liabilities are reasonably liquid and diversified. More importantly, for the commercial banking system as a whole, ultimate liquidity is provided by the Federal Reserve. Certainly sensible monetary-fiscal policy, the FDIC, and the Fed's judicious use of discounting for members needing liquidity have increased overall bank liquidity regardless of what the usual measures indicate.

Time Trend

Finally, it is useful to see the time trend of commercial bank assets, liabilities, and capital since 1950. Table 5-2 shows the major trends in the sources and uses of bank funds for 1950, 1960, and 1970 for all insured commercial banks.

As mentioned earlier, this table shows, on the liabiliity side, the enormous growth in time and savings deposits vis-à-vis demand deposits in the 1950–1970 period. If we separate time and savings deposits, we can see that the former—consisting mainly of certificates of deposit with a scheduled maturity date—have been primarily responsible for the growth since 1960. In fact, passbook savings accounts of individuals and nonprofit organizations declined percentagewise since 1960. On the asset side, banks have apparently shrunk their cash assets (vault cash, deposits at the Fed and other banks) and their holdings of government securities from about 60 percent in 1950 to less than 30 percent in 1970.[18] In place of these assets, banks have increasingly turned to state and local securities, mortgages, and various types of loans.

---

[16]Typically, commercial and industrial loans of various duration constitute 20–25 percent of a commercial bank's total assets in recent years.

[17]For example, in 1950, it was 34 percent; in 1960, 52 percent; in 1970, 62 percent; and in 1974, it was 72 percent for all insured commercial banks. Part of this rise is deceptive since banks were excessively liquid in 1950 through vast purchases of government securities.

[18]Actually, banks would have even less government securities today but for the legal requirement that they hold such securities as collateral against government (federal, state, and local) deposits. By statute these "pledged assets" must be U.S. government or high-grade municipal bonds and they must be equal to the dollar total of U.S. government deposits. State and local governments often impose these same requirements. It has been estimated that at least one third of all the securities in commercial bank portfolios are "pledged assets." See Charles F. Haywood, *The Pledging of Bank Assets* (Association of Reserve City Bankers, 1967).

Table 5-2   Assets, Liabilities, and Capital Accounts
                    Percentages of Insured Commercial Banks, 1950, 1960, 1970
                           (All figures are shown as percentage of total)

Assets				Liabilities and Capital			
	1950	1960	1970		1950	1960	1970
Cash assets	24	20	16	Demand deposits	70	61	43
U.S. government				Passbook savings			
securities	36	24	12	deposits	17	22	17
Municipal				Time deposits			
securities	5	7	12	proper	5	7	24
Business loans	13	17	19	Other liabilities	2	2	9
Mortgages	8	11	13	Capital accounts	6	8	7
Consumer loans	6	10	12				
Other loans	4	8	8				
Other assets	4	3	8				
Total	100	100	100	Total	100	100	100

Source: FDIC *Annual Reports*. All figures are as of year end.

SUMMARY AND CONCLUSION

The first bankers in the modern sense were the goldsmiths, who frequently accepted bullion and coins for storage. The goldsmiths promised to return the same number of coins they received, but were under no obligation to return the identical coins left with them. Two important consequences followed. They found they could use some of this gold to make short-term loans. They also found that their promissory notes, issued in exchange for the gold, were soon preferred to the gold itself due to their convenience.

Originally the notes were representative money, with a dollar in gold in the vaults for every dollar of notes held by the public. When the goldsmiths began to lend part of the gold, the reserves became fractional rather than full, for these early loans decreased the vault cash reserves, but left the number of notes in circulation unchanged. The notes were then credit money, backed by a partial reserve.

Later the goldsmiths learned a more efficient way to put their credit money into circulation. They lent by issuing additional notes, rather than by paying out gold. In exchange for the interest-bearing note received from their customer, they gave their own noninterest-bearing note. In effect, each was borrowing from the other. Everybody was happy. The customers were satisfied because they could use as money the notes they received. The goldsmith bankers profited because they were drawing interest on loans made with money they were printing. As had been true since they began lending some of the gold left with them, their notes were credit money. The advantage of the later procedure of lending notes rather than gold was that, on the basis of a given gold stock, more notes could be issued if the gold remained in the vaults. If it was paid out, it might presently return and be re-lent; but there was no certainty that it would return from circulation or that it would return to the institution that had lent it. As long as the public was willing to use the notes as money, the goldsmiths had no reason to want to encourage the public to go back to using gold.

The notes would never have become credit money and the principle of fractional reserves would never have been practical except for one fact. Once gold was left with the goldsmiths, there would ordinarily be very little of it demanded on any day or in any week. The notes, being more convenient, took over the money functions formerly performed by the gold. Usually as much or more gold would be brought in by some as might be demanded by others. The goldsmiths found that only a partial reserve was necessary as long as the public felt the gold was there to be had whenever it was wanted.

Thus, through the principle of bank note issue the banks learned to create money in the form of their own liabilities. When banks were later prohibited from issuing notes, they found that they could create deposits that, as we shall discover in the following chapter, would similarly increase the money supply. This monetization of private credit is the traditional function of the commercial bank.

Capital or net worth is the difference between assets and liabilities. The two major functions of capital are to foster managerial efficiency and to protect creditors. Capital stock, preferred stock, common stock, surplus, and undistributed profits have each at times been sources of capital for banks.

The fact that bank capital ratios are near their lowest level in history is not proof that they are too low. When we consider the purpose of the capital accounts and the diversified and liquid nature of bank assets and liabilities today, the capital ratio does not appear to be alarmingly low. There is certainly no objection to a greater measure of protection if capital ratios can be raised, but the present level of bank earnings suggests that any increase in capital is more likely to come through the gradual process of reinvestment of earnings than through the sale of more capital stock. Even a high capital ratio will not protect a bank from the consequences of poor management. The quality, diversification, and liquidity of its assets are important to a bank's solvency. Even more important is the posture of the Federal Reserve, which is the most important determinant of liquidity for the entire banking system.

Discussion Questions

1. "What is truly unique about commercial banks relative to other financial institutions is not on the asset side, but on the debt side." Explain.
2. If you stored gold with the goldsmith, what was the advantage of receiving his note specifying payment to your order rather than to bearer? Why were his notes later made payable to bearer?
3. How did bank notes come to be considered as money? Was it primarily the result of legislation, of rules by the goldsmiths, or of other causes?

4. When the goldsmiths issued notes in excess of the gold they held, did this mean they were no longer able to redeem all their notes? Explain.
5. Explain why it was impossible for the goldsmiths to create money without the public's cooperation.
6. For any economic entity, what are assets? liabilities? net worth? How are these concepts related?
7. "Banks must be concerned with both profitability and liquidity." Briefly explain why you agree or disagree.
8. What is the difference in nature between a loan you would make and a loan a bank makes? Of what significance is this difference to the economy?
9. Since banks in the U.S. today (except Federal Reserve Banks) no longer issue notes, why is an understanding of the nature of bank note issue important?
10. Is note issue a less important or more important function of commercial banks in the United States today than it was a century ago? Why?
11. To what extent, if at all, does the capital of a bank (or other corporation) help protect its creditors?
12. What are three reasons why bank stocks no longer carry double liability?
13. In the event of liquidation, is the protection of short-term creditors of non-bank corporations likely to be increased or decreased if the corporation has borrowed on long term? Is this important? Briefly explain.
14. List the principal reasons that the ratio of banks' capital to their assets has declined from about 70 percent in 1800 to less than 10 percent today.
15. "By most measures bank liquidity has declined substantially since World War II." Explain.

Chapter 6   Creation and Transfer of Deposits

What is a bank deposit? A simple question, isn't it? Anyone can answer it. Unfortunately most people will answer it incorrectly or, at best, inexactly. If, without reading further, you can accurately define bank deposits, you are the exception.

There is a persistent confusion respecting deposits.

1. Deposits are our most important money. Yet to the bank, the deposits of its customers are not money at all.
2. You take a handful of currency to the bank and deposit it. However, under no circumstances whatever do the bank's deposits consist of currency.
3. Most people suppose that a bank lends the deposits of its customers. In fact, however, no bank ever lends its deposits.

These apparent contradictions result from the fact that we regularly use the word *deposit* in two entirely different, and completely inconsistent, ways. Ambiguity is inevitable unless we clearly specify which meaning the word is to have. We cannot possibly, in an analysis of bank operations, follow the common practice of allowing *deposit* to mean one thing one moment, something entirely different a moment later.

Specifically, we must decide whether we are going to consider a deposit as being the thing that is turned in to the bank—the actual checks on other banks and pieces of silver and currency—or as being the sums owed to depositors. These two things are not the same at all, for one is an asset, the other a liability of the bank.

Logically, perhaps, the term *deposit* should refer to the physical asset that one surrenders to the bank. There is no difficulty in understanding what has taken place if we say someone deposited $50 of currency or made a deposit of $300. The customer turned in that amount to the bank, and the word is used in accordance with the first definition.

But then we say, "The customer has a deposit of $300," and we have swung over to the second definition. The deposit is an asset of the customer. It cannot possibly be at the same time an asset of the bank. Exactly what is the customer's deposit asset? Certainly it is not the handful of currency or the check the customer turned over to the bank teller, for these are now assets of the bank. The asset the customer received in exchange was a claim on the bank. From the bank's point of view, this deposit, as such, is a liability. When the bank increases its assets (currency, checks on other banks, other negotiable instruments), it increases its liabilities by an equal amount (or sometimes

144

gives other assets in exchange). In this respect it is no different from any other firm.

Two hundred years ago, banks gave their notes in exchange for coin (and other assets) rather than giving deposit credit for it as they do today. The increase in the bank's liability, offsetting the increase in its assets, was in the volume of its notes outstanding. There was no chance for ambiguity, since the promissory notes that one has given to others are clearly and unmistakably a liability for the giver. The item "Deposits" did not appear on the bank's balance sheet at all.

But as present-day banking techniques evolved, especially in the United States, the banks ceased to issue notes. Instead, when a customer brought in specie or other forms of money, the bank simply made a record in its books that it owed that sum to the individual. Probably some word other than "deposits" would have been less troublesome. If at the outset the banks had called these "Customer Accounts," perhaps, or "Public Credits," much confusion might have been avoided. Unfortunately they termed the liabilities "Deposits" because in a great many instances it was a deposit (asset) that created the liability.

But the importance of deposits (in the sense of liabilities) lies in the very fact that they do not necessarily result from deposits (in the asset sense). The particular asset that customers leave with the bank is not important. So although we may agree that, logically, *deposits* should refer to bank assets, we shall use this term only to refer to the bank's liabilities to its customers. This choice is not an arbitrary one. Bankers themselves universally agree in drawing up their balance sheets to list as deposits the sums that they owe. A bank never lists as deposits its holdings of currency and coin. These holdings of currency and coin are classified as Vault Cash and appear, quite properly, on the asset side of the sheet.

A bank's deposits, then, are the amounts that it owes to its customers. Most individuals whom the bank owes at any particular moment will be individuals who have brought some sort of money to the bank. These specific dollars then belong to the bank, which may use them in any way it wishes—as a basis for lending or for paying current expenses or as a pool of idle funds. The bank agrees in return to make the same number of dollars (but not the same pieces of currency) available to the customers at any time they may wish to have them.

But some individuals to whom the bank is in debt may never have brought any form of money to the bank. The bank's employees, the telephone company, the firms from which the bank buys its office supplies, all have claims of one sort or another on the bank. Periodically, usually the first of the month, the bank will change the form of most of these miscellaneous liabilities. Many of these creditors then hold deposits in the bank instead of their bills for goods and claims for wages. (Creditors who bank elsewhere will instead be paid by a cashier's check, which is another form of bank liability.)

As a result the bank owes no more and no less. It has simply changed the form of its liabilities. The process is somewhat akin to that of a corporation that sells bonds (borrows on long term) and uses the receipts to pay off its short-term indebtedness, except that the bank, instead of converting short-term liabilities to long-term, is converting them to demand liabilities. These deposits are, of course, completely indistinguishable thereafter from deposits originating in other ways.

Still a third and extremely important group has claims upon the bank because its members have borrowed from the bank. There has been an exchange of liabilities. The bank holds the borrower's promissory note and the borrower holds a deposit in the bank. It is very important to realize that the deposits of these borrowers as well as the deposits provided for the employees and business creditors mentioned in the preceding paragraph are not "borrowed" from the first group of deposits. They are in addition to those deposit liabilities. And this power to create deposits is the reason banks are so important to the economy.

CREDIT EXPANSION BY THE INDIVIDUAL BANK

Usually a commercial bank makes a loan by crediting the borrower's account. There is no need to pass currency back and forth. It is more convenient for the borrower to spend the proceeds of the loan by drawing checks against his new deposit. These checks are received by other people, who can either:

1. cash them, forcing an increase of currency in circulation outside the banks; or
2. deposit them to their own accounts, possibly in the same bank, more likely in other banks.

So far as the total money supply is concerned, the interrelations between an increase in deposits and the resulting drain of currency into circulation are more significant for the banking system as a whole than for the individual bank. We shall consider them later in this chapter.

If the loan-created deposit is transferred to other accounts in the *same* bank, the bank's total deposits are unaffected by the transfer. The bank owes less to the person who has written the checks (in this case, the borrower) and more to those who have received them.

However, as the borrower writes checks against the new deposit, the bank that lent the money will most likely lose reserves and deposits to other banks. Total deposits of the banking system are unaffected by the transfer of deposits from one bank to another, but the shifts are of vital significance to the individual banks.

Old Deposits and New

Interbank transfers of funds go on continuously, whether banks are expanding credit, contracting credit, or simply maintaining the volume of their loans. Every day a bank receives from its depositors checks drawn on other banks. These checks increase its deposit liabilities and at the same time equally increase its reserves, drawn from the banks upon which the checks are written. Every day a bank also loses deposits and reserves as its own depositors write checks that are deposited in other banks.

Take the case of a bank with deposits of $2,500,000 and vault cash reserves of $500,000. If a substantial part of these deposits were transferred all at once to other banks, this bank would have insufficient reserves. The bank's management knows that such a transfer would be most unlikely, however. It expects to retain this $2,500,000 deposit total, with increases in some deposit accounts offsetting decreases in others. On the other hand, it quite rightly expects that if it were to make a loan by creating a new deposit, it would probably lose to other banks nearly that amount of deposits and reserves.

Why can the total of the old deposits be expected to remain in the bank when most of the newly created deposits are expected to disappear? The reason is simple. The old deposits are part of the existing money supply, the new are not. Over a period of time the bank has succeeded in building up its deposits to a certain figure. It has from time to time created deposits by its own lending and investing, but nearly all those deposits that it created itself have long since been transferred to other banks. In turn it has received deposits as the result of the spending of deposits created by other banks. Most of the bank's existing deposits are the result of past lending and investing by approximately 14,500 other commercial banks. Daily transfers of the existing money stock will ordinarily cause little change in its total of deposits. Since the bank has many depositors, the law of large numbers applies. Some will be withdrawing funds, but others will be depositing funds. The results will usually average out, and the bank can expect to receive from other banks about as much as it pays out to others. But of new money, whether created by itself or by others, it can expect to hold or gain more or less permanently only its proportionate share.

Suppose, for example, there are two banks in a community. For the moment we shall ignore all other banks. One of these banks has deposits of $1 million, the other of $5 million. As long as neither is increasing the money supply, both banks might expect their deposits and reserves to remain relatively stable. There may be five times as many people depositing checks in the large bank, but there are also five times as many writing checks on that bank. There is no reason for the larger bank to gain deposits from the smaller or to lose deposits to it.

But if now either bank makes a loan of $6,000, where are these $6,000 likely to lodge after they have changed hands a few times? We should expect that they will become merged with the money previously existing, which was divided between the two banks on a 5 to 1 ratio. The smaller bank should gain about $1,000, the larger bank about $5,000.

In reality, of course, it is not one bank versus another, but one bank versus approximately 14,500 other banks. A bank that makes a loan may retain some of the new deposit that it has created, but the chances are that it will not retain much of it.

Bank Reserves—Required, Legal, and Excess

The goldsmith bankers understood the importance of maintaining a fractional reserve in gold against their notes. They would never have attempted to operate with no assets except the promissory notes of the borrowers to whom they lent their own notes. Banks today hold no gold, but most banks are required by law to hold a fractional reserve of liquid assets against their deposit liabilities.

The specific reserve requirements for Federal Reserve members are set by the Board of Governors within a range specified by Congress within these limits: (1) between 3 and 10 percent against time and savings deposits, and (2) between 7 and 14 percent (10 and 22 percent) against demand deposits up to (over) $400 million. Basing reserve requirements on deposit size rather than geographical location began in 1966 (1968) for time (demand) deposits. The present arrangement favors small banks since reserve balances earn no interest and hence are not profitable.

If regulations call for a reserve of 16 percent against deposits, a bank with deposits of $1 million will be required to hold a minimum of $160,000 of reserves. *Required reserves* are the amount of reserves that a bank must hold, as determined by the amount of its deposits and the percentage that the law specifies must be held against those deposits.

Can we say the bank is holding some of the deposits as reserves? Certainly not. Not a dollar of the deposits can possibly be reserves. The deposits, we have seen, are liabilities of the bank. The reserves must be assets.

Now if bank regulations merely stated that a bank should hold a certain percentage of assets as reserves against its deposits and stopped there, obviously the requirement would be meaningless. The bank's officials could claim that any and all the bank's assets were serving as reserves. So the regulations also state what kind of assets may be counted as reserves. For all banks, vault cash meets the reserve requirement. For member banks of the Federal Reserve system, legal reserves are also deposits in a bank's regional Federal Reserve Bank. *Legal reserves* are all assets that the bank holds that the law permits to be used in meeting reserve requirements. If the above-mentioned bank, with *required* reserves of $160,000, is holding $175,000 of vault cash, its *legal* reserves are $175,000. In short, required reserves are the minimum amount that the bank *must* hold (some percentage of its deposits); legal reserves are the total amount of qualifying funds the bank is *actually* holding (for example, its total vault cash).

It is unlikely that a bank's required reserves and legal reserves will be exactly equal. Its legal reserves must, of course, be at least as much as its required reserves, and they usually will be somewhat greater, as shown in the example. This difference between legal reserves and required reserves is the bank's *excess reserves*.

In all the discussion of bank credit expansion in the following paragraphs, and in later discussion of the Federal Reserve Banks and monetary and fiscal policy, we shall be constantly referring to the importance of changes in banks' reserves. Be sure you have the three types of reserves clearly distinguished. Excess reserves = legal reserves − required reserves. Anything that changes either legal or required reserves necessarily changes excess reserves.

Excess reserves are the key to the banks' lending power. No matter how many billion dollars of deposits a bank may be liable for, and no matter how large its capital, it cannot lend a cent unless it has excess reserves. If it does have excess reserves, it may lend approximately the amount of the excess. For even if the entire proceeds of the new loan should shortly be withdrawn (decreasing legal reserves by the same amount), the bank will still have the necessary minimum reserves required against its remaining deposits.

Result of Lending a Multiple of Excess Reserves

Suppose a bank, subject to a minimum reserve requirement of 20 percent, is holding:

Assets		Liabilities & Net Worth	
Vault Cash	$ 500,000	Deposits	$2,000,000
Loans	1,600,000	Capital	100,000
	$2,100,000		$2,100,000

It is required to hold $400,000 of reserves against the $2,000,000 of deposits. It is at this moment holding $500,000. With excess reserves of $100,000, why can't this bank immediately lend, in the form of deposits, $500,000? Its accounts would then appear:

A		L & NW	
Vault Cash	$ 500,000	Deposits	$2,500,000
Loans	2,100,000	Capital	100,000
	$2,600,000		$2,600,000

The reserves of $500,000 would be 20 percent of deposits of $2,500,000. It might seem that the bank had followed a sensible policy in creating $5 of deposits against every dollar of excess reserves that it held at the outset.

But now what happens as the borrowers begin to spend their new deposits? They write checks, and the checks are deposited in other banks as this net addition to the total money stock is distributed around the banking system. The bank that created the deposits might possibly lose them all. Its balance sheet would then show:

A		L & NW	
Vault Cash	$ 0	Deposits	$2,000,000
Loans	2,100,000	Capital	100,000
	$2,100,000		$2,100,000

Disaster! Something would have to be done, and fast, to secure the $400,000 of reserves needed against the $2,000,000 of deposits. Perhaps by hustling around to other banks and rediscounting $400,000 of its loans the bank might raise the cash required.[1]

A		L & NW	
Vault Cash	$ 400,000	Deposits	$2,000,000
Loans	1,700,000	Capital	100,000
	$2,100,000		$2,100,000

Bankers know their business too well to commit any such blunder. Since every banker is aware that at least the major part of any newly created deposits will be quickly withdrawn, no banker would ever get in such a jam. Bankers know better than to lend $4 or $5 against each dollar of excess reserves.

Result of Lending Only Excess Reserves

Now suppose the bank discussed above decides to lend only $100,000, the amount of its excess reserves when it is holding $500,000 of vault cash as legal reserves against $2,000,000 of deposits. After lending $100,000 in the form of deposits, its balance sheet shows:

A		L & NW	
Vault Cash	$ 500,000	Deposits	$2,100,000
Loans	1,700,000	Capital	100,000
	$2,200,000		$2,200,000

For the moment, the bank still has excess reserves. Against the $2,100,000 of deposits, $420,000 of reserves are required. The $80,000 of excess reserves are only temporary, however. As the new deposits are spent and, along with vault cash, gradually transferred to other banks, the bank's balance sheet will presently show:

A		L & NW	
Vault Cash	$ 450,000	Deposits	$2,050,000
Loans	1,700,000	Capital	100,000
	$2,150,000		$2,150,000

Required reserves against $2,050,000 are $410,000; excess reserves are now only $40,000.

Even if every dollar of the newly created deposits were transferred to other banks, the first bank would not find itself with insufficient reserves, for its required reserves would continue to drop as its deposits fell. The bank's balance sheet would finally show:

---

[1]The so-called federal funds market, operated through brokers and dealers, buys and sells claims against deposits—on a one-day renewable basis—at Federal Reserve Banks at rates which are usually at or below the Fed's discount rate. In essence, those banks with excess reserves loan to banks with deficient reserves. See Chapter 7.

A		L & NW	
Vault Cash	$ 400,000	Deposits	$2,000,000
Loans	1,700,000	Capital	100,000
	$2,100,000		$2,100,000

Compare this T-account with the original account shown on page 149. Notice that deposits (and capital) are now the same as they were at the outset. Because $100,000 of newly created deposits was lost to other banks, $100,000 of vault cash was also lost to other banks. And since this cash exceeded what the bank was required to maintain against $2,000,000 of deposits, the loss of the cash creates no problems, now that deposits are again down to $2,000,000.

Part of New Deposits Retained

Although they certainly will not lend several times the amount of their excess reserves, bankers may feel justified in lending a little more than exactly the amount of their excess reserves. This statement may appear to contradict what we have just been saying. It does not. It simply drops the assumption that every dollar of deposits that a bank creates will, in the normal course of events, disappear from that bank.

We have already seen that two strong forces tend to pull such deposits away from the bank that creates them. Some of the deposits will be converted into cash at the demand of the public, and a much larger part will be redistributed to other banks. However, to suppose that every dollar will flow out of the bank is unrealistic for the following reasons:

1. Most city banks have a rule that the borrowers' average balances must be at least 20 percent of the amount of their loans. An average balance is not a minimum balance. Nothing prevents the borrowers from spending immediately the full amount of the loans. They may even spend more than that amount, drawing on their previous deposits. However, if the average of 20 percent is to be maintained, then the lower the deposits fall at one time, the higher they must rise at another.
2. The borrowers must, in rural banks as well as in city banks, build up their deposits between the time they spend the borrowed money and the time they are to repay it.
3. In many cases borrowers obtain a loan because they may need additional funds for some transaction and want to have them ready. The opportunity to use them may never materialize, and the deposit never has a check drawn against it.
4. In many other instances borrowers hold all or part of the funds for days or weeks before spending them.

For all these reasons, the average deposits of customers, after the bank lends to them, will tend to be larger than before, until the loans are repaid.[2]

---

[2]See also the discussion of derivative deposits below.

To that extent the bank can lend a little more than if every dollar of deposits that it created were to disappear forever from it.

Continued Lending Ability

Suppose that from past experience the bank knows that, on the average, 75 percent of any deposits that it creates disappear, either to other banks or in the form of currency. With $100,000 of excess reserves the bank will be justified in lending more than exactly $100,000, for if it does lend only that amount, it finds, after the dust has settled, that it has retained $25,000 of the new deposits. If the reserve requirement is 20 percent, the bank would need to hold $5,000 against these deposits. It still has excess reserves, though now they are down to $20,000, and it can lend again. But every time it lends, if it lends only the amount of its excess reserves, the bank ends up with some unused lending power.

Of course, this lending potential becomes steadily and rapidly smaller, approaching zero as a limit. If the bank lends just the $20,000, it soon finds itself holding $5,000 of the new deposits and $5,000 of the reserves with which it began. The bank then has $4,000 of excess reserves. In this particular example the bank will be able, each successive time, to lend 20 percent of what it lent before. This figure of 20 percent results from our assumptions that:

1. Each deposit the bank creates at the outset is backed dollar for dollar by reserves; that is, it is reserve-backed 100 percent.
2. The required reserves are 20 percent. Consequently, for every dollar of deposits that is backed by reserves of $1, excess reserves are $.80, or 80 percent.
3. The bank "retains" 25 percent of each dollar it creates; that is, its total deposits are, on the average, increased more or less permanently by 25 percent of the amount it lends in the form of deposits.
4. The bank therefore ends up, each time it lends, with excess reserves of 80 percent against 25 percent of the deposits it has created; 80 percent of 25 percent is 20 percent.

Primary v. Derivative Deposits

Most of us think of our deposit as the account we regularly carry with the bank for convenience in making payments. We leave with the bank currency, perhaps, or more likely checks we have received. The bank becomes the owner of the cash or the collection item. In return, the bank owes us that amount. These *primary deposits* let us write checks to pay our bills. They reduce our need for currency. They are, basically, a currency substitute.

Primary deposits tend to be stable. Certainly you may deposit your paycheck the first of the month and find by the end of the month that your account is painfully low, but your average balance will be about the same each month, even if it varies from day to day during the month. We ordinarily do not maintain a checking balance that is some months only about as large as our monthly bills and other months is ten times that large. Usually if we have much more money than we need to handle our monthly transactions, we are likely to exchange some of it for earning assets. Business firms follow the same policy, so their primary deposits also are fairly stable.

In contrast to primary deposits are *derivative deposits*. These are deposits that are loan created or accumulated by the borrower in anticipation of a loan repayment.[3]

When a commercial bank makes a loan, it credits the depositor's account.[4] Thus, a deposit is derived from the loan made by the bank. Ordinarily most of this deposit will soon be spent. Part of it may remain in the borrower's account. This part is a derivative deposit. As the time approaches when the borrower is to repay the loan, he or she builds up a larger balance with the bank for the specific purpose of repaying the loan. This part of the deposit is also a derivative deposit.

City National Bank

A		L & NW	
		Deposits	
Loans		Nichols Hardware	$10,000
Nichols Hardware	$200,000		+$200,000

Suppose Nichols Hardware has been maintaining a balance of about $10,000, from which it pays its regular monthly bills. This is a primary deposit, permitting checks to be used instead of currency. The company now needs a short-term loan to finance a shipment that is arriving. A bank loan increases its deposits from $10,000 to $210,000, of which $200,000 is, by definition, a derivative deposit.

City National Bank

A		L & NW	
		Deposits	
Reserves	−$185,000	Nichols Hardware	$ 210,000
			− 185,000
			$ 25,000

Union Trust Co.

A		L & NW	
Reserves	+$185,000	Deposits	
		Wholesalers, Inc.	+$185,000

---

[3]The classification of deposits as primary and derivative was initially stressed and analyzed in detail by C. A. Phillips. The analysis here is based upon his *Bank Credit* (New York: Macmillan Company, 1931), pp. 40–54.

[4]Very small loans may be made in cash, but such loans are an insignificant part of the total dollar volume of bank loans.

When Nichols Hardware writes a check for $185,000 to Wholesalers, Inc., the $185,000 is transferred to Union Trust Co., where Wholesalers keeps its account. We cannot say whether this $185,000 is now a primary or a derivative deposit. It might be either, depending on whether Wholesalers, Inc. plans to use this money to pay off a bank loan of its own (derivative deposit) or to pay its ordinary bills (primary deposit). We can say, however, that $15,000 of Nichols' present $25,000 balance is a derivative deposit.

City National Bank

A	L & NW
	Deposits
	Nichols Hardware $210,000

Three months later, when the loan is due, Nichols Hardware will have rebuilt its balance to about $210,000. $200,000 of this is earmarked for loan repayment, and is, therefore, a derivative deposit.[5] Whether this $200,000 resulted directly from increases in the reserves of City National or from decreases in its other deposits is irrelevant. Most likely both factors were involved, as well as vault cash. But the point is that the $200,000 is, by definition, a derivative deposit since it was accumulated for the specific purpose of repaying the bank loan.

In the individual account, derivative deposits are less stable than primary deposits. Typically a customer's derivative deposit is high on the day the loan is made. In a few days, most of and possibly all the deposit has been spent. Gradually the derivative deposit recovers to the original figure as the borrower accumulates the funds to repay the loan. When the borrower does write a check to pay off the loan, the derivative deposit disappears altogether. On an average, the amount of the customer's derivative deposit may be perhaps 10 or 20 percent of the amount borrowed.

From the bank's standpoint rather than the customer's, derivative deposits are fairly steady. By the time a bank has set up a well-diversified loan portfolio, some loans will be maturing every day. Derivative deposits will tend to be at a minimum for the majority of the loans made most recently, although some borrowers may find they do not need to spend the money as soon as they anticipated or, perhaps, to spend it at all. In the loans nearing maturity, derivative deposits will be close to 100 percent of the amount of the original loans. All these derivative deposits together average perhaps 10 or 20 percent of a bank's loans outstanding.

The distinction between primary and derivative deposits, as defined above, is admittedly of little importance to the banking system. The system as a whole can expand credit by several times the amount of its excess reserves, and can do so whether each bank finds its derivative deposits are 100 percent of its loans or are zero. The only difference is that the higher the percentage of derivative deposits, the more quickly the loan expansion would be completed. As shown later, the percentage of its derivative deposits to its loans is an

---

[5]This discussion disregards interest or discount to avoid confusing the issue with accounting techniques.

important determinant of the amount the individual bank can lend at any one time. The more each *individual* bank can lend, the more quickly the *system* can expand credit.

To the individual bank the distinction between primary and derivative deposits is of strategic importance. The higher the percentage of its derived deposits to its loans, the more it can lend. If its derivative deposits average 25 percent, it should be able to lend at once about $125,000 on the basis of reserve requirements of 20 percent and excess reserves of $100,000. But if its derivative deposits average only 10 percent, it can lend only about $109,000.

Coefficient of Credit Expansion by the Individual Bank

If the bank knows all along that it can reasonably count on holding on to about 25 percent of the deposits that it creates, it does not have to spread this lending over a period of time. It can immediately lend the same amount. It can be shown mathematically[6] that the final result of the decreasing series of loans is represented by the formula:

$$L = \frac{E}{kr + (1-k)}$$

where L = total amount which may be lent

E = excess reserves

k = percentage of the bank's loan-created deposits that it ordinarily retains

r = percentage of reserves required against deposits

In the case we were previously considering on page 152,

$E = \$100,000$
$k = 25\%$
$r = 20\%$
$$L = \frac{\$100,000}{.25\,(.20) + (1 - .25)} = \frac{\$100,000}{.05 + .75} = \$125,000$$

So with $100,000 of excess reserves, the bank could at once lend $125,000 on the basis of the above values for k and r. Or we may say that, with these values of k and r, the bank can lend 1.25 times the amount of its excess reserves.

When the bank lends $125,000, it should find .25 ($125,000) or $31,250 remaining on deposit. It loses $93,750 of deposits and reserves. The bank, therefore, is left with $6,250 of the original excess reserves, which is just what is required against the retained deposit liabilities.

The coefficient of 1.25 is simply illustrative. It might be a little more or, more probably, it would be somewhat less. Its value depends upon the percentage of deposits retained and upon the ratio of reserves to deposits, mainly the former. The coefficient would, however, fall as low as 1.00 only if every dollar were withdrawn, which we have seen is unlikely. We conclude that a

---

[6]Phillips, *op. cit.*, p. 71.

bank may usually lend, on a given date, somewhat more than the amount of its excess reserves.[7]

Seasonal Clearing Gains and Drains

Thus far we have tacitly assumed that a bank might be losing deposits and reserves only because of the loans that it was making. For various reasons, however, a bank may find that it is, at least temporarily, steadily gaining reserves and deposits from other banks, or losing reserves and deposits to other banks.

Often this is due to a seasonal factor. A bank in a farming community will usually find in the fall, as the farmers sell their crops to out-of-town buyers, that its deposits and reserves rise steeply. Through the winter, spring, and summer the farmers draw checks against their accounts. Some of these checks are deposited immediately in banks elsewhere. Others may be deposited in the same bank by local merchants; but as the merchants rebuild their inventories, they write checks that are deposited out of town. The bank finds its deposits and reserves gradually falling. Finally the harvest season comes around, and again reserves and deposits flow into the bank.

In like manner, the banks in a small town where a large university is located find their reserves and deposits abruptly raised every fall as students descend upon the campus with their checks from home. Some of these checks are deposited with the local banks by the students themselves, opening local checking accounts. Others may be deposited by local merchants, to whom the students have endorsed them. As the bookstore pays for more books, the movie theater pays rent on films, and the stores restock their shelves, the reserves and deposit liabilities gradually move out of the local banks to the banks of the publishers, film companies, and manufacturers.

Changes from Expansion or Contraction by Other Banks

Besides the seasonal gains and drains, a bank's position will change as a result of the rate at which other banks are expanding or contracting credit. If Bank A is neither expanding nor contracting its loans at a time when other banks generally are expanding theirs, Bank A will gain reserves and deposits from the other banks. If the other banks are contracting loans, Bank A will lose reserves and deposits to them. More generally, if Bank A is expanding loans more rapidly (or contracting credit more slowly) than most other banks, it will probably lose reserves to them. It will probably gain reserves if it is expanding credit more slowly, or contracting it more rapidly, than the rest of the banks.

---

[7]It is, of course, not compelled to lend at all. At times a bank may choose to hold excess reserves. Ordinarily, however, to maximize its profits, it will try to keep excess reserves at a minimum.

Effect on Expansion by the Individual Bank

If a bank is subject to a seasonal drain of reserves and deposits, the bank may find that it cannot possibly lend more than the amount of its excess reserves. Indeed, the bank might feel any lending would be imprudent if its excess reserves are small and it has reason to believe that in the weeks ahead it will be losing reserves even if it makes no loans whatever. Conversely, it may feel safe in lending freely if it is sure that it is shortly to experience its usual seasonal inflow of reserves.

Suppose, however, that the bank is not subject to seasonal movements, and that it is expanding credit neither more nor less rapidly than are other banks. How much could it then lend for every dollar of excess reserves that it held?

If each bank could be sure that the only deposits it would lose of its newly created deposits would be to the currency drain, and that so far as clearings are concerned it would neither gain nor lose, then each bank might lend $2 or $3 for each dollar of excess reserves held. Quite rightly, no bank follows such an optimistic policy. Any bank that did would find itself completely out of step with the general pace of credit expansion. It would quickly be in the embarrassing situation described earlier.[8]

Instead, the bank might lend to the extent permitted by its coefficient of credit expansion. According to our example earlier, it might lend $1.25 for every dollar of excess reserves. However, although we found when we first discussed this coefficient that the bank's lending power would then be exhausted, we see now that under the abnormal conditions involved, it would not. For since we are now assuming that all other banks are expanding credit at the same rate as is this bank, this particular bank does not, in fact, lose 75 percent of its deposits and reserves to them. It gains as much as it loses.

It finds, therefore, that even after it has lent $1.25 for each $1 of excess reserves, it still has excess reserves, though now smaller in amount. Because other banks are also expanding loans and deposits, this bank's only net losses of deposits and reserves as a result of its own lending operations will be, as for all other banks, to currency in circulation. Over a period of time and by repeated lending it may eventually lend around $2.50 or $3 for every $1 of excess reserves it held at the outset. If its reserve requirements are 20 percent, it will then have, when its excess reserves are finally fully utilized and some of its reserves have been paid out to increase the currency in circulation, $5 of deposit liabilities against every $1 of reserves that it still holds.

Secular Change in Deposits

In addition to the short-run variations in deposits, the individual bank may find that its total deposits are showing a fairly steady trend over which

---

[8]In other words, an individual bank is automatically limited in its ability to create new deposit money by the necessity of maintaining reserves to meet adverse clearing balances.

the bank itself may be able to exercise little control. If a bank's deposits (and reserves) are declining daily or weekly, the management will probably decide that the adverse clearing balance is due to an overexpansion of credit, which can quickly be corrected. Likewise, a persistent and substantial increase in its deposits and reserves may be evidence that the bank is out of step with other banks and should be lending more freely. But clearly, there are limits to the extent to which a bank can control the volume of its deposits. If it restricts credit too severely in the attempt to gain deposits created by other banks, its own customers may become dissatisfied and transfer their accounts elsewhere. If the decline is due to a change in the relative importance of the community itself to the rest of the economy, there may be little that the bank can do to offset the slow transfer of deposits to other banks.

Under more favorable circumstances a bank may find, again for reasons largely outside the field of its own policies, that it is enjoying a steady growth. An alert bank management is aware of these changing conditions and by taking advantage of them may be able to secure a sizable increase in deposits.

Geographical Shift of Deposits

Of much the same nature are the shifts of deposits from one area of the country to another. As noted elsewhere, such shifts may be seasonal deposits in banks in farm areas, increasing when the farmers sell their crops, decreasing as the deposits are spent and the money is transferred to manufacturers of automobiles, farm machinery, clothing, and so on. In addition to these regular changes there may also be other movements of a more permanent nature.

During World War II deposits flowed profusely from New York to other areas of the country. A great volume of government securities was bought in New York, both by the banks and by the general public. In either case, as the Treasury spent the money, the New York banks lost deposits (and reserves) which were transferred to industrial areas, air bases, army camps, and similar regions.

CREDIT EXPANSION BY THE BANKING SYSTEM

Now we turn from the individual bank to the entire banking system. How many dollars can the system as a whole lend against every dollar of excess reserves?

If the logic of the preceding analysis is clear, we should have no trouble with this question. When we are dealing with the banking system rather than with a single bank, we can ignore clearing drains and gains. Total deposits and reserves of the system as a whole are unaffected by shifts among the individual banks.[9] There are, however, as we shall discuss, some other drains of currency into circulation that need to be taken into account.

---

[9]To the extent that shifts occur between banks subject to different reserve requirements, there will be a change in excess reserves, here disregarded. For further discussion, see Chapter 7.

Potential Expansion, Ignoring Currency Drain

The expansion process will be clearer if we ignore at first the effect on currency in the hands of the public. Suppose all banks are subject to a reserve requirement of 20 percent and that all banks except Bank A are fully loaned up.[10] Bank A alone has excess reserves, totaling $100,000.

At this point it matters not in the least, as far as the system is concerned, whether Bank A lends exactly $100,000 or a somewhat higher figure. It does not matter, either, whether all the new deposits are checked out of Bank A into other banks or whether part (or, for that matter, all) of them stay in Bank A. Whatever bank eventually finds itself holding any of the new deposits, accompanied by the same amount of reserves, will be able to lend 80 percent of the amount received.

If Bank A does lend exactly $100,000, and if all the new deposits check into Bank B (or in a group of banks that we shall symbolize by Bank B), then Bank B's accounts are changed as below:

A		L & NW	
Vault Cash	$100,000	Deposits	$100,000

B's required reserves have increased by $20,000 due to additional deposits of $100,000. Since its legal reserves have simultaneously increased by $100,000, it now has $80,000 of excess reserves.

Note, too, that if only part of the new deposits were transferred, the total excess reserves of the system would be unaffected. Suppose that $25,000 of the deposits remained in A and $75,000 were transferred to B. Bank A began with $100,000 of (excess) reserves and $100,000 of new deposits. It is left with $25,000 of these reserves and $25,000 of deposits, against which only $5,000 of reserves are required. Therefore, there are $20,000 of excess reserves in Bank A. Bank B has in this case received $75,000 of deposits, against which .20 ($75,000) or $15,000 of reserves are required. Since it received at the same time $75,000 of reserves, its excess reserves are $75,000 minus $15,000 or $60,000. The system still has $80,000 of excess reserves, just as it did when all the new deposits were transferred from Bank A.

Since it makes no difference to the system whether we assume that part or all the loan-created deposits are transferred, we shall make the simplifying assumption that the entire amount is transferred, and that, therefore, a bank lends only the amount of its excess reserves. Therefore, we assume that Bank A loses $100,000 of deposits and the same amount of reserves and is loaned up. Bank B has $80,000 of excess reserves and lends that amount. The $80,000 is transferred to Bank C, changing its balance sheet by the following amounts:

A		L & NW	
Vault Cash	$80,000	Deposits	$80,000

---

[10]For a more realistic situation, taking into account the amount of member bank indebtedness to the Federal Reserve Banks, see discussion of *free reserves*, Chapter 11.

With $80,000 more deposits, Bank C's required reserves are increased by $16,000. With an increase of $80,000 in its legal reserves, Bank C has excess reserves of $64,000. This amount it lends.

We might continue this infinite series of loans, making each time a loan of 80 percent of the preceding loan. We can see that the amount that can be lent will steadily decrease. If we go far enough, it would be down to a fraction of a cent. The series would begin:

Bank A lends	$100,000.00
" B "	80,000.00
" C "	64,000.00
" D "	51,200.00
" E "	40,960.00
" F "	32,768.00
" G "	26,214.40
" H "	20,971.52
" I "	16,777.22

The total of deposits created by the first nine banks thus far against the $100,000 of excess reserves is about $433,000, and the expansion process is not yet fully worked out.[11]

But we need not go on and on with these re-lending effects. Obviously if required reserves are one fifth of deposits, then when deposits are five times the amount of reserves there will be no excess reserves. In this case we assumed the expansion began with $100,000 of excess reserves for the system. By the time $500,000 of deposits have been created against this $100,000, the entire amount of reserves will be required, and no further expansion of loans can take place against them.

To sum it up, we may say that, for the banking system as a whole:

1. where r = the percentage of reserves required against deposits;
   E = the excess reserves held by the banking system; and
   L = the total loans that the banking system may make over a period of time on the basis of these reserves, that is, the total new deposits the system may create;
2. and when we are disregarding the effect of the increased deposits upon the public's demand for currency, then:[12]
3. $L = \dfrac{E}{r}$

---

[11]Strictly speaking, it could never be fully worked out, if we were to consider the possibility of bank loans of a few cents or a fraction of a cent.

[12]Actually this elementary coefficient of credit or deposit-expansion equation makes three other simplifying assumptions besides that of no currency drain—i.e., that the public prefers to hold a fixed quantity of currency irrespective of the level of their deposits or of the transactions within the economy. They are: (1) all bank deposits—whether demand or time—are subject to the same reserve requirements; (2) all banks are subject to the same regulations, e.g., all belong to the Federal Reserve System and it does not differentiate among classes of banks; and (3) banks are always fully loaned up and do not hold any excess reserves. See Jerry L. Jordan, "Elements of Money Stock Determination," *Review*, Federal Reserve Bank of St. Louis (October, 1969), pp. 10–19. The complete monetary multiplier which takes most of these various factors into account explicitly is derived in the Appendix to this chapter.

Thus, through the process of credit expansion the banking system is able by repeated lendings to create several dollars of deposits against every dollar of excess reserves. By this time it should be thoroughly clear that the banking system as a whole cannot as a general rule increase its loans and investments without increasing deposits.[13] Notice particularly that the money supply increases regardless of whether the public wants more money as such. The public will have to hold the added funds, whether it wants them or not. The public's deposits will be determined by, and roughly equal to, the total reserves and earning assets held by the banks. Someone has to hold the additional money resulting from an increase in bank lending. Spending it merely transfers it to another owner. The only decision the public makes concerns the form in which it will hold the money.

Besides the increase in deposits that is the direct result of the activities of the banks themselves, there are other possible increases with respect to which the banks play a passive role:

1. Member deposits and reserves are affected by Treasury purchases of gold and silver. (See Chapter 7.)
2. Movements of currency into and out of circulation affect deposits (and reserves). When a large volume of new deposits is created, some will naturally tend to be exchanged for currency. Many individuals who receive the added money do not maintain checking accounts. Also, as prices begin to rise, it becomes convenient to carry around a little more currency.
3. An increase in the amount of Treasury currency (coin and United States notes) outstanding tends, other things being equal, to increase bank deposits.[14] The fact that the Treasury issues more currency does not require the public to hold more currency. Until and unless the public does decide it wants more currency, the effect of the additional Treasury currency is simply to increase bank deposits and reserves. Since Federal Reserve notes at present constitute by far our most important currency, the increase in Treasury currency in circulation would cause a decline in Federal Reserve notes in circulation. The public, finding itself holding more currency than it wished, would exchange excess currency for deposits. The banks, finding their vault cash (and, therefore, their insurance premiums) unnecessarily high, would exchange currency for deposit credit at the Federal Reserve Banks. And the Federal Reserve Banks would retire Federal Reserve notes from circulation, reducing their note liability as they increased their deposit liability. Note that excess reserves of member banks would increase, permitting a further increase in deposits. As a result of the initial increase in deposits (as the excess currency was turned in to the banks) and the secondary increase in deposits, if it materializes, the public will probably wish, finally, to hold more currency. But with the exception of this consequence of an increase in deposits, the issuance of additional Treasury currency would not increase the total currency in circulation.

---

[13]Exceptions: by increasing bank capital or by purchasing securities from the Federal Reserve, exchanging reserves for earning assets.

[14]In particular, if there is no simultaneous increase in the demand for currency. Neither the Treasury nor the Federal Reserve can force the public to hold more currency than the public wishes.

Effect of Currency Drain

We must explicitly take into account the drain of cash repeatedly referred to previously. Some of the new deposits will inevitably disappear from the system as their holders demand currency instead of deposits. Given existing public tastes and preferences and the institutional framework, people want to hold a certain amount of currency for every dollar of deposits they hold or for every dollar of transactions in the economy. In truth, the optimal ratio is influenced by such factors as income levels, credit card use, and uncertainties regarding general economic stability. A change in the amount of deposit money is accompanied by a roughly proportionate change in the amount of currency held by the public.

Table 6-1 lists for several years (1) currency outside the banks, and (2) demand deposits (other than interbank and United States government, less cash items reported as in process of collection). The ratio of currency to demand deposits (c) has been fairly stable over the last quarter century, and in normal times has usually been not far from 25 to 31 percent.[15]

Table 6-1   Ratio of Currency to Demand Deposits

Year (December)	Currency Outside Banks (billions)	Demand Deposits (billions)	$\dfrac{\text{Currency}}{\text{Demand Deposits}}$ Ratio = c
1930	3.7	21.7	17%
1933	5.1	14.4	35%
1940	6.7	32.3	21%
1945	25.3	73.9	34%
1950	25.0	91.2	27%
1955	27.8	107.4	26%
1960	29.0	115.2	25%
1965	36.3	134.9	27%
1970	49.1	172.2	28%
1974	67.9	216.5	31%

Source: *Economic Report of the President* (Washington: U.S. Government Printing Office), various issues. These figures are seasonally adjusted.

The significance of this ratio between currency and demand deposits held by the public is that it limits the ability of the system to create deposits. Just as the individual bank cannot possibly, on the basis of 20 percent reserve requirements, lend five times the amount of its excess reserves, neither can

---

[15]The high value in 1933, during the banking panic, needs no explanation. In 1945 the high ratio resulted from several factors. In general, the extremely rapid increase of demand deposits during the war was not immediately matched by a corresponding willingness to hold deposits, and an unusually large proportion was exchanged for currency. Later the more normal ratio reappeared. In the 1970s the ratio rose again, to a slight extent because coins were being hoarded (increasing currency "in circulation"), but mainly because many demand deposits had been exchanged for time deposits. Values of c from 1929 to 1974 can be calibrated from the figures shown on the endsheets of the book.

the banking system. The single bank ordinarily loses most of any new deposits it creates, for the deposits are transferred to other banks. The system does not lose deposits from interbank deposit transfers, for regardless of which banks hold deposits, total deposits of all the banks together are unchanged. But the system can and does lose some newly created deposits to currency. If the public has been holding $1 in currency to every $4 of demand deposits, it will quite likely wish to continue this proportion. So, if the banking system creates $5 million of new deposits, the public will probably insist on exchanging $1 million for currency. As they pay out this currency, the bankers will lose a million dollars of legal reserves.

This limitation imposed by the cash drain is very often overlooked. Frequently financial columns state that, with 20 percent reserve requirements, the system can create about $5 for every dollar of excess reserves it holds. The true figure is much less—more nearly $3. For example, where reserve requirements for the banking system are 20 percent and the public wishes the proportion of currency to demand deposits to be 25 percent, on the basis of $1,000,000 of excess reserves the system can create $2,777,777 of deposits. Of these newly created deposits the public exchanges one fifth, or $555,555, for currency. This leaves deposits of $2,222,222, which is four times the amount of the added currency in the hands of the public. Bank reserves are decreased by the currency outflow. The original $1,000,000 of excess reserves is reduced to $444,445, now required against the retained deposit liabilities of $2,222,222. Using what at the present time are the most realistic approximations of $r = .15$ and $c = .30$, the monetary multiplier would allow the system to create $2,888,888 of deposits. In short, an induced currency drain decreases the value of the monetary multiplier.[16]

Especially note that the banking system cannot expand credit at all unless the system has excess reserves. If the system has no excess reserves and one bank gains $100,000 of reserves from another bank, the system as a whole still has no excess reserves. The possible credit expansion on the part of the individual bank that has excess reserves will be offset by the credit contraction necessary for the bank that has lost the $100,000 and consequently has a reserve deficiency.

---

[16]For any who may be interested, the formula for credit expansion by the banking system is stated below. There is no reason to remember it but be sure you remember its significance.

Where L_1 = the amount the banking system can lend
E = excess reserves of the banking system
r = average reserve requirements of the banking system
c = ratio of currency to demand deposits

Then $L_1 = \dfrac{E(1 + c)}{r + c}$

In our first example, $L_1 = \dfrac{E(1 + .25)}{.20 + .25} \approx E(2.78)$ and in the second, more realistic example,

$L_1 = \dfrac{E(1 + .30)}{.15 + .30} \approx E(2.89)$. An even more comprehensive monetary multiplier is derived in the Appendix to this chapter.

Effect of Induced Time and Savings Deposits Changes

There are several other factors, discussed in more detail in the Appendix, that, as with the currency drain, can affect the numerical value of the monetary multiplier. One that is particularly important in recent years is the rapid growth in time and savings deposits (which are examined in detail later in this chapter). The ratio of time and savings deposits to demand deposits has risen sharply in recent years (see Table 6-4, page 175, and endsheet), and the range of fluctuation has been much wider for time deposits. The fact that the reserve requirements against time and savings deposits are much smaller (but are still not zero) than against demand deposits and that there may be induced changes in time and savings deposits as banks expand (and contract) is significant. The ratio of time to demand deposits depends on such factors as their relative yields as well as yields on other claims, the level and the rates of change in people's incomes, savings, and consumption levels, etc.

The general effects of some proceeds of a bank expansion (through the purchase of loans and investments) going into time deposits are fairly easy to isolate. The total amount of combined deposits—time and demand—and of loans and investments which can be generated will be larger with the induced time deposits since their reserve requirement is lower. Demand deposits and the money supply will expand less because of the induced time deposits. Since the "reserves" which could be used to support demand deposits are used to support time deposits, the former must be smaller than they otherwise would have been without the inducement effect. Since time deposits are not included in the narrower M_1 definition of the money supply, their expansion does not change the money supply, but the accompanying restriction in demand deposit expansion does decrease it.[17]

Effect of Idle Excess Reserves

Finally, the above monetary multipliers assumed that banks are willing and able to expand their loans or security purchases by the full amount of their excess reserves. This is not always true. Certainly in the Great Depression of the 1930s, unused excess reserves were commonplace. However, in the post-World War II period, most banks have been near the limit of their potential expansion. Only a few small rural banks have held a modest amount

---

[17]For an excellent algebraic derivation of changes in time deposits on the monetary multiplier, see Lester V. Chandler, *The Economics of Money and Banking* (New York: Harper & Row, 1973), Chapter 7. The monetary multiplier with currency drain was $L_1 = \dfrac{E(1+c)}{r+c}$. If we add this induced time deposit effect to it, defining $r_d(r_t)$ as the average demand (time) deposit requirement and t as the ratio of time and savings deposits to demand deposits, the new monetary multiplier is:

$$L_2 = \frac{E(1+c)}{r_d + c + (t)(r_t)}$$

Thus, given ballpark approximations such as $c = .30, r_d = .15, r_t = .04$, and $t = 1.5, L_1 = 2.89, L_2 = 2.55$. The demand deposit multiplier, as opposed to the total deposit multiplier, falls from 2.22 with only the currency drain to 1.96 with both the currency drain and the induced time deposit effect. The values of t for selected years from 1947 to 1974 are shown in Table 6-4, page 175.

of idle excess reserves. The value of any of the monetary multipliers is reduced if there are idle excess reserves.

Effect of the Combined Factors

Taking into account all the possible modifying factors—currency drains, induced time deposit changes, possible excess reserves—a perhaps more realistic estimate of the true monetary multiplier operating in the United States today would be between 2.0 and 2.5.

These modifications show that the Fed's ability to control the money supply is limited by this lack of precision as to the exact value of all these factors at any one time. Our central bank must keep close tabs on our currency drains, time deposit growth, level of excess reserves, etc., if it is to effectively manage the money supply to achieve economic stabilization.

CONTRACTION OF CREDIT

So far we have discussed possible credit expansion on the basis of excess reserves. There also may be occasions when there is a deficiency instead of an excess of reserves.

If the system has a reserve deficiency of $100 million and there is no source of additional reserves, credit must be contracted by several times $100 million. The necessary contraction is given by the same formulas we used to find the coefficient of credit expansion for the system. We simply write E as a negative number, for example, − $100 million.

An Individual Bank

If an individual bank has a reserve deficiency, it will naturally try to get reserves from another bank—by borrowing, by selling some of its securities to other banks, or by other means. So if Bank A, subject to a 20 percent reserve requirement, finds that it has:

A		L & NW	
Vault Cash	$19,000,000	Deposits	$100,000,000

it will attempt to obtain $1 million of reserves to meet its requirements.

If the Treasury retires bank-held debt with tax surpluses or with funds borrowed from the public, the public's deposits will decline as people pay their taxes or buy government securities. The funds are transferred to the deposits held by the Treasury; and when they are later used for debt redemption, the banks are left with fewer assets and fewer liabilities. To be sure, if such a reduction occurs at a time when businesspeople and consumers are eagerly seeking bank loans, as in the postwar years, it may be simultaneously accompanied by a loan expansion. The decline in deposits caused by the reduction in bank-held government debt lowers the level of required reserves without affecting legal reserves. Hence, excess reserves and lending power of the banking system are increased.

All Banks

What can be done by any one bank individually, however, cannot be done by all the banks simultaneously. Note that if all banks, at the same time, have deficient reserves, they may all be trying to gain reserves from each other. This will not increase by a dollar the total reserves to be distributed among them, and they will have to contract their deposits (and their assets) by several times the amount of the reserve deficiency. Before 1914 this was a frequent cause of depression and financial panic. We will see later how the organization and development of the Federal Reserve System have helped to solve this problem.

COLLECTION AND CLEARING

We need to understand the easy way in which demand deposits are transferred from one account to another and from one bank to the next. Demand deposits could never have acquired their present importance if clearing arrangements had not been devised to permit prompt, safe, and economic transfer of deposits. Although final explanation of this activity must be postponed until the operation of the Federal Reserve is discussed, the process of local clearing will be analyzed. Clearing on a national or an international scale is somewhat more complicated in that it involves additional steps, but the principle involved is the same as in the simple procedure by which several banks in a community handle their collections.

Every day each bank in a large city may receive thousands of checks from its depositors. Laborers deposit the checks with which their employers paid them; landlords turn in the checks with which their tenants have paid their rent; manufacturers deposit checks that they have received from their customers; retail stores deposit checks that they have received; and so on. It is exactly because so many payments are made by transferring the ownership of demand deposits that these deposits are by far the most important part of our money supply.

In the case of checks drawn on the same bank in which they are deposited, there is no collection problem. The amounts are deducted from the accounts on which the checks are drawn and are credited to the accounts in which they are deposited. Obviously, this transfer of liabilities is all there is to the matter. Currency need not be handled at any point.

When the check is drawn on one bank and deposited in another, the case is not quite so simple. Most depositors feel that they have deposited "money" when they endorse a check and deposit it in their bank. In fact, they have authorized the bank to collect a sum that is due them but that they find inconvenient to collect in person.

The check may be an order by Ms. Stein instructing the City National Bank to pay the sum of $50 to Mr. Fitzgerald or to anyone whom Fitzgerald designates. Fitzgerald, instead of going to the City National Bank and demanding payment, endorses the check and leaves it with his own bank, the First National, for the bank to collect.

The First National has at this point received no money, but it has taken over Fitzgerald's claim on the City National for $50. Accordingly, the First National credits Fitzgerald's account for $50 but tells him that he must wait a day or two before drawing on this amount, for the First National has as yet received only a non-interest-bearing claim on money. When the claim is collected, Fitzgerald may draw checks against this amount.

First National could collect by sending a messenger to City National with the check. City National would then turn over $50 to the messenger and deduct that amount from its vault cash and from Stein's account. First National, which briefly carried the check as an asset under the heading "Items in Process of Collection," would decrease that asset classification by $50 and increase "Vault Cash" by the same amount. The collection process would be complete.

Banks did at one time collect checks in this manner. As the use of checking accounts became more common, a more expeditious method of collections evolved. Since 1853 in New York and since 1775 in London, clearinghouses have been organized to eliminate the necessity for each bank messenger to go to each of the other banks in the city. In addition to saving time, the clearinghouses eliminate the need for the messengers to carry currency, thus eliminating a former inviting opportunity for robbery.

Need for a Clearinghouse

A *clearinghouse* is a central meeting place where all bank messengers come at a certain hour of the day with checks to be collected. Each bank will have claims on the other banks and the other banks will have claims upon it. Instead of passing currency back and forth, it is simpler to find the total favorable or unfavorable balance for each bank and pay only the balance. A bank may have claims of $100,000 on other banks, but if the other banks have claims of $98,000 on the first one, the entire total of $98,000 is settled by the payment of $2,000.

Even for this small amount the messengers need not handle currency. Years ago bank officials ordinarily provided the clearinghouse with a moderate amount of cash out of which the bank's adverse clearing balances were paid. The sum did not need to be large, for if the bank was to remain in business, it would not and could not have a continuously adverse clearing balance. In the long run it should have received about the same amount from other banks as it paid out to them. When the bank originally made this deposit with the clearinghouse, the bank received in return clearinghouse certificates. These certificates were used instead of money in the settlement of balances. If a particular bank did have a sustained unfavorable balance, all its certificates presently passed into the possession of the other banks, and the first bank would have to make a new deposit at the clearinghouse.

Today neither cash nor clearinghouse certificates are involved to any extent. Settlement is usually made through the Federal Reserve Banks, which directly debit or credit the accounts that banks carry with them, partly for this very purpose.

Mechanics of a Clearinghouse

The mechanical details of clearing will vary somewhat, depending upon how many banks are involved. In a small town with only two banks, clearing might be handled in a back room in either of the banks, with a single representative from each bank. In larger towns there is likely to be a separate establishment with a manager who meets with the messengers and ascertains the claims of each bank on the other banks, finally paying the balances as indicated above. In still larger associations each bank will have two representatives: a delivery clerk and a settling clerk. At the clearing hour all settling clerks take their appointed positions and receive from the various delivery clerks the bundles of checks drawn upon their banks. They add the totals to find the total amount that their banks owe and compare this with the total, previously ascertained, of the claims of their banks upon all the others. Since the clearinghouse will collect these sums, the first total is the amount their banks owe to the clearinghouse; the second total is the amount their banks are owed by the clearinghouse. When all the settling clerks have ascertained their net debit or credit balances with the clearinghouse, the totals are added. Their algebraic sum must be equal to zero or a mistake has been made. The clearinghouse itself can neither "gain" nor "lose," for the total amount owed by the banks with an unfavorable balance must necessarily equal the total amount owed to the banks with a favorable balance.

This point is obvious if we consider the case of a clearinghouse that serves just two banks. If one bank owes the other $37,000 more than it is owed, then the other bank must be owed $37,000 more than it owes the first.

This relationship may also be seen in a little more elaborate form in the following illustration. Before going to the clearinghouse, the settling clerk of Bank A will have found that it has total claims of $24,000 against the clearinghouse, as represented by the checks drawn against the other banks and deposited in Bank A. Likewise, the settling clerks of Banks B, C, D, and E will have found their claims against the clearinghouse to be $28,000, $20,000, $16,000, and $22,000 respectively.

At the clearinghouse Bank A's settling clerk is presented with $7,000 of checks drawn against A and deposited in B, $9,000 deposited in C, and so on for a total of $21,000. In a similar way, the settling clerks of B, C, D and E are presented with checks against their banks. After all these figures are properly set down, they appear as shown on page 169.

The clearinghouse is owed $110,000 by the five banks, and it owes them the same amount. The *net* balances of the five banks are quickly ascertained as A, $3,000; B, $10,000; C, −$7,000; D, −$11,000; and E, $5,000. These figures check, $18,000 equals $18,000, and the individual banks are debited and credited accordingly, usually by the Federal Reserve Banks, which are notified of the necessary entries by the clearinghouse. The clerks return to their respective banks with the bundles of checks from the clearinghouse, and the accounts on which the checks were drawn are then debited. The transaction is now completed and the checks are set aside to be returned to the customers who issued them, together with their monthly statements.

(In thousands of dollars)

Claims of	Against					Clearinghouse "owes"
	A	B	C	D	E	
A	—	5	7	8	4	24
B	7	—	8	10	3	28
C	9	4	—	2	5	20
D	1	3	7	—	5	16
E	4	6	5	7	—	22
Clearinghouse is "owed"	21	18	27	27	17	110

As long as the banks are all expanding or contracting credit at the same rate, no one bank is likely to have a persistently favorable or unfavorable balance. By the end of the year its claims on other banks will be about equal to the claims that other banks have presented against it. But if it is expanding at a faster rate, it will probably have a persistently unfavorable balance; and if it is expanding more slowly than the others, it will regularly gain from them, increasing its excess reserves.

INTERBANK DEPOSITS AND BALANCES WITH DOMESTIC BANKS

All commercial banks in the United States hold more than $700 billion of deposits. Currently a little more than half of this total is in time and savings deposits. (This figure excludes the approximate $400 billion in deposits at nonbank thrift institutions.) The deposits are owed primarily to the general public—corporations and individuals. However, about 1 percent are Treasury deposits. About 7 percent are interbank deposits.

Many of the larger commercial banks, especially in the big cities, include banks among their customers. The deposits owed by banks to other banks are called *interbank deposits* (or demand, time, and savings deposits—commercial banks in the United States). They are also called *balances with domestic banks* (or demand and other balances with banks in the United States). The terminology depends upon which bank is listing the deposit—the bank owing the deposit or the bank owning it.

Balances with domestic banks are assets belonging to the customer banks. Ordinarily more than 95 percent of these deposits are payable on demand. They are almost as liquid as vault cash. At any time they can be exchanged for vault cash or for balances at the Federal Reserve Banks.

The banks that owe these deposits list them as *interbank deposits*. For all banks together, interbank deposits and balances with domestic banks will necessarily be equal, since the deposits for which some are liable are the same deposits that are assets to other banks. For most of the groups of banks listed in the *Federal Reserve Bulletin*, however, the liability, "Interbank deposits, domestic," regularly exceeds the assets, "Balances with domestic banks." The nature of these deposits causes this situation. Before taking up the specific reasons for banks to carry balances with other banks, we may note in a little more detail the difference between these two items according to class of banks.

As Table 6-2 shows, the contrast between "all other" (for convenience, hereafter called "small") banks and the "large" banks could not be more clear.[18] The former hold a relatively small volume of deposits for other banks, but hold large sums with others. The latter follow the opposite course. This suggests the explanation for the inequality of these items in the case of insured commercial banks. Evidently the noninsured banks, generally small institutions, are carrying larger balances with other banks than they are holding for other banks, just as the (insured) small banks are doing. Generally, interbank deposits are held by "large" (metropolitan) banks for their correspondent banks located elsewhere.

To the "large" banks these deposits are, like any other funds that they can secure, a means of increasing their reserves and hence increasing their lending potential. They formerly paid interest on them, as on other demand deposits. Since such deposits were ordinarily as liquid as cash or as reserves with the Federal Reserve, neither of which paid any interest, they were an attractive liquid asset for the "small" bank. The bank in which the deposits were held, however, knew that such deposits were subject to large fluctuations, partly but not entirely predictable. To pay interest on these deposits and at the same time stay as liquid as possible, the New York banks, which then as now held a large portion of total interbank deposits, made many call loans with securities as collateral. Large withdrawals by correspondent banks were met by liquidating these call loans, frequently resulting, as explained in Chapter 7, in abrupt declines in stock prices. Partly to discourage the speculation that resulted from this alternate excess and deficiency of investment credit and partly to strengthen the banks by reducing their expenses without affecting their ability to compete with each other, the Banking Act of 1933

Table 6-2   Interbank Deposits and Balances with Other Banks
June 30, 1974
(In billions of dollars)

	Balances with Domestic Banks	Interbank Deposits, Domestic
Insured commercial banks	31.9	40.9
Member banks	21.0	39.4
New York City and Chicago banks	8.5	25.2
Other large banks	4.0	10.6
All other banks	8.6	3.5

Source: *Federal Reserve Bulletin* (November, 1974), pp. A18–A19.

[18]Before November 9, 1972, "large" and "small" (i.e., "all other") banks were called "reserve city" and "country" banks, respectively. After that date, designation of banks for reserve-requirement purposes was based on the size and not the geographical location of banks. Today a "reserve city" bank is any bank with demand deposits exceeding $400 million.

prohibited the payment of interest on interbank (or other) demand deposits by any bank insured by the FDIC.

Changing Importance of Balances with Other Banks

If some banks had refused to pay interest while other banks still paid interest, the former would probably have found it difficult to retain their deposits. But when all were restrained from paying interest on these deposits, no bank was placed at a disadvantage. In fact, paradoxically, the volume of interbank deposits thereafter increased both absolutely and, until after Pearl Harbor, relatively. The explanation of this anomaly lies in the fact that the banks were loaded with excess reserves during the thirites, so that they lost nothing by keeping balances with other banks even though they no longer gained any interest. The banks had plenty of vault cash; their reserves at the Federal Reserve were far larger than required; and by keeping large balances with other banks, they obtained certain benefits. After our entry into the war, interbank balances became less important. As banks supplied more currency for circulation, they had to reduce their legal reserves by drawing currency from the Federal Reserve Banks.[19] Also, as they invested in government obligations, their deposits increased, eventually increasing their required reserves and, consequently, decreasing their excess reserves still more. Interbank deposits today are greater than before World War II, but their relative importance has declined to about the level of fifty years ago.

Functions of Balances with Other Banks

Even though all member banks and many nonmember banks maintain balances with the Federal Reserve Banks, the smaller banks still find that for a number of reasons it is convenient to maintain balances with other banks.

Legal Reserves. In the days of the National Banking System, a portion of the legal reserves of "small" (country) banks might be held as a deposit with "large" (reserve) city banks, and a portion of the latter's reserves might be held as a deposit with the New York, Chicago, and at one time St. Louis (so-called central reserve city) banks. This is no longer true for the national banks and other members of the Federal Reserve System, but the thousands of nonmember banks may still hold some of their legal reserves in this form. Probably interbank deposits declined in relative importance principally because balances with other banks no longer constitute legal reserves for most larger banks. During the first year or two of the Federal Reserve's operation, when few state banks had applied for membership, interbank deposits were about 25 percent of total deposits, a level not attained after 1916.

Clearings and Collections. Before the establishment of the Federal Reserve, banks had to maintain balances with other banks for clearing and collecting checks. Since this function is now handled more rapidly and efficiently

---

[19]At the time vault cash did not count as legal reserves.

by the Federal Reserve, and since nonmember banks may avail themselves of this service of the Federal Reserve, correspondent balances are less useful than they once were. However, many banks still do clear all or a part of their checks through correspondents. Nonmember banks that do not wish to remit at par for checks drawn against themselves cannot collect through the Federal Reserve and must use correspondent banks. Correspondent banks cannot collect these checks through the Federal Reserve; but as part of their service, they absorb any exchange charges so that the nonmember correspondent is able to collect at par on all items that it presents, even though it does not remit at par itself and although some of the items may be collected from other banks following the same practice. Also, some small banks, members as well as nonmembers, send their out-of-town collection items to their city correspondent for immediate credit. In some instances, particularly when a bank is receiving checks on a nearby city in which it has a correspondent, collection may be faster through a correspondent there.

Borrowings. Banks often find it convenient to be able to borrow from other banks, especially from the large banks in the financial centers.[20] The latter expect their correspondent banks to hold, like any other borrower, a minimum average balance of, perhaps, 20 percent of the amount they borrow. Although the increased availability of credit from the Federal Reserve makes such borrowing less necessary than formerly, banks still borrow frequently from correspondents rather than from the Federal Reserve.

Foreign Exchange. An explanation of the technique of foreign exchange cannot be given in this chapter.[21] However, it may be noted that banks in this country that do not operate branches abroad or maintain accounts with foreign banks must operate through a bank in this country that does one or the other if they are to be able to supply their customers with foreign exchange. Few interior banks have direct access to foreign funds. Although they might purchase foreign exchange from a New York bank by means of a bank draft, they often find it more convenient to maintain a balance with the New York bank through which such purchases may be handled.

Services. Finally, the "large" banks can provide various useful services for the interior banks that are among its customers. The small bank ordinarily does not have the facilities for critical investment analysis. It can obtain investment advice from its city correspondent. Also, through its correspondent it can make call loans in New York; it can purchase or sell securities or open market paper; it can obtain credit information; and it can secure other helpful services.

Classification of Demand Deposits

Demand deposits other than interbank are broken into a fourfold classification in the *Federal Reserve Bulletin*, as shown in Table 6-3.

---

[20]See footnote 1 on the federal funds market.
[21]See Chapters 26 and 27.

Table 6-3   Demand Deposits of All Member Banks
(In billions of dollars)

Year (December)	United States Government	States and Political Subdivisions	Certified and Officers' Checks	Individuals, Partnerships, and Corporations
1939	0.7	2.3	0.6	24.6
1945	22.2	4.2	2.5	63.0
1965	4.9	10.8	5.4	115.9
1970	6.5	13.3	7.3	147.5
1974	3.2	13.1	8.4	180.8

Source: *Federal Reserve Bulletins.*

The Treasury maintains demand deposits (Tax and Loan Accounts) in thousands of banks, although it does not write checks on those accounts. When it is ready to spend the money held there, it instructs the Federal Reserve Banks to transfer a portion of its balances with individual banks into its account with the Federal Reserve. The Federal Reserve Banks do this by charging the accounts that the member banks maintain at the Federal Reserve and crediting the amount to the Treasury account. By spending the money immediately thereafter, the Treasury returns the funds to the banking system, avoiding the alternate excesses and deficiencies of bank reserves that would occur if it held all its idle funds in the Federal Reserve Banks.[22]

The deposits of states and political subdivisions are like those of any other depositors. Their higher level today reflects the increase in the expenditures of these agencies due to the higher price level and to their expanded scale of operations.

Officers' checks outstanding (checks of the bank drawn on itself—see Chapter 11) are classified by the Federal Reserve as demand deposits. Such a check is simply a bank officer's order that the bank pay a certain amount. The bank acquires assets in exchange. Or the bank decreases a deposit liability if the officer's check is given to a customer in exchange for the customer's check, which is less widely acceptable. Eventually the officer's check will result in an addition to a customer's deposit account or a loss of reserves. Meanwhile, as long as it is outstanding, it is a liability, payable on demand, hence certainly very similar to a demand deposit.

In the strict sense of the term it is hardly a demand deposit. We ordinarily understand a demand deposit to be credit, any part or all of which the owner may transfer by check to others. One cannot draw checks against an officer's check. The officer might transfer the entire amount by endorsing the check, but cannot transfer some part of it, as can be done with a demand deposit, until he or she has converted it into a true demand deposit (or, possibly, cashed it). Then, however, the officer's check is no longer listed as a liability, since it is no longer outstanding. In contrast to a depositor's check charged

---

[22]See also Chapter 12.

against the depositor's account, the officer's check, when deposited, will increase deposits without decreasing any existing deposit account (other than "officers' checks outstanding"—if for convenience we agree to classify that liability as a deposit).

Certified checks represent earmarked deposits. A customer may write a check and have the bank stamp it as certified, thereby guaranteeing that the bank will honor the check when it is presented. The check's acceptability is increased since the recipient has the bank's signature as well as the individual's. At the time the bank certifies the check, it deducts that amount from the depositor's account so that from the bank's point of view the customer has already paid. But until the check is presented for payment, the amount for which it is written appears in no deposit account nor has it as yet caused a reduction in reserves. Consequently, such amounts are considered as deposits, temporarily without an owner.

Interest and Service Charges on Deposits

Bankers are anxious to attract new depositors because of the addition to reserves and increase in lending power that will result. They may attempt by convenient and beautiful buildings to add to their deposits. Large accounts may be obtained sometimes as a result of direct personal salesmanship. Advertising and publicity may help. There is a danger, however, that this competition among bankers may lead to unsound banking generally.

Before the Depression banks generally paid interest on demand deposits, and outside the large cities they made no service charges. In the indiscriminate scramble for deposits, the public was invited to use the banks as a free bookkeeping agency, paying for even small items by check to have a record later. Many of these small accounts were unprofitable to the banks, since the work involved in keeping track of the account and making up monthly statements more than offset the earnings that the bank might expect from the small increase in its reserves. The payment of interest on demand deposits further reduced the banks' net earnings and encouraged the banks to make risky investments that paid a high rate of return.

As cited earlier, the payment of interest on demand deposits was prohibited by the Banking Act of 1933. At about the same time the banks began to weigh more carefully the worth of individual accounts and to put service charges into effect. Previously some banks, especially in the cities, imposed service charges but usually only by making a flat deduction from all accounts that were below a certain figure. Today most banks apply measured service charges to their regular accounts, taking into consideration the customers' average or possibly minimum balance during the month, the number of items they have presented for collection, and the number of checks they have written. Smaller depositors who might find the cost of such an account excessive are encouraged to open special accounts. With these special accounts, the depositor pays the bank $2 or $3 for each book of 25 checks or pays a small monthly charge that permits the customer a number of free checks.

The importance of service charges to the banks is greater than is indicated by the fact that they account for around 5 percent of total bank earnings. They have resulted in less bookkeeping for the bank despite the necessity to make up statements of charges, for thousands of small depositors reduced their checking account activity after they began to pay for the bank's services. By holding more currency, they could get along writing fewer checks.

TIME DEPOSITS

Time deposits have increased enormously since World War II (see Tables 5-2 and 6-4). Since 1945, while demand deposits have approximately doubled, time deposits have risen to over seven times their earlier level. Twenty-five years ago time deposits were about two fifths as large as demand deposits. Today they well exceed demand deposits (interbank deposits excluded). For the first time in 1965 time and savings deposits of commercial banks were larger than demand deposits. Presently commercial banking savings deposits ($419 billion) are approximately twice as large as demand deposits ($216 billion). Although only selected values of t from 1947 to 1974 are shown in Table 6-4, any value of t from 1929 to 1974 can be calculated from the data provided on the endsheet.

Table 6-4   **Ratio of Time and Savings Deposits to Demand Deposits at Commercial Banks**

Year (December)	Time and Savings Deposits (Billions)	Demand Deposits (Billions)	$\dfrac{\text{Time and Savings Deposits}}{\text{Demand Deposits}} = t$
1947	35.4	86.7	41%
1950	36.7	91.2	40%
1955	50.0	107.4	47%
1960	72.9	115.2	63%
1965	146.3	134.9	108%
1970	229.3	172.3	133%
1974	419.4	216.5	194%

Source: *Economic Report of the President* (Washington: U.S. Government Printing Office, February, 1975), Table C-52, p. 310 and *Federal Reserve Bulletin* (June, 1975), p. A12. These figures are seasonally adjusted.

Savings Deposits

Savings deposits are a type of time deposit. The bank has the legal right to require notice of withdrawal 30 days or more before it makes payment. The accounts in mutual savings banks and many of the time accounts in commercial banks are held as savings accounts, all payments and withdrawals being made by passbook. Savings accounts may be held by individuals and nonprofit organizations only, and ordinarily may not exceed a certain amount, usually from $5,000 to $25,000.

There are two reasons for these restrictions. In the first place, until recently interest paid on savings accounts was higher than on other time deposits. The purpose of savings accounts was to bring in as depositors many people, especially in the low-income sector, who would otherwise have had no relations with the banks, since they could not afford or did not wish to maintain checking accounts. There was no need to offer as high an interest rate for the temporarily idle balances of corporate treasurers or wealthy individuals.

In the second place, savings deposits have always been more liquid than other time deposits. A corporate treasurer who transfers a million dollars of idle demand deposits to a 90-day time deposit would hesitate to ask for the funds to be reclassified as demand deposits before the 90 days were up. This action would reflect seriously on the treasurer's business reputation. If an emergency arose, he or she would borrow somewhere until the corporation's funds could be drawn upon again. For savings accounts, however, the banks almost never enforce the rule regarding 30 days' notice.[23] Enforcement is unnecessary under normal conditions because banks are sufficiently liquid. During a period of financial strain, the banks fear that imposing the requirement will lead to a loss of confidence and further heavy withdrawals, intensifying the very problem that it is supposed to solve.

Other Time Deposits

Time deposits unlimited as to amount may be held by business firms as well as individuals. These deposits are of two types, certificates of deposit and time deposits, open account.

Certificates of deposit (CDs) have long been used to indicate that specified sums are payable 30 or more days after deposit or 30 days after notice has been given. Since 1961 many banks have turned to *negotiable* certificates of deposit to increase their resources. The advantage to the bank is that such certificates can readily be issued for periods of six months or a year or even longer. The negotiable feature makes these certificates especially desirable. The certificates are issued in denominations of $100,000 to large industrial and commercial borrowers. The latter know that if they should need money before the certificates mature, they can sell the certificates to anyone looking for a high-grade, short-term investment. The attribute of negotiability gives the certificates a high degree of liquidity.

These instruments have been the fastest growing component of time deposits since their introduction. In fact, these large negotiable CDs have become so important that in 1975 the *Federal Reserve Bulletin* began publishing two new measures of the money stock: $M_4 = M_2$ plus large negotiable CDs, and $M_5 = M_3$ plus large negotiable CDs. Within five years some of the New York City banks found these negotiable certificates accounting for more than 50 percent of their total time deposits. Banks elsewhere have less occasion to

---

[23]Since 1964 some banks have offered "savings certificates" with a higher yield than regular savings accounts. (These certificates are nonnegotiable and not to be confused with the negotiable certificates of deposit discussed below.) However, customers agree to leave their money with the bank for six months or a year when they buy the savings certificates.

use them. However, the nation's largest banks (holding half the total time deposits of the banking system) hold a quarter of their time deposits in the form of these negotiable certificates of deposit. In 1974 the Federal Home Loan Bank authorized its savings and loan association members to offer negotiable certificates of deposit.

Time deposits, open account, refer to time accounts other than the two preceding. The depositor enters into a written agreement with the bank that no part of the sum will be withdrawn prior to the maturity date, which must be at least 30 days after the deposit is made, or without giving notice 30 days before withdrawal. Besides the large time deposits of business firms, these include "Christmas savings" and special accounts to provide funds for taxes, vacations, or other future events.

Origin

Although the mutual savings banks had previously held savings accounts, time deposits were not established as a separate category for commercial banks until 1913 when the Federal Reserve Act authorized members to hold lower reserves against such deposits than against their demand deposits. The reason for this distinction lay in the belief that time deposits were more stable than demand deposits so the bank could reasonably expect that its time deposits would remain constant or gradually increase. Hence, it appeared there was less need for liquidity, which at that time was considered the principal function of reserves.

Interest on Time Deposits

Since the banks felt that time deposits would seldom be withdrawn, they considered using them for investment in less liquid assets which often would yield a higher return. For this reason and to attract such deposits, the banks paid higher interest on them than they paid on demand deposits. Interest is still paid on time deposits, although the payment of interest on demand deposits is now prohibited. Maximum rates are set by the Board of Governors and on most time deposits may currently be as high as 7.5 percent.[24] From 1936 to 1956, however, banks were not permitted to pay more than 2.5 percent even on long-term deposits, nor, as late as 1964, more than 1 percent (annually) on time deposits of less than 90 days.

Time Deposits Distinguished from Demand Deposits

In practice time deposits are often very nearly the same as demand deposits. Some large time deposits are, in fact, merely reclassified demand deposits. A corporation with demand deposits that exceed its needs for the next month

---

[24]In consequence of their greater liquidity, savings deposits are currently limited to a return of 5 percent (effective July 1, 1973. From January 21, 1970, until then it was 4.5 percent, and 4 percent before that). Effective July 16, 1973, maximum interest rates were suspended on all maturity time deposits in denominations of $100,000 or more.

by $100,000 may exchange them for a 30-day certificate of deposit which at 6 percent will yield $500. Such a return is better than nothing, and it can be had with less trouble than would be involved in finding a safe, liquid short-term investment. Especially since depositors have been unable to receive interest on demand deposits, such temporary reclassifications have been common.

Furthermore, many small depositors treat their savings accounts very much as though they were demand deposits. If they are unable to keep a large enough average balance to make a regular checking account practical, they may prefer a so-called savings account to a thrift-service checking account. On the latter they would receive no interest and would usually pay ten or fifteen cents for each check written. By sacrificing the convenience of checks, they may instead deposit their salaries in their savings accounts and withdraw cash from time to time as they require it. Although they may deposit $400 the first of the month, the account may regularly be down to $50 by the end of the month. On the basis of their average balance they will receive $2 or $3 of interest during the year and will save about the same amount by avoiding the expense for checks. To be sure, this is hardly the purpose that savings accounts supposedly are designed to serve; but since the banks do usually pay such deposits on demand, many are being used in this way. These practices have made time deposits much more active than their name implies. Accordingly, banks cannot safely make too much distinction between demand and time deposits in forming policies.

Short-Term Notes

Short-term unsecured notes, introduced in 1964 by the First National Bank of Boston and since then used by some of the larger banks, are not, strictly speaking, deposits. Neither are they capital, however.[25] Since they are a close substitute for time deposits, we shall briefly summarize them here.

In the increasingly intense competition for funds, banks in 1963 and 1964 found themselves handicapped by Regulation K of the Board of Governors. According to the Regulation at that time, commercial banks could pay on time deposits of less than 90 days a maximum interest rate of 1 percent per year. By 1964 short-term funds invested in 91-day Treasury bills were yielding more than 3 percent. Naturally the banks were being shut out of the short-term borrowing market.

At this point some banks began to sell their own promissory notes to large institutional borrowers, just as commercial and industrial firms had often done. (See Open Market Commercial Paper, Chapter 7.) The notes were usually in $500,000 or $1,000,000 denominations, and matured in from 30 days to a year. Since the notes were not specifically deposits, they were not subject to Regulation K (nor were they subject to reserve requirements). The banks could pay whatever rate necessary to attract funds.

---

[25]Do not confuse them with capital notes (more often called debentures) discussed in the preceding chapter. Capital notes usually are of 25-year maturity.

Frequently we find that regulations lead to innovations. Ingenious lawyers can often find a way to get around a regulation if it becomes oppressive. It is safe to assume the banks would not have turned to short-term notes if Regulation K had not made it impossible for them to attract time deposits of less than 90 days. In any event, the Board of Governors, which disapproved of the notes without actually prohibiting them, promptly raised the maximum rate payable on short-term time deposits. From 1936 to 1964, through depression, war, and postwar prosperity, the rate had been held constant at 1 percent. Two months after the first short-term notes appeared, the maximum rate was abruptly raised to 4 percent, and to 5.5 percent a year later.

Notes may be summarized as follows:

1. Banking began several hundred years ago with the issue of *bank notes*—demand obligations, redeemable in gold or silver. These notes were discontinued a generation ago by the national banks, a century ago by the state banks. Only the twelve Federal Reserve Banks still issue (demand) bank notes in the United States.
2. *Capital notes*, or debentures, usually of 25-year term, have been issued by some banks since 1964.
3. *Short-term notes*, of a year or less, have also been issued by some banks since 1964.

DEPOSIT INSURANCE

A few bank deposits were first insured more than a century ago. However, although the importance of demand deposits increased rapidly after the Civil War, the banking collapse of the 1930s was required to bring about a nationwide program of deposit insurance.

Local Attempts

As early as 1829 deposits were insured in the state of New York, but after a few years the insurance coverage was limited to notes. For about a century noteholders continued to benefit from protection not available to depositors. Under the free banking laws and under the national banking system, bank notes, although not insured, were protected by the pledge of specific assets. In the event of bank failure depositors received what was left, often very little. (See Chapter 8.)

The great increase in the use of demand deposits together with the many bank failures resulting from our unit system of banking slowly aroused interest in the insurance of bank deposits. Many bills for protecting bank deposits were introduced in Congress but defeated. A number of states instituted deposit insurance programs early in the 20th century, but none of these were successful. They included only the state banks, often not the strongest or the most conservatively managed; they admitted banks regardless of condition, thereby including bad risks; and the banks that were included were not sufficiently diversified.

Necessity for Nationwide Deposit Insurance

The failure of more than a third of the nation's banks in a 12-year period culminating in the banking debacle of 1930–1932 suggested that the restoration of confidence in the banks and the provisions of a sound banking structure would require drastic treatment. One possibility might have been to revolutionize our banking system and eliminate its inherent evils. The other possibility was to retain the system, modified in some particulars, and to provide a government guarantee of deposits. If it did nothing else, such a program should at least create more confidence in the banks and eliminate the hardships resulting from bank failures. It was hoped, however, that it would also help prevent failures and encourage the development of sounder banking, particularly among banks not members of the Federal Reserve System.

Organization of the Federal Deposit Insurance Corporation

The guarantee of deposits was provided by the organization in 1933 of the Federal Deposit Insurance Corporation to insure deposits, originally up to $2,500. Over the years the coverage has been gradually increased to the present $40,000. Ninety-nine percent of all depositors are fully protected; but due to the very large size of some business deposits and government deposits, only about two thirds of total deposits are covered. (Government deposits ordinarily have the additional protection of surety bonds or securities pledged by the bank.)

All members of the Federal Reserve System are insured. So also are all other banks that wish coverage and can qualify for membership in the FDIC. Less than two percent of the nations's banks, holding only one half of one percent of total deposits, have not joined the FDIC. (Many of these are Massachusetts-chartered mutual savings banks, covered by a Massachusetts insurance program.)

An unusual feature of the FDIC is that it has no capital stock. Its original capital was provided by the Treasury and the Federal Reserve Banks. This stock was retired and canceled in 1947 and 1948. Today the FDIC holds only its surplus, officially termed the Deposit Insurance Fund.[26] Most of the Corporation's income today comes from the securities in which the Fund is invested. The balance results from the assessments of, nominally, one twelfth of 1 percent on all deposits of insured banks.

Question of Proper Assessments. Note particularly that assessments are based on *total* deposits, not on insured deposits. At the outset some of the large metropolitan banks protested that they were being required to pay a disproportionate share of the cost of the program. They objected to paying an assessment based on their total deposits when perhaps only a small proportion of their total deposits was fully insured. Many small banks with no large corporate accounts were obtaining a guarantee of total deposits. In short, the

---

[26]However, the Corporation is authorized to borrow up to $3 billion from the Treasury, if necessary.

large banks paid more than the small banks per dollar of *insured* deposits. Further, the large banks claimed that they were in a stronger financial position than the average bank, and, as preferred risks, merited a lower assessment rate. To these objections it was replied that rate differentiation would be impractical, that it would make deposit insurance prohibitively expensive for the smaller banks, and that the city banks' savings from the discontinuance of interest on demand deposits would more than suffice to cover the insurance premiums.

Later the banks argued that assessments should be decreased. Especially since World War II, deposit insurance losses have been very low, in most years a small fraction of 1 percent of the investment income alone. Total losses incurred by the Corporation since 1934 are a little more than one fourth of its current annual receipts from its investments alone. And the Corporation's annual total payout for losses and all administrative expenses has been running recently at from 20 to 25 percent of its investment income. The Corporation, therefore, has been adding to surplus three fourths of its investment income and the entire amount of its receipts from assessing the banks. Some bankers have protested that instead of adding indefinitely to its ever-growing surplus, the FDIC should recognize that its assessment rate is excessive.

The Corporation has not been convinced. Although in its first thirty-three years of operation the FDIC was able out of income to repay the subscribed capital and create a deposit insurance fund of over $3 billion, the ratio of the fund to insured deposits is lower today than it was before World War II. The ratio had been rising slowly during the prewar years, but the great surge in bank deposits during and after the war was not matched by a proportionate increase in the deposit insurance fund. Corporation officials have pointed out that if the assessment were to be dropped entirely, the ratio of the fund to insured deposits would again decline. Compromising, Congress decided in 1950 to reduce the contribution by the banks by about one half.[27]

Activities of the FDIC. The FDIC has improved banking standards by requiring the improvement of banks that examination shows to be managed improperly. In such instances the Corporation first reports the unsatisfactory conditions to the proper regulatory authority. If corrective action is not promptly taken, the bank's insurance is terminated. Loss of its insurance would require a national bank to give up its charter and a state bank to withdraw from the Federal Reserve. More importantly, banks realize that knowledge that they were no longer insured would probably lead to a rapid deposit loss and quite likely to eventual failure.[28] Also, the FDIC has persuaded state banking authorities to withhold charters for new banks until the Corporation has studied the prospects for the proposed bank and determined whether it could qualify for insurance.

---

[27]The rate of one twelfth of 1 percent was retained, but the banks were given a rebate of two thirds of the preceding year's assessment income remaining after the Corporation's expenses and losses. This rebate reduces the effective rate to about one thirtieth of 1 percent.

[28]For the public's protection the existing accounts, although not new accounts, in such a bank continue to be insured for two years.

The FDIC may take over and liquidate the assets of an unsound bank or it may lend to the bank. Since 1944, however, the Corporation has often followed the policy of promoting a merger of a weak bank with a stronger neighbor, and if necessary, purchasing some of the assets or lending against them. This procedure has two advantages over outright liquidation:

1. FDIC losses are less since liquidation expenses are avoided.
2. Large depositors as well as small are protected since total deposits, not just insured deposits, are transferred to the new institution. Under this procedure no depositor has so far lost a dollar.

Mergers are, however, impractical when the extent of the bank's liabilities is in doubt. It was not clear in 1965, for example, whether certificates of deposit should be considered as equivalent to regular deposits.

In summary, the FDIC insures deposits in 14,457 banks in the U.S., including all national banks, but it is not the agency that examines, supervises, or presses corrective action on either national banks or state-chartered members of the Federal Reserve System. That job belongs to the Comptroller of the Currency (4,710 national banks) and to the Federal Reserve System and state banking departments (1,072 state-chartered "member" banks). The FDIC's examination responsibilities are confined to the nation's 8,675 state-chartered banks which are not members of the Federal Reserve System. The FDIC's insurance activities, as distinct from its examination responsibilities, are designed to minimize the impact of bank failure on depositors.

It is, of course, much too early to attempt a final evaluation of the FDIC. Certainly it would be a great mistake to assume that its record to date proves that banks are now safe or that the Corporation can prevent losses from bank failures. Remember that, although the FDIC was organized in a very black hour of banking history, its members were the survivors of the panic and presumably more sound than the thousands that had failed in the preceding months. Also, throughout most of the life of the FDIC, the nation has been enjoying a high level of prosperity. Admitting these qualifications, we may still concede that if the FDIC and other agencies continue to work for improvement in banking policies, it seems unlikely that the banking situation will again become as chaotic as in 1932. Deposit insurance should greatly reduce the likelihood of bank runs, which probably forced the closing of many essentially sound banks. The Federal Reserve has greater power today to help the banking system. Finally, if the resources of the FDIC should prove inadequate under stress, Congress could increase them by authorizing additional borrowing power or by other means.

SUMMARY AND CONCLUSION

The deposits of greatest importance to the general economy are demand deposits. People in this country make 90 percent of all payments with these deposits. Changes in these deposits are the principal cause of changes in the total money supply. By controlling demand deposits Federal Reserve authorities control the quantity of money and, to some extent, the value of money. Changes in demand deposits may also affect the level of income and employment.

Deposits are the debts that banks owe their customers. Some of these debts result from currency turned over to the bank by its depositors; some result from checks drawn on other banks and turned over to a bank for collection; and some result from the lending activities of the bank and of other banks. When a bank lends, it ordinarily credits the borrower's checking account. No currency changes hands. These loan-created deposits are the means by which the banks increase the economy's money supply. Their control over the money supply places the banks in a strategic position. Prices, employment, and the income level may all be affected by bankers' decisions to increase or decrease their loans and deposits. The broad social significance of bank loans is that when the system as a whole is increasing (decreasing) its loans, the money supply is also increasing (decreasing).

Loans and investments comprise most of a bank's assets. These assets cannot be paid out to depositors and no bank can possibly pay off all its depositors at once. The management knows that the bank will not be called upon to do so, and that the inflow of funds will usually be about equal to the outflow. The reserve of vault cash (or other specified assets) need be only a fraction of the bank's deposit liabilities.

Legal reserves are the assets a bank *is* holding that according to law may be used to meet its reserve requirements. *Required reserves* are the amount of reserves the bank *must* hold, as determined by the amount of its deposits and the percentage of reserves specified by the regulations. *Excess reserves* = legal reserves − required reserves. Excess reserves determine the lending power of the bank or system, as summarized below.

The individual bank's lending power is equal to its excess reserves divided by $kr + (1-k)$. This formula takes into account the fact that when a bank does create new deposits, it ordinarily loses most of them. Otherwise the bank could lend several dollars for every dollar of excess reserves (for if $k = 1.00$, the expression $\frac{E}{kr + (1-k)}$ would reduce to $\frac{E}{r}$). If, on the other hand, the bank ordinarily kept no part of the deposits it created, it could lend only the amount of its excess reserves. Normally it can safely lend a little more unless, for reasons not directly connected with its current loans, it finds it is losing reserves to other banks or wishes to maintain idle reserve balances larger than the required minimum.

For the banking system as a whole, transfers of deposits and reserves from bank to bank cancel out. However, as the volume of deposit money is increased, the public demands that part of it be converted into currency. This currency demand limits the possible credit expansion. If there were no currency drain, a banking system subject to 20 percent reserve requirements could, over a period of time, create $5 of deposits for every $1 of excess reserves. But since the banks do have to pay out additional currency as the volume of deposits rises, part of their legal reserves disappears. As shown by the monetary multiplier $L_1 = \frac{E(1 + c)}{r + c}$, the banking system can create only about \$2.89 of demand deposits against \$1 of excess reserves if the average reserve requirement is 15 percent and if the public requires that its currency holdings be about 30 percent of its holdings of demand deposits.

If we modify the monetary multiplier to take account of induced changes in time and savings deposits as well as the currency drain, we find that $L_2 = \dfrac{E\,(1 + c)}{r_d + c + (t)\,(r_t)} = 2.55$. This formula recognizes that while both total and time deposits will be greater, the multiplied expansion of demand deposits and the narrowly defined M_1 money supply will be reduced. The multiple credit expansion takes place whether individual banks lend a little more than or exactly the amount of their excess reserves. As a result of the re-lending that takes place over a period of time, each bank finally has no excess reserves and, for the system as a whole, \$2 or \$3 have been lent for each dollar of originally excess reserves.

It is always possible that excess reserves will not be fully utilized. There are times when banks prefer to hold some excess reserves rather than to be fully loaned up. Holding excess reserves would tend to bring the monetary multiplier down closer to 2. If there should be an actual deficiency of reserves for the system and there were no additional sources of reserves, a multiple contraction of credit would be necessary.

The banking system smoothly handles the daily transfer of billions of dollars of deposits through clearing arrangements. Clearinghouse officials make book entries of the net amounts gained and lost by the various banks. Clearinghouses facilitate check collection and eliminate the need for currency in the collection process.

There are a number of reasons why smaller banks find it convenient to maintain balances with other banks. In return for these *interbank deposits* (or balances with domestic banks), a number of useful functions have been and continue to be performed.

Time deposits have increased dramatically since World War II and are now larger than demand deposits. Savings deposits and certificates of deposits are two of the more important types of time deposits.

Although there were local attempts to insure deposits in the United States as early as 1829, the banking failures of the late 1920s and early 1930s pointed out most dramatically the necessity for a nationwide deposit insurance program. The Federal Deposit Insurance Corporation was organized in 1933 and has been very successful in minimizing the impact of bank failures on depositors and providing sound examination procedures.

Discussion Questions

1. Your bank statement shows you that your bank never lends any of your deposit. Because of the nature of deposits, banks cannot possibly lend them. Explain both statements.

2. You cannot determine a bank's excess reserves unless you know both its legal reserves and its required reserves. Moreover, once requirements have been set, it is necessary to define legal reserves. Explain.
3. "The specific reserve requirements for Federal Reserve members are set by the Board of Governors on the basis of size rather than geographical location." Briefly explain whether you agree or disagree.
4. If a bank were convinced that, whenever it created new deposits to lend to its customers, it would lose every dollar of those deposits to other banks, would it have any incentive to expand credit when it found itself holding excess reserves? Explain.
5. Are derivative deposits more stable from the point of view of the bank or of the individual borrower? Why?
6. Banks ordinarily refuse to let a customer draw immediately against newly deposited checks drawn on other banks. Why?
7. If someone asked you, "Just what does the bank do with the money when a typical business loan is repaid?" how would you answer?
8. On the basis of the formula $L = \dfrac{E}{kr + (1 - k)}$, how much could a bank with $1,000,000 of excess reserves lend:
   a. If $k = 100\%$, $r = 10\%$?
   b. If $k = 50\%$, $r = 20\%$?
   Explain the reason for the difference in the two answers.
9. What determines, at any time, the maximum amount of loans a bank may make?
10. Sometimes bankers tell their customers, "Since we must maintain a reserve of 20 percent against our deposits, we require that, when we lend $1,000, the customer keep at least $200 of it in the bank at all times." Critically comment.
11. The elementary coefficient of credit or deposit expansion equation $L = E/r$ makes four simplifying assumptions. What are they?
12. Although everyone is familiar with money, few people realize that most of our money is invisible, intangible, and abstract. Explain.
13. What is the immediate, direct effect on the quantity of money when the public draws $10 billion of currency from the banks? What is the indirect effect on the quantity of money?
14. Suppose that as a result of repeated surpluses the government is able to pay off most of the national debt over the next thirty years. Do you think this would have any effect on currency in circulation? Explain.
15. What is the difficulty in trying to measure monetary policy quantitatively by studying the changes in currency plus demand deposits? Can you suggest a more satisfactory approach?
16. What is the net clearing balance of each bank in the example below? Is it by coincidence or necessity that the total owed by Banks B and D is exactly equal to the total owed to Banks A, C, and E? Why?

Owed by	Owed to				
	A	B	C	D	E
A	—	40	20	30	20
B	30	—	60	40	20
C	50	20	—	40	50
D	30	30	40	—	50
E	40	10	50	30	—

APPENDIX: THE COMPLETE MONETARY MULTIPLIER[29]

The monetary multiplier m_1 shows how the money supply M_1 is related to some reserve measure, typically the monetary base B; that is, $M_1 = m_1B$. The monetary base (base money) is the net monetary liabilities of the federal government (i.e., the Fed and the U.S. Treasury). This so-called "high powered money" consists of commercial bank reserves plus currency held by the nonbank public. The narrow definition of the money supply M_1 consists of the net demand deposits of commercial banks plus foreign demand balances at Federal Reserve Banks plus currency outside banks. The Federal Reserve controls B essentially by its open market operation, since Federal Reserve holdings of U.S. government securities are the major component of B.

To control the money supply M_1, the Fed must know the complete monetary multiplier which applies to any change in B. Since 1950, m_1 has varied within the narrow range of approximately 2.52 to 2.77. (See Figure 6-1.) Since this ratio is stable and reasonably predictable, the concept of a monetary multiplier is useful to the monetary authorities.

MONEY STOCK/MONETARY BASE

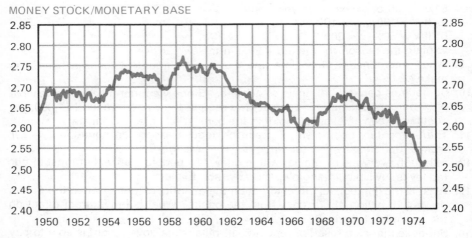

Source: Federal Reserve Bank of St. Louis.

Figure 6-1   The Monetary Multiplier

There are four key ratios that affect m_1. The first three of these were discussed in Chapter 6, but a fourth was not.[30] According to Robertson and Phillips, the monetary multiplier depends on the following ratios:

---

[29]This appendix draws on the lucid, straightforward expositions of Jerry L. Jordan, "Elements of Money Stock Determination," *Review*, Federal Reserve Bank of St. Louis (October, 1969), pp. 10–19, (available as Number 46 in their Reprint Series); and more especially Ross M. Robertson and Almarin Phillips, "Optional Affiliation with the Federal Reserve System for Reserve Purposes Is Consistent with Effective Monetary Policies" (Conference of State Bank Supervisors, 1974), pp. 15–20.

[30]Chapter 6 does take up a fifth factor which is not discussed in the Robertson and Phillips paper—the possibility of idle excess reserves. No doubt the reason they did not take up this factor is that as an empirical matter, in the last two decades, there have been few instances of idle excess reserves.

1. *The r-ratio.* The "r-ratio" is defined as a weighted-average reserve ratio against all deposits of commercial banks. It is computed by dividing total reserves by total deposits. In making this computation the monetary authorities must make estimates for nonmember banks on dates between benchmark call-date data presently available four times each year. Nevertheless, the "r-ratio" is the least volatile of all the ratios that determine the money multiplier.

2. *The k-ratio.* The "k-ratio" is defined as the ratio of currency outside banks to total demand deposits. If the nonbank public always held a fixed proportion of currency to demand deposits, this ratio would be constant. The fact is, however, that at certain times of the year and at certain points in the business cycle the public wishes to hold more or less of its assets as cash. If, with a given increase in the monetary base, the amount of currency the public desires to hold remains unchanged, the new base money remains in the banking system entirely to support an increase in deposits. Thus, the "currency drain" that accompanies an increase in the base must be estimated in determining the amount of base money that must be supplied to achieve a desired increase in the money stock.

3. *The t-ratio.* The "t-ratio" is defined as the proportion of time deposits to demand deposits of all commercial banks in the system. Although time deposits are not included in the narrow definition of the money supply, banks must keep reserves against them. As we have observed, the reserve requirements of member banks are much lower against time deposits than against demand deposits, and in general the different state jurisdictions require lower reserves against time deposits than against demand deposits. Because a given amount of reserves permits more time deposits to be supported than demand deposits, Federal Reserve officials must be able to estimate the public's desire to hold time deposits relative to demand deposits in order to determine how much the money supply will change following a change in base money. In some respects the variables affecting the "t-ratio" are more complex than those affecting either the "r-ratio" or the "k-ratio." For the growth of time deposits depends not only on competition among banks and the nonbank intermediaries for household and business savings but also on the legal ceilings on rates payable by these institutions as imposed by Federal Reserve, the Federal Deposit Insurance Corporation, and the Federal Home Loan Bank Board.

4. *The g-ratio.* The "g-ratio" is defined as the proportion of U.S. government deposits in commercial banks to the total of private demand deposits. None of the definitions of the money supply includes U.S. government deposits. Yet commercial banks are required to hold the same proportion of reserves against federal deposits in the Treasury tax and loan accounts as against private demand deposits. Thus, changes in the amount of U.S. government deposits in commercial banks affect the amount of private deposits the banking system can support with a given amount of base money. Fluctuations in the "g-ratio" are primarily the result of shifts in Treasury balances from the tax and loan accounts in commercial banks to the Treasury's checking accounts with Federal Reserve. Although changes in this ratio are

predictable on the basis of information from the Treasury, the "g-ratio" is the most volatile of the four we have just considered.[31]

The historical trend of these ratios since 1950 is shown in Figure 6-2. In algebraic terms, the value of the monetary multiplier m_1 is the following quotient (which is plotted in Figure 6-1):[32]

$$m_1 = \frac{1+k}{r(1+t+g)+k}$$

Recalling that in the text we used the letter c for what above is labeled k, we can derive the text's less complete banking system expansion multiplier $L_1 = \frac{(1+c)}{r+c}$, which includes the currency drain, but not changes in the t-ratio or g-ratio. Since these two factors are not included in the text's formulation, the value of t and g in m_1 above would be zero. This gives the simplified text version.

One final point on trends. The r-ratio has been relatively stable with a slight downward trend, whereas the t-ratio has exhibited pronounced short-run variability and a sharp upward trend. The t-ratio movements mostly result from shifts of funds within commercial banks from demand to time deposits, from disintermediation from time deposits to the money market (as in 1969), and from the higher rate of long-term growth of time and savings deposits over demand deposits.

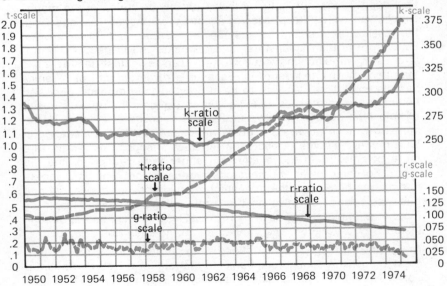

Source: Federal Reserve Bank of St. Louis.

Figure 6-2   Monetary Multiplier Ratios

[31]Robertson and Phillips, *op. cit.*, pp. 16–17.
[32]The r-ratio depends upon the estimation of seven ratios and is further complicated by lagged reserve requirements. See Jordan, *op. cit.*, especially pp. 15–16. If the money supply is more broadly defined to include time deposits (M_2), the new monetary multiplier is:

$$m_2 = \frac{1+k+t}{r(1+t+g)+k}$$

Chapter 7   Bank Assets

By far the most important bank assets are reserves, loans, and invest-ments. The various kinds and amounts of these assets held vary from bank to bank. But a combined statement of these assets for all banks provides a good idea of the (weighted) average asset mix. Table 7-1 shows the composition of bank assets for all commercial banks.[1]

Loans and investments are a bank's principal earning assets. Table 7-1 shows that these loans and securities comprised over 80 percent of all bank assets in June, 1974. (A discussion of the enormous variety of these debt claims held by banks against others is found in the latter portion of this chapter.)

RESERVES

Reserves are a bank's most liquid assets and are mostly nonearning assets. The majority are so-called *cash items*, which include not only vault cash but also deposits that the bank holds with other banks (including the Federal Reserve Bank) and collection items that will normally be converted into a balance at the Federal Reserve within a day or two. Since these items are not profit-making, banks usually keep them at the minimum legal limit. The balances due from other banks generally result from banks using other banks for various correspondent services as described in the previous chapter. Most banks lump together their cash items under the heading "Cash and due from banks," thus avoiding a specific statement of how much vault cash they hold and how large a balance they are carrying at the Federal Reserve Bank.

To avoid confusion in discussing the various types of reserves, we may profitably review our definitions. Reserves under discussion in this chapter do not include valuation reserves, similar to those maintained by other business organizations. (Such items are frequently the only reserves specifically listed as such on the bank's balance sheet.) We are here concerned only with re-serves maintained against deposits. These reserves may be classified as legal and other. The legal reserves may be subdivided into required and excess. Reserves may also be classified as primary and secondary according to the nature of the component assets.

---

[1]The time trend of major assets, liabilities, and capital from 1950 to 1970 is shown in Table 5-2, p. 141.

Earlier we defined *legal reserves* as those funds that according to law may be counted as a part of the reserves that the bank must keep against its deposits. *Required reserves* are the product of the bank's deposits multiplied by a

Table 7-1   Total Commercial Bank Assets
June 30, 1974
(In millions of dollars)

Cash bank balances, items in process		$126,487
Currency and coin	$ 8,378	
Reserves with Federal Reserve Banks	30,146	
Balances with banks in the United States	34,370	
Balances with banks in foreign countries	1,386	
Cash items in process of collection	52,207	
Total loans and securities		719,173
Total securities held—book value	189,762	
U.S. Treasury	$ 52,114	
Other U.S. government agencies	31,359	
States and political subdivisions	99,870	
All other securities	6,420	
Federal funds sold and securities		
resale agreements	35,307	
Commercial banks	31,612	
Brokers and dealers	2,658	
Others	1,037	
Loans	494,104	
Real estate	126,173	
Commercial and industrial	177,184	
Individuals	102,615	
Farmers	18,444	
Financial institutions	56,211	
All other loans	13,477	
Other (net)		39,095
Fixed assets-buildings, furniture, real estate	14,168	
Other assets	24,927	
TOTAL ASSETS		$884,755

Selected ratios:
Percentage of total assets:

Cash bank balances, items in process		14.3%
Total loans and securities		81.3
Total securities held	21.4%	
Federal funds sold and securities resale agreements	4.0	
Loans	55.9	
Other (net)		4.4
TOTAL		100.0%

Source: *Federal Reserve Bulletin* (March, 1975), pp. A18–A19. (Details may not add to totals because of rounding.)

percentage figure stated by law or authority. *Excess reserves* are the difference between legal reserves and required reserves. Thus, if a bank's deposits are $10,000,000 and it is required to maintain reserves of 16 percent, its required reserves are $1,600,000. If it is holding a total of $1,900,000 that may legally be counted as reserves, its excess reserves are $300,000 and it may safely lend slightly more than that amount.

Other reserves are highly liquid assets other than legal reserves. Together with legal reserves they compose primary and secondary reserves. *Primary reserves* are cash and its immediately convertible equivalent. They include legal reserves, balances with other banks, and items in process of collection. *Secondary reserves* are assets that will or can be quickly converted into cash with little or no loss. They include short-term government paper and commercial paper of highest quality. More broadly, they consist of assets that may be discounted or sold, without appreciable loss, to the Federal Reserve Banks if not to other buyers.

LEGAL RESERVE REQUIREMENTS

Nearly all banks in the United States are required by law to hold a certain portion of their assets in the form of legal reserves. This requirement arises from the nature of American banking specifically, rather than from the nature of banking generally. Banks in England and Canada have no specific reserve requirements imposed by law, nor do state banks in Illinois that are not members of the Federal Reserve. Our unit system of banking, made up of thousands of banks, requires more supervision than does a branch system composed of five or six banks. Legal reserve requirements were first imposed to make sure that banks would maintain the primary reserves that their own self-interest required. Today they are a control device important to our decentralized banking.

Review of Requirements

Originally state banks had no legal reserve requirements. After the panic of 1837, state legislatures, feeling that part of the banks' difficulties was due to their inadequate reserves, began slowly to formulate requirements. Usually these reserves were held in specie, although sometimes a part or all might be held as deposits with other banks.

When the national banking system was organized, country banks were required to hold reserves of 15 percent against their total deposits. These reserves could be in the form of vault cash, or as much as three fifths might be held as deposits with reserve city and central reserve city banks. Similarly, the reserve city banks were required to hold reserves of 25 percent, of which half might be in the form of deposits with the two (once three) central reserve city banks. The central reserve city banks held reserves of 25 percent, entirely in vault cash.

With the organization of the Federal Reserve System came a gradual change in the reserve requirements of national banks and state member banks. For the first time a distinction was made between demand and time deposits, with lower reserves required against the latter.

In 1935 the Board of Governors received the power to vary reserve requirements. They increased them in the three classes of banks from 13, 10, and 7 percent against demand deposits and 3 percent against time deposits to as high as 26, 20, 14, and 6 percent. For a few months in 1948–1949 they were authorized to raise requirements a little above the usual maximums. The extent of this discretionary control over reserve requirements was somewhat reduced in 1962, when the distinction between central reserve cities and reserve cities was abolished. New York and Chicago banks are now subject to the same reserve requirements as banks in the other reserve cities.

Existing Requirements

By law a member bank of the Federal Reserve holds about a sixth or seventh of all demand deposits as nonearning reserves, mainly as deposits with its regional Federal Reserve Bank, but also as vault cash. The specific permissible requirements are set by the Board of Governors with the limits set by Congress, which today are: 3–10 percent against savings and time deposits, 7–14 percent against demand deposits up to $400 million, and 10–22 percent against demand deposits over $400 million.[2] The actual level of required reserve ratios, effective as of May 31, 1975, is shown in Table 7-2.

It was only in 1968 (1966) that demand (time) deposits' reserve requirements began to be based on deposit size. Before that, legal required ratios

Table 7-2   Legal Reserve Requirement Ratios for
                  Federal Reserve Member Banks
                  (In effect as of May 31, 1975)

Size of Bank's Deposits	Reserve Ratios Required (Percent)
Demand Deposits:	
$0–$2 million	7.5
$2–$10 million	10.0
$10–$100 million	12.0
$100–$400 million	13.0
Over $400 million	16.5
Time and Savings Deposits:	
$0–$5 million	3.0
Over $5 million, maturing in 30–179 days	6.0
Over $5 million, maturing in 180 days and over	3.0

Source: *Federal Reserve Bulletin* (June, 1975), p. A7.

[2]Today banks with reserves over $400 million are reserve city banks, irrespective of their geographical location, while banks with reserves of less than $400 million are called "other banks."

were based solely on geographical location—*viz.*, banks in larger cities (called reserve city banks) had higher required ratios than banks in small cities (called country banks). From 1966 to 1972 both geographical location and deposit size were used, and in November, 1972, requirements began to be based exclusively on deposit size.

The setting of lower ratios for small banks increases their profitability by tying up a smaller percentage of their assets in non-interest-earning legal reserves. This practice has helped slightly in arresting the trend toward nonmembership, but nonetheless the percentage of member banks has been falling gradually but steadily since World War II. In 1945 about 49 percent of all commercial banks were members and they held about 87 percent of total bank deposits. By 1974 only about 40 percent were members and they held about 78 percent of total bank deposits. Today there are approximately 14,500 commercial banks in the United States. All of the approximately 4,700 national banks are members, but only about 1,100 of the 9,750 state banks are members. (Never have as many as 25 percent of the state banks been members.)

The major advantage in state reserve requirements comes not so much from the lower level of reserve requirements as from the more favorable composition of permissible required reserves. Most states have about the same level of reserve requirements as the Fed. However, nonmembers profit from being allowed to count earning assets, such as U.S. government securities and correspondent balances (including in some cases uncollected items), whereas Fed members can mostly count only sterile balances on deposit at the Fed and vault cash as reserves. Since the major function of these requirements is to enable the Fed to control the money supply and not to make deposits liquid and safe, many feel that all banks should be subject to the same legal requirements.[3] They feel that either uniform reserve requirements or the payment of interest by the Fed on reserve deposits of member banks can make monetary policy more effective and more equitable.

Definition of Legal Reserves

Over the years there have also been changes in the definition of legal reserves. For a few years member banks were allowed to count as legal reserves not only their balances at the Federal Reserve Banks, but also their vault cash and their balances at reserve city and central reserve city banks. In 1917 an amendment to the Federal Reserve Act redefined legal reserves to include only balances at the Federal Reserve Banks. Reserve requirements were simultaneously lowered, so that the size of the required balances at the Federal Reserve Banks was little changed by the ruling that vault cash and balances with correspondent banks no longer counted as legal reserves. Since, however, there was no longer any advantage in holding vault cash in excess of what was needed for till money, and since such excess vault cash was often in the form of gold certificates due to their large denominations,

---

[3]An excellent discussion of the pros and cons of this proposal is contained in *Business Review* of the Federal Reserve Bank of Philadelphia (June, 1974).

banks were encouraged to ship gold certificates to the Federal Reserve Banks. By thus increasing their excess reserves, the banks increased their lending power. At the same time they increased the lending power of the Federal Reserve Banks, for which, at that time, the gold certificates (and gold) were legal reserves. Though banks could no longer count as legal reserves the balances they held with correspondent banks, they were permitted by later legislation to deduct such deposits from their gross demand deposits in computing their required reserves.[4]

In 1959 the Federal Reserve Act was again amended. The Board of Governors was now authorized to permit member banks again to count part or all of their vault cash as legal reserves, and to permit the inclusion of balances with correspondent banks, as was done before World War I. The Board has not yet given permission to include balances with correspondents, but does now allow the banks to count all vault cash as legal reserves.

It is amusing sometimes to compare the alleged and the real reasons for changes in policy. Emphasized at the time was the fact that there had been an element of inequity in the requirement that banks maintain adequate vault cash in addition to their legal reserves, which were entirely in balances at the Federal Reserve Banks. Banks in cities where Federal Reserve Banks or branches were located could get by with a minimum of till money. More remote banks had to carry larger amounts of vault cash, so were holding a larger percentage of nonearning assets. In effect, they had been subject to higher reserve requirements. Now, counting their vault cash as legal reserves, they can somewhat reduce their balances at the Federal Reserve Banks.

One might wonder why this inequity had been permitted to continue for more than 40 years. In the earlier years it did strengthen the Federal Reserve System by encouraging banks to exchange their gold certificates for deposits at the Federal Reserve Banks. After 1933, however, the banks were legally required anyway to surrender all gold certificates to the Federal Reserve Banks. Not until a quarter of a century later were the banks permitted to count vault cash as part of their legal reserve. Why wasn't the inequity corrected in 1934?

Excess reserves grew rapidly and to record heights in the 1930s. There was no clear need to create still more reserves, and there was concern that the banking system's reserves were already dangerously high.

It was a different story in 1959. At that time the Federal Reserve Banks were still required to maintain gold certificate reserves against both their notes and their deposits. Their gold certificate holdings were rapidly shrinking as gold continued to drain abroad. Simultaneously, their required reserves were rapidly increasing. To permit credit expansion by member banks, the Federal Reserve Banks were obliged, through open market purchases, to create new deposits of their own as legal reserves for the member banks. Also, credit expansion by member banks led to an increase of currency in the hands of the public. Most of this currency consisted of Federal Reserve notes. On both fronts the Federal Reserve Banks found their reserve requirements

---

[4]Banks could also deduct cash items in the process of collection.

increasing. Their power to create more credit was nearly exhausted as their excess reserves approached zero.

By allowing the banks to count vault cash as legal reserves, the Federal Reserve Banks temporarily reduced the total of their deposits and notes. Their excess reserves were somewhat increased, and the final solution—the elimination of all reserve requirements for the Federal Reserve Banks—could be postponed a few years.

FUNCTION OF LEGAL RESERVES

Since reserves against deposits evolved historically from reserves against bank notes, there has been a persistent confusion concerning their modern function. In the early part of the 19th century when demand deposits were unimportant and a bank's liabilities were primarily in the form of its notes, many banks were expanding their note issues far beyond any reasonable relation to their stock of specie. The early state regulation of reserves was based on the conviction that banks must be sufficiently liquid to meet any possible demand for note redemption.

Reserves as a Source of Liquidity

Today, many people still believe that reserves are required to provide liquidity. Yet required legal reserves are the one asset that the bank cannot possibly convert into cash for its depositors if the bank is to continue as a going business. To be sure, the bank may pay out excess reserves, and by borrowing the bank may increase its legal (and excess) reserves. But the idea that a certain percentage of reserves that must be held against deposits constitutes a liquid asset is simply a contradiction in terms. Unless the bank closes its doors, it must hold the legal reserves required as long as it is holding deposit liabilities.

Primary reserves are another story. Given the amount of its legal reserves, the greater a bank's other primary reserves, the more readily it can meet depositors' demand for currency. But note carefully, the liquidity depends upon the fact that the bank is not required by law to hold these additional reserves. If need be, the entire amount can be paid out. Even if (as with collection items and balances with other banks) some of these assets do not qualify as legal reserves, they can quickly be converted into vault cash if necessary. The moment that particular assets are required against deposits, these assets are, for the most part, frozen. Only $10 or $20 of required legal reserves are available to meet withdrawal demands of $100.

Reserves as a Means of Monetary Control

The modern function of bank reserves is to limit bank credit expansion. The reserve requirements of commercial banks relate only to their deposits, since these banks no longer issue bank notes. A specie reserve would today be meaningless, since even our coins are today credit money. There is no longer much point, as far as liquidity is concerned, in requiring banks to hold large reserves in the form of either currency or deposits with the Reserve Banks. Most individual deposits are fully covered by insurance. Their owners would probably not feel safer in time of panic with Federal Reserve notes than with the deposits guaranteed by a government agency.

The owners of large deposits, uninsured except for the first $40,000, might prefer currency in a period of financial strain, but they should have little trouble obtaining it. The Federal Reserve, as a central bank, can issue whatever amount of currency the system demands.

Two fundamental principles are involved here:

1. As central banks, the Federal Reserve Banks can create additional reserves to provide liquidity when needed by the banks.
2. As central banks, the Federal Reserve Banks can also issue currency whenever the public wishes more currency.

Thus, the Reserve Banks can, if necessary, purchase all the assets currently held by the commercial banks. By crediting the accounts of the member banks, the Reserve Banks can increase the liquidity of member banks, which would then hold legal reserves instead of loans and investments. Since no reserves are required against their deposits, the Federal Reserve Banks can buy any amount of assets.

When the banks can promptly secure unlimited additional balances (or, if they wish, currency) by borrowing from the Federal Reserve Banks or by selling assets to those Banks, they need not hold large reserves to provide liquidity. A strong central bank makes large reserves superfluous to the liquidity of the member banks.

Reserve requirements do, however, serve a useful purpose in restraining credit expansion. In fact, they always served in this role, although previously their connection with liquidity obscured this function. Long before the organization of the Federal Reserve, a bank that was lending excessively found that the consequent drain on its reserves forced it to contract its loans. Likewise, banks that had been following an overcautious lending policy were encouraged by the increase in their reserves to lend more freely. The establishment of the Federal Reserve provided a central organization with the responsibility for credit control and the power by various means to affect the reserves of the banking system as a whole.

ORIGIN OF RESERVES

Reserves originate in two quite different ways, depending upon whether we are speaking of individual bank reserves or reserves of the banking system as a whole.

Reserves and the Individual Bank

Obviously, the individual bank's reserves will increase when the bank receives currency from its depositors or when it deposits with the Federal

Reserve Bank checks drawn on other banks. However, unless the Treasury has issued new currency, the currency received by one bank will have been paid out by another bank.[5] The system's total reserves are unaffected. Likewise, there is no net increase in legal reserves when, through clearing operations, balances at the Federal Reserve Banks shift from some banks to others.

Factors Affecting Total Reserves of the Commercial Bank System

In earlier chapters we have touched upon various factors affecting reserves of the banking system as a whole. In general, whenever one bank receives additional reserves while no other bank loses reserves, total reserves of the banking system increase. This occurrence may result from gold purchases, government spending, currency movements, open market operations of the Federal Reserve Banks, and so on.

First, consider the effect of gold imports:

1. Gold purchases ordinarily increase both deposits and legal and required reserves of the member banks.[6] The Treasury checks received by gold sellers are deposited in their banks and, when collected, result in the transfer of credit from the Treasury's account with the Federal Reserve to the Federal Reserve accounts owned by the banks in which the checks are deposited. The Treasury restores its balance by issuing more gold certificates to the Federal Reserve (or crediting the Federal Reserve gold certificate account).
2. If, however, the Treasury issues no certificates and instead sterilizes the gold imports by paying for them out of taxes or by borrowing from the nonbank public, there will be no net effect on deposits or reserves of the member banks.
3. If the Treasury were to borrow from the member banks to pay for the gold, bank deposits would be increased, but there would be no effect on legal reserves. Required reserves would rise, excess reserves fall.

Second, member reserves will increase as a result of the spending, by either the Treasury or foreign banks, of deposits held with the Federal Reserve. Thus, if the bank's nonmonetary liabilities decrease, such as by decreasing foreign deposits or the Treasury's holdings of cash and deposits, the money supply and member reserves will increase.[7]

Third, a decrease in currency in circulation outside the banks will lead to an increase in member reserves. Reserve requirements and legal reserves automatically rise when the public exchanges currency for deposits or the Treasury releases currency, increasing deposits in either case. Since the increase

---

[5]Theoretically, the Federal Reserve Banks might push additional currency into temporary circulation to effect an increase in member bank reserves. Most of this currency, the amount not desired by either the public or the banks, would find its way back to the Federal Reserve Banks. This possibility is of no practical significance, since the Federal Reserve can more simply increase member bank reserves directly, through open market operations.

[6]The effects of Treasury issues of Special Drawing Rights (SDRs) are similar to that of monetary gold purchases. When the Treasury purchases gold or issues SDR Certificates, it typically issues an equal amount of gold or SDR Certificates to the Federal Reserve Banks in return for deposit credits.

[7]A similar effect is produced by a decrease in the public's holdings of time deposits.

in legal reserves is equal to the entire amount of currency deposited, but the increase in required reserves is only a fraction of that amount, excess reserves are increased and banks have more lending power.

Fourth, member reserves will be increased by an increase in the float or fictitious reserves. Anything that causes a greater difference between uncollected items and deferred availability items creates additional reserves for the system. Bad weather, for example, delaying airmails, or a higher level of checking account activity will cause uncollected items to increase by more than the increase in deferred availability items, and therefore will increase reserves.[8]

Fifth, by far the most important cause of increases in member reserves since 1941 has been the Federal Reserve's purchase of government securities. Only occasionally and for short periods of time does the Federal Reserve lend directly to the Treasury.[9] When the Federal Reserve buys securities from member banks, either directly or on the open market, the banks' legal and excess reserves are increased and their investments decreased. When the Federal Reserve buys securities from nonbank holders, the sellers deposit with their banks the checks received from the Federal Reserve. By collecting these checks, the banks increase their legal reserve, just as though they had themselves sold securities to the Federal Reserve. But since the receipt of these checks from their customers has increased the banks' deposits as well as their reserves, legal, excess, and required reserves will all rise, although by different amounts. In either case the Federal Reserve's lending power is unchanged, since it is not required to maintain reserves against its deposits.

Sixth, member bank required, legal, and excess reserves will ordinarily be increased by a shift of deposits from nonmember to member banks. Such a transfer might be effected through the clearing balances carried by some nonmember banks with the Federal Reserve, thus directly increasing member reserves. Or it might be handled through currency shipments.

Seventh, total legal reserves of member banks will tend to be increased by any loans made by the Federal Reserve Banks.

Finally, although deposit reclassification will not change total reserves of the banking system, required reserves will decrease and excess reserves increase if demand deposits are reclassified as time deposits. Also, a shift of deposits from larger banks to smaller banks will cause required reserves to fall due to the lower reserve requirements of smaller banks. For example, if reserve requirements in the larger banks are 15 percent and in smaller banks are 10 percent, a shift of $100 million from the larger banks to the smaller will increase excess reserves by $5 million. If the smaller banks retain these reserves, they can, by acting together, expand loans and deposits by around $30 or $35 million, the final amount depending on the amount of the currency drain.

---

[8] See also Chapter 9 for a detailed discussion of the float.
[9] By law, the Federal Reserve Banks may not hold at any one time more than $5 billion of securities purchased directly from the Treasury. Usually they hold none, lending directly only in an emergency.

GROWTH OF LEGAL RESERVES SINCE 1920

Total legal reserves increased enormously between 1930 and 1940, as can be seen in Table 7-3. The increase in excess reserves was even more spectacular, roughly 10,000 percent. During this period our gold stock increased, partly as a result of devaluation, from $4 billion to $22 billion, although the resultant increase in reserves was somewhat less than $18 billion because some of the gold was sterilized at the time it was purchased.[10] Also, part of the devaluation profits did not affect member reserves because the Treasury held most of the money in a special exchange stabilization fund, later transferred to the International Monetary Fund. The gold purchases were, however, the dominant factor affecting member reserves.

Table 7-3   Member Bank Reserves (In billions of dollars)
Average of Daily Figures (December)

	1920	1930	1940	1950	1960	1970	1974
Total Legal Reserves	1.8	2.4	13.2	17.4	19.3	29.2	36.9
Total Excess Reserves	*	0.06	6.5	1.0	0.8	0.2	0.2

Source: Federal Reserve Board of Governors, *Banking and Monetary Statistics; Federal Reserve Bulletins.*
*Not available before 1929.

Between 1940 and 1945 excess reserves melted away as the banks bought large amounts of government securities. As deficiencies appeared, the banks secured more reserves—sometimes by borrowing from the Federal Reserve on the security of government obligations, more often by selling some of their portfolio to the Federal Reserve. This was especially true of the central reserve city banks. In many other parts of the country the banks were generally well supplied with reserves as in the course of the Treasury's spending for army installations and war materiel they received deposits and reserves that had originated in the lending by New York and Chicago banks.

It may seem strange that total reserves were not much greater after the war than they were in 1940, in spite of the fact that Reserve Bank credit outstanding increased from $2.4 to $25.1 billion, principally as a result of open market purchases by the Reserve Banks. The added reserves, however, created for the banking system during the war years were almost entirely offset by the increase in the amount of currency that the public wished to hold. The drain of currency from the banks forced them to obtain more currency from the Federal Reserve, drawing on their deposit balances. Hence, the net increase in member reserves during the war was only about 15 percent.

---

[10]This sterilized gold served as an "ace in the hole" for the Treasury. In the fall of 1953, when Congress refused to raise the ceiling on the national debt, the Treasury was able to finance a small deficit by monetizing $500 million of gold bought in 1935 and paid for at the time out of taxes and loans.

RATIO OF EXCESS RESERVES TO TOTAL RESERVES

When the banking system is lending freely, few banks will hold any large amount of excess reserves. Rather, they are more likely to be protesting concerning the amount of reserves that they are required to hold. If required reserves were computed on a daily basis, a bank would necessarily hold at least a small quantity of excess reserves at all times, since the bank would find it almost impossible to hold its reserves exactly at the level required against deposits with both deposits and reserves changing daily. Since, however, requirements are based on the average deposits over a "reserve period," the banks can operate with almost no excess reserves.[11] For several days they may have a slight reserve deficiency; but by the end of the averaging period, they will either contract their credit slightly or borrow additional reserves from the Federal Reserve or from a member bank that has excess reserves. Hence, for the period as a whole their legal reserves may be almost exactly equal to their required reserves.

Although statistics of excess reserves prior to 1929 are not available, as a proportion of total reserves they probably did not differ widely from excess reserves in 1930, which stood at $60 million as compared with $2,400 million of total reserves. The combination of massive gold imports and interest rates so low that banks were reluctant to lend caused excess reserves to mount during the 1930s until they amounted to almost 50 percent of total reserves. Since World War II the ratio of excess to total reserves has gradually fallen. As a result of the tight monetary policies instituted in 1965, excess reserves have recently been less than 1 percent of total reserves. Net free reserves of the system have been replaced by net borrowed reserves. (See Chapter 11.)

PROPOSED CHANGES IN RESERVE REQUIREMENTS

A number of drastic changes in reserve requirements have been proposed at one time or another, especially when banking problems have been unusually difficult. To date, however, the changes have been minor.

Quantitative Changes

The nature of reserve requirements indicates two or three possible ways in which the requirements may be modified. The first is by changing the percentage of reserves that a bank must maintain against its deposits.

100 Percent Reserves. Among other proposals for changes in reserve requirements is the recommendation that all banks be required to maintain reserves of 100 percent.[12] Three advantages are claimed for such banking.

---

[11]Until 1968, smaller (country) banks computed their required reserves twice a month, larger (reserve city) banks once a week. Today both compute required reserves weekly, on the basis of average deposits over the previous two weeks. By permitting banks to average their deposits over two weeks, the Board hopes to smooth random fluctuations and enable the larger banks to forecast their reserve requirements more accurately.

[12]Probably the most cerebral of the arguments for 100 percent reserves can be found in Milton Friedman, *A Program for Monetary Stability* (Bronx: Fordham University Press, 1959), especially pp. 65–76.

1. Bank runs and bank panics would be prevented. Knowing that against every dollar of their deposit liabilities the banks held a dollar in vault cash or as a balance at the Federal Reserve Banks, the public would know their deposits were safe. There could never be a repetition of the disastrous banking breakdown of 1932 and 1933.

   This argument has lost most of its force since the establishment of the Federal Deposit Insurance Corporation. However, adherents of the 100 percent reserve proposal point out that federal insurance of bank deposits would be unnecessary under their plan, and argue that the banking system itself should provide for the safety of deposits rather than delegating this responsibility to the government.

2. With a fractional reserve system, currency movements force an inherent instability. If at any time the public chooses to hold more currency and less deposits, member bank excess reserves are reduced. Conversely, a preference for deposits rather than currency increases excess reserves. If banks maintained reserves of 100 percent, then no changes in the total money supply would be made possible or necessary by the public's choice between currency and deposits.

3. The institution of 100 percent reserves would properly and completely separate the function of lending from the function of money creation. The unplanned and accidental development of fractional reserve banking turned over to lenders the power, rightly belonging to the government, of controlling money. If banks were required to maintain reserves of 100 percent, a decline in business activity, leading to a contraction of bank loans, could not force a contraction of the quantity of money. Similarly, a monetary inflation could not result from an expansion of bank loans in prosperity. The lending and investing now done by commercial banks would be taken over by new investment firms, which would lend funds raised by selling their own stocks or bonds. These new firms would be unable, however, to create money, so the quantity of money would be entirely independent of the volume of loans and investments. It would be equal to the amount of the reserves and would be governed solely by the Federal Reserve's open market operations and by the Treasury's gold transactions.

The gradual increase to 100 percent reserves would be accompanied by massive open market purchases by the Federal Reserve Banks to prevent a contraction of the existing money supply. Eventually the member banks' assets would all be vault cash or deposits at the Federal Reserve Banks, except for a few loans and investments they might make on the basis of their own capital and surplus. A bank would no longer find its lending power affected in any way by an increase or decrease in either its deposits or its reserves. Its functions would be exclusively the transferral of funds and the exchanging of deposit money for currency money. Its income would be from service charges, which might be supplemented by requiring the Federal Reserve Banks to pay interest on member reserve balances held with them.

Although there is considerable logic to the proposal, it has not received much support. There is some feeling that the cure might turn out to be worse than the disease. Granted that normal seasonal currency movements do interject some slippage in a fractional reserve banking system, Reserve authorities appear able to cope with it. Also, with the passing of the real bills theory of bank credit, the quantity of money is linked much less closely to commercial loans than it was a generation ago.[13] Today we should expect a decline in bank loans to cause not a decrease in deposits but an increase in investments. To turn to 100 percent reserves would require an entirely new approach to lending, which would almost certainly present entirely new and unforeseen problems. (Recall that when, a century ago, state bank notes were taxed out of existence, it was supposed the state banks would be forced to obtain national charters. The unexpected result was the rapid growth of demand deposits and the continued profitability of state banks.)

A minor objection is that 100 percent reserves might well cause a higher level of short-term interest rates. The new investment firms would do business in the same way that savings and loan companies operate. They would lend money that had been lent to (or invested with) them, and on which they themselves were paying interest (or dividends). A savings and loan association can pay 5 or 6 percent for money that it lends at long term at 8 or 9 percent, but it is not easy to see how investment firms could profitably lend at 5 percent or less for short-term needs.

The emphasis of the proposal appears rooted in the conviction that it is exclusively the *quantity* of money that needs to be controlled. As has been pointed out elsewhere, all financial institutions create credit, although commercial banks are the only firms whose credit is classified as money. Some of these firms have been growing more rapidly than the commercial banks. The indirect credit that they create is to some extent preferred to money and substituted for money, reducing the desire to hold cash balances. Although the *quantity* of money would be unaffected if a depositor exchanged $1,000 for shares of an investment firm, which then lent the money, the *velocity* of money would be increased if otherwise the depositor would be holding the money idle. Even with 100 percent reserves, the money *flow* would continue to be affected by loan expansion and contraction. Reserve authorities would have to work out new control policies. There is at least a reasonable doubt that they would be more successful in this completely changed environment than they would be in continuing to regulate a system with which they have acquired over a half century of experience.

There is, at any rate, no indication that the monetary authorities are currently contemplating a transition to 100 percent reserves. Since 1948 the trend of reserve requirements has been downward.

Ceiling Reserves. In contrast to the proposal that commercial banks be required at all times to maintain 100 percent reserves against all their demand deposits is the more modest suggestion that in time of emergency the banks might be required to maintain a larger percentage of reserves than usual against that portion of their deposits in excess of some specified figure. If gold inflows, for example, or war finance caused bank reserves to shoot up to dangerously high levels at a time when, or on a scale such that, the Federal

---

[13]The real bills theory of bank credit is also known as the commercial loan theory of banking. See the discussion below.

Reserve could not effectively control them through open market sales, the additional reserves might be partially or entirely sterilized.

A number of foreign countries do require that deposits in excess of a certain figure be accompanied by additional reserve requirements, in some instances as high as 100 percent. Such a program in this country would have prevented the development of the threateningly high excess reserves during the 1930s, when each additional billion dollars of gold, resulting as it did in an increase of a billion in reserves and a billion of deposits, created around $800 million of excess reserves. If the ceiling reserve plan had been in effect and deposits in excess of those prevailing in another year, such as 1935, had been made subject to 100 percent reserve requirements, there would have been little increase in excess reserves. Also, it would have aided in the postwar control of credit when the Federal Reserve, in attempting to support the market for Treasury obligations, found itself unable to prevent the member banks from gaining reserves whenever they wished by selling government securities. Although there has been some objection that such a control might be kept in force too long, unnecessarily restraining the banks, it is difficult to see why such a result would be any more likely than the Board of Governors, under their present powers, insisting that regular reserve requirements be consistently maintained at maximum levels, to the detriment of the member banks.

Supplementary Reserves. On a number of occasions it has been suggested that the Board of Governors be given the authority to raise reserve requirements temporarily above the usual maximum rates, which would have much the same effect as the proposal discussed above. Both are open to the obvious objection that the increased requirements would decrease the earning power of the member banks. Unless the requirements were made applicable to nonmember banks as well, banks might be induced to give up their membership in the Federal Reserve. Even if the requirements were made to apply to nonmember as well as to member banks, they might still weaken the banks by seriously reducing their earnings.

A possible solution would be the requirement of a special, supplementary reserve. This reserve could be held in the form of short-term interest-bearing government securities unless the bank found it more convenient to hold this supplementary reserve in vault cash or with the Federal Reserve.

As we found after World War II, when the Federal Reserve Banks were buying all government securities offered to help enforce a pattern of low interest rates, and when member banks have large quantities of government securities to exchange for reserves, the Federal Reserve cannot control bank credit expansion. At such a time the Federal Reserve cannot check credit by raising the discount rate, for a high discount rate is incompatible with the low rate the Federal Reserve is helping to maintain for the Treasury's benefit. Also, member banks are not borrowing, so the discount rate has little significance. Anytime the banks need additional reserves, they can obtain them by selling some of their government securities to the Federal Reserve. In supporting the market price of the securities, the Federal Reserve is prevented from discouraging these sales by the banks. Its principal tools of control are useless. Even in 1965–1970, when the Federal Reserve was permitting bond prices to sag and encouraging a rise in interest rates, banks sold bonds and continued to expand their loans.

The advantage of the supplementary reserve plan would be that a large part of the bank-held securities would be immobilized since they would be required against deposits. A little flexibility for the individual bank would result from the provisions that supplementary cash reserves might be substituted for the securities if the bank did not possess the necessary short-term obligations; but ordinarily, for the sake of earnings, the banks could be expected to hold the securities.

In effect, however, what would be accomplished would be discrimination in favor of the Treasury over all other borrowers. Regardless of what rates might be required of other borrowers, the Treasury would be in a position to pay low interest rates. The only alternative of the banks to holding more United States government obligations would be to hold additional sums of vault cash or balances with Federal Reserve Banks, yielding no interest at all. There appears to be a serious question whether the best interests of the nation would be served by largely freeing the Treasury from the necessity of considering interest costs. Although not so extreme a step, it would be much the same in effect as permitting the Treasury to print money to pay its bills. This consequence would result, of course, not from the higher reserve requirements as such, but from the fact that the banks would be encouraged to hold increased reserves in the form of Treasury obligations.

Qualitative Changes

In contrast to the preceding plans, which are primarily concerned with increasing requirements determined on the present basis, are suggestions for changing the basis of reserve classification. Reserves might be based on something other than the amount of deposits. One such proposal is to base reserves on the turnover or the velocity of deposits rather than on their level. A more recent proposal bases reserves partly on the type of assets the bank holds.

Reserves Based on Velocity. Under our present system, if demand deposits are reclassified as time deposits, required reserves are decreased. Yet if the deposit was previously an idle demand deposit, its reclassification as a time deposit is largely technical. Its rate of turnover may have been unaffected. In this respect the velocity reserve requirement would have the merit of determining reserves on the basis of what was actually happening to deposits, rather than on the basis of their technical classification.

We realize that money affects the economy not simply in proportion to its quantity. It is the money flow, rather than the money stock, that is significant. Fifty billion dollars turned over 20 times a year will do the same work as $100 billion turned over 10 times during the same period. Specifically, during the years between the Second World War and the Korean War, the increasing turnover of money contributed to the postwar inflation, for during those years the total monetary stock showed little change. Earlier, in the final months of the speculative orgy that culminated in the stock market crash in the fall of 1929, required reserves would have been increased by this method of establishing requirements instead of remaining stationary as they did. Reserve requirements based partly on velocity of circulation are a logical development.

Computation of required reserves would probably be a little more difficult under a velocity reserve requirement plan, and not all banks would be affected to the same extent. These objections are unimportant. However, such a basis of requirements would be subject to one serious weakness. The turnover of bank deposits increases for two quite different reasons.

Velocity increases when there is general optimism and great confidence in future economic prospects. For such increases the requirement of higher reserves might be a wholesome restraint, discouraging speculative excess.

But velocity increases also at times when there is a lack of confidence in the currency. If nearly everyone is trying to get rid of money by exchanging it for other assets, turnover becomes much more rapid. Although the banks can control the volume of deposits through their lending operations, they can do little to control velocity. To increase reserve requirements at such a time of strain would involve hardships for the banks, especially if, as might well be the case, they were at the same time faced with heavy withdrawals from depositors who feared bank failures.

Reserves Based on Type of Asset. More recently it has been proposed that reserves be based in part on the type of assets held by the bank. At present, two member banks with the same amount of deposits are required to keep the same percentage of legal reserves against their deposits. Yet conceivably the earning assets of the one bank might be government securities only, while the earning assets of the other might be entirely in the form of corporate bonds and business and consumption loans. It has been argued that the Board of Governors should have the power to check credit expansion by the ability to raise reserve requirements in accordance with the type, as well as with the quantity, of loans that banks are making. Bankers are understandably unenthusiastic about this recommendation for qualitative credit control. The proposal is interesting in its clearcut recognition of the essential function of reserves as being that of credit control rather than (as it still appears to many) that of providing funds to permit the withdrawal of deposits. At the same time such a step may not be necessary. The Federal Reserve already exercises considerable control over the lending activities of its member banks. If the banks are to continue to operate within the private enterprise framework, it seems desirable to permit bank management some latitude in their lending policies rather than to enforce a general pattern for all to follow. Also, this kind of supervision, like the supplementary reserve plan discussed above, could possibly have the effect of separating the borrowing market into two separate spheres—the United States Treasury and all other borrowers. The wisdom of such a policy is far from evident.

LOANS AND INVESTMENTS

Loans and investments (or securities) are the banks' stock-in-trade. Banks must maintain primary reserves to meet demands for cash and for payments to other banks and to meet legal requirements imposed to regulate the volume of bank credit. But if banks were to hold only such assets, they would have no income. Long ago bankers learned that they need hold only a fractional reserve of cash against their liabilities. Banks hold, against the largest part of their deposits, assets that will pay their expenses and yield a profit to their owners.

These earning assets are listed on bank statements as "Loans and Investments." The distinction between the two types of assets is blurred and somewhat arbitrary. A generation ago, loans tended to be short term, investments long term. This was, however, never the basic difference, and today is a much less valid generalization than it once was. Now maturities completely overlap. Many loans run for 30 to 90 days, but loans are also made for longer periods, for 10 years or more in the case of real estate loans. Although some bonds may run for 30 years or more, banks invest more heavily in securities of shorter term, including especially the 91-day bills sold by the Treasury.

In general, loans involve a direct relationship between the borrower and the bank; investments involve an indirect relationship.[14] Typically a loan results from a conference between the borrower and the bank. Usually, although not always, the bank is the only lender involved. Investments, by contrast, are ordinarily acquired on the open market. A corporation or a government agency may borrow by issuing bonds. The bonds are bought by banks, other financial institutions, nonfinancial firms, and individuals. Also, many of these bonds change hands many times between the time they are first issued and the time they mature. They are traded in the open market. The relationship between borrower and lender is completely impersonal.

LIQUIDITY

Since most commercial bank liabilities are payable upon demand, bankers must carefully walk a tightrope. The more liquid their assets, the more easily they can meet unexpectedly large deposit losses to other banks or to cash. But also, the more liquid their assets, the lower their earnings. Either too much or too little liquidity may push their institution into receivership. The problem of maintaining a reasonable liquidity and at the same time earning a satisfactory income is as old as commercial banking.

Short-Term Loans

At one time bankers felt that their security lay in making short-term loans almost exclusively. They lent for periods of one to three months. After a bank had been in business for a while, it could expect to have some of these loans

---

[14]Note that the word "investment" is now being used in the everyday sense. It must not be confused with the special meaning of "investment" as we use the term in income analysis to denote one of the components of national income.

maturing every day. As the loans were repaid, the bank sometimes received funds—perhaps specie, perhaps notes of other banks, or, later, deposits in other banks. Or the bank's own liabilities—its notes or its deposits—decreased. Either way its liquidity increased, and it would be less likely to be embarrassed by deposit withdrawals (or note redemption) than if its assets were frozen in long-term loans. Also, the bankers were in a position where they could continuously reappraise business conditions. As long as the outlook appeared favorable, they could continue making new loans as fast as the old ones were repaid. But if there appeared to be clouds gathering on the business horizon, they could refrain from making new loans. In three months they could expect to be almost entirely liquid, with most of their assets in cash or the equivalent.[15]

Commercial Loan Theory

The emphasis on short-term lending together with the fact that most bank loans were made originally to businesses led to what was known as the *commercial loan* (or *real bills*) *theory* of bank credit. A generation ago it was generally agreed that the primary field of bank credit was to supply businesses with working capital. Besides being short term, such loans were alleged to be self-liquidating, and they were claimed to be largely self-regulating.

Self-Liquidating. Much importance was once attached to the argument that loans that supplied working capital to business were self-liquidating. The manufacturer, to whom the bank advances the funds to complete goods that will immediately be sold, is able to repay the bank with the proceeds of the sale of the bank-financed goods. Inventory loans to manufacturers and dealers likewise carry with them the means of their own payment, for when the goods are sold, the borrowers can repay the bank the funds that it lent to permit them to handle the goods. Although loans for fixed capital would eventually be self-liquidating also, they would not be self-liquidating within the short period that should limit the length of bank loans. Therefore, they appeared less suitable for the banks than loans for working capital and inventory.

In contrast to commercial loans, real estate loans tied up bank funds for longer periods. Also, a real estate loan did not necessarily liquidate itself by means of the production that it had facilitated. It might be eventually repaid from sale of the property or out of the borrower's income. Such loans, it was claimed, were no substitute for self-liquidating commercial paper.

Self-Regulating. Also, it was claimed that banks making only short-term working capital loans to business would automatically extend at all times the proper amount of credit. Under such a policy, fixed capital would increase only through savings of the public. As the tempo of business activity quickens in the short run, from one year or one month to the next, business requires more working capital. As the banks supply this additional money, there is a

---

[15]Naturally, if they expected to stay in business, they would not entirely liquidate. They would not, for example, sell the building and equipment.

corresponding simultaneous increase in the flow of goods to the market.[16]
Thus, at all times the amount of money is supposed to be kept proportionate
to the requirements of trade. Without the intervention of any monetary authority, the price level should be stable as a result of free market forces, much
as, under the automatic gold standard, the value of gold was supposed to tend
toward the same level everywhere without supervision.

Weaknesses of the Argument. The commercial loan *policy* was not without
some justification under the conditions of the time. In the 19th and early 20th
century, real estate loans were seldom regularly amortized. The borrower
paid nothing on the loan before maturity, and often expected to renew the
loan. If real estate values meanwhile declined, neither the original lender nor
any other lender might be willing to accommodate the borrower. When towns
and cities were springing up in the wilderness, land speculation was enormously attractive. Real estate loans tended to cause an inflation and a crash of
real estate values. Under such conditions, banks could lose heavily on loans
made when real estate values were high. Also, when money was tight, the
banks found it difficult to find other lenders to take over some of their real
estate loans. With such frozen assets, they were in no position to meet deposit withdrawals. They were doubtless better off with commercial loans.

The argument was partly rationalization. Few other fields of lending were
open to the banks. Consumers ordinarily paid cash for their purchases in
those unenlightened days; and when they did borrow, they did not borrow
from the commercial banks. The federal government borrowed little, except
in wartime. Except for working capital loans, there were really few short-term
loans that the banks could make.

The logic of the commercial loan *theory*, however, must be rejected. The
argument that commercial loans were self-liquidating was true to the extent
that only a single bank was concerned. But when we consider such loans for
the entire banking system, we realize that they are no more liquid than any
other type of loan. For the system as a whole, no loan can be self-liquidating.
The inventory does not somehow become changed into money. It simply
changes hands, and frequently the new owner has borrowed to acquire the
inventory. As was from time to time all too painfully clear, banks occasionally
found their customers could not pay because they could not move the inventory. Unless a second bank was willing to lend to someone else, it might be
impossible for the first borrower to pay the first bank. Self-liquidity was an
illusion, created by confusing the individual bank with the banking system as
a whole.

---

[16]Note that if the banks provided long-term funds for expanding plant and equipment, the
supply of goods would eventually increase when the new equipment came into operation. This is
hardly the same thing, however. It may be several years before any additional goods are produced by the added equipment; and when they do appear, they will require additional financing to
move them to market. When banks supply long-term credit, they increase the amount of money
at a time when there is no increase in the amount of goods in the market. The later repayment of
such loans forces a reduction in the quantity of money that is not accompanied by a reduction in
the amount of goods. Thus, the amount of goods and the amount of money are not in step,
according to the argument.

Nor can we accept the proposition that the proper amount of credit will necessarily be provided as long as banks make only commercial loans. The argument is not altogether wrong. There are times when such a lending policy might provide the proper amount of credit. If the goods financed are moving to market at the same rate as the loans are moving to maturity, the price level should be unaffected by the amount of bank credit created to finance them. That is, if the goods are sold at the end of 30 days and the loan against them is paid off, with the purchaser paying for them with borrowed funds or funds received as income, there is no net inflationary effect. There may be several consecutive loans against the goods as they move toward the market, each loan being used to pay off the preceding loan until the goods are at last paid for by the consumer. Then the goods are no longer part of the stream of goods for sale, and the money no longer exists to float them on to the consumer.

But business could possibly be supplied with too much or too little credit when banks make only commercial loans. Even though new money may be created only as new goods are being produced, the money and the goods are not tied together. They circulate separately. If they circulate at different speeds, prices will be affected. More specifically, the loans will tend to result in rising prices if the new money circulates more rapidly than the new goods.

First, more than one loan may be outstanding against a block of goods. If the loans are paid at maturity and the goods sold before that time, two or more loans created against the same goods may exist simultaneously. The money created by the first loan continues temporarily to circulate through the economy with the rest of the money supply. At times of full employment such an increase in the money supply would tend to be inflationary. There likewise exists the deflationary possibility that if goods cannot be sold for enough to pay off loans at maturity, businesses may have to resort to distress sales. Such sales might be the occasion for a general decline in the price level, depending on whether the money that the public saves on these goods is spent to drive up prices of other goods or is held idle.[17]

Second, there is no necessary connection between the form of the loan and the way in which the proceeds of the loan are spent. Firms with adequate resources might borrow, not to increase their inventories, but to free for long-term investment their own funds with which they had previously been meeting their working capital requirements. At times when the outlook was less promising, businesses might similarly reduce the level of short-term loans without necessarily reducing their current level of operations. By selling securities to the public, by retaining profits, by selling government bonds that they had been holding as a reserve against emergencies, or by other means, they might continue spending as much as before for working capital purposes after their bank loans had been reduced to a small fraction of their former level. To the extent that the price level is responsive to changes in the quantity of money, it might be forced either up or down during a period in which banks were making only commercial loans.

---

[17]These problems of price levels and the velocity of circulation of money are taken up in detail in Chapters 13 and 15.

Third, the bankers had at all times a discretionary, nonautomatic control over the volume of bank credit. If they were pessimistic, they granted loans less freely. Not only did this violate the alleged automatic adjustment of commercial loans to the requirements of trade, it also was likely to cause the earlier credit expansion to be excessive, for unless new loans were being made the maturing loans could not be repaid. This is not to say that the bankers were wrong in using their judgment rather than acting as automatons. It is simply that if credit control is to be discretionary, by definition it cannot simultaneously be automatic.

Sixty-five years ago the commercial loan theory was unquestioned. The framers of the Federal Reserve Act subscribed without reservation to the proposition that commercial banks should do most of their lending in this area. The Act required banks to make such loans if they expected to get help from the Federal Reserve Banks. Members could borrow from the Reserve Banks only by discounting commercial paper. Also, this discounted paper was necessary collateral for the issue of Federal Reserve notes. (Exceptions were at the time insignificant.) Today, a depression and two world wars later, the theory is no longer taken seriously.

Shiftability

It was occasionally argued that liquidity could be had, even with long-term assets, as long as these assets were readily marketable. High-grade bonds, it was claimed, were far more liquid than their distant maturities might suggest. True, they were not repaid as quickly as were commercial loans. Even with a well diversified portfolio of varying maturities, a bank could not expect to have more than a small fraction of a percent of them maturing daily. The bank would have to wait not 90 days, but perhaps 20 years or more for all its investments to mature. But, it was argued, if the bank did need more cash, it need only sell the bonds. As long as it bought only high-grade securities, it should have little difficulty liquidating them.

Like the commercial loan theory, this analysis was more applicable to the individual bank than to the banking system. If one bank needed more reserves and other banks did not, the first bank could usually with little difficulty liquidate part of its portfolio. But at a time when all banks were trying to become more liquid, there were few buyers. The banks themselves were selling, not buying. And the public was not eagerly buying either; for since the banks were selling, the money supply was contracting. Little money was available for the purchase of bonds.

Need for a Central Discounting Agency

Before the establishment of the Federal Reserve System, all that banks could do in a period of strain was to contract credit drastically. Each bank might try to increase its reserves, but total reserves held by all banks not only could not be increased at such a time, but would be decreased if the public became alarmed and began withdrawing currency and the country banks withdrew deposited funds from reserve city banks. For the system as a whole, the repayment of loans or the sale of securities to the public added not a dollar of reserves. All that could be accomplished was a reduction in liabilities. On the basis of reserve requirements of 20 percent, the banks were obliged to liquidate about $5 million of assets for every million dollars of the unavailable but needed reserves. At such times, losses were heavy both because liquidation was on so large a scale and because the banks were dealing with the public. The banks were either attempting to collect loans that frequently could not be repaid at such times, or they were inducing the public to take over securities and give up money in the form of bank notes or deposits. The latter course required an increase in interest rates, that is, a fall in the price of fixed income bonds, or the public would have no reason to prefer to hold more bonds and less money.

These difficulties disappeared with the development of the Federal Reserve System. Today the banks can all gain reserves simultaneously. When the Federal Reserve Banks buy the assets of the member banks, or lend to the member banks, new reserves are created. It is no longer necessary to trim the liabilities to fit the reserves. A reserve deficiency of a million dollars (for the banking system) no longer forces a contraction of several million dollars of bank credit. The banks may repair the deficiency by offering for discount or by selling a million dollars of assets to the Federal Reserve Banks. Or they may obtain a million dollars of advances from the Reserve Banks, leaving the total of their earning assets unchanged.

Also, heavy losses need not be sustained on sound assets. The Federal Reserve Banks are not operated to make profits but to serve the banks and, through them, the public. They can, when conditions require, take over billions of dollars of assets from the banks without lowering the market value of those assets. We realize today that liquidity does not depend upon maturity nor upon the possibility of selling securities to other banks or their customers. For the system, the fundamental guarantee of liquidity lies in the availability of discounting facilities. As long as there is a central bank that can create more reserves when necessary, the banking system as a whole can have the necessary liquidity, regardless of the maturity of any of the assets that individual banks may hold in their portfolios.

We should not, however, jump to the conclusion that the maturity of a bank's assets makes no difference. It makes less difference than before. But the fact that the Federal Reserve has increased the liquidity of the banking system does not mean that the individual bank can ignore the maturity element and make only long-term investments. The Federal Reserve is under no obligation to rescue individual banks from the consequences of their folly. Nor can the individual bank count certainly on disposing of any of its assets at cost or higher to the Federal Reserve. Reserve authorities may feel that credit is generally overexpanded. At such times they are likely to encourage higher interest rates and a decline in bond prices. A bank that must sell securities to the Federal Reserve at such a time might do so only at a loss. However, banks that are following the broad policies encouraged by the Federal Reserve and generally adhered to by most other banks need be less concerned than formerly with concentrating their loans primarily in the short-term field to be relatively liquid.

CHANGING LOAN-INVESTMENT RATIO

Even when the commercial loan theory was most generally accepted, banks made some investments. Investments were supposed to be a sort of residual outlet for the banks' lending power. After they had made all the short-term loans they could, banks with excess reserves usually bought bonds rather than hold idle funds. However, loans were consistently several times the amount of investments until the Depression of the 1930s. For the 60 years between 1870 and 1930, loans ranged from about twice to six times the volume of investments.

Recent Changes

Then a striking development occurred. The relative importance of loans and investments was reversed. For 20 years, investments exceeded loans, and at one time were four times the volume of loans.[18] Many felt that the character of American banking had undergone a structural and permanent change.

This violent reapportionment of loans and investments was the result of two circumstances—the Depression and the Second World War. During the Depression, business firms were borrowing little. As bank loans declined to half their former volume, banks gradually increased their investments to supplement their meager earnings. This expansion of their portfolios was facilitated by the repeated federal deficits during the Depression, which increased the available supply of Treasury securities. Later, purchases of Treasury securities by all commercial banks in the United States during the war sent their investments skyrocketing to $98 billion in 1945, in striking contrast to the average of less than $14 billion of investments held during 1924–1929.

Immediately after the war there was some sober discussion of the future of American banking. If bankers were to surrender their traditional role as credit rationers and become simply monetizers of the national debt, there was some question whether banks were really needed any longer. The Federal Reserve Banks or even the Treasury itself might perform this service equally well and at no interest cost to the Treasury.

The concern was premature. Immediately the ratio of loans to investments began to rise. Investments declined, partly because some of the bank-held securities were retired or refunded by the Treasury, partly because the banks themselves were disposing of government securities so they could make more loans. Business was clamoring for credit, and so were consumers. The banks were anxious to accommodate their customers, especially since loans carried a higher interest rate than (short-term) government securities.

---

[18]In 1945, national banks held $14 billion of loans and $55 billion of investments.

By 1955 loans once more exceeded investments; in 1974 loans were considerably more than double total investments. (See Table 7-1.)[19]

Future Outlook

Despite the steady rise in the loan-investment ratio since 1945, it seems improbable that in the near future loans will again be five or six times as great as investments. Since World War II the United States has been operating with few exceptions at or near full employment, with a correspondingly high demand for loans. Any slackening of our industrial pace, such as in the early 1970s, is typically accompanied by a decline in the demand for loans as well as by a reluctance to lend on the part of the banks. A fall in the volume of loans causes the ratio of loans to investments to fall unless the volume of investments also decreases proportionately. In fact, however, at such times the level of bank investments would doubtless rise; for as bankers found the demand for loans contracting, they would be likely to buy securities to hold up their own earnings. This increase in investments would further lower the ratio of loans to investments. This is exactly what bankers did during the 1930s. Buying securities will be all the easier in the future because of the large national debt, which in this respect will help to stabilize the volume of the nation's deposit money. Approximately a third of bank investments today is in Treasury obligations. Furthermore, only about 20 percent of the marketable government debt is at present held by the commercial banks. Even if the national debt were reduced, the banks could still add to their portfolios by purchasing government securities that are presently held by insurance companies, other corporations, and individuals. Similar statements may be made respecting the tax-exempt state and municipal obligations which represent the other principal investment area of the banks today. All indications point to the probability that investments will continue to make up a much more important component of bank assets than they did before 1930.

RISKS OF LENDING AND INVESTING

The lower the apparent risk in lending money or buying a bond, the lower the interest rate. Although some loans and investments are less risky than others, all have at least some element of risk. Loans and investments usually contain some degree of these three types of risks: credit risk, money risk, and purchasing power risk.

Credit Risk

With any investment or loan, there is the chance of default. The risk is ordinarily negligible in the case of investment in Treasury securities, for a government can always pay its domestic debts even if it has to print the

---

[19]The time trend of loans and investments from 1950 to 1970 is shown in Chapter 5, Table 5-2, p. 141.

money to do it. But when money is lent to other organizations or to individuals, the borrower may be unable to pay by the time payment is due. The longer the maturity of the loan or investment, the more difficult the evaluation of the risk factor. It is easier to judge a firm's financial condition for the next 60 days than for the next 60 years. By the time a long-term bond matures, the firm and possibly even the industry may have passed into history.[20] Also, the longer term obligations must face the hazards of the business cycle. The credit risk involved in a loan or investment of distant maturity may greatly change as the nation passes from prosperity to depression. Although short-term obligations may also be influenced by cyclical movements, they are likely to be less affected than long-term obligations, because business conditions do not ordinarily change a great deal during the short time the credit is outstanding.

Money Risk

Long-term loans and investments are subject to another type of risk which is negligible for short-term credit. This is the possibility that before repayment, interest rates may rise. A change in the interest rate level will cause a change in the price of even the highest grade bonds, but will have little effect on the value of short-term assets.

The price of high-grade bonds or other assets yielding a fixed income over a long period of time varies inversely with current interest rates. A perpetual bond (or loan) bearing no maturity date but promising an income of $80 a year to the owner will sell for $1,000 only when the long-term interest rate currently prevailing on loans of similar credit rating is 8 percent. If the current long-term rate falls to 4 percent, the price of the bond (still paying $80) rises to $2,000, to yield 4 percent. If the current market rate rises to 16 percent, the bond will sell for $500. The bond must sell at such a price that the buyer can obtain the same yield available elsewhere.

Few perpetual bonds have been issued. The principle, however, is the same for all long-term loans and investments, although complicated slightly by the necessity to take into account the eventual repayment of the principal. In general the closer the maturity date, the less the effect of a change in interest rates.

For two reasons, then, short-term credit involves little money risk. The shortness of the time until maturity makes even a substantial change in interest rates of little effect. Also, the short space of time between the granting of the credit and its repayment makes large changes in interest rates unlikely.

It was due to this money risk that banks permitted massive excess reserves to accumulate during the 1930s. The extremely low interest rate level prevailing at the time made an eventual rise of interest rates appear almost certain. Bankers were willing to lend on short term, but the supply of sound

---

[20]Fifty years ago the bonds of city and interurban trolley car lines were considered a very sound investment. Today few of these lines still operate.

short-term investments and loans was limited. Rather than lend on long term, bankers held idle reserves. Fully understanding that the probable eventual rise in interest rates would necessarily cause a decline in the price of high-grade bonds,[21] bankers preferred to hold unnecessarily large balances at the Federal Reserve Banks rather than increase their investments.[22]

Purchasing Power Risk

Loans are subject to the risk that before repayment the purchasing power or value of money may change. If there has been substantial inflation, the lender will be paid back in dollars of reduced purchasing power. Again, there is a greater risk of changes in the value of money for long-term investments than for short-term. And as shown in the endsheet, any of the popular price indexes will disclose a substantial inflation in the post-World War II period.

LOANS

If you lend $50 to someone whom you trust absolutely, you probably will not ask for security. To someone else, either someone you do not know or someone whom you know to be careless about debts, you will be unlikely to lend without some kind of security.

Secured Loans

Many individuals and business firms would find it impossible to borrow at the bank if they did not have property that could be pledged as security that the loan will be repaid. Others find that they can borrow at a lower rate when they offer security. Secured loans are especially common in the case of smaller borrowers whose credit is limited.

Many types of property are pledged as security for loans. In the case of real estate loans, the bank holds a mortgage giving it the right to seize and sell the property to recover any unpaid balance on the loan. Many consumer loans, particularly those made to finance the purchase of automobiles and major household equipment, are secured by a chattel mortgage on the property purchased. Most agricultural loans are secured, some by livestock, others by crops or farm machinery. In addition, stocks and bonds are often put up as

---

[21]The price of low-grade bonds rose with the return of prosperity, if the issuing company succeeded in surviving the Depression, for their credit risk was then less. However, banks seldom intentionally buy such securities.
[22]It is due to this kind of possibility that some have recommended in recent years that interest rates always be kept at a low level, regardless of the condition of business. If there is no expectation that rates will presently rise, the money risk is eliminated and banks during depression will invest more freely than they have done in the past. The proposal would have more appeal if we could rely on restrictive fiscal policies during inflations, regardless of their political implications.

security.[23] Mortgages are often given against plant and equipment, or inventories are pledged as security.

As earlier observed, inventory loans were long considered to be the most suitable loans a bank could make. They have been popular also with businesspeople who can use their own funds for the expansion of plant and equipment and still, by obtaining a secured loan, have cash for the purchase of goods. They find it important to pay cash to take advantage of the discounts that many sellers offer for payment within 10 days or less after the buyer has received the goods. A discount of even 1 percent for immediate payment rather than payment at the end of the month is a highly attractive inducement to buyers, since it involves an annual rate of more than 12 percent. If they can possibly borrow from their bank at a rate of perhaps 10 percent, they will do so. In fact, their bank will consider them poor financial risks if they fail to take the discounts for cash.[24]

Unsecured Loans

The greater part of the dollar volume of a bank's business loans and some of its other loans are unsecured. The term is a little misleading. Naturally a bank does not lend unless it feels the loan is sound. But if a borrower has a sufficiently high credit rating—large companies are especially favored for this reason—the bank may feel that the borrower's general credit is sufficient guarantee that the loan will be paid and that it is unnecessary to require the deposit or pledge of security.

Maturity of Loans

The development of banking over the last half century and in particular the evolution of the Federal Reserve Banks have modified the banks' former attitude toward loan maturity.

Call Loans and Short-Term Loans. Traditionally, a bank's loans fell in one of two categories. Just as the bank's deposits might be payable upon demand or only after a specified short period of time, so its loans were due either upon demand or after a few months had elapsed.

---

[23]We are not here concerned with loans made for purchasing and carrying securities, which are subject to margin requirements. The secured loans referred to here are made for other purposes, in general for providing short-term working capital. Margin requirements do not apply. It must be admitted that, strictly speaking, the loans are made to permit the borrowers to carry the securities, for if the borrowers were to sell them, they would probably not need to borrow. But if the securities were purchased some time ago and they appear to be holding them as a long-term investment, or if perhaps the securities are currently selling at twice what the borrowers paid for them and they do not want to take the profit and pay a capital gains tax, they may pledge them as security for the loan. If the loan is for a short period and for a purpose clearly associated with the borrowers' business, bankers do not consider such loans to be in the same category with those obviously associated with the securities market.

[24]In passing, we might note that the bank's right to seize the goods if the borrower defaults does not insure the bank against loss. The inventory might spoil in storage or it might fall in market value. Also, a dishonest borrower might set a fictitiously high value on the goods. Further, the goods may have been acquired by an innocent purchaser, leaving the bank with no security. But for reliable customers who are themselves financing a part of the cost of goods of reasonably stable market value, the banks are glad to provide funds for carrying inventories.

Demand or call loans bear no maturity date. At any time the bank may require that they be paid, or at any time the borrower may pay them off. Although call loans are sometimes secured by other assets, they are particularly suitable for financing the purchase of securities. Investors may borrow part of the money needed to buy stocks, pledging the stocks as security for the loan. From the bank's point of view, such a loan is ideally liquid. As there is a continuous market for securities accepted as collateral for call loans, the loan can be collected at any time either by repayment or by sale of the collateral. If the collateral securities decline in value while the loan is in force, the bank requires the borrower to repay part of the original loan so that the remaining part will be as well secured as was the original loan.

Years ago, when banks were lending on stocks as much as 90 percent of the value of the security, call loans were much more important than they are today. Again, although such loans may be safe from the bank's viewpoint, they tend to increase the fluctuations in the stock market. They provide the funds for additional purchases in a bull market, driving high prices still higher. When prices begin to fall and many borrowers cannot supply additional margin, the distress selling resulting from call loans drives falling prices down still further.

Other than call loans, all loans have a definite maturity date. Banks prefer that they be short term, so that the individual bank's assets will be reasonably liquid. Most bank loans are made for periods of a year or less, frequently for one to three months. Loans secured by or for the purpose of carrying inventory are typically of such maturity. At the end of the specified time the entire amount of the loan is due. Sometimes a part or all of the loan is renewed at maturity, and it may be agreed when the loan is made that renewal will be possible. Under such circumstances, what is apparently a 90-day loan may become, in effect, a loan for a year or more.

Term Loans and Long-Term Loans. In many instances borrowers, especially business firms, need to borrow for periods longer than a year. At one time such borrowers found it difficult to borrow from the banks. Large concerns might succeed in obtaining long-term loans by selling their bonds to banks (or to other buyers). Bankers justified a limited amount of such investing, in contrast to lending, because the borrowing firm's well-known name would make their bonds easily marketable if need for liquidity should arise. Small firms, however, could not issue bonds. For them there was one other possibility. Banks might make short-term loans, periodically renewing the loans until they were finally repaid, possibly some years later.

As a substitute for these two kinds of earning assets, banks today are making a considerable volume of so-called *term loans*. (A more accurate name would be *intermediate term loans*, but unfortunately they are regularly referred to by the less descriptive title.) Term loans run from 1 to 10 years or occasionally for longer periods. They usually provide for repayment on an installment basis. Thus, they are intermediate between the ordinary (short-term) business loan and the long-term loan. They may be either secured or unsecured, but in either case a borrowing agreement is drawn up specifying the payments to be made and requirements to be met by the borrower. In making loans of this type, the bank is less interested in the concern's current position than in its possibilities to continue showing a profit over a number of years and its ability to make the payments set forth in the agreement. Also, the bank requires assurance that the corporation will incur no further indebtedness that might weaken the claims of the bank as, for example, through the pledge of the corporation's assets.

For large corporations, a term loan is quite similar to an issue of short-term bonds, privately placed. If the loan is too large to be handled by a single bank, as many as 20 or 30 banks may jointly participate. The advantage of the term loan over bonds is that the corporation need not comply with the regulations and requirements that surround a publicly offered bond issue.

Although small businesses will usually be required to deposit security and to pay higher interest rates than large businesses on their term loans, they benefit, perhaps more than any other group, from the opportunity to borrow on this basis. They do not have the alternative sources of credit that are available to large borrowers. Short-term loans are not always the answer to their requirements. To the extent that small businesses can borrow for a period of two or three years, they have a longer time to make arrangements for repayment and to plan their financial program.

Besides making short-term loans and term loans, banks make also a limited volume of long-term loans, which may run for as long as 20 to 30 years. These are ordinarily secured by real estate, and are discussed below that heading.

Purpose of Loans

In an economy that depends more and more on credit, banks find themselves lending for a variety of purposes, sometimes directly, sometimes through agencies. Some loans commonly made by banks today would have been summarily refused by the same banks 50 years ago. This wider variety of loans is not due merely to a change in the banks' attitude. It reflects also more fundamental changes such as shifts in the public's consumption patterns and in financial investment policies.[25]

Commercial and Industrial Loans. The largest single category of bank loans includes those made to business, traditionally for the purpose of supplying working capital to handle inventory, to permit the extension of more credit to customers, or for other short-term needs. It is from these commercial loans that commercial banks get their name. The volume of these commercial loans has recently been around $180 billion.

There is no such thing as a typical commercial loan. It may be secured by some kind of asset or it may be unsecured. It may be for five or ten years, for one or two months, or callable at any time. It may be for a hundred dollars or less, or it may be for more than a million dollars. Although frequently for the

[25]Table 7-1, page 190, shows the exact composition of all commercial bank loans as of June 30, 1974.

purpose of supplying working capital, these loans in recent years have also been made to supply intermediate-term capital, especially for improvement and modernization. The characteristics of any particular commercial loan depend upon bank policy, the borrower's financial resources and bargaining power, and the specific purpose for which the funds are borrowed.

Loans for Purchasing or Carrying Securities. Before the Depression, loans on securities were second only to commercial and industrial loans, and at their peak exceeded $10 billion. By 1940 they were down to about $1 billion.

Banks lend both to investors directly and to brokers, who lend to their customers. Toward the close of World War II both these classes of security loans shot up to about five times their 1939–1942 level, largely in consequence of the speculation that developed in the market for government obligations. (See Chapter 23.) As the opportunity for sure profits on government securities disappeared after the war, the volume of these loans declined. Then, with a revival of interest in common stock as a hedge against inflation, they climbed back to about $9 or $10 billion. Today most of them are made for purchasing or carrying securities other than obligations of the United States government. They are generally referred to as call loans.

Agricultural Loans. Typically farmers have faced the usual difficulties of small businesspeople in applying for bank credit. To provide more adequately for their needs, a number of special farm credit agencies have been set up. (See Chapter 5.) Member bank agricultural loans rose from a little under $1 billion before 1945 to about $20 billion by 1974.

Real Estate Loans. Member bank loans on real estate before World War II never greatly exceeded $3 billion but climbed steadily and rapidly after the war. Today they are over $125 billion, second only to commercial and industrial loans. About two thirds of these loans are on residential property, about 5 percent are on farm land, and the balance are on "other property," including office buildings, hotels, theaters, stores, and other business property.

Bank policy with respect to real estate loans has varied. The settlement of the nation and the growth of cities offered almost limitless opportunity for speculation in real estate. Canals and, later, railroads transformed crossroads hamlets into thriving towns, creating fortunes for those who had bought land before the period of rapid growth. The possibilities of enormous profits in land operations led to excessive speculation and occasional drastic decline in inflated land values. The many failures experienced by the state banks due to real estate loans led the framers of the national bank system to withhold from the national banks the right to make such loans, although in the rural regions where there was little demand for commercial loans, real estate loans might be almost the only secured loans the bank could make.

The organization of the Federal Reserve in 1913 led to permission for national banks to lend against real estate. State banks could not be attracted into membership if regulations were too strictly drawn and if joining the System was to mean the banks would be entirely prohibited from lending policies that, for some, were necessary if they were to lend at all. On the other hand, it was inconsistent for the Federal Reserve to deny to those members with a national charter the rights that it permitted to those with state charters. Accordingly, national banks may now make real estate loans subject to certain regulations.[26]

Consumer Loans. As late as 1929 almost the only banks making installment loans to consumers were the Morris Plan banks which later evolved into commercial banks. Two circumstances contributed to the lack of consumption loans by commercial banks. In the first place, the growth of consumer credit, from whatever source, is a fairly recent phenomenon. It was little used until the end of the First World War, when the rapid increase in the market for automobiles encouraged its growth. In the second place, the commercial banks did not immediately enter this new lending field, perhaps due to the contrast between consumer loans and business loans. Business loans increased the borrower's earning power and were often regarded as self-liquidating. The consumer loan merely permitted the consumer to buy goods before he or she had put aside enough money to pay for them, a financial policy doubtlessly heartily deplored by traditionally conservative bankers. But viewing the increasing volume of such credit being handled by sales finance companies, small loan companies, other lenders, and by retail firms selling goods on time payments, the banks finally entered the field during the Depression. Since then they have been actively increasing their share of this business. By 1974 banks were providing 40 percent of the total of $102 billion of consumer loans. In addition, they were providing funds that other lenders made available to consumers.

Most consumer credit is repaid in installments.[27] Some, however, is in the form of charge accounts and single payment loans. During World War II, when consumer durable goods were unavailable, installment credit dropped below noninstallment credit. In the last few years installment credit has mounted rapidly, pushed up not only by the large volume of automobile sales but also by tremendous sales of household appliances and equipment purchased for modernization or to equip new homes.

Open Market Loans

To this point we have been considering the loans a bank makes directly to its customers. Besides such loans the banks, especially in the larger cities, make a relatively small volume of loans that are similar to investments in that there is no personal relation between the bank and the borrower. The so-called money market deals in these highly liquid, short-term loans as well as in bank acceptances and, most importantly, short-term Treasury securities. (As of March, 1975, there were about $124 billion of Treasury Bills outstanding, $89 billion of negotiable, large denomination bank CDs, $51 billion of

---

[26]Mortgages guaranteed by the Federal Housing Administration or the Veterans' Administration are not subject to these regulations. More than a quarter of real estate loans made by commercial banks are guaranteed.

[27]*Consumer debt* includes home mortgages. The term *consumer credit* does not.

commercial paper, and $19 billion of bankers' acceptances.) There are four classes of open market loans: commercial paper, bankers' acceptances, brokers' loans, and federal loans.

Commercial Paper. The term *commercial paper* often refers to notes and drafts that a bank discounts for its own customers to supply them with short-term funds to finance inventories, meet payrolls, or meet similar working capital requirements. *Open market commercial paper*, however, refers to short-term promissory notes issued by large corporations themselves (especially finance companies) to hundreds of investors looking for a high-grade investment. These obligations are sold on a discount basis in denominations of from $5,000 to $100,000.

For well over a hundred years commercial paper has been sold in the United States. During the Depression it almost disappeared. From the billion dollar level after World War I it declined to less than a hundred million in 1932. Businesses had little occasion to borrow, and banks were glad to lend at very low rates. Even during World War II open market borrowing was less than $200 million. But since 1945 it has climbed rapidly. By 1950 it stood again at nearly a billion dollars, from which it climbed steadily and rapidly to its all-time high of over $50 billion by early 1975. Banks are among the buyers of this paper, but corporate treasurers with temporarily surplus funds have in recent years been supplying the bulk of the funds. Also, insurance companies, colleges, mutual funds, and other institutional investors buy commercial paper.

Open market lending is unlikely to usurp the traditional role of the banks. Most firms will continue to depend on their banks for their working capital. If a firm is to borrow successfully on the open market, its credit rating must be unquestioned and widely known. There is not the opportunity for the detailed credit investigation that would accompany a typical bank loan. For this reason, small firms can seldom utilize this method of borrowing. Even if their credit is excellent, it is not sufficiently well known for their unsecured promissory notes to be publicly marketed.

Larger firms gain two important advantages by borrowing some of their funds on the open market. There is the immediately obvious advantage that it is less expensive. If money is easy and banks are trying hard to make loans, this may be of little importance. But when, as in 1975, banks were charging 8 to 8½ percent to their most favored customers and in addition requiring that the borrower keep a compensating balance with the bank proportionate to the loan, and when the borrower may, instead, borrow on the open market at 6 to 7½ percent with no compensating balance required, the interest saved on a loan of several million dollars is substantial.

The additional advantage is that, by demonstrating its ability to borrow on the open market, the corporation is establishing clear proof of its high credit rating. This evidence may be useful in later negotiations with its banks, with other creditors, or in the flotation of a bond issue.

To corporate treasurers with temporarily idle funds, open market commercial paper is an attractive short-term investment. It is safe. Since 1936 there have been no losses in this field, and there have been very few instances when time extensions were required. And it offers a somewhat higher yield than is obtainable on government securities of comparable maturity. Because the commercial paper is so safe, the rate differential is not great, but it may be as much as .5 percent. A difference of .5 percent certainly is not to be ignored by a treasurer with $10 million to invest. Over a six-month period, the .5 percent amounts to $25,000.

There still remains this question. If a bank's prime rate, the rate at which it lends to its best customers, is 8 percent, why will it buy open market paper yielding only 6½ percent? The answer is simple. If it can place all its funds safely at 8 percent, it will not buy the commercial paper. But there will almost always be some banks that have excess reserves. They may be hundreds or thousands of miles from the firm that issues the paper, and there would be little chance for the borrower to tap this source of funds through the usual bank-and-customer relationships. By borrowing on the open market, a firm obtains funds wherever money is easiest.

Also, a bank may feel the need for greater diversification. Located, perhaps, in a farming area, it recognizes that the soundness of its local loans is closely related to agricultural prosperity. Not only its loans to farmers, but its loans to retailers in the area and its real estate loans and consumption loans will be affected by agricultural prices and profits. The bank may be happy to invest in the paper of a finance company or perhaps of an industrial borrower to avoid an overconcentration of risk.

In addition, open market paper is suitable for secondary reserves. It is readily marketable if the bank wishes to dispose of it before maturity, and it will almost certainly be repaid promptly at maturity. A bank customer may ask to renew a loan, entirely or partially; the corporation that has borrowed by publicly issuing short-term notes would have to be in desperate circumstances before it would fail to pay the entire amount at maturity.

Bankers' Acceptances. Bankers may also buy acceptances from either dealers or bill brokers. This type of paper, arising principally in connection with foreign trade, is available primarily to the metropolitan banks.

Brokers' Loans. Earlier we took up loans made against stocks and bonds. Such loans may be on a customer basis, either to the individual purchasing the stocks or to the person's broker. But banks also make open market loans to brokers, placing them through specialists called loan brokers. The loans may be on either a call or time basis.

Federal Funds. Elsewhere, in studying the question of member reserves, we observed that ordinarily the banks attempt to keep excess reserves at as low a level as possible. An unexpected drain of reserves may, therefore, cause a bank's legal reserves to fall below the required level. Rather than increase its reserves by borrowing from or selling assets to the Federal Reserve, a bank may prefer to borrow reserve funds from other banks temporarily holding excess reserves. These transactions in reserves are termed dealings in federal funds. Such loans are ordinarily made for a single day, in multiples of $1 million, the interest rates being close to the discount rate currently prevailing.[28] The exact rate at any time depends on the abundance or scarcity of federal funds.[29] The lender benefits by receiving interest on funds otherwise idle. The advantage to the borrowing bank is that it need not refer to the Federal Reserve and it obtains conveniently, immediately, and at minimum cost, the funds required for the brief time that it needs them.

REGULATION OF BANK INVESTMENTS

National banks and to a lesser extent state banks have been subject to considerable regulation respecting their investments. Both are forbidden to buy stocks, with minor exceptions.[30] Some states refused to permit commercial banks to buy bonds, and national banks were not originally given explicit authority to buy bonds other than those of the United States Treasury. Neither state nor national banks are permitted to own real estate, other than that required for carrying on the work of the bank.

National banks were not only permitted but required to buy government bonds, for these were required as collateral against their note issue. By a ruling of the Comptroller of the Currency, the state power of the banks to purchase "notes, drafts, . . . and other evidences of debt" was interpreted to give them the power to purchase other bonds. But it was not until 1927 that, by the McFadden Act, specific authority to buy bonds was granted the national banks. This Act required that not more than 10 percent of the bank's unimpaired capital and surplus be invested in the obligations of any one borrower. This rule applies, however, only to securities issued by private corporations. It is inapplicable to obligations of, or guaranteed by, the United States Treasury or to obligations of states and municipalities.

According to the language of the McFadden Act, the banks were authorized to purchase "marketable obligations evidencing indebtedness . . . in the form of bonds, notes, or debentures commonly known as investment securities, under such further definition of the term 'investment' securities as may

---

[28]Small-town bankers are not concerned with the federal funds market. Because their deposits are relatively stable, they can usually adjust their reserves without last-minute borrowing. If necessary, they can borrow from one or another of their correspondent banks. For the larger (formerly reserve city) banks, it is a little more difficult to accomplish a full utilization of reserves without occasionally finding themselves a little short. For such giants as the Chase Manhattan, required reserves are around a billion dollars. Certainly the bank could avoid a reserve deficiency by holding at all times a little more than the required amount. But a constantly maintained cushion of $50 or $100 million of excess reserves would be an expensive insurance indeed. Where there is an active demand for loans, the big banks watch their reserve position very closely to hold excess reserves to the bare minimum. If, two or three hours before the end of the week they find they have an excess or a deficiency of $20 or $30 million for the week, they contact other banks and lend or borrow that amount.

[29]When money is easy, federal funds are plentiful and the federal funds rate will be a little below the discount rate. When money is tight and banks are trying to avoid borrowing from the Federal Reserve Banks, the federal funds rate rises a little above the discount rate. It has only been since the mid-1960s that the latter has regularly been the case. This is mainly because banks are now using federal funds not only to meet temporary reserve shortages, but to bolster their regular lending powers.

[30]Members of the Federal Reserve System buy stock in the Federal Reserve. Also, banks may buy stock in a subsidiary corporation that they organize to handle their safe deposit business or to administer the details of operation of the bank building, leased, perhaps, to hundreds of tenants. The amount in the safe deposit business may not exceed 15 percent of the capital and surplus; the amount invested in their building may not exceed the amount of the capital stock.

. . . be prescribed by the Comptroller of the Currency." Nine years later the Comptroller of the Currency attempted to define the terms of the McFadden Act. "Marketable obligations" were stated to be issues that were sufficiently large and well enough distributed that marketability would be assured. In defining "investment securities," he prohibited the banks from purchasing speculative securities. This definition in itself is, of course, meaningless unless a definition of speculative securities is provided. The Comptroller at this point referred to the bond ratings issued by private companies specializing in such work. Where there was any doubt concerning a security's eligibility for purchase, it was to be supported by at least two rating services.

This ruling was not popular with the bankers. It restricted the use of their own judgment and permitted them to buy only the bonds that, with a satisfactorily high rating in the manuals, were in the greatest demand and consequently were selling at the highest prices. However, the banks' previous record with respect to their bond purchases seemed clearly to indicate that restrictions of some kind should be imposed.

Why Regulation Was Required

The growing importance of investments caused the price of bonds to have a material effect upon the solvency of the banks. Before World War I, when investments totaled about the same amount as capital accounts, bond prices could vary widely without greatly affecting solvency. But by 1928 investments were nearly double the total of capital accounts, and six years later they were three times as much as the banks' capital. A decline of 30 percent in bond prices in 1934 would in itself have nearly eliminated total capital accounts, forcing the banks into receivership.

Bond prices did, in fact, vary considerably during these years. The price of high-grade corporate bonds declined by more than a third between 1928 and 1932 and rose by two thirds between 1932 and 1936. Between 1920 and 1932 the banks held more corporate than government obligations; and although many banks bought only high-grade bonds, some banks had large holdings of speculative issues. For this there were two principal reasons:

1. Some of the larger banks were carrying on both investment and commercial banking, underwriting the issue of new securities in return for a commission on their sale. Consequently, issues that met a poor reception with the investing public gravitated into these banks, which agreed with the selling corporation to take over any part of the issue that could not be sold.
2. Also, some banks, especially during the Depression, were tempted into purchasing speculative issues. The low price made the yield attractive; and if the corporation's affairs improved, the price of the bonds rose, providing a nice capital gain.

Regulation of Bank Investments—Conclusion

The first situation was corrected by the Banking Act of 1933, which required that all commercial banks sever their connections with their affiliates in security marketing and prohibited them from underwriting new issues other than government issues.

The second problem was the one that the Comptroller of the Currency was attempting to solve by spelling out which securities the national banks might purchase and how bank examiners should evaluate them. Finally, securities were classified under these three headings:

1. *Substandard:* Bonds in the four highest grades (Aaa, Aa, A, and Baa) established by rating agencies, and unrated securities of equivalent value.[31]
2. *Doubtful:* Lower rated bonds or their unrated equivalent but excluding any securities in default.
3. *Loss:* Bonds in default and all corporate stocks.

Banks are permitted to purchase only bonds in the first group listed. However, they will often hold a few securities of the two lower groups. These securities may have come to the bank through default on a collateral-secured loan. Or the bank may have purchased bonds when they qualified as "Substandard" but, while the bank was still holding them, the bonds declined in quality until they were classed "Doubtful" or "Loss."

As a result of these rulings as well as other factors, the quality of the banking system's bond portfolio has notably improved. It appears most unlikely that the banks as a whole could suffer any real difficulties today from a decline in bond prices due to credit risk, for nearly all their holdings are in government or municipal bonds. In contrast to the great increase since 1929 in deposits, total assets, and capital accounts, banks' holdings of corporate securities have shown little change. Holdings of Federal Reserve members changed as shown in Table 7-4, detailed records of which are available.

Management of the Bond Account

Proper handling of the bond account requires a high degree of skill and experience. Country bankers who may be excellently qualified to handle loan applications of their local customers and to judge the general state of local affairs often do not invest frequently enough or on a large enough scale to be qualified as investment experts. They are likely to rely on the advice of a city correspondent bank or of rating services or bond salespeople, for they are not trained in security analysis. Nor can they dispose of the problem simply by confining their purchases to Treasury obligations, for there is more to it than the avoidance of credit risk. A successful bond portfolio must take into account the probable future level of interest rates and carefully weigh the higher returns available on some issues against the possibility of loss from a change in market interest rates.

---

[31]It may appear paradoxical that the highest classification—including bonds rated Aaa—should be "Substandard." Remember, though, the banks' right to buy federal government securities was never questioned. This classification pertains to other investment securities. In contrast to Treasury securities, which carry no credit risk, even the highest grade corporate and local government bonds carry some credit risk. Unlike the federal government, these other borrowers cannot, if necessary, print the money to retire their obligations. There does appear to be an element of semantics in the nomenclature. The terminology seems to imply that in the opinion of the Comptroller of the Currency commercial banks should buy only federal government bonds.

Table 7-4   Deposits, Capital, and Securities Held by
Federal Reserve Member Banks
(In billions of dollars)

| Date | Deposits (Time + Adjusted Demand Deposits) | Capital Accounts | Securities | | |
			U.S. Government	States and Political Subdivisions	Other
Dec., 1929	29.5	6.7	3.9	1.4	4.5
Dec., 1974	493.3	48.2	59.8	74.3	4.9

Source: *Banking and Monetary Statistics* (Washington: Board of Governors of the Federal
Reserve System, 1943); *Federal Reserve Bulletin* (June, 1975), pp. A16–A17.

The handling of the bond portfolio is further complicated by tax considerations. The officer in charge must be not only a good judge of investments,
he or she must also be familiar with the details of and the changes in the tax
laws relating to bank investments. The rapid and massive increase in bank
investments since 1940, reinforced by changing tax laws, has made the management of the bank's investment portfolio more important than formerly.

SUMMARY AND CONCLUSION

The most important assets of a bank are its reserves, loans, and investments (or securities). Loans and investments constitute over 80 percent of all
bank assets and are its principal earning assets. There is considerable variety
in the composition of a typical commercial bank's loans and securities.

A bank's reserves are its most liquid assets and are mostly nonearning
assets. The primary function of legal reserve requirements today is to control
the money supply, not to provide liquidity, because required legal reserves
are the one asset that a bank can never pay out to depositors as long as it
remains in business.

The Board of Governors has been empowered to vary reserve requirements within the permissible limits set by Congress. These reserve requirements are lower for time than for demand deposits and are today based on
deposit size.

Both the level and composition of required reserves have tended to discourage state banks from becoming members of the Federal Reserve System.
Unlike the Federal Reserve, the states allow nonmember banks to count several earning assets as legal reserves.

Reserves originate in two quite different ways for individual banks than
for the banking system as a whole. The individual bank's reserves increase
when it receives currency from its depositors or when it deposits with the
Federal Reserve Bank checks drawn on other banks. However, the banking
system as a whole can only gain reserves when one bank receives additional
reserves while no other bank loses reserves.

It has been suggested that reserves be based on the velocity of deposits or on the type of assets held rather than on the level of deposits. Others have suggested that all banks be required to maintain reserves of 100 percent or at least maintain ceiling reserves larger than usual in time of emergency. It has also been proposed that there be a requirement of a special, supplementary reserve. While each suggestion has advantages, it also has shortcomings.

The commercial loan theory emphasizes that banks should make only short-term, self-liquidating loans to businesses; however, this philosophy has been largely discredited. Today the Federal Reserve serves as a central discounting agency and is the final arbiter of liquidity.

Over the years there has been a dramatic change in the loan-investment ratio in banking. While once investments dominated, now loans do. Loans and investments usually contain some degree of credit risk (default), money risk (interest rate decline), and purchasing power risk (decline in the value of money).

Banks make a much wider variety of loans today than 50 years ago. While the largest single category of bank loans is commercial and industrial loans, banks also lend substantial sums to parties in real estate, agriculture, banks and other financial institutions, etc. Banks also loan directly to customers and indirectly through the open market. The so-called "money market" deals with four classes of open market loans: bankers' acceptances, brokers' loans, commercial paper, and federal funds.

National banks and to a lesser extent state banks continue to be subject to considerable regulation of their investment portfolio. For instance, they are limited in their ability to purchase common stocks, real estate, and even corporate bonds.

Discussion Questions

1. What are a typical bank's three most important assets?
2. Why has there been a trend toward nonmembership in the Federal Reserve System? Why might this trend reduce the effectiveness of monetary policy?
3. Briefly contrast the effect on the excess reserves of both the commercial banks and the Federal Reserve Banks when member banks withdrew Federal Reserve notes from the Banks to hold more vault cash:

   a. In 1914   c. In 1960
   b. In 1917   d. Today
4. Since a continued expansion of member bank deposits appeared desirable, the 1959 ruling that vault cash would count as legal reserves, and the 1965 ruling that reserves were no longer required against Federal Reserve deposits were both alternatives to a reduction in member bank reserves. Explain.
5. "Since the Federal Reserve Banks no longer are required to maintain reserves against their deposits, logic suggests that member banks also be freed of reserve requirements." Explain why you agree or disagree.

6. Since coins, Federal Reserve notes, and deposits at the Federal Reserve Banks are all credit money and are also the legal reserves of member banks, is there really any purpose in continuing to require the banks to hold legal reserves? Explain.

7. How can the banking system operate with excess reserves amounting to only a fraction of 1 percent of deposits?

8. A 100 percent reserve requirement would take the control of money away from the banks and give it to the Federal Reserve. It would not, however, control the money flow. Explain why you agree or disagree.

9. Briefly discuss two proposed bases for reserve requirements, other than the amount of deposits. What is the principal disadvantage of each?

10. The basic difference between loans and investments is that loans tend to be short term, investments long term. True or false? Explain.

11. Although the operation of the Federal Reserve System was originally based on the commercial loan theory of bank credit, the organization of the Federal Reserve was in part responsible for the decline in importance of that theory. Explain.

12. The Federal Reserve Banks are not operated for a profit. What is the consequence of this, if any, for shiftability?

13. Briefly describe the three types of risk in lending money or buying a bond.

14. To what extent has the increase in open market commercial paper since World War II resulted in an increase in the velocity of money? How, if at all, are these two variables related to changes in interest rates and in the quantity of money during this period? Explain.

PART 3
Central Banking

Chapter 8   Predecessors of the Federal Reserve

American colonists never had much money. As late as the 18th century money was primarily in the form of gold or silver coins. There were no mines of importance in the colonies; for that matter, there never has been much gold or silver discovered along the Eastern Seaboard. And although the Indians of Central America had huge stores of gold and silver, the natives around New England and New Amsterdam, unfortunately for the colonists, were getting along with wampum.

Finding no precious metals either in mines or in the hands of the Indians would not have been serious if the colonists had brought plenty of coins with them, or if they had regularly had a favorable balance of trade. But they did not bring much money with them, partly because many of them came to this wilderness only because they were poor and partly because even those who did have money naturally spent most of it before they left the mother country to stock up on all the things they knew would be unavailable in the New World. Also, the little money that did come to this country tended to flow rather quickly back to England and Europe. The colonists were so busy trying to survive that they had little time to produce goods for export. At the same time there were necessities of all sorts, and an occasional luxury for the fortunate, obtainable only from the Old World. Naturally the colonists usually had an unfavorable balance of trade, pulling gold and silver out of the colonies.[1]

---

[1]Remember that not until 1776, with the publication of Adam Smith's *The Wealth of Nations*, did English writers and statemen seriously question England's mercantilistic colonial policies. Until then it was generally assumed that a principal goal of sound colonial policy should be to enrich the mother country by draining gold and silver from the colonies and, therefore, to require the colonies to have an unfavorable balance of trade.

The money situation grew worse instead of better. In the earliest colonial period the settlers were busy clearing land, building cabins, and pacifying or liquidating Indians. They were largely self-sufficient. But as the settlements developed into villages and towns, specialization replaced self-sufficiency. Specialization requires exchange, and exchange is far easier if there is an adequate money supply. Lacking gold and silver, the colonists used various other commodities as money, including tobacco, corn, and beaver skins. Often these commodities were made legal tender. They were far from satisfactory, and the colonists found paper money irresistibly attractive.

Even in England and Europe there were frequent efforts during the same period to develop credit money, although specie was relatively much more plentiful there. That the colonial efforts were generally unsuccessful was due in part to irresponsibility, but to a greater extent the unsuccessful efforts were the result of a lack of experience and a misconception of the nature of money.

During the colonial period there were no banks at all in the modern sense. A few "public banks" were established as early as the 17th century, and a number of "private banks" were formed during the 18th century. But both the public and the private institutions were entirely unlike banks as we know them today. They did not receive the public's deposits nor did they regularly make loans. They did not even have any capital. A bank in colonial times simply issued paper money. The function of a bank, public or private, was supposed to be to supply notes to the community. Once the bank was organized, such lending as might thereafter be done was handled by private individuals, entirely apart from the bank.

BRANCH BANKING v. UNIT BANKING

After the Revolution, when successful private banks were first established, there were two possible lines of development—*branch banking* and *unit banking*. Branch banking operates in most of the world but failed to survive in this country to any important extent until recent years.

With unit banking, each bank is a separate organization, serving primarily its immediate area.[2] A branch banking system may have hundreds or even thousands of banking offices, but all are part of the same institution.

No bank in this country operates nationwide. In fact, almost no bank operates in more than one state, although a few of the largest banks operate branches abroad.[3] The regulations concerning domestic branches are drawn up by the 50 states and apply without distinction to state banks and national banks alike. Banks may operate domestic branches, if at all, only in the state in which their head office is located. Most states permit banks to operate branches; some fail to authorize branches or expressly forbid them.[4] Of those

---

[2]The 15 states allowing only unit banking are primarily in the Midwest.

[3]The New York banking firm of Brown Brothers Harriman & Co., on the strength of an old charter, does maintain branches in Boston and Philadelphia. Likewise, the Bank of California operates branches in Washington and Oregon, established when the region was the Oregon Territory. The 12 Federal Reserve Banks are not commercial banks but central banks, necessarily serving much wider areas than do the commercial banks.

[4]Nineteen states, mostly in the West, allow unlimited state-wide branching; whereas 16 states, largely in the East, permit only limited branching.

states where branch banking is permitted, only half authorize banks to organize branches anywhere in the state. Elsewhere the states allow branches to open only in a certain part of the state.

Hence, certain paradoxes appear regarding branch banking in the United States. A few very large banks operate 50 or more branches. In recent years a number of banks have rapidly expanded by starting new branches or buying existing banks and converting them into branches, so that the number of branches now exceeds 20,000, an increase of 100 percent during the last ten years. On the other hand, many of our branch bank "systems" consist of one or two branches only. Their head offices are often small banks, not affiliated with the Federal Reserve, and located in towns of 50,000 or less. Since nearly 4,000 banks are operating branches, the average system contains only about 5 branches. "Systems" of this kind have little in common with the nationwide systems of branch banks that have developed in other countries.

True branch banking is in many ways superior to unit banking. It permits a greater diversification of assets. Better credit facilities are provided, since, with the system's resources behind it, no branch need refuse a loan as being too large to handle. Management is likely to be superior, and there are better opportunities for training personnel. Also, branch banking permits some economies; branch banks find it less necessary to erect imposing structures of marble and bronze as evidence of financial stability.

But distrust of Wall Street and fear that branch managers brought in from outside would be less sympathetic to local business than would a local person in a local bank prevented the development of nationwide branch banking in this country. States' rights also played a part. In the critical, formative years of American banking the conservative and sound policies encouraged by branch banking were in many quarters highly unpopular. Certainly the nature of banking and credit were not thoroughly understood even by the leaders of the time. When banking became a political football, branch banking ended.

The first successful private bank organized in the United States was the Bank of North America, chartered in Philadelphia in 1781. A handful of other state chartered banks were later organized but were not of great importance until the 19th century.

Bank of the United States

Branch banking dominated the scene in the early years after the Revolution. Alexander Hamilton argued successfully that rather than continue to encourage the development of state banks, Congress should charter a federal bank to serve the entire nation.[5] This was soon done. The Bank of the United States began operations December 12, 1791, in Philadelphia, and by 1804 had opened eight branches to serve the rest of the nation. One fifth of its capital

---

[5]Hamilton and his friends also established a private bank in 1784, the Bank of New York. This firm is still in business, although it has never made any attempt to attract hordes of depositors and borrowers. Conservative and rather aloof, it has specialized in serving only large accounts. In fact, it was not until 1965 that the management was persuaded to adopt the innovation of stockholders' meetings!

was contributed by the government, which, establishing a thoroughly bad precedent, borrowed from the Bank itself to pay for its stock.

The Bank of the United States was highly successful. It held most of the Treasury's deposits and at its own expense transferred funds from one part of the country to another. Also, the Bank aided the government with loans, collected revenues promptly, and maintained a sound note issue. Furthermore, by refusing to receive the notes of non-specie-paying banks, it discouraged the state banks from overissue. This enforcement of conservative banking practices provided the public with sound currency but also aroused the enmity of the state banks, which found their credit-creation powers, and hence their profits, considerably checked by the necessity of redeeming their notes. In addition, these banks were bitterly opposed to the Bank of the United States due to its great size and power, which they felt gave it an unfair advantage over the state banks.

The Bank's charter expired in 1811 and renewal failed by a single vote, partly as a result of the determined opposition of the state banks. From 3 in 1790, the number of state banks had increased to 28 by 1800 and to 88 by 1811. Only the restraining policies of the Bank of the United States had stood between these banks and the high profits they were anxious to secure. Only this same restraint had prevented still more state institutions from arising, as is shown by their rapid increase after the fall of the Bank of the United States. In the three years following the charter's expiration 120 state banks were chartered.

At war within a year, the government was forced to turn to the state banks, most of which suspended specie payment in 1814. The suspension would probably not have been necessary if the Bank of the United States had continued in operation and had restrained the enthusiastic note issue policies of the state banks. In any event, agitation began almost immediately for the rechartering of such an institution.

The Second Bank of the United States

In 1816 the Second Bank of the United States opened its doors. Less than 20 years later it went down, a victim of politics. It was managed by Nicholas Biddle, a Philadelphia aristocrat whose economic outlook and business philosophy were diametrically opposed to those of the Jacksonian democracy in which he was trying to operate. Biddle felt that the administration was trying to have bank officers appointed by the "spoils" system, an interference he considered unwarranted and intolerable. President Jackson, on the other hand, claimed that the bank was dominated by Biddle, run for private interests, and operated to thwart government policies. He opposed the concentration of so much power in one institution and in one man. In the passionate literary style of the day, Jackson referred to the bank as "the monster" and insisted that it was really insolvent as well as unconstitutional.

The Bank's charter was to expire in 1836, but in 1833 Jackson decided not to wait for the Bank's charter to expire but to transfer public funds immediately out of the Second Bank of the United States and into the state banks.

He so instructed the Secretary of the Treasury, who disagreed and was transferred to another position. His successor also refused to withdraw the government's funds from the Bank and he, too, was replaced. The third Secretary complied with Jackson's wishes, spent the funds that were held in the Second Bank of the United States, and placed current receipts in selected state banks, which naturally enough quickly became known as "pet banks." The Bank attempted to remain in business as a state institution but failed a few years later, partly as a result of making speculative loans encouraged by the Bank's overcapitalization.

Adoption of Unit Banking

The disappearance of the Bank of the United States committed the nation to a unit banking system. In contrast to the rest of the world, which adopted branch banking and developed a handful of giant banks, the United States encouraged the formation of thousands of small, independent banks, many of which were undercapitalized or improperly managed. Thus, while big branch banks are normally more profitable and efficient, small independent banks have survived under the umbrella of state antibranching statutes. Unit banking still predominates today in terms of numbers, but not in terms of total assets. Branch banking since World War II has grown rapidly.

STATE BANKS

The passing of the Second Bank of the United States left the nation with only the state banks. Some of these, especially in the New England area, were competently managed, but in many parts of the country banking conditions were shockingly bad. In an earlier period there had been an era of so-called "silk-stocking banking," during which banking was thought to be an occupation appropriate for distinguished, trained, and public-spirited gentlemen. Later banking came to be regarded as simply another business, open to anyone who could raise the necessary capital, and offering extraordinary profits if managed cleverly.

One characteristic of banking was readily understood from the beginning. When a bank fails, not just the owners lose money. The general public, finding its bank notes (or its bank deposits) are worthless, often loses far more than do the stockholders. To be sure, creditors of other bankrupt businesses often lose substantially, but there is this important distinction. No one is obliged to lend to a farmer or a merchant and presumably will not unless the lender has thoroughly investigated the borrower's credit standing. But when bank notes are the principal means of payment, the public is practically obliged to accept these bank debts and hope for the best.

From the outset it was recognized that somehow the public should be protected from the consequences of bank failures. For about 60 years no bank was permitted to begin operations until a special act of the state legislature had granted its charter. The purpose of this requirement was to prevent incompetent and dishonest men from organizing banks. Unfortunately, as might have been guessed, it soon encouraged bribery and corruption. Bank promoters knew very well that the cost of buying votes in the legislature could quickly be made up if—but only if—they got their charter allowing them legally to print all the money they wished. They could afford to be generous. If they were not, then someone else would get the coveted charter. The legislators also quickly became aware of this important fact of economic life. They often made out quite well when several groups were competing for the right to charter a bank in a good location.

Free Banking

In 1837 Michigan dropped the requirement of a special act of the legislature and ruled that the field of banking should be free to all. Shortly thereafter other states also adopted the so-called free banking legislation. Any person or group of persons was now permitted to organize a bank as long as they complied with certain provisions of the law. One of the most important provisions required banks to deposit specified collateral with a state official who would then issue them notes that they could sign and place in circulation. The mortgages, railroad bonds, state bonds, or similar collateral were supposed to insure that the notes would be secured at all times, regardless of the bank's success or failure. In theory, the public was to be protected at the same time that the field of bank operation was opened wide to all. Also, there were requirements relating to specie reserves and paid-in capital.

Free banking eliminated the evils associated with the special chartering of banks, but introduced new weaknesses. By facilitating entry into the field, it encouraged the formation of many new banks, often irresponsibly managed and operated primarily or only for the purpose of issuing notes.[6] Also, the legal provisions that were supposed to insure proper management were all too often evaded or ignored.

As has been repeatedly emphasized, the country's money supply was inadequate. There was so little specie that foreign coins were legal tender until the middle of the 19th century. The frontier especially was not very critical of the quality of money as long as it had money of some kind. In issuing a mass of paper money, much of which was of doubtful value, the bankers faced little opposition from the public except when banking crises and panics swept the nation, forcing nearly all banks to suspend specie payment. Most of the time the public was quite willing to tolerate the kind of banking with which it was provided. When action was threatened against the banks, they could often avoid it by announcing that they would call in all their loans.

Evasion of Capital Requirements

The banks ignored the paid-in capital requirements and brazenly flouted the reserve specie rules. Thus, it was discovered that two banks in North

---

[6]In New York, 76 new banks began operations in the 20 months following the passage of the free banking bill. Three years later only 46 were still in operation, and during the next two years 26 free banks failed.

Carolina that had issued more than $3 million of notes, lent at 6 percent, had never required their stockholders to pay specie for their stock as required by law. These banks were drawing around $200,000 annually from the community for supplying it with these practically worthless notes.

As was true in many other institutions, the stockholders had given their own promissory notes to pay for the stock in the new bank. In fact, they insisted that as stockholders they had a special right to borrow from the bank the amount necessary to pay for their stock. For the stockholders it was "heads we win, tails you lose." If the bank succeeded, the stock dividends were more than sufficient to pay the interest on the loan. If the bank failed, the bank's creditors had little real security, for the stockholders, with no desire to pay for a dead horse, made every effort to avoid repaying their loans. When the authorities attempted to halt this practice by allowing a bank to open only after the full amount of the capital had been paid in specie, the banks easily evaded the requirement by arranging with other banks to lend the new stockholders the required amount of specie. The stockholders would bring the specie to the new bank, pay for their stock, immediately borrow the specie, and return it to the first bank.

Note Redemption

The Georgia legislature permitted the state chartered bank in Darien to require all people presenting notes for redemption to sign a written oath that the notes belonged to them and that they were not, as agents, collecting them for anybody else. The bank saw it could improve on this. It required that the oath be signed in the presence of five bank directors, the cashier, and a justice of the peace, a collection of witnesses that would ordinarily be quite inconvenient if not impossible to assemble. In the South and West generally, anyone from out of town who brought notes to the bank and demanded specie redemption was considered a public nuisance and sometimes threatened with tar and feathers. Specie redemption was considered to be a legal technicality, something that a bank must promise to do but that it must make every effort to avoid doing.

If the banks had regularly and freely redeemed their notes, the banks would have been safer for two reasons. First, such redemption would have restrained them from overissue. Secondly, in order to redeem, the banks would have had to require their subscribers actually to pay in cash, as the law vainly attempted to prescribe.

The Michigan banking commissioners found, when they set out in 1838 on an inspection of the state's banks, that the banks kept track of the commissioners' movements and sent the stock of specie on ahead. At each bank the commissioners found an adequate stock of specie, which bank officers were ready to swear was the sole property of the bank. But at that time most of the specie was in the form of foreign coins, and any particular stock of specie was easily recognizable from the proportionate distribution of the many varieties of coins. After they had checked it a few times, the commissioners recognized that it was actually the same stock that they had already gone through several times in the banks they had just visited. On one occasion a box of specie was found to contain nails and glass, with a top layer of gold and silver. It is hardly surprising to find that 36 of the 40 free banks established in Michigan in 1837 failed within two years. In other states there were similar evasions, for the desire to enter banking was too frequently unaccompanied by the resources appropriate for such an undertaking.

A major cause of the period's banking evils was the confusion of security with redemption. Many believed that currency secured by pledged collateral should be safe—that is, should retain its value—whether or not it was regularly redeemed in specie. Banks, they argued, were performing a public service in converting stocks, bonds, and mortgages into the currency needed for commerce. People did not understand the fallacy of issuing money against the monetary value of the security with no check on overissue other than eventual disaster. Only repeated and bitter experiences taught them that an excess of money could cause a rise, not only in prices generally, but specifically in the prices of the real estate and securities used as note collateral. The rise in the money value of the collateral permitted the issuance of still more bank notes, which pushed prices still higher, until finally the inflated credit structure collapsed. There were no brakes to slow credit expansion to a gradual halt.

Wildcat Banking

During the state banking period the term *wildcat banking* came into use, describing banks established in the wilderness where there were more wildcats than settlers. The advantage of such location was that for notes to be redeemed they had to be brought to the bank, and by locating in remote parts of the country the bank could easily keep its notes in circulation. The notes did not need to be placed in circulation at that same location. On the contrary, a bank officer would use the notes to make loans in distant cities. Likewise, many Chicago banks issued notes through agent banks in the South.

NOTE SECURITY

The state bank notes did have security of a sort behind them, for they were backed by the stocks, bonds, or mortgages that the banker had pledged with the state banking authorities. However, the cushion of capital provided by the stockholders was so thin, if it existed at all, that the slightest decline in the value of the bank's assets reduced it to insolvency. The nation's banking structure was at all times in an extraordinarily delicate state of balance. The failure of a few banks and the sale of their assets tended to reduce the value of similar assets held as security behind the notes of other banks, and hence to reduce the other banks also to insolvency.

The Safety Fund System

In New York and New England, banks operated more conservatively than in most of the rest of the country. New York introduced a safety fund system similar to our modern deposit insurance system. The banks, all of which at the time were chartered by special act of the legislature, were required to establish a mutual safety or guarantee fund out of which the creditors of insolvent banks would be paid. The assessments were based on the banks' capital rather than on their liabilities, which would have been a more sound arrangement. Each bank paid in annually an amount equal to one half of 1 percent of its capital until it had paid in a total of 3 percent.

As originally set up in 1829, both noteholders and depositors of banks were protected. By 1842 it was evident that the fund was insufficient to provide such complete coverage, and it was amended to protect noteholders only. The reason for this preferred treatment for the noteholders was that they did not stand in as close relationship to the bank as did the depositors. Today the only bank notes we use are those issued by the Federal Reserve Banks, and we can take for granted that the notes are sound. At that time the public was constantly handling notes issued in many instances by unknown banks. For that matter, the condition of all the banks even in the immediate vicinity could hardly be known to the general public, especially the poorer people who had no direct dealings with banks but who through bank failures could lose what little they had. People maintaining checking accounts, however, would ordinarily need to investigate the reliability of their own banks. Depositors could more reasonably be expected to look out for themselves than could the noteholders.

If the chartering of banks had not become so tainted by political corruption, the safety fund system might possibly have been adopted elsewhere, contributing to the soundness of the banking structure. But it was an alternative means of providing security for noteholders; it applied to the notes of the specially chartered banks only. Note issues of the rapidly multiplying free banks were supposedly made safe by the pledge of specific securities. No attempt was made to apply the safety fund system to note issues of the free banks, and the safety fund system disappeared when the last of the special bank charters expired in 1866.

The Suffolk System

An innovation in New England banking was the result of private rather than public regulation. The banks outside Boston in the early 19th century were often located as inaccessibly as possible, just as, later in the century, wildcat banks were organized in the frontier territories. Some banks even exchanged notes with each other, each bank lending the notes of the other, located at some distance, and each thus minimizing the redemption problem. As an apparent accommodation to their customers, and incidentally in an unsuccessful attempt to reduce the note circulation of the out-of-town banks, the Boston banks presently offered to accept country bank notes and redeem them, charging the noteholder the redemption cost. These costs averaged one half of 1 percent on notes of Massachusetts banks and from 1 to 5 percent on those of other New England banks.

Thus, country bank notes were accepted by the Boston banks only at a discount, whereas notes of the Boston banks were accepted at par. Meanwhile the country banks continued to place their notes in circulation in Boston by making loans in that area. Since merchants were willing to accept the country bank notes at par, although the Boston banks did not, these notes remained in circulation. Anyone in Boston wishing to hold specie or bank deposits presented the notes of the Boston banks, which due to this operation of Gresham's Law found it difficult to keep their notes in circulation. Although the Boston banks held more than half the banking capital of New England, their notes were only one twenty-fifth of the total New England issue.

To facilitate the circulation of their own notes and incidentally to bring all the New England bank notes up to par in Boston, in 1818 the Suffolk Bank of Boston announced a plan whereby the note redemption cost was to be borne by the issuing banks instead of by the noteholders. In essence, country banks were invited to utilize the Suffolk Bank as a Boston redemption agency. To compensate the Suffolk for redeeming their notes, the country banks were to keep a deposit of $5,000 in the Suffolk Bank. The earnings from the assets deposited would cover the administrative expenses of the Suffolk's redemption department. In addition, the country banks were to keep such further deposits with the Suffolk as might be necessary to redeem their notes.

Understandably, the country banks were hostile to the plan. They had no desire to make the redemption of their notes easier and felt that the Suffolk's proposal, if put into effect, would certainly reduce their profits. Lacking their cooperation, the Suffolk Bank began collecting their notes and presenting them for redemption in specie. On some occasions, when the Suffolk Bank held a large volume of its notes, a country bank could be forced into bankruptcy if obliged to redeem immediately such a large fraction of its total issue. The majority of the country banks were gradually forced into the Suffolk System, and the other banks in Boston cooperated with the Suffolk Bank in enforcing the program. The result was that New England was provided with an elastic currency, for the ease of redemption prevented notes from remaining in circulation when there was no longer any demand for them. The currency was also uniform, since the notes of all the banks in the System circulated at par.

Currency Outside New York and New England

In other parts of the country the currency was all too easily expanded but difficult to contract. With no safety fund to guarantee the notes and no clearinghouse such as the Suffolk Bank, the notes outside New England and New York frequently circulated at discounts that increased with the distance from the redemption point. And as a result of the multitude of designs of bank notes, counterfeiting became widespread. In some instances the notes of sound banks were counterfeited; in other instances denominations were raised; and at times notes were printed for nonexistent banks. Also, notes of banks that had failed often remained in circulation. The difficulty of distinguishing genuine notes from counterfeit was enormously increased by the lack of standardization as well as by the fact that notes tended to remain in circulation so long that they became worn, torn, and almost illegible. Bulletins were periodically issued listing worthless notes, both those of banks that had failed and those that were counterfeit. A *Counterfeit Detector* of 1839 lists 1,395 issues of altered or counterfeit notes in circulation at the time. More than 5,000 of such notes were described in a *Bank Note Reporter* in 1859.

Such was the state of banking and currency at the outbreak of the Civil War. By 1861 there were 1,601 state banks holding a total of $257 million of deposits and with $202 million of notes in circulation, issued according to one or another of four different principles. Some of these notes were secured by general assets, as in the case of the New England banks; some were secured by collateral pledged with a state official, as in the case of the free banks. In New York the notes of the specially chartered banks were secured by the safety fund. Also, some notes were secured by state credit, for, although the Constitution forbids the states to issue paper money directly, the Supreme Court ruled that states could own note-issuing banks.[7]

THE INDEPENDENT TREASURY SYSTEM

The Treasury, along with the public, had frequently sustained losses through bank failures when it was obliged to rely on the state banks. Finally, Congress ruled that the Treasury would accept only coin.[8] Henceforth, all payments due the government were to be made in specie, which the Treasury held in its own and subtreasury vaults. This policy subjected the banking system to new strains, for on tax collection dates the banks found their specie reserves being drained off to be locked up in the Treasury. As the government later spent the money, the banks found their reserves again restored, regardless of whether there was then a demand for credit. To alleviate the pressure upon the banks, the Treasury later, after the organization of the national banks, began to carry its balances with these institutions so that the specie would remain at all times in the banking system.[9] The Independent Treasury System was finally discontinued in 1920, when the 12 Federal Reserve Banks, organized in 1913, proved to be capable and efficient fiscal agents of the government. Still more recently the Treasury has followed the policy of carrying large balances with insured banks and drawing on them through the Federal Reserve.[10]

---

[7]In Ohio, Indiana, Louisiana, Virginia, and Missouri these state-owned banks were quite successful. Elsewhere the results were disastrous.

[8]In 1840; repealed in 1842; passed again, 1846.

[9]These deposits were of two varieties: (1) regular deposits, on which no interest was paid, that were maintained for the convenience of the government where no subtreasury office was located; and (2) special deposits, on which at least 1 percent was paid, that were made for the purpose of returning funds to the banking system.

[10]See Tax and Loan Accounts, Chapter 12.

THE NATIONAL BANKING SYSTEM

The first national bank was opened June 20, 1863, in Philadelphia, as authorized by legislation passed that year. The original National Currency Act proved unsatisfactory in some particulars and was replaced by the Act of June 3, 1864, commonly known as the National Banking Act, and by related legislation through 1866.

The national banks must be clearly distinguished from the Banks of the United States that we have previously surveyed. They were not, like those two earlier institutions, to do a nationwide branch banking business. Rather, they were essentially the same as the free banks that had been chartered under state laws except that they received their charters from the federal government and secured their currency by the pledge of securities only of the United States government.

Two principal reasons were urged for the establishment of national banks: (1) to provide sounder banks and a safe and uniform currency, and (2) to provide a source of loans to the federal government, borrowing heavily to carry on the Civil War. Also, government leaders may have hoped that the establishment of national banks might help to hold wavering states in line, under the threat that the security for the bank note issues of seceding states would be seized by the government, throwing such states into immediate financial difficulties.

Earlier we have noted the issue of greenbacks as a result of the government's reluctance to tax. In 1861 Secretary Chase lightheartedly recommended that the entire war expenditures for the year be borrowed. Although Congress provided more adequate tax revenues than Chase recommended, the Treasury still found it necessary to borrow large sums and realized that bond sales could be greatly facilitated by requiring the (national) banks to deposit as security for their note issues the bonds of the federal government only.

The national banks were organized too late to have much effect on the government's borrowing program, providing less than 4 percent of the funds borrowed to finance the war. But they did greatly improve the status of American banking and they provided the country with its first safe and uniform bank currency since 1833.

The Act provided that any group of at least five persons might establish a national bank or that existing state banks might become national banks as long as they complied with specified requirements, the most important of which concerned capital, note circulation, and reserves. There were also restrictions on the types of loans that they might make, and they were subject to the control of a newly created administrative officer, the Comptroller of the Currency.

Capital Requirements

The capital requirements fixed then are the same today. Banks in cities of 50,000 and over are required to have a minimum capital of $200,000. In towns of from 6,000 to 50,000, $100,000 capital is required; in towns of less than

6,000, at least $50,000.[11] These figures seem low when compared to the capital of many of the state banks, but the important difference is that the national bank cannot begin operations until at least 50 percent of the capital has been paid in, the remainder to be paid up within the first five months of operation or the shares surrendered and sold to others. The stock originally carried double liability, so that in the event of the bank's failure the stockholders could be called upon to contribute an additional amount equal to the par value of the stock for which they had already paid.[12] Not less than one third of the capital and in any case at least $30,000 was to be invested in government bonds.[13]

Note Circulation

The bonds were to be deposited with the Comptroller of the Currency, who would in return issue notes imprinted with the name of the bank to the amount of 90 percent of the par value of the bonds or 90 percent of their market value, whichever was lower. This feature of the law, requiring that the notes be secured by government bonds rather than by general assets, guaranty fund, or state credit, was copied from the free banking laws except for the provision that federal government bonds only were eligible note security.[14]

In addition to the bonds, the banks were required to keep on deposit with the Comptroller of the Currency a redemption fund amounting to 5 percent of their note circulation. Since the government was at the time on a greenback standard, the banks were permitted to redeem in greenbacks. As a result, redemption was seldom demanded, for the ultimate security behind either the bank note or the United States note was the same. No national bank could issue notes in excess of its capital, and each was to receive at par the notes of all other national banks. The notes were subject to a circulation tax of 1 percent per year when secured by bonds carrying a rate higher than 2 percent, otherwise to a tax of one half of 1 percent, in either case recapturing for the Treasury a portion of the interest it paid to the banks.

Reserves

The percentage of reserves required against deposits was determined by the location of the bank. Banks in the central reserve cities, New York, Chicago, and at one time St. Louis, were required to maintain vault cash reserves

---

[11]Reduced to $25,000 between 1900 and 1933, then restored to $50,000.

[12]This provision was designed not only to provide additional assets out of which the bank's creditors might be paid, but to encourage stockholders to insist upon conservative bank management. It was dropped during the 1930s, when the Federal Deposit Insurance Corporation was organized.

[13]No longer required after 1900.

[14]The record of American banking is marked by considerable veering back and forth between bond security and general asset security for notes. Notes of the New England banks were secured by general assets, notes of the free banks and national banks by bonds. When the Federal Reserve was organized, notes could be secured by discounted paper but not by bonds. As a result of later legislation, more than 95 percent of the credit behind Federal Reserve notes today is government obligations.

amounting to at least 25 percent of their total notes and deposits.[15] Banks in certain cities of 500,000 or more inhabitants, specified as reserve cities, were also required to maintain 25 percent reserves against their liabilities, but half of these reserves might be in the form of a deposit with a central reserve city bank. Elsewhere, reserves of 15 percent were required, three fifths of which might consist of deposits in reserve city banks. If a bank's legal reserves dropped below the statutory minimum percentage, the bank was forbidden to make further loans or to pay dividends until reserves were at a satisfactory level. If a bank's reserves remained deficient for more than a month, the Comptroller of the Currency might force its liquidation.

Restrictions and Control

National banks were forbidden to make real estate loans or to lend to any one borrower an amount in excess of 10 percent of their capital. They were prohibited from withdrawing any of their capital in dividends. They were subject to examination and were required to make periodic reports of their condition. Any impairment of capital due to losses was to be corrected within three months by additional capital subscription.

The existing state banks had been expected to promptly apply for national charters. However, most state banks preferred to be governed by the looser regulations of the state banking authorities. To induce them to join the national bank system, their notes were subjected to an annual tax of 10 percent, beginning July 1, 1866. Results were not entirely as expected. The state bank notes were rather quickly driven from circulation, improving the standard of the nation's currency. But the state banks continued to operate, finding that the growth of deposit banking made note issue no longer the great advantage that it once had been.

Even for the national banks the note issue privilege was not a tremendous advantage, for they could issue notes only to the amount of their capital. The state banks had been able to continue issuing more notes as long as by one means or another they could keep them in circulation (except that in a few states the banks were not allowed to issue notes in excess of some multiple of their capital). Hence their notes, secured by general assets, might amount to a great deal more than their capital, and their earnings would reflect the additional assets acquired through the large note issues. The state banks found, after the tax on their note issues, that only through demand deposits could they lend anything more than the amount of their capital. The national banks similarly found that through deposit banking they could increase their lending activities far more than through note issue, since there was no required capital-deposit ratio.

Advantages

The organization of the national banks constituted a great step forward. The hodgepodge of state bank notes, some good, most discounted, and some

---

[15]The reserve requirement was amended in 1874 to apply to deposits only.

worthless, was replaced with a uniform and safe currency. Although depositors might still suffer losses from bank failures, noteholders were amply protected. Also, the more conservative banking standards imposed by national regulation and examination lessened bank failures. Furthermore, a measure of correspondent banking was introduced by the provision relating to the redeposit of reserves in the reserve city and central reserve city banks. Banks found it somewhat easier to make distant collections through the system of correspondent banks. Also, country banks with surplus funds found that they could readily place them in the financial centers through their correspondent banks with which they regularly carried reserves.

Limitation—Difficulty of Collecting Checks

At the same time there were serious shortcomings. The national banks were a system in name only. There was no centralization, no unification nor coordination. Except as noted above, there was not even provision for the collection and clearing of checks. As deposit banking replaced note circulation, this lack became steadily more costly. Remember, a check is not, in itself, money. It is an order, signed by a depositor, instructing the bank to pay a certain sum either to "cash" (or "bearer") or to the order of a designated payee. If the payee comes to the bank and presents the check for payment, the bank is obligated to pay the face amount of the check. But few checks are collected in this manner. Ordinarily the payees deposit the checks in their own banks for collection. Their banks enter that amount to the payees' credit but usually deny them the right to draw against the checks until the funds have been collected, for at the moment the banks have received no money, only items for collection.

Before the organization of the Federal Reserve, if a national bank (or state bank) mailed checks directly to the banks against which they were drawn, the latter might refuse to remit at par and might deduct an exchange charge that varied from one tenth to one fourth of 1 percent. They justified charging an exchange fee on two grounds. First, since the bank, not the payee, submitted the check, the paying banks maintained that they were acting as agents of the collecting banks and were thus entitled to compensation.

Second, the paying banks also claimed that the cost of transmitting the funds should not fall upon them, for it was not their concern that the payees found it inconvenient to come to them for payment. If the payees wished the bank to transfer to them $1,000 of the deposit of one of the bank's customers, the bank had the right to deduct a dollar or two or cover the cost of sending them the money. This cost might be represented by the packaging, shipping, and insurance charges involved in shipping currency. More likely, however, payment would be made by sending to the collecting bank a draft on another bank, usually in a large city, acceptable to the collecting bank. A bank in Georgia, for example, might keep an account with a correspondent bank in Chicago. When the out-of-town banks presented checks for payment, the Georgia bank might make payment in the form of drafts (checks) against its account in Chicago. If the collecting banks also held accounts with Chicago banks, they could deposit these drafts with them and thus increase their assets at the same time that they increased their liabilities by crediting their customers' accounts.

However, to maintain these out-of-town balances involved certain costs for the banks. They might establish and maintain such an account by several means—by shipping currency, by discounting paper with their correspondent, by borrowing from the correspondent bank, by selling securities to the correspondent, or by sending it items for collection, the proceeds to be retained by the correspondent. However they handled it, there would be some administration costs.

Roundabout Collection to Avoid Exchange Charges. The collecting bank did not want to absorb the exchange charges except, perhaps, for a few customers who held unusually large accounts with them. Neither did they wish their customers to be forced to bear the cost, for the customers might conclude that the bank was not serving them satisfactorily and transfer their accounts elsewhere. Hence, the collecting banks went to considerable effort to try to collect at par, which required usually that the checks be forwarded to correspondent banks in the neighborhood of the drawee bank. If, for example, a bank in Memphis received a check drawn on a bank in Seattle, the Memphis bank might pass the check along to a correspondent in, perhaps, Atlanta. The Atlanta bank might forward the item to its correspondent in New York, from which it might go to a bank in Chicago which would forward it, perhaps, to San Francisco. Ultimately it would be presented, perhaps by another Seattle bank, to the Seattle bank on which it was drawn, and the transaction would be completed.

An additional reason for collecting through correspondent banks was that the courts held the drawee bank to be an unsuitable agent for the collecting bank, since the drawee bank would be collecting a claim against itself. Consequently, a bank that mailed checks directly to the banks against which they were drawn might suffer substantial losses if any difficulty arose, because depositors could claim that their bank had been negligent in its choice of agent.

The slower the collection process, the greater the cost to the depositor, implicitly or explicitly. Suppose that by roundabout routing a bank did succeed in collecting a check at par—eventually. What was its customer supposed to use for money while waiting a week or two for the check to be collected? Banks in the major cities usually required that out-of-town checks be actually collected before their customers start drawing against them. If they permitted depositors to treat such items as immediate credits to their accounts and draw checks against them at once, the banks were really making interest-free loans since, for a week or more, they themselves were holding only collection items, not money. Even if merchants received their customers' checks a few days after they had shipped the goods, they might wait weeks until the checks were collected and they could draw against them. The result was about the same as if the merchants were selling for credit. They had to wait for their money. So they had to do one of two things:

1. They might keep a large amount of working capital on hand. This was expensive, since otherwise the merchants might have used these funds to expand their business or to increase their income in other ways.
2. They might borrow from their bank, repaying their loans as checks were collected and credited to their account. The interest on loans of this kind was at one time a considerable expense to merchants.

Shifting Exchange Costs to the Buyer. The sellers could avoid this loss by requiring in advance that payment be made in New York funds or Chicago funds. On these terms the buyers had to purchase New York or Chicago funds from their local bank, which might charge them $1 or $2 per thousand dollars in the same manner in which it handled foreign exchange. The bank claimed that the exchange fee, like the right to remit at less than par, was justified by the costs it incurred in maintaining a balance elsewhere.

Anyway, whether the buyer paid the domestic exchange costs or the seller bore the costs involved in collection delays and sometimes nonpar remittance, the burden of this inefficient collection system was primarily upon business, not upon the banks. It caused the banks' operating expenses to be unnecessarily high, however, due to all the paperwork involved in shuffling the checks from one bank to another.

Slow Collection and Fictitious Reserves. A country bank was to some extent compensated for its work by the fictitious reserves that appeared while the checks were "afloat in the mail." It could count as part of its legal reserve not only the balance it held with its reserve city correspondent, but also collection items it sent to that correspondent. If a bank in Athens, Georgia, sent to the Chase National Bank of New York a check for $1,000 drawn on a bank in New Orleans, the Athens bank was immmediately credited with $1,000 of reserves. Yet it might be weeks before collection was made from the New Orleans bank. Meanwhile there were $1,000 of phantom reserves. For weeks both the New Orleans bank and the Athens bank would be claiming ownership of $1,000 that, in fact, could have belonged to either one but not to both at the same time. Although this double counting of reserves was temporarily advantageous for the individual bank, it increased the instability of the banking system.

Limitation—Unsatisfactory Nature of Reserves

The second basic weakness of the national banking system was the unsatisfactory system of reserves, which regularly broke down in times of strain. This weakness resulted partly from the fictitious reserves, but even more from the practice of holding some reserves in the form of balances with other banks. As long as times were good and business and credit were still expanding, the partial pooling of reserves permitted a greater credit expansion than would otherwise have been possible. Obviously if cash reserves of 25 percent are required and the banking system holds $100 million of vault cash, it may hold $400 million of liabilities.

But now (slightly simplifying the national banks' requirements) suppose that one half the reserves of both reserve city and country banks were permitted to be in the form of deposits with their correspondent banks in the cities. The system could have held more than $400 million of liabilities, the exact amount depending upon how the currency was distributed and also upon how the country banks (and reserve city banks) acquired deposits with their city correspondents. Whether country banks established reserve city balances by shipping currency or by borrowing from their correspondents, total reserves of the system were increased. Yet each bank individually considered itself fully as liquid as before. Each regarded the deposit that it held with another bank as the equivalent of cash and convertible into cash at any time.

As we study the reserve structure of the system, however, we see the fallacy. The individual bank's assumption that its city balances were readily convertible into cash was justified only as long as there was no general demand for cash. There is no escaping this simple, basic fact. There was still just $100 million of actual currency, no matter how it was distributed and in spite of the fact that deposits were considerably greater than when vault cash was the only legal reserve.

Inability to Expand Reserves. Also, this currency set a limit on the possible total of reserves. The total might vary somewhat, depending upon how the currency was distributed and how the "deposit reserves" were created. But once the total was attained, there was no way in which additional reserves could be provided. At such times money became tight, and banks everywhere tried to increase their reserves. In the first place, increased reserves would permit them to extend more credit to their customers; and in the second place, increased reserves would permit them to take care of any demand of their depositors for more currency. But although the banks might be able to gain reserves from one another, they could not possibly all increase their reserves at once if credit had already been expanded to the limit. At such times there was just a general scramble for the reserves already existing. The system as a whole held no more reserves than it had before.

Currency Drains and Reserves. Worse yet, currency movements depleted reserves at the very time when the banks were fighting to gain reserves. In prosperity, there were more cash transactions as well as more credit transactions, and a greater amount of currency was needed for hand-to-hand circulation. The public drew the currency from the banks, where much of it had been serving as legal reserves. Also, to meet customer demands for currency, the country banks withdrew currency from the reserve city banks and the latter withdrew it from the central reserve city banks. Even if the public did not actually demand cash as their banks expected them to do, the mere expectation of a currency demand was enough to upset the financial equilibrium. It decreased reserves by reducing the balances that banks carried with their city correspondents.

To sum it up, in prosperity the currency drain from the banks to the public directly decreased reserves; the currency drain from city banks to country banks indirectly decreased reserves at the same time. At the very time the system needed added reserves, it lost reserves.

This defect might not have been too important except that the banks usually followed the policy of being completely loaned up, so there was little margin to meet emergency requirements. The city banks were competing actively for the deposits of the country banks, on which at times they were paying interest as high as 4 percent. To cover their expenses they had to reduce their nonearning assets (of which their legal reserves were most important) to the legal minimum. Also, they tried to keep their loan portfolio as liquid as possible. Many of their loans were to brokers. Since these loans were secured by listed stocks, for which there was ordinarily a continuous market, and since they could be called by the bank at any time, the city banks felt they were maintaining a properly liquid position. If one or two city banks wished to gain reserves, they could easily do so by calling some of their loans. The brokers would borrow elsewhere and settle with the banks demanding payment.

But when all the banks were calling loans and none were making them, brokers had to call their own loans. Their customers were forced to sell their securities to repay the loans. A fall in security values was the result, for everyone was selling and few had the money to buy. Also, despite the sometimes violent pressure on the securities market, there could be no increase in reserves from this churning around of accounts. The most that could be accomplished would be a reduction in loans and deposits. Such reductions would reduce the amount of reserves required by about 25 percent of the decline in deposits and would be accompanied, perhaps, by a panic, touched off by a stock market collapse. Such panics occurred in 1873, 1884, 1893, and 1907 and threatened on other occasions.

Limitation—Unsatisfactory Nature of Notes

A third major weakness was the unsatisfactory nature of bank notes. They were safe, and that was a great improvement over the state bank notes. But they were inelastic, responding to the price of government bonds rather than to the needs of trade.

Seasonal Inelasticity. A nation's currency should be capable of expansion to meet seasonal and cyclical needs. Every year the amount of currency in circulation increases in December as people withdraw currency for Christmas spending. Generally the currency in circulation declines in January as spending patterns return to normal.[16] Under the operation of the national banking system the country banks met these demands for added currency by withdrawing their deposits from the reserve city banks, promoting seasonal monetary stringencies every fall in the cities and encouraging easy money conditions there in the spring and summer. Every dollar of cash the country banks

---

[16]Similarly, currency in circulation tends to increase in the fall when farmers are harvesting their crops. This movement was more pronounced 50 years or so ago when fewer farmers carried checking accounts and agriculture constituted a larger proportion of our total economy than today.

withdrew tended to force the city banks to reduce their earning assets by an added $3. In Canada, however, total bank notes regularly increased in the fall and decreased in the spring, avoiding the necessity for a periodic redistribution of bank reserves. Such a policy was impractical under the national banking system. The individual bank simply had no incentive to increase and decrease its note issue during the year. If a bank did find its stock of vault cash regularly too large at certain times of the year, it would send the cash to a city correspondent and draw interest on the deposit. This practice was much more profitable than expanding and contracting the issue of its own notes, a creakingly slow operation at best with the bond-secured currency. Seasonally, therefore, the note issue remained relatively constant.

Perverse Cyclical Elasticity. Cyclically, the total volume of notes outstanding tended to vary inversely with the level of business activity. Instead of expanding in prosperity, the national bank notes tended to decline. This troublesome *perverse cyclical elasticity* resulted from the fact that the profitability of note issue depended upon the price of government bonds, which rose in prosperity, when Treasury surpluses were used to retire bonds. The competition of banks and other investors for the gilt-edged security represented by government bonds drove up their price. As a result, when times were good and Treasury revenues substantial, the price of 4 percent bonds rose as high as $1,280. These bonds had around 18 years to run. Although the bank was drawing $40 a year in interest from the government and could, in addition, lend $900 of notes issued against the bond as security, many banks found it advantageous to sell their bonds.[17]

Likewise, when bond prices fell in depression, with the government no longer actively supporting the market, the banks might find it profitable to buy bonds again and reissue notes, regardless of whether added currency was required at such a time. As long as the price of government bonds determined the note issue, the country could not expect to have a currency that would expand and contract in accord with the cyclical needs of trade.

Limitation—Unsatisfactory Relations with the Treasury

Finally, the national banking system provided inadequate banking machinery for the federal government. Although the Independent Treasury System was still in effect, the Treasury was permitted to keep funds with certain

---

[17]If the bank lent the $900 at, say, 5 percent, its total receipts were $40 (from bonds) plus $45 (from loans), or $85. This $85 was reduced to $75, however, by a tax of 1 percent on the bonds securing its note issue. More importantly, the bank could get a $280 premium if it sold the bond. If it held the bond 18 years until maturity, it received only the par value of the bond. It sacrificed $280 by retaining the bonds. This amounted to a yearly charge of more than $15. The bank's net receipts yearly from the double lending would be $85 less $10 tax less $15 yearly depreciation in the value of the bond itself, or about $60. If instead the bank were to sell the bond for $1,280 and lend that amount at 5 percent, its receipts would be around $64. Even in 1907, by which time banks were allowed to issue notes up to the full value of the bonds instead of 90 percent as formerly, the bank's profit on note issue, after deducting all expenses, was only 1 percent greater than what it could get by selling the bonds and investing the proceeds at 6 percent. It was hardly worthwhile to trouble with issuing $100,000 of currency to gain an added $50 or $60 of income.

national banks that qualified as depositaries of government funds. By 1914 the Treasury was keeping part of its funds in the vaults of the Treasury and nine subtreasuries and part in 1,584 national banks. The exact amount of funds to be held by any bank and by the banks in general was subject to the Secretary of the Treasury's discretion. The banking system was regularly in trouble when large sums were transferred to the Treasury vaults, draining the banks of their reserves. At other times, especially when the Treasury's expenditures exceeded its receipts, the banks were flooded with reserves. The alternating scarcity and abundance of reserves frequently led to sharp changes in call loan rates and considerable fluctuations in the stock market. In addition, since the Treasury could frequently relieve the pressure by transferring funds to the banks, the banks came to depend largely on the Treasury to rescue them when they found themselves overextended. A sound banking system should be able to take care of itself without appealing to the Treasury for help.

Reform

Growing dissatisfaction with the national banking system crystallized in the determination to institute major banking reforms. A system that permitted a banking panic every decade was intolerable. Banking principles evolved from a predominantly agricultural economy were found quite unsuited to the needs of our rapidly growing industry and commerce. From time to time various proposals were made for the establishment of a central bank, for improved check collection, for a more elastic currency based on commercial paper, and for a more efficient method of pooling reserves. The panic of 1907 brought matters to a head. The Aldrich-Vreeland Act of 1908 authorized the banks to issue emergency currency, subject to a tax to encourage its retirement as soon as the emergency was past. The Act also called for the organization of a monetary commission to investigate and recommend further legislation. This commission's work produced the passage on December 23, 1913, of the Glass-Owen Bill, better known as the Federal Reserve Act.

Result

The unintended result of the National Currency Act of 1863 and its related legislation in 1864 to 1866 was to make the American banking system a "dual" system in which both federal and state chartering (and supervising) of commercial banks coexist. This dual system, which is unique to the United States, has worked fairly well although the membership in the Federal Reserve System has been dropping in recent years. The legislation intended to drive out state-chartered banks with a stiff tax on their bank note issues. But state banks increasingly turned to demand deposits in place of currency and flourished.

Table 8-1 shows the structure of banking in the United States as of December 31, 1974. Most banks are state chartered, but the federally chartered banks (supervised by the Comptroller of Currency in the U.S. Treasury) are generally larger. In fact, about two thirds of all commercial banks are state banks. Table 8-1 also shows that the majority of banks are not members of the Federal Reserve System, although most are insured. While the Federal Reserve System has never had as many as one quarter of the state banks as members, the membership has been dropping in recent years and now stands at about 11 percent of all state banks. Table 8-1 also shows that only about 35 percent of the commercial banks maintain branches or additional offices.

One relevant aspect of the banking structure not shown in Table 8-1 is the wide range of fluctuations in the number of banks in the last 75 years. The number of banks peaked in the late 1920s at about 29,000, up from about 9,000 in 1900, only to retreat to about 14,000 in 1940. The figure has remained rather close to 14,000 since 1940.

Table 8-1   **Structure of Commercial Banking**
December 31, 1974

	Number of Banks	Percentage
All Commercial Banks	14,457	100.0%
National Banks	4,710	32.6
State Banks	9,747	67.4
State Banks with Federal Reserve Membership	1,072	11.0
State Banks without Federal Reserve Membership	8,675	89.0
Federal Reserve Member Banks	5,782	40.0
Nonmember Banks	8,675	60.0
FDIC Insured Banks	14,220	98.4
Noninsured Banks	237	1.6
Commercial Banks Maintaining Branches or Additional Offices	5,123	35.4

Source: *Federal Reserve Bulletin* (April, 1975), p. A76.

SUMMARY AND CONCLUSION

The banking system that developed in the United States is unlike that of any other country. We have thousands of individual banks; most other countries have only a handful of banks, each with many branches. However, in the post-World War II period branch banking has grown rapidly in the United States. American banking is also unique in that it is a "dual" system in which there are both federal and state chartering and supervision of banks.

Branch banking is likely to be safer banking. The pages of the financial history of the United States are blotted with thousands upon thousands of bank failures, a record not approached by that of any other country. Unfortunately banking became a political issue in this country, and politicians pulled down the successfully developing Bank of the United States.

For several decades, during the period of the state banks, banking in the United States was the poorest in the civilized world. One of its worst features was the lack of a safe, uniform currency.

To be sure, in the earlier settled, more conservative, and usually creditor area from New York to New England, sounder banking and safer currency prevailed. In Massachusetts, the Suffolk System kept bank notes circulating at par. In New York, the Safety Fund System once protected bank notes. Later, with the change to free banking, an attempt was made to protect noteholders by requiring the banks to pledge specific assets against their notes.

But the frontier, generally, a debtor area, was much less eager for sound money and a stable price level. Nineteenth century bankers and legislators generally believed that as long as bank notes were specifically secured, redemption was unnecessary if not actually contrary to the public interest. Certainly the fewer of its notes presented for redemption, the more notes the bank could issue and, of course, the more interest it could draw from the public. It is not hard to see why wildcat banking developed and why various ingenious dodges and devices were worked out to minimize the number of notes a bank would redeem.

The national bank ''system'' did provide a currency that circulated at par and that involved no loss for the noteholder, even if the bank failed. It also improved somewhat the regulation of banking and encouraged more interbank relationships. But, the system:

1. still failed to provide an adequate organization for check collection;
2. failed to come to grips with the basic problem of reserves, namely, the impossibility of supplying new reserves when needed if the entire banking system is at all times fully loaned up to maximize profits;
3. failed to provide a currency that would expand and contract with the needs of trade; and
4. was too often and too easily upset by Treasury operations.

The economy staggered from one financial crisis to another until finally, just before World War I, the Federal Reserve Act was passed to plug some of the holes and gaps in our banking structure.

Discussion Questions

1. Why did unit banking develop in this country instead of branch banking which developed in Great Britain and most European nations?
2. Briefly summarize the advantages of nationwide branch banking. Why was it unpopular in this country, especially in the South and West?
3. How is a major function of capital largely nullified when a bank's organizers are permitted to borrow from the bank the money to pay for their shares of bank stock?
4. In trying to prevent the redemption of their bank notes, perhaps the early bankers in this country had the right idea but were ahead of their time. Comment on this statement.
5. Can you suggest any reasons why more than a century elapsed between the establishment of the Safety Fund System and the establishment of the Federal Deposit Insurance Corporation?

6. The fact that national bank notes were secured by government bonds was at the same time an advantage and a disadvantage. Why?
7. Was the Independent Treasury System in accordance with or in conflict with the public interest? Briefly explain.
8. By what regulations were the national bank notes made a safe currency, circulating at par everywhere in the country? Could the same regulations have been applied just as well to the state banks years earlier?
9. Why was the development of the national banking system expected to create a market for Treasury securities, and why was this eventually unimportant?
10. How did the organization of the national banking system encourage the growth of demand deposits?
11. What were the three great weaknesses of the banking system around 1900? Why was it believed they could be overcome by the organization of some kind of central bank?
12. If deposits in some banks are to be counted as legal reserves of other banks, it is imperative that the first banks do not attempt to maximize their profits. Explain.
13. The less money there is in circulation, the harder it becomes for most firms to borrow money, but the easier it is for banks to borrow, in effect, from the public. Explain.
14. Assuming the government decides to require a reserve against bank liabilities, there is a world of difference between requiring that behind every $100 there must be an ounce of gold and requiring that behind every $100 there must be, for example, $35 of marketable securities. Explain, including a brief discussion of the bank notes of the mid-nineteenth century.
15. What was an unintended result of the various national banking acts from 1863 to 1866?
16. Which are more important today, state banks or federal banks? Why?
17. Are most banks today members of the Federal Reserve? What percentage of the state banks are members? Are they insured?
18. "There are more commercial banks in the United States now than ever before in our history." True or false? Explain.

Chapter 9

The Federal Reserve: Structure and Routine Operations

By 1913 American bankers had been lending money for over a hundred years. Now, finally, with the creation of the Federal Reserve System, they had a bank of their own from which they could borrow. Previously they often borrowed from each other, as they still do. This works very well when some banks are in a position to lend. But when credit is tight everywhere and nearly all banks need funds, they obviously cannot supply each other's requirements. At such times they need a separate institution, a bankers' bank, lending only to banks and—like the banks themselves—able to create the money that it supplies. Thus, when the banking system as a whole needs more reserves, a central bank can supply them, and the banks can avoid the multiple credit contractions they found necessary so often in pre-Federal Reserve days. The United States was one of the last major powers to establish a central bank, trailing Sweden by almost 260 years and England by almost 220 years. Moreover, not until many years after the establishment of the Fed did the American people want their central bank to monitor and regulate their monetary and credit conditions continuously and systematically.

The Federal Reserve System was organized to supply reserves when needed and help control bank credit. It occupies a distinctive position in our economic structure because, although privately owned, it is operated not for profit but in accordance with the public interest. The System is composed of 12 Federal Reserve Banks, each controlled by its own board of directors; the Federal Reserve Board of Governors, to which the banks are responsible; a number of special committees; and approximately 5,800 member banks. Figure 9-1 indicates the boundaries of the Federal Reserve districts and their branch territories, and Figure 9-2 depicts the organizational structure of the Federal Reserve System.

THE FEDERAL RESERVE BANKS

The 12 Federal Reserve Banks are central banks, similar to the central banks in other countries. No reserves are required against their deposits. They do not hold deposits of the general public, nor do they ordinarily lend directly except to banks. Recognizing the antagonism that twice prevented the permanent establishment of the Bank of the United States, the creators of the

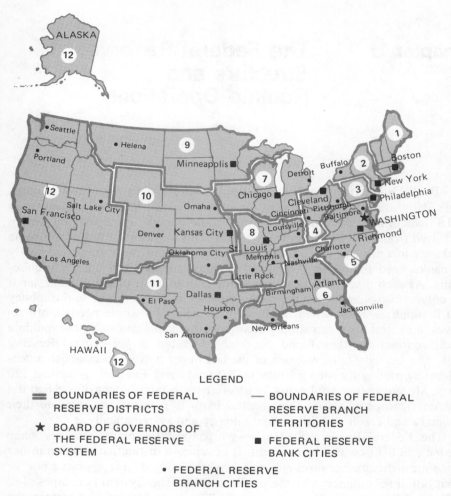

LEGEND

══ BOUNDARIES OF FEDERAL RESERVE DISTRICTS

★ BOARD OF GOVERNORS OF THE FEDERAL RESERVE SYSTEM

• FEDERAL RESERVE BRANCH CITIES

─ BOUNDARIES OF FEDERAL RESERVE BRANCH TERRITORIES

■ FEDERAL RESERVE BANK CITIES

Source: *Federal Reserve Bulletin.*

Figure 9-1   The Federal Reserve System

Federal Reserve made no attempt to set up again a great branch banking system. The Federal Reserve Banks were to cooperate, rather than compete, with the thousands of existing banks.

Regional Organization

In other countries the central bank is a single institution rather than a number of banks. That arrangement appeared politically inappropriate for this country. Mindful of the opposition to a "monopolistic" bank and of the criticism that the Bank of the United States was more concerned with Wall Street than with Main Street, the legislators settled for the political compromise of

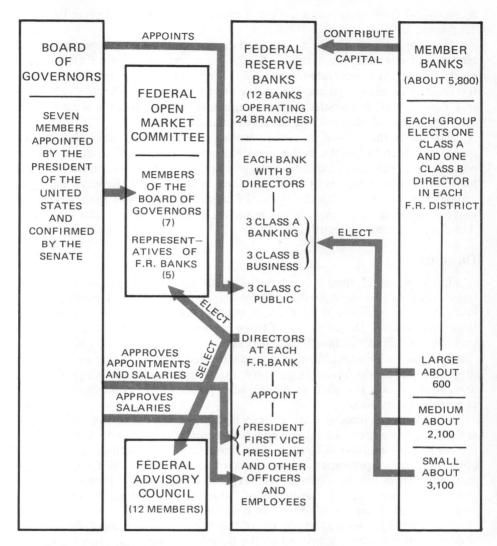

Source: *The Federal Reserve System: Purposes and Functions*
(6th ed.; Washington: Board of Governors,
September, 1974), p. 18.

Figure 9-2   Organization of the Federal Reserve System

regional banks rather than the more logical single central bank. The country
was divided into 12 areas, each of which would be served by its own Bank. In
this manner the particular needs of each part of the country would, it was
claimed, receive individual and sympathetic attention. The financial requirements of a predominantly agricultural region differ from those of a manufacturing area. For that matter, deposits, currency in circulation, and loans vary

more widely from month to month in a one-crop agricultural section than in a diversified farming region.

Geographical variations of this kind do not really require separate central banks, and over the years the 12 Banks have come to operate more like a single Bank than as separate institutions.[1] But in 1913 the nation was probably too financially unsophisticated to accept the philosophy of a single Bank. Central banking was sugarcoated with the regional feature. No doubt we are lucky that we ended up with only 12 Banks instead of 50 or 100.[2]

To serve their districts better, some of the Banks have established branches.[3] Member banks in the Twelfth Federal Reserve District, for example, may find that they can more promptly secure currency when they need it and can avail themselves of other services of the Federal Reserve because, rather than deal only with the Federal Reserve Bank in San Francisco, they may instead deal with one of the branches located in Salt Lake City, Los Angeles, Portland, or Seattle.

Directors

Each of the 12 Banks is controlled by a board of 9 directors, selected ingeniously to represent lenders, borrowers, and the general public, and to insure that the interests of the small banks will not be set aside in favor of the larger institutions. Directors are of three classes, A, B, and C. Class A directors may be bankers. Class B directors represent borrowers and must be chosen from businesspeople, farmers, or people in other nonbanking occupations; they may not be stockholders, officers, or directors of banks. Class C directors, representing the general public, also must not be connected with the operation of any bank.

The A and B directors are chosen by the member banks of the district, each bank voting for one A and one B director. For purposes of this voting the banks are classified as large, middle-sized, and small, so that each of these groups has two representatives on the board of directors. The Class C directors are chosen by the Board of Governors of the Federal Reserve, one of them being designated by the Board of Governors as Federal Reserve Agent and Chairman of the Bank's board of directors.

The directors choose the officers of the Bank, of whom the President and Vice-President must be approved by the Board of Governors. They also select the majority of the board of directors of any branch that the Bank may have in the district, the remainder being appointed by the Board of Governors. Subject to the direction of the Board of Governors, the directors are responsible for the conduct of their Bank.

---

[1]To be sure, there are reasons other than geography that would make the regional American system of central banking more logical than would appear at first. For instance, our unique "dual" banking system of federal and state chartering and supervision and our lack of nationwide branching make regionality a bit more sensible.

[2]These 12 Banks vary enormously in size, from the New York Bank with nearly one fourth of all Bank assets and the Chicago Bank with about one sixth of all Bank assets to the Minneapolis Bank with just a little over two percent of the total assets. Even these figures fail to reflect the actual relative influence of the New York Bank. It exerts an inordinate amount of influence on our money supply.

[3]These 24 branches are not distributed evenly among the 12 districts.

THE BOARD OF GOVERNORS

The Federal Reserve Board of Governors coordinates and directs the activities of the System. These 7 people are appointed by the President and serve 14-year terms staggered so that one person's term expires every other year.[4] To make the Board generally representative of the country as a whole, not more than one person may come from any one Federal Reserve district. The President is required to give due representation in the selections to the country's various industrial, financial, commercial, and agricultural interests.

The Board of Governors has the right to examine the 12 Banks and the thousands of member banks and to pass on applications for membership. It issues a weekly statement summarizing the condition of each of the Banks. Also, it publishes the *Federal Reserve Bulletin* monthly and submits an annual report to Congress. These publications contain, in addition to a wealth of statistics concerning national and international conditions of money and banking, the results of the economic research carried on under the Board's direction. It is the function of the Board of Governors to manage the banking system in such a way as to encourage sound banking and sound credit conditions. The Board, in carrying out this objective, has the power to raise or lower member bank reserve requirements or to suspend them.[5] The discount rates set by the Banks, determining the cost to the member banks of borrowing from the Banks, must be approved by the Board.[6] And through its majority control of the Open Market Committee, the Board can determine whether member bank reserves shall be increased or decreased through open market operations. It also supervises the international operations of the Federal Reserve Banks and issues regulations on a broad range of topics, some of which, such as the occasional regulation of consumer credit, are effective outside as well as inside the System.

FEDERAL OPEN MARKET COMMITTEE

Today the Federal Open Market Committee is composed of 12 people consisting of the Board of Governors and 5 representatives chosen by the 12 Banks in the following manner:

One is chosen by the Federal Reserve Bank in New York.
One is chosen by the Banks in Boston, Philadelphia, and Richmond.
One is chosen by the Banks in Cleveland and Chicago.
One is chosen by the Banks in Atlanta, Dallas, and St. Louis.
One is chosen by the Banks in Minneapolis, Kansas City, and San Francisco.

---

[4]Formerly there were eight people appointed, plus the Secretary of the Treasury and the Comptroller of the Currency as *ex officio* members. In a reorganization in 1935 the number of members was reduced to seven and the two government officials were removed to make the Federal Reserve more independent of the Treasury. At the same time the name of the group was changed from the "Federal Reserve Board" to the "Board of Governors." To date, a woman has never been selected as a member of this august body.

[5]As will later be apparent, the Board will probably never need to suspend reserve requirements, at least as long as the member banks can increase their reserves by borrowing from the Federal Reserve Banks or by selling them government securities.

[6]Although these rates may remain unchanged for several years, each Bank is required to establish its discount rate at least once every 14 days.

Open market operations are the purchases and sales of securities that the Federal Reserve Banks make through security dealers and on the initiative of the Banks themselves, in contrast to transactions with and on the initiative of member banks. The member banks may sometimes take no direct part in such operations, but cannot prevent the Federal Reserve Banks from buying and selling as decided by the Open Market Committee. The Committee makes all its purchases and sales through the Federal Reserve Bank of New York and requires that each of the 12 Banks be responsible for a percentage of each transaction in proportion to its assets. Like other banks the Federal Reserve Banks create deposits when they add to their investments, extinguish deposits when they shorten their portfolio. There is this important difference: the deposits that fluctuate in response to lending operations of member banks are the deposits held by the public. The deposits over which the Federal Reserve Banks have control are for the most part the reserves of the member banks, which maintain most of their legal reserves in the form of deposits at the Federal Reserve Banks. Hence, regardless of whether or not the member banks cooperate, the Reserve Banks can exercise considerable control over bank credit by increasing or decreasing the supply of member bank reserves. (See also Chapter 11.)

The nature and importance of open market operations were not understood at the time the System was organized.[7] As it began to be apparent that the Banks could make funds available to or take funds away from the member banks by purchasing or selling government securities in the open market, it became apparent also that for such a policy to be effective it would have to be coordinated.[8] Little would be accomplished if some Banks were trying to add to member reserves at the same time that other Banks were trying to reduce them. At one time an informal open market committee, with a representative from each of the Banks, attempted to set the policy, but some Banks refused to be bound by its recommendations. Amendments to the Federal Reserve Act in 1933 and 1935 created the Federal Open Market Committee as now constituted. All open market purchases and sales are under this committee's control. Although the Board of Governors constitutes the majority of its membership, the Committee is aware of the Banks' views as expressed by their five representatives.

OTHER COMMITTEES

At least three times a year the Conference of Presidents of the Federal Reserve Banks meets with the Board. There is also a Federal Advisory Council made up of a representative from each district selected by the boards of directors of the Banks. This council meets at least four times a year with the Board of Governors for general discussion and to keep the Board informed of

[7]The discount rate was considered the Fed's main instrument as the "lender of last resort" until the Great Depression of the 1930s. Since open market operations were unknown and reserve requirements were controlled by Congress, the only instrument contained in the original Federal Reserve Act was the discount rate.

[8]While the buying and selling of any financial assets, including both private and public securities, would accomplish the same end, the Banks have felt it judicious to refrain from dealing in private securities.

the particular problems of the various districts. Ordinarily the people chosen for the Advisory Council are prominent bankers, well acquainted with credit conditions in their area.

THE MEMBER BANKS

Completing the System are the thousands of member banks. They buy stock in the Federal Reserve Banks and agree to abide by the rules of the Federal Reserve authorities and to be subject to examination by Federal Reserve officials. Most importantly, they agree to meet the reserve requirements imposed by the Board of Governors. These legal reserves were once kept in the form of cash and by nonmember banks may still be kept in the form of cash, balances with other banks, or even (in some states) federal or state securities. Now they are held by members of the Federal Reserve either as vault cash or (mainly) as deposits with the Federal Reserve Banks.[9] No interest is paid on these deposits. As members of the System, banks may avail themselves of the services of the Federal Reserve Banks, to be discussed in the following chapters.

All national banks are members of the Federal Reserve. State banks are not required to join, but are eligible for membership if they can comply with the requirements. Of the nearly 14,500 commercial banks, about 40 percent are member banks. They include, however, most of the larger banks, for their demand deposits are more than four times as great as those of nonmember banks and in total constitute about 77 percent of all bank deposits.

Membership in the System yields several privileges:

> For example, member banks may (1) borrow from the Federal Reserve Banks when temporarily in need of additional funds, subject to criteria for such borrowing (customarily called discounting) set by statute and regulation; (2) use Federal Reserve facilities for collecting checks, settling clearing balances, and transferring funds by wire to other cities; (3) obtain currency as needed; (4) share in the informational facilities provided by the System; and (5) participate in the election of six of the nine directors of the Federal Reserve Bank for their district.[10]

REASONS FOR NONMEMBERSHIP IN THE FEDERAL RESERVE SYSTEM

It may appear surprising that over half the banks of the country are operating outside the Federal Reserve System. Some fail to meet the requirements for membership; others prefer not to join.[11]

---

[9]Besides its legal reserves, a member bank keeps other liquid assets to permit it to make payment on the checks drawn by its depositors. These assets include balances a bank holds with other banks and items in process of collection. (See discussion of primary reserves, Chapter 7.)

[10]*The Federal Reserve System: Purposes and Functions* (6th ed.; Washington: Board of Governors, September, 1974), p. 20.

[11]Most disturbing to some Fed officials is that membership has been declining in recent years. In 1945, 49 percent of all banks controlling 87 percent of total bank deposits were members; whereas in early 1975, 40 percent of all banks controlling 77 percent of deposits were members.

Freedom from Control

Nonmember banks are less closely supervised and regulated than are members of the Federal Reserve. They have more freedom in lending, investing, and other bank activities and policies and with respect to charges they may wish to impose. To join the System, they must comply with various federal laws, regulations, and conditions of membership including adequacy of capital, mergers with other banking institutions, establishment of branches, relations with bank holding companies, interlocking directorates, loan and investment limitations, etc.

Insufficient Capital or Managerial Experience

To meet the requirements for membership, a bank must possess enough capital to satisfy the Board of Governors, which takes into account at the same time the character and condition of the bank's assets and liabilities.[12] This capital requirement automatically excludes some banks which are operating under state charters partly for the reason that capital requirements are low. Furthermore, the applying bank must convince the Board of Governors that it is under competent, experienced management.

Comparable Services from Competing Sources

Banks often find it necessary to carry balances with correspondent banks even though they are maintaining their legal reserves at the Federal Reserve Bank. A correspondent bank in the city is necessary if a bank is to buy or sell foreign exchange, foreign securities, or commercial paper. The Federal Reserve Banks do not provide these services. Furthermore, the correspondent bank is able to provide the same services that a bank might otherwise obtain from the Federal Reserve Bank. It can discount or lend to its customer, collect checks, and supply currency.

Even the Federal Deposit Insurance Corporation, which insures deposits in banks that are not members of the Federal Reserve as well as in banks that are members, is in a sense competing with the Federal Reserve Banks. A generation ago depositors felt a little safer in dealing with a Federal Reserve member bank than with a nonmember bank. After their deposits were insured, they no longer were as interested in whether their bank was a member of the Federal Reserve System.

Many banks feel they have nothing to gain by joining. Their needs can all be met by other agencies. Also, by keeping a balance at a Federal Reserve Bank they can have most of the services available to member banks without joining the System and becoming subject to its regulations and restrictions.

---

[12]Until July 15, 1952, a state member bank had to have the same amount of capital as a national bank in the same community. In other words, its capital requirement was automatically determined by the population of the town where it was located. The new rule substitutes the discretion of the Board for the former arbitrary criterion. However, if its capital is less than that required for a national bank in the same location, it may not be approved for membership by the Board unless it is approved for federal deposit insurance.

Greater Profits

It boils down to dollars and cents. Many banks that could join prefer to remain outside the System because they can show higher profits. Their loan policy is subject to less regulation. Perhaps most importantly, their idle funds are smaller, for as members all their legal reserves must be vault cash or deposits at the Federal Reserve Banks. In some states nonmember banks may hold part of their reserves in the form of interest-bearing assets. In addition, nonmember banks are sometimes, but not usually, subject to lower reserve requirements.

Besides having to hold a larger proportion of nonearning assets, member banks must remit at par for all checks drawn against them. Nonpar remittance is no longer as important an issue as it used to be, for today more than 90 percent of all banks remit at par. Still, of the nonmember banks, about 8 percent do continue to collect exchange charges. They are generally small institutions in the South or Midwest. Many of these smaller banks insist that they cannot afford to give up the revenue from their exchange charges. If they can have most of the advantages of belonging to the Federal Reserve System without the direct and indirect costs of membership, they are satisfied.

DESIRABILITY OF UNIVERSAL MEMBERSHIP

The fact that an individual bank may be better served by a correspondent bank than by a Federal Reserve Bank does not mean that the bank is, in reality, receiving no benefit from the Federal Reserve. If the correspondent bank itself were not able to borrow from the Federal Reserve and to secure from the Federal Reserve the additional currency that sometimes is required, it would often be in no position to accommodate the nonmember bank that is its customer. To some extent the nonmember bank is getting a free ride, benefiting from the Federal Reserve without accepting the responsibility of membership. For this reason there have occasionally been unofficial proposals to require all commercial banks to join, strengthening the control of the Federal Reserve by making all banks subject to its regulation.[13] To date, however, there has been no coercion stronger than moral pressure brought to bear on nonmember banks.

CAPITAL OF THE FEDERAL RESERVE BANKS

The capital of the Federal Reserve Banks reflects the dual nature of the organization as a private institution serving the general public interest. Although the member banks own all the stock, the Treasury receives most of the profits. A member bank buys stock to the extent of 3 percent of its capital and surplus in the Federal Reserve Bank of its district. It can be called on to double its investment, but thus far the additional 3 percent holdings have not

---

[13]It has alternatively been suggested that to make monetary policy more effective and more equitable either reserve requirements should be uniform for members and nonmembers or the Fed should pay interest on reserve deposits of members. (See Chapter 7.)

been required. If a bank's capital and surplus changes, it must adjust accordingly its holdings of stock in its Federal Reserve Bank. The stock bears double liability, so that according to the provisions of the Federal Reserve Act the banks might be called on to pay in an additional amount equal, altogether, to three times what they have paid thus far. Such a possibility appears remote; but should it occur, it would be no misfortune for the member banks. The stock, paying 6 percent, is ordinarily the best security they own. The dividend is earned many times over and is cumulative so that, if for any reason it was skipped, it would be paid later.

Treasury Ownership of Federal Reserve Surplus

There is one unusual provision regarding Federal Reserve stock. Ordinarily a corporation's surplus belongs to the stockholders. Profitable operation of the business results in increased earnings, which are the property of the stockholders, whether distributed as dividends or retained by the corporation. But the Federal Reserve is not organized for profit. No matter how high its earnings may rise, its stockholders cannot receive more than 6 percent on their investment. The retained earnings of the Federal Reserve Banks belong to the Treasury. In other words, if the Federal Reserve Banks were ever liquidated, the member banks would be entitled to a return of what they paid for their stock. Any funds remaining after other liabilities had been paid would be turned over to the Treasury on the theory that this surplus should somehow be returned to the nation as a whole rather than to the member banks which, as we shall see, had very little to do with creating that surplus.

Disposition of Earnings

The Federal Reserve Banks currently turn over the greater part of their profit directly to the Treasury, rather than let it pile up in a surplus account that the Treasury would eventually take over if the System were liquidated. Once this policy of sharing with the Treasury was mandated by law. The Banks were at one time required to pay 90 percent of their net profits as a franchise tax to the Treasury. Congress removed the tax in 1933 when it directed the Federal Reserve Banks to subscribe to stock in the Federal Deposit Insurance Corporation to the extent of one half their surplus. No one doubted that the stock of the FDIC was more of an assessment than an investment and would soon be written off the books.

A few years later the Banks' wartime earnings were very large; they continued high after the war. Congress might appropriately have restored the franchise tax. But this was one of those times when Congress did nothing. Consequently, the Board of Governors themselves in effect restored it in 1947 by imposing an interest charge on all notes the Banks issued over and above the amount of gold certificates the Banks held.[14] The interest receipts, two or

---

[14]When the legislators provided, thirty-odd years earlier, that the Board of Governors might tax the note issues of the Banks, it did not occur to them that the interest charge could be a substitute for the franchise tax. The provision was originally inserted as a possible means of disciplining Banks that might, in the Board's opinion, be expanding credit excessively.

three billion dollars a year, are turned over to the Treasury, and the interest rate is adjusted so that the Treasury will receive about 90 percent of the Banks' net earnings over expenses and dividends. The other 10 percent is credited to surplus.

Reasons for Surrendering Profits

The reason for this generosity on the part of the Board of Governors is that they really do not know what to do with the Banks' net income. During World War II the Federal Reserve Banks purchased billions of dollars of Treasury securities—not for income, but to create plentiful member bank reserves and to support the bond market. (Never forget that when a Federal Reserve Bank buys a million dollars of Treasury bonds, it is not spending its own money or the money of the member banks. It is creating money which will flow into the member banks, increasing their legal reserves.) Since 1945 they have gradually doubled their security holdings. The reason, again, has been to supply the member banks with reserves sufficient for the volume of deposits judged appropriate to the needs of the economy. Quite incidentally but necessarily the Banks' income greatly expanded—to a level that the Board of Governors felt could not be justified.

After all, what can be done with profits if the law limits the amount the stockholders may be paid? Earnings may be reinvested; but the purpose of plowing back earnings is not to find a drain down which to pour current profits, but to increase future earnings. The Board of Governors feels that the capital and surplus of the Federal Reserve Banks are adequate, and their earnings far more than adequate. In their opinion, retaining most of their present earnings would accomplish nothing useful.

It is a little unfortunate that the inaction of Congress causes the Board of Governors to indulge in games like this. The example is poor. When we could have the same results without any evasion or distortion of the law, it seems too bad that, because of Congressional inaction, we must rely on such tortured construction of the Federal Reserve Act.

The interest turned over to the Treasury has occasionally been attacked on other grounds. Some of the criticism has been based on the claim that the earnings of the 12 Federal Reserve Banks belong rightly to the member banks, which own their stock. Such an argument loses sight of the basic principle that a central bank is not supposed to be operated for the sake of making a profit. Also, it ignores the fact that the profits a central bank may make are attributable primarily to its unique powers rather than to clever management on the part of its owners, the member banks.

Another objection has been that the Federal Reserve Banks are undercapitalized and should be increasing their surplus rather than making large payments to the Treasury. Admittedly total capital accounts of $2.2 billion offer little protection against a possible decline in value of assets totaling nearly $110 billion. A shrinkage of 2 percent in asset values would wipe out the capital accounts. However, this point cannot be taken seriously. About one tenth of the assets of the Federal Reserve Banks are gold certificates, the money value of which cannot shrink. Most of the remainder is made up of government securities. The Federal Reserve Banks are in no danger of becoming insolvent.

The operations of the Federal Reserve Banks will be easier to understand if you can clearly picture their balance sheet, as summarized in Table 9-1. This consolidated statement underscores the fact that the Federal Reserve Banks' main assets are largely investments (primarily U.S. government obligations) and to a lesser extent gold certificates. Their major liabilities are Federal Reserve notes and member bank deposit holdings. Typically, the net worth or capital account is less than 2 percent of the total assets.

Table 9-1   Consolidated Balance Sheet of All Federal Reserve Banks
February 28, 1975
(In billions of dollars)

Assets		Liabilities	
Gold certificate account	11.6	Federal Reserve notes	68.1
SDR certificate account	0.4	Deposits:	
Vault cash	0.4	Member bank reserves	28.5
Loans	1.1	United States Treasury—	
Investments	86.4	general account	2.9
Cash items in process		Foreign and other	1.3
of collection	5.8	Deferred availability cash	
Other	2.7	items	4.3
		Other liabilities	1.1
		Capital Accounts	
		Capital paid in	0.9
		Surplus	0.9
		Other capital accounts	0.4
Total	108.4	Total	108.4

Source: *Federal Reserve Bulletin* (March, 1975), p. A12.

ROUTINE OPERATIONS OF THE FEDERAL RESERVE BANKS

The activities of the Federal Reserve Banks fall into two general categories. A great part of their operations is concerned with routine chores that have no relation to policy. Such work is handled in the same manner today as it was when the Banks first began operation, except to the extent that it has been modified to permit greater speed and efficiency. In this chapter we shall discuss operations of this kind. The Banks and the Board of Governors are also concerned with other activities that implement the policies established by the Board and the Banks. These will be reviewed in the following chapters.

FISCAL AGENTS OF THE UNITED STATES GOVERNMENT

Although the Federal Reserve Banks are, in general, banks for the member banks, they carry two other sets of deposits. One of these is composed of the deposits of foreign banks, foreign governments, the International

Monetary Fund, and the International Bank for Reconstruction and Development. The other is the deposits of the United States Treasury (and of other government corporations), which keeps most of its checking accounts with the Federal Reserve. As noted earlier, the Treasury was permitted, after the establishment of the national banking system, to deposit funds with the national banks, even while the Independent Treasury System was still legally in effect. Section 15 of the Federal Reserve Act provided that the Secretary of the Treasury might deposit funds in the Federal Reserve Banks as well. On January 1, 1916, the Banks received their first Treasury deposits and provided such satisfactory service that the Independent Treasury System was discontinued four years later. Besides handling checking accounts for the Treasury, the Federal Reserve Banks handle a tremendous volume of paper work for the Treasury in connection with the issuance, refunding, and retirement of debt. Detailed discussion of the relation between the Treasury and the Federal Reserve will be deferred until Chapter 12.

COLLECTION OF CHECKS UNDER THE FEDERAL RESERVE SYSTEM

The clearing and collection of checks has been greatly changed by the services of the Federal Reserve, which employs more than one fourth of its personnel for this function. Local checks may still be cleared through clearinghouses, and banks may still collect checks through correspondent banks if they wish to do so. About 500 of the smaller banks that do not wish to remit at par (referred to as nonpar banks) collect through correspondent banks. Also, about half the member banks prefer to clear out-of-town checks through a city correspondent, especially if they are not located near a Reserve Bank or Branch Bank. This procedure has the advantage that the bank can send out all its checks together, without sorting out the checks on nonpar banks, not accepted by the Federal Reserve. The city correspondent sorts the checks and depends on the Federal Reserve to collect all items drawn on par banks.

The collection services of the Federal Reserve are available to all member banks and to nonmember banks that will agree to remit at par and maintain a clearing balance at the Federal Reserve Bank of its district. Collection may be *intradistrict* or *interdistrict*.

Intramural Collection

The services of the Federal Reserve Banks, or of any other outside agency, are not needed in the case of *intramural collections*, which are checks written by a bank's customers and turned over to the bank for collection (that is, "deposited") by other customers of the same bank. This kind of collection is simple. Yet if you understand it clearly, you will have no trouble with more complex collections. The bank's bookkeepers merely shift the ownership of the bank's liabilities. Carmela Gonzales deposits a $30 check from Stanley Johnson, who carries his account with the same bank. The bank collects the $30 by adjusting its accounts. It owes Miss Gonzales $30 more, Mr. Johnson $30 less.

Other types of collection follow exactly the same principle, but bring additional accounts into the operation. In every case, the trick is to avoid passing currency around and instead to transfer the ownership of bank deposits.

Intradistrict Collection

Intradistrict collection is almost as simple as intramural. We just add another level of banks. The Federal Reserve Bank is the bank with which every member bank (and many nonmember banks) of the district will carry an account. From the point of view of the Federal Reserve Bank, collections between members banks of its district are intramural. Any member bank or any nonmember bank that keeps a clearing balance at the Federal Reserve Bank can collect from another such bank in the district as easily and in the same way that Miss Gonzales collects from Mr. Johnson above. More specifically:

1. Terry Chen deposits with the First National Bank of Hamilton, Ohio, a $50 check he has received from Betty De Lorme, drawn on the Covington National Bank of Kentucky. He receives deferred credit, and is allowed to draw against it a day or two later.
2. The First National Bank forwards the check to the Federal Reserve Branch Bank of Cincinnati, where both the First National and the Covington National Banks maintain reserve balances.
3. The Federal Reserve Branch Bank credits $50 to the account of the First National Bank and charges $50 to the account of the Covington National. It then sends the check to the Covington National.
4. The Covington National Bank receives the check, reduces by $50 the amount it owes Mrs. De Lorme and reduces by $50 the amount of its claim against the Federal Reserve Branch Bank. Finally, it puts the check aside to be returned to Mrs. De Lorme with her statement.
5. The whole collection operation was completed by simple bookkeeping entries. The Federal Reserve Branch Bank shifted the ownership of its deposit liabilities, just as in our first example the individual bank shifted $30 from Mr. Johnson's account to Miss Gonzales'. The First National added $50 to the amount of its claim against the Federal Reserve Branch Bank and added $50 to the amount of its liabilities to depositors. The Covington National similarly subtracted $50 from its assets and from its liabilities.

Interdistrict Collection

Interdistrict collection follows the same general techniques, although still another level of accounts now is required. In this case, the two member banks carry their accounts in different Federal Reserve Banks. The Federal Reserve Banks settle differences among themselves through the Interdistrict Settlement Fund. This impressive title relates to a set of accounts maintained in Washington. It shows how the ownership of gold certificates is distributed among the 12 Banks. Daily, millions of dollars are changed from one Bank to another by the adjustment of their respective accounts in the Interdistrict Settlement Fund. It is so easy to collect checks from banks thousands of miles apart that today we take the whole process for granted. The smoothly running machinery of interdistrict collection includes several transfers:

1. Ted Patton deposits in the North Adams National Bank in Massachusetts a $500 check he has received from Judy Griffin, drawn on the Oakland National Bank in California. He receives deferred credit and is allowed to draw against it about a week later.
2. North Adams National passes the check to the Federal Reserve Bank of Boston, which allows North Adams National to count the check as collected after two days. The Federal Reserve Bank of Boston forwards the check to the Federal Reserve Bank of San Francisco.
3. The Federal Reserve Bank of Boston also includes the amount of this check in its daily telegram to the Interdistrict Settlement Fund, in which it lists the total amounts received drawn against banks in the 11 other districts. Since a similar claims statement is made by all 12 Banks, the Interdistrict Settlement Fund, like any clearinghouse, has only to make up a summary of the amounts owed to and owed by each Bank, find the net change, plus or minus, for each Bank, and credit or charge the appropriate amount to each Bank's account in the Fund. (The effect of this $500 item by itself will be to add $500 to the account of the Federal Reserve Bank of Boston and subtract $500 from the account of the Federal Reserve Bank of San Francisco.) The total amount of the Interdistrict Settlement Fund is unaffected by these transfers.
4. The Federal Reserve Bank of San Francisco charges $500 to the account of the Oakland National Bank and sends the check to the Oakland National, which reduces by $500 the amount it owes to Ms. Griffin, reduces by $500 the amount it is owed by the Federal Reserve Bank of San Francisco, and puts the check aside to be returned with Ms. Griffin's statement.

The telegram from the Federal Reserve Bank of Boston to the Interdistrict Settlement Fund is a form of draft. In effect, the Boston Bank is ordering the Federal Reserve Bank of San Francisco to pay this $500 (along with millions of dollars of other checks drawn on banks in the Twelfth District).

This draft is different from the checks individuals write, ordering the bank with which they have an account to make a payment to someone else. Through the Interdistrict Settlement Fund the Boston Bank is ordering the San Francisco Bank to make a payment to the Boston Bank itself. Payment will be made not in ordinary bank deposits but in the very special accounts in the Interdistrict Settlement Fund, maintained expressly for the purpose of facilitating interdistrict collections. Despite the technical differences the transaction is fundamentally the same as is involved in an ordinary clearinghouse operation, and the basic principle of the draft as an order to pay is the same whether it pertains to this daily settlement telegram or to an ordinary check.

The Federal Reserve insists that banks using its facilities remit at par because there is today no longer the justification for imposing exchange charges. Bankers no longer have to make payment at distant points. They pay at the nearest Federal Reserve Bank or branch, usually out of their accounts there or by sending in their own collection items for credit. In the event a bank does decide to ship currency, the Federal Reserve pays the shipping cost.

The Federal Reserve has reduced the average collection time by about one half. Checks drawn on and deposited in banks in or near cities where there are Federal Reserve Banks or branches can be collected in one day. In a week checks can be collected from the most distant parts of the country. The increased speed of collection is due in part to the telegraphic settlement between the Federal Reserve Banks, in part to the elimination of roundabout routing, and in part to better transportation arrangements and more efficient sorting and handling procedures. Member banks may arrange to send checks directly to the Federal Reserve Banks of other districts if they regularly have many items from outside their own district and especially if they are located near the district boundary. Banks in a city may use the local clearinghouse, which telegraphs daily the clearing figures to the Federal Reserve Bank so that the banks' balances may be promptly adjusted.

Mechanization of Check Collection

Since 1960 rapid progress has been made in mechanizing the banks' paperwork. Something had to be done. The processing of checks has long been banking's biggest routine operation. The average check passes through $2\frac{1}{3}$ banks and may be handled up to 20 times. With steadily rising labor costs, personal sorting and posting of checks were becoming constantly more expensive. Besides, the volume of checks has been expanding rapidly. By 1975 almost 30 billion checks a year were being written, nearly double the number of only 10 years earlier. (Taped end to end they would reach to the moon and back over 4 times.) In 1974 the Reserve Banks cleared over 11 billion of the estimated 28 billion checks drawn on banks in the United States. Unless the cost of check processing could be reduced, service charges would necessarily rise. Today most checks are generally encoded in magnetic ink in the lower corner of the check. This ink, together with the specially designed, "blocky" numerals used, permits the numbers to be read automatically and at high speed. As the mechanization of check processing is more completely developed, the amount of each check will be encoded by the first bank receiving the item for collection. For intermediate and paying banks subsequently handling it, the process will be almost entirely mechanical.

Float

In Chapters 7 and 8 we referred to the *float* or fictitious reserves which once resulted from our uncoordinated, disorganized way of collecting checks. Although it might be supposed that with our faster, more efficient check collection today we have eliminated the float, the fact is that the float today is generally higher than in pre-Federal Reserve days.

This is not a matter of any concern. If the Board of Governors wished to reduce the float, it easily could. The Board may just as well let this particular element of reserves stand, even if it is fictitious. The Board can easily offset it by a little less credit expansion in some other area—perhaps a few less securities bought in the open market. The significant thing, after all, is not the amount of change in member bank reserves that results from every individual action of the Federal Reserve Banks, but rather the *total* change in reserves effected by the Federal Reserve Banks.

Once the float was the result of inefficiency. Today it is the result of kindheartedness. The Federal Reserve Banks give credit for many items before they can be collected. This means that the reserves of some banks are increased before the reserves of other banks have been reduced. Total reserves are, therefore, overstated. The float would disappear if the Federal Reserve Bank would require depositing banks to wait a day or two longer before receiving reserve credit on items deposited for collection from banks outside the district. The chances are, however, that reserves would then be understated. As explained below, reserves of the drawee bank are reduced only when the collection process is actually complete. But reserves of the depositing bank are credited in accordance with a schedule based on the estimated collection time. The actual and the estimated collection time will often differ. Hence, a difference appears between Deferred Availability Cash Items and Uncollected Cash Items.

On the balance sheet of Federal Reserve Banks the float is not stated separately but appears as the difference between the asset, "Uncollected Cash Items," and the liability, "Deferred Availability Cash Items." *Uncollected Cash Items* are checks a Federal Reserve Bank has received from member banks but not yet collected from the banks on which they are drawn. The collection process may take a day or two or even a little longer.

Deferred Availability Items are checks the Bank has received for which it has not yet credited the depositor. Each Bank prints an availability schedule showing the number of days that must elapse before items will be credited to the account of the bank that submits them. This schedule permits member banks to know exactly when they will receive credit for items they are turning in for collection. The member banks can accordingly permit their customers to draw against these checks shortly after they have deposited them, often a necessity to businesses. Checks on banks in the immediate vicinity or checks on any Federal Reserve Bank are credited to the depositing bank's account the same day they are received. Checks from more distant banks will be given credit in one day or, at the most, in two days—even if collection is not actually completed for three or four days. If availability were always deferred until collection was completed, there would be no float. But since, by the availability schedule, reserves are often made available to some banks before the collection process has reduced the reserves of other banks, total reserves are overstated by this float.

SUPERVISION OF BANKING

The Federal Reserve's supervision of banking is complicated by the fact that, on the one hand, some of its supervisory functions are delegated to other authorities and, on the other hand, some of its regulations govern the activities of institutions whether or not they are members of the System.

The primary purpose of supervision is the maintenance of sound banking conditions. In this connection most people are likely to think first of bank examinations, which serve several purposes. Revealing unsatisfactory conditions may serve as a guide to the establishment of required general regulations. It may lead the management to correct the situation, and it may lead to disciplinary action. This disciplinary action might involve the removal of officers and directors of member banks that are found by Reserve authorities to have been following unsound banking practices. Also, member banks may find their right to credit from the System suspended if they have been making excessive use of bank credit to finance speculation.

Each Federal Reserve Bank examines the state member banks in its district. Since the national banks are examined at least twice a year by a representative of the Comptroller of the Currency, from whom they secure their charters, they are not examined separately by the Federal Reserve. The examinations occasionally reveal embezzlements and errors, but ordinarily their principal result is an appraisal of the bank's assets and an evaluation of the bank's current lending activities.

The Federal Reserve also requires regular reports from the member banks, the number varying with the bank's location. Statements of deposits are submitted semimonthly, weekly, or semiweekly. Several hundred member banks submit each week a condensed statement of condition from which the Board of Governors makes up a summary for publication. In addition, the member banks submit earnings and dividend statements twice yearly.

The Federal Reserve also authorizes national banks to establish branches in foreign countries and to invest in the stock of corporations engaged in international banking. Seven large banks have been permitted to operate about 75 branches situated in 21 countries. Also, the Federal Reserve authorizes national banks to operate trust departments and grants permits to holding companies to control the affairs of member banks whose stock they own.

CURRENCY

Most of the time the banks find that, as some depositors are withdrawing currency, others are bringing it to the bank. For this reason the bank does not need to keep a major portion of its assets in the form of vault cash. There is no need for the banks to carry large reserves of vault cash, for they can promptly secure from the Federal Reserve any additional currency that they may need to meet the demands of their depositors.

Neither the Federal Reserve Banks nor the member banks can directly control the volume of currency in circulation, which is determined by the public. In general, the public's desire to hold currency is governed by two circumstances. There is a regular seasonal fluctuation, with more currency demanded in the fall and before Christmas and returned to the banking system after the first of the year. Also, the amount of currency in circulation is roughly proportionate to the volume of demand deposits; so that when bank credit has been expanded, the volume of currency will increase, reflecting in part the fact that many individuals do not maintain checking accounts and if paid by check they go to the bank and ask for cash.

Between 1941 and 1945 total demand deposits (excluding interbank deposits) for all banks increased from $44 billion to $107 billion.[15] During the same period currency in the hands of the public increased from a little under $10 billion to more than $26 billion. The public received this currency from the banks, which in turn drew currency against their own deposits in the Federal Reserve Banks. Member banks were supplied directly by the Federal Reserve: over the counter in the case of banks located in the same cities as the Reserve Banks; by mail or express in the case of other banks. Nonmember banks depended upon their correspondent banks, which ordinarily were members of the Federal Reserve.

Ultimate Source of Additional Currency

Where did the Federal Reserve Banks secure this currency in response to the public's demand for almost three times as much paper money as had ever previously been in circulation? Not from their own vault cash, certainly, for the Reserve Banks, like the member banks, do not hold a great deal of cash in proportion to their liabilities.[16] Nor did the needed currency come primarily from an increase in Treasury currency, which increased by less than a billion dollars during this period.

Primarily the public's demand for additional currency was satisfied by the issuance of additional Federal Reserve notes, of which there were $8 billion outstanding in December, 1941, and $25 billion in December, 1945. When a Reserve Bank found its stock of cash insufficient, it requested an additional supply of notes from its Federal Reserve Agent, submitting at the same time the required collateral in the form of gold certificates and eligible short-term paper or government securities.[17]

This power of note issue is one of the distinguishing features between the Federal Reserve Banks and the member banks. Nearly all of our circulating currency—some 90 percent of it—is issued by the Federal Reserve Banks in the form of Federal Reserve notes. The issuance of additional Federal Reserve notes does not increase the liabilities of the issuing Bank, which is exchanging one liability for another. As notes in circulation increase, member bank deposits with the Federal Reserve decrease until such time as the Federal Reserve may take action to restore them by open market operations or by lending.

---

[15]This particular period is used as an illustration because of the record increase of 150 percent in demand deposits and other money during these four years. The same procedures are effective today but operate much more gradually. Over the last four years deposits increased only 15 to 20 percent.

[16]Specifically, the Federal Reserve Banks held $260 million of vault cash (excluding gold certificates) at the beginning of World War II. Over the next four years they paid out more than 60 times that amount of vault cash.

[17]The reason for this transfer from the Bank's general assets to the assets held by the Agent is that the Agent has the express responsibility to maintain custody of all collateral against which notes are issued. The collateral is still the property of the Bank, but as long as notes are outstanding this particular part of the Bank's property is in the possession of the Agent to guarantee that the notes are properly and adequately secured.

Seasonal Currency Movements

Less spectacular than this impressive increase that the Federal Reserve creates in the supply of currency is the day-to-day activity of the Federal Reserve in accommodating the seasonal demands for currency. In recent years the growth of currency in circulation has been so great that the seasonal movement has been overshadowed for the System as a whole. However, in particular areas there may be a greater or lesser demand for currency which, due to offsetting tendencies in other regions, has little effect on the total amount of currency in circulation. In the cities demand for currency will likely increase in the summer, when workers are taking their vacations, and again in December for Christmas shopping. In agricultural regions the demand for currency will usually increase in the fall, when farmers are harvesting their crops. The banks, supplied by the Federal Reserve, provide this additional currency for their customers. Later, as the public's demand for currency lessens and the currency flows back to the banks, the banks return it to the Federal Reserve, since there is ordinarily no reason for the banks to hold unnecessarily large stocks of vault cash.[18] They face the risk of loss when the cash is in their own vaults.

Inspection of Currency

When currency is returned to the Federal Reserve Banks, it is inspected to see whether it may be reissued or whether other disposition should be made of it. Any currency that is in process of retirement, such as silver certificates and Federal Reserve Bank notes, is permanently withdrawn from circulation. Currency that is unfit for further circulation is cancelled and sent to Washington, along with lightweight and mutilated coin which is melted down for recoinage. The Federal Reserve bears all costs of printing, handling, shipping, and redeeming of currency.[19]

---

[18]In recent years some banks hoarded the old silver coins. If they were able to obtain, for example, $100,000 of the old dimes, quarters, the half dollars, they put it away in their vaults, not to pay out to customers but, hopefully, to sell some day at a good profit. They were permitted to count this as part of their legal reserves, which they had to maintain anyway. Therefore, unlike all other silver hoarders, banks had no interest cost on their silver investment.

[19]Until a few years ago, the Federal Reserve Banks were forbidden to pay out the notes issued by any other Federal Reserve Bank. They were required to return such notes to the issuing Banks and were subject to a 10 percent tax on any notes issued by other Banks that they returned to circulation.

This regulation was logical when the Federal Reserve first began operations as 12 regional Banks. Each was supposed to issue notes only in accordance with the currency requirements of the Federal Reserve District that it served, and any excess of notes was to be returned to the issuing Bank.

In recent years the System has become more unified with much less emphasis on its regional nature. With nearly $27 billion of Federal Reserve notes in circulation after World War II, a great volume of currency shipments was constantly required to comply with the regulation. By an act of Congress, approved on July 19, 1954, the tax was removed and the Banks were no longer prohibited from paying out notes issued by other Banks.

SUMMARY AND CONCLUSION

The Federal Reserve System is composed of the Board of Governors, 12 Federal Reserve Banks with 24 branches, and about 5,800 member banks.[20] The 7 Governors are chosen by the President of the United States. This Board of Governors is the apex of the Federal Reserve System's organization, for it supervises and coordinates the activities of the Federal Reserve Banks, permitting them to operate more nearly like a single central bank. The Board of Governors is in charge of overall credit policy. Member banks (and sometimes other institutions and individuals) are subject to its regulations. It is assisted by a number of committees, the most important of which is the Federal Open Market Committee.

The 12 Banks are bankers' banks. Their only depositors are banks, the United States Treasury, and other government agencies, foreign and domestic. The Federal Reserve Banks, like other banks, create new deposits when they increase their loans and investments. Since most of the deposits of the Federal Reserve Banks constitute legal reserves of member banks, the Banks usually can, by increasing or decreasing their deposits, encourage credit expansion by the member banks or force credit contraction. The member banks own the capital stock of the Federal Reserve Banks, but the Treasury owns the surplus. Ninety percent of the Reserve Banks' earnings, after payment of expenses and the 6 percent dividend on the stock, goes to the United States Treasury. The remainder is added to the Banks' surplus.

All national banks and some state banks are members of the System. Members buy stock in the Federal Reserve Bank of their district. They keep most of their legal reserves in the form of deposits at that bank, and they are subject to inspection by Federal Reserve authorities and to regulation by the Board of Governors. Many banks, especially the smaller ones, find it more profitable to remain outside the System. Their credit policies are less closely controlled and for other reasons their incomes may be higher. Also, they have most of the advantages of membership without actually joining the System.

The Federal Reserve Banks have greatly accelerated check collections. The extra "layer of banks" they provide permits collections between banks anywhere in the United States to be handled very much like collection of items deposited in and drawn on the same bank. The float is an element of member bank reserves caused by the policy of the Federal Reserve Banks in the collection of interdistrict items. The Banks often give reserve credit to one bank before they have reduced the reserves of the other bank. The float is the difference between Uncollected Cash Items and Deferred Availability Cash Items.

---

[20]To see how the Federal Reserve views its purposes and functions, see its publication, *The Federal Reserve System: Purposes and Functions* (6th ed.; Washington: Board of Governors, September, 1974). This edition is changed substantially from the 5th edition of December, 1963. The first edition is dated May, 1939.

The Federal Reserve Banks supply most of the currency in circulation. Seasonally they absorb currency from and release it to the member banks, which receive it from or pay it out to the public. In addition, the Banks print more money when it is required. The principal collateral behind Federal Reserve notes today is credit instruments—certain short-term commercial or agricultural paper or, more probably, securities of the federal government. Gold certificates are also used as note collateral.

Discussion Questions

1. Briefly discuss the origin and structure of the Federal Reserve System.
2. Where do the Federal Reserve Banks get the money that they lend or with which they buy securities?
3. "The nature and importance of open market operations were not understood at the time the Federal Reserve System was organized." Explain.
4. Explain the difference between open market operations and loans of the Federal Reserve Banks. Can commercial banks also engage in open market operations?
5. Open market operations, once left to the discretion of the 12 Federal Reserve Banks, are now all handled by the Federal Open Market Committee. Why? And how does the Committee operate?
6. What are the important obligations members of the Federal Reserve System must assume?
7. Is it possible for banks to hold earning assets as part or all of their legal reserves? Why or why not? What are the legal reserves of the banks that are members of the Federal Reserve System?
8. If the Federal Reserve Banks are not organized for the sake of making a profit, why are their profits so high that they feel impelled to give them away?
9. What would be the major assets and the major liabilities in a consolidated balance sheet for all Federal Reserve Banks?
10. List what you feel are the most important differences between a Federal Reserve Bank and a commercial bank.
11. Could Deferred Availability Items possibly be greater than Collection Items? Explain.
12. What effect would you expect an airline strike to have on the Federal Reserve float?

Chapter 10 The Federal Reserve: Original Powers and Their Modification

The nation into which the Federal Reserve was born on December 23, 1912, was very different from the United States of today. This country was a debtor nation as far as the rest of the world was concerned. England was still the greatest creditor nation, and sterling was the most important and the most stable currency used in international transactions. Although giant corporations had made their appearance on the American scene, they had not achieved the dominant position that they were later to enjoy. The United States was little concerned with what might happen in Europe thousands of miles away. For a hundred years we had been at peace with the rest of the world, with the exception of short wars with Mexico and Spain. Our concern was almost entirely with domestic problems as we proceeded with the development of our industries and the utilization of our resources. The interest-bearing government debt was less than a billion dollars. Seldom did the Treasury borrow, and then usually by selling long-term bonds to refinance existing debt, most of which had been incurred during the Civil War. Governmental controls such as we know today were almost nonexistent.

Although in the past there had been periods when business was poor and frequent periods of panic, they were attributed primarily to defects in our banking system. The business cycle as such was little understood. The Federal Reserve was organized as a direct consequence of the banking panic of 1907 to provide better bank regulation, a more satisfactory currency, and a source of credit for the banks. The broad controls that it later was to exercise were not specified at the time because the need for them was not evident.

Six years later the government debt had shot up to 25 times its earlier level. The quantity of money had doubled. In the United States as in other countries World War I had led to inflation, which was followed by a sharp deflation in 1921. Gold imports had swollen our gold stocks. The dollar had become an important international currency. Our position had changed to that of a creditor nation, although many of our policies continued to be those appropriate to our traditional position as a debtor nation. The great increase in the sale of automobiles had expanded consumer credit. Tractors and trucks were beginning to mechanize American farming. These and other great changes in our economy, many of which resulted from the war, caused the desirable range of the activities of the Federal Reserve to appear much wider than it had in the more placid prewar era.

The purpose of the Federal Reserve System, as stated in the Federal Reserve Act, makes no specific reference to controlling inflation or deflation, preventing excessive speculation, curbing consumer credit, stabilizing interest rates, or aiding the Treasury's borrowing operations except as these responsibilities are included in the four-word catchall at the end of the preamble.

> An Act to provide for the establishment of Federal reserve banks, to furnish an elastic currency, to afford means of rediscounting commercial paper, to establish a more effective supervision of banking in the United States, and for other purposes.

However, from early statements of the Federal Reserve Board (as the Board of Governors was then called) it appears that from the beginning a basic objective of Federal Reserve policy was the maintenance of stable business conditions. As we began to be more aware of the potentialities of monetary and credit controls, the Board of Governors was gradually given further powers and responsibilities to increase its effectiveness.

In the preceding chapter we discussed the establishment of the Banks and their supervisory (and service) functions. We now take up the provisions that were made for lending to the member banks and for supplying a more elastic currency. In the following chapter we shall see the additional powers and responsibilities later acquired. Especially note in these chapters the changing philosophy of the proper role of the Federal Reserve, as shown by the repeated changes broadening the scope of its powers.

LOANS TO MEMBER BANKS

Just as the public borrows from the banks, so the banks themselves may borrow from the Federal Reserve Banks (and also from each other). One technique by which the Federal Reserve Banks may lend to member banks is called *discounting*.[1] The interest rate charged to member banks for this temporary loan of reserves is called the *discount rate*.

Nature and Significance of Discounting

Ordinarily when a business borrows, the bank takes the interest out in advance. (You do the same thing when you buy a savings bond, giving the Treasury less money than it agrees to repay you later.) The business doing the borrowing may give the bank its note, promising to repay $10,000 after 90 days. The bank, discounting the note at perhaps 6 percent simple interest per annum, credits the borrower's account with $9,850, the present value of $10,000 payable in 90 days and discounted at 6 percent. During the following

---

[1]When the Fed was started, it was thought that member banks would "rediscount" their customers' promissory notes in return for new cash, and hence the technique was referred to as "rediscounting" and the price charged as the "rediscount rate." However, since 1935 most member banks borrow on government securities. Thus, the Fed's asset term, "Discounts, loans, and acceptances," is primarily loans or advances to member banks which are charged the discount rate.

three months the note gradually ripens to maturity, increasing in value by $50 a month or approximately $1.67 a day.

The effective interest rate paid by the borrower is a little higher than the simple interest rate. In this illustration the business is paying $150 for the use of $9,850 for one fourth of a year.

Meanwhile if the bank itself should need funds before the borrower's note is due, it can have that note discounted, provided it can find a lender. The original borrower's note was discounted by the first bank; it may be discounted again by another bank. (Technically, a note that has been discounted more than once has been *rediscounted*. We find that in practice rediscounts are often referred to as discounts, and that the Federal Reserve authorities usually refer to their *discount rate* rather than their *rediscount rate*.)

In the illustration above, if the first bank needs funds a month after it discounted a $10,000 note for its customer, it may endorse that same note and have it discounted by another bank. In effect it is selling to the second bank a $10,000 asset, payable in 60 days. The amount that the second bank will pay for it is determined by the rate at which it discounts the note. If the second bank is discounting at 6 percent per annum, this note, with two months to run until maturity, will be purchased for $9,900. If the second bank is discounting at 8 percent, it will give $9,867 for the note; and if it is discounting at 4 percent, it will give $9,933. If a bank is able to have notes discounted at a lower rate than the rate at which it has discounted them, it will profit from the transaction, just as it loses if the notes are discounted at a higher rate than the rate at which it discounted them.[2]

Banks seldom apply for discounts to profit from a favorable spread between the interest rate and the discount rate, but rather to obtain funds needed to repair reserve deficiencies. Such funds are, like the proceeds of any other bank loans, in the form of deposit credit. The money placed at the disposal of the borrowing bank is created by the bank that discounts the note, just as the money received by the original maker of the note is created by the bank when it discounts the maker's note. In either case, of course, the lending bank must have excess reserves.

Before the establishment of the Federal Reserve, banks could discount with other banks as, of course, they still may do. Such discounting presented no particular problem when only a few banks were pressed for funds, but it was impossible in periods of general credit stringency. At such times no banks were in a position to lend. There was no way by which new reserves could be created.

If the central reserve city banks had followed the policy of maintaining massive excess reserves in normal times, then they would have been able to

---

[2] In the example the bank supplied $9,850 to the borrower. Later, discounting at 8 percent, it sold the note for $9,867. How does the bank "lose" by discount at this higher rate? It loses because it has received only $17 income for the month in which it held the note. In effect, discounting the note at 8 percent has caused the bank to lose two thirds of the expected yield for the month during which it held the note. Observe, also, that if the bank were to find it necessary to discount the note at 8 percent only a week after it had made the loan, it would receive approximately $9,815—although it credited the original borrower with $9,850.

create additional reserves in emergencies. At such times they could have made loans to other banks, just as the Federal Reserve Banks do today. But they did not customarily maintain large excess reserves because they were private institutions operated for profit. During their first half century the Federal Reserve Banks could usually create new reserves for the member banks when necessary because, not trying to maximize their own earnings, they were not nearly loaned up. Today, with a reserve no longer required against their deposits, the Federal Reserve Banks' power to make loans is limitless.

The Federal Reserve Banks have been authorized from the outset to discount for the member banks. In fact, originally a bank could only borrow from the Federal Reserve by endorsing short-term paper which it held. Yet in spite of the importance of discounting by a central bank, the nature of the process was not clearly understood when the Federal Reserve began operations. To many it appeared that the significant fact was that the Federal Reserve was pooling reserves. All member banks were required to hold their reserves with the Federal Reserve. From this pool of reserves, it was asserted, the Federal Reserve could shift funds to those banks in need of them.

This reasoning involved the same confusion we observed earlier in the statement that a bank lends its deposits. The Federal Reserve is a bankers' bank. It can no more lend its deposits, which are the reserves of the member banks, than can the member banks lend their deposits, which are the balances due to their customers. Rather, the Federal Reserve creates additional deposits when it discounts, just as the member banks similarly create deposits by lending and discounting.

There are two important differences: unlike the individual member bank, the Federal Reserve Bank is not required to maintain reserves against its deposits; and unlike the member bank, the Federal Reserve Bank has the power of note issue. If member banks wish to withdraw their deposits, Federal Reserve authorities may furnish them currency in place of the deposits. The Reserve Banks need not liquidate their assets as, to some extent, would be necessary for a member bank faced with heavy deposit withdrawals. The Reserve Banks simply replace one liability with another liability, creating the currency as they extinguish the deposits.

However, when the Federal Reserve began operations, it was required to maintain reserves against its deposits, and its notes were redeemable in gold. At that time there was some truth in the contention that the Federal Reserve's lending power resulted from its holding reserves of member banks. To be sure, it certainly did not lend those reserves. On the other hand, it could make loans by creating additional reserves only as long as the banking system continued willing to hold those added deposits with the Federal Reserve. If the banks had insisted on withdrawing reserves as fast as they were created, either gold or Federal Reserve notes in circulation would have rapidly increased. If the Federal Reserve notes were presented for redemption in gold or if reserves were withdrawn in the form of gold, the reserves of the Federal Reserve Banks themselves would have decreased and the Federal Reserve might have been obliged to contract its credit. As long as the Federal Reserve was required to redeem its obligations in gold, there was this possibility of its own reserves being drained into circulation.

One of the most important consequences of our present system is precisely this freedom that it permits the central bank. Because the public no longer can demand gold, the Federal Reserve Banks (and also the Treasury) have far more freedom in policy determination. For better or for worse, this is the reason there has been so little official support of proposals for a return to the pre-1933 gold standard.

The Discount Rate as an Instrument of Control

The discount rate permits the Federal Reserve to restrain or encourage discounting by changing the cost of acquiring reserves through discounting. Earlier we saw that if a bank has to have paper discounted at a higher rate than the rate at which it originally discounted the paper, it will be reluctant to discount.[3] True, banks seldom discount with the Federal Reserve Banks to increase loans to their own customers. They know that the Board of Governors expects them to stay out of debt to the Federal Reserve Banks except in emergency and that borrowing is considered a privilege, not a right, which is to be done for need, not profit.

But they do watch the discount rate as an indication of Federal Reserve policy and the availability of credit. When the Banks lower the discount rate, member banks conclude that money will be easy; when the discount rate is raised, member banks begin to restrict credit, considering loan applications more critically and raising their own rates. The discount rate is an important business barometer. In fact, because the discount rate is more widely publicized and better understood by the public than are open market operations, the "announcement effect" from changes in the discount rate affects expectations. While the interest rate is only indirectly related to the discount rate, the evidence does suggest that the interest rate on short-term money market instruments, such as Treasury bills and the prime rate, is associated with the discount rate, with the discount rate typically trailing the interest rate.

In the Federal Reserve's early years the discount rate was related primarily to the Federal Reserve Banks' reserve ratio. Just as the Bank of England and the central banks of other nations raised their discount rates when their reserve ratios fell, so the Federal Reserve Banks watched the ratio of their gold to their total liabilities. (At that time the Banks were required to maintain a reserve in gold certificates or gold against both their notes and deposits.) As this ratio approached the legal minimum, they raised the discount rate. Such an increase tended to reduce liabilities of the Federal Reserve Banks. Banks that had borrowed from the Reserve Banks tightened credit more severely, increased their excess reserves, and drew against their reserve balances to get

---

[3]This is obvious enough if we remember that a bank can lend only about the amount of its excess reserves and that regardless of what the system as a whole can do a bank never lends several times that amount. A bank definitely cannot borrow $1 million at 6 percent and lend $5 million at 5 percent.

out of debt even more promptly than ordinarily. As Federal Reserve Bank deposits fell, there was a proportionate decrease in the amount of gold required as reserves against deposits. At the same time there was an increase in the amount of gold actually held. The rise in the discount rate tended to attract gold from abroad, since the general interest rate level in this country would then tend to be higher than elsewhere. Some of this gold would be deposited with the Reserve Banks. With gold reserves increasing and deposits decreasing as loans were repaid to the Reserve Banks, the ratio of reserves to deposits quickly rose.

But as early as 1922 the reserve ratio had become unimportant as a guide to credit policy. By that time the Federal Reserve Banks held so much gold that the reserve ratio was far above the legal minimum. For nearly 40 years thereafter the discount rate level was determined less objectively, on the basis of general credit conditions.

Originally in keeping with the plan to establish regional Banks, each Bank seems to have been expected to set its own rates, appropriate to conditions in its district. For a short period in the 1920s the Banks tried a system of graduated rates, charging higher rates as member banks' borrowings increased in proportion to their contributions to the capital and surplus of Reserve Banks. With the expiration of the authority to establish rate differentials on that basis, each Bank charged the same rate to all borrowers in its district except that by law it was required to charge slightly higher rates on certain types of advances. Also, during both World Wars the Banks established preferential rates on loans secured by government obligations.

Since 1942 the basic rate on eligible paper has often been the same in all districts, as though there were only 1 central bank instead of 12. There have been occasional differences of one fourth or even one half of 1 percent among Banks; but usually if one Bank changes the generally prevailing rate, all other Banks quickly follow suit.

It has never been entirely clear whether rates should be set by the Banks or by the Board of Governors. The Act states that the Banks shall at least every 14 days, and more often if instructed by the Board of Governors, "establish" discount rates "subject to review and determination by the Board of Governors." The Board interprets this language to give them much more power than merely to approve the rates established. The Board of Governors maintains that the authority to "demand" that rates be established and the authority to "determine" rates gives them power to set the rate level and to initiate rate changes.

Restrictions on Discounting

Along with the desire to establish a discounting agency that could lend to banks in need of funds was also the fear that such discounting might lead to excessive credit expansion and inflation. Accordingly, both Congress and the Federal Reserve Board established several checks to insure that the credit created would be in proportion to the legitimate needs of the economy and backed by adequate cash reserves for the Federal Reserve Banks. Besides the discount rate, these included the provisions regarding reserve requirements, redemption, eligibility, and acceptability. Over the years most of these checks have been weakened or removed entirely.

Reserve Requirements. At the outset the Federal Reserve Banks were required to maintain reserves against both notes and deposits, originally in gold or gold certificates, and since 1934 in gold certificates only. (For convenience we shall refer only to gold certificates.) From 1945 to 1965 the requirement, as set by Congress, was 25 percent against both liabilities.[4]

Thus, although the Federal Reserve Banks could create credit, there was a limit to the amount they could create. In lending to member banks they increased the amount of their own deposits. Also, if gold flowed out of the country, the Federal Reserve lost gold certificates. If at any time, whether because of an increase in liabilities or a decrease in gold certificates, the Federal Reserve Banks had found their liabilities were four times as great as the amount of their gold certificates, they would then have been unable to expand credit further. They could make new loans only as old loans were paid off, decreasing their liabilities and required reserves and thereby creating excess reserves.

The Federal Reserve Banks were never intended to follow a policy of expanding credit as far as their gold certificate reserves would permit. A maximum credit expansion would result in maximum earnings, of course, but the Federal Reserve Banks were not organized for that purpose. Only by maintaining excess reserves would they be able to lend freely when the banking system and the economy needed more credit.

There were, however, three occasions when the reserve requirements threatened to become restrictive. In 1933, gold withdrawals reduced the reserves of the Federal Reserve Banks to the point that the Board of Governors was forced briefly to suspend the requirement. By 1945 the wartime increase in both notes and deposits of the Federal Reserve Banks had become so great that Congress lowered the percentage of reserves required to the 25 percent figure. Twenty years later Congress removed the reserve requirement against deposits. The purpose of this change was to release the gold certificates tied up as a reserve against deposits and thereby make more gold available to meet foreign demand. The gold outflow continued, and in March, 1968, the reserve requirement against notes was also abandoned. Finally, in August, 1971, gold convertibility was terminated even for foreign treasuries.

It would be unreasonable to charge that in any of these cases the suspension, reduction, or removal of required reserves was due only or even primarily to a mistaken and reckless overexpansion of credit by the Federal Reserve Banks. They can hardly be held responsible for World War II and its

---

[4]Originally the reserve requirements were somewhat more complicated. Reserves of 35 percent were required against deposits, and 40 percent against notes. Also, while the reserves against notes had to be entirely in the form of gold or gold certificates, the reserves against deposits might be in the optional form of "lawful money," which included greenbacks and silver certificates, but not Federal Reserve notes. The option of "lawful money" reserves may have been necessary 50 years ago, when the Federal Reserve's stock of gold certificates was less than $2 billion and when reserve requirements were higher. It would serve no useful purpose today, especially since silver certificates have been withdrawn from circulation.

financial requirements. Perhaps the panic in 1933 might have been avoided by more skillful monetary management, but this is uncertain; the collapse of credit at that time was not primarily domestic but worldwide. The gold losses during the 1960s were the result of a number of factors. For the Federal Reserve System to have prevented the gold outflow would have called for a monetary policy so restrictive that the government would have refused to tolerate it.

This evaluation is not to imply that the Federal Reserve never makes a mistake.[5] It is to suggest that the requirement of a gold certificate reserve against Federal Reserve liabilities has proved to be considerably less useful than was originally expected. In normal times it is unnecessary. Most of the time the Federal Reserve Banks have expanded credit far less than their reserves would have permitted. The judgment and discretion of the monetary authorities, rather than the amount of the Federal Reserve's legal reserves, have set the limits to the country's money supply.

By removing the reserve requirement against deposits, we have indicated that we are no longer going to even pretend that our gold stock will govern our credit policies. In 1913 we had great confidence in the gold standard's efficacy and its automatic regulation of domestic money and credit, directly or indirectly. Today we place much more emphasis on the importance of discretionary management. Gold has apparently even lost its traditional significance as a convenient means of making international settlements.[6]

Redemption Requirements. Today the Federal Reserve Banks are not only not required, they are not permitted to redeem their notes in gold or gold certificates. They may "redeem" their notes in any form of currency, including their own notes.

In 1913, however, gold certificates were the principal legal tender. All banks were required to redeem their notes in gold or gold certificates upon demand, and the Federal Reserve Banks were no exception. It was hoped that this provision for currency redemption would help check excessive credit expansion. Federal Reserve Banks that were following too liberal a credit policy would find their reserves slipping away as the public presented for redemption the notes that the Banks had been issuing.

Effect of Relaxed Requirements. Lowering reserve requirements and removing redemption requirements has increased greatly the independence of the Federal Reserve. When the Federal Reserve Banks lend (or buy securities

---

[5]See Milton Friedman and Anna J. Schwartz, *A Monetary History of the United States* (Princeton: Princeton University Press, 1963).

[6]This subject of reserve requirements for the Federal Reserve Banks is one on which opinion is divided. Many competent people in the field of money and banking continue to distrust a banking system based entirely on credit with no reserve requirement limiting the possible expansion. They are disturbed by the possibility of limitless inflation. This is an old area of disagreement. More than a century ago English writers were debating almost the same question.

Our own feeling, shared by many but certainly not all economists, is that modern monetary and fiscal policies are incompatible with a credit policy limited by the amount of gold certificates held by the Federal Reserve. The limit seems meaningless anyway, since on the rare occasions when it might have become effective, it was relaxed.

in the open market[7]), they increase their deposit liabilities, which are legal reserves of the member banks. If the Federal Reserve Banks today buy a million dollars (or ten million or ten billion dollars) of securities, their lending power is completely unaffected. Whether or not the credit expansion leads to an increase in Federal Reserve notes is immaterial. With, now, no reserve requirements against either deposits or notes, the term "excess reserves" is meaningless as applied to the condition of the Federal Reserve Banks. Obviously the Federal Reserve is much more free to decide on credit policies today than when it had to consider carefully the probable effects on its reserve position.

Eligibility Requirement. The only paper that member banks originally could present for discount had to meet the standards of eligibility as prescribed in Section 13 of the Federal Reserve Act and determined by the Board of Governors (then called the Federal Reserve Board). The criteria of eligibility were based on the *real bills theory of bank credit,* which asserted that the amount of credit would be properly adjusted to the requirements of the economy if bank loans were made only to supply working capital for business.[8] Such loans were short-term and, it was claimed, self-liquidating. As the level of business activity rose, the banks could expect businesses to increase their borrowing. And as the banks' discounting for businesses caused their reserves to be insufficient in proportion to their deposits, they could discount with the Federal Reserve some of the commercial paper they held. To be eligible for discount, the paper must have arisen out of actual commercial transactions; that is, it might consist of notes, drafts, or bills of exchange issued for industrial, commercial, or agricultural purposes. In cases of agricultural paper its maturity might run to nine months.[9] Otherwise its maturity could not exceed 90 days. In either case the loan should be for the purpose of producing the goods or moving them to market, so that in the normal course of operations the loan would, within the specified time limit, be repaid out of the proceeds of the transaction in connection with which it was made.

One other type of paper was also eligible for discount: notes issued in connection with the purchase or carrying of United States government securities. At the time the Federal Reserve Act was passed, this provision was not of much importance since the total amount of such securities was less than a billion dollars.

The Federal Reserve was not allowed to discount, however, paper arising out of the purchase of securities other than those of the government, or from the purchase of fixed assets, or from loans to consumers. These restrictions on the type of paper eligible for discount at the Federal Reserve were supposed to encourage the member banks to concentrate their lending on commercial paper (real bills), and the restrictions on maturity were supposed to keep both the member banks and the Reserve Banks liquid. If the Federal

---

[7]See Chapter 11.
[8]This theory was also known as the commercial loan theory. See Chapter 7.
[9]Originally six months, later amended to nine.

Reserve were to remain able to lend, it appeared necessary that borrowing banks promptly repay their loans.

Acceptability Requirement. Paper presented for discount had to be acceptable to the Federal Reserve Banks. The Banks reserved the right to refuse paper that met the technical eligibility requirements if, in their opinion, the loan was unsound or the bank attempting to discount had been borrowing too frequently from the Federal Reserve. Also, if Reserve officials felt that, although the paper presented was technically eligible, the borrowing bank intended to use the proceeds of the loan for purposes not in accordance with eligibility standards, they declared such paper nonacceptable.[10] Even though the discounting bank was liable to the Federal Reserve in the event that the borrower could not pay, the Reserve Bank insisted that, to be acceptable for discounting, commercial paper had to be of the very highest grade.[11] The concerns whose paper was presented for discount were to be sound and liquid, and statements had to be furnished for the makers of any individual notes or drafts for more than $5,000. Likewise, the Federal Reserve considered the condition of the bank that wished to discount and the extent to which the bank had borrowed previously.

From the outset, Federal Reserve authorities insisted that discounting was a privilege, not a right. The Banks stood ready to supply reserves temporarily. When member banks found their reserves deficient, they would find the Reserve Banks ready to help them. Member banks should not, however, discount for the deliberate purpose of increasing their own lending ability, the Board of Governors insisted. If a bank's reserves were low, the bank should contract credit somewhere else before making new loans. Or the bank might increase its reserves by selling more capital stock or reinvesting its profits. But it should not depend upon the Federal Reserve Banks to increase its lending potential.

Some of the member banks argued that they were entitled to Federal Reserve credit because they were supplying the capital and carrying their reserve accounts with the Federal Reserve. To this, the Federal Reserve replied that it had been organized to meet temporary needs for additional reserves and thus to benefit the banking system as a whole. If some banks were permitted to remain continuously in debt to the Federal Reserve, other banks could not be accommodated. Rather than rely on the Federal Reserve to supply them with reserves permanently, member banks should either contract their credit or raise additional capital. The banking reforms of 1933–1935 settled the argument and upheld the Federal Reserve's right to refuse to discount eligible paper if, in the opinion of the Bank authorities, such extension of credit would be inadvisable.

---

[10]For example, a bank might present $500,000 of eligible paper for discount; then on the basis of its increased reserves it might lend money to stock speculators.

[11]Exception: paper discounted in emergencies under the provision of Section 10 (b) of the Federal Reserve Act. See p. 286.

These restrictions of reserve requirements, redemption requirements, and eligibility and acceptability requirements reveal the banking philosophy of the Federal Reserve System's creators. Only limited discretion was to be permitted Reserve authorities. The economy was to be guarded against unwise credit expansion by allowing the Banks to lend (1) only when their gold reserves permitted and (2) only to member banks making (3) short-term commercial and agricultural loans. Banking could hardly go far wrong, it was believed, when conducted according to these rules. With their power to determine the discount rate, Reserve authorities were free to change the cost of borrowing; but even here their policy was originally dictated by the their gold position. The only area where they were given any real discretion lay in the acceptability requirement; they could refuse to accommodate perennial borrowers.

Little of this philosophy survives today. As will presently appear, we now give far more responsibility to the people in charge and rely less upon a policy inflexibly dictated by regulations and formulas. Of the five restrictions discussed above, two were restraints over which the Federal Reserve Board and the Board of Governors had no control. The law required them to redeem their notes in gold and to maintain a fractional reserve against their notes and deposits. Both these requirements have been eliminated. Also, Reserve authorities have become more free to use their judgment in setting the discount rate, and as explained below, they now have the right to discount noneligible paper. The condition of acceptability has always been a restraint only on the member banks, never on the Federal Reserve. This restraint is the only one of the five that has not been relaxed or eliminated.

Advances

On September 7, 1916, Section 13 of the Federal Reserve Act was liberalized by granting member banks the right to obtain advances from the Federal Reserve. The difference between an advance and a discount is this: when a bank discounts, it is really selling some of its assets at less than their maturity value; when a bank obtains an advance, it gives to a Reserve Bank its promissory note, secured by the same kind of collateral that otherwise it might have discounted. An advance corresponds more closely to a loan as we ordinarily use the term. Funds are received in return for the specific promise to repay that sum, plus interest, at a later date. In the case of a discount, the bank may collect from the original maker of the note and pass the funds along to the Federal Reserve, but it has not made a specific promise to repay. The distinction between discounts and advances is, however, more in form than in significance. The bank is contingently liable on discounted paper. If the borrower does not pay, the bank must reimburse the Federal Reserve Bank. In this respect the discount does represent, like the advance, a promise.

Direct or indirect obligations of the United States government could also be used as collateral for advances. (Indirect obligations are those issued by federal government corporations rather than by the United States Treasury.)

This provision was not of great importance until the United States entered World War I.

The banks did very little discounting after they were permitted to get advances by giving their collateral notes. On several counts they preferred advances. Some of their customers objected to having their paper discounted, feeling that their affairs were being publicized. They were unaware if their notes were used as collateral for an advance. Also, some customers, especially in a period of financial tension, might have less confidence in the bank if they knew it was forced to obtain funds from the Federal Reserve. Finally, advances were more convenient because the exact maturity of the paper was unimportant. If a bank needed reserve funds for a week or ten days, it would make out a note for that period of time and attach eligible collateral such as commercial paper, agricultural paper, or government securities. It paid interest only for the time that it needed the loan, and at the end of that time it regained the assets it had pledged. When it presented for discount, that is, sold eligible paper, the bank was obliged, if it wished to minimize the cost of this credit, to go through its portfolio carefully and select for discount only that paper that was within a few days of maturity. If, for example, it needed reserve credit for a week and the shortest maturity of eligible paper it held was 30 days, the bank was paying four times as much interest as it would pay by securing a one week advance. If the demand for loans was keen, the bank might be able after a week to make new loans to replace those that had been discounted; but it was simpler to get an advance and retain title to the collateral. As provided by the 1916 amendment, banks could obtain advances of up to 15 days. Later changes now permit advances of up to 90 days.

Ineligible Paper Accepted. The Reserve Banks were also authorized in 1932 to make advances of up to four months on collateral technically ineligible but satisfactory to the Bank. These advances, provision for which is made by Section 10(b) of the Act, permit the Federal Reserve to assist banks that may be fundamentally sound but that cannot present eligible collateral. Such advances are required to carry an interest rate at least ½ percent higher than the basic discount rate then prevailing at the Bank, applicable to discounts of eligible commercial paper and to advances secured by such paper or by government obligations. This penalty rate is a carry-over from the real bills doctrine of a generation ago, upon which the requirements of eligibility were based. There is considerable question as to whether the best interests of banking and the public are served by increasing borrowing costs at a time when the banks are already operating under difficulties. If the bank's condition is sound enough to justify a loan at such a time, there seems to be little point in applying a penalty rate, especially since banking authorities are no longer convinced that a bank's lending activities should be confined primarily to commercial loans as required by the real bills doctrine. Moreover, there is really no reason to require any collateral behind commercial bank loans from the Fed.

Discounts and Advances Today. Most loans the Federal Reserve Banks make today are in the form of advances, and most of the time the only collateral is eligible paper rather than the paper permitted by Section 10(b), discounted at a higher rate. However, borrowing from the Federal Reserve, in whatever form, is usually much less significant today than it was in earlier years. During the decade of the 1920s, discounts and advances totaled, on an average, anywhere from about half a billion to a billion dollars. Today, with total bank deposits over eight times as great as they were then, advances and discounts have seldom been above a billion dollars in the last 20 years and peaked at about $2 billion. As long as the Federal Reserve Banks supply ample reserves through their open market purchases, the banks need not borrow. Besides, with the commercial banks themselves holding about $50 billion of Treasury securities, those banks that do need funds can easily dispose of some of their securities rather than ask for loans.

On April 19, 1973, the Federal Reserve System established a seasonal borrowing privilege through an amendment to its Regulation A governing the lending process of Federal Reserve Banks. Prior to this, borrowing by a member bank on a prearranged basis to meet seasonal loan demands or deposit declines was considered an inappropriate use of the discount window. This change was made in response to the growing awareness that many banks maintained a high level of liquid assets to meet these seasonal flows since they lacked access to external sources of funds, such as the sale of money market instruments. Retaining an excess of liquid assets, however, reduced the volume of long-term credit banks could make available. Thus, the seasonal borrowing privilege would help banks meet both the seasonal and nonseasonal credit needs of their communities. A large proportion of small, rural, and agriculturally oriented member banks are expected to qualify for and use the new seasonal borrowing privilege.[12]

Shortcomings of the Discount Mechanism. There are at least four major shortcomings of the Fed's discount mechanism for injecting and withdrawing reserves.

1. The discount rate or price of borrowing from the Fed applies only to member banks, which now constitute only about 40 percent of all commercial banks.
2. The quantity and availability of lending by the Fed is not indicated by the discount rate and can be altered significantly by such things as changes in collateral requirements.
3. The initiative for borrowing rests with the member banks. If excess reserves are plentiful as in the 1930s and 1940s, lowering the discount rate will elicit little or no additional borrowing and the Fed is helpless to inject new reserves into the system. Today with few excess reserves available, changes in the discount rate are more meaningful.

[12]See Margaret E. Bedford, "The Seasonal Borrowing Privilege," *Monthly Review* of the Federal Reserve Bank of Kansas City (June, 1974), pp. 10–16.

4. A change in the discount rate affects reserves and the money supply much less than do open market purchases and sales and changes in reserve requirements. For instance, in the post-World War II period discounting on average provided about 2 to 3 percent of total bank reserves and never reached as high as 10 percent.[13]

THE NEW CURRENCY

Earlier we noted that in the period of state banking the New England banks issued notes secured by general assets. Free banking laws required that notes be secured by specified collateral for the better protection of noteholders. The National Banking Act adopted the same principle in requiring that notes be secured by obligations of the United States. This bond-secured currency, although safe, turned out to be inelastic; and the frequent shortages of currency were often inconvenient and sometimes disastrous. To replace the national bank note currency, the Federal Reserve Banks were authorized to issue two distinct types of currency: Federal Reserve notes and Federal Reserve Bank notes.

Federal Reserve Notes

The principal currency that the Federal Reserve was to provide was the Federal Reserve note. The legislators hoped this currency would be an elastic currency, expanding and contracting with the needs of trade.

Discounted Commercial Paper as Collateral. To insure the elasticity of Federal Reserve notes, the Federal Reserve Act provided that the new currency should be backed entirely by short-term commercial paper that the Banks had discounted for the member banks. There was one exception which at the time appeared unimportant. According to Section 13 of the Federal Reserve Act, the Reserve Banks could discount notes made for the purpose of purchasing or carrying United States government securities; and since, according to Section 16, the collateral behind Federal Reserve notes was to consist of "notes and bills, accepted for discount under the provisions of Section 13 of this Act," it would have been possible for Federal Reserve note collateral to consist of the discounted promissory note of an individual or business concern backed by government securities. Since the total interest-bearing debt of the federal government was less than a billion dollars at the time the Federal Reserve Act was passed, this possibility appeared to be of little significance. It was to contribute in 1932, however, to the complete contradiction of the original principle of Federal Reserve note issue.

This policy of commercial paper as note collateral involved a direct reversal of the principle of bond-secured currency introduced by free banking and maintained by the national banking system. Backed only by discounted commercial paper, the new currency was supposed to be sufficient at all times for

---

[13]See Robert H. Rasche, "A Review of Empirical Studies on the Money Supply Mechanism," *Review* of the Federal Reserve Bank of St. Louis (July, 1972), pp. 11–19.

the needs of trade. At a time when business was slow, businesses would be borrowing little from member banks which, in turn, would be doing little discounting at the Federal Reserve.

An upper limit was set on note issue by requiring that Federal Reserve notes in circulation be backed by a 40 percent reserve in gold (or gold certificates). This reserve requirement was in addition to the requirement of 100 percent collateral. Regardless of how much collateral (discounted paper) they might hold, the maximum volume of notes the Banks could have in circulation would be 2½ times the amount of such gold as was not required as legal reserve against their deposits. But on the other hand, regardless of how much gold they held, the Banks could issue notes only when they held the necessary collateral in the form of discounts.

Gold Substituted for Commercial Paper as Collateral. In spite of all the fanfare about the benefits of the new currency, the Federal Reserve note did not long remain automatically elastic. The Federal Reserve Banks themselves scuttled the concept by evading the requirement that the notes be backed 100 percent by discounted commercial paper.

According to the law, Federal Reserve notes could be issued only when backed 100 percent by discounts. But issuing notes does not mean placing them in circulation. Notes are issued to the Bank by the Federal Reserve Agent. (See Chapter 2.) The Agent issues notes when other officials of the Bank turn over the prescribed collateral. Later the Bank places the notes in circulation. Only then does the reserve requirement become effective.

Remember that this discounted paper was short-term paper. When, in a month or so, it was due, Bank officials had to get it back from the Agent so they could turn it over to the original borrowers for payment. Then the question arose: what about the Federal Reserve notes that had been issued against that paper?

1. One obvious possibility would have been for the Bank officials to give the Agent a fresh batch of discounts in exchange for the maturing commercial paper. This practice would have been in harmony with the idea of an automatically elastic currency. It would have indicated that, with new borrowing replacing old borrowing, the needs of credit and commerce were unchanged, and therefore there should be no change in the amount of currency.
2. Another obvious possibility would have been for the officials to surrender to the Agent Federal Reserve notes, equal in amount to the value of the discounted commercial paper they were receiving from the Agent. This practice, too, would have been in harmony with the concept of an elastic currency. It would have implied that the officials lacked newly discounted paper because businesses were borrowing less—and with this drop in the level of business activity, the supply of currency was being reduced by pulling Federal Reserve notes out of circulation.

The Reserve Banks soon began, however, to follow neither of the above policies. Instead, they redeemed with gold (or gold certificates) the collateral held by the Agents. This did not violate the letter of the law, but certainly violated its spirit. It permitted the Banks to keep their notes in circulation in spite of a decline in business and even if they currently held no discounted paper. As long as they discounted occasionally, they could meet the requirements of the law by using that paper as collateral for newly issued notes, later replacing it with gold and leaving their notes in circulation.

Federal Reserve authorities may have lacked central banking experience, but they were learning fast! They had discovered how to pay for gold by issuing their own notes. When member banks turned in excess currency, the Reserve Banks sorted out the gold certificates and gold and used them to redeem the collateral they had pledged with the Agents. When member banks requested currency, the Banks paid out their own notes, retaining the gold and gold certificates. The law may have been stretched and twisted a bit, but our banking was improved. Although this procedure was not intended by the framers of the Federal Reserve Act, it did greatly strengthen the Federal Reserve System. The more gold the Federal Reserve Banks held, the greater the volume of discounting they could do if the need arose. It did decrease the cyclical elasticity of Federal Reserve notes, but the authorities felt that the benefits outweighed the damage to the original concept of an automatically elastic currency.

For these reasons the Federal Reserve Board rebuked one Bank that was returning gold certificates to circulation to avoid the cost of printing and issuing its own notes, pointing out that, "while the Board recognized the importance of small economies in the operation and administration of the Federal Reserve Banks," the Banks should not lose sight of the larger goals. The Board stressed the desirability of keeping as much gold as possible in the Federal Reserve Banks and the Treasury.

The Board urged that the need for this roundabout procedure be eliminated by amending the Act to permit the Banks to issue notes secured by gold so that, if required, notes might be backed 100 percent by gold, with no corresponding short-term paper whatever.

By an amendment of June 21, 1917, the principle that the collateral behind Federal Reserve notes must be discounted paper was abandoned. The Federal Reserve Banks were permitted to use either short-term paper or gold to meet the requirement of 100 percent collateral. Any gold used as collateral, moreover, would be counted as part of the 40 percent reserve required against notes in circulation. The gold, in short, was to serve as both reserve (necessarily) and collateral (optionally). If the Banks were doing enough discounting, notes in circulation could be backed, as before, 100 percent by commercial paper and also by the 40 percent gold reserve. Alternatively, however, they might now be backed only 100 percent—as long as gold was at least 40 percent of the total. It could be as much as 100 percent of the total. Henceforth notes might be backed entirely by gold, if the Federal Reserve held no discounted paper. Granting that this change strengthened the position of the Federal Reserve, we must recognize at the same time that it was a complete short circuiting of the basic philosophy of an automatically elastic currency as earlier stated in the Act. It was also a stricture on the operation of the "automatic" gold standard, permitting the Federal Reserve to offset the effects of gold movements.

Government Securities Used Indirectly as Collateral. The amendment of 1916 permitted the Reserve Banks to make loans to member banks by taking their promissory notes, which were eligible as collateral against Federal Reserve notes. Since the promissory notes might be secured by federal government obligations and since the government debt was shooting up from less than $1 billion in 1916 to more than $25 billion by 1919, the Federal Reserve began to use government securities as a kind of indirect collateral for Federal Reserve notes. The government obligations were not in themselves eligible collateral, but they could serve as the basis for the bank advances which were eligible.

Government Securities Authorized as Collateral. During the 1920s and early 1930s the Federal Reserve continued this policy of issuing notes backed by member banks' notes secured by either commercial paper or government obligations or backed by gold in excess of the 40 percent reserve required. By 1932 it was apparent that the rules must be changed if the Federal Reserve was to be able to help meet the banking crisis.

The situation was this:

1. The member banks needed large additional supplies of currency to pay off frightened depositors who were withdrawing their accounts.
2. Gold withdrawals by the public in the fall of 1931 had reduced the Federal Reserve's gold reserves from about $3.7 billion to less than $3 billion.
3. The Federal Reserve was attempting by open market operations to get the member banks out of debt and to supply plentiful bank reserves. In July, 1929, the Reserve Banks held less than $150 million of government securities and $1,100 million of bills discounted or bought in the open market. By the end of 1931 they held nearly $800 million of government securities. As a result the total of bills discounted or bought had fallen to about $250 million by July of 1931.
4. The Federal Reserve found that its efforts to continue providing the banking system with additional currency and reserves were hampered by the lack of eligible collateral. The policy of reducing member bank indebtedness was diametrically opposed to the policy of issuing more currency, since according to the Federal Reserve Act currency could be backed only by gold or by paper resulting from the borrowings of member banks (or by commercial paper bought in the open market). In supplying additional currency, the Federal Reserve was obliged to tie up considerably more gold than the minimum requirement of 40 percent, since other than gold it held little eligible collateral. In February, 1932, the Reserve Banks held approximately $1.4 billion of excess reserves but, lacking other collateral, were obliged to tie up $1 billion of this gold as collateral against Federal Reserve notes. The total of $2.9 billion of notes was supported by $.9 billion of commercial paper and $2 billion of gold. This left the thin margin of $.4 billion of "free" gold to pay out upon demand or to use as the basis for further note issue.

To free their gold by substituting other collateral, Reserve authorities requested permission to back their notes directly with government securities, subject to the usual requirement that the notes be backed by a 40 percent gold reserve. As an emergency measure the Glass-Steagall Bill of February 27, 1932, permitted the Banks to issue notes secured by government obligations purchased in the open market. Permission in each instance had to be specifically granted by the Board of Governors, and the authority was to terminate March 3, 1933. The effects of this legislation were promptly felt as the Federal Reserve undertook what were up to that time the largest open market operations in its history. By the end of 1932 the Reserve Banks held nearly $2 billion of government securities, and the total of paper discounted or purchased had dropped from $1.1 billion to about $.3 billion. Member reserves during the same period had increased from $1.9 to $2.4 billion. However, the greatest effect of this authorization was not felt until later. Subsequent legislation extended the authority, and in 1945 the Federal Reserve Act was amended to permit the Banks to use government securities as collateral at any time and without applying to the Board for permission. In urging the passage of this legislation, Reserve authorities pointed out that the risk factor of government securities is little affected by the consideration of whether they are endorsed by member banks. However, this point had never been the issue. The reason that government securities were not, from the outset, made eligible collateral for note issue was that the monetary experts were at that time attempting to break away from precisely that kind of currency.

In consequence of the massive gold inflow during the latter 1930s and the concentration of gold certificates in the Federal Reserve vaults, the permission to use government securities as note collateral was, after the panic, not again important until World War II. The great increase that occurred at that time in currency in circulation necessitated an extensive and constantly increasing reliance on this method of note issue. The historical trend of the actual collateral used in selected years is shown in Table 10-1.

As observed earlier, the nature of the Federal Reserve note today disturbs some thoughtful bankers and economists. In effect, the Federal Reserve note has become irredeemable government debt.

1. The Federal Reserve Banks may, if convenient, issue Federal Reserve notes to buy Treasury securities.
2. The Federal Reserve Banks are not required to redeem their notes (other than by the meaningless gesture of exchanging other Federal Reserve notes for them).
3. The Treasury obligations, when due, may be paid in these same Federal Reserve notes.

The whole operation would be much simpler and more obvious if instead of selling a billion dollars of bonds to the Federal Reserve Banks and receiving irredeemable Federal Reserve notes (or deposits) in exchange, the Treasury itself simply printed a billion dollars of irredeemable notes. Admittedly either policy, carried to excess, opens the door to the kind of inflation that swept Germany in the 1920s. We have lost the safeguard of gold as a limiting factor to credit expansion.

Table 10-1 Collateral for Federal Reserve Notes Outstanding

Year (December)	Government Securities (% of Total Collateral)	Commercial Paper, etc. (% of Total Collateral)	Gold or Gold Certif. (% of Total Collateral)
1928	0	46	54
1930	0	23	77
1932	14	7	79
1934	7	0.2	93
1936	2	0.1	98
1938	0	0.1	100
1940	0	0.03	100
1942	3	0.02	97
1944	52	0.6	47
1946	58	0.05	42
1948	47	0.2	53
1950	46	1.0	53
1960	68	0.07	32
1970	94	0.00	6
1974	95	0.00	5*

Source: Adapted from *Federal Reserve Bulletins*.
*Includes Special Drawing Rights Certificate account.

On the other hand, the ability to issue notes against government securities, along with other changes in the original Act, strengthens the powers of the Federal Reserve and permits the exercise of more discretion. Experience indicates that the attempt to prescribe rigid rules with respect to lending and currency issuance is likely to cause difficulties in times of emergency and that, rather than improvise solutions at such times, it may be better to repose greater confidence in the ability and discretion of the monetary authorities by increasing the powers at their disposal. Finally, as will be shown in Chapter 22, inflation does not necessarily result if, instead of levying taxes, the government pays part of its bills with newly created money. There are times when an increase in the money supply (whether caused by the government or the banking system) will encourage a rise in prices. However, there are also times when it will not and circumstances under which it would be a serious error not to expand the money supply.

Federal Reserve Bank Notes

At one time Federal Reserve Banks were authorized to issue a second type of currency, Federal Reserve Bank notes. In contrast to Federal Reserve notes, hedged with restrictions, Federal Reserve Bank notes required no gold reserve and from the outset could be secured by government bonds. Later (in 1933) they could also be secured by discounted paper. This possibility, however, was never of practical significance.

They never achieved the importance of Federal Reserve notes, nor were they expected to. On several occasions they were temporarily useful. When the Federal Reserve began operations, Federal Reserve Bank notes were used to some extent to replace national bank notes withdrawn from circulation. They were used again during World War I to replace silver certificates pulled out of circulation when the Treasury sold silver to England. Their issuance was authorized during the bank holidays in 1933 because the authorities feared that when the banks reopened bank runs might resume, and other currency was becoming scarce. They were last placed in circulation in World War II to help meet the public's demand for more currency.

The 1945 amendments to the Federal Reserve Act (1) reducing the minimum reserves required against Federal Reserve notes, and (2) permitting Federal Reserve notes to be issued directly against government obligations, made it apparent that there was no longer any need for a special type of emergency currency. Any remaining differences between Federal Reserve notes and Federal Reserve Bank notes were of technical rather than practical significance, especially as, since 1933, the public no longer had the right to demand that Federal Reserve notes be redeemed in gold. Consequently, Congress terminated the Federal Reserve's authority to issue Federal Reserve Bank notes.

GRAPHICAL SUMMARY OF CREDIT POLICY INSTRUMENTS

Figure 10-1 shows the relationship of the various credit policy instruments which are available to the Federal Reserve to achieve its goals of promoting long-run growth in the economy and dampening short-run fluctuations. The thrust of general monetary policy is made effective through the coordinated use of its three complimentary instruments: open market operations, member bank discounts, and member bank reserve requirements. While the initial impact of the Federal Reserve actions is on the cost and availability of bank reserves, the effects of these changes rather quickly spread to the supply of money and credit, interest rates, and overall liquidity. Ultimately, after time lags of varying lengths, these financial factors in turn affect expenditures, employment, output, and prices.

SUMMARY AND CONCLUSION

Legal reserves of a member bank are vault cash and, primarily, the deposits it holds with its Federal Reserve Bank. When its reserves are too low, it secures additional reserves by borrowing from the Federal Reserve Bank. The latter does not lend the excess reserves of some other bank nor lend, somehow, from the "pool" of member reserves. It creates new member reserves when it lends.

The central reserve city banks did the same thing in the pre-Federal Reserve days. However, the central reserve city banks ordinarily made all the loans they could, so they had no room to expand credit in emergencies. The Reserve Banks, not operated for profit, customarily maintained large excess

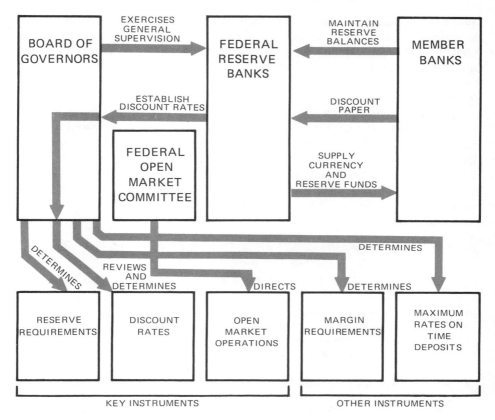

Source: *The Federal Reserve System: Purposes and Functions*
(6th ed.; Washington: Board of Governors,
September, 1974), p. 50.

Figure 10-1   The Federal Reserve—Relation to Instruments of Credit Policy

reserves. When member banks needed more reserves, the Reserve Banks could easily create them by expanding their own loans. Today, of course, no longer subject to any reserve requirements, the Federal Reserve Banks have unlimited lending power.

From the beginning, Reserve authorities emphasized that credit at the Reserve Banks is a privilege, not a right. Member banks are not supposed to borrow to increase their owns loans and investments, but only to correct a reserve deficiency. They are expected to take prompt steps to correct this deficiency and repay the Federal Reserve Bank.

Originally banks obtained reserves only by discounting when dealing with the Federal Reserve Banks. Later, advances replaced discounts almost entirely, although the term "discount" is still used in a broad sense to refer to any loans by the Reserve Banks to member banks.

The Banks together with the Board of Governors set the rate at which the Banks will discount commercial paper or make advances to member banks.

While the discount mechanism has some serious shortcomings, by raising and lowering the discount rate, Federal Reserve authorities can exercise some control over credit expansion by member banks. Changes in the discount rate not only change the cost of borrowing, but also are an indicator of official opinion regarding the soundness of business and credit.

Federal Reserve notes have gone through a kind of reverse evolution. Originally introduced as a currency backed by discounted commercial paper, the Federal Reserve note was supposed to replace the bond-secured national bank notes. For the last 35–40 years commercial paper has seldom been more than a fraction of 1 percent of the collateral, and the principal collateral has frequently been government securities, as with the old national bank notes.

Because of the changes in Federal Reserve notes, there is no longer any need for the former emergency currency, the Federal Reserve Bank note, now being retired.

Discussion Questions

1. Why is the term "discount rate" used instead of the older term "rediscount rate"?
2. Would you ordinarily expect that after a member bank borrows at a Federal Reserve Bank the member bank will increase its loans or decrease them? Why?
3. How was the usefulness of discounting greatly increased by the organization of the Federal Reserve?
4. Why did the Federal Reserve Banks find it impossible during the Depression to help member banks get out of debt and at the same time supply the member banks with the additional currency being demanded by frightened depositors? How was the difficulty overcome?
5. Briefly explain the three restrictions on the lending power of the Federal Reserve Banks when they began operations.
6. "Since member banks know that the Board of Governors expects them to stay out of debt to the Federal Reserve Banks except in an emergency, the discount rate is a seldom-considered instrument of control." True or False? Explain.
7. Are member bank reserves today larger or smaller than they were 50 years ago? What is the principal direct means by which this change was brought about?
8. During the early years of the Federal Reserve System, might a banker be holding paper eligible but unacceptable for discount at the Federal Reserve Bank? Might the banker be holding paper ineligible but acceptable? Briefly explain.
9. The real bills theory of bank credit was the basis of the eligibility requirement for discounting. Explain.
10. What is the difference between an advance and a discount, and why did the banks usually prefer advances?

11. "Borrowing by a member bank from the Federal Reserve to meet seasonal loan demands or deposit declines is considered an inappropriate use of the discount window." True or False? Explain.

12. Briefly discuss four major shortcomings of the Fed's discount mechanism for changing member bank reserves.

13. By what regulations did the framers of the Federal Reserve Act attempt to provide an elastic currency?

14. What is the principal advantage and the principal disadvantage of requiring the Federal Reserve Banks to maintain in gold certificates a fractional reserve against their note and deposit liabilities?

15. What exactly were the Federal Reserve Banks trying to accomplish when they began substituting gold certificates for the maturing discounted paper held against notes the Banks had issued? Why?

16. What is the principal collateral today behind Federal Reserve notes? When did we have a similar currency? Why is it more satisfactory today than it was then?

17. The Federal Reserve note of today is close to, and possibly will soon become equivalent to, the original Federal Reserve Bank note. Explain.

18. Can you see any advantages in having the Federal Reserve Banks issue their notes, as they do, backed by government securities, rather than having the Treasury itself issue the same volume of notes instead of issuing securities? Any disadvantages?

Chapter 11 The Federal Reserve: Further Development and Redirection

We have touched on the original responsibilities and powers of the Federal Reserve, observing that over the years the responsibilities have eroded and the powers have increased. Removal of the obligation to redeem notes and deposits in gold, removal of the obligation to maintain reserves against liabilities, permission to lend directly rather than only through discounts, permission to lend against technically ineligible collateral, permission to back Federal Reserve notes with Treasury securities—all of these were steps in the gradual establishment of a strong and independent central bank. In this chapter we shall continue to trace the changes in the Federal Reserve, studying the additional powers it has acquired and the change in the credit control philosophy that they reveal.

INCREASING THE AVAILABILITY OF CREDIT TO BUSINESS

Remembering the opposition that finally destroyed the Bank of the United States, the framers of the Federal Reserve Act took care to prevent the 12 Banks from competing with private banks. No provision was made originally for the Federal Reserve Banks to supply credit to business except indirectly as member banks discounted their customers' notes at the Federal Reserve Banks. After the Federal Reserve System had become thoroughly established and its importance recognized by everyone, the precaution against competition seemed less necessary. The Depression emphasized that there might be occasions when direct loans to business by the Federal Reserve would be helpful.

Direct Loans to Business

In 1932 the Federal Reserve Banks received for the first time the authority to make loans directly to business, but only if the borrowers were unable to obtain credit elsewhere. That the Federal Reserve should be permitted, under any circumstances, to lend directly to business suggests general public acceptance of the Federal Reserve. On the other hand, at least as matters turned out, it appears doubtful that this power was needed. It was authorized during the bank holidays, when there was apprehension that, with the banks closed, employers might be unable to meet their payrolls. The rapid reopening of the banks made it unnecessary. Also, there was some feeling at the time that business needed credit that the banks were unable or unwilling to supply. In retrospect, it appears that the banks were able to accommodate most of the legitimate credit requirements. Provision for these direct loans was in part repealed by the Small Business Investment Act. (See Chapter 4.)

Guarantee of Industrial Loans

Much more important were the World War II V loans, on which guarantees were arranged by the Federal Reserve Banks on behalf of government procurement agencies. President Roosevelt had instructed the War Department, Navy Department, and Maritime Commission to provide guarantees for loans that they considered essential to the war effort, and directed the Federal Reserve Banks to act as the agents of these agencies. In Regulation V, the Board of Governors spelled out the procedure. After a loan to finance war production had been certified as essential by a representative of the War Department, Navy Department, or Maritime Commission, a Federal Reserve Bank arranged the guarantee on behalf of that agency. With this guarantee, usually to 90 percent of the amount of the loan, the borrower had little difficulty in obtaining a loan from a bank. For the bank, it was almost as safe as buying Treasury securities. Later, VT loans appeared as a variation involving the termination of military contracts at the end of the war. Although the program has been repeatedly extended, it is currently of little significance.

Evaluation of Federal Reserve Loans and Guarantees

A policy of guarantees by the Federal Reserve, either directly or as agent for the government, may be necessary in war or a period of financial crisis. It appears undesirable under normal conditions. It would encourage bankers to look for risk-free loans, demanding guarantees on loans that involved any degree of uncertainty.[1] The principal risk taker would be the government or the Federal Reserve. It is hardly appropriate to the needs of a free economy that risk funds should be supplied by a governmental or quasi-governmental agency. Also, the banks would probably suffer in the long run; for there seems little doubt that if bankers were to abdicate their traditional role as arbiters of credit, considerable demand would develop for the nationalization of the banks.

OPEN MARKET OPERATIONS

The most outstanding development of the Federal Reserve has been its use of open market operations.[2] To be sure, the power to engage in open

---

[1]Possibly guarantee fees might discourage lenders from excessive reliance upon loan guarantees. This does not really face the issue, however. With V loans, the guarantee followed automatically if it was requested and if the loan was certified as essential to the war effort. But to extend the principle of loan guarantees to ordinary business loans in peacetime would place upon the shoulders of the Federal Reserve Banks the necessity of evaluating the risk and desirability of the loan. This is the proper responsibility of the commercial banks.

[2]See Chapter 9.

market operations was authorized to the Reserve Banks by the original provisions of the Federal Reserve Act. But the consequences of such operations were not apparent to the framers of the legislation or to the Reserve authorities during the first years of the System's operations. In part, the reason may have been that the extent of such operations was restricted in 1914. The interest-bearing public debt totaled less than a billion dollars and to a large extent was held as collateral against the note issues of the national banks. The Federal Reserve might have purchased county and city warrants as well as bank acceptances and other commercial paper, but there was no possibility of acquiring billions or even hundreds of millions of dollars of U.S. government obligations.

Quite apart from the limited possible scope of open market operations, there was simply a failure to understand the real significance of such transactions. At the time the System was established, it was feared that some Banks might have trouble earning enough from discounts to pay their expenses.[3] The reason the Federal Reserve Act authorized the Banks to purchase assets in the open market was to allow them to increase their earnings at such times as member banks might not offer paper for discounting. There was complete failure to understand that by open market operations the member bank reserves would be affected, and that when the Federal Reserve increased its open market purchases, the member banks might use the addition to reserves as a means of getting out of debt to the Federal Reserve Bank, thus defeating the possibility of increasing the Federal Reserve's earning power.

As the public debt began its rapid rise in 1918, supporting purchases by the Reserve Banks greatly increased the scope of their open market operations. Even earlier, however, there appeared a trend to purchase government obligations. By June, 1915, only six Banks reported earnings from such assets, the total of their income from that source for their first eight months of operation being $58,000. But between January and December, 1916, the Banks reported more than $1,000,000 of earnings from government obligations, an amount that was 22 percent of their total earnings.

Yet as late as 1920–1921, the Reserve Banks were still attempting to use open market operations to increase their earnings. At the time, there was a postwar return of currency from the public to the banks. Here was the sequence of events:

1. The public brought excess currency to the banks.
2. The banks increased their legal reserves by sending the currency to the Reserve Banks. (At that time they were not allowed to count vault cash as legal reserves.)
3. As their reserves increased, the member banks were able to pay off their loans at the Reserve Banks.
4. Therefore, the earnings of the Reserve Banks dropped.
5. The Reserve Banks then bought securities in the open market in the confused hope of increasing their earnings.

---

[3]As a matter of fact, four Banks did fail to cover their operating expenses until the middle of 1916.

But the Reserve Banks discovered that as they bought securities in the open market, borrowing by member banks declined still further in approximately equal volume to the amount of open market purchases. Member banks had been advised from the outset to borrow only in emergencies and to get out of debt to the Federal Reserve at the first opportunity. They did as they had always been told to do. Any open market purchases by the Federal Reserve Banks, whether of warrants, commercial paper, or government securities, necessarily increased the member bank reserves. The purchases were therefore promptly followed by a reduction in the volume of Reserve Bank loans to member banks. Total assets and total income of the Federal Reserve Banks were little affected.[4]

Effect of Federal Reserve Purchases Illustrated

Suppose the Federal Reserve Bank of New York is buying government securities. Normally it would make its open market purchases through a dealer who, as middleman, would supply securities bought from some individual, bank, or other corporation. For simplicity we may eliminate the dealer and consider only the buyer (Federal Reserve Bank) and the seller. The Bank pays for the securities with a cashier's check. If the seller happens to be the Chase Manhattan Bank, the balance sheet of the Federal Reserve Bank and the balance sheet of the Chase Manhattan Bank will show the changes indicated below.

Federal Reserve Bank of New York

A		L & NW	
(1) Government securities	+$1,000,000	(1) Cashier's checks	+$1,000,000
		(2) Cashier's checks	−$1,000,000
		(2) Deposits (Chase Manhattan)	+$1,000,000

Chase Manhattan Bank

A		L & NW
(1) Government securities	−$1,000,000	
(1) Collection items	+$1,000,000	
(2) Collection items	−$1,000,000	
(2) Reserves	+$1,000,000	

---

[4]Since 1933 member bank indebtedness to Reserve Banks has represented a very small percentage of total Federal Reserve credit, seldom higher than 3 or 4 percent and often less than 1 percent. When, today, Reserve Banks buy government securities, their earnings do increase, for member banks do not, as a result, get out of debt—they are not (much) in debt to begin with. The increased earnings are purely incidental today. Easier credit for the economy, not high profits for the Federal Reserve Banks, is the motive for the purchases.

302 Part 3 Central Banking

The Federal Reserve Bank:

1. increases its assets as it acquires $1,000,000 of government securities. Simultaneously, its liabilities are increased by the cashier's check (or "officer's check") that it issues in payment for the securities. This check is an order on the Bank to pay, signed by an officer of the Bank. It will continue to be listed as a Bank liability until it has been presented for payment.
2. receives the cashier's check from the Chase Manhattan Bank, which has endorsed it and presented it for deposit. The liability "cashier's check" is transformed to the liability "deposits."

The Chase Manhattan Bank:

1. turns over the securities and receives the cashier's check, which it classes temporarily as a collection item; then
2. exchanges the cashier's check for reserve credit by depositing it at the Federal Reserve Bank.

If the securities are purchased from some individual or nonbank corporation, the effect on the legal reserves of member banks will be the same, although the effect on excess reserves will differ.[5] The Federal Reserve balance sheet will be affected in the same way as though it had purchased the securities from a member bank. But there will be a difference on the books of the member bank.

Suppose the securities bought by the Federal Reserve Bank are sold by the New York Life Insurance Company, which banks at the Chase Manhattan Bank.

Chase Manhattan Bank

A		L & NW	
(1) Collection items	+$1,000,000	(1) Deposits (New York Life)	+$1,000,000
(2) Collection items	−$1,000,000		
(2) Reserves	+$1,000,000		

1. The New York Life Insurance Company, which sold the securities to the Federal Reserve Bank, endorses the check it receives from an officer of the Federal Reserve and deposits it with the Chase Manhattan for collection, increasing the assets and the liabilities of the Chase Manhattan by $1,000,000.
2. The Chase Manhattan sends it to the Federal Reserve Bank and gives up the check in exchange for an addition to its legal reserves, held as a deposit with the Federal Reserve.

---

[5] The seller deposits with the bank the check received from the Federal Reserve Bank. If the seller's bank is a member of the System, it passes the check on to the Federal Reserve Bank at which it holds its account, as in the example above. If the bank is a nonmember bank and does not keep a balance with a Federal Reserve Bank, it may send the check to a correspondent bank, thus increasing its own reserves. But since the correspondent bank will almost certainly be a member of the System, its reserves will also increase when it deposits the check at the Federal Reserve Bank.

In this case deposits as well as legal reserves increased. Excess reserves of the Chase Manhattan increased by $1,000,000 in the first example. In the second case they increased by $835,000. The increase of $1,000,000 deposits increases the required reserves by $165,000.[6]

Some authors distinguish between "dynamic" and "defensive" open market sales and purchases, where the former is undertaken to affect member bank reserves and the latter to halt undesired changes in member bank reserves.[7] The defensive operations are used to defend "target" levels of reserves from exogenous influences. Rather than offset outside influences, dynamic open market operations aim at changing member banks' lending power by changing their reserve level. It has been estimated that most, perhaps 80–90 percent, of the Fed's open market operations are defensive, offsetting outside influences.[8]

Difficulties from Lack of Coordinated Policy

The effect of open market operations was complicated by the fact that their results might be felt in districts other than those in which the Banks were directly engaged in such operations. In particular, the effects were likely to be noticeable in New York City. When, during the depression of 1921, the Federal Reserve Banks outside New York City turned to the purchase of government securities to increase their earnings, the Federal Reserve Bank of New York City found its earnings decreased, since many sellers of securities deposited in New York City banks the funds they received. These deposits increased member reserves and decreased member borrowing in New York City. It was undesirable that the Banks should have been competing for earnings. Also, the Treasury's financing program was jeopardized if the Banks were buying and selling government securities in a disorganized manner, with consideration only of their individual portfolios.

Discovery of Usefulness of Open Market Operations

The possibility of credit control through unified open market operations was finally recognized. In the annual report for 1923 the Board explained:

> The fact that the reduction of the open market holdings during 1923 was accompanied by an increased amount of discounting by member banks in a volume approximately equal to the funds withdrawn by the reduction of open market holdings showed that the total volume of reserve bank credit outstanding was not in excess of the demand for such credit.
>
> In view of the influence which the open market operations of any Reserve Bank in the general money market may have on the credit situation, the

---

[6]Assuming reserve requirements are 16½ percent, as they were for large reserve city banks with demand deposits of more than $400 million on June 30, 1975.

[7]This distinction was first articulated by Robert V. Roosa, *Federal Reserve Operations in the Money and Government Securities Markets* (Federal Reserve Bank of New York, 1956).

[8]John Wood, "A Model of Federal Reserve Behavior," *Monetary Process and Policy*, edited by George Horwich (Homewood: Richard D. Irwin, 1967).

Board regarded it as essential that the purchases and sales of securities by Reserve Banks should be made with primary regard to the broader consequences and in accordance with the credit policy of the system. The following was the principle laid down by the Board in this matter: "That the time, manner, character, and volume of open market investments purchased by Federal Reserve Banks be governed with primary regard to the accommodation of commerce and business and to the effect of such purchases or sales on the general credit situation."

Gradual Centralization of Operations

As a first step toward the unification of their open market transactions, the first Open Market Committee was established in 1922, consisting of the governors (today called presidents) of five of the Federal Reserve Banks. This Committee had, however, no power over policy. Its function was merely to act as a central agency for the systematic execution of all open market operations of the 12 Banks. Spokesmen for the group made it clear that the establishment of this committee was not intended to interfere in any way with the autonomy of the individual Banks, which were free to buy and sell as they chose as long as their transactions were handled by the Committee.

As the consequences of such operations became more clearly evident, it was recognized that coordinated action was necessary. When the new policy was enunciated, an open market investment account was established in 1923. The Open Market Committee was authorized, with the approval of the Board, to add to or sell securities from this account in which each of the 12 Banks held a share proportionate to its size. Individual Reserve Banks might still buy or sell independently, but such operations became less important.

Further centralization was introduced by the Banking Acts of 1933 and 1935, which established the Federal Open Market Committee. Membership was changed to include the seven members of the Board of Governors and five representatives of the 12 Banks, thus insuring a majority control to the Board. The individual Banks no longer had any choice in the matter. Their participation in open market operations was required. From now on, open market operations would represent the 12 Banks acting as a single organization. Like the separate states which a century and a half earlier had eventually united to form a single nation, the Banks were losing their individual sovereignty to become a powerful central bank.

THE NEW CONCEPT OF RESERVES

Recognition of the potentialities of open market operations depended not only on a realization of their effect upon reserves but also upon a clear understanding of the nature of reserves. Historically, banks had always kept, or at least were supposed to keep, some of their assets in the form of vault cash. These funds permitted them to pay depositors on demand. The member bank reserves held by the Federal Reserve Banks were at one time regarded in the same light, and in fact are still so considered by many people. Yet a little reflection reminds us that *required* reserves are certainly not available for the payment of depositors. As long as a bank has *excess* reserves, it may draw currency from the Federal Reserve Bank of its district and pay it out to its depositors. But as long as the bank continues as a going concern, it cannot permit its vault cash plus its balance with the Federal Reserve Bank to fall below the minimum required by law against its deposits. Its required reserves are its least liquid asset, rather than its most liquid.

Reserves, the Limit to Credit Expansion

In losing their original function as a pool of liquid assets, reserves have acquired an entirely different importance. They control the banks' lending power. The individual bank, if it is not in debt to a Federal Reserve Bank, can lend a little more than the amount of its excess reserves. The system as a whole can lend several times the amount of its excess reserves less its indebtedness to the Federal Reserve Banks.

Suppose excess reserves of the banking system are $500 million but that banks are currently borrowing $490 million from the Federal Reserve Banks. Although some banks would have excess reserves, others would have a reserve deficiency if they had not obtained advances. Taking all the banks together, we would expect to see very little credit expansion. The banks with excess reserves may expand their loans and deposits, but the banks trying to get out of debt to the Federal Reserve will simultaneously be contracting credit. For the system as a whole, there is only a net $10 million base for credit expansion.

Net Free Reserves

The difference between excess reserves and member borrowing at the Federal Reserve is called *net free reserves*. If borrowings are greater than excess reserves, we can show the difference as *negative free reserves*, or we can call it *net borrowed reserves*. It has been suggested that when net free reserves are large and positive, banks have a predilection to expand; and when they are large and negative, the incentive is to contract to maintain either a constant or minimal level of excess reserves.

As has been repeatedly emphasized, no member bank is supposed (except perhaps in wartime) to borrow at the Federal Reserve for the purpose of increasing its own loans and investments. Similarly, the system as a whole finds that its ability to expand credit depends not on excess reserves alone, but on net free reserves.

Thus, the Federal Reserve, through its power to affect the volume of member bank reserves, can frequently exert a powerful influence upon the total volume of deposits, encouraging the banks to expand their loans and investments or forcing them to contract their credit. Taken in conjunction with the discount rate, open market operations have at times been an effective means of control. Open market purchases make it possible for member banks to expand credit, although they may choose not to take advantage of the opportunity. Also, by open market sales the Federal Reserve can reduce the volume of member reserves. Usually this will force the banks to borrow or otherwise repair their reserve deficiency. If a high discount rate is put into effect at the same time, the banks will be obliged to raise their own lending rates and to restrict credit. Since a high discount rate is in itself ineffectual when the member banks are not borrowing from the Federal Reserve Banks, it is frequently said that open market operations make the discount rate effective. Perhaps it would be just as accurate to put it the other way around. The discount rate makes the open market operations effective in that it links these activities with the banks. The transferring of securities in open market operations need not have anything to do with the banks. However, the discount rate directly concerns the banks. Because of the Federal Reserve's open market sales, the banks must borrow from the Federal Reserve at the rate the Federal Reserve sets—the discount rate.

Shortcomings of the Net Free Reserves Measure

The historical movement of net free reserves for selected years is shown in Table 11-1. The figures suggest that the Fed was pursuing a more expansive policy generally in the 1940s, early 1950s, and early 1960s, and a more contractive policy in the late 1960s and early 1970s. But this simplistic interpretation and use of net free reserves is now regarded as naive. Federal Reserve officials now use several different measures in formulating policy: interest rates, the money supply, the volume of business loans, bank credit, etc. The problem with using net free reserves exclusively as an indicator of what the Fed is doing is that it does not bear a fixed relationship to the money supply or bank credit. For example, from 1950 to 1970 net free reserves fluctuated within a rather narrow range of $\pm$ $1 billion, while at the same time the money supply, bank credit, and the interest rate each exhibited a strong upward trend. Differently stated, the optimal level of net free reserves from the banks point of view is not invariant but depends on a number of factors.[9] Yet, to be a precise measure of expansionary or contradictory pressures, the optimal quantity of net free reserves demanded by banks should be a constant.

Astute observers of the monetary scene now recognize the limitations of net free reserves as a surrogate for Fed policy actions and employ a subtle blend of several different measures in reaching a final assessment. In fact, since 1970 the Fed has looked more to the reserves available to support private nonbank time and demand deposits as an operating target and a monetary indicator. These reserves available for private deposits (RPDs) are determined by deducting from total reserves those reserves required against U.S. government (Treasury) deposits and interbank deposits. (These two items are not included in the money supply.) Unfortunately, to this point the Fed has openly acknowledged its inability to control its RPD target. Nor has the

---

[9]Michael W. Keran and Christopher T. Babb in "An Explanation of Federal Reserve Actions, 1933–1968," *Review* of the Federal Reserve Bank of St. Louis (July, 1969), pp. 7–20, conclude (p. 9) that: "The evidence marshalled against free reserves as an important causal link in the monetary process is impressive."

Table 11-1   **Net Free Reserves of Member Banks**
(Millions of dollars)

(1) Year (December)	(2) Member Bank Excess Reserves	(3) Member Bank Borrowings	(4) Net Free Reserves* (2)−(3)
1929	48	801	−753
1930	73	337	−264
1935	2,893	6	2,887
1940	6,646	3	6,643
1941	3,390	5	3,385
1942	2,376	4	2,372
1943	1,048	90	958
1944	1,248	265	983
1945	1,491	334	1,157
1946	900	157	743
1947	986	224	762
1948	797	134	663
1949	803	118	685
1950	1,027	142	885
1951	826	657	169
1952	723	1,593	−870
1953	693	441	252
1954	703	246	457
1955	594	839	−245
1956	652	688	−36
1957	577	710	−133
1958	516	557	−41
1959	482	906	−424
1960	756	87	669
1961	568	149	419
1962	572	304	268
1963	536	327	209
1964	411	243	168
1965	452	454	−2
1966	392	557	−165
1967	345	238	107
1968	445	765	−320
1969	257	1,086	−829
1970	272	321	−49
1971	165	107	58
1972	219	1,049	−830
1973	262	1,298	−1,036
1974	339	703	−364

Source: *Federal Reserve Bulletin* and *Economic Report of the President*, various issues.
*Called "Net Borrowed Reserves" if (2)–(3) is negative.

money-to-RPD "multiplier" been sufficiently stable to permit fine tuning. The multiplier declined gradually in the 1960s, largely as a result of shifts in the composition of bank deposits, as time deposits grew faster than demand deposits. While the downward drift stopped temporarily during the tight-money period of 1969, over the long-run it has fallen, offsetting three upward influences:[10] (1) a rising proportion of demand deposits at smaller banks, outside large cities, with low reserve requirements; (2) the long-run tendency of banks to hold a smaller quantity of excess reserves; and (3) the long-run propensity of the Federal Reserve to reduce legal reserve requirements more often than it increases them.

INADEQUACY OF CREDIT CONTROL BY FORMULA

At the same time the monetary authorities were beginning to realize the potentialities of credit control by a combination of open market operations and changes in the discount rate, they were also beginning to lose confidence in the argument that total bank credit expansion would automatically be correctly related to the legitimate needs of the economy as long as the Federal Reserve Banks followed the policy of discounting only eligible paper. The framers of the Federal Reserve Act believed that as long as member banks could borrow only by discounting high-grade, short-term commercial and agricultural paper, overexpansion of credit was unlikely. The lending power of the Reserve Banks, they reasoned, could hardly lead to excessive credit or be used as the basis for speculation when the only loans they could make would be those resulting from legitimate business activity. Gradually it came to be realized that it is often difficult to be sure how the proceeds of a loan will be used, regardless of the nature of the collateral supplied, and that it is impossible to know what use will be made of the funds as they continue to be transferred through the economy.

Frequently the issues involved are so complex that even in retrospect it is far from clear what action should have been taken. Years later monetary experts were still debating whether the Federal Reserve policies in 1929 and during the Depression were correct.[11] Yet somehow the Board of Governors must decide at the time what action should be taken and when and to what extent, realizing the importance of their decisions to the national welfare. An attempt to aid the Treasury's borrowing program by enforcing low interest rates may lead to inflation. A recession may be touched off by a policy of restraint applied with too heavy a hand. Even if the direction of the action required is unmistakable, the decision of how much is enough is likely to be extremely difficult. Rules of thumb are hardly adequate.

---

[10]See *Monthly Economic Letter* of the First National City Bank of New York (January, 1973).

[11]In particular, Milton Friedman and Anna J. Schwartz, in *A Monetary History of the United States, 1867–1960* (New York: National Bureau of Economic Research, 1963) and *Monetary Statistics of the United States: Estimates, Sources, Methods* (New York: National Bureau of Economic Research, 1970), argue that the Fed has not been very successful in using monetary policy either to control the business cycle or to promote economic growth. They further aver that since the Fed is not fully aware of its powers and purposes even yet, it has great difficulty in setting an appropriate course of action even when the proper direction of change is agreed upon.

RESERVE REQUIREMENTS OF MEMBER BANKS

Besides having the ability to change the total volume of reserves held by the banking system through open market operations, the Federal Reserve, by action of the Board of Governors, can change the reserve requirements, increasing or decreasing the volume of excess reserves. The Federal Reserve Act specified that reserves against time deposits should be 3 percent in all banks and that reserves against demand deposits should be 7 percent for banks outside the central reserve and reserve cities, 10 percent for banks in reserve cities, and 13 percent for banks in the two central reserve cities.[12] Banks in the outlying districts of reserve cities and central reserve cities might, with the permission of the Board of Governors, be subject to lower reserve requirements than the downtown banks; the total of banks classified as reserve city and country banks in New York City in 1961 was almost as great as the number of central reserve city banks. The classification "central reserve city banks" was dropped in 1962.

In 1933 when considerable inflationary legislation was being passed, Congress felt it would be wise to give additional power to the Federal Reserve so that it might be able to halt an inflation if one should develop. Accordingly, the Board was temporarily given the power to increase reserve requirements according to its discretion, with no limits specified. Before such action could be taken, however, the Board had to secure the approval of the President and declare a state of emergency. The Banking Act of 1935 reaffirmed the Board's right to control reserve requirements, eliminated the necessity for the declaration of an emergency and the approval of the President, and set as maximum reserve requirements 6 percent against time deposits in all banks, and 14, 20, and 26 percent against demand deposits in country, reserve city, and central reserve city banks respectively. The present legal limits are: net demand deposits, reserve city banks, 10 to 22 percent; net demand deposits, other banks, 7 to 14 percent; and time deposits, 3 to 10 percent.

At the outset the Board of Governors unhesitatingly increased reserve requirements steeply. In the first exercise of their new power, in 1936, they increased by 50 percent the required reserves of the banking system.[13] A few months later requirements were raised again, and a third raise shortly thereafter brought requirements to the legal maximums. No obvious hardship resulted, for the banks' excess reserves were at that time so great that they were not eliminated even though requirements were doubled within nine months.[14] In normal times, however, banks try to hold almost no excess reserves. Drastic changes in reserve requirements would cause disturbance and confusion

---

[12]As amended in 1917. (During the three-year transition period from 1914 to 1917 a rather confusing arrangement prevailed. It was swept aside by the 1917 amendment.)

[13]From 7, 10, and 13 percent against demand deposits of the three classes of banks to 10½, 15, and 22¾ percent.

[14]It is quite possible that the increase in reserve requirements was an entirely mistaken policy, intensifying the Depression and causing severe and unnecessary hardships for the whole economy. The Board was excessively concerned in 1936 with the dangers of inflation. Member banks, after the disasters of 1932 and 1933, may have felt that only by maintaining large excess reserves could they be in position to meet heavy deposit withdrawals if they should rematerialize. By raising reserve requirements the Federal Reserve decreased excess reserves and may have more successfully warded off recovery than inflation. See Friedman and Schwartz, *op. cit.*

for the banking system. An increase of only two percentage points in reserve requirements may require a bank to hold perhaps 15 to 25 percent more legal reserves. If its excess reserves were previously nearly nonexistent, it must borrow and it must sharply contract credit to offset its sudden reserve deficiency. Since World War II, changes in reserve requirements have been made less frequently and more gradually than in the 1930s, in recognition of the powerful leverage of this control device. Increases have not exceeded one percentage point, and have often been less.

When reserve requirements are changed, the Fed usually dampens the impact with open market operations. The Fed seldom changes reserve requirements because the effects are so powerful and because such changes are discriminatory, penalizing member banks. Although members hold approximately 80 percent of all bank deposits, changes in reserve requirements are used sparingly to avoid increases in nonmembership that would impair the efficiency (and equity) of the Fed's operations. From 1951 to mid-1974 reserve requirements against demand deposits were changed only about 17 times, being raised about 7 times and lowered 10 times.

LIMITATIONS OF QUANTITATIVE CONTROLS

Although it may appear that through open market operations, changes in the discount rate, and the control of reserve requirements the Federal Reserve should be able at all times to control the credit expansion of the member banks, the fact is that there are times when the Fed is relatively powerless. The difficulty that the Federal Reserve experienced after World War II will be discussed in a later chapter. The problem at that time was, in a sense, one that it had created itself, although not entirely willingly.

But the situation in the years just before World War II was one for which it was not responsible. The flood of gold from the rest of the world to the United States increased bank deposits and also increased reserves. Since the banks were not making many loans during the 1930s, their excess reserves and net free reserves began to climb. In previous years the banking system had ordinarily fully utilized its lending power in order to maximize its earnings, so that total excess reserves were ordinarily in the neighborhood of $200 or $300 million. By 1940 member banks held over $6.6 billion of excess reserves, creating a tremendous inflationary potential. (See Table 11-1.) Even with reserve requirements at the maximum permitted by law, these excess reserves might be used as the basis for a credit expansion of around $15 or $20 billion. In 1940 reserve requirements were a little below the authorized maximum, but an increase to the maximum would have reduced only slightly this mass of excess reserves. At the time the Federal Reserve held about $2.5 billion of government securities, the result of purchases on an unparalleled scale during 1932 and 1933. Even if the Federal Reserve had sold all the securities it held, simultaneously increasing reserve requirements, it could not have mopped up as much as half the excess reserves in 1940. In any event, such a course of action would hardly have been practical even if it had succeeded in eliminating the excess reserves. The Federal Reserve Banks would then have had no source of earnings; and if their sales had touched off a decline in the bond market, many member banks might have found themselves in difficulties. We might note, in passing, that under the circumstances the discount rate could not be used to restrain credit since the banks were not borrowing from the Federal Reserve and would have no need to borrow until they had used up the excess reserves they already possessed. Thus, Reserve authorities found in 1940 that the $6.6 billion of excess reserves held by member banks could not be materially reduced either by raising reserve requirements or by open market sales, and that the discount rate was meaningless. If, without World War II, inflationary pressures had developed that Reserve authorities felt should be checked, their quantitative controls would have been useless.

SELECTIVE CREDIT CONTROLS

The sweeping changes in banking after the reopening of the banks in 1933 included a credit control innovation by the Federal Reserve. Until this point, the Board of Governors had exerted some control over the total quantity of money, but had had little to say about particular areas of credit. A Federal Reserve Bank could refuse to lend to a member bank if it disapproved the latter's credit policy. By statements to the press, Reserve authorities could let it be known that they were opposed to speculation and credit excesses. That was about it. There was no effective way to rein in credit in particular areas without also checking and possibly choking credit generally.

In a laissez-faire economy there will be, by definition, a minimum of government regulation of and policy determination for business. The Federal Reserve System was created at a time when faith in free enterprise was high and when few dreamed of the increasingly important role that government was shortly and permanently to assume.

Selective controls permit the Board of Governors to control credit more effectively and with some discretion. Also, these controls extend the Board's authority far beyond the limits of the Federal Reserve System. Not too surprisingly, they have been regarded with considerable distrust by the public and, in two cases, accepted only as emergency measures. To many, the selective controls were gloomy mileposts on the road to the welfare state.

Margin Requirements

The first selective control, margin requirements, has caused less unhappiness. In this case at least, the medicine was less unpleasant than the fever. The excess of speculation that preceded the stock market crash in 1929 was encouraged by the widespread practice of buying and selling stocks on margin. The Federal Reserve's attempts to control this area of credit were hampered by the fact that at times as much as half the loans for this purpose were being made by individuals and nonbanking institutions, not subject to its authority. In some instances speculators were trading on margins as low as 10 percent, using the stock purchased as the basis for a loan of 90 percent of the amount of the transaction. The advantage was that as long as prices continued to rise, speculative profits were multiplied. When a speculator bought $10,000 of stock, paying $1,000 and borrowing $9,000 with the stock as security, the $1,000 would be doubled by an advance of 10 percent in the stock's price. Losses were multiplied in the same way. If the $10,000 of stock declined to a value of $9,000, the loan was no longer adequately secured. Unless the borrower could put up more margin, the stock was sold before a further decline would result in a loss to the lender.

Since ordinarily buyers could not advance much additional margin because they had already put most of their available funds into buying as large a block of securities as they could handle, an otherwise mild decline in the stock market was likely to set off a flood of sales, especially since the possibility of selling short on margin added to the selling pressure. Transactions on margin thus contributed to rapid advances and steep declines. Feeling against them as being contrary to the public interest was so strong after 1929 that a bill outlawing all margin transactions was narrowly defeated in the Senate. The Securities Exchange Act of 1934 authorized the Board to set margin requirements that should apply both to member banks and to any other institutions or individuals lending funds for the purchase or carrying of listed securities. As later amended, the same margin requirements now apply also to short sales; they are the same for banks as for brokers and dealers.

The higher the margin requirement, the less that can be lent. A margin requirement of 100 percent allows no loan at all against stocks when the loan is for the purpose of buying or holding stocks; the investor must supply 100 percent of the funds required. (Margin requirements do not apply to loans made against stock collateral when the loans are for purposes other than investment in securities.)

It is not easy to assess the effectiveness of margin requirements. Too many variables are involved. It might be supposed that stock market prices would be inversely related to changes in margin requirements. However, changes in margin requirements change the demand itself by affecting the public's expectations. When requirements are raised (lowered), the public may interpret the action as unmistakable evidence that inflationary (deflationary) conditions are imminent.[15]

We might similarly expect that the number of shares traded daily would increase when margin requirements are lowered and fall when margin requirements are increased. However, sales volume increased about 10 percent in 1955 when, in two jumps, margin requirements were increased from 50 percent to 70 percent. We cannot tell, of course, whether, if margin requirements had not been raised, average daily sales would have increased by even more or perhaps by less. Again in 1958 when requirements were reduced to 50 percent as Reserve authorities were encouraging an easy money policy, average daily sales in the three months following the reduction were lower

---

[15]There have been several empirical studies which conclude that changes in margin requirements typically have had trivial and sometimes perverse influences on stock price behavior. See James A. Largay and Richard R. West, "Margin Changes and Stock Market Behavior," *Journal of Political Economy* (March/April, 1973), pp. 328–339.

than they had been in the preceding three months. The increased margin requirement in July, 1960, was followed by the heaviest trading activity since 1929, as was also the increased requirement in 1963.

We cannot arrive at a certain conclusion even on the much broader question as to the general effect on sales volume over 40 years of margin controls. Through 1929 and much of 1928 the average daily volume of shares traded on the New York Stock Exchange was more than four million. In the years since margin requirements have been set by the Board of Governors there were, until 1959, few months when daily sales averaged even three million. For 25 years they averaged around two million (as they did as far back as 1925–1927), and often were much less. Not until 1961 did daily sales again average four million.[16] By then, however, there were more companies listed on the New York Stock Exchange, and many older companies had far more shares of stock outstanding than they had in 1929. The total of listed shares by 1961 was more than six times as great as it was in 1929. Also, the population had increased since 1929. Making allowance for the increase in population and the increase in number of shares listed, we find the trading volume today proportionately much less than it was a generation ago. But is this lower sales volume today due solely or even mainly to the margin requirements? American investors learned a hard lesson in 1929. Besides, much of the frenzied finance and market manipulation by professional speculators has been curbed by the Exchange itself and by the Securities and Exchange Commission.

Nevertheless, this power to control margin requirements is significant on three counts:

1. It represents the first control exercised by the Board of Governors over individuals and organizations outside the Federal Reserve System.
2. It was the first selective control given to the Board of Governors to control the quality as well as the quantity of credit. Previously the Board had sometimes hesitated to check credit that was leading to excessive speculation, fearing that credit restraint might prove injurious to legitimate commerce and industry. Henceforth it could, when necessary, reduce the availability of speculative credit without interfering with the availability of funds for other areas of trade and without affecting the total of available credit.
3. It is the only permanent selective control given to the Board of Governors. Other selective controls were on an emergency and temporary basis only.

Wartime Selective Controls

Even before the United States was actively engaged in World War II, strong inflationary pressures were accumulating. As the industrial production level rose due to defense production, individual incomes increased. But since a great deal of the production concerned planes, ships, the construction of military installations, and the like, the volume of consumer goods was not increasing in proportion to the increase in incomes. Under such conditions an

---

[16]The year's total of 1,124,800,410 shares traded in 1929, however, stood as an all-time record until 1963. Since then, volume has risen as high as nearly four billion shares a year.

upward-spiralling price level was almost inevitable unless steps were taken to prevent it. Price ceilings are one possible line of action at such a time, but they do not strike at the cause of the difficulty, namely the increase in purchasing power.

Moreover, in this country a substantial increase in consumer incomes is likely to exercise its greatest effect in the particular field of consumer durable goods. Ordinarily the sale of food and clothing is not as likely to show marked change when incomes rise as is the sale of cars, radios, washing machines, and the like. It is, however, particularly difficult to increase or even maintain the supply of these durable goods when war production is making heavy demands upon industry. Under more normal competitive conditions price increases may serve the usual functions of:

1. rationing the presently available production,
2. calling forth increased production, and
3. reallocating the factors of production in accordance with the public's wishes.

When overall production cannot be increased, price rises cannot serve the second purpose, although they can the first. Also, when the goods that must be produced are those the military requires, not those the public would like to have, an increase in the price level of consumer goods is futile in attempting to fulfill the third function. During war there are better ways to maximize total production and reallocate production to wartime needs than by letting prices spiral upward. An effective way to restrain such price increases is to check the demand for the goods. Since often these goods are purchased on credit, an obvious solution is the control of consumer credit.

Control over Consumer Credit. By an Executive Order of the President dated August 9, 1941, the Board of Governors was directed, during the emergency, to regulate consumer credit other than for housing. On August 21 the Board issued Regulation W, to go into effect September 1, 1941. In it the Board specified minimum down payments and the maximum length of time that might be involved in installment purchases. Although there were many modifications, the general requirements were:

1. down payments of at least one third;
2. installment contracts that should run not longer than a year; and
3. charge accounts that should run not longer than two months.

These restrictions reduced demand by eliminating those would-be purchasers who had sufficient funds to make down payments of perhaps only 10 percent and required contracts of two or three years. Or to put it a little differently, the average consumer might, under these terms, still be able to buy one or two items but would have difficulty in financing a number of them at once. The volume of consumer credit outstanding declined steeply during the war, the greatest decrease being in installment credit which had risen to more than $6 billion in 1941 and by 1943 had fallen to $2 billion, where it remained until the war was over. To what extent this decline was due to Regulation W would, however, be impossible to say. To a considerable extent the decline may have been the result of the scarcity of consumer durable goods, the imposition of price ceilings, and the fact that higher incomes reduced the public's dependence on credit.

The Board's authority to regulate consumer credit expired in November, 1947, but was twice renewed. The first occasion was September 20, 1948, when the Board was authorized to resume control until June 30, 1949. Then after the outbreak of the Korean War the Board was again given power to regulate consumer credit, and Regulation W was reissued September 8, 1950, and suspended May 7, 1952, shortly before the Board's authority to impose it expired.

Control over Real Estate Credit. A new type of qualitative credit control was introduced October 10, 1950, when the Board issued Regulation X (suspended two years later), restricting the credit available for residential construction. Similar restrictions were applied to all government guaranteed home loans. (See Chapter 5.) By the Voluntary Credit Restraint Program which followed in March, 1951, member banks were encouraged to restrict their lending. In particular, they were asked to require substantially larger down payments and shorter maturities in the transfer of existing houses so that, like new houses, they would be in less demand. Minimum down payments were set as high as 50 percent for more expensive homes (from $24,250 and up), so that buyers would need thousands of dollars in hand, rather than the $500 or $1,000 that had frequently been sufficient earlier. According to the regulations, down payments had to come from the buyer's funds, not from personal loans or second mortgages.

The necessity for this tightening up of real estate credit on both new and existing homes was an outgrowth of the housing boom that had resulted from the easy credit during the postwar years. First, the tight credit would discourage new construction, freeing materials and manpower for war production. The authorities hoped to reduce by one third the number of new houses being built. This applied, of course, to Regulation X only.

Second, Regulation X would hold down the increase in the effective money supply by checking the growth of both the quantity and the velocity of money. The terms of sale of existing houses may appear to make little difference to the national welfare. But if the demand for them (as well as for new homes) can be restrained by the requirement of substantial down payments, houses are less likely to rise in price. In the absence of such legislation the increased difficulty of buying new homes may encourage an inflationary increase in the price level of existing houses. Furthermore, with fewer houses sold, a smaller amount of savings return to the income stream, so velocity of circulation does not rise as rapidly as otherwise. Also, with larger down payments required, the banks create considerably less additional money, both because the amount lent on the individual transaction is less and because there are fewer transactions.

Evaluation of Qualitative Controls

The possibilities of qualitative credit control have not been exhausted with the regulation of stock market, real estate, and consumer credit. Other credit could conceivably be specifically controlled, especially in such fields as inventory accumulation and industrial spending for plant and equipment, which, like the preceding three sectors, are highly volatile. However, although there has been some support for a broader use of selective credit controls, no move has been made in this direction. For a number of reasons a wide spectrum of qualitative credit controls appears both unnecessary and unpromising:

1. The government has other selective controls at its disposal through its tax and expenditure policies, its subsidies, and its credit agencies.
2. Due to their differential effects, quantitative controls exercise also some qualitative control. A rise in the general level of interest rates is more likely to restrain housing expenditures than expenditures for industrial inventories and equipment, and to reduce more the spending on consumer durables than the spending on nondurables.
3. Enforcement difficulties might well prove formidable. True, in the case of mortgage credit and credit for purchasing securities and consumer durables, the purpose of the loan is usually closely related to the collateral offered. These are the easiest areas to control effectively. But in many instances it is not easy to identify the purpose of the loan, especially in the case of business borrowing. Evasion might make the control ineffective.

The consensus today is that, except for its control over stock market credit, the Federal Reserve can in normal circumstances adequately control credit by general, quantitative techniques.

SUMMARY AND CONCLUSION

Originally the Federal Reserve Banks were expected to be passive institutions, operating within a fairly precise and detailed framework of legislation. When member banks presented for discount commercial paper that met the carefully drawn eligibility provisions, the Banks would ordinarily provide the credit requested. Both the Federal Reserve's lending power and its power to issue currency depended upon the level of commercial activity (and also upon the Federal Reserve Banks' holdings of gold and gold certificates). It was supposed that, just as the automatic gold standard involved self-correcting mechanisms, credit control that was geared to self-liquidating commercial and agricultural paper would necessarily prevent both shortages and excesses of credit. For several reasons this theory was incorrect.

First, there is no necessary relation between the nature of the paper discounted and the purpose for which the loan is made, whether we are speaking of loans to the bank customers or to the bank itself. The customers may have liquid funds to use for working capital; but when the bank lends them working capital, they are free to put their own funds into plant expansion, real estate, the stock market, or whatever they please. Although in a narrow sense such a loan may be said to provide working capital, its effect may be to provide funds for quite different purposes. Moreover, even if the original loan is unquestionably for the purposes specified by the eligibility provisions, there is no guarantee when the bank presents the paper for discount that the bank is restricting its loans to that particular field. Banks do not borrow to make new loans and investments; they borrow because their reserves are deficient, frequently as a result of their past lending operations. If credit is available only through discounting certain types of paper, such paper will naturally be presented, regardless of whether it represents the bank's major field of lending.

Second, quite apart from the limitation discussed above, an excess of credit may develop even if all loans are of the self-liquidating variety favored by the framers of the Federal Reserve Act. During a period of full employment, an increase in such loans may cause an inflationary rise in prices by making it possible for entrepreneurs to bid against each other for factors of production already fully utilized.

Third, an increase in reserves permits a multiple increase in loans and deposits. Although the individual bank securing the loan from the Federal Reserve is unlikely to expand its loans at all in consequence of the loan and certainly will not expand by some multiple, the loan does increase the total reserves available to the banking system, which can so expand credit. Thus, although on the basis of the short-term paper presented there may be indicated a need for $3 billion of additional credit, there is no indication of a need for the $10 or $20 billion of additional deposits, depending on reserve requirements, that are made possible by an added $3 billion of reserves.

Reliance on eligibility could not prevent excesses of credit, and restriction of eligibility made it difficult for the Federal Reserve to be of assistance in emergency. As a result the Federal Reserve authorities acquired much greater powers of discretionary action. These additional powers are of three classes.

The first has to do with the relaxation of legal restrictions and controls over the Federal Reserve Banks, discussed in the preceding chapter. The most important was the removal of the redemption requirement and (later) of the reserve requirement against Federal Reserve deposits and notes.

The second group concerns the quantity of credit. By open market operations and by varying the percentage of required reserves, the Federal Reserve can directly affect the volume of excess reserves, which determines the banks' lending power.

The third concerns the quality of credit. By their control over stock margin requirements and the control that they sometimes exercise over consumer credit and real estate credit, the Board of Governors has attempted to exert influence over three specific, important areas without affecting credit conditions elsewhere. All three of these controls apply to everyone, not just to members of the Federal Reserve.

Finally, to meet the abnormal strains imposed by depression and war, the Board now has the authority to take almost any action that the Board might deem necessary or advisable.

We have seen that this growth of responsibility was inevitable. The banking system is too complex an organization and too subject to evolutionary development for its management to depend upon a mechanical formula or upon rigid and restrictive legislation, no matter how carefully drawn. Constantly changing problems require new solutions, more easily obtainable by the authorities when they have freedom to act as the circumstances of the time appear to require. Any attempt to prescribe in advance is likely to fail because whenever conditions indicate that the prescription is no longer appropriate, it will be set aside.

Discussion Questions

1. "Because member banks pay interest on their borrowings at the Federal Reserve, the Federal Reserve Banks cannot appreciably increase their earnings by open market operations as long as member banks are in debt to the Federal Reserve." Explain.
2. At one time Federal Reserve authorities advised the Federal Reserve Banks to buy only readily marketable securities, easily liquidated if member banks needed to borrow. Explain why you agree or disagree with this policy.
3. Briefly explain the difference between "dynamic" and "defensive" open market operations.
4. What is the primary function of reserve requirements? Compare this with the function of gold in the early banks.
5. "An increase in net free reserves might be evidence of either an easier or a tighter monetary policy." Explain.
6. The money-to-RPD multiplier declined gradually during the 1960s and early 1970s despite three upward influences. What were these three influences?
7. The framers of the Federal Reserve Act would have had less reason to specify eligibility requirements for paper discounted at the Federal Reserve Banks if they had really understood the nature and consequences of loans by these Banks. Explain.
8. When undertaking a program of gradual credit restraint, the Federal Reserve often makes open market purchases at the same time that it is raising reserve requirements. Why the apparent inconsistency?
9. Why are changes in reserve requirements used so seldom by the Fed?
10. Is it consistent that the member banks should be subject to reserve requirements set by the Board of Governors when the Federal Reserve Banks themselves are not subject to reserve requirements against their own deposits? Explain.
11. Would you expect that the average commercial bank in the United States would be most likely to increase its loans immediately as a result of a lowering of reserve requirements by the Federal Reserve, open market purchases by the Federal Reserve, or an advance from the Federal Reserve? Explain.
12. "From the point of view of the individual bank the question is: Can we profitably increase our loans? From the point of view of society the question is: Should the money supply be increased at this time? It is likely to be the first question which is answered directly, thereby determining the answer to the second." Critically discuss.
13. What are the three areas in which the Federal Reserve has exercised selective credit controls?
14. Summarize the principal ways in which the Federal Reserve's powers have been increased since 1914.

Chapter 12   The United States Treasury and the Banking System

There was a time when the United States Treasury was required to perform some of the functions of a central bank. Fortunately most of that was ended by the establishment of the Federal Reserve System. Yet even though the Federal Reserve Banks have taken over the specific responsibility of providing for the regulation of the member banks and the establishment of sound credit conditions, Treasury operations still exert a tremendous impact upon the banking system. This has always been true, but it has become increasingly important as the flow of the Treasury's funds has swollen from the trickle of a generation ago to the torrent of today. The banks might easily see most of their reserves and deposits disappear when the Treasury borrows money and collects taxes. When the Treasury repays loans and pays the current government expenses, reserves and deposits of the banks might be greatly increased. Without careful planning, the Treasury's policies might make the job of the Federal Reserve authorities impossible, and the position of the commercial banks would often be desperate.

INTEREST RATES

The most obvious and at the same time the least important point concerns interest rates. If the Treasury is currently borrowing a great deal of money (as is almost always the case today), Treasury officials probably will favor cheap money. Yet to avoid excessive credit inflation, perhaps interest rates should be higher. If it ever came to a knockdown, drag-out fight between the Treasury and the Board of Governors, we should place our bets on the Treasury. It is an official, governmental agency; the Federal Reserve is not. The government can always have the last word.

Nevertheless, although there have been occasional disagreements between Reserve and Treasury officials, the final word on credit policy has thus far always been had by the Federal Reserve. In wartime the Board of Governors and the Federal Reserve Banks have given all possible support to the Treasury and encouraged extremely easy money conditions. But on some other occasions when the Treasury would have liked low interest rates continued, the Federal Reserve has insisted on raising interest rates and has placed overall credit requirements ahead of the Treasury's wishes.

This state of affairs may not continue forever. A good case can be made for turning over to the Treasury the control over monetary policy via interest rates as well as by other means. If the administration is to be held responsible for maintaining a high level of employment, perhaps it should hold all the necessary powers including those of controlling the money supply. But until such a change is decided upon, the effect on monetary policy of the Treasury's interest rate manipulations may generally be disregarded as being more potential than actual.

POWER TO REDUCE RESERVES AND DEPOSITS

When the Treasury receives checks in payment of taxes or checks to pay for savings bonds or other government securities, reserves and sometimes deposits of the banks may be reduced. The effect depends upon what the Treasury does with the checks.

Payment of Taxes

In 1800 the Treasury received $11 million in taxes. Million, not billion. By 1850 its tax receipts were $44 million. Increasing with gathering speed, total receipts climbed to $567 million by 1900. By 1975 they had soared to over $200 billion, roughly 400 times as high as at the turn of the century.

Taxes flood into the Treasury at the rate of more than $20 million an hour, 24 hours a day. The outflow, as the Treasury spends these funds, does not usually vary by more than 20 percent from one month to the next. If the inflow were equally steady, taxes and government expenditures might cancel out, as far as their effect on the banks is concerned. But the inflow is far from constant. In the highest months it may be more than three times as much as in the lowest month of the same year. How does this affect the banks?

We are considering the effects only of the tax payments, remember. The spending of these funds is something else entirely, and will be studied later. Here we are looking at what happens to deposits and reserves at the time the taxes are paid.

Under the Independent Treasury System, as we saw earlier, the Treasury could withdraw specie from the banks as taxes were paid, then lock it up in the Treasury vaults until the Treasury was ready to spend it. Fortunately we have come beyond that primitive stage. Results today would be, however, almost as bad if the Treasury followed the policy of carrying its bank balances exclusively with the Federal Reserve Banks. Then tax payments would automatically drain reserves from the member banks, just as tax payments drained their specie in earlier days.

To settle the balance due on his income tax, William Flewellen writes a $5,000 check on his account with the First National Bank. Suppose the Treasury deposits this check in a Federal Reserve Bank, to be collected and added to the Treasury's account.

Federal Reserve Bank

A	L & NW	
	Deposits	
	Member Banks	
	First National	−$5,000
	U.S. Treasury	+$5,000

First National Bank

A		L & NW	
Reserves	−$5,000	Deposits	
		Flewellen	−$5,000

The check is in this case immediately collected by charging the account of the First National Bank and crediting the Treasury's account.

1. From the point of view of the Federal Reserve Bank, an intramural collection has been made: $5,000 has been transferred to another account.
2. From the point of view of the First National Bank, its deposits have declined by $5,000. If it is required to maintain reserves of 20 percent of its deposits, its required reserves are decreased by $1,000. But its total legal reserves have been decreased by $5,000. Net result: its excess reserves are reduced by $4,000. Because Flewellen has paid his taxes and because of the way the Treasury is handling the payment in this particular instance, the First National Bank is going to have to tighten up on its loans. Since a bank can lend somewhat more than the amount of its excess reserves, the First National's lending power has been reduced by a little more than $4,000.
3. From the point of view of the banking system, there also has been a decline of $4,000 in excess reserves. The funds that were checked out of the First National's account at the Federal Reserve Bank went into the account of the Treasury. No other bank receives the reserves lost by the First National as long as the Treasury continues to hold the tax receipts. So deposits for the system and legal reserves for the system were reduced by $5,000, just as they were for the First National. Excess reserves were decreased by $4,000 for the system, as for the First National. For the system as a whole, this reduction in excess reserves reduces the lending potential by around $12,000 or $13,000. For the banking system, credit will be tighter.

Borrowing

Besides taxing the public, the government borrows. Billions of dollars of government securities mature every year and are refunded by the issuance of new securities. These new securities may be sold to the general public or to the commercial banks.

If the Treasury sells securities to the public and deposits with a Federal Reserve Bank the checks it receives, the effects on the banks will be the same as we have seen above with tax payments. The only difference is that Flewellen has a government bond instead of a tax receipt.

But if the Treasury sells securities to the banks, results are not quite the same. Suppose the First National Bank buys $5,000 of Treasury bonds and the Treasury immediately deposits the check with the Federal Reserve Bank.

1. The balance sheet of the Federal Reserve Bank will be changed as in the previous two cases. Deposits owed to the First National will be reduced by $5,000; the deposit owed to the Treasury will be increased by $5,000.
2. The balance sheet of the First National Bank will not be changed exactly as before. In this case, deposit liabilities of the First National Bank are unaffected and investments increase.

First National Bank

A		L & NW
Reserves	−$5,000	
Investments	+$5,000	

With no reduction in deposits there is no reduction in required reserves. Total legal reserves have decreased by $5,000, so excess reserves of the First National Bank have shrunk by $5,000 and its further lending potential has shrunk by a little more than $5,000.

3. Likewise, the system's excess reserves have dropped by $5,000. If reserve requirements average 20 percent, the banking system's lending power has been reduced by around $15,000 because of the way a $5,000 loan to the government was handled.[1]

POWER TO INCREASE RESERVES AND DEPOSITS

When the Treasury writes checks, whether to pay its current bills or to pay off maturing obligations, bank reserves and sometimes bank deposits may increase. Again the effect depends upon how the transactions are handled.

Government Spending

The Treasury writes a $5,000 check to pay for an official automobile. Capitol Motors deposits the check in the Riggs National Bank. Riggs National passes the check on to the Federal Reserve Bank of Richmond, which collects it and returns it to the Treasury.

Federal Reserve Bank of Richmond

A		L & NW	
		Deposits	
		Member Banks	
		Riggs National	+$5,000
		U.S. Treasury	−$5,000

---
[1]See the discussion in Chapter 6 of the coefficient of credit expansion.

Riggs National Bank

A		L & NW	
Reserves	+$5,000	Deposits	
		Capitol Motors	+$5,000

1. The Federal Reserve Bank has made an intramural collection in the usual way, changing the amounts it owes to individual depositors but not affecting its total liabilities or assets.
2. The Riggs National Bank owes $5,000 more to Capitol Motors. Against this increase of $5,000 in its deposit liabilities, it will be required to hold $1,000 more reserves, if its reserve requirement is 20 percent. It has gained $5,000 of reserves, since the Federal Reserve Bank has credited its account by that amount. So the Riggs National has $4,000 of excess reserves because the Treasury spent $5,000 of its balance at the Federal Reserve Bank. It can lend more freely, since it has somewhat over $4,000 more lending power than before it received the Treasury's check.
3. The system, too, has gained $4,000 of excess reserves. The $5,000 of added reserves the Riggs National gained came straight from the Treasury account. Other banks did not, as a result of this Treasury expenditure, lose any reserves at this time. The gain of the Riggs National was a net gain for the system as a whole. Because of this government expenditure and the way the funds were handled, the system has around $12,000 or $13,000 more lending power.

Repayment of Debt

If the Treasury draws on idle balances at the Federal Reserve Bank to repay $5,000 borrowed from the public, the books of the Federal Reserve Bank and the Riggs National Bank will be changed as in the previous case. If the Treasury is repaying bank loans, the effect will be the same for the Federal Reserve, but for the Riggs National Bank we would find:

Riggs National Bank

A		L & NW
Reserves	+$5,000	
Investments	−$5,000	

In this instance excess reserves are increased by $5,000 instead of $4,000, for there has been no change in deposits and required reserves. The Riggs National can lend possibly $6,000 or thereabouts. On the usual assumption of a 20 percent reserve requirement, the banking system can lend around $15,000 or $16,000.

Other Treasury Activities

We could go on to trace the effects of other Treasury operations. The Treasury's purchases and sales of gold and silver and its debt refunding operations have important implications for the banks.[2] But it should be evident, from what has already been said about the effects of taxes, borrowing, and government expenditures, that Treasury policies may have an enormous impact upon the banks, especially through their effect upon bank reserves.

Neutralization by Federal Reserve Banks

Conceivably the Federal Reserve Banks could handle the problem created by various Treasury activities by taking offsetting open market action to supply reserves when needed and absorb reserves when the Treasury was returning funds to the banks. Such operations would necessarily be on a massive scale and would involve a great deal of churning about in the securities market. Also, they would probably make the stabilization of interest rates more difficult. If the Reserve Banks were to absorb reserves, they would have to sell securities. To be sure that the securities were sold, the price would be marked down, raising their yield. This procedure might make it difficult for the Treasury to borrow at low rates. Investors might sensibly decide to wait and buy these securities later from the Federal Reserve Banks at a lower price and a higher yield. Investors might be encouraged, also, to speculate in government bonds. If it became evident that, because the Reserve Banks were frequently buying and selling government securities, the prices of these securities were fluctuating fairly predictably, there would be plenty of money ready for a quick ride on a sure thing. For all these reasons, open market operations by the Reserve Banks would be an unsatisfactory way to offset the daily routine of the Treasury's operations.

Possibly the Board of Governors might attempt to offset the movement of Treasury funds by raising or lowering reserve requirements. The trouble here is that all the banks will not be losing or gaining Treasury funds at the same rate. An increase in reserve requirements when the Treasury is releasing funds to the banks would heavily penalize those banks that were drawing little of the Treasury funds, but for some other banks would be quite ineffective in offsetting the inflow of reserves. The problem is one for which the Treasury is responsible and one that the Treasury can most effectively solve.

DEPOSITARIES

While the Treasury maintains a regular checking account with the Federal Reserve Banks, it also holds deposits at thousands of other banks to dampen the effects of its fiscal operations. These banks are classified as general depositaries and special depositaries. To qualify as a Treasury depositary, a bank today must be insured and it must deposit with the Treasury United States government bonds or other prescribed collateral as security against all deposits not covered by insurance.

---

[2]"Debt refunding" means making new loans to pay off old loans.

General depositaries are the older and less important of the two categories. About 1,900 banks are currently used to supplement the Federal Reserve Banks as receiving and paying agents. The relation between the Treasury and the general depositaries is the ordinary customer-bank relationship. Against its deposits the Treasury draws checks directly, as a matter of convenience. The Treasury does not ordinarily transfer its deposits from the general depositary banks to the Federal Reserve Bank.

More important than the general depositaries are the approximately 13,300 banks serving as *special depositaries*. Tax and Loan Accounts with special depositaries comprise the bulk of the funds the Treasury holds with commercial banks. Tax payments and payments for government securities are temporarily transferred to the Federal Reserve Banks, from which the Treasury returns them promptly to the commercial banks. During World War II these accounts (then called War Loan Accounts) were exempted from reserve requirements. Today the Tax and Loan Accounts are no longer given preferential treatment. Using the special depositaries minimizes the strains of the Treasury's spending, taxing, and borrowing activities on the banking system.

SECURITIES OFFERED BY THE TREASURY

The Treasury has to borrow staggering amounts of money. Like other borrowers, the Treasury does not want to pay any more interest than necessary. So the Treasury has invented all kinds of securities. Some of its innovations have been highly successful; others have presently disappeared. By having on its shelves securities with all kinds of provisions, the Treasury hopes to have an investment to appeal to every possible purchaser.

There is another even more weighty reason for the diversification of securities. It helps the Treasury determine the placement of the debt. Some kinds of securities appeal principally to private individuals, some to nonfinancial corporations, some to pension funds, insurance companies, and savings banks, and some to commercial banks. By far the most important decision for the Treasury to make when it is about to borrow large amounts is whether it will borrow from the banking system or from the public. There are advantages and disadvantages to both. The deciding factor is or should be the general state of business.

In depression it is usually most effective for the Treasury to borrow from the banks. When the borrowed money is spent and passes into the hands of the public, there is more money in circulation than before, and there is an increase in money income, tending to increase output and employment.

At a time of full employment, an increase in bank loans is likely to be inflationary. If the banks are holding large excess reserves at such times, the Treasury should market securities that are more attractive to the public than to the commercial banks. But if excess reserves are low, as they are likely to be in inflation, and if the Reserve Banks are not supplying additional reserves, any loans that the banks make to the Treasury will simply replace loans they would otherwise be making to private industry. Here there would be no net inflationary effect, since the total of loans is not increased.

MARKETABLE SECURITIES

Banks, other financial institutions, corporations with more cash than they currently need, and some wealthy individuals may buy one or another of the Treasury's various marketable issues, available in all maturities. These are securities which may be freely traded in the market.

Treasury Bills

Treasury bills are sold weekly on a discount basis.[3] Most of them are sold to the highest bidders, that is, those willing to accept the lowest discount rate; but to encourage sales to smaller banks, about 10 percent are sold on noncompetitive bids at the average of the bid prices.

Bills are the Treasury's most flexible instrument because:

1. The amount offered can be increased or decreased from one week to the next, as conditions require.
2. The competitive basis on which they are sold ensures that the rate paid by the Treasury will be immediately responsive to any changes in the interest rate pattern.

Besides the regular bills there have been occasional issues of Tax Anticipation Bills (TABs). TABs are receivable in payment of taxes and may be freely traded in the market, but are not redeemable in cash. They are not of great importance quantitatively, nor are they a regular constituent of the debt. Often there are none outstanding.

Certificates of Indebtedness

Certificates of indebtedness (not to be confused with the special certificates by means of which the Treasury occasionally borrows overnight from the Federal Reserve) were usually a one-year security. They were once an intermediate security between the 91-day bills and the longer term notes and bonds. They have been little used since the introduction of the one-year bills, and from 1967 to 1974 there have been none outstanding.

Certificates were a less flexible monetary instrument than bills, for they were sold, like bonds, at a fixed price and interest rate. The Treasury tried to set an interest rate that would be high enough to guarantee that the entire issue would be sold. The auction technique used with bills helps minimize the Treasury's interest costs.

---

[3]For years the bill invariably had a 91-day maturity. In December, 1958, the Treasury introduced the 26-week bill. Five months later the Treasury marketed an issue of 340-day bills. In August, 1963, the Treasury instituted the policy of selling one-year bills every month, supplemented by the weekly offering of 13-week bills. It appears that the former concept of the bill as a 91-day instrument is being replaced by the more flexible concept of a security running for anywhere from three months to a year.

Treasury Notes

Unlike Treasury bills, notes are not issued on a discount basis. Instead, the Treasury sets a specific interest payment that it believes will be sufficiently attractive that the issue will be somewhat oversubscribed, offers it to the public, and fills orders on an allotment basis. (With bills, the buyers themselves determine the yield by their bids.) Occasionally, to avoid an awkwardly large clustering of maturities, a 13-month note has been issued instead of a one-year bill. Other note issues, until 1967, ran for as long as five years. There is no legal limit on the interest rate the Treasury is permitted to pay on notes, as there is on bonds. In 1969–1970 the Treasury had to offer as high as 8 percent on its new issues. Bonds were out of the question. In a transparent effort to circumvent the interest ceiling and place at least a small amount of the debt in securities of more than five years' maturity, the Treasury introduced seven-year notes. In August, 1974, people mobbed the Federal Reserve Banks trying to purchase a Treasury issue which required a $1,000 minimum purchase and had the highest coupon rate since the Civil War. The $4 billion auction included 9 percent notes due in 33 months and 9 percent notes due in six years.

Treasury Bonds

Quite unlike the much publicized and widely distributed savings bonds are marketable Treasury bonds. They are not redeemable upon demand, and the buyer assumes the risk that their market price may fall due to a rise in interest rates.[4] Issued in $1,000 denominations, they carry various interest rates, depending on the current interest rate level at the time the bonds are marketed and on the length of time before the bonds mature. The Treasury is forbidden, however, to issue bonds with coupons higher than 4¼ percent. Bonds have been issued for periods as short as five years and as long as 30 years.

Treasury bonds were for a time classified as bank restricted and bank eligible. The distinction was one of maturity. To prevent the banks from loading up on long-term securities, paying (at that time) a higher interest rate, the longer term issues during World War II were ineligible for bank ownership until within 10 years of maturity.[5] Bank-restricted bonds reached their peak of $53.4 billion in 1946 but rapidly declined a few years later. Today no Treasury bonds are bank restricted.

For many years the Treasury marketed its bonds the same way it sold its certificates and notes. It stated the maturity and set an interest rate that it hoped would insure that the issue would be oversubscribed. It then allotted the bonds to the subscribers. After a few experiments the Treasury did not use the auction technique, employed with bills, for two principal reasons:

1. It is much more difficult to evaluate the true market worth of a long-term security than of a security maturing within a year. Too many things can

---

[4]In 1975, prices of several longer term Treasury bonds fell to less than $700.
[5]In May, 1942, the banks were forbidden to buy the long-term issues until 10 years after date of issue, when, of course, the securities might still have 15 years or more to run. In June, 1945, the rules were tightened to require that the security be within 10 years of maturity.

happen in 20 or 30 years. The great number of banks, insurance companies, and other corporations that eagerly and independently bid for short-term securities could not be expected to be equally active in the long-term market. When the Treasury did, on a few occasions, attempt to auction bonds, it found nearly all the bonds being awarded to the very large financial institutions, which alone were qualified to evaluate them confidently. Smaller firms bid on the first occasion, but when they found their bids were higher than those submitted by the big banks they refrained, thereafter, from the auctions.

2. A possible alternative would have been to permit competitive bidding by financial groups that wished to underwrite the issue. The successful bidder would then distribute the issue at a slight profit if all went well. The Treasury did not employ this method of auctioning securities either, feeling that it implied that the Treasury needed professional help in marketing its securities, conceivably casting some reflection on the Treasury's credit or financial acumen.

However, there were difficulties also with the allotment technique. If the Treasury set too low a rate on a new bond, the issue was undersubscribed, and this had undesirable implications. On the other hand, if it set too high a rate, it had the satisfaction of seeing the issue oversubscribed, but the satisfaction was tempered by the realization that the Treasury was paying a higher interest rate than necessary and also was encouraging speculation in government bonds.

For these reasons Treasury officials decided finally to try auctioning their bonds to underwriting groups, as state and local governments have long been doing. In January, 1963, competitive bidding on a 30-year bond issue was invited from banking syndicates. About two hundred firms formed into three underwriting groups, looking toward not only the potential profit but also the prestige of being recognized as banker for the government. There was, in addition, one dealer who, individually, bid for the issue, having previously organized a group of investors who would take over the bonds from him if his bid was successful.

The winning syndicate offered $998.511 per $1,000 bond, one tenth of a cent higher than the next highest bid. This price gave the Treasury an interest cost six millionths of 1 percent lower than that of the next bidder, or about $15 less per year on the entire issue of a quarter of a billion dollars. Obviously the professionals were figuring very much alike. Treasury officials were pleased with the results, feeling that if they had placed the bonds in the usual way, they would have been obliged to offer a higher interest rate to insure that the issue would be fully subscribed.

A similar, slightly larger operation was successfully carried out a few months later. This also involved a long-term (31-year) bond issue, which, as previously explained, could not possibly have been successfully marketed by ordinary auction techniques.

Since then there have been no further bond underwritings for the Treasury. In fact, from 1965 until 1971 there were no more sales of bonds. (On several occasions holders of maturing obligations were offered bonds of 25- to

30-year maturities in exchange for their securities — so-called refunding operations — but no cash changed hands.) With interest rates at their highest level in more than a century, the Treasury has not been able recently by any marketing technique to sell bonds with coupons of 4¼ percent or lower, as required by law, with minor exceptions.[6]

NONMARKETABLE SECURITIES

When buying Treasury securities, the average citizen purchases nonmarketable issues, the current price of which can never be affected by rising or falling interest rates in the marketplace. These securities may be held until maturity or, at the holder's option, presented at any time to Treasury agents for redemption. They may not be sold by one individual or corporation to another.

Savings Bonds — General Considerations

The sale of savings bonds began during the Depression. At that time the public was not urged, as at a later date, to reduce its consumption and buy bonds, for one of the principal problems at the time was the excessively low level of consumption. Bonds were sold at this time, rather, to promote a wider ownership of the public debt. Individuals who were going to save anyway were encouraged to invest in government bonds.

As deficits continued to add to the national debt, increasing attention was paid to debt ownership. It was pointed out that, although a debt that we owed to ourselves would not in itself involve future burdens, there might be some difficulties from transfer payments involved. In particular, if only the banks and a small group of wealthy individuals were buying government bonds and if the public were to be later taxed to pay interest upon and retire the bonds, the eventual result would be the establishment of a privileged class supported by taxes. The more widely the debt was held, the fewer frictions would arise.

If small investors were to be successfully encouraged to buy government bonds, three conditions were essential:

1. The bonds should bear a higher interest rate than the Treasury (during the Depression) was paying on other types of borrowing. A safe 2 percent

---

[6]The Treasury has repeatedly asked Congress to remove the 4¼ percent interest ceiling on bonds, but so far with little success. Over a period of years the government's interest costs obviously will be least if the Treasury borrows on long term when interest rates are low and issues short-term securities when rates are high. Presumably the ceiling was imposed to prevent some Secretary of the Treasury from absentmindedly issuing a few billion dollars of long-term bonds while interest rates were temporarily high.

Unfortunately when rates continue high for 10 years or more, the arbitrary policy causes the average maturity of the debt to shrink steadily, for maturing bonds are being constantly replaced by short-term issues. By 1971 almost half the Treasury's marketable securities were due within 1 year. In 1971 Congress grudgingly authorized the Treasury to issue up to $10 billion of intermediate term bonds (up to 10-years' maturity) without regard to the 4¼ percent ceiling. The first issue, with a 7 percent coupon, appeared in July, 1971. As of January, 1973, the Treasury had issued about $7.5 billion of bonds bearing coupon rates greater than 4.25 percent. In August, 1974, it offered $400 million of 8½ percent bonds due in 1999.

might appeal to the wealthy individuals who had already acquired a fortune and were interested primarily in protecting it by the most conservative investments possible. If their principal was large enough, they might live very comfortably in spite of the low rate of return. To small investors, 2 percent would hardly be exciting. It would offer them little stimulus to save; and, even if they did save, it would give them so little return that they would be tempted to accept a little more risk in return for a more generous income from some other investment.

2. There should be no repetition of the unfortunate episode of 1920, when the market price of bonds fell to about 80 percent of their par value. Seasoned investors might understand the reasons for such a decline and might accept that possibility as one of the risks of investment. The public would not understand. A panic might be touched off in the bond market, and political repercussions would be probable.

3. The bonds should be available to the small investor. A wide market could never be reached through sale of the customary denominations of $1,000 and higher. At the same time it would be necessary to arrange the issue in such a way that the cost of servicing it would not be too great, in spite of the multitude of small holders.

Savings Bonds, Series E

The bonds sold to the smallest investors were successively termed A, B, C, and D series savings bonds; but after the fifth year, when Series E was introduced, there was no further change in name. For economy of administration they were issued as discount bonds. Instead of receiving a few cents every six months in interest, the public bought the bonds at less than their face value. When the bonds matured 10 years later, the holder received a sum that included interest at the rate of 2.9 percent, a figure considerably exceeding what the Treasury was then paying on other securities of similar maturity.

The bonds could be redeemed before maturity by surrending them to the Treasury. But redemption prices were so arranged that the effective yield would be lower if the buyer did not hold them for the full term. The bonds were made nontransferable, so were immune to market fluctuations.

Since the Series E bonds could be bought in denominations as low as $25 (the discounted price of which was $18.75), they were within the public's reach. Although at one time available to all subscribers and at another time available to individuals only, today the Series E savings bonds are available to all investors except commercial banks. Their terms were gradually liberalized. A $100 (face value) bond continues to sell for $75, but today it matures in five years to yield 6 percent.

To prevent heavy purchases of these securities by wealthy individuals who do not need the incentive of the (ordinarily) comparatively generous interest rate, the Treasury limits the amount that may be bought in a single year.[7] The limit was originally $5,000, face value. Later it was raised to $10,000 and then to $20,000 face value, but in 1969 it was lowered to $5,000 issue price ($6,667 face value).

---

[7]There is a $100,000 denomination savings bond offered, but only to trustees of approved employee savings programs.

When the limit was still $20,000, there were occasional objections that if savings bonds were supposed to be for the benefit of small investors, the limit on annual purchases was unrealistically high. Few people are ever going to accumulate bond portfolios of $100,000. However, the lower the limit, the fewer savings bonds will be sold and the more the Treasury must borrow from banks, corporations, and wealthy investors. Also, while a $100,000 portfolio is beyond the reach of most individuals, it is small in comparison with portfolios of millions of dollars. Moreover, assuming that when the bonds begin to mature, the investor uses $15,000 of the maturing bonds to buy another $20,000, face value, of new bonds, the $6,000 annual income the portfolio would generate is rather modest. The Treasury can scarcely be charged with allowing the savings bonds to become a major source of assured and comparatively liberal income for privileged millionaires.

The original yield, 2.9 percent on a savings bond held for 10 years, was, in the 1930s, well above the yields available on marketable Treasury bonds of similar maturity. By 1969, however, the yield on savings bonds, by then 4¼ percent, was far below the yields on marketable issues, which had climbed to 7 percent. Some investors switched from savings bonds to marketable bonds, notes, and bills. For many, however, the savings bonds continued to be the most attractive investment, especially after their rate of return was raised to 5 percent. Even if they yielded $15 or $20 less interest a year per $1,000 than marketable issues, they had two distinct advantages:

1. They were immune from loss in market value from a rise in market interest rates, since the Treasury would always redeem them for at least as much as the buyer had paid for them. (The higher interest rates went, the less advantageous this distinction became; rates still higher began to appear less probable than, eventually, lower rates—which would result in a premium on outstanding marketable bonds but not on savings bonds.)
2. Holders were permitted to postpone paying income tax on the interest until the savings bonds matured. For many purchasers this permitted the tax to be postponed until they retired and were in a lower tax bracket.

These Series E savings bonds have been the most important of the nonmarketable obligations.[8] By the end of World War II nearly $30 billion of the debt was in this form. Since that time there has been a gradual increase to about $52 billion, although more bonds have been redeemed in some recent years than have been sold. Interest accruals, however, have caused the total dollar volume of savings bonds to increase, despite the excess of redemptions over new sales.

Savings Bonds, Series H

The Series H savings bond was introduced in 1952, to be sold under much the same restrictions and to provide the same yield as the Series E. The difference is that the Series H is a current income bond. Not everyone finds it convenient to wait 5 years for the interest. Series H bonds are sold at par in

---

[8]A number of other series of savings bonds—F, G, J, K—were temporarily offered but are no longer available.

denominations of from $500 to $10,000, the larger minimum denominations being required for economy of administration. Their volume is only about 20 percent of the size of the Series E volume.

Miscellaneous Nonmarketable Securities

The most important component of this category is the block of special securities, most of them payable in foreign currencies rather than in dollars, sold to foreign countries. The Treasury had not borrowed abroad since 1918, until in 1962 it began a policy of borrowing directly from foreign official agencies. The reason was not that the Treasury had exhausted its credit at home. Rather, these borrowings were a part of the Treasury's operations in foreign exchange to support the dollar. Often central banks and treasuries from which the U.S. Treasury was borrowing were simultaneously borrowing from the Treasury. In effect, the monetary authorities were swapping currencies.

Summary of Nonmarketable Issues

The average person is likely to exaggerate the importance of savings bonds, particularly the well-advertised Series E. Savings bonds of E and H series together amount to less than a seventh of the debt. Still, the savings bonds and other nonmarketable securities do represent a significant innovation in Treasury finance. By guaranteeing the holder against market fluctuation and by agreeing to redeem most of them upon demand, the Treasury placed within a few years' time an amount of securities greater than the total public debt as late as June, 1942. Most of these securities are held by investors other than banks, to that extent restraining the increase in the money supply. For the Treasury to have borrowed to the same extent from nonbank sources without offering them the advantages of the redeemable securities, it would probably have been obliged to offer considerably higher interest rates. Losses to investors have been avoided, and the public has confidence in such securities.

Three criticisms of the policy may be noted. In the first place, redeemable securities are a demand liability of the Treasury. Together with the large volume of short-term securities and of bonds currently maturing, redeemable securities comprise an enormous floating debt. In the second place, securities that are redeemable upon demand are very close to a greenback issue. They cannot actually be spent so are not quite money. But the dividing line is a fine one from the viewpoint of both the holders, planning their expenditures, and the Treasury, committed to redeem the securities upon demand. In the third place, the administration's failure to restrain inflation has caused substantial losses to the holders of any bonds, money, or claims for specific amounts of money. The holders of savings bonds are no worse off in this respect than other bond holders. However, the Treasury, which frequently calls attention to the fact that no one has ever lost a dollar buying savings bonds, cannot overlook the fact that the $25 paid to retire a savings bond often will not buy what could have been bought several years earlier for the $18.75 invested in the bond.

SUMMARY AND CONCLUSION

The flow of Treasury funds could seriously disrupt the economy through its effects on bank credit and the volume of money. When the Treasury spends its balances at the Federal Reserve Banks, commercial banks find their excess reserves increased. Credit is easy. When the Treasury is building up its balances at the Federal Reserve Banks, by either taxes or loans, the excess reserves of commercial banks disappear. Money becomes tight.

To avoid these alternations of excess reserves and reserve deficiencies, the Treasury keeps most of its bank accounts with commercial banks rather than with the Federal Reserve Banks. However, most of its checks are drawn against the Federal Reserve Banks.

To help dampen the effects of its fiscal operations, the Treasury holds deposits with commercial banks. General depositaries are the older and less important of these banks. Special depositary banks, through Treasury Tax and Loan Accounts, are useful in connection with Treasury borrowing and taxing operations.

The Treasury can to some extent control the placement of the national debt by the types of securities it offers. With billions of dollars of debt being refunded yearly, the Treasury is in a strategic position to encourage an increase in the money supply through an expansion of bank loans or to encourage a contraction of bank credit.

However, the Treasury has continued to let the Federal Reserve authorities carry the principal responsibility of deciding monetary policy. Neither by deliberate shifts of its balances between commercial banks and Federal Reserve Banks nor by refunding securities has it seriously challenged the leadership of the Federal Reserve.

Discussion Questions

1. The Treasury is far more sensitive to and influential upon the level of interest rates today than in 1900, not only because its debt is greater, but because it now is borrowing not only every year but every week. Explain.
2. The Treasury is not permitted to regularly borrow directly from the Federal Reserve Banks. Why not? Give two reasons why the Treasury does occasionally sell securities directly to the Federal Reserve Banks.
3. Why does the Treasury find it necessary to keep deposits with thousands of member banks, in addition to its balances at the Federal Reserve Banks?
4. Which is the more common type of depositary? Why?
5. Are excess reserves of the banking system made more stable or less stable when Tax and Loan Accounts are exempted from reserve requirements? Briefly explain.

6. What effect, if any, would there be on the money supply if the Treasury sold $1 billion of savings bonds and with the proceeds retired the same amount of 91-day bills? Briefly explain.
7. What is the important distinction between the marketing of Treasury bills and the marketing of most other Treasury obligations? What is the reason for the distinction?
8. When the Treasury occasionally markets a new issue of intermediate or long-term bonds, there is often a considerable amount of speculative buying, usually on 5 percent margin. Explain why.
9. Why are Series E savings bonds "nonmarketable"?
10. Explain how the Treasury might, by its fiscal policies (taxing, borrowing, and spending):
    a. increase the velocity (rate of turnover) of money.
    b. increase the quantity of money through debt-refunding.
    c. increase the quantity of money by deficit-financed expenditures.
11. During both the Revolutionary War and the Civil War the Treasury printed great quantities of paper money. Give two reasons why, during World Wars I and II, there were no comparable issues of Treasury currency.

PART 4
The Value of Money

Chapter 13 Changes in the Value of Money: Significance and Measurement

Money, we observed earlier, is an inconstant standard. Suppose that all our rulers were made of a material that in cold weather shrank to one half, in summer expanded to twice its original length. If everything measured with these varying standards also contracted and expanded to the same degree as the standards, there would not only be no problem, we would not even be aware of the variations. But if the measuring standards alone were fluctuating, a man who was 6 feet tall on a mild day in spring would be 3 feet tall in summer and 12 feet tall in winter. If we were used to this we probably would not find it too confusing, but it would present some problems of measurement. We would expect to qualify any measurements that we were stating, making allowance for the temperature. Otherwise we would have no way of knowing whether a man described as 6 feet tall was a fairly tall fellow, a giant, or a midget.

Money behaves in very much this way. At times it appears that almost everything has grown in terms of the dollar; at other times almost everything has shrunk. During World War I, prices in the United States shot up to, on the average, twice their 1914 level. A steep decline in 1920–1921 canceled most of the wartime rise. During the Depression many prices fell back to and even below their 1914 level. Since 1941 we have seen an almost uninterrupted rise in prices. Climbing slowly during World War II, while price ceilings were in effect, prices began to soar in 1946. Today they are, in general, more than triple what they were in 1941. Perhaps partly as a result of these recent great changes people understand what is happening a little better. It is not that somehow nearly everything has suddenly become more or less valuable than before. Rather, the value of money itself has changed.[1] It takes almost four times as many dollars today as it took in 1933 to buy a given collection of goods because our dollars have less value today, not because the goods are less available or somehow of greater worth.

CHANGES IN INDIVIDUAL PRICES AND IN THE PRICE LEVEL

Of course, prices may change without a change in the value of money. Every day prices are changing, some rising, some falling, even when the value of money is constant. As a result of shifts in demand or of new productive methods, new discoveries, new marketing policies, or other causes, individual prices will constantly be shifting. These changes, however, will often tend to offset each other. The price level rises or falls only when prices in general are moving in the same direction.

It is sometimes claimed that a fall in the price of one commodity must lead to a rise in the price of other commodities because less will now be spent on the first commodity and the funds released from purchases in that area will be available to drive up prices elsewhere. Accordingly, it is argued, movements of individual prices will cancel out and there will be no general movement of the price level unless the value of money changes. This proposition is a little misleading.

In the first place, if the price of a good falls, there will not necessarily be more money to spend on other goods. If the demand for the good is elastic, the total amount spent for it will be greater after the price is reduced.[2] Less money, not more, will be available for spending on other goods. There is no reason for prices elsewhere to rise because a particular price has declined. They may remain unchanged, rise, or fall.

In the second place, a movement of the general level of prices may possibly be due to a change in the value of money. Less equivocally, it *is* a change in the value of money. Rather than say that a change in either is the cause of a change in the other, we should say that a change in either is a change in the other; the price level and the value of money are two ways of looking at the same thing.

SIGNIFICANCE OF CHANGES IN THE VALUE OF MONEY

Changes in the value of money are important for three reasons:

1. They distort many of our measurements.
2. They exercise some influence on business conditions.
3. They exercise a great influence on the redistribution of income and wealth.

Distortion of Measurements

We live in a money economy. Every part of our economic system is related to money. As individuals, we receive and spend our money incomes. As a

---

[1] Of course the denominational value of money never changes—"a dollar is a dollar is a dollar." The expression "value of money" is used to refer to the purchasing power of money.
[2] See the Introduction.

nation, we necessarily estimate our total national income in money since money provides the common denominator by which we may add locomotives and office buildings and apple pies and haircuts and all the other goods and services that go into our total production. By setting money values on all these diverse commodities and services, we can arrive at a single figure that sums up the whole collection. Only by such a procedure can we make any meaningful comparison between the production of one year and that of the next, since the exact amounts of each specific good or service will almost certainly vary from year to year. If it were necessary to express the total in physical terms, each year we would have thousands of subtotals of production, defying any simple comparison with other years.

On the much smaller scale of an individual business, a firm buys raw materials; hires labor; incurs selling expenses, transportation costs, and the like; and sells its product. By expressing all these activities in terms of money, the businessperson can make up a simple summary statement showing whether the business is operating at a profit or a loss. Also, the businessperson can learn about business conditions in other sectors of the economy by studying current statistics, many of which are expressed in money terms.

All these measurements are alike affected by the fact that they are expressed in terms of a standard that varies. Unless we also know what has happened to the value of money meanwhile, we have no way of knowing whether we are better or worse off if our incomes, after taxes, have risen from $10,000 to $15,000, or whether the nation is producing more goods and services if total national output has risen from $1,000 billion to $1,500 billion. There may be more residential construction, automobiles, or machine tools, or there may be less; we cannot be sure simply by comparing dollar amounts of these items unless we know to what extent the value of the dollar has changed.

Effect on Business Conditions

Changes in the value of money are often associated with cyclical changes in business and employment. Businesspeople seem generally to find it easier to make profits during a period of rising, rather than falling, prices.[3] That is largely due to the fact that profits are a residual element. They are what is left after all expenses have been met. Many business costs tend to be relatively stable in the short run. Certainly interest on bonded indebtedness already incurred does not increase during a period of rising prices. Rent, also, may be a contractual item, periodically revised perhaps, but not subject to change from month to month and in many instances fixed for several years. The rates on power and light may be unchanged for years at a time. In some instances

---

[3]However, G. L. Bach and J. B. Stephenson in "Inflation and the Redistribution of Wealth," *Review of Economics and Statistics* (February, 1974), pp. 1–13, found that during three strongly inflationary periods in the past two and one half decades, 1950–1952, 1955–1957, and 1965–1971, the distribution of national income shifted dramatically to wages and salaries and away from business profits. The reverse was true during the intervening stable and falling price periods, 1953–1954 and 1958–1964.

wage rates may also show little immediate change if contracts have been made setting the level of wages for a year or more.[4] If enough of a business's costs lag behind the general advance in prices, its sales at advancing prices will result in gratifying profits.

These stimulating profits may be increased still further by accounting practices, particularly in regard to inventory and depreciation. The practice of first-in, first-out computes the cost of the raw materials consumed in the manufacture of current output on the basis of the cost of the original inventory at the beginning of the period. In a period of rapid price advances, that cost may be substantially below the current prices for those same raw materials; the profit accordingly may be greater than if the raw materials were valued at current price, by the last-in, first-out procedure. Also, when depreciation charges are based on the original cost of the equipment rather than on the current, higher cost, the charges will be smaller and profits accordingly greater when prices are rising.

Some of these profits may be more apparent than real; but they may encourage a business to expand production, employ more laborers, increase purchases from other firms, and perhaps add to plant and equipment. All this leads to increased orders for other firms, both those that supply the business directly and those that provide goods and services demanded by the laborers added to the payroll. Nearly everyone finds business is good. To be sure, a few businesses may not share in the general prosperity encouraged by the falling value of money. Public utilities, in particular, are likely to find their profit margin squeezed by rising costs and an inflexible rate structure, since they may raise their prices only with the approval of the regulating authorities. But a large proportion of the costs of utilities are fixed costs. They can expand their output substantially with very little addition to their variable and total costs. If the demand for their products increases sufficiently, their average cost may drop and their profits increase.

When the value of money is rising, however, almost all businesses find it more difficult to show a profit. Many of their costs are relatively stable when prices in general are falling, just as they are slow to move when the general level of prices is rising. Rents, wages, interest, and some other cost elements are not immediately revised when wholesale prices drop. Some concerns may be able to lay off workers, cut down their purchases, postpone expansion, and hold their losses down to the point where they can handle them. Other enterprises, particularly those burdened with heavy fixed costs, may be forced into bankruptcy. All these individual situations tend, as before, to set in motion cumulative forces, but with the falling prices leading to progressively reduced employment and falling national output.

Statisticians have found that prosperities are stronger and longer and recessions are milder and shorter in periods when there has been a long-term

---

[4]Wages are probably less stable today than in former years, due to the frequency with which automatic cost-of-living increases are written into current wage contracts. Even so, however, businesses, especially manufacturers, have some opportunity for a windfall profit since the cost of living may rise more slowly than wholesale prices. However, economic theory does not imply nor does the empirical evidence support the common misconception that wage rates typically, if not inexorably, lag behind consumer goods prices.

(25 to 30 years) upward drift in prices, and that recessions are more severe and prosperities are shorter and milder during periods when the price level has been in a long-run decline. These findings, although they do not contradict the line of reasoning presented above, admittedly cannot be said to prove it either. Perhaps the falling price level is a result rather than a cause of recession, or perhaps both are the result of some other cause. Nothing is proved by the mere fact that recessions and a rising value of money go hand in hand. But it seems reasonable to assume that the line of causality may flow in both directions with the result that each intensifies the other. Likewise, the falling value of money may stimulate prosperity that in turn encourages a further fall in the value of money.

Effect on Redistribution of Income and Wealth

Changes in the value of money may cause a violent and arbitrary redistribution of income and property.

Falling Prices. Who are the people who suffer when prices are falling? This is a complex question. If the falling price level is the only change (which is unlikely), then those who feel it most keenly are probably debtors. Take the case of the person who for 10 years has been paying the interest and a little on the principal of the mortgage on a house. Perhaps by now the homeowner's equity has increased by $5,000; in other words, that much of the original loan has been paid off. If real estate prices are falling along with everything else, the house may have declined several thousand dollars in value. Possibly the $5,000 equity has been wiped out entirely. Whether the homeowner continues to pay off the mortgage or decides to give up the house, the savings that have been invested in the house have disappeared.

A business which has borrowed to purchase various assets may find itself in an even more unfavorable position. In the example above, we implicitly assumed that the homeowner's income was not affected by the rising value of money. We can hardly make the same assumption for the business. Besides seeing the fall in the value of its assets, the business is likely to find that it becomes progressively more difficult to pay interest and sinking fund charges on its debt. Even if the business is doing the same physical volume of business as before, it is taking in less receipts at the lower price level. A debt that could easily be serviced when the corporation is doing an annual business of $100 million may force the concern into bankruptcy when sales amount to $60 million or less.

If only the value of money changes, it is apparent that creditors are enriched when prices are falling. One who lent $20,000 a few years earlier, when prices were high and the money bought little, may receive a great deal more purchasing power than was given up. For that matter, suppose the creditor lent the $20,000 to the home-buyer above. Let us say the buyer put in $5,000 at the time and paid an additional $5,000 in monthly payments since. If the buyer now gives up the house, in discouragement or because of inability to make the payments, how does this affect the lender? Assume the market value of the house is now $15,000.

The lender, who gave up $20,000 a few years ago, has recaptured $5,000 and in addition now owns a house that, at the time of the loan, could not have been bought for less than $25,000. Perhaps the house will and perhaps it will not ever have that value again. The point remains that the lender has profited because of being a creditor. The house has cost $15,000, $10,000 less than it would have cost to buy it outright. The $10,000 was transferred to the lender from the debtor.

Furthermore, anyone on a fixed income, such as from interest, annuities, or pensions, can buy more and more with that income as prices fall. People on relatively fixed salaries, provided they can keep their jobs, tend to benefit in the same way as creditors at such times.

Effect of Rising Prices. When prices are rising, that is to say when the value of money is falling, the debtor is benefited and the creditor is injured, if other conditions remain the same. During the German inflation after World War I, farmers were able to pay off the mortgages on their land with a dozen eggs or a pound of butter. Many of the well-to-do middle class who had invested their life savings in high-grade bonds and mortgages found that, when the bonds were retired and the mortgages paid off, the money they received would hardly buy them a sandwich. In fact, by 1923 all the mortgages in Germany, 20 years earlier originally worth $10 billion, could have been paid off with one American cent![5] Conversely, those who had borrowed heavily and bought property at the beginning of the inflation found little trouble in paying off their debts as prices mounted to millions and billions of times their prewar level. Because of inflation the property cost them virtually nothing.

In this country we had a somewhat similar situation during the Revolution, although the inflation did not go as far as in Germany after World War I. More recently, Americans as well as people in other countries have been subjected to the same kind of redistribution of income and property as a result of the decline in the value of money caused by World War II and its aftermath. Those on fixed incomes have been obliged to lower their living standards substantially. An American who lent $10,000 in 1940 gave up a sum of money that would have bought a comfortable home. If the money were repaid 20 years later with 3 percent compound interest, the lender would have received about $18,000—an amount that, even ignoring income taxes, would have been insufficient to buy the house that might have been bought in 1940 for $10,000. The citizen who invested money in real estate or common stocks during World War II probably fared much better than a more patriotic neighbor who bought as many savings bonds as possible.

In all these illustrations the principle is the same, whether the value of money is changing by 10 percent or 80 percent. Higher prices tend to make it easier for debtors to pay off their debts and to effect a redistribution of property from creditors to debtors and to reduce the share of those who are on a fixed income. Falling prices have the opposite effect.

---

[5]Severe as the German inflation was, it pales in comparison with the inflation in Hungary in 1946. The German mark declined to the point that four trillion marks were worth $1. The Hungarian government issued the highest denomination of currency in the world's history—the 100 quintillion (100,000,000,000,000,000,000) pengo note. It was worth less than $0.01!

To any such generalization there will always be many exceptions. A fall in the value of money will not benefit every debtor. Take the case of a person who has gone heavily into debt, with a large part of monthly income earmarked for payments on a house, a car, a television set, and a new furnace. What is left must be spread over the bills for food, utilities, clothes, doctors, gasoline, repairs, and so forth. As the prices of these latter items rise, it will become increasingly more difficult to stretch a paycheck if it is no larger than before. There is no benefit here in being a debtor; it may be impossible to keep up all the payments. A business might be in similar difficulties, although this is less likely as long as the business's products can be sold at higher prices.

To this point we have simplified our analysis by the assumption that only the value of money changes, and that employment levels and real income remain unchanged. In fact, these are very likely to be changing along with the changes in the value of money, as we observed earlier in this chapter. This considerably complicates the redistribution of property that takes place.

Complications Introduced by Accompanying Changes in Production. Debtors may find it harder than ever to pay off their debts when prices are falling, not only because they are giving up a greater purchasing power than they received, but because in many instances a fall in the price level is accompanied by a decline in the level of output. Debts that appeared modest in relation to income may prove unbearable when one has lost one's job.[6] And although creditors who are paid at such times benefit from the rise in the value of money, many find that they will not be paid. If a corporation cannot pay the interest on its bonds, the bondholders may foreclose; but this action may result in nothing more than their becoming the owners of a company that is running further in debt every year. Conversely, although creditors are repaid in smaller dollars when the value of money is falling, their chances of repayment may be substantially greater. Borrowers who have been unable to pay interest or principal during a severe recession may be easily able to meet their obligations with the return of prosperity. The holders of all but the very highest grade bonds were probably quite happy to see the steadily quickening industrial tempo beginning in 1939, even if it did mean that the value of money would probably fall. They now were more certain to receive the interest to which they were entitled but which perhaps they had not been receiving.

THE PROBLEM OF INFLATION TODAY

Inflation occurs because the supply of money increases relative to the demand for money (which in turn is based on peoples' income and wealth, their tastes, preferences, and expectations, the institutional structure of the economy, etc.). While this most typically occurs because of an absolute

---

[6]The disturbing thing about the enormous growth of consumer debt in the postwar period— from less than $6 billion in 1945 to more than $180 billion by 1974, accompanied by an 18-fold increase in consumers' mortgage debt—is the possible effect it might have if a depression or even a very serious recession should occur. This concern was quite evident in 1974 and 1975.

increase in the supply of money, it could result from a decrease in the demand for money because of a decrease in wealth, say, from a natural disaster.

Inflation is insidious. At the same time that it is eating away the value of our insurance policies, savings bonds, pensions, and similar assets, it charms us into a kind of trance because it allows rapid increases in many money incomes. Wages and profits rise more rapidly than would be possible with a stable value of money. We look at our paychecks or at the profits we are making in our business (or the capital gains we have picked up in the stock market) and delude ourselves by thinking we are better off than we were a few years ago when we received less money. In many instances, however, we may be worse off because of the more than proportionate increase in our income taxes as our incomes rise. We are likely to take the complacent attitude that "something should be done" about inflation, but we may resist bitterly any policies that will actually restrain the rapid increases in our own incomes or our own spending.

A fashionable economic philosophy since World War II has been that a slow but constant inflation is really desirable. It is supposed to stimulate the economy, encouraging full employment, a high rate of growth, and a rapidly increasing total output. Not all economists support this thesis, although it has attracted some highly persuasive and internationally renowned advocates. The opposition has maintained that the steady, gradual erosion of the value of money would be inequitable and undesirable even if it were possible. Moreover, the conservatives insist that a policy of sustained inflation must eventually require prices to rise faster and faster to prevent business decline. A continuous gentle inflation is, therefore, a logical impossibility.

Beginning in 1968, however, the administration took strong measures in an attempt to check further price increases. This change of emphasis mainly resulted from the fact that another old monetary truth had been proved once more: continuous inflation is likely to pose eventual serious international problems for inflated currency. Any attempt to control prices would necessarily be accompanied by rising unemployment and falling profits and incomes. Unfortunately in spite of the administration's attempts, prices since 1968 have continued to rise.

Trying to halt the forces of inflation requires political courage. Voters will seldom throng to the polls to support anti-inflationary policies. Yet even in the uncertain event that inflation could indefinitely prolong a prosperity, we must recognize the accompanying problems that perpetual inflation would present. The entire program of Social Security and private as well as public pension and retirement systems become meaningless if by the time workers retire the purchasing power of the dollar has become so little that they do not have the financial security they believed they were establishing.[7]

---

[7]Again, Bach and Stephenson, *op. cit.*, challenge this conventional view, as they found that Social Security benefits actually rose rapidly compared to other shares of national income in the three inflationary periods.

One of the most recent suggestions to correct, but not halt, the deleterious effects of inflation is indexing. *Indexing* ties the amount of the payment in any contract to some form of price index. This method requires payments to vary directly with price variations. As prices rise (fall), the size of payments also rises (falls). Thus, indexing protects the person receiving the payment against the declining value of the dollar.

While indexing is widely used in some countries, such as Brazil, it exists in the U.S. only haphazardly. The best known form is the cost-of-living escalator clause in labor contracts and the cost-of-living adjustments by the federal government in some employee wages and in Social Security. A crude form of indexing has been tried with interest rates as lenders have insisted on higher rates to protect against anticipated inflation.

Proponents of indexing would like to see it used in federal finances. For instance, they advocate indexing the tax system—individual exemptions, the standard deduction, and rate tables—to reflect rising prices; exempting capital gains if they reflect only inflation; and changing corporate depreciation allowances in line with rising prices. A simpler change would be to require the Treasury to issue purchasing power securities, on which interest would rise in line with inflation. (Short-term Treasury notes and bills which are close to cash might be excluded.)

There are a number of logical as well as practical objections to indexing. For one thing indexing can make the first flareup of inflation worse. It may also lessen the governmental will to end the inflation. At best it is only a crude form of protection against inflation. This much is certain: we already have some indexing and we surely will get some more.

In any event, whether prices are rising slowly or rapidly, and whether they are rising or falling, changes in the value of money vitally concern us all. They affect our investments and savings, our living standards, our incomes, and even our jobs.[8] As a first step to the understanding of these changes, we want to be able to measure them as accurately as is possible.

Many of our time series are expressed in terms of dollars. We would like to correct these series for changes in the value of the dollar, that is, convert our series from current dollars to dollars of constant purchasing power. Also, in studying the inflationary and deflationary aspects of trends and policies, it is not enough to say, "Many prices rose (or fell)." We want an objective and quantitative measure giving some idea of the amount of change in the value of money. For these and similar purposes we use *price indexes*.

MEASUREMENT OF CHANGES IN THE VALUE OF MONEY

Values are ordinarily expressed in money. How can we measure the value of money itself? We can measure it only *relatively*, not absolutely. All we can do is compare the value of money at one time with its value at another time.

---

[8]To be precise, inflation does not decrease the value of all saving, but reduces the value of monetary holdings. Clearly savings need not be held in the form of monetary wealth.

Even this comparison will be made *indirectly*. For convenience, we attack the problem backward. Because money itself is the standard of value, we cannot directly compare money values as we do with other commodities. For example, if we are comparing the value of wheat at one time with its value at another time, we simply compare wheat prices of the two periods. If a bushel of wheat once cost $1 and now costs $2, its price, or money value, has doubled. The current price of a dollar, however, is always a dollar.

We could, if we wished, directly express the value of a dollar in terms of wheat and other commodities. In the example above, a dollar is worth half as much wheat as it used to be. We might similarly find a dollar is worth a third as much coal as it was earlier, 80 percent as much iron, and so on. And we might, somehow, average these values. But it is simpler to work out some kind of average of *prices*. Since we can buy less when prices rise and more when prices fall, when we have measured the price level we have the *reciprocal* of the value of money. If prices are now, on the average, 125 percent of what they were, the value of money must be 80 percent of what it was.[9] We can then say, "We have a dollar that is worth 80 cents in terms of the earlier dollar." It takes a dollar now to buy what could have been bought for 80 cents then.

CONSTRUCTION OF A PRICE INDEX

For our change in price level to be most useful as a measure of the change in the value of money, we shall show the changes in individual prices as percentages rather than as absolute amounts; that is, we shall use price relatives. We divide the price an article is selling for today by the price it was selling for in some earlier period. This price relative tells us what percentage the present price is of the earlier price.

Even if there were only a single commodity being bought and sold, a price relative would most conveniently show us what has happened to the value of money. Suppose that we were in an economy where the only good for which money was exchanged was coffee. Also suppose the price of coffee rose from $1 a pound to $3. In this simple case we hardly need construct a price relative to know that our money buys just one third as much as it did before. A dollar is now worth only a third of a pound instead of a full pound of coffee.

But suppose the price rose from $1.20 to $1.50. Here it is not quite so easy to say, from looking at the two prices, how much the value of money has changed. But if we use a price relative, we see that the price today in relation to the earlier period is $1.50/$1.20, or 1.25, or 125/100. The purchasing power of money must, therefore, be 100/125, or 80 percent of what it was. Both price relatives and index numbers, incidentally, are usually written without the decimal point, as percentages—in this case as 125 and 80.

The use of price relatives is all the more important when we are working with many different prices. Some items cost a few cents, others cost hundreds

---

[9]The reciprocal of 1.25, or 5/4, is 4/5, or .80.

of dollars. If we try to compute the change in the "average price" of bread and automobiles, for example, we find that what happens to the price of bread makes very little difference. A very slight change in the price of cars would outweigh any conceivable change that might occur in the price of bread.

But when we use price relatives to show what has happened, the size of individual prices makes no difference. If for cars the price has risen by $1,000, from $3,000 to $4,000, and for bread the price has declined by $.05, from $.15 to $.10, we see that $4,000/$3,000 = 133 and $.10/$.15 = 67. The average of the two price relatives is 100.

Prices to Include in an Index

If our index is to measure changes in the value of money, it should relate money to all the things for which it is exchanged. All prices should be taken into account in our index, each expressed as a percentage of the corresponding price in the base year. (The *base year* is the year against which all other years are compared for changes in the average price level. Base year average prices are always given an index number of 100.)

Since it is obviously impossible to compute a price index that will include all prices, we must use the sampling method. We shall take a large number of prices and assume that their behavior is characteristic of prices in general. The first question to be settled, then, is this: Just what prices shall we include? Shall we use wholesale prices or retail? Shall we include both finished goods and raw materials, producer goods and consumer goods, and real estate and security prices along with commodity prices?

There is no single answer to these questions. It depends upon the purpose for which the index is to be used. If we are interested in measuring changes in the value of money generally, a general price index is required. Such an index should be as comprehensive as possible. If we are interested primarily in measuring changes in the value of the consumer's dollar, an index of the retail prices of the principal items bought by consumers is the appropriate measure. Such an index is regularly computed by the Department of Labor. It is often referred to as an index of the cost of living, and is the basis of many wage contracts. Perhaps we wish a sensitive price index that will exaggerate price movements, or we may wish an index of those prices that usually move earlier than prices in general. Again, we may be interested in the price level of certain types of goods, such as building materials, producers' goods, or farm products. Indexes relating to prices in specific areas are helpful in the analysis of current economic problems. Sometimes they will reveal changes concealed by the more general type of price index which, by its very generality, may fail to show significant changes among different groups of prices.

Recent emphasis on the analysis of income formation has somewhat lessened our interest in the all-inclusive general price index, which, however, still has some usefulness as a theoretical tool. At any rate, the general price index is helpful as a first approach to the theory of the value of money.

Simple Average of Price Relatives

Having decided what prices to include, we compute our price relatives and average them. If we were using a simple, unweighted average, we would just add the price relatives and divide by the number of items. For a general price index we would probably be using a hundred or more commodities.

Weighting of Price Relatives

By averaging price relatives rather than the prices themselves, we have made each commodity equally important. This method is better than making all changes in low priced commodities of little or no consequence, so that the changes in high priced commodities are the determining ones. Yet it is still unsatisfactory. Why should all commodities be equally important when we are trying to measure what has happened to the purchasing power of money? We are much more affected by what happens to some prices than by what happens to others. A doubling of the price of meat or gasoline hits our pocket-book much harder than a doubling of the price of olives or dictionaries. We should attach a greater weight to what happens to the prices of the goods on which we spend larger amounts. This is the same principle you observe in figuring your grade average. The grade in the five-hour course is given five times the weight of the grade that you received in the one-hour course.

The simplest, most objective weights are the actual amounts spent, that is, the values of the various commodities. The amount spent is of course given by the price of the commodity and the quantity sold.

We might use as weights the base year values[10] or the given years values. The former are more convenient and more readily available. They are also much better when we are comparing prices over a period of years (rather than comparing two years only), for they are constant over the period, whereas given year value weights change each year. All we are doing is comparing with the total amount spent in the base year the total amount that would have been spent in the current year if all physical quantities had been the same as they were in the base year.

Dilemma of the Weighting Technique

The method above is commonly used in the computation of price indexes. It is not the only appropriate method, nor is it entirely satisfactory. The use of base year weights introduces some bias. In fact, any fixed weights offer the disadvantage that over a period of time they become less and less representative of the prices to which they correspond. Entirely new commodities appear that may account for major portions of our expenditures. We cannot attach the same weight to automobile expenditures in 1976 as in 1920. Private television sets were unknown before World War II.

---

[10]The statistically inclined may be interested to note that this method is often described as a *base year quantity weighted aggregative index.*

Yet in comparing one year with another, we must have the same weights in the numerator as in the denominator if our index is to measure the change in price only. Otherwise it would be a composite, a value index, showing the combined effect in any particular year of a change in price and quantity.

In practice this dilemma is resolved by a periodic change of weights, perhaps once in 10 or 20 years. The earlier index is then recomputed on the new base or sometimes left as a separate series. This compromise is required by the fact that, strictly speaking, an index number is most significant when it involves a comparison of two years only. In practice we are not satisfied with comparing one year with one other year. We want to work out a series of figures that will show us the value of money over perhaps a century or more. However elaborately such a series may be calculated, it must be recognized as no more than an approximation. The shorter the period under consideration, the more significant the price index.

Subject to this limitation, changes in the value of money in recent years are indicated by the indexes of consumer prices and of wholesale prices computed by the United States Department of Labor, each of which is shown in the endsheets of this book for the years 1929 to 1974. These are two of the most commonly used indexes. Neither attempts to show *the* value of money. One measures (inversely) the buying power of the consumer's dollar; the other measures average wholesale prices, which are considerably more sensitive than retail prices. General price indexes, such as the Implicit Price Index (GNP deflator) also shown in the endsheet, have occasionally been computed but are not widely used.

Price Indexes and Quality Changes

Too many people, looking at the official price indexes carried out to a tenth of a percent, assume that indexes are precision measuring devices. So also do some students after studying the construction of price indexes. The mere fact that there is an equation for the price index seems to suggest a mathematically "right" answer.[11] The fact is, no price index today can possibly be anything more than an approximation.

If the necessary data had been available at the time, economists three or four hundred years ago could probably have constructed price indexes subject to less qualification than today's indexes. It was not only that the problem of weighting, discussed earlier, would have been less important. In addition, the quality of goods remained about the same from one decade to the next. Today qualitative changes are very important—but there is no way to give them an exact mathematical formulation.

The quality of some goods and services has deteriorated. Railroad passenger service, commuter service, and urban public transportation, when available at all, are much inferior to those services 30 or 40 years ago. Probably

---

[11]The formula for our base year weighted index of price relatives is: $p = \dfrac{\Sigma p_1 q_0}{\Sigma p_0 q_0}$ where $p_0 q_0$ are the base year values and $p_1 q_0$ are the given year values.

more frequently, however, the quality of goods is better today. The air-conditioned Ford of 1976 is a far cry from the Model T of 1925. It has more power, speed, and comfort than the luxurious Pierce Arrow of 1925, which sold then for about the price of the Ford today. To a considerable extent the price of cars is higher today not simply because money is worth less, but because cars are better today.

Our attempts to measure the changing value of money cannot provide us with exact answers when we cannot mathematically allow for the continuous changes in the quality of goods and services. Often we are comparing the prices of entirely different items rather than of the same items. Thus, there is a spurious accuracy in the official figures, presented as computed to a tenth of a percent.

SUMMARY AND CONCLUSION

There is no way to measure directly the value of money. All we can do is compare its purchasing power in one period with its purchasing power in another period, called the base year. Even this measurement is made indirectly by comparing the level of prices at one time with the price level in the earlier period. The higher our price index, the lower the value of money. They are reciprocals of each other. If prices are twice as high as they were earlier, our money will buy half as much. If prices fall by one third, the value of money is greater by one half—for if $P = 2/3$, the value of money must be 3/2.

A price index is computed by:

1. selecting a sample of the goods on which we spend most of our money and
2. computing a base year value weighted average of the price relatives of the goods included in our sample.

The result will be a fair indication of whether our money is buying more or less. There is no way to measure exactly the changes in the value of money over a period of years, even if we used a much more elaborate technique. Neither this formula nor any other can be regarded as best. This one is simpler to compute than many and more satisfactory than most, so it is widely used.

Discussion Questions

1. The term "value of money" is foolish since the denominational value of a dollar never changes. True or False? Explain.
2. Can we safely conclude that the value of money has fallen (a) if the prices of some consumer goods and services have risen? (b) if the prices of all consumer goods and services have risen? Explain.
3. G. L. Bach and J. B. Stephenson in their studies obtained some empirical results which are not widely acknowledged. What are they?

4. Is it primarily the rich or primarily the lower income groups who are likely to be hurt by rising prices? Briefly explain.

5. Disregarding income taxes, what would mainly determine whether a debtor would be benefited or injured by a rise in prices?

6. "Inflation results from an increase in the supply of money." True or False? Explain.

7. Briefly describe the nature and significance of indexing.

8. Money is used as a standard of value to measure the value of everything else. How can we measure the value of money itself?

9. Although we cannot construct a satisfactory price index without using weights, the use of weights makes it impossible to construct an accurate index. Explain.

10. By the time economists had the necessary data and had learned how to combine them to construct price indexes, the problem of accurately measuring changes in the value of money was rapidly becoming more impossible than ever before. Explain.

11. The reaction of banks and other financial institutions to increases in the price level is quite different from the reaction of individual lenders. Explain. What possible consequence might this have if prices continued to rise until almost everyone took for granted that they would go on rising indefinitely?

Chapter 14   Commodity Theory of the Value of Money

In this chapter and the next we shall review older theories of the value of money. This is not an idle exercise in tracing obsolete and discredited theories. They are less popular today, not because they are based on error, but because they are dependent upon assumptions that are today often unrealistic. However, they do contain a measure of truth. They do still have some support. They have been the basis of important monetary policies during the 20th century, including devaluations of the dollar and (with respect to the quantity theory) the attempt since 1968 to check inflation. We shall better understand why certain policies were adopted in the past if we know the reasoning of the people who supported these policies. Also, we shall be able to evaluate more intelligently the probable effects of current monetary policies if we have some understanding of what can be accomplished by changing the gold content of the dollar or changing the quantity of money.

Most of us will never find ourselves on the advisory staff of the Board of Governors or the President. But all of us do have a personal, vital stake in what happens to the value of money. Who wants to hold money if its value will be falling? Who wants to hold real estate or stocks if the value of money will be rising?

It is seldom wise to be so dazzled by the latest fashions, whether in architecture, furniture, or economic theory, that we throw out all the inheritance of the past. Too often we later realize that it really had some usefulness after all, and that, perhaps with some qualifications, it can still be of service.

EARLIER THEORIES IGNORED INCOME CHANGES

The early theories of the value of money were basically simple because they were concerned with a very narrow question. They were trying to explain changes in the value of money only. They were not concerned with consumption, investment, saving, growth rates, or even the level of income. Why were they so interested in price levels and so unconcerned about other matters, some of which we feel today are more important than changes in the value of money? Basically there were two reasons.

Lack of Adequate Statistics

Not until the 20th century were reliable statistics available except for a few series, usually specialized or localized and not very significant. In the

days before computers, calculating machines, and typewriters, it was impractical to collect the wealth of figures compiled today. Besides, the importance
of such figures was not recognized, and even if it had been, there was no
agency responsible for collecting them. Governments were exercising little
supervision over business. Giant corporations had not yet replaced the small
firms and individual proprietorships, many of which kept only sketchy records. There was, however, some information on prices, enough to make it
quite evident that money had been worth more at some times than it had at
other times.

Assumption of Full Employment

Secondly, most economists assumed until shortly before World War II
that the equilibrium level of income was at full employment. If this were true,
then a study of the determinants of income would have no practical value.
The economy would be at full employment most of the time. Unemployment
would be a temporary phenomenon, quickly corrected by natural forces with
no need for assistance from the government or the banking system. This assumption of full employment was based partly on theoretical considerations
and partly on conditions generally prevailing.

Say's Law. Classical economists believed that general overproduction was
impossible. This point of view was summed up early in the 19th century by
the French economist, Jean Baptiste Say (1767–1832) in his law, "Supply
creates its own demand." Certainly, he said, society would never produce
more goods than people wanted, for people's wants are insatiable. Too much
might sometimes be produced of particular goods, leading to overproduction
in some industries, but this was a temporary maladjustment, quickly corrected by normal market forces.

Nor could production be greater than demand or ability to buy. The more
that was produced, the more income would be created and, therefore, the
more buying power there would be. This is an interesting point, made more
than a century before Lord Keynes (1883–1946) introduced his income
theory.[1] It is true, as far as it goes. What it overlooks—and this is a fatal
oversight—is that we live in a money economy, not a barter economy. Production creates income, true enough. But incomes are received as money.
Money may be used as a store of value. People are not forced to spend. If
nearly everyone is trying to sell but almost no one wants to buy, even if
people do have the money, then supply certainly may exceed demand, and
general overproduction and overcapacity result. To be sure, Say and the Classics were interested in long-term relationships. The longer the time frame, the
less incorrect is the Classical position.

Decrease in Demand Resulting from General Price Decline. The second
oversight of Classical economists was inconsistent with their acceptance of

---

Say's Law. They forgot that costs were simultaneously income. Therefore, they believed that depressions, if they should occur, would quickly correct themselves. As prices fell, sales would increase and production would expand. They quite forgot that a fall in prices was at the same time a fall in incomes, and that, with less money in their pockets, people might buy less than before, even if prices were lower.[2] They assumed, in other words, an unchanged demand schedule.

If 10,000 units could be sold at a price of $5, a $4 price should increase sales to perhaps 12,000 or 13,000. This reasoning is correct if we assume that demand is unchanged, still represented by D_1 in Figure 14-1. But a general fall in prices requires a general fall in incomes—and the demand schedule, therefore, shifts to the left. At all prices, less is demanded than before.

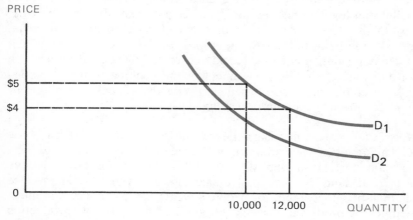

Figure 14-1   Change in Demand

Full Employment Encouraged by Circumstances. Although the 19th century equilibrium theory was unsound, conditions during that period were generally favorable to the maintenance of full employment. For one thing, less was being produced. Most production was needed for consumption. Besides, this period of rapid industrialization and expansion required enormous amounts of investment. There was no lack of opportunities for profitable additions to capital. In fact, the demand for funds for capital expansion was so strong that often it required forced saving. Frequently bank credit was created, at full employment, to supply businesses with purchasing power. The result was that factors of production were bid away from the production of consumption goods to the building of factories and railroads. This led to a rise in prices. Also, during wars prices rose. At some other times, and especially after wars, prices fell.

As economists of the period saw such price changes, they tried to explain them in terms of money itself. What had happened to money that it now bought less or more than before?

_____

[2]However, if demand is elastic, a fall in wages will be associated with a higher level of total wages paid. See the Introduction.

THE COMMODITY THEORY OF MONEY

The oldest theory of the value of money is that it depends upon the value of the commodity out of which it is made. This appeared particularly obvious and, in fact, was largely true when money was almost entirely in the form of coins. But a number of difficulties appear when we attempt to apply this theory to modern money.

As long as a government freely redeems its money with a fixed quantity of gold (or other metal), the value of the money cannot differ from the value of its metallic content by more than the cost of coining the metal or melting coins and the value of the seigniorage charge, if any. To this extent the commodity theory is unmistakably correct. This necessary condition of equality does not, however, answer the question of why either the gold or the money has value. It merely states that the value of the money and of a certain quantity of gold will be the same. Naturally their value must be equal if either one may be exchanged for the other. But should we conclude that money has value because it can be converted into gold, or that gold has value because it can be converted into money?

The answer is not quite as simple as the commodity theory implies. According to the theory, money derives its value from the gold for which it may be exchanged. But gold has an intrinsic value apart from its use as money. Even if it were not used for money, gold is in demand for ornamentation and for use in the arts and industry.

It is important to realize that we can claim no more for gold than that. It would not be correct to add that gold is also desired because its relatively high value makes it easy to store or because it is portable, for such statements beg the question that we are trying to solve. Gravel can also be easily stored as far as spoilage is concerned, but it would not be a practical store of value because it does not have the high value per ounce that is characteristic of gold. Likewise, the portability of gold is a consequence, not a cause, of its high intrinsic value.

Nor, as elementary economic theory reminds us, can we evade the question by stating that the high value of an ounce of gold is due to the scarcity of gold. Certainly scarcity and value are two aspects of the same thing, but both are also relative concepts. Why should gold be worth over five million dollars a ton when the Treasury holds thousands of tons of it? Again we return to the question of the demand for gold. Ten or 12 thousand tons represent considerable gold, but it is not really very much in comparison with all the possible uses to which gold might be put. Here we begin to come to grips with the problem. What are these uses to which gold might be put? Why is gold so universally desired?

Demand for Gold for Ornamentation

Two thousand years ago perhaps it was true that gold was desired almost entirely because of its usefulness for decoration. The world's stock of refined gold was small. Gold is easily worked, and even a fairly primitive society could produce rings, bracelets, and necklaces by which the wealthy might display their fortune. Apart from gold and jewels, the rich had few outlets for consumption expenditures. Today gold is much less important for this purpose, especially in the more industrialized nations. Rather than wear 10 or 12 pounds of golden chains or bracelets, a prosperous person today would rather drive a new car. And rather than eat food from a golden plate, a modern person would rather get food from a new freezer. There is such a multitude of things produced today, many of them undreamed of a century or even a decade ago, that we cannot become greatly interested in building up a large stock of ornamental gold. Most people get far more satisfaction from a television set, swimming pool, or luxury cruise than they would derive from a pound or two of golden jewelry. It is not a question of not being able to afford the gold but of preferring other things. Although a few people may wear solid gold watches and carry cigarette cases and lighters of solid gold, the majority are satisfied with gold plate, silver, or other metals, spending the difference in ways that bring them more satisfaction.

Also, people today are ready to buy earning assets to increase their income. Centuries ago most wealth was inherited, and aristocrats did not soil their hands with trade. They had their fortunes and were expected to enjoy them with distinction and elegance. (The royal coat of arms of France was particularly explicit with its *fleur-de-lis*, signifying the lilies of the field, and its motto, "They toil not, neither do they spin.")

Because it resists corrosion, gold is an excellent material, when hardened by the addition of other metals, to make into pen points. Except for a wedding ring, that pen point is the only item of solid gold that the average person is likely to want, at least as long as gold sells at anything like its present price.

Even though in the Orient gold is in greater demand for purposes of personal display, the total world demand for gold as ornamentation cannot begin to explain the general demand for gold.[3] The reason for this conclusion is simple. Most of the world's gold today is used as monetary reserves. If the people of the modern world wanted more gold for personal adornment, they could have it. National treasuries would simply hold that much less. But today there is relatively little demand for gold products. The demand for gold at, say, $200 an ounce must lie largely outside the field of ornamentation.[4]

Demand for Gold for Hoarding

A demand for gold undoubtedly exists, in spite of the fact that it is no longer greatly desired for ornamentation. One of the most compelling arguments against a return to our earlier form of gold standard with its provision that the government freely sell gold is the claim that our gold reserves, massive as they are, would be insufficient to meet the public demand for gold. Perhaps this assertion is true and perhaps it is not. But whether the Treasury would lose all or only part of the gold it now holds, how can we explain

---

[3]To some degree, however, his wife's gold (or silver) bangles represent the merchant's reserve funds. They are, to a limited extent, functioning as money.
[4]Despite the fact that gold also has wide usage in industry, such as in the space programs, as well as for personal adornment, this statement holds. And of course, since December 31, 1974, U.S. citizens for the first time in 41 years are allowed to purchase gold freely for investment.

people's desire to hold gold in addition to what they are already free to hold in the form of pen points, watchcases, and jewelry?

Suppose a government declares war or embarks on irresponsible financial adventures. Many people consequently will expect that prices will soon rise rapidly. If they are right, then the longer one holds paper money—deposits or notes—the less it will buy. By the same token, anyone holding commodities will find them steadily rising in monetary value. In terms of other commodities, the person's hoard of goods, if wisely chosen, will retain approximately its present value, even if the value of paper money falls almost to zero. Obviously, the sooner one can exchange money for a stock of something, the better.

If the value of money falls sharply, almost any commodity is better to hold than paper money. Some commodities, however, are better stores of value than others. What is the best commodity to hold? One consideration is the ease of storage and the loss or shrinkage through spoilage of a commodity. In light of this consideration, gold is convenient, although platinum might be considered still more convenient when one is assessing these problems.

Another far more important consideration is that the commodity chosen must be one that will retain its value with respect to other commodities. If money is losing its value, commodities will be expected to increase in value in terms of the depreciating currency. Some commodities will rise less in price than others, however, and hence will lose in value as compared to commodities in general. Apart from spoilage problems and storage costs, holding stocks of cotton, potatoes, or copper might prove unsatisfactory because of a subsequently lessened demand for these products or an increased supply.

Gold is far superior to any other commodity as a store of value because, directly or indirectly, it is the basis of most of the world's money. Until very recently the treasuries of many nations would buy all the gold they were offered.[5] The demand was limitless. Remember, treasuries of gold-standard nations print the money to pay for gold. The gold costs the treasury nothing, and it can buy all it is offered. As we saw in Chapter 2, the market price in any country cannot fall below the price offered by the treasury of that country. Consequently, except in the unlikely event of an upward revaluation of the currency, there is no possible chance that the price of gold will drop. Of course, if a nation's money falls in value with respect to other currencies, it will lose gold. Then it must either force other prices down or set a higher price for gold, either of which will profit the person holding gold.

If the gold hoarders are mistaken and their government is able to keep the value of money from falling, those who have exchanged their currency for gold may convert back to currency and recover the entire amount they originally "invested" in gold. If the treasury is unsuccessful, it will ultimately abandon the gold standard, at least temporarily, and currency will be at a discount with respect to gold. Regardless of the severity of monetary inflation that may follow and of the losses that will be sustained by creditors and by

---

[5]From 1968 to 1971 governments freely bought gold from each other and stayed out of the private market. Now governments can sell gold, but not buy it, in either the private or the official market.

those holding paper money, the people who hold gold have the same command over all other goods and services as when they converted to gold. Their protection has been absolute.[6]

Those who have bought commodities other than gold are taking a chance. Those commodities, relative to other goods, may be either more or less valuable when one later converts back to currency. Such possibilities are of interest to the speculator, who hopes to guess the course of particular prices. They are not the concern of the person trying to guard against loss due to a fall in the value of money. As long as treasuries continue to buy gold at a fixed price in unlimited quantities, gold is the one commodity for which the demand cannot weaken.

Thus, we arrive at the rather surprising conclusion that *the demand for gold is largely a result of the fact that gold is used for money*. Of course, we cannot say that the value of gold as a commodity is determined entirely by the demand for gold as money. But still less can we suppose that the value of gold as money is determined by its value as a commodity for nonmonetary use, as the naive form of the commodity theory maintains. Gold is in demand for two purposes—for monetary uses (which is today the principal purpose) and for use in the arts and industry. The value of gold reflects this joint demand for gold. It is not the result of either demand by itself. It is quite wrong to suppose that gold has value as money simply because gold has value in nonmonetary uses.

Relation between Price Level and Cost of Gold Production

A more carefully formulated version of the commodity theory admits that, to a considerable extent, the demand for gold is derived from its association with money rather than the other way around. But the theory still maintains that money's value or purchasing power is regulated by the amount of gold it represents. This approach relates the general price level to the cost of gold production. It attempts to show the effect of supply as well as demand upon the value of gold and therefore of money. When new, rich gold strikes are made, gold production rises and the value of gold relative to other commodities falls. Also, in a period when the general price level declines, an increase in gold production should verify the appreciating value of gold in terms of other goods. The value of gold, it is asserted, like the value of any other commodity, is governed by the relation between supply and demand. And with the value of gold thus determined, market prices of other goods represent our comparative valuations of these goods in terms of gold, the valuations expressed for convenience in monetary units.

This version of the commodity theory of money, although superior to the naive theory discussed earlier, is not entirely satisfactory. It is true that gold

---

[6]We are here assuming, of course, that their right to hold gold is not denied by the government, as it was in the U.S. from 1933 to 1974.

production will tend to increase when the cost of gold production is falling due to a decline in the price level. At such a time mining companies can profitably mine ores of lower grade since their operating costs are falling, but the price for gold remains unchanged.

In the case of most commodities we should expect an increase in production to result in a decrease in the value of the commodity. Such a decrease would ordinarily be indicated by a fall in the price of the commodity. In the case of the commodity used as the monetary standard, the price will be changed only by government action. A decline in its value will be shown by a rise in the general price level. If gold is our monetary standard and the value of gold is declining, more gold will be required in exchange for a given amount of other commodities. An automobile tire, for example, once considered equal in value to an eighth of an ounce of gold may later be considered as equivalent in value to a fourth of an ounce of gold.

We cannot assume that the value of gold, as measured inversely by the general price level, will closely correspond to the cost of gold production. In the first place, there is a wide variation in the production costs of an ounce of gold, depending on the richness of the ore, transportation and labor costs, and other factors. As with any commodity, the relation between production costs and market price will determine the extent to which production will be carried on, but only the marginal producers will find that the price is just equal to their cost of production.

In the second place, the changes in production induced by changes in the value of gold will not be immediate. In the case of a rising value of gold, it frequently takes time to obtain and put into operation the additional equipment required for processing lower grade ores. Likewise, if the value of gold is falling, some producers are likely to continue producing for years, even if they cannot recover their full costs. If they cover all their direct costs and obtain some return on the capital invested in machinery and equipment, they will usually be better off than if they close down completely and have no return at all on their invested capital. Eventually, as their equipment wears out, they cease producing, but the readjustment is delayed.

In the third place, gold is unlike most commodities in that the total available stock is affected very little and very slowly by changes in output. Much of the gold held today was produced in earlier centuries. Current yearly gold production probably amounts to less than 2 percent of the world's gold stock.[7]

Finally, the value of gold is affected by the extent to which other forms of money are substituted for gold. Let us suppose that a cheap process was discovered for recovering gold from sea water. Gold would become far more abundant than ever before. If there were no monetary demand for gold, it

---

[7]Though the records are obviously incomplete, up to Columbus' voyage, 160 tons of gold were produced. From 1493 to 1900, gold production amounted to 15,000 tons and from 1900 to 1971 about 57,000 tons. The grand total comes to about 85,000 tons, including estimates of Communist area production.

would decline in value. But if it was the monetary standard and the Treasury continued to buy it at the same price, (or, as today, continued to maintain a price floor), then its value could decline only if there was a fall in the value of money. And the value of money might be unaffected. The results would depend upon the significance of gold to the nation's money supply. The following three cases may be distinguished:

1. If the only money in circulation was gold currency, then a drop in the value of gold and of the dollar would be almost inevitable under the circumstances. Prices of most goods and services would rise.
2. Or if every dollar of gold used as monetary reserves was always the basis of the same amount of bank credit so that an increase of 300 percent in gold reserves resulted in an increase of 300 percent in demand deposits and bank currency, a general rise in prices would, again, be likely.
3. But suppose nearly all the money in circulation was credit money and that the increased gold hoards were held by the Treasury. If the gold certificates were held by the Federal Reserve Banks, and member banks were at the same time required to hold larger reserves against their deposits, anything might happen to the value of money.[8] It might rise, fall, or remain constant at the same time that the cost of gold production fell. The gold-extraction plants might be making handsome profits, but as long as the government continued to absorb at a fixed price per ounce all the gold offered, the greatly increased supply of gold would not necessarily affect the value of gold or money.

Assumption That Pricing Involves Valuations in Gold

The assumption that our price system is the result of our constantly evaluating all other goods in terms of gold does not seem realistic. It seems most doubtful that people pay $5,000 for a car because they decide the car has the same value to them as approximately 25 ounces of gold. Still less do they buy a shirt because they value it as worth a twentieth of an ounce of gold.

The argument in 1933 that the domestic price level could be raised almost immediately to any desired level by regulating the gold content of the dollar was not supported by the results of the experiment.[9] There was no prompt marking up of wage rates, real estate values, or prices in general in consequence of the fact that a dollar, after the devaluation, contained about 40 percent less gold than before.

The devalued dollars were in just as great demand as the former dollars had been. People still tried to get as many dollars as they could for their labor or whatever else they were selling. But no one was willing to pay more dollars than before. The gold content of the dollar was not that important. The evolution of money had gone beyond the point that a dollar was simply a piece of

---

[8]You will recall from Table 3-1 that from 1914 to 1974 there was no significant relationship between the domestic money supply and the gold stock and there was no inevitable relationship between the wholesale price level and the gold stock.
[9]See Chapter 3.

gold or exchangeable for a piece of gold. The dollar was now an abstract standard of value. The connection between gold and money was still convenient in settling international balances and in limiting the possible expansion of the money supply. Otherwise its importance was largely historical.

SUMMARY AND CONCLUSION

The various shortcomings of the commodity theory limit its usefulness in explaining changes in the value of money; and because of its theoretical weaknesses, it does not provide a good guide to monetary policy. It comes closest to reality when it deals with the effect of changes in the monetary stock caused by changes in gold production and changes in the distribution of gold between monetary and nonmonetary uses. The value of money may be investigated more satisfactorily, however, by directly analyzing changes in the monetary stock, taking into account also the turnover of money, which is ignored by the commodity theory. To this approach we now turn.

Discussion Questions

1. Why were pre-Keynesian economists more interested in price levels than in the determinants of income?
2. Although Keynes demolished Say's conclusion that overproduction is impossible, part of the Keynesian framework was first set forth by Say. Explain.
3. Until about 45 years ago, economists believed that production and income were in equilibrium only at full employment. Explain their reasoning.
4. The error of Say's Law resulted from the failure to recognize one of the essential functions of money. Explain.
5. What does price elasticity of demand have to do with the Classical economists' belief that depressions correct themselves automatically?
6. How were falling prices and falling costs in depression viewed:
   a. by Classical economists?
   b. by Keynes?
7. "The high value of an ounce of gold is due to the scarcity of it." Explain why you agree or disagree with this statement.
8. The "penny" mentioned in the New Testament was the Roman silver denarius, which contained a little less silver than the U.S. quarter did until a few years ago. After a few centuries the silver denarius was withdrawn from circulation and replaced by a new denarius of a copper alloy. The new denarius had only a fraction of the value of the old. Did this decline in value prove the validity of the commodity theory? Does it suggest that since we followed the Roman example and replaced our own silver coins with copper we, too, can expect prices to rise? Justify your answer.
9. Commodity theorists believed that, in a gold-standard country, falling prices would automatically be corrected partly because of their effect on gold production. Explain and evaluate.

10. Some commodity theorists have recommended that the price level be stabilized by continually adjusting the price of gold rather than by holding it constant for years at a time. How would the changes in gold prices affect the general price level, if these theorists are correct? Would you expect the price level to be more or less stable than with the automatic gold standard, according to the commodity theory?

11. During the 19th century, as tons of gold and silver were taken from the New World, prices in Europe rose.
    a. Was this in accord with what commodity theorists would expect? Explain.
    b. Did it prove the validity of the commodity theory? Explain.

Chapter 15   Quantity Theory of the Value of Money

The quantity theory of the value of money is a cousin of the commodity theory. The quantity theory represents, however, a broader case and is less subject to criticism.

We saw that, according to the commodity theory, the value of money is determined by the amount of gold it contains or represents. The value of the gold itself would depend, as with any other commodity, upon its scarcity relative to other goods.[1] An increase in the supply of gold, other things being equal, would cause a decline in the value of gold, that is, a rise in the price level. Or an increase in the demand for gold, that is, an increase in the supply of goods and services offered in exchange for gold, would cause a fall in the price level.

CHANGES IN QUANTITY OF MONEY AND CHANGES IN PRICES

The quantity theory generalizes from this more exclusive case. According to the quantity theory, an increase in the supply of money (of any kind) would cause the value of money to fall and prices to rise. An increase in the demand for money would cause prices to fall.

At an earlier stage of monetary development, when most money was in the form of gold or silver coins, the commodity theory carefully stated and the quantity theory amounted to the same thing. An increase in the quantity of gold was in fact an increase in the quantity of money. But as gold faded into the background as hand-to-hand money, there was no longer the same identity of gold and money. It became necessary to distinguish between the effects of an increase in gold and an increase in money. The supply of gold could be increased or decreased without the quantity of money being necessarily affected. Also the quantity of money could be changed without necessarily affecting the gold stock. Although under the automatic gold standard there was still a strong link between gold and the value of money, the interrelations between gold movements and changes in the price level could be explained as working themselves out through the changes that they caused in the quantity of money.[2]

---

[1]Only the crudest form of the commodity theory ignored changes in the demand for and supply of gold.
[2]See Chapter 2.

History gives some support to the quantity theory. The price level rose in Europe in the 16th century as the Spanish treasure ships carried the gold and silver of the New World to the Old, swelling the money supply. During the Revolutionary War, the Civil War, and both World Wars, an increase in prices accompanied the increase in money in circulation in the United States. Of course, even if changes in the price level were always strictly proportionate to changes in the quantity of money (as they are not), we could not jump to the conclusion that changes in quantity must be the cause, changes in value the effect. It might be the other way around.

Causal Connection between Prices and Money

Two hundred years ago, the causal connection was obvious. Money was almost entirely in the form of coins. The only way the quantity of money could be increased was by acquiring more gold and silver. The quantity, not the value, of money would necessarily be the independent variable.

Today the relation is less obvious. The banking system can increase the quantity of money at any time. Suppose prices did rise without, as yet, the quantity of money increasing. Businesses, borrowing more to carry stocks of higher priced goods, would secure larger loans from the banks, total deposits would be increased, and P (the price level) might still be proportionate to M (the quantity of money in circulation). In this instance, the change in the price level would have induced the change in the quantity of money. Instead of having a quantity theory of the value of money, we would have a value theory of the quantity of money.

Short-Run Relationship

More importantly, "P is proportionate to M" is of little value in explaining short-run changes in the value of money. In most instances we are less interested in the price level of one century as compared to another than we are in the price level from year to year and even from month to month. During these periods we find, through study of the statistics, that there is no unvarying relationship between the quantity of money and the price level. As a short-run statement, "P is proportionate to M" is untrue. If we are to set up a valid relationship between M and P, we shall have to take other variables also into account.

Expenditures Equal Receipts

The amount of money spent will necessarily and at all times equal the amount of money received. We could write this as $E = R$. This is a definitional identity. We do not have to worry about possible exceptions or study the statistics to find whether expenditures and receipts have always been equal. They have to be equal.

On the other hand, even if it is necessarily true, this equation is not very useful in its present form. We want to break down both sides of the equation to find what determines expenditures and receipts.

VELOCITY APPROACH

Both the quantity of money and the price level enter into the level of money receipts and expenditures. It seems most logical to associate total money spent with the quantity of money and relate total receipts to the price level.

Expenditures—Quantity and Velocity of Money

Total expenditures depend upon not only the quantity of money but also how often it changes hands. What happens to prices is determined not so much by the quantity of money in existence at some particular moment as by the amount spent over a period of time. A $1,000 bill hidden in a mattress is technically money in the hands of the public, but it can have little effect on prices. Or if it is spent once during the year, it will have no more effect on prices than will a $100 bill that changes hands 10 times. Similarly, if, after the banks have increased deposits by making loans, the deposits are spent once or twice and then settle down in idle balances, prices will not be affected to the same extent as they would be if the deposits continued to pass from one account to another.

We shall represent total money expenditures by MV, where M stands for the quantity of money in the hands of the public[3] and V stands for its yearly turnover, or velocity. If the nation's total stock of demand deposits, paper money, and coin is $100 billion and the yearly velocity is 20, MV is $2,000 billion a year.

In other words, changes in M are a means of expressing changes in the supply of money, and changes in V relate to changes in the demand for money (or in the Keynesian income approach, the spending function). Significant (3 percent or more annually) changes in M show a high correlation with the rate of output, prices, and unemployment. The association between M and P becomes stronger at high levels of employment.

Receipts—Total Transactions

At one time it was customary to symbolize receipts by PT, where P represented a price index and T represented total transactions. National income figures had not yet been computed. It was easy enough to estimate total money expenditures. Banks reported total debits (volume of checks drawn). This figure was increased by about 10 percent to allow for the estimated expenditures in currency. Thus, if bank debits were reported as $1,800 billion, it could be assumed that total expenditures (MV) must have been in the neighborhood of $2,000 billion. Since $PT = MV$, PT would also equal $2,000 billion. On both sides of the equation the $2,000 billion could then be broken down into two components and their interrelationships studied. With both M and MV known, V could be determined. PT was known, since it was defined

---

[3]This includes demand deposits and currency, exclusive of interbank deposits, vault cash, and balances at the Federal Reserve Banks. In short, it is the M_1 definition of money.

as equal to MV. With the price index, P, computed, transactions could be determined by dividing PT by P.

Receipts—Total Income

Today, with national income figures available, it is usually more convenient to include only income-creating expenditures rather than all transactions.[4] We write $MV = PO$, where O is real national income and PO is national income in current dollars.

The most important advantage is this: At full employment there cannot be much increase in output. On the other hand, there could conceivably be an increase of 100 percent or more in transactions, especially if widespread speculation developed. Suppose that during a period of full employment the quantity of money was increased by 20 percent. With the equation, $MV = PT$, we could only say that V or P or T, or some or all of them would necessarily change. With $MV = PO$, we can be more definite. Real output cannot be increased by much more than 4 or 5 percent at full employment. Most of the adjustment to a 20 percent increase in M would have to be in V or P.

Either formulation is equally correct; but since more qualifications are necessary with the earlier form, we shall concentrate on $MV = PO$. The logic of the analysis is the same, whether we use $MV = PT$ or $MV = PO$.

Of course, since PO is equal to the current value of national income, MV and PO cannot be determined by bank debits. Instead of starting on the left-hand side of the equation, as we did before, we start on the right, with PO. We find the current value of national income.[5] Suppose this is $1,000 billion. Then MV, which equals PO, must also equal $1,000 billion. Since we know M and can compute P, we can find the other variables easily enough. $V = MV/M; O = PO/P$.

Income Velocity and Transactions Velocity

At this point one question might well suggest itself. Since PT includes all payments, it will always be several times as large as PO. The latter includes only payments made for final goods and services. The former includes also all intermediate payments and all transfer payments. How, then, can MV be equal to both?

The quantity of money is naturally the same whichever equation we use. But the velocity is not the same. In $MV = PT$, V tells us how many times the average dollar was *spent* during the year. In $MV = PO$, V tells us how many times the average dollar *became income* during the year. Of course, the transactions velocity will always be higher than the income velocity, since dollars spent for intermediate goods and transfer payments are not creating income. In recent years, transactions velocity has typically been around 20 or 30, while income velocity has been around 4 or 5. (See endsheet.) From here on,

---

[4]See Chapter 16.
[5]See Chapter 16.

V will refer to income velocity, unless transactions velocity is specifically stated.

Definition of Price Level and Output

The concepts of P (price level) and O (real income, or output) are a little deceptive. Their product, PO, must be expressed in dollars if it is to be equal to MV. At first glance it may appear obvious that all we need do is total the output and multiply this sum by some average price in dollars. It is not quite that simple. There is no possible way to add 3,000 pencils and 5,000 quarts of milk directly. We have to give them a common denominator by expressing them both in terms of money: $150 of pencils plus $1,250 of milk is $1,400.

If the value of money never changed, we could write $MV = O$. But price levels do change. The very point we are investigating is the causes of changes in the value of money. We know that a price index measures reciprocally the value of money (see Chapter 13), so we include a price index in our equation.

What, then, is O, exactly? Evidently it is national income in base-year dollars. We find this figure by dividing PO, national income in current dollars, by P, the current price index. If we know the current dollar value of national income is $1,000 billion and that prices today are 125 percent of what they were in the base year, the value of national income in base-year dollars is $800 billion. A trillion dollars is the amount that was actually spent, $800 billion the amount that would have been spent for the same quantity of goods and services if prices had remained at their earlier, lower level.

Note particularly that P is not an average price; it is not a dollar figure of any kind. It is a percentage. The dollar sign refers to output.

Ideally for P we would use a general price index, taking all prices into account. A great deal of work would be required to construct such an index by the usual technique. However, we can quite easily approximate such a figure. If we divide the consumption section of national income by an index of consumer prices and similarly divide other income components by appropriate specialized price indexes, the total of these separately adjusted amounts should be about what we would get if we had instead divided total national income by a general price index. Thus, we find this "implicit" index by dividing our deflated total of national income into total national income in current dollars. If national income is $1,200 billion in terms of current dollars, and after separately correcting the various components for price changes we find their total is $1,000 billion, we can conclude the general price index is about 120.

We are not interested in trying to work out specific values for P and O to see whether the product of P and O really does equal MV. $PO = MV$ is a truism. They are equal by definition. Empirical proof and statistical verification are irrelevant. We are exploring changes in the value of money and would like to know approximately the amount of that change over a period of time. We know from our earlier study of price indexes that it is mathematically impossible to construct an index that will measure such changes exactly. The approximate result that we get by using the "implicit" price index or, for that matter, by using an index of wholesale prices or even consumer prices, will be satisfactory and convenient.

IMPLICATIONS OF $MV = PO$

In itself the equation $MV = PO$ tells us nothing whatever as to the relations between cause and effect. There is no indication of which variables are dependent, which independent. Although it is termed a quantity equation because it contains a term referring to the quantity of money, it is not quantity theory nor has anyone ever claimed that it proves the quantity theory of money. To be sure, we may rewrite it as $P = MV/O$, but in so doing we have not proved that changes in P are the result rather than the cause of changes in other factors. We could just as easily write $M = PO/V$, $V = PO/M$, or $O = MV/P$.

The equation only sets down for our consideration four variables that are related in a certain way. On the basis of the equation itself we cannot say that a change in any one term must lead to a change in another specified term. We can say only that if one term changes there must necessarily be a change or changes elsewhere—in one, two, or three of the other terms.

It is not very helpful to say, "If the quantity of money is increased, something else will change—perhaps the velocity of its turnover, perhaps the level of income, perhaps the price level, or perhaps two or three of these factors." Quantity theorists have attempted to narrow the range of possibilities and show that changes in the quantity of money will be reflected in the price level, that is, reflected entirely in the price level, according to rigid quantity theory, or reflected primarily in the price level, according to the more qualified version of the quantity theory.

P Assumed to Be a Dependent Variable

In any equation of the form $ab = xy$, if ab is always and necessarily equal to xy, then one or more of the variables must be dependent. If all four variables were independent, ab would not always equal xy. At least one of the four terms must passively adjust to changes in the other terms. (Of course, it would be possible that at one time the dependent variable would be one term, another time it would be a different one. Also, there might be more than one dependent variable.)

Working with $MV = PO$, quantity theorists assume that P is always the dependent variable, so that it can change only as a result of changes in the other terms. Most of our money today is in the form of demand deposits, increased whenever banks expand loans and investments. Increases in productivity and in the level of employment will increase output, and we shall shortly see why velocity may change. None of these changes in M, O, or V requires a prior change in the price level. They are the independent variables. On the other hand, the value of money, or its reciprocal, the price index, will not spontaneously change. A change in P is a result, never a cause, of a change in the other terms, according to quantity theorists. The possibility is ruled out that costs may begin spontaneously to rise, pushing up prices and forcing a corresponding change in M, V, or O. Certainly some manufacturers may raise their prices, but according to the quantity theorists, this will not affect M, V, or O. In consequence, the increase in individual prices must be offset by a decrease in other prices.

Expected Changes in *P* May Cause Changes in Other Terms

Quantity theorists admit that expected changes in prices may affect M and V in such a way as to result in a realized change in P. This development is frequently encountered in a period of rapidly rising prices, sometimes alleged to be the cause of increased borrowings by businesspeople and, therefore, the cause of an increase in bank deposits. Quantity theorists insist that to suppose the increase in money results from the rise in prices is to confuse expected prices with realized prices. The expectation of higher prices cannot possibly be fulfilled unless M and/or V (or conceivably O) move in such a way as to permit the higher level of prices. Something, of course, must cause M and V to change or they will remain constant. The originating cause may well be the expectation of higher prices. But only if M or V (or O) changes first can P change.

Determination of *P*

If P remains constant until one of the other variables changes, our analysis must proceed along two lines. First, we must decide what conditions will cause M, V, or O to change; for unless they change, by our first assumption, P cannot change. Second, we must decide what the probable response will be to a change in each of these factors. To say that P will not change unless V (or some other term) changes is not at all the same as saying that P will change if V changes. As far as the equation is concerned, a change in V could just as well be offset by changes in M or O or both as by a change in P.

CHANGES IN OUTPUT

The level of output is affected by several factors, some of mainly long-run, some of short-run importance. The long-run factors may be of somewhat more importance, however.

Long-Run Changes

Output will increase as a result of improved methods of production and additions to the labor force. Since 1800 national output has increased by about 3 percent a year, even though the length of the work week has been shrinking. This annual increase is a highly significant long-run factor. It permits in about 20 years a doubling of output at full employment levels. Professor Hansen, who by no stretch of the imagination can be classified as a quantity theorist, had this rising output in mind when shortly after World War II he advised that we not attempt to pay off the national debt as rapidly as possible, for most of it might soon be required as backing for a money supply adequate to our productive potential. As Hansen observed, "An adequate money supply is a *necessary* but not a *sufficient* condition for economic expansion."[6] As Hansen and others have shown, the principal effect of such an increase in output would probably be upon P. There is no reason for either M or V to increase spontaneously in consequence of this long-run increase in O; but unless one or the other is, somehow, increased, P must fall as O increases.

Short-Run Changes

Both population growth and improved productive techniques are secular trends, of importance in long-run analysis and long-range planning but of limited effect in the short run. From one year to the next their effect may be greatly overshadowed by cyclical movements. When millions lose their jobs, output may be reduced by considerably more than 3 percent. During a period of rapid recovery, output will rise rapidly.

In the short run the relations between O and the other variables are not quite the same as in the long run, in which they are being influenced by a different set of factors. This should be clear when we complete our observation of O and study the behavior of M and V. Common sense tells us that if, in recovery, output increases but money and velocity remain unchanged, the price level would necessarily drop. Common sense also tells us that such a state of affairs would be quite surprising. One of the typical circumstances of a recovery movement is that prices have finally halted their earlier downward movement and, if they are not rising, at least they are firm. It appears from this that the effects of the increase in O at such a time must be more than offset by increases in either M or V. Likewise, after the recovery has passed into prosperity and on into recession, the decline in O during the recession is, we know from experience, not characterized by an increase in P as it would necessarily be if there had been no change in M or V.

P and *O* Related in the Long Run Rather than the Short Run

The behavior of the terms of the equation during periods of cyclical change suggests that changes in O at such times may be more closely linked to M and V than to P. Logic suggests the same conclusion. In a typical recovery movement, output increases because for various reasons people are making more purchases. In the case of many durable goods, purchases may have been deferred for a number of years, but eventually can be postponed no longer. The roof that leaks and the car that breaks down must at last be replaced, just as manufacturers may finally be forced to replace obsolete equipment which, except for the recession, would have been abandoned before.

---

[6]A. H. Hansen, *Monetary Theory and Fiscal Policy* (New York City: McGraw-Hill Book Company, 1949), p. 198.

Also, when the public becomes convinced that prices will fall no further so that they have nothing to gain by waiting longer, there may be a resumption of purchases that had been temporarily postponed. Public works undertaken on a large scale may cause a substantial increase in O, both in direct consequence of the initial purchases and as a result of subsequent purchases by those who receive the funds. As optimism replaces pessimism, O may rise as buyers increase their purchases to escape higher prices later.

In all these instances, however, it appears probable that either or both M and V will be directly affected by the decision to increase purchases. The additional goods must be paid for. Some buyers will borrow from the banks, causing deposits to increase. Others may spend money they had been holding idle, causing V to rise.

In recession, on the other hand, O declines as fewer purchases are made. And the general decision to buy less, held by consumers and producers alike, will result in less borrowing and also in a slowing of the velocity of circulation of money. The connections between O, M, and V appear quite direct. During a process of cyclical change it seems altogether likely that a change in O will be accompanied by similar changes in M and V. At such times P is likely to change in the same direction as O rather than in the opposite direction, as it would if there were no change in M or V.

In short, changes in O appear more likely to influence P alone and directly in the long run, rather than the short run. We are making some progress, since we have narrowed to M and V the factors that in the short run are likely to cause variations in the value of money. If now it can be shown that changes in V will result primarily in changes in O, and also that changes in M will affect neither V nor O, the quantity theory of money is established.

CHANGES IN VELOCITY

Earlier we defined V as the number of times money is turned over during a period. What normally decides whether money will have a velocity of twice a year or twice a month? Would it be possible for velocity to average twice a day? What determines velocity?

The word itself is a little misleading. To most of us "velocity" suggests speed. We speak of the velocity of a falling object or the orbital velocity of a satellite. The velocity of circulation of money, however, has nothing to do with miles per hour. Since the only "movement" of money with which we are concerned is the movement from hand to hand, to measure its speed we would have to measure it in terms of inches per year. However, this is not at all the kind of measurement in which we are interested.

The income velocity of circulation of money is nothing more than the ratio between the total money income during a period and the amount of money on hand. In terms of our equation this should be obvious. MV/M equals V. MV is defined as equal to PO, total current money income. If income is \$1,500 billion and the total stock of money is \$300 billion, the yearly velocity must be 5. This stock of \$300 billion belongs, at every moment, to millions of owners. Suppose we classify these owners as consumers and business enterprises and investigate the behavior of their cash holdings, a subject to which we shall return in a little more detail at the end of this chapter.

Velocity and Financial Institutions

One determinant of velocity is the availability of credit. If consumers and businesses know they can easily borrow funds when necessary, they will tend to hold small idle balances. Without well-developed credit institutions, people will need to hold large amounts of money in proportion to their incomes. They will need to keep large sums idle to be sure they have money when they need it. As they find it easier to obtain credit, and as they increase their holdings of other fairly liquid assets (created by nonbank financial institutions), they keep less cash on hand and depend on the banks and other lending agencies to accommodate their temporary requirements.

Financial institutions do not spring up overnight. Changes in velocity as a result of the evolution of credit systems have a long-run significance, but may generally be disregarded in the short run.

Velocity and the Frequency of Receipt of Income

Another important determinant of the average amount that most consumers hold with relation to their incomes is the frequency with which they are paid. It is a little easier to see this relationship if we relate cash balances to yearly expenditures rather than yearly income. There will be little difference anyway between a typical consumer's income and consumption.

The number of times a year that people spend their average balance depends primarily upon how often they receive their income. A farmer, for example, may receive all his income for the year on one day in the fall when he sells his crops. Let us say that his income at that time is $6,000. That sum of money must last him for a year, and we shall suppose that he spends it at an even rate during the year. The yearly velocity of the money that he holds is, therefore, 2. It is not 1, as might appear at first glance, for he is spending $6,000 a year but his average balance for the year is only $3,000.

Suppose, now, that he sells his farm and goes to work for a monthly salary of $500, and that he continues to spend $6,000 yearly. Although his income and his expenditures are the same as before, velocity has changed. If he invests the proceeds from the sale of the farm in Series E savings bonds, his cash balance, dependent entirely on his salary, will probably be quite low by the end of every month. His average balance might be around $250 and the yearly velocity of his average money stock would then be 24. Or if we assume that he sold the farm for $12,000 and holds this sum in the form of cash, still spending his current income of $6,000, the yearly velocity of his money will be a trifle under one half.

The yearly income velocity of the nation's stock of money is the sum of all incomes (national income) divided by the total of all balances held (quantity of money). Changes such as this in the frequency of income receipt appear, for the nation as a whole, to be of little importance in the short run. In the course of a century the nation changed from a predominantly agricultural to an industrial economy, but there was little change from one month to the next or even from one year to the next in the timing of income payments and resulting size of desired cash balances. Also, changes in frequency of income receipt are largely independent of changes in the quantity of money. Neither increases nor decreases in the quantity of money will cause farmers generally to market crops weekly, nor factory workers to be paid on a yearly basis.

We cannot entirely rule out the possibility of this kind of relationship, however. Many crops can be stored. If an increase in the quantity of money leads to an expectation of rising prices, the farmer may sell part of his crop to meet his immediate needs and store the rest to await more favorable prices. Thus, he may receive his yearly income in three or four installments rather than one, increasing the velocity of his average balance. Also, while the transition from an agricultural to an industrial economy is normally a gradual process, there may be periods when the movement is accelerated or retarded. During the Depression there was a back-to-the-farm movement by many who could not find employment. The movement was reversed when the defense program got well under way. But the total effect of such changes will probably ordinarily have little effect in the short run upon the magnitude of V.

Velocity and the Business Cycle

In the short run a much more important factor affecting V is likely to be the general state of business. During recession V declines as everyone tries to avoid making any except the most necessary expenditures. In prosperity people spend more freely and V rises accordingly. We shall return to this topic later when we consider the motives that impel people to hold cash balances of varying size.

Velocity and Interest Rates

By far the most important cause for the sustained and rapid increase in velocity over the last 10 years (see Table 15-1) has been the rising level of

Table 15-1 **Annual Velocity of Turnover of Demand Deposits (Excluding interbank and U.S. government demand deposits)**

1941	19.4	1951	18.4	1961	26.2	1971	57.3
1942	18.4	1952	18.4	1962	27.7	1972	61.8
1943	17.4	1953	18.9	1963	29.0	1973	75.8
1944	17.3	1954	19.2	1964	33.4	1974	86.7
1945	16.1	1955	20.4	1965	37.5		
1946	16.5	1956	21.8	1966	39.7		
1947	18.0	1957	23.0	1967	40.8		
1948	19.2	1958	22.9	1968	43.4		
1949	18.7	1959	24.5	1969	48.4		
1950	20.3	1960	25.7	1970	52.4		

Source: *Federal Reserve Bulletins*. Figures are for December for 232 SMSAs (excluding New York).

interest rates. After a generation of easy money, and destroying the widely held expectation that low interest rates should and could be maintained forever, the cost of borrowing money shot up to the highest level in more than a hundred years. Naturally, velocity increased.

Individuals and corporations were willing, when interest rates were very low, to hold unnecessarily large checking accounts. The individual might plan to spend two or three hundred dollars in two or three months. Why bother to lend it meanwhile? The person lost little by holding the money temporarily idle. Similarly, a corporate treasurer had little incentive to look for someplace to lend or invest 10 or 15 million dollars that would not be needed for a month. In 1950, as in 1975, the treasurer might have invested for a month in Treasury securities. If the securities were bought within a month of maturity (or if the bond dealer agreed to repurchase longer maturities a month later at a specified price), the treasurer was taking no risk. In 1950, however, a $10 million 30-day transaction would have netted the corporation only about $10,000. It might be overlooked. By 1975 the same operation would net more than $60,000. It could not be overlooked. Thus, tight money and high interest rates encourage a more intensive use of the existing stock of money, as holders of temporarily idle funds transfer them to eager borrowers who promptly put them into active circulation.

Effect of Changes in Velocity

The short-run changes in V appear to be related to changes and expected changes in P. This necessary qualification is a serious weakness of the quantity theory. If P, responding generally to movements in M, induces changes in V, we cannot be sure what the effect on P will be of a given change in M unless we know how the effect of the subsequent change in V will be dissipated. To be sure, if the change in V would be canceled out by a corresponding change in O, we could ignore both changes in analyzing the relationship between M and P. Often this will be the case, but not invariably. Particularly in periods of rapidly rising prices, V may increase considerably more than O, driving up P still further.

Three examples will illustrate the effect that V may exercise upon P. Toward the end of the inflationary whirlwind that swept through Germany after World War I, there was about 245 billion times as much money in circulation as in 1913, but the index of wholesale prices was 1,380 billion times as high as in 1913.[7] Again in the United States total deposits and currency declined from $55 billion to $45 billion, or about 18 percent, between 1929 and

---

[7]F. I. Graham, *Exchange, Prices & Production in Hyper-Inflation: Germany, 1920–1923* (Princeton: Princeton University Press, 1930), pp. 105–106. (Also, see Chapter 13.) Germany's experience also points out the dangers of using "real money balances" (i.e., money divided by an index of prices) as an indicator of the thrust of monetary policy. From June, 1922, to November, 1923, the German money stock rose by almost 2 trillion percent, the price level rose by 10 trillion percent, and "real money balances" fell each month at an annual rate of over 50 percent. Although the monetary authorities may (at times) be able to control M, P will adjust to frustrate any changes in real balances which are inconsistent with public demand. See Denis S. Karnosky, "Real Money Balances: A Misleading Indicator of Monetary Actions," *Review* of the Federal Reserve Bank of St. Louis (February, 1974), pp. 1–10.

1932 while during the same period the all-commodity index of wholesale prices declined from 95 to 60, or nearly 37 percent.[8] Finally, in the period between June, 1946, and June, 1950, total currency in circulation and demand deposits (not including interbank and United States government deposits and less cash items reported as in process of collection) showed little change, increasing from $106 billion to $110 billion, while the index of wholesale prices increased from 113 to 157.[9] Almost the entire postwar rise in prices in this country up to the outbreak of the Korean War was due to the increase in V rather than to any change in M.[10]

Velocity and the Trend of M

It has been suggested that if the quantity of money were properly regulated, changes in V would have little or no effect upon P.[11] We have not been properly measuring our terms, says Warburton. He suggests that our results will be more meaningful and more certain if, instead of measuring the absolute amounts, we measure their deviations from their respective trends. According to his analysis, a gradual increase in the quantity of money will be in accordance with its past trend and with its proper trend for the future. A *change* in M will be represented by a quantity of money that is larger or smaller than the *trend* value of M for that date. Similarly, trend values for V may be computed and deviations from the trend observed. By this kind of analysis he concludes that deviations of M from trend will be followed later by deviations of V from trend. Presumably if the quantity of money could be increased by just the "right" amount to accord with the current trend value, the changes in M would have no effect upon V.

It does seem possible that a sudden and marked increase in the quantity of money such as we experienced during World War II may at times be accompanied by a drop in velocity until people have revised their spending

---

[8]Federal Reserve, *Charts on Bank Credit, Money Rates, and Business*.

[9]*Federal Reserve Bulletin*.

[10]The changes in the value of P were probably not as great as indicated by the above changes in the indexes of wholesale prices. As observed earlier, the changes in this abstract P correspond to changes in a *general* price index, which would include wholesale prices and also retail prices. The latter generally fluctuate less than wholesale prices.

[11]C. Warburton, "Business Stability and Regulation of the Cost of Money," *American Journal of Economics and Sociology* (January, 1954), pp. 175–184; "Bank Reserves and Business Fluctuations," *Journal of the American Statistical Association* (December, 1948), pp. 547–558. See also Milton Friedman, *A Program for Monetary Stability* (New York: Fordham University Press, 1959); idem (ed.), "The Quantity Theory of Money—A Restatement," *Studies in the Quantity Theory of Money* (Chicago: University of Chicago Press, 1958), pp. 3–21; idem, *Dollars and Deficits* (Englewood Cliffs: Prentice-Hall, 1968); idem, *The Optimal Quantity of Money and Other Essays* (Chicago: Aldine Publishing Co., 1969); idem, "The Demand for Money: Some Theoretical and Empirical Results," *Journal of Political Economy* (August, 1959), pp. 327–351; idem, "A Theoretical Framework for Monetary Analysis," *ibid.* (March/April, 1970), pp. 193–238; idem, "A Monetary Theory of Nominal Income," *ibid.* (March/April, 1971), pp. 323–337; idem, "Comment on the Critics," *ibid.* (September/October, 1972), pp. 906–950; idem, "The Role of Monetary Policy," *American Economic Review* (March, 1968), pp. 1–17; idem, "Interest Rates and the Demand for Money," *Journal of Law and Economics* (October, 1966), pp. 71–86; Milton Friedman and David Mieselman, "The Relative Stability of Monetary Velocity and the Investment Multiplier in the United States, 1897–1958," in Commission on Money and Credit, *Stabilization Policies* (Englewood Cliffs: Prentice-Hall, 1963); Milton Friedman, *et al.*, "A Symposium on Friedman's Theoretical Framework," *Journal of Political Economy* (September/October, 1972).

habits to take into account the increased stock of money, and that later, when the quantity of money has ceased to grow, velocity may rise to or beyond its former level. The annual velocity of turnover of demand deposits (excluding interbank and government deposits) since 1941 is shown in Table 15-1.[12] (The income velocity of money, M_1, from 1929 to 1974 is shown on the endsheet of this book.)

The evidence in Table 15-1 is suggestive although not entirely convincing. Probably the decline in V between 1941 and 1945 was largely due to price controls and rationing rather than solely or even primarily to the unusually large increase in the quantity of money that occurred during those years.

What stands out most in Table 15-1 is the rapid increase in velocity since 1956. As will be explained in Chapters 24 and 25, the monetary authorities in 1956 ended the 25 years of easy money and progressively tightened the monetary screws. It may well be that if a more stable monetary policy had been followed (as recommended by Friedman), velocity would also have been more stable.

Changes in Velocity—Conclusion

The fact is that we cannot say positively whether changes in V will influence P or O. The results depend upon the circumstances. In general, when there is full employment and V is increasing, corresponding changes in O become progressively more difficult. At such times an increase in V is most likely to cause a fall in the value of money. Increases in V are unlikely to affect P when there is large scale unemployment, but decreases in V will probably help to depress prices at such times.

CHANGES IN THE QUANTITY OF MONEY

When full employment exists, there appears to be no reason for changes in M to cause changes in O. Increasing the quantity of money will not directly increase the productivity of labor or other productive factors. During periods when V is stable, changing only slowly and gradually as a result of changes in the method of wage payments and in monetary institutions, the result of substantial changes in M at a time of full employment will probably be changes in P.

The increasing importance of demand deposits once generated high hopes of regulating the value of money. It appeared that by appropriate changes in reserve requirements and discount rates and by open market operations of the Federal Reserve Banks, the quantity of money and, therefore, the price level could be regulated at will. Disenchantment with this quantitative relationship

---

[12]For the years 1940–1950, 100 cities are included; for 1951–1963, 337 cities; since 1964, from 224 to 232 cities. To avoid the effect of the high turnover typical of financial centers, New York City is excluded throughout. (For example, velocity of demand deposits in New York City in 1970 rose to 176.) For the same reason six other major cities were also excluded, 1951–1963. (These official figures pertain to transactions velocity. Income velocity was much lower, but showed a similar rate of increase.)

set in during the Depression when it became apparent, as someone remarked, that you can't push on a piece of string. Two difficulties appeared:

1. The quantity of money will not necessarily be increased when the banks are holding excess reserves.
2. Even if the quantity of money is increased, the price level may not be affected.

Effect of Excess Reserves

Ordinarily commercial banks do not hold large excess reserves.[13] If they find their excess reserves increasing, they make more loans and investments; and the increase in deposits causes required reserves to rise and excess reserves to evaporate. If the Treasury or the Federal Reserve Banks cause an increase in excess reserves of commercial banks, we should normally expect an increase in loans and deposits.

But the banks are not forced to lend. By 1940 excess reserves, which had totalled about $100 million in 1930, had climbed to the staggering sum of almost $7 billion. During this period, there had been a great increase in our gold stock, the result of our nationalization of gold and the flight to our shores of a large part of the world's gold. The Treasury held a little over $4 billion of gold in 1933. By 1940 it held almost $20 billion. Excess reserves of the Federal Reserve Banks and the commercial banks were enormously increased.[14] However, there was little demand from businesses for loans during this period. Interest rates were low, and the banks hesitated to tie up their funds in long-term investments, certain to decline in market value if interest rates should rise again. They bid eagerly for the limited volume of short-term obligations available, driving up their price and forcing the yield on such securities as 91-day Treasury bills down as low, at times, as zero. There were not enough high-grade, short-term lending opportunities to absorb the unused lending power of the banks. So, although their excess reserves would have permitted the banks to create an additional $20 to $25 billion of deposits, the banks preferred to remain liquid. The modest increase in the money supply was far less than permitted by the excess reserves. Had the Treasury and Federal Reserve Banks created still more reserves, the banks probably would not have used those reserves either. The banking world's earlier optimism that the monetary authorities could, at will, bring about an increase in the quantity of money was unjustified.

Effect of an Increased Quantity of Money

But suppose the banks do expand credit on the basis of their excess reserves. If businesses and consumers are not borrowing, the banks might buy

---

[13]In Chapter 11, Table 11-1 showed the historical trend of excess (and net free) reserves from 1929 to 1974.

[14]In 1940 Federal Reserve Banks were still required to maintain reserves, in gold certificates, against their liabilities.

bonds on the open market. The nonbank public would then hold less bonds and more deposits.

Unfortunately an increase in the quantity of money will permit, but will not necessarily cause, a change in the price level. When there is widespread unemployment and a general lack of confidence, everyone tries to hold on to any extra money. Velocity falls so that even if M rises, MV may be no greater than before. Between 1933 and 1940, demand deposits of United States commercial banks (excluding interbank deposits) increased from about $28 billion to about $54 billion. But while the quantity of money doubled, its velocity declined. As a result, the index of wholesale prices rose from 65.9 to only 78.6. The increase of nearly 100 percent in the quantity of money was accompanied by an increase of less than 20 percent in the price level.

Note, too, that even if V remained unchanged, the initial impact of an increase in M in depression would almost certainly be on O, not P. It is highly unlikely that, with widespread unemployment and excess plant capacity, prices will move up as soon as the public begins to spend more freely. More probably, idle workers and machines will gradually be drawn back into production. Eventually if spending continues to increase, the economy may approach full employment, and prices would then begin to rise.

Decreases in Reserves and Quantity of Money

The quantity theory is on firmer ground when it analyzes the braking, rather than the accelerating, effects of monetary policy. A reduction in their reserves can force banks to contract loans and deposits. The consequent reduction in the quantity of money will have some tendency to cause an increase in the value of money. Quantitative controls are more effective in restraining a boom than in overcoming recession or depression.

Even in inflation, however, there is no precise relation between the quantity of money and the price level. If the quantity of money is reduced, an increasing velocity of circulation may permit the price level to remain constant or continue rising. Or possibly O will decline while prices remain unchanged. About all we can safely say is that changes in the quantity of money will often result in changes in the value of money.

EVALUATION

There is some relation between the quantity of money and its value. The velocity type of quantity equation summarizes the relationship by the statement that the money flow, MV, is equal to the current value of national income, PO. M, V, and O may all change regardless of whether P changes. M depends primarily upon the banks' lending policies. V depends upon the willingness of the public to spend the money they hold. O depends upon the level of employment. P, however, according to quantity theorists, depends upon the other three variables. The price level cannot rise by itself. There must be a greater money flow to force the change.[15] Nor can the price level decline

---

[15]Or conceivably a decline in output.

unless something else forces a decline in MV, or an increase in O without a proportionate change in MV.

Quantity theorists have tried to show that changes in V and O will cancel out, and that a change in the quantity of money will cause a proportionate change in the price level. At times this may be true, especially if full employment exists. But quantity explanations of the value of money must be extensively qualified. The "pure" quantity theory is easily disproven. The question arises: Is the theory still useful when sufficiently qualified to be defensible? Before answering this question we shall explore a different formulation of the relation of money to the price level.

CASH-BALANCE APPROACH

There is another way to look at the flow of money expenditures which many people prefer to the velocity approach discussed above. It is helpful in getting to the basic explanation of what really determines velocity. Paradoxically, although this explanation does not contain a term for velocity, it offers a better analysis of why velocity changes than does the approach that specifically includes a term for velocity. In this section we shall turn our attention to people's desire to hold cash. In using the term "cash" we are including both currency and demand deposits.

The amount of cash you hold is related to your income.[16] If you are earning $3,000 a year, your average balance might be $100. But if your income is $30,000, you will probably keep a balance of nearer $1,000. In the examples above, the suggested cash balance is one-thirtieth of the year's income. It would therefore be turned over 30 times during the year. Evidently there is a reciprocal relation between the size of a cash balance in proportion to income and the velocity with which it is turned over.

Since the amount of cash we desire to hold will bear some relation to our incomes, we want to relate these variables somehow, so that we can see how changes in income, changes in our desire to hold money, and changes in the stock of money are interrelated and how they affect the value of money. We can summarize these relationships in the equation $M = PKO$, in which M represents the quantity of money; P represents the price level; K represents the proportion desired between the stock of money and income; and O represents income, expressed in base-year dollars.

K and V are necessarily reciprocals since $M = PKO = PO/V$. However, this must not lead us to think of either one as being merely the reciprocal of the other. K and V direct our attention to two entirely different things. V, the velocity, is the number of times the stock of money becomes income during a period of time. K, the proportion we wish to maintain between our stock of money and our incomes, determines what the velocity of money will be but is not itself a rate of turnover.

---

[16]It is also related positively to the physical stock of goods and the price level, the product of which is wealth. For convenience, in the ensuing discussion the term "income" is used for both income and wealth.

CONSIDERATIONS RELATING TO CASH BALANCES

The cash-balance approach concerns people's desire to hold cash.[17] This desire is governed by, on one hand, the advantages that cash balances offer and, on the other hand, the costs they entail.

Advantages of Holding Cash

A cash balance permits fairly regular expenditures out of income received only at certain times. People may be paid only once a month or, in the case of many farmers, once a year. If they are going to be able to continue making purchases until the next time they receive income, they must set aside a stock of cash. The more infrequent their receipts of income, the larger must be the fraction of their year's purchases over which they wish command in the form of cash.

A second reason to hold cash is as a safeguard against possible emergencies such as fire, theft, sickness, loss of employment, and the like. A third reason is to make provisions for unusually large expenditures, either consumption or investment, that people plan to make when they have set aside sufficient funds. Even if they expect to borrow most of the money, they cannot buy a house, for instance, until they have first accumulated the necessary down payment.

A very important consideration has to do with the expected future level of prices and income. Both individuals and corporations are likely to reduce their cash holdings at a time when they expect prices to rise rapidly, and both will try to increase their holdings if they feel prices are going down, especially if they fear their incomes may fall also.

Costs of Holding Cash

Although cash balances are necessary, they also involve a certain sacrifice. Apart from the question of a general flight from money, the public never wants its cash balances to be unnecessarily large. For one thing, there is usually an appealing stock of consumer goods and services which one must voluntarily go without if one is to hold cash. Only a miser will prefer to add indefinitely to cash holdings. In the second place, cash is a nonearning asset; after a certain amount of cash has been set aside, most people will prefer to purchase income-yielding investments rather than continue to add to their holdings of idle cash. Rather than hold demand deposits (or currency) totaling $20,000, most people will exchange some of this cash for earning assets.

ATTEMPTS TO CHANGE CASH BALANCES

It is important to understand that decisions involving the amount of cash to be held relate basically to K, the proportion one wishes to maintain between the money one is holding and one's income. They are not related primarily to M, the quantity of money, even though in trying to change K one

---

[17]See also transactions demand and asset (speculative-precautionary) demand for money, Chapter 19.

will usually attempt to change M. This is the crux of the matter. To be sure, any one individual may succeed in increasing the amount of money being held by building a cash balance at the expense of the cash balances of the rest of the community. But obviously unless the total stock of money is increased, it is impossible for all to increase their cash balances at the same time. Yet K, the proportion of money held to income, may be increased for the community as a whole even with no increase in the total stock of money.

Attempts to Increase K

Suppose that for a typical individual $2,000 = $12,000 \times 1/6$ and that the person wishes to increase the value of K from 1/6 to 1/4. The direct way to accomplish this is to increase M from $2,000 to $3,000. However, the total stock of money in the country is nothing more nor less than the sum of all the money held in cash balances; every dollar is in a cash balance somewhere. The individual can successfully increase his cash balance only if others are willing to see their cash balances slightly reduced, as may often be the case. There is no reason why everyone else would have the same desire as this individual to increase K and M.

But if the person's decision is made at a time when practically everyone else is also attempting to increase their cash balances, matters work out differently. Some may gain a little, others lose a little cash; but if the total monetary stock has not increased, the person who had $2,000 before may have $2,000 still, after the community has for some time been vainly attempting to build up individual cash balances. As a result, however, of the universal effort to increase cash balances by reducing expenses, there will be a fall in either the price level or real income, or more probably both. In any case PO falls. For our typical individual, formerly holding $2,000 and receiving an income of $12,000, income may decline to $8,000, for example. With $2,000 = $8,000 \times 1/4$, the original attempt to increase K will have succeeded, although certainly not in the manner intended.

In this illustration we assumed that the total quantity of money was unchanged in this period in which everyone was attempting to increase cash balances. But in fact, the total quantity of money would probably be reduced at the very time when everyone was trying to get into a more liquid position.

An expectation of falling prices and incomes would be characteristic of such a period. The same pessimism that impels people to try to build up their cash reserves drives them also to pay off their debts. It is entirely a matter of a desire for increased liquidity. No one would satisfy a desire to hold cash by going to the bank and borrowing, for the person would then be no more liquid than before. Instead the individual would try to get out of debt as fast as possible for two reasons. It is easier to repay debt when the value of money is low than when it is high, and the debtor gives up less in purchasing power. More importantly, a sharp drop in income may make debt retirement not merely unpleasant but impossible, resulting in bankruptcy. Many a concern has been forced into receivership through a debt structure that it could easily service as long as times were good but that it could not handle in recession. In the course of the liquidation of debt, many bank loans would be paid off, with a consequent shrinkage of the money supply. Therefore, the typical individual might hold, finally, not $2,000 = $8,000 × 1/4 but $1,500 = $6,000 × 1/4.

Attempts to Reduce K

Similarly, if the public generally wishes to reduce K, for example from 1/6 to 1/9, the obvious procedure for each acting individually is to reduce the size of his or her cash balance. Although this can easily be done at a time when others are attempting to increase their cash balances, a general attempt to get rid of cash is destined to fail because money is not destroyed by spending it. As fast as one person's cash balance is reduced, someone else's balance is increased. Thus, as long as the total quantity of money is unchanged, the only way K can finally be forced to the desired value is, as before, by changes in PO. In terms of our earlier illustration, this might be at the point where $2,000 = $18,000 × 1/9. Or possibly the desire to decrease K from 1/6 to 1/9 may gradually be weakened as PO rises, and the public would then decide to settle for a value of 1/8 or 1/7, accordingly forcing PO to $16,000 or $14,000 for the average individual. Consequently, the total PO for the society will, of course, be the sum of all these individual incomes.

Furthermore, just as we earlier noted the paradox that the total quantity of money would decrease at a time when everyone was attempting to hold more money, we now must recognize that at a time when people generally are trying to get rid of money and reduce their cash balances, there will be an increase in the total stock of money and, consequently, in the size of the average cash balance. When there is a general attempt to reduce cash balances, people desire goods and services rather than money. Consequently, borrowing increases. The purpose of borrowing is not to permit people to hold more money, for ordinarily one does not borrow money and pay interest on it for the purpose of holding it idle. Rather, by borrowing money one is able to spend more money than ever. The more firmly convinced one becomes that prices and incomes are going to rise, the more eager one becomes to borrow money and spend it now, repaying it later when the value of money is less. A consumer expecting prices to rise may borrow to buy a home or car before prices have advanced. A business anticipating higher prices and profits will borrow to increase plant capacity or to purchase additional inventory. In either case the banks will be expanding their loans, the borrowers will spend the proceeds of the loan, and consequently, the public will find the size of their cash balances increasing.

Hence, society's attempt to reduce a $200 billion total cash balance to $133 billion in order to reduce K from 1/4 of $800 billion to 1/6 may easily result in a $250 billion total cash balance. If, with M increasing to $250 billion, the community resolutely persists in its attempts to reduce K to 1/6, PO would finally settle at $1,500 billion, nearly double its former level. At this point the public's desire for less liquidity would be satisfied. At the higher dollar level of PO, cash balances held, although larger in terms of dollars than at the outset, would represent only that fraction of the year's income over which the public wished control in the form of cash.

The speculative changes associated with expected changes in income and the price level may assume great importance. If enough people become convinced that the price level is going to change, it will change, if for no other reason than that the public thought it would and acted accordingly.

Efforts to Gain Liquidity during Depression

As prices and incomes dropped in 1930, both businesspeople and consumers became alarmed, and each one tried to increase K, that is, to get in a more liquid position. Instead of buying a new car as usual, people decided to make the old one do for another year or two and to try to put aside a little money. When most workers are afraid that they may lose their jobs and that it may be impossible to find another, even those who have money are not willing to spend it. And when some people attempt to increase their cash holdings by disposing of their real estate or securities, they find few buyers. At the same time businesses, operating their plants at half capacity or less, realize that their best chance of survival lies in their building up cash reserves out of which to pay the losses that appear likely in the period ahead and to pay off any short-term debt that may soon be maturing. As businesspeople and consumers alike attempt to reduce their expenditures, PO necessarily declines. The historical trend of K from 1929 to 1974 is shown on the endsheet of the book.

Effect of World War II on Liquidity

During the war years consumer income rose steeply. The hard core of unemployment which had persisted for a decade melted away. Women who ordinarily did not work outside their homes took jobs in defense plants. About 12 million men were put in uniform; to meet the enormous demand for military equipment as well as the needs of the civilian economy, every available person was needed. Furthermore, to facilitate the shifts that were required in production, a considerable amount of inflation was permitted which involved, among other things, rising profits, high bonuses, rising wages, and a great deal of overtime. By borrowing heavily from the commercial banks and spending the money, the Treasury forced an increase in the quantity of money and in the flow of money incomes. For the duration of the war, however, there was not a great deal that could be done with this extra income. In fact, the whole secret of keeping the inflation under control lay in making it difficult to spend the added income. Rationing and price controls distorted the economy from the lines along which it would have developed under normal, peacetime conditions. The kinds of things on which we ordinarily like to spend additional income once our basic wants are provided for—new cars, refrigerators, homes, and the like—were not available for most people at any price. Unable to spend their incomes, people added to their cash balances and also bought defense bonds, many of which were later converted into cash. Businesses followed a similar policy. In many cases it was impossible for them to spend their profits for plant expansion. They knew that when the war ended, it would be necessary to convert back from war production to peacetime goods—and, like the consumers, they accumulated cash and bonds.

After the war, there was a rush to get rid of cash. On the part of consumers this was, at the outset, prompted less by the fear that prices would rise than by the feeling that they had been waiting a long time for these things that were now again available. They had more money on hand than they had ever had before. They were out of debt on the goods they had purchased in the 1930s on the installment plan, and they wanted the postwar goods as fast as they could get them. As businesses saw this demand materializing, they attempted to expand their plants as rapidly as possible. Nearly everyone was trying to reduce cash holdings. But spending merely transfers money. It does not destroy it. The total amount of money to be held was as large as before. K was reduced, nevertheless, through a little increase in O and a substantial increase in P. The outbreak of the Korean War gave a new impetus to the movement. Remembering the shortages of World War II, millions decided they would not be caught a second time with an old car, old tires, a worn-out furnace or refrigerator, or, in the case of businesses, with an inadequate stock of raw materials. At this time people were probably buying to escape the expected shortages and higher prices rather than for the reasons of the period immediately after World War II. The result was the same for PO, especially since M began now to increase rapidly so that the public held more money than ever.

Interest Rates, Changing Price Levels, and Desired Cash Balances

Earlier in this chapter we analyzed the effect of rising interest rates on velocity. Suppose we look at this again, this time concentrating on desired cash balances rather than velocity.

When interest rates are very low, the cost of holding idle funds is minimal. One would gain very little from lending them. If at the same time prices are falling (or are expected to fall), both businesses and consumers have an incentive to postpone expenditures as long as possible. Falling national expenditures result in falling incomes. The ratio (K) of money to income rises.

On the other hand, when interest rates are rising, it becomes increasingly expensive to hold idle funds, for one sacrifices more interest income by not lending the money at a high interest rate. Also, since borrowing is costly, businesses and consumers will try to avoid borrowing if they can. At other times they might get an inexpensive loan when their bank balances are low. Now they will try to do without, attempting to reduce their balances to the minimum. As already emphasized, the total quantity of money is unaffected by these efforts to reduce individual cash balances. P or O (or both) will rise, so that an unchanged M will become a smaller fraction (K) of PO.

COMPARISON OF CASH-BALANCE AND VELOCITY EQUATIONS

These examples show the usefulness of the cash-balance type of equation. By concentrating on the cash-balance aspect, we are studying the variable that determines velocity. The advantage of the cash-balance equation is exactly this emphasis upon individuals and their motives. Individuals are not concerned with velocity. They do not ponder whether to spend their money faster or more slowly, whether to turn over their average balance more or less often during the year. Although, on the other hand, they almost certainly cannot be said to think in terms of our K, yet they do decide whether they wish to hold more or less cash, which comes to the same thing. The decisions that they make relative to their cash balances determine K and therefore V. Hence, the cash-balance approach seems the more fundamental of the two, throwing light on the psychological determinants of velocity.

Nevertheless, in this country the velocity form of monetary equation is more widely used. Instead of emphasizing the effect of changes in the desire to hold cash, we more generally refer to the rate of turnover of the money stock. Most people seem to find V a less abstract concept than K.

It really makes little difference whether we write $M = PKO$ or $MV = PO$. The only reason for presenting the two versions is that they describe the same thing from two points of view and give us a more complete explanation than either can supply by itself. When we have nailed down the concept of K, we really begin to understand what is meant by V. The rate of turnover (V) of the money stock depends upon the ratio (K) of money held to money income.

Whichever way we write the equation, we can see that the value of money is related, through either V or K, to the quantity of money and the level of income. We can see why an increase in the quantity of money, not accompanied by an increase in output, will permit a rise in prices. At the same time we can understand why it will only permit, not force, such a rise. We can better realize the potentialities and also the limitations of monetary policy to control the business cycle. Similarly, from either of these equations we can see why, without a gradual increase in the quantity of money, a long-run increase in output will encourage (but not compel) a secular fall in the price level.

No equation, simple or complex, can be used to grind out infallible answers to our economic problems. These equations do help us attack questions of monetary policy by pointing out significant elements to watch.

EVALUATION

We have seen that the quantity approach to the theory of the value of money rests on two basic assumptions:

1. The price level is the dependent variable in the equation $MV = PO$.
2. Changes in output and in income velocity tend to cancel, and the price level therefore tends to respond to changes in the quantity of money.

Is Price Level Dependent? Possible Effect on Velocity

The first assumption could be accepted with least reservation in the analysis of price changes in a highly competitive society. When we are studying developments in an economy characterized by widespread monopoly elements and the prevalence of administered prices, the assumption is questionable. Suppose that in a basic industry, such as steel, labor wins a substantial wage increase and management raises the price of steel. Quantity theorists emphasize that the price increase: (1) will not force banks to increase their loans, thereby increasing the quantity of money; (2) will not force people to wish to hold less money relative to their incomes, thereby increasing the income velocity of money; and (3) will not force a decline in output. Accordingly, unless one of these three variables just happens to change, the only effect of the higher price of steel must be a decline in prices in other sectors, leaving the general price level unchanged. This seems hardly realistic.

Suppose for a moment that the monetary authorities sternly prevent any increase in bank credit. What would be the most likely result from a rise in steel prices—an exactly proportionate decline in other prices, as the quantity theory assumes, or an induced change in velocity or output?

Consider first velocity. True, higher steel prices are not going to make the public wish to hold less money in proportion to their income. But isn't it possible that, whether they wanted or planned it, the public might find their incomes somewhat higher while they were holding the same amount of money as before? If we assume that, especially due to price rigidities in an industrial economy, other prices do not fall and some even rise along with steel, the public may decide to draw down their average balances rather than lower their living standards. As they spend this extra amount, they are simultaneously creating income, so national income rises. Moreover, the transfer of money does not leave the public as a whole with any less money than before. As money moves from hand to hand the public finds itself holding the same amount of money as before. However, since income has risen, there has been an increase in income velocity caused by the independent and initiating increase in the price level.

Effect of a Changed Price Level on Output

Still on the assumption that no increase in the quantity of money is to be allowed, might the higher steel prices lead to a decline in total output? There seems to be no justification for ruling out this possibility. If, instead of temporarily trying to reduce their idle balances as we assumed above, the public spends exactly as much as before, the outcome is going to depend on the elasticity of the demand for steel. If it is highly inelastic, the public will spend a larger total amount for steel than before and will have less to spend on other goods. Conceivably this might work out in such a way that there would be no changes in either P or O, but this would surely be a very special case. True, we are now assuming no change in either M or V, so, of course, the product of P and O cannot change. However, the net result of the changed composition of output could certainly be that the general price level would be a little higher (or a little lower) than before, with an offsetting change in the future for output.

If, on the other hand, the demand for steel is highly elastic, the total amount spent for steel will be less than before, and the public will have more to spend on other goods. Prices elsewhere would tend to rise along with the price of steel. With M and V assumed constant, the result in this instance would be a rise in the price level and a decline in output. People would be spending as much as before, but at the higher price level they would be receiving less for their money. Particularly in this case it seems doctrinaire to assert that the price level must be a dependent variable and to claim that changes in V or O such as we have described could not be caused by a change in P.

Effect of a Changed Price Level on the Quantity of Money

Finally, we relax the assumption of an unchanged quantity of money. For two reasons the rise in steel prices would tend to call forth an increase in the money supply. In the first place, steel-using industries would need more working capital to carry their steel inventories and would depend to a considerable extent on the banks for the additional funds. Loans and deposits would increase accordingly.[18]

In the second place, both the Treasury and Federal Reserve authorities would probably be concerned lest the money supply be inadequate to permit full employment at a higher price level. Fearing that the combination of higher steel prices and a tight money policy might be the cause of a decline in output, they might encourage credit expansion. This seems to be mostly what happened during the 1950s and early 1970s. The authorities permitted the money supply to increase despite rising prices. It was not that they wanted inflation, but that they wanted to avoid a decline in production. It may be noted, incidentally, that if the monetary authorities accepted the quantity theorists' proposition that the price level is a dependent variable, they would not have feared that individual price and wage increases might raise the price level, forcing output to fall.

To sum it up, the assumption that the price level is necessarily the dependent variable appears unwarranted, especially in a modern economy with important areas of price administration. At times it may be the dependent variable. At other times a change in the price level may be the cause of changes elsewhere in the equation.

---

[18]An uncompromising quantity theorist would insist here that it is the increase in M that makes possible the increase in P. This becomes rather tenuous. If one or more prices rise, something else has to change: either other prices fall by just enough to leave P unaffected, or M, V, and/or O will change. Quantity theorists' emphasis on the first possibility seems unwarranted.

The New Monetarism

In recent years a more sophisticated approach to the quantity theory, largely championed by Milton Friedman, has come to challenge the Keynesian income framework discussed in Chapters 16–19.[19] The pros and cons of the theoretical aspects of the monetarists' revolution will be taken up at the conclusion of Chapter 20 after we have analyzed the income approach. For now we only wish to underscore that monetarists have consistently emphasized that monetary policy should be conducted in terms of controlling the rate of growth of monetary aggregates rather than controlling interest rates or money market conditions as Keynesians have urged. Then too, monetarists feel that monetary policy is more important in controlling business cycles, whereas the Keynesians believe that fiscal policy is more important.

The monetarists also believe in having the Federal Reserve System governed by "rules" rather than by "discretion" or "authority." The monetarists feel that the 19 identifiable people who comprise the Federal Reserve Board and who sit around a table in Washington are primarily responsible for the sustained inflation since the mid-1960s. In fact Professor Friedman believes that there have been more severe crises since we have had a Federal Reserve System than in the years from the Civil War through 1914. Even discounting the war years, he feels the Fed has failed in its basic mission of keeping the economy on a steady plane. He feels the Fed has made its decisions in good faith, but with incomplete knowledge. He sincerely feels that the Fed is a system of power and not of rules, and people are fallible. For example, he points out that during the Great Depression the Fed managed to shrink the total money stock by a third and raise the discount rate at a time when banks were closing all around the country! They did this for the most honorable of reasons. Friedman wishes to take away some of the discretionary power from the Fed and make it into a system that operates according to rules. In particular, he suggests that to have economic growth without inflation, the stock of money should increase at a steady rate of about four percent a year—roughly matching the growth in the real output of goods and services which has occurred in our country over the last 25 years. A disciple of Professor Friedman recently said facetiously on a local television show that the Fed should increase the money supply by 3.65 percent a year. When asked why, he replied that this should be done because there are 365 days in a year! This

[19]In addition to all the Friedman citations given in footnote 11, the *Review* of the Federal Reserve Bank of St. Louis is a particularly useful, albeit largely sympathetic to the monetarists' viewpoint, organ for discussing this controversy. For example, see the July, 1968, November, 1968, January, 1972, September, 1973, and January, 1974, issues. In the same vein, see Karl Brunner and Alan H. Meltzer, "Mr. Hicks and the Monetarists," *Economica* (February, 1973). An excellent collection of readings which also lean more to the monetarist position is William E. Gibson and George G. Kaufman, *Monetary Economics: Readings on Current Issues* (New York: McGraw-Hill Book Co., 1971). An excellent analysis supporting the Keynesian position that fiscal policy is important is contained in Alan S. Binder and Robert M. Solow, "Does Fiscal Policy Matter?" *Journal of Public Economics* (November, 1973), pp. 319–337. For a balanced view see the series of articles contained in Part Five, "The Role of Money," *Macroeconomics: Selected Readings*, edited by Walter L. Johnson and David R. Kamerschen (Boston: Houghton Mifflin Co., 1970), pp. 141–206; and the papers by Stanley Fischer, W. C. Brainard, and R. N. Cooper, and the comments by Milton Friedman and Franco Modigliani in the session entitled "25 Years After the Rediscovery of Money: What Have We Learned?" *American Economic Review* (May, 1975), pp. 157–181.

would allow the strictest of rules—the Fed could increase the money supply by .01 percent a day.[20]

SUMMARY AND CONCLUSION

Unquestionably there is a basic truth in the quantity theory of the value of money. We are always confronted with the question, "How much is enough?" If money were issued without limit, it would be valueless. At the other extreme, if there were very little money, prices would tend to be extremely low.

However, the quantity theory must be extensively qualified. Theorists who use the quantity approach realize very well that there are many exceptions to the proposition that an increase in the quantity of money will result in a proportionate decrease in its value. In fact, because he believes these qualifications lead to such unpredictable relationships in the short run, one of today's most sophisticated (and influential) quantity theorists, Milton Friedman, recommends that the goal of monetary policy, at least until we know a great deal more about the subject, should be directed primarily at controlling the quantity of money rather than the price level. We shall succeed only in rocking the boat, he believes, if we attempt to control either interest rates or prices by changes in monetary policy.[21]

Most writers agree that as a guide to monetary policy the quantity theory is likely to be useful at times of full employment, when a tight money policy may help check inflationary price increases. Political considerations tend to prevent the effective use of fiscal policy at such times. In recession or depression any addition to the money supply is likely to be added to idle balances. At such a time fiscal policy can be very helpful in raising income, as will be explained in the next several chapters.

Quantity equations are subject to two general criticisms. They are too general, and at the same time they include too little. The price level and the income level are both very broad concepts. The general price level, because it does cover everything, may conceal highly significant but offsetting price changes in particular areas. Possibly agricultural prices are falling and, simultaneously, prices of manufactured goods are rising. Such a change would have important implications for the economy but could be entirely concealed by a general price index. Similarly, the figure for output tells us only the base year value of total current output with no indication of its composition or distribution or of the level of employment. It tells us nothing about how that income was created.

Although quantity theory must be qualified, and although it has its limitations, it is far from being worthless. Over a generation ago, when the income approach was introduced, many economists too quickly concluded that, clearly, money did not matter. Monetary policy went into eclipse. Today we realize that both quantity theory and income theory can help us understand the

---

[20]During his discussion of various arcane subjects during the broadcast, he did not take up the complications with his formula during leap years!
[21]Milton Friedman, "The Role of Monetary Policy," *American Economic Review* (March, 1968), pp. 1–17.

causes of inflation and recession and how to control them. Neither is a useless guide, and neither is infallible.

Discussion Questions

1. Answer the following questions true or false and explain. With the $MV = PO$ version of the equation of exchange:
   a. M measures the demand for money.
   b. M measures the change in the quantity of money.
   c. V measures the number of times each component of the money stock is used to transact exchange.
   d. V measures the average number of times that the money stock is used for purchasing final goods and services.
   e. P is a price index.
   f. O is real national income.
   g. PO is national income in current dollars.
2. a. What explanations can you suggest for the almost uninterrupted increase in the velocity of money over the last 20 years and its accelerated rate of increase since 1968?
   b. For what reasons would you expect the velocity of circulation of money to be higher today than it was a century ago?
3. "When we write $MV = PO$, we deny that wars, for example, can affect the value of money. According to the equation, only M, V, and O can cause the value of money to change." Discuss.
4. In the equation $MV = PO$, which of the four values will always be the last two to be determined? Explain.
5. "The more convinced the public becomes of the validity of the quantity theory, the less proportionate will changes in the price level be to changes in the quantity of money, especially at full employment." Explain.
6. In a dynamic and progressive economy, which of the terms in the equation of exchange, $MV = PO$, would most likely have a rising secular trend? Why?
7. If the equation $MV = PO$ is applied to an individual rather than to society, over which of the variables would the individual have much control in the short run? Explain.
8. Assuming there is no change in the total stock of money, what difference, if any, is there between the attempt of some individuals to increase the transactions velocity of their average cash balances and the attempt of the society as a whole to increase the transactions velocity of money?
9. Summarize the monetary developments during the 1930s which led to the loss of confidence in monetary policy as a weapon against the Depression.
10. "Real money balances (i.e., the money supply divided by an index of prices) provide a reliable indicator of the thrust of monetary policy." Evaluate.
11. The cash-balance approach, with no mention of velocity, is more helpful in explaining changes in income velocity than the formula $MV = PO$. Explain.
12. How is it possible that K may be increased even though the quantity of money in circulation decreases?
13. In depression, by what means could the government cause an increase in M? Why might there be no change in PO, and how might the government bring about an increase in PO without an increase in M?
14. What are the basic differences between the monetarists and the Keynesians?

PART 5
Money and the National Income

Chapter 16   Money and Production: The National Income

Once *money* meant pieces of metal (or other commodities) and, later, paper exchangeable for the metal. The significance of money today is that it is a claim on goods and services in general, with gold and silver being two of the goods with which, in daily usage, money is the least concerned.

PRODUCTION AND MONEY FLOW

The modern economy, no longer primarily agricultural and self-sufficient, is incredibly interdependent. There is interdependence not only between nations, but also within the nation, by occupation as well as geography. The wheat farmer depends upon the cattle rancher and the automobile manufacturer not only to provide their products but also to take the farmer's own production. A breakdown in the process of production and exchange — that is, a breakdown in the expenditure circuit — can quickly lead to national disaster. As was so evident 45 years ago, when something happens to the money flow and the production flow, millions are out of work, our standard of living falls, and our productive machinery rusts away. In an age of mass production and specialization, the proper functioning of our money system and the proper flow of money expenditures are not matters of idle academic interest. They determine whether we lose our jobs, our homes, possibly our economic system, and conceivably even our national existence. They are by far the most important aspect of money and credit.

In earlier chapters we have seen how, with the development of the banking system and the Federal Reserve, we learned to control, within limits, the quantity of money and the level of interest rates. This was a great advance over the haphazard monetary fluctuations before the 20th century, but it was far from sufficient. It is not enough to be able to regulate the amount and the rental price of money, although these are important first steps. At best, however, they are a means to an end. Basically, we need to know how to control the total level of expenditures, increasing it in slack periods and restraining it when inflationary pressures are eroding the value of money. We need to know how to redirect it, when necessary, to attain desirable social goals. For answers to questions such as these we look to theory, that is, to a logical analysis of what determines the level and composition of expenditures.

Theory is especially necessary due to the abstract nature of money itself. What could possibly be more abstract than a loan-created demand deposit — a debt passing from hand to hand? There is a record of the debt, but the record is not the money. Checks transfer the debt, but the checks are not money either. Most of our payments are made with a pure abstraction. Precisely because it is itself abstract, we cannot even begin to understand money without a careful theoretical analysis.

Expenditures and National Income

Once the analysis of expenditures included all monetary transactions, for whatever purpose. Today we have found a more helpful approach. Since we want to study the relation between money and economic activity, we look only at expenditures directly concerned with the production of goods and services. The total of these expenditures we call the national income. It summarizes simultaneously the total of money incomes received and the total value of what we are producing. It is in many ways the most useful monetary figure we have, and it is basic to the modern theory of monetary and fiscal policies.[1]

In real terms, rather than in terms of money, the national product (or income) is the total of final goods and services that are produced during the year.[2] This collection is the sum total of what the nation is turning out to be consumed during the period or to be added to the existing stock of previously created goods, called capital.[3] Of course, there is no way that we can directly add houses, magazines, and movies, or any unlike goods. But we can add up the total value of all final products for the dollar total of national income. This single monetary statistic summarizes the nation's entire economic activity from several points of view.

Income—Both Receipts and Costs

The money incomes created are the sum of the costs of production. They are necessarily equal to the total value of what has been produced.[4]

A word of warning here. In accounting terminology, profits are defined as the difference between receipts and costs of production. There is nothing wrong with the accounting concept of profits, but economists find it more logical and convenient to include profits as part of the cost of production on the grounds that (in a free economy) there must be profits or there will be no

---

[1]Fiscal policies relate to government expenditures and taxes.
[2]Intermediate products, such as the peaches sold by the farmer to the cannery, are not separately listed since they eventually appear elsewhere as final products—in this instance as canned peaches.
[3]For the moment we shall disregard exports and imports.
[4]Other than depreciation allowances and indirect business taxes.

incentive for firms to remain in business. Farmers, for example, will not continue to cultivate their land if they know that each year they will sell their crop for only enough to cover their operating costs. Like anyone else they expect an income for their work. They are not being paid wages, and if they are farming their own land they are not receiving rental income. Nor are they receiving interest from their farming operations. Their income is in the form of profits (or losses). In the long run they must receive profits or they quit farming. In this sense profits are a part of production costs.

Since profits and losses specifically measure the difference between market receipts and income created up to the point just before the goods were sold, when we list them as income, we are, by definition, equating the market value of production with the dollars of income created. If, at the end of the year, the business has paid out $40,000 to others and has taken in $50,000, total income created was $50,000 ($40,000 to others plus the $10,000 of profits which is the business's income). If the business took in only $38,000 and paid out $40,000, total income would be $38,000 ($40,000 less the $2,000 of losses).

Total value of production, total costs, total expenditures on final goods, and total incomes are just four different aspects of the same thing. We may say that in a particular year the nation produced $1,500 billion of final goods and services. This was the market value of the goods—the amount for which they sold. At the same time, it was the total cost of the goods, it was the total amount of money income received by the factors of production, and it was the dollar total of the real income that the nation may consume or save. It is the same income whichever way we look at it.

INCOME FLOW

It is imperative that from the outset we thoroughly understand the concept of the circular flow of income. Figure 16-1 presents a highly simplified illustration of this process. Later we shall take into account the important factors here omitted—savings, investment, government expenditures, and taxes.

As shown in Figure 16-1, the public receives money income in the form of wages, rent, interest, and profits. To earn this income they supply factors of production—in many cases their labor, in some instances natural resources, capital goods, or managerial ability. The first point to realize is that the total dollar value of the productive services, in Channel 2, must necessarily be equal to the total money income paid out in wages, rent, interest, and profits in Channel 1. The money that businesses pay out as costs becomes income sooner or later to someone or to some organization. This is obvious in the case of wage payments. In the case of purchases of raw and semifinished materials, the income creation is perhaps a little less apparent. But a little reflection reminds us that the individuals who supply materials to businesses have usually incurred costs of their own. The money that they receive from their own sales is used to pay for labor and materials that they in turn employed, and any amount remaining becomes income for themselves. All

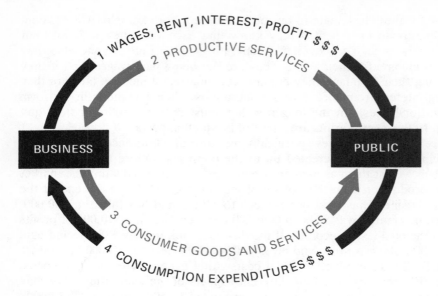

Figure 16-1   Circular Flow of Income

money spent for current production eventually becomes income to someone, whether an individual, partnership, or corporation.

There are two principal points to be kept in mind:

1. Channel 1 relates to income from current production only. Relief checks, veterans' bonuses, inheritances, and the like are excluded, for we are measuring the value of total production, or national income, by summing up the individual incomes paid out in creating that national product. For the same reason we exclude the money received by people who sell their car, house, or stocks, for payments of this kind merely transfer the ownership of existing assets; they are not received for current production.
2. Channel 3 relates to final products only. We must not count both the value of the final product and the value of the products out of which it is made. That would be counting the same thing twice. For the same reason we are not including the value of machines produced to replace worn-out equipment, as the value of these, too, is included in the value of the final product that they help to produce.

None of these payments drifts off into a vacuum, for a payment cannot be made unless there is someone to be paid, whether individual or corporation. We must summarize by observing that Channels 1 and 2 are both concerned with the creation of income and have the same monetary value, Channel 2 showing the factors that are combined in the process of creating real income, and Channel 1 showing the money income paid out for those factors.

Likewise, Channels 3 and 4, which relate to the disposition of income, are necessarily equal. The money the public pays out for its consumption purchases is equal to the dollar value of the goods and services provided the public by business.

Finally, as here drawn, Channel 4 must equal Channel 1. At this stage we are not recognizing any source from which additional funds may be injected into an income stream, nor any outlet into which income might be drained off, not to appear on subsequent circuits. No one is trying to increase his or her stock of goods. No one is trying to save. Whatever the level of money income may be, it will continue indefinitely in this closed system. Income is at an equilibrium level. Note specifically, however, that the fact that, as drawn, income is necessarily in equilibrium tells us nothing as to whether this system has full employment or mass unemployment. All that we can say is that, in our illustration, the money income, 1, received by the public is equal to the money value of the services, 2, contributed by the public; and that 1 is also equal to the money income, 4, spent by the public which in turn is equal to the money value of the real income, 3, received by the public.

Furthermore, according to our illustration total capital is being maintained at a constant level. The stocks of goods cannot increase as long as Channels 1, 2, 3, and 4 are equal, for by these assumptions the nation is consuming goods and services as fast as it produces them. Nor can there be a decrease, or we would have to show consumption exceeding income. For similar reasons there can be no saving or dissaving, and we are ignoring government receipts and expenditures.

Simultaneous Creation and Consumption of Income

This highly simplified example brings out the important fact that the creation of income and the spending of income may be thought of as a simultaneous process with no time lag. Goods are being consumed as fast as they are being produced.

This concept sometimes is difficult to grasp at first. As individuals, we must receive income before we can spend it. Our first impression may be that a nation also must first receive its income before it can spend it. But when some members of a group are spending income, they are creating income for others. If you pay the barber or the dentist, you are consuming your income. In the process you are creating income for the people you pay. If you buy goods, the same principle is involved less obviously. The merchant does not receive $15 of net income when you buy a pair of shoes for $15, but the entire $15 does eventually break down into income for the long line of producers—cattle raisers, leather companies, shoe manufacturers, transportation workers, salespeople, and others who have cooperated to bring you the shoes. It is not necessary to insert a time lapse between the earning and the spending of national income, and usually it will be helpful to regard the two activities as simultaneous.

Note, incidentally, that when we are using a timeless analysis, we are necessarily dealing with rates of consumption and income rather than with the amounts actually occurring over a period of time. We are saying, "Income (or consumption) is running at a rate that, if maintained for a year, would amount to $1,500 billion." It is exactly the same as when we say, "We're traveling 60 miles an hour." At the end of an hour we may or may not have gone 60 miles, depending on what happened to our rate of travel in the meantime. Or to use a dollar comparison, at the end of a successful month a salesperson may have earned $5,000 in commissions. This income is currently running at the rate of $60,000 a year, but by the end of the year the salesperson's total earned income may be entirely different.

Income, Origin, Distribution, and Disposition

So much for the total income flow. There are several ways in which we can profitably break down this overall aggregate.

With respect to income source, the shares of income created by the production of consumer goods and capital goods have important implications for monetary policy, income growth, economic stability, and the standard of living, as will appear in the course of our analysis. We find there are wide swings in the production of capital goods, and we look for the reasons. We see also that the consumer goods category may be broken down into durable and nondurable goods, production of which does not proceed at any constant ratio. Further, a considerable part of our real income is in the form of services, and those who supply the services receive a corresponding part of our money income. Shifts from capital goods to consumer goods, shifts from consumer durable goods to consumer nondurable goods, and shifts (as we have seen since 1960) from consumer goods to consumer services necessarily change the composition of national income. More importantly, they usually also change the total level of income and employment, and they may change the value of money.

Along a little different line, we observe that if more income is paid out for the creation of goods, the supply of which may readily be increased, and less income is paid out for goods in inelastic supply, the price level is less likely to rise than would be the case under the opposite conditions.

Level of National Income

If the flow of income were really as simple a process as shown in Figure 16-1, there would be few problems. The money level of income would be constant, no matter what changes might occur in its composition as a result of shifting consumer preferences. With consumers turning back to business, in the form of purchases, the same amount of money that they received for their productive services, and with businesses again making this same sum available as income to the public through the productive process, money income could neither rise nor fall.

To be sure, relative prices could still change as a result of shifts in demand. The general price level could also change. If the population were increasing and the economy remained at full employment, the total output would increase and, with money income assumed constant, this output would necessarily be produced and sold at a lower level of costs and prices. Furthermore, the amount of unemployment could change even in this highly simplified income model. If consumers began to spend a larger part of their incomes for personal services and less for other products embodying relatively little labor, more workers would be employed and the wage component of income would rise at the expense of rents, interest, or profits. Much more importantly, if we assume a constant price level and either or both an increasing labor force or an increase in productivity per person, then a constant dollar value of national income necessarily requires increasing unemployment unless offset by the shift to services mentioned in the preceding sentence.

However, changes such as the above are insignificant, in the short run, in comparison to other changes that occur in national income. Usually the public will spend less for consumption than it is currently receiving as income, reducing the stream as it appears as income for business. Occasionally the public consumes more than its income. Businesses, in turn, may spend less or more than the funds they are currently receiving from the public as it spends its income. Income levels will be driven up or down by additions and subtractions of this kind. Only as long as, on balance, no income is being either withdrawn or added, the income in one period will be the same as in the preceding period. Usually, however, income does change from one period to the next.

These changes in economic activity and expenditures are of signal importance. They change the money incomes and the real incomes of the factors of production. They reflect changes in the levels of output and employment. Often they affect the value of money and the level of interest rates. They are often the cause and frequently the result of changes in credit and in monetary and fiscal policy. In the following chapters we shall explore the factors that determine the level and are responsible for changes in the level of total productive expenditures, which economists have learned to measure fairly well.

Measures of National Income

There are several measures of national income. The one we shall generally use is *national income at factor cost,* usually shortened to *national income* (or *NI*). As the term implies, this is the total of wages, rents, interest, and profits received for current production.

It also approximately, but not exactly, equals the market value of all final goods and services produced. There are two reasons for this discrepancy:

1. The market value of goods includes *indirect business taxes,* such as sales taxes and excises. It is assumed, not entirely accurately but as a rule of thumb, that all such taxes increase market price and that all other taxes (such as personal taxes and corporate profits taxes) do not. On this assumption the market price will be the total of what the factors of production receive plus any indirect business taxes. When a person pays $10 for 20 gallons of gasoline, including state and local excises of $.20 a gallon, there has been only $6 of income created. The national output at market value is called *net national product* (*NNP*) and exceeds national income by the total of indirect business taxes.
2. Included in the total market value of final goods may be capital goods that merely replace, rather than add to, our stock of goods. Logically, we

should exclude these replacements. The value of the capital goods consumed in the process of production is included in the value of the final product. We are counting the same thing twice when we include in the national product both the value of the electricity produced and the value of the generators replaced during the year. Yet the most common measure of national output is the *gross national product* (*GNP*), which makes no allowance for depreciation. Gross national product, then, exceeds net national product by the total of depreciation allowances. Currently, *NNP* is approximately 10/11 of *GNP*. Put differently, depreciation is about 1/11 of *GNP*.

Other Measures

Besides the overall measures of national income, there are several subsidiary measures, all of which are helpful in tracing the flow of money expenditures through the economy. There is *personal income* (*PI*), which omits from *NI* all corporate income other than that paid to individuals as dividends, and which adds in the transfer payments people receive from the government.

If personal taxes are subtracted from personal income, we have *disposable personal income* (*DPI*). The latter finally breaks down into *consumption* (*C*) and *personal savings* (*S*), the topics with which most of the rest of this chapter will be concerned. Since 1950 *S* has been 5–10 percent of *DPI*, and therefore *C* has been 90–95 percent of *DPI*.

In recent years economists have become disenchanted with counting only "goods" or material goods and services and using *GNP* as a measure of economic welfare. They have turned to an adjusted *GNP* concept called *measure of economic welfare* (*MEW*).[5] Proponents of *MEW* feel that it better measures what is happening to the "quality of life" or "social welfare" by modifying the present *GNP* measure primarily in three ways: (1) by subtracting certain unmet costs or "bads," such as pollution and other ecological costs; (2) by excluding some "regrettable" and "intermediate" services, such as police and national defense, which represent unpleasant necessities of modern urbanization and industrialization; and (3) by adding certain items, such as household activities (housework, home repair, etc.) and the value of leisure. The result is that *MEW* has been growing in the United States since, say, 1930, but at a slower rate than has *GNP*.

These six measures illustrate a simple but basic point to which we shall repeatedly return. One can do just three things with one's income: pay taxes, spend it for consumption goods and services, or abstain from consuming it.

Comparative Evaluation. All these estimates are useful, each in its own way. None is exact. When we want a measure of overall productivity, we use one of the first three. Of these, *NI* is the most logical choice when we are

---

[5]This measure was formally proposed by William Nordhaus and James Tobin, "Is Growth Obsolete?" *Economic Growth,* Fiftieth Anniversary Colloquium, Vol. V (New York: National Bureau of Economic Research, 1972). An excellent short summary can be found in Kenneth Stewart, "National Income Accounting and Economic Welfare: The Concepts of *GNP* and *MEW*," *Review* of the Federal Reserve Bank of St. Louis (April, 1974), pp. 18–24.

studying the circular flow process. The value of the flow of goods and services is identical with the incomes created in their production. On the other hand, for measures of general economic activity *NNP* and *GNP* are more commonly used. Of the three measures, *GNP* is the most popular. As a broad measure of production it is easily understood. It is a little more reliable than *NNP*, for it involves one less estimate; we cannot state positively the amount of depreciation during the year. Also, if we are interested in our maximum potential output, we may not be much concerned with the question of how much capital we are currently consuming. We want to know our total productivity, disregarding the estimate of capital consumption.

The various breakdowns of personal income are helpful in studies of economic welfare and living standards. They may reveal facts concealed by the broader totals. It would be possible, for example, that as a result of higher taxes *DPI* would fall even though *GNP* was rising. A change in corporate policy concerning dividend distribution would affect *PI*, even if there were no change in *GNP*. Decisions concerning monetary and fiscal policies appropriate to counter inflation or recession will certainly take into account the estimates of *PI, DPI, C,* and *S*. Such estimates are useful also in forecasting sales of consumer goods. The number of cars, television sets, and outboard motors that will be sold in a year depends largely upon the disposable personal income in the hands of the public and whether they are increasing or decreasing the proportion currently saved. Finally, if we are interested in a measure of "quality of life," *MEW* is best, since it subtracts from *GNP* the estimated costs in maintaining clean air and water, moderating urban congestion, and utilizing police and national defense services, and adds to it the estimated value of nonmarket activities, such as household work and leisure time.[6]

Corrections for Changes in the Price Level. The real value of income by any of these measures will be distorted by changes in the value of money. To eliminate the effect of changing price levels, it is customary to divide the dollar values of national income by a price index.[7] This is particularly important in comparing the national income of one period with that of another. By "deflating," the incomes will be stated in terms of the same dollar rather than in current dollars. For some purposes, however, and especially in studying inflationary processes, the uncorrected series are superior to the deflated figures. The *GNP* in current and constant dollars for selected years from 1929 through 1974 is shown in Table 16-1.

Adjustment for Changes in Population. Also, if we are comparing national incomes over a long span of years, our comparisons may have more significance if we place them on a per capita basis by dividing by total population.

---

[6]In truth, *MEW* does not measure welfare but consumption. A true welfare measure would need to quantify the amount of satisfaction or utility received from consumption and would depend, in part, on the distribution of income.

[7]More exactly, by a number of price indexes. Rather than divide *GNP* by a single index, the statisticians deflate a number of components of *GNP*, each by its appropriate index, and then total these corrected components to derive *GNP* in deflated dollars.

Table 16-1   Gross National Product in Current Dollars
and Constant Dollars (1958=100)
(In billions)

	1929	1933	1941	1945	1950	1955	1960	1965	1970	1974
GNP, current dollars	103.1	55.6	124.5	211.9	284.8	398.0	503.7	684.9	977.1	1,397.4
GNP, constant dollars	203.6	141.5	263.7	355.2	355.3	438.0	487.7	617.8	722.5	821.2

Source: *Economic Report of the President*, 1975.

This is not so important when comparing two adjacent years, for the change in population from one year to the next is so small that it will not greatly affect the results. But if we are comparing national income of 1900 with that of today and wish to draw any conclusions as to either the productivity or the economic welfare of individuals, we should certainly compare the deflated incomes on a per capita basis.[8]

DISPOSITION OF INCOME

For the time being we shall concentrate on a closed economy, disregarding imports and exports. We shall also for the present disregard government spending and taxes. Finally, in the balance of this chapter we shall be concerned primarily with what we do with income received. Later we shall take up income creation.

As individuals, what do we do with the income we receive? Obviously either we do or we don't consume it. Simple enough. Yet when we begin to study the causes and consequences of this consumption and nonconsumption, we have taken a giant step toward understanding the causes of changes in national income and employment.

Consumption and Saving

We shall define as *consumption* (C) all spending by individuals when they are buying goods for their own (or their familes') personal use. Why can't we say, more briefly, "all spending by individuals"? The shorter definition would include too much. It would grossly violate the meaning of consumption as the term is generally used. A farmer may spend $5,000 for a tractor, but it would be nonsense to say that this was a consumption expenditure. But if the farmer spends $500 for a color television for family entertainment, by the above

---

[8]And also take into account changes in income distribution, which have been marked during the last 45 years. Alternatively, today many economists would simply use per capita *MEW* in discussing economic welfare.

definition we unhesitatingly classify it as a consumption expenditure. (Note that the same television set, if bought by a hotel to attract more trade, would not be a consumption expenditure. We shall go into this in more detail in the next chapter.)

All income that is not consumed we shall define as *saving* (*S*). This is a treacherously simple definition. All unconsumed income is saved. Perhaps this seems only common sense and, in a way, it is. But remember this definition! Note carefully that it says nothing whatever about what is finally done with this nonconsumed income, nor does it explain why and how consumption is less than income. Later we shall analyze these variations more closely, but for the present merely note that there are three general sources or causes of saving:

1. A person may spend only part of his income, holding the balance unspent. He holds more money or perhaps exchanges money for other financial assets, such as time deposits, bonds, or stocks. This might be called *obvious saving* and corresponds fairly closely with everyday usage of the word.
2. He may spend all his income, but partly on nonconsumption goods. Perhaps he buys a truck or builds a warehouse. He has saved, but his bank account and savings account do not reflect it. Also, neither the truck nor warehouse nor the money spent for them is itself saving, even though it is the result of saving. Be sure you understand this point, for it is of critical importance to later analysis! The saving is only the nonconsumption of income, whatever the reason may be.
3. He may even spend all his income on consumption; but because prices are rising faster than his income, he is consuming less than the value of what he produced. In this situation, commonly referred to as *forced saving,* neither his financial assets nor his stock of capital goods has been increased.[9] Nevertheless, in real terms this consumer has by definition saved, for he has failed to consume all his (real) income.

Typically, not only the saving of society as a whole but also the saving of many individuals will contain all three of the above elements. Unspent income, expenditures for nonconsumption goods, and rising prices together cause total consumption to be less than total real income.

Clearly we must avoid confusing saving with the amount of money held at a period of time, with savings deposits, or with savings bonds. We cannot even say that the increase in any or all the above will measure the aggregate saving of the year. Obviously all these and other assets may be increased by saving, but they are not in themselves saving.

There is an important difference between consumption and saving. Both refer to what we do with money income received. But only consumption creates income. The act of saving in itself is a leakage out of the money stream of income payments.

We may conveniently summarize our definitions in the form of simple equations. In the simplified picture of the income flow presented earlier in this chapter, we assumed all income was consumed. Under this condition,

---

[9]Taxes are sometimes also included under the heading of forced saving, since they certainly cannot be classified as consumption. At this point we are disregarding taxes; later we shall usually treat them as a third, separate disposition of income.

$NI = C$. Such a state of affairs would be possible.[10] There have been times when the entire income of the United States has been consumed, and even times when this country consumed more than its current income. And there are other countries that tend regularly to consume all or practically all their income.

Most of the time, however, we would expect that our income would not be entirely consumed. Usually we try to save something. Of course, other people may be digging into past savings to supplement their present income. But if total savings exceed total dissavings, we cannot say that $NI = C$. We shall write $NI = C + S$.

In 1932, 1933, and 1934, the worst years of the Great Depression, consumption exceeded national income; in 1931 consumption exactly equalled national income. In all other years, as shown in Table 16-2, part of our national income was not consumed. It was, by definition, saved.

Interrelation of Consumption and Income

Later we shall look at the statistics to see how consumption and income are, in fact, related. But before we go any further, suppose we just think a

Table 16-2   Consumption and Income
(In billions of current dollars)

Year	Consumption	National Income	Year	Consumption	National Income
1929	77	87	1952	217	291
1930	70	75	1953	230	305
1931	60	60	1954	237	303
1932	49	43	1955	254	331
1933	45	40	1956	267	351
1934	51	50	1957	281	366
1935	56	57	1958	290	368
1936	62	65	1959	311	400
1937	66	74	1960	325	415
1938	64	67	1961	335	427
1939	67	73	1962	355	458
1940	71	81	1963	375	482
1941	81	104	1964	401	518
1942	88	137	1965	433	564
1943	99	171	1966	466	621
1944	108	183	1967	492	654
1945	120	182	1968	536	711
1946	143	182	1969	580	766
1947	161	199	1970	618	801
1948	174	224	1971	667	858
1949	177	218	1972	729	946
1950	191	241	1973	805	1,066
1951	206	278	1974	877	1,142

Source: *Economic Report of the President,* 1975.

---

[10]In fact, as Table 16-2 shows, it occurred in the United States in 1931.

little about how we would expect them to be related. Specifically, would we expect that:

1. a society would tend to consume about the same amount every year, regardless of the level of its income?
2. total consumption would fall when income is rising?
3. consumption would rise when income rises?
4. consumption and income would vary independently, so that some years a rising income would be accompanied by a rising consumption, some years by a falling consumption?

We can use simple diagrams to illustrate each of the above possibilities. On the vertical axis we measure consumption, on the horizontal axis national income. We shall set down points, showing for 10 or 12 years possible combinations of income and consumption. Corresponding to the four cases above, we might have something like what is shown in Figure 16-2.

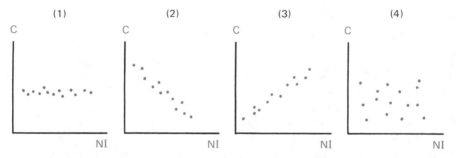

Figure 16-2   Four Possible Consumption and Income Relationships

Common sense suggests that the third relationship would be what we might most reasonably expect. From personal experience we know that, as individuals, we tend to consume more, at least up to a point, as our income rises. To some extent we buy more goods than before. To some extent we buy better goods—choicer foods, better made clothes, more spacious and more convenient houses. Either way we are consuming more. Forget for a minute about income in the dollar sense. Think of real income. We are consuming goods and services. These goods and services are the result of productive effort. More labor and other productive factors have been employed in importing a fabric and hand-tailoring it into a suit than were necessary to turn out a ready-made suit, mass-produced and hung on a rack. More income has been created in the production of the first suit. Our consumption of real income is increased when we buy such goods just as it is more obviously increased if we buy twice as much gasoline or twice as many movie tickets as before.

The Consumption Function—General

When one variable is found to depend upon another, we may say that it is a function of the other variable. This term *function* seems to throw some students into an immediate state of panic. Yet all we are saying is that one variable is determined, at least in part, by the other. We say that the gasoline mileage a car will deliver is a function of the speed at which the car is driven and also the weight of the car. Both speed and weight have something to do with miles to the gallon. Again, your grades are a function of the amount of studying you do, and, of course, of your native intelligence.

Similarly, we refer to the consumption function, sometimes called the *propensity to consume*. This is a tool of fundamental importance to income analysis. In its most general sense the *consumption function* states simply that consumption depends directly upon income. That is the relationship shown by diagram 3 of Figure 16-2, which indicates that consumption and income move together. It seems reasonable to assume that the most important single factor determining whether you spend $5,000 or $50,000 a year will ordinarily be your current income. Whether a nation's consumption is $90 billion or $900 billion will depend, we may confidently assume, primarily upon its income.

Qualifications

Of course, your current income is not the only factor. Your spending will be affected by such considerations as your previous and your expected future income, the stock of assets held, the level of advertising by businesses, your own subjective tastes and preferences, and your wealth.[11] If you already own a million dollars of property, you probably will not be trying so hard to put something aside out of current earnings for a rainy day. Also, the income you have been making in previous years has something to do with how much you spend this year, and so too, probably, does the rate of change in your income. So does the income you expect to make in later years. And your spending will be affected, too, by changes in the price level, by whether you think prices are going to rise or fall, and by whether you think goods are going to be scarce (as during World War II) or plentiful, as well as by the importance you attach to keeping up with the Joneses.

The total consumption for a nation will reflect all these factors influencing consumption decisions of individuals. It may be influenced, too, by government policies. Yet with all these other considerations, it appears reasonable to assume that the most important single determinant of total consumption is national income.

A Guess at the Equation of the Consumption Function

Before we turn to the statistics to check upon our analysis of how things ought, logically, to be, we might consider one more point. If we are correct in assuming that the consumption function is best represented by the relationships shown in diagram 3 of Figure 16-2, can we go one step further and

---

[11]A comprehensive review of the factors influencing consumption is given in Daniel Suits, "The Determinants of Consumer Expenditure: A Review of Present Knowledge," *Macroeconomics: Selected Readings*, edited by Walter L. Johnson and David R. Kamerschen (Boston: Houghton Mifflin Co., 1970), Chapter 8, pp. 59–92; and Robert Ferber, "Consumer Economics: A Survey," *Journal of Economic Literature* (December, 1973), pp. 1303–1342.

attempt a guess at the general nature of the equation of a line that might reasonably well fit the points of the scatter diagram? Assume, for simplicity, that we decide arbitrarily to use a straight line rather than some kind of curve. What can we guess about the nature of that line?

Consider first the slope of the line, which will show how much change in consumption is associated with a change in income. Since we are assuming that as income increases consumption also increases, we have shown the points rising from left to right; that is, the slope is positive. Can we be more specific? A positive slope might be anything from just over zero to just under infinity.

What does common sense suggest? If income increases by $100, should we expect most often to find that consumption increases by $100, more than $100, or less than $100? Individual cases will differ, but can't we safely assume that in the majority of instances the increase in consumption is more likely to be $70 or $80 than $100 or more? If so, we are assuming that the slope of the line we are considering is less than 1.0—perhaps 0.7 or 0.8, maybe a little more or a trifle less—but certainly less than 1.0.

CONSUMPTION

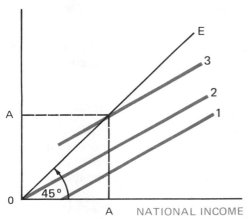

Figure 16-3   Three Alternative
Consumption Functions

In Figure 16-3 we draw *OE* purely for reference. It is not supposed to represent a consumption function, but it will help us decide how to draw a reasonable guess at what the consumption function might look like. *OE* is a guideline drawn starting at the origin, where both consumption and income are zero; it is drawn with a slope of 1.0, so that at every point on *OE* the values of consumption and income are equal to each other. To draw guideline *OE* with a slope of 1.0, it is necessary to draw *OE* at a 45° angle from the origin, thus bisecting the origin, and therefore making every point on line *OE* equidistant from both the vertical (consumption) and horizontal (national income) axes.

We decided that the slope of the consumption function is most likely to be less than 1.0, so it will rise less steeply than *OE*. Three such possible lines might be sketched in to represent different assumptions:

1. Assume that at all levels of income part, or possibly all, would be saved, and that consumption would be zero at very low levels of income. Only as income rises do people finally begin to consume. Obviously this would be a fantastic state of affairs.
2. Assume that part of income is always saved, no matter how small the income, and that consumption would be zero if income were zero. This is nearly as unrealistic as the preceding case. At very low levels of income, saving becomes not merely difficult but impossible. With zero consumption everyone quickly starves to death.
3. Assume that there would be some consumption even if income were zero. The individual (or the society) would be consuming goods on hand if none were being currently produced. Capital is being consumed, rather than income. Or we may say that at low levels of income savings are negative. As income rises, the dissaving becomes less until at *A* consumption is exactly equal to income and there is neither dissaving nor saving. If income rises still further, consumption becomes less than income, as shown by the fact that consumption function 3 has crossed *OE* and now lies below it. (Remember that only on *OE* will consumption be equal to income at every point.)

Can there really be any doubt that consumption function 3 is the only one of these choices that we could possibly expect might describe the consumption-income relationship?

The Evidence

Let's check our theory against the facts. Table 16-2 presents consumption and income data for the 46 years between 1929 and 1974. We see that from 1932 to 1934, when income was very low, consumption exceeded income; in 1931 consumption was equal to income; in other years consumption was less than income.

Figure 16-4 presents the same information in the form of a scatter diagram such as we constructed by guess in Figure 16-2. If we work out by the method of least squares the equation of the regression line that most closely fits this data, we have line *CC*.[12] The equation of this line is $C = \$4.8$ billion $+ .76$ (*NI*);[13] that is, it is a line with a positive slope; the slope is less than 1.0; and the line, if projected to the vertical axis (i.e. the *y*-intercept), would indicate a consumption of \$4.8 billion if income were zero. Our common sense analysis is completely verified by the statistics, for these are exactly the characteristics

---

[12] The method of least squares is a technique used by statisticians in fitting a trend line to data such as these. The procedure can be found in any statistics text.

[13] Other equations might be used to express the relationship between consumption and national income, both expressed in deflated dollars, or between consumption and disposable personal income, or gross national product, or per capita income. Any of these equations would be consumption functions. If, for example, the equation between consumption and disposable income were calibrated over these same years, the slope would be closer to 9/10 than to 3/4. Put simply, a regression coefficient, such as .76 in the above regression equation, is a statistically determined measure of the quantitative effect of a change in one variable upon another.

CONSUMPTION
(Billions of Dollars)

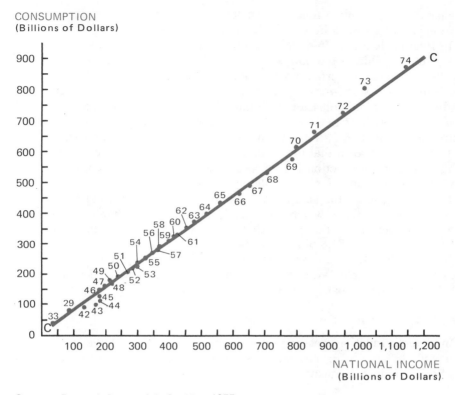

Source: *Economic Report of the President,* 1975.

Figure 16-4   Historical Consumption Function

that logic suggested—a positive slope, less than 1.0, and crossing the guideline *OE* from above.

Consumption Function Independent of Income

Note particularly that the consumption function does not depend upon income. The amount of consumption will vary with the amount of income; but the equation itself, or the line that it represents, is not affected by changes in income. The consumption function is changed only if at all levels of income there is more (or less) consumption than before, that is, a change in the equation itself.[14]

Although the consumption function may change, Figure 16-4 suggests that it is unlikely to shift. All the points lie close to the same regression line.[15]

---

[14]This is the same distinction that is made in economics between a change in demand and a change in the quantity demanded. Demand is not increased when the price is lowered and more goods are taken. Demand would increase if more goods were taken without a price reduction.

[15]A standard measure of goodness of fit, the coefficient of determination (R^2), is equal to .98. The regression equation for the consumption function for the 15 years between 1960 and 1974 is $C = \$6.1$ billion $+ .76(NI)$.

Because the consumption function is stable, it is a highly useful piece of analytical apparatus, as will be shown in the next chapter.

   In Figures 16-5 and 16-6 we have drawn again the function C = $4.8 bil-
lion = .76(NI), which we found best described the relation between consumption and income over certain past years. Suppose, however, that as we continued to plot consumption-income combinations over the next 10 years, we
found the new points consistently falling above the regression line. It would
appear that there had been an increase in the consumption function. If, as
illustrated in Figure 16-5, the new points appear to lie on a line parallel to our
first line, it would seem that the slope of the new function is the same as that
of the first, but the function is at a higher level. The new function might be
found to be, for example, C = $6 billion + .76($NI$).[16]

   Possibly, instead, the later points would lie above (or below) the original
line, but along a new line which rose more (or less) steeply than the first, as in
Figure 16-6. Here it would appear that the new consumption function might
be, for instance, C = $4.8 billion + .80($NI$).

   Shifts such as these are possible. They are, however, infrequent. Until the
data give unmistakable evidence to the contrary, we are justified in assuming
there has been no change in the consumption function.

Significance of the Consumption Function

   In general, functions relating one variable to another all have in common
this useful characteristic: they help to explain changes in the dependent variable. So it is with the consumption function.

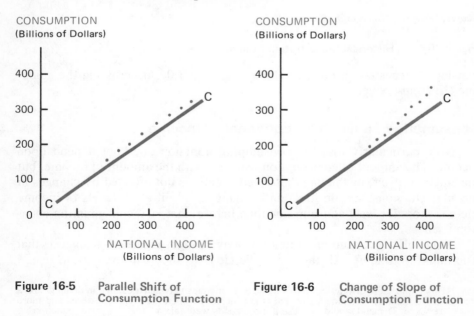

| Figure 16-5 | Parallel Shift of Consumption Function | Figure 16-6 | Change of Slope of Consumption Function |

---

[16]As mentioned in the previous footnote, this is approximately what did happen if we compare 1960–1974 with the longer 1929–1974 relationship.

However, if this were its only significance, it would merit little attention. Why have we stressed it in such detail? The dependence of consumption upon income is admittedly a remarkably stable relationship, but also remarkably obvious. The fact is, however, this apparently simple relation is basic to the whole analysis of income determination, as will appear in the following chapter. The level of economic activity and the total flow of money incomes are, we shall see, dependent in part on the value of the consumption function. Some of the most helpful guides to the analysis of monetary and fiscal policy are in terms of the consumption function. Changes in interest rates or the value of money may shift the function, with important consequences for total economic activity. Likewise, changes in taxes or government spending, by affecting disposable personal income, will generally drive consumption and income to new levels. The consumption function is the key to understanding the interrelated developments of changes such as these, and, simple though it is, it is the foundation of much of modern monetary analysis.

The Saving Function

Since we are defining saving as all nonconsumed income, we can easily find from Table 16-2 the amount of income saved at various levels of income. It is hardly surprising to find that saving increases as income increases, just as consumption does. What is surprising is that for a long time economists overlooked this obvious relationship, arguing instead that saving increased when interest rates rose. The fact is that the relationship between interest rates and the amount saved is obscure at best. Some people may try harder to save when interest rates rise. Others may feel there is no need to save so much, since $10,000 at 6 percent will bring in the same revenue as $20,000 at 3 percent. On the other hand, what could be more obvious than that you cannot save $5,000 a year unless your income is more than $5,000? Or that if your income dropped from $20,000 last year to $6,000 this year, you are likely to save less than last year? The most important single factor governing the amount saved is the level of income.

Saving, then, is a function of income, as indicated by Figure 16-7. We could, again, use the least squares technique to work out the equation of this trend. However, since we have already worked out the equation of the consumption function, we know what the saving function must be, without any additional computation. Saving is nonconsumed income. According to our consumption function, .76 of any addition to income is consumed. Then, by definition, .24 of any addition to income is not consumed; it is saved. Also, according to our consumption function, total consumption will be $4.8 billion *more* than .76 of national income. Total saving, then, must be $4.8 billion *less* than .24 of national income. Over the period of years shown, $S = -\$4.8$ billion $+ .24(NI)$. It has to have this value if consumption is $4.8 billion $+ .76(NI)$, for at all levels of income, $C + S = NI$, and:

At any level of income, $C = \$4.8 \text{ billion} + .76(NI)$
At any level of income, $\underline{S = -\$4.8 \text{ billion} + .24(NI)}$
At any level of income, $\quad\quad C + S = NI$

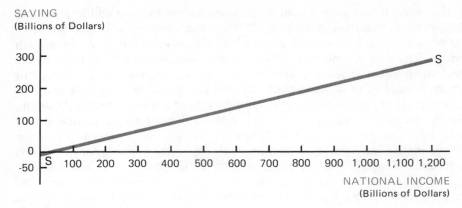

SAVING
(Billions of Dollars)

Figure 16-7   Saving Function

Of course, we are not saying that in any year saving will be exactly $4.8 billion less than 24 percent of national income. On the basis of past experience, this would be our most reasonable estimate. Because income is such an important determinant of saving, and because the saving function, like the consumption function, is a stable relationship, the estimate will be fairly close. But we can hardly suppose that nothing except the income level will effect saving. As with consumption, saving may to some extent be affected by other variables. Primarily, however, it will be governed by income.

Since the saving function is the complement of the consumption function, it evidently has the same analytical importance. This will be developed in the next chapter.

SUMMARY AND CONCLUSION

Money is significant today, not as pieces of metal, but as the abstract means of settlement necessary for specialization and exchange in modern society. The stream of money, or volume of money payments, is the most useful approach to an understanding of money. In particular, the flow of total money incomes gives us a monetary measure of total economic activity. It shows us, on one hand, the returns to the factors of production and, on the other, the total value of the economy's current production. After allowance for indirect business taxes and for replacement of capital goods worn out during the year, total expenditures are equal to total wages, rents, interest, and profits.

Part of these incomes is consumed. The part that is not consumed (other than taxes, ignored for now) is defined as saving. Saving, as such, is a leakage, reducing the flow of income.

Income consumption and income creation are synchronous, since the consumption expenditures of buyers are income to the producers. The level of consumption depends primarily upon the level of current income. The stable relationship between consumption and income, known as the consumption function, will be shown to be one of the key factors determining the income level and often the value of money.

Changes in national income reflect changes in employment, in the growth of the economy, in living standards, and in the level of economic activity. They also cause redistribution of property and real incomes when they lead to changes in the value of money. They may even, as in the 1930s, contribute to the collapse of the banking system. The national income has become the usually dominant consideration in the selection of appropriate monetary and fiscal policies.

Discussion Questions

1. Which of the following payments are included in national income? Explain.
   a. tips received by a waiter
   b. wages received by a carpenter
   c. interest received by a bondholder
   d. Social Security check received by a retired worker
   e. money you receive when you sell your car
   f. dividends received by a stockholder
   g. profits earned by a corporation but not distributed as dividends
   h. rent you pay for your apartment
2. Why do economists include profits as a production cost in the long run?
3. "Since *GNP* is the sum of the market values of the final goods and services (excluding intermediate goods and services) produced by a nation's resources during some period of time, a businessperson's clothes or the gasoline used to drive to work should be excluded." (Final goods are normally not resold, whereas intermediate goods are sold.) True or false, and explain.
4. In measuring national income at factor cost, we deduct from net national product indirect taxes, such as sales taxes, but we do not deduct direct taxes, such as income taxes. Why do we treat these two types of taxes differently?
5. How would you measure yearly depreciation for a corporation? Would you measure yearly depreciation for the economy as a whole in the same manner? Briefly explain.
6. In what ways does the concept "measure of economic welfare" (*MEW*) differ from *GNP*?
7. Which of the following measures would probably be most important to a government engaged in a major war: *GNP*, *NNP*, or *NI*? Why?
8. Give at least three reasons why there might be no change or a decrease in *DPI* at the same time there was an increase in *GNP*.
9. Is a business saving, in the national income sense of the word, when it spends $10,000 for additional productive equipment? Explain.
10. In which of the following instances may an individual be saving? Explain.
    a. spending only part of income
    b. spending all income, but only partly on consumption goods and services
    c. spending all income on consumption goods

11. Although we can and should verify our conclusions statistically, common sense should tell us the general appearance of the consumption function, represented graphically. Explain.

12. What factors other than income may affect the level of consumption?

13. Which of the following would be most likely to cause an increase in the consumption function? Explain.
    a. rising prices
    b. rising income
    c. rising interest rates
    d. an increase in the saving function
    e. falling interest rates

14. If you have carefully fitted a freehand straight line of regression to a scatter diagram of consumption and income, you could immediately show the saving function on the same graph without preparing a scatter diagram of saving and income. Explain fully.

15. What connections can you suggest between national income and the functions of money? Can you see any possible relationships between the consumption function and money?

16. If it is true that $NI = C + S$, is it correct to say that national income is caused by consumption and saving? Explain.

Chapter 17   Investment and Income Determination

The spending of income received, we observed, simultaneously creates income. Wherever we break into the stream, it is still the same income. We began by studying what might be done with income received, and decided that either it would be consumed or it would not. Defining nonconsumed income as saving, we necessarily defined income as the sum of consumption and saving. This equation relates to the *disposition* of income.

INCOME CREATION

Now we want to look at income *creation*. Income is created by the production of goods and services. Refer to the diagram of income flow, Figure 16-1, if this point is not absolutely clear. When we are studying the national income, we may think of it as either the sum of the money incomes being received or the total flow of final goods being produced. The money income is what is received by the factors of production. The real income is what is produced. We measure it, to be sure, in terms of money, since we cannot add directly the goods and services themselves.

Investment—Additions to Capital

In the simplification of our income-flow diagram we assumed that all goods produced were consumed. Now, more realistically, we shall divide income into two parts.[1] One part is goods taken by purchasers for their personal use. We have already defined this part of income as consumption. We shall now define as *investment (I)* all other final goods produced plus (or minus) changes in business inventories. By this definition investment, if positive, as is ordinarily the case, necessarily involves an addition to our stock of goods, which we call *capital*.

This addition to capital may be in the form of additional plant facilities, machine tools, buildings, and the like. It also may be in the form of additions to inventories. Note this point! A manufacturer of men's shirts is producing,

---

[1]For the time being we shall ignore a third component, expenditures by government.

we may agree, a consumer good. However, if sales are slow and the manufacturer presently finds that inventory has increased by 10,000 shirts, for the time being these shirts represent investment, not consumption.[2]

Final goods include, in addition to consumer goods, such items as factory buildings, machinery, rolling stock, and other producer goods. Any additions to this equipment, after allowing for replacement of machinery worn out during the year, are part of the nation's net production during the period and have been the source of money income. (The value of replacements is already included in the value of the final products.) If, on the other hand, producers' equipment is less than it was at the beginning of the period, because the total of such goods produced was less than the amount worn out during the year, then this (major) component of net investment is negative.

Just as we count additions to producer durable goods as part of the national income, so also must we make an adjustment to include any changes in producers' inventories of goods and raw materials. If our shirt manufacturer has 10,000 less yards of cloth at the end of the year than at the beginning, we must subtract the value of this cloth from the current national income total. To include it would be to overstate the value of current production, for the cloth was produced in an earlier period. And if the manufacturer is holding more cloth than at the beginning of the period, we must add this inventory accumulation. This cloth is not a final product, true. However, in this case the cloth is not included in the value of the final product (shirts) turned out this year, for it was not made into shirts. Neither does it merely replace the cloth that was made up into shirts, for it is in addition to the replacement cloth. At the same time, the production of this cloth did result in money incomes, and the cloth itself is an addition to the total stock of goods held by society. In short, to arrive at the true total of money incomes created (and net production of goods and services) we must make an adjustment for changes in business inventories, adding any inventory increases, subtracting any decreases.

Before going any further, be sure you thoroughly understand this concept of investment. We are discussing *real investment*. This is something entirely different from investment in the financial sense. Everyone knows what you mean if you say you invested in real estate or made an investment in the stock market. You exchanged one asset (money) for some other asset. But these exchanges of assets are not investment in the sense in which we use the word in income analysis. In terms of national income, investment means additions to capital; in other words, goods currently produced but not sold to consumers for their personal use. Every dollar of investment of this kind creates a dollar of income. Or to put it the other way around, every dollar of income is represented by a dollar of spending for either consumption or investment. The total market value of what is produced is the national income; consumers take part of what is produced; the rest is left over: $NI = C + I$.

---

[2]If these shirts retail at $5, do the 10,000 shirts represent $50,000 of investment? Certainly not. In effect, the manufacturer has "bought" them for whatever was paid to make them—perhaps $30,000. If and when the shirts finally move into the hands of consumers, additional income of $20,000 will be created. This income will be shared by wholesalers, railroads and truck lines, retailers, and others who helped get the shirts to the consumers.

Realized Savings and Realized Investment

With our present definitions, the amount of saving actually accomplished, or realized, will necessarily equal the amount of realized investment.[3] Remember, we are using a timeless analysis, so the income being spent is identical to the income simultaneously being created. Both saving and investment are equal to the difference between national income and consumption. However, they are not at all the same thing, even if they are necessarily equal. Saving is the failure to consume income. It is passive and a leakage out of the income stream. It tends to cause prices to fall or to restrain their rise. Investment is expenditure other than for personal consumption. It is active and an injection into the income stream. It tends to cause prices to rise or to restrain their fall. When we are thinking about *what is done* with income, we write $NI = C + S$. When we are studying the *formation* of income, we write $NI = C + I$. Consumption and investment are the expenditures that *create* income.

PLANNED SAVING, INVESTMENT, AND INCOME DETERMINATION

Although realized saving and investment are necessarily equal, there is no reason whatever that planned saving and investment will be equal. Usually they will not be equal, for planned saving relates to the existing level of income. If income rises, the saving actually realized will be greater than the amount the public had planned to save. To put it another way, if the economy is at a high level of income, the public may plan to save $60 billion. But these plans cannot be fulfilled if, during the same period, investment is only $10 billion. In this instance the attempt to save will only force income down so that the saving actually realized at the lower income level will be less than was originally planned. Since the level of planned saving depends upon income, there would be little change in planned saving if income remained the same from one year to the next. If investment were equally stable, there would be little variation in the income level. In fact, however, investment is highly unstable, often changing greatly from one year to the next, depending on various nonincome factors, such as interest rates, the money supply, growth rates, innovation, expectations, etc. In 1929 we were adding more than $8 billion to our capital; three years later our capital stock was shrinking about $6 billion a year.[4] In 1948 we added $25 billion, in 1949 we added only $14 billion, and a year later we added $29 billion. After only $17 billion of investment in 1958, we had $32 billion in 1959. From $54.5 billion in 1966, net capital formation dropped 30 percent by the second quarter of 1967 to an

---

[3]Later in this chapter we shall add two terms to include the effects of taxes and government spending.

[4]Figures here refer to domestic net investment. Total expenditures by business for additions to inventories, plant, and equipment are listed as gross investment. Part of these purchases are not really additions, however, but are to replace worn out equipment. Since in our national income analysis we are interested only in the final goods and services, we do not add in separately the cost of goods consumed in the production process. Hence, we subtract from gross investment the estimated replacement of capital to find net investment.

annual rate of $38.7 billion. By 1975 annual investment outlays were over $90 billion. These changes in investment are, in fact, the principal cause of the changes in the level of national income, for income must rise (or fall) to drive planned saving up to (or down to) the constantly changing level of investment.

This is another of those places where we can easily avoid unnecessary confusion if we will just remember that our analysis runs in terms of national income, not the individual's income. An individual must, of course, save something out of income before he or she can invest that saving. But it does not work that way when we are thinking of saving and investment by society. True, without saving there cannot be investment. If a nation consumes all its income, it has nothing left to add to capital. But it is equally true that without investment there can be no saving. If a nation adds to its capital (invests), it is saving. If it increases its investment, its saving will increase as a necessary result. But if it is adding nothing to its capital, it is consuming all that it produces, saving nothing.

Equilibrium Level of Income

Income is said to be at an equilibrium level if there are no forces present to push it to a higher or lower level. By definition, realized saving and realized investment are always equal, whether or not income is at the equilibrium level. But only at the equilibrium level will planned saving and planned investment be equal. (Note, we can also say that only at the equilibrium level of income will planned saving equal realized saving. At any other income level, people will be planning to save either more or less than, in fact, they will actually save.) If at any income level planned saving and investment are not equal, that income level cannot be maintained. It will rise or fall until planned saving and investment are equal. Then there is no force operating to drive income further up or down. Income is then, therefore, at an equilibrium level, until investment changes again.

Income Changes Equate Planned Saving and Investment

The solid line *SS* in Figure 17-1 approximately represents the saving function discussed in Chapter 16. It tells us that, on the basis of past relationships between saving and income, we may expect saving to be about $10 billion less than 25 percent of income.[5] Its upward slope indicates that saving depends in a passive way upon income. By itself, it gives us no clue as to what the level of either income or saving will be.

However, this saving function and the amount of investment, between them, determine the level of income. Since realized saving must equal realized investment, a given amount of investment will force income to a level that will generate saving equal to the investment.

In Figure 17-1, we show investment measured, like saving, on the vertical axis. Since investment depends on nonincome factors, it is drawn horizontally

[5]We have modified the equation because $10 billion and 25 percent are more convenient to handle than $4.8 billion and 24 percent. These changes will not affect the logic of the analysis.

SAVING, INVESTMENT
(Billions of Dollars)

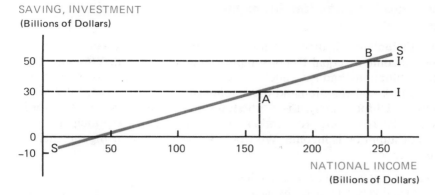

Figure 17-1 Investment, the Saving Function, and Income

and is therefore independent of income. If investment is $30 billion, as shown by the lower of the two dashed lines, investment equals saving only where they intersect, at point A. The equilibrium level of income must, therefore, be $160 billion; for only at an income level of $160 billion will saving be $30 billion according to the relation we have found between income and saving.

It should be unnecessary to add that we are using this equation as a matter of convenience. It describes fairly well the income-saving relationship for the few years we plotted, but we would not be justified in assuming that we would get exactly the same equation if we were to plot, for example, the figures for 1950–1980. Nor should we assume that it is impossible for the saving function to vary, even slightly.

Of the $160 billion, the public will save $10 billion less than one fourth of $160 billion, or $30 billion. Any other income level would be a disequilibrium level, for saving would not meet these two conditions:

1. $S = -\$10 \text{ billion} + .25 \, (NI)$;
2. $S = I = \$30 \text{ billion}$.

For similar reasons, if investment increases to $50 billion, income must rise to $240 billion. The $20 billion increase in investment requires an equal increase in saving. With the saving function that we are assuming, an $80 billion increase in income is required to generate the $20 billion increase in saving.

Why is the increase in income so much larger than the increase in investment or in saving? One possible way to explain it is to concentrate on the fact that the increase in saving must equal the increase in investment, in this instance $20 billion. Only if all additional income were saved could we expect that a $20 billion increase in saving could result from a $20 billion increase in income. But according to our saving function, we save only one fourth of any addition to income. If we are to save $20 billion more, we shall have to have $80 billion more income. This is the reason that income is not determined by investment alone, but by investment and the saving function.

The Consumption Function, Investment, and Income Determination

Now let's look at this theory of income determination from another angle. We defined income as equal to consumption plus investment. Why can't we forget about functions and say much more simply that income is determined by the amount of consumption and the amount of investment. We could make this statement. Unfortunately it is a little too simple. It explains nothing, for it involves circular reasoning. Remember, we decided that the principal determinant of consumption is income. We would arrive nowhere using the analytical framework:

1. Income is determined by consumption (and investment).
2. Consumption is determined by income.

Each determines the other.

However, we saw that the consumption *function* is *not* dependent on income. Whether income rises or falls, the consumption function tells us approximately how much income will be consumed. Can we say that the consumption function is a determinant of income? We saw in the last chapter that the saving function and the consumption function are necessarily related. If we know either one, we know the other, for the sum of the two functions must be 1.00 *(NI)*. This certainly implies that, if we can say income is determined by investment and the saving function, we ought to be able also to say income is determined by investment and the consumption function. Suppose we look into this.

When we were studying the saving function and investment as determinants of income, we defined the equilibrium level of income in terms of planned saving and planned investment. Now we shall redefine it, this time in terms of consumption and investment.

Income will be neither rising nor falling if current spending, as determined by the amount of investment and the consumption *function*, is equal to national income. Of course by definition national income is the sum of consumption and investment, whatever the income level. But if the level of income is to be maintained, it must be equal to that dictated by the consumption *function* and the amount of investment. Otherwise—given the amount of investment—consumption will increase (or decrease) until income does arrive at the equilibrium level. And if investment then changes, income must move to a new level of equilibrium.

Note particularly that the change in investment does not cause an instantaneous change in consumption. The initial change in income is equal only to the change in investment. However, this initial change in income calls forth a somewhat smaller change in consumption, which causes income to increase again, inducing another increase in consumption. Thus, an increase of $10 billion in investment leads to a whole series of increases in consumption and income, each smaller than the one before. The former level of consumption will no longer be maintained, for it is not in proper accord with the changed level of income as determined by the consumption function. This is why income will be at a disequilibrium level until the total of consumption plus investment, or national income, is equal to the amount of investment plus the amount of consumption *normal* with respect to that income—that is, until national income equals investment plus consumption as determined by the consumption function.

In Figure 17-2 the consumption function is drawn to show that, at all levels of income, consumption is $10 billion more than three fourths of income.[6] This is the solid line marked *CC*.

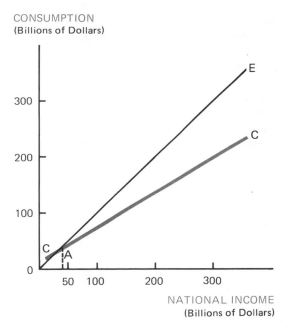

CONSUMPTION
(Billions of Dollars)

NATIONAL INCOME
(Billions of Dollars)

Figure 17-2   Consumption Function

For convenience we draw the guideline *OE* from the origin and with a slope of 1.0. This is not a consumption function; it is merely a visual aid. At any point on *OE* the values of consumption and income will be equal.

Since our consumption function has a slope of only .75, it rises less steeply than does the guideline *OE*. Also, when we worked out the equation for the consumption function we found that it did not start at zero, but at a point about $10 billion above zero. So, starting at a higher level than the guideline but rising less steeply, the consumption function crosses the guideline at point *A*. This intersection shows that at this income level, and only at this income level, consumption is exactly equal to income.

---

[6]As it must be, if saving is $10 billion less than one fourth of income.

To the left of A, where income is less than $40 billion, consumption ex-
ceeds income, as shown by the fact that the consumption function lies above
the guideline. At these very low levels of income, society is not only unable to
save, it has to consume part of what it has saved in the past. The amount of
dissaving at any income level is measured by the distance between CC and
OE when CC lies above OE.

When income exceeds $40 billion, society is consuming only part of its
income. The amount saved at any income level is represented by the distance
between CC and OE when CC lies below OE.

Do you see, then, that between them, the consumption function and the
amount of investment may also be said to determine the income level? In
Figure 17-3 we draw the guideline and the consumption function as before,
but this time we add on the investment spending. Suppose there is going to be
$30 billion of investment. We do not yet know what the income level will be,
but we do know that at the equilibrium income level the total of consumption
plus investment spending will be $30 billion more than consumption spending
alone will be. So we draw a second line, $C + I$, parallel to CC but $30 billion
above it. $C + I$ intersects the guideline at point B, where the total of consumption plus investment equals national income, which equals $160 billion.

With income defined as consumption plus investment, there is only one
possible equilibrium income level consistent with a particular investment level
and a particular consumption function. In the example above, income could
not be more than $160 billion, for then total consumption and investment

CONSUMPTION, INVESTMENT
(Billions of Dollars)

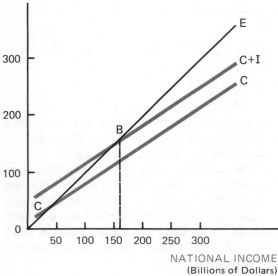

NATIONAL INCOME
(Billions of Dollars)

Figure 17-3   Investment, Consumption Function,
and Income

would be less than income. Nor could income be less than $160 billion, for total consumption plus $30 billion of investment spending would then be greater than income. Only at an income level of $160 billion can consumption (assumed to be $10 billion more than three fourths of income) be $130 billion and investment be $30 billion. If investment were $50 billion instead of $30 billion, $C + I$ would be shifted up by $20 billion, intersecting guideline OE at an income level of $240 billion. At this higher income level, consumption would be $190 billion.

Incidentally, since in Figures 17-2 and 17-3 saving is indicated by the distance between CC and OE, only at point B is saving equal to investment when investment is $30 billion. This illustrates a little differently the point brought out in Figure 17-1 that at the equilibrium income level planned saving must be equal to planned investment.

Shifts in the Consumption Function

The consumption function is a stable relationship. We saw in Figure 16-4 that all the consumption-income combinations lay close to the line that we computed to state their general relationship.[7]

We should not overlook the possibility that income might change as a result of a change in the consumption function—without a change in investment. A relationship may be stable without necessarily being absolutely constant. The public may become more confident than before. Or people may spend more at all income levels because they anticipate inflation. Or they may spend less, fearing depression. It is possible that if, because banks have increased their loans and investments, the public is holding more money than before, the consumption function will be increased. We should expect that controls over consumer credit, as during World War II, will temporarily lower the consumption function, and their removal tend to increase it. In any event, a relatively small change in the consumption function will cause a surprisingly large change in income.

The consumption function might change in either of two ways, or in both. One possibility would be that the new function would be parallel to the old but a little higher or lower. Suppose that, with investment still at $30 billion, the consumption function should change to $C = \$12$ billion $+ .75 \, (NI)$. The equilibrium income level would now be $168 instead of $160 billion. The other possibility would be that the slope of the consumption function would change. It may seem as though it would make very little difference whether the slope were .75 or .76. Yet if the consumption function were $C = \$10$ billion $+ .76 \, (NI)$, then with investment of $30 billion income would be almost $167 billion.

Although changes in the consumption function will cause changes in the income level, we generally concentrate on the effects of changes in investment rather than shifts of the consumption function. The reason for emphasizing the role of investment is that the amount of investment is volatile and

---

[7]Since a shift in the consumption function necessarily means also a shift in the saving function, you should be able to adapt these paragraphs easily to show how income would be changed by a shift in the saving function.

varies widely from one year to the next; also, it can be measured fairly well. It is not so simple to show that there has been a short-run shift of the consumption function, even if the relation between consumption and income varies a little from year to year.

Consumption Function v. Saving Function

Why should we talk about both the consumption function and the saving function if either of them, along with investment, may equally well be said to determine income? In the first place, by looking at both functions we will probably more easily understand the relationships with which we are concerned. Why will a certain income level result from a given amount of investment, whether we relate the investment to the consumption function or to the corresponding saving function? Only because $C + S = NI$. If we know how much of a given income is consumed, we automatically know how much is saved and vice versa.

Secondly, the logic of the analysis is clearer to some in terms of the consumption function, to others in terms of the saving function. Consumption is active, saving passive. Consumption creates income, saving does not. In this respect it seems more natural to think of income as the result of total expenditures for consumption and investment, and we use the consumption function rather than the saving function.

On the other hand, use of investment and the saving function has its own advantage. It emphasizes that, by changes in income, saving is kept equal to investment. The adjustment is in just the opposite direction to what is frequently assumed. Investment is often popularly supposed to adjust to saving. "The more is saved, the more investment there will be." Figure 17-1 shows that things work quite differently. The amount of saving is determined primarily by income. Investment may be at any level and is determined primarily by nonincome factors.[8] But whatever the investment level, saving will adjust to it. Hence, the higher is investment, the higher will be saving—and necessarily also the higher will be income. If investment exceeds planned saving, income will increase.

With higher incomes, people decide to save more. When income has increased enough, the amount people are planning to save will be equal to investment (and to realized saving). Income is then at an equilibrium level. It will neither rise nor fall unless there is a change either in the percentage of income saved at all income levels or in the amount of investment. (Refer again to Figure 17-1 to see that income must increase if investment increases, or if SS moves to the right, indicating less will be saved at all income levels.

The saving function (and consumption function) may change so that, of a given income, more or less will be saved than before (and correspondingly less or more consumed). More often, however, there is a change in the

---

[8]To be sure, some texts recognize that investment may in part be a function of income, thereby making the investment function, such as in Figure 17-1, slightly upsloping and not horizontal. However, this change would not affect the general tenor of the analysis presented here.

amount of investment. These changes in investment are ordinarily the most important causes of changes in national income.

CHANGES IN NONCONSUMPTION SPENDING

It will be easier to study the reasons for changes in nonconsumption spending if we subdivide this category into two parts. The most important breakdown is into public and private spending. The public component refers to all government payments for goods and services. To keep the main outline of the analysis as simple as possible, these public expenditures have to this point been ignored. Hereafter we shall consider government expenditures, designating them as G. Investment will refer only to nonconsumption expenditures by the private sector of the economy. With this terminology, $NI = C + I + G$.[9]

Government Expenditures—G

Forty-five years ago government expenditures for goods and services were relatively unimportant. State and local governments were spending $6 or $7 billion a year, but the federal government spent only $2 billion for goods and services in 1933 and that was the highest peacetime level ever reached to that point.[10] With the federal government today spending over $2 billion a week for goods and services, and state and local governments spending over one and one half times as much again, the total value of goods and services purchased by government today is more than triple the total national income of $87 billion in 1929 and almost eight times as high as the national income of $40 billion in 1933, as can be seen from Figure 17-4.[11]

To be sure, a billion dollars today buys less than in 1933. The government spends more because the value of money is less, but money buys less partly because these government expenditures, added to the public's consumption and investment expenditures, swell money incomes and, when the economy is operating at or near full employment, tend to force prices up. A relative comparison is more significant. Government expenditures comprised about 10 percent of national income in 1929, about 20 percent in 1933 (when consumption and private investment were very low), and 25–30 percent today. Government purchases made up about one third of total nonconsumption expenditure in 1929 but today run from two thirds to more than three fourths of the total. In

---

[9]Some writers prefer to distinguish further. If we like, we may show separately private domestic investment and private foreign investment by writing $NI = C + I + G + F$. We shall not make that distinction on the practical ground that foreign investment is seldom as much as 1 percent of national income.

[10]Total payments by the federal government were $3.9 billion, but approximately half of these were transfer payments, including veteran expenditures and interest on the federal debt. Since such payments do not create income but only transfer it, they are not included with the payments for goods and services.

[11]It took the federal government from 1789 to 1956 to spend its first trillion dollars. Now it takes only 9 or 10 years.

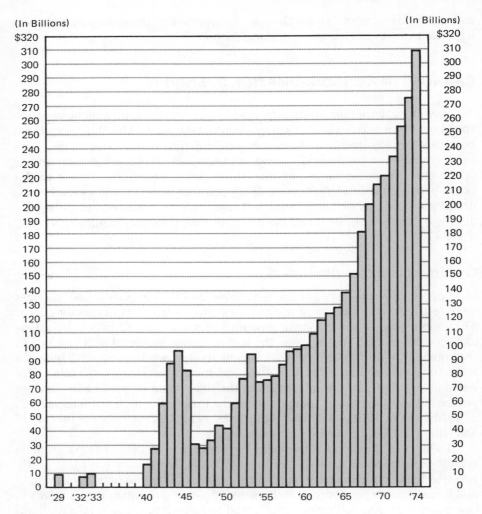

Source: *Federal Reserve Bulletins.*

Figure 17-4   Government Expenditures for Goods and Services
1929, 1932-1933, and 1940-1974

this day of big business, government is by far the biggest business. Its purchases between 1951 and 1975 dwarfed total net investment during the same period.

Changes in Government Expenditures

Government expenditures increase enormously in wartime. At other times there is no inherent instability in this component of national income.

For a number of reasons there tends to be a persistently increasing total of government purchases of goods and services over the years:

1. Inflation is partly responsible. As the value of money declines, the government must spend more to buy the same amount of goods and services as before. The dollar bought less in the 1920s than it did before World War I, and it buys much less today than it bought in the 1920s.

2. Increasing urbanization requires the expansion of government services. More money must be spent for police and fire protection, sanitation requirements, traffic control, and the like.

3. More government services are also required as a part of our rising standard of living. We can afford and we demand better roads, more educational facilities, more swimming pools and parks, more adequate inspection of foods and drugs, and many other facilities not supplied 50 years ago. Roads alone have accounted for billions of dollars of government expenditures in recent years. It is difficult to realize that only 40 years ago at least 90 percent of the main highways outside city limits were two-lane gravel roads.

4. It is notably difficult to turn off a faucet of government expenditure once it has been turned on. Even if there is little justification for continuing a particular governmental function, the only people who are likely to be much concerned are those who are working in that particular governmental bureau.

5. In recent years national defense has assumed a new and critical importance. New weapons have destroyed for all time the comfortable safety once provided by our location. At the same time weapons and counter-weapons have become tremendously more complex and staggeringly expensive. Worse yet, the rate of technological progress seems to make them obsolete almost as soon as they are in production and sometimes before.

Government expenditures, however, do not ordinarily contribute to the ups and downs of the business cycle. Governments are not operated to make a profit. They do not have to reduce their spending because the business outlook is dark. To be sure, government receipts will fall in recession or depression. Tax receipts will decline, even if tax rates are unchanged. But the government at such a time can still borrow, as consumers and private industry usually cannot or should not. The amount the government should spend in any year is determined by the needs of the economy, not by the possibility of profit. Today it is generally agreed that in a recession the government should spend more rather than less, and that it should reduce its expenditures in prosperity when consumption and investment are at high levels. This is, in fact, one of the important discoveries we have made with the help of income analysis. An effective policy of counter-cyclical government expenditures is a powerful tool for maintaining a continuously high employment level in the economy.

Investment

Investment involves additions to our accumulated stock of goods (capital). Sometimes you see the term *capital formation*, which means the same thing. It is only common sense to say that any goods that are produced *(NI)* and neither consumed by the public *(C)* nor taken by the government *(G)* are "left over" *(I)*, so they add to our stock of goods. These additions may be to plant and equipment or to inventories. Investment is by far the most unstable component of income.

Especially notable in Figure 17-5 are the several negative entries. These represent net capital losses. Not only were no additions being made to our total of plant, equipment, and inventories in the mid-1930s and from 1943 to 1945, but industry was not even replacing some of the capital consumed. During the Depression there was little incentive for business to expand. Rather, with much plant and equipment standing idle, businesses postponed replacing worn-out but temporarily unneeded plant and equipment.

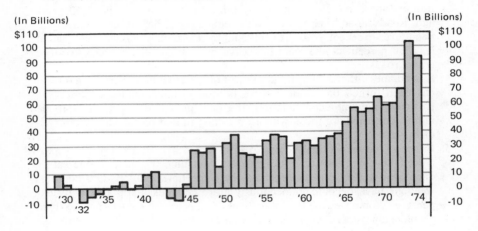

Source: *Federal Reserve Bulletins.*

Figure 17-5   Net Investment, Foreign and Domestic, 1929-1974

World War II and Investment

The decline in investment during World War II was a special case. Investment was held down during that period, as was consumption, so that the share of national income taken by the government could be larger. When we are at full employment, as we were then, we are producing all we possibly can. There is only so much national income that can be created. Since $NI = C + I + G$, the less there is of C and I, the more there is for G.

Also, the investment figures for the war years were reduced as a result of our unfavorable trade balances. This point requires a little clarification. Goods that we export are all classified as investment, regardless of whether they are producers' equipment or consumer goods.[12] The point is that in producing these goods we create income in this country (wages, rents, interest, and profits), but the goods do not show up as consumption for this country. For example, the wheat we export is consumed abroad. Since there is no domestic consumption expenditure on this wheat to be included in our national income,

---

[12]For another definition of foreign investment, see Chapter 26.

we classify the exported wheat as investment. The money spent to produce the wheat was, for this country, nonconsumption spending, exactly like the money spent to build a steel mill.

The significant figure, of course, is exports minus imports. Our imports count as investment for foreign countries but as disinvestment for us.

During World War II we needed all our production for ourselves and our allies. We could not spare the resources to produce much to sell to other countries. At the same time we were buying whatever we could from them to increase our total stock of supplies at a time when we desperately needed everything we could get. Thus, our unfavorable private trade balance of from $1.4 to $2.2 billion from 1943 to 1945 was investment for other countries. For us it appeared as a negative item, reducing our total investment by those amounts.

DETERMINANTS OF INVESTMENT—MARGINAL EFFICIENCY OF CAPITAL AND INTEREST RATES

The most important factor determining the amount of investment is the marginal efficiency of capital *(MEC)*.[13] By the *marginal efficiency of capital* we mean the rate that, when used to discount the future earnings expected from a capital asset, will make the sum of their present values equal to the supply price of the asset.

Supply Price and Market Price Distinguished

Note that the marginal efficiency of capital refers, not to the market price, but to the *supply price*, by which we mean the price at which the producer of the asset is willing to continue producing it. The current market price of an asset might be $1,000, but to induce the manufacturer to produce another unit, possibly $2,000 or more might be required. For example, the supply price of a particular lathe might be $15,000. At the same time the same lathe might be available for $10,000 or less from someone who had ordered it and did not want it after all. Or if pressed for cash, the manufacturer may temporarily sell at a loss equipment already produced. If the purchaser is simply buying a surplus lathe, whether from the manufacturer or from someone else, there is an exchange of assets—cash and the lathe—but there is no economic investment. The investment occurs when a new lathe is made, constituting an addition to the total stock of goods and in the process creating income for the factors of production. This is the investment process with which we are concerned, and the supply price that it involves is the price that is related to the marginal efficiency of capital.

---

[13]Some writers prefer to distinguish further between the stock concept *MEC* and the flow concept marginal efficiency of investment *(MEI)*. Although we do not do so here, the interested reader may consult Gardner Ackley, *Macroeconomic Theory* (New York: Macmillan Co., 1961), Chapter 17, especially pp. 481–485. The factors influencing investment are also summarized in Robert Eisner and Robert Strotz, "Determinants of Business Investment," Commission on Money and Credit, *Impacts of Monetary Policy* (Englewood Cliffs: Prentice-Hall, 1963), pp. 60–337.

Future Incomes Discounted

There are always potential investments promising some return over and above the price at which the property will be currently produced. Suppose we are considering the purchase of a machine that will be worn out in a year with no scrap value. Suppose also that the manufacturer will produce and sell us this machine for $1,000. If we believe that the use of this machine will net us an additional $1,200 of profit by the end of the year, we equate the $1,000 cost with the future $1,200 by the formula $1,000 = $\frac{\$1,200}{1+r}$. In this instance $r = 20$ percent.

Suppose we expected an additional $1,200 of profit, but in two sums of $600, one at the end of one year, one at the end of the second year. Total cost of the machine is the same ($1,000), total eventual profit is the same—but we must wait longer for it. We are discounting part of the expected profit for a longer period of time. In this case we set $1,000 = $\frac{\$600}{1+r} + \frac{\$600}{(1+r)^2}$. The discount rate would now be approximately 13 percent.[14]

Ordinarily the arithmetic of the problem is not so simple. Machines usually last more than a year or two, and buildings last a long time. The principle is the same. Over its lifetime of 10, 20, or more years the asset is expected to bring in something each year over and above all operation costs including depreciation of the asset itself. Otherwise there is no reason for buying it. Perhaps an eventual total of $5,000 of such incomes is anticipated. The present value of this series of incomes is less than $5,000. We are not willing to give up a dollar today for the return of a dollar sometime in the future. We discount future incomes. Also, to repeat, the discount rate that equates the sum of the future expected returns with the present supply price of the asset is the marginal efficiency of capital.

Various rates will be in effect simultaneously. In some industries an expansion of capital may promise an annual return of 10 percent of the cost. In others, returns of 12 percent or more may appear probable.

The earning power of existing capital is irrelevant. It is entirely a question of what can be expected from new, additional capital, which is what we mean by investment. This marginal efficiency of capital may have very little relation to the overall earning power of existing capital. Existing capital may have been created when prices were low and may be yielding much higher returns than could be expected on current investment. Or it may represent equipment that is obsolete, with a lower efficiency than that obtainable from investment in modern capital assets. In any case the purchase of existing capital is not investment. No real income is created when you buy a piece of used machinery or a factory already in operation. Investment is defined as part of current production and, therefore, as a part of current income.

---

[14]The general formula is $C = \frac{y_1}{1+r} + \frac{y_2}{(1+r)^2} + \frac{y_3}{(1+r)^3} + \ldots + \frac{y_n}{(1+r)^n}$, where C is the asset's cost, $y_1, y_2, y_3, \ldots, y_n$ is the asset's gross dollar yield at the end of 1, 2, 3, $\ldots$, n years, and r is the discount rate which will reduce the sum of the series of expected dollar yields from the use of the asset to equal the cost of the asset; i.e., r is the MEC.

Expectations and Marginal Efficiency of Capital

It is never possible to know in advance the total future income that a capital asset will produce. There are too many uncertain factors. In the case of some types of capital, machinery in particular, we may be able to make a fairly good estimate of the amount of physical product that it will turn out in a year. Similarly, we know that an apartment house will provide each year a year's shelter for a certain number of families. But we want to know the dollar profit, not the quantity of goods or services provided. To arrive at the profits figure, we must make various estimates. We cannot possibly work out answers that we know are correct. We have to guess the best we can.

To know eventual profits we must know future costs and future receipts. The future costs are in doubt. There will be expenses to provide supplementary factors of production or goods and services required, for we cannot expect a capital asset to produce in a vacuum. Labor will probably be required, and perhaps fuel or raw materials, selling expenses, and various other requirements. There also will be depreciation of the equipment itself. The fact that we may arbitrarily decide to write off its full cost over a 10- or 20-year period does not guarantee that it will not be obsolete before that time and have to be replaced. Nor does it guarantee that we shall discard it at the end of 10 or 20 years.

Future receipts are even more a matter of guess work. Even if we were able to decide how much physical product could be turned out and also, somehow, to know what our total costs would be, we still could not know what our net receipts would be. If we are selling in a highly competitive market, we may have to take the price as established by general market forces. We have no way of knowing what that price will be in 10 or 20 years. If we are selling a highly differentiated product, we may be able to set our own price; but we still will not know in advance what the most profitable price will be or in fact whether, over the years, we can sell at any profitable price.

Instability of Marginal Efficiency of Capital

Because the marginal efficiency of capital is based on expectations, which may be suddenly and drastically revised, it is far from stable. When business is good, businesses are optimistic. Their markets have been expanding, their profits have been rising, and their estimates of the future are rosy. A few months of business recession and the optimism evaporates. Fundamentally there may have been little actual change, but all the future prospects are now viewed through dark glasses. Plans for expansion are shelved. Also, of course, as investment falls, national income falls, and the outlook becomes still more gloomy. Changes in public psychology thus tend to intensify changes in investment. But they are not the only cause of variation in the marginal efficiency of capital.

A factor of great importance to the marginal efficiency of capital is the development of new industries and improved productive techniques. In a stationary state the marginal efficiency of capital might fall close to zero. The more capital that was acquired, the less profitable would each additional application of capital become. More capital would just increase the production of the same goods being sold to the same market as before. But if something new is invented, like the railroad or the automobile, the marginal efficiency of capital may temporarily rise very high until enough capital has been attracted to the new industry to expand it to the desired volume of output.

Any sudden market expansion would have the same stimulating effect. A change in tariffs or a new colonial policy might open up great markets to the nation's producers. Likewise, an increase in the rate of population growth would increase demand, although for many types of goods there might be a lag of 10 or 20 years. (An increase in the birth rate will not immediately increase the sale of bicycles, cars, and houses.) Sometimes the market may increase as a result of changes in customs; cigarette sales were relatively small in the United States prior to World War I, when any person who smoked them was regarded with a little suspicion. As their sales mounted steeply during and after the war and again climbed a decade later as it became fashionable for women to smoke, it was for a while highly profitable to build more tobacco warehouses and cigarette factories.[15]

Marginal Efficiency of Capital and the Interest Rate

Ordinarily investment will be continued to the point that the marginal efficiency of capital is equal to the interest rate. Entrepreneurs will purchase more equipment if its expected rate of return is more than, or at least equal to, the interest they must pay on borrowed money or forgo on their own funds. They will certainly not borrow at 10 percent for an expected return of 6 or 8 percent.

If the interest rate were zero, funds would be available for all projects that promised any net return over cost. However, investors must compete for funds. Only so much investment will be made. Interest serves, like any other price, as a guide to production and to the allocation of productive resources. The more profitable investments are undertaken, the less promising are not, just as a piece of land or a day's labor will tend to be allocated to that area of production where its marginal productivity is greatest.

Schedule of Marginal Efficiency of Capital

We can show the marginal efficiency of capital in the form of a demand schedule.[16] The lower the interest rate (price of money), the more funds will be demanded for investment. If at a particular time the marginal efficiency of capital is shown, as in Figure 17-6, by a linear *MEC* and the interest rate is *i*, investment will be *OM*. If the interest rate falls to *i'*, investment will increase to *OM'*.

---

[15]See the discussion of the accelerator, Chapter 18, where the relation between investment and an increase in consumption is discussed in greater detail.

[16]As discussed in the Introduction, a demand schedule shows the amounts of a good that will be demanded at various prices. The lower the price, the more will be demanded. The entire schedule is called the demand. An increase in demand is shown, not by a movement along the curve, but by a movement of the curve itself.

Relative Importance of Changes in Marginal Efficiency of Capital and Interest Rates

Although with a given schedule of the marginal efficiency of capital a decline in interest rates should lead to more investment, changes in interest rates probably have less effect on the amount of investment than do changes in the marginal efficiency of capital, that is, shifts in the *MEC* schedule. As we have seen, the marginal efficiency of capital is based on uncertain estimates. Businesses can do little more than make an intelligent guess as to their future income from a possible expansion of their capital. It seems improbable that most businesses would borrow at 9 percent for expansion but would not borrow at 10 percent, other things remaining equal. More likely, they would expand when they feel there is a good chance of making 15, 20, or 30 percent, and the interest rate they pay would be of little importance to their decisions.[17] If the marginal efficiency of capital in the project under consideration is no more than 10 or 11 percent, businesspeople would be in no hurry to authorize the expansion. The chance of gain is too slight to outweigh the risk of loss.

A number of surveys have been made to see what businesspeople themselves have to say on this point. In general the evidence supports the reasoning above. They replied that they paid little or no attention to interest rates when making their investment decisions.

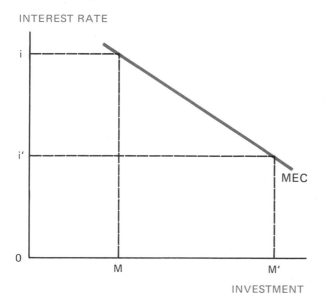

Figure 17-6   Linear Marginal Efficiency
             of Capital Schedule

---

[17] For corporations, paying 48 percent tax on net profits above $25,000, the interest rate is of still less importance. Since interest is a cost, deductible in computing profits, the effective rate paid by corporations is approximately half the nominal rate. If higher interest rates force them to pay 12 percent rather than 8 percent, their effective rate has been raised from 4 to 6 percent.

Exceptions

There are certainly some fields in which interest rates may be important. Low interest rates ordinarily stimulate residential construction. Also, interest rates are an important consideration in the spending plans of public utilities and railroads. Since their charge for services is regulated, these concerns cannot expect very high rates of return per dollar of investment. With good management and luck they may clear around 8 percent. Interest rates would certainly be relevant to expansion programs in this area. These are the most important exceptions. In general, the interest rate appears to be a minor consideration in private investment decisions.

Investment, Interest Rates, and Marginal Efficiency of Capital—Summary

All this is summarized in Figure 17-7. We draw *MEC* and *MEC'* to represent nonlinear *MEC* schedules that are highly inelastic within the range of ordinary variations in interest rates, around 6 to 10 percent.[18] A 50 percent

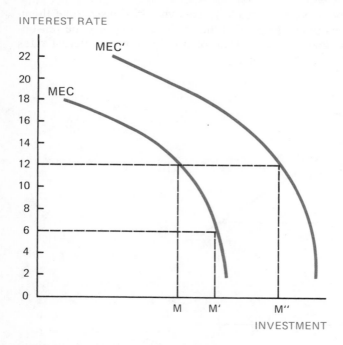

Figure 17-7   Nonlinear Marginal Efficiency
of Capital Schedules

[18]As discussed in the Introduction, any demand curve is said to be inelastic at a certain price if at a slightly lower price the increase in the quantity demanded is less than proportionate to the decrease in price. The demand for eggs is inelastic at $.50 a dozen if the quantity demanded increases by less than 10 percent when the price falls to $.45. For evidence on the interest-elasticity of *MEC* see William H. White, "The Changing Criteria in Investment Planning," *Macroeconomics: Selected Readings*, edited by Walter L. Johnson and David R. Kamerschen (Boston: Houghton Mifflin Co., 1970), pp. 95–115.

decrease in the interest rate, from 12 percent to 6 percent, will cause invest-ment to increase by only *MM'*. On the other hand, an increase in the marginal efficiency of capital to *MEC'* with the interest rate remaining at 12 percent would cause investment to increase by *MM''*. Such a shift in the schedule of the marginal efficiency of capital might result from any of the causes dis-cussed earlier. It might be caused merely by a more optimistic outlook. What-ever the cause, additional investment would result.

It should be obvious that Figure 17-7 is drawn only to illustrate our as-sumptions, not to prove them. We could just as easily draw the *MEC* sched-ule as highly elastic around 10 percent, perhaps rising to no higher than 12 percent or 14 percent at its highest point. We could also show only a single *MEC* schedule, implying that changes in the marginal efficiency of capital were unlikely. But from what has already been said it should be clear why we choose to represent the marginal efficiency of capital schedule as inelastic in the range of lower interest rates and why we expect that changes in the mar-ginal efficiency of capital (shifts of the curve) will probably be important.

Between them, the level of interest rates and the marginal efficiency of capital determine the amount of investment. Of the two determinants, the changing marginal efficiency of capital is probably the more effective in caus-ing volume of investment to change.

NONCONSUMED INCOME—*C + S + T*

In the last chapter, ignoring taxes, we defined all income that was not consumed as "saved" and wrote $NI = C + S$. For the same reasons that we broke down nonconsumption spending into the two components, *I* and *G*, we shall now separate nonconsumed income into private savings *(S)* and the dis-posable income of the government *(T)*. Hereafter, when we refer to income disposition, $NI = C + S + T$.

Private Saving—*S*

The greater part of net private saving is in the form of personal saving.[19] The rest is represented by undistributed corporate profits and, to a lesser extent, by entries of an accounting nature with which we are not concerned. The effect of *S* upon income will be seen to be the same as the effect of *T*. Income is decreased by an increase in either, for remember we are now look-ing at what is done with income already created. An increase in the portion of a given income that is not consumed *(S + T)* requires a decrease in the part that is consumed *(C)*. Since consumption is the only one of these three com-ponents that also creates income, the result must then be a fall in income. Both *S* and *T* refer to income received but not consumed. (In the case of *S*, however, the nonconsumption is more likely to be voluntary.)

---

[19]Gross saving includes, also, business depreciation charges, just as gross investment in-cludes the cost of replacing worn out equipment. Since it is net saving (and investment), not gross, that is a component of (net) national income, we shall not include depreciation allowances.

Government's Disposable Income—*T*

The letter "*T*" suggests a reference to taxes. *T* does, in a general way, relate to taxes, and we sometimes loosely identify it with taxes. But specifically, *T* is not the total tax receipts of government. It is the government's *disposable income*, which is the surplus of its taxes (and miscellaneous receipts from fees and fines) over and above transfer payments. The federal government is paying billions of dollars for interest on the national debt and billions more to veterans and for Social Security benefits. These amounts must be subtracted from its total receipts to find its disposable income *(T)*, which is the amount of its current revenue that it is free to spend on goods and services. It amounts to the same thing as counting as a reduction from our personal income only that part of taxes that is not going to be handed back to us automatically as a transfer payment, with no sacrifice on our part. There is no reduction in private consumption required by the fact that the government collects $30 billion in taxes from us and hands it back to us as interest on the bonds we hold. We have just as much income as we had before. There is, therefore, no need for consumption to be reduced.

It is quite different with tax receipts over and above what may be required for transfer payments. Perhaps these funds reappear as income, perhaps they do not. If this money returns to us as income, it is only because the government pays it out for goods and services *(G)*. If, instead, the government simply holds part of its disposable income as an unspent balance, national income will be reduced by that amount. Similarly, if the government uses some of its income to retire some of its debt, this operation in itself will also reduce income. The second policy is less deflationary than the first, however, due to the likelihood that some of the bondholders will decide to spend part of what they are paid by the government, resulting in the return of this money to the income stream.

Taxes, like savings, are leakages out of the income stream. The funds that the government removes from the income stream as taxes may or may not reenter the stream as transfer payments or as payments for goods and services, but the tax itself does not create or transfer income any more than saving does. It is a leakage only.

The government's disposable income *(T)* depends primarily on the tax rates set by the government. It will also be affected in several ways by the national income. At a high level of national income, a given tax rate structure will yield more revenue than the same rates will produce in recession or depression. Also, the amount of transfer payments to be deducted from receipts to give the government's disposable income will be affected by the level of the national income. In prosperity interest rates may rise and the government will have to pay more interest when it borrows to refund maturing bonds. In recession it may be paying more in other transfer payments. When we bring in the effect of government transactions, equilibrium is attained when $C + I + G = C + S + T$ or $I + G = S + T$, where I and S refer to planned investment and planned saving, respectively.

SUMMARY AND CONCLUSION

The payments stream which makes up the total money incomes from current production and simultaneously constitutes the total expenditures for currently produced goods and services is a helpful approach to understanding the role of modern money. Chapters 16 and 17 have been devoted to an outline of the income analysis framework and an explanation of terms used. The usefulness of these terms in practical policy will appear in the following chapter, together with some supplementary concepts useful in the study of income changes.

Before going further, you should be sure that you understand the logic of the argument to this point. If there is any confusion concerning the points listed below, it will be difficult to follow the later analysis.

1. A nation's real income is the total flow of final goods and services that it produced during the year. Raw materials consumed, equipment worn out, and other intermediate goods and services are not counted separately, for they are embodied in the final products.
2. The total of this real income is expressed in dollars. This is the national income *(NI)*, the value of all final goods and services produced during the year.
3. *NI* is equal also to the total incomes received by all factors of production. What appears to one as a cost appears to another as a receipt of income.
4. $NI = C + S + T$. We consume part of our income, save part of it, and pay the rest to the tax collector.
5. $NI = C + I + G$. The national income is created by expenditures for personal consumption, the goods and services taken by the government, and for "other" goods. The latter *(I)* adds to our stock of goods, that is, increases our capital.
6. *C* depends primarily upon the level of *NI* and is a fairly stable relationship. We call this relationship between *C* and *NI* the consumption function. (The same relationship is also called the propensity to consume.)
7. *S* also depends primarily upon the level of *NI* and is a fairly stable relationship. We call this relationship between *S* and *NI* the saving function (or the propensity to save).[20]
8. *G* depends upon government's decisions.
9. *T* depends partly upon government's decisions and partly upon *NI*.
10. *I* depends upon the marginal efficiency of capital and to some extent upon the level of interest rates.
11. The marginal efficiency of capital is highly unstable. It depends upon the relation between the supply price of assets and their expected eventual net income, which in turn depends on various factors.
12. The consumption function and investment determine national income.[21]

---

[20]As used earlier in this chapter, the saving function referred to the relation between total nonconsumed income and national income. Either formulation is correct, but naturally their equations will not be identical. It is a little more precise to define savings *(S)* as $(NI - T) - C$ rather than as $NI - C$.

[21]This applies when we ignore taxes and government expenditures, or, alternatively, when we include them as a part of saving and investment respectively, both defined broadly to include all nonconsumed income. This comment applies also to points 13 through 16.

13. National income may alternatively be said to be determined by the saving function and investment.
14. Realized saving will always equal realized investment.
15. When planned saving equals planned investment, national income is at an equilibrium level.
16. When planned saving is not equal to planned investment, national income will rise (fall), causing realized saving to be greater (less) than planned saving. The rise (fall) in income will also cause planned saving to rise (fall) until it equals investment.
17. When we consider the effect of government transactions, national income is at an equilibrium level when $C + S + T = C + I + G$ or $S + T = I + G$, where $S(I)$ refers to planned saving (investment).

Discussion Questions

1. What is meant by "investment" as the term is used in income analysis? Although we may tend to think of investment as being the result of careful planning, businesses often find that they have been investing when they neither planned nor wished to do so. Explain.
2. Broadly defined to include the government's disposable income and government expenditures for goods and services, saving and investment are necessarily separate but necessarily equal. Explain.
3. Where there are no government transactions, will planned saving equal planned investment? Will realized saving equal realized investment? Explain.
4. How might a change in investment cause realized saving to be less than planned saving? How might realized saving and planned saving finally be equated?
5. If the income level is determined solely by the consumption function and the amount of investment, must we concede that a change in monetary policy cannot possibly change the income level? Explain.
6. Do you think consumption is more related to temporary (or transient) income or to long-run permanent income (i.e., wealth)?
7. Why might disinvestment in some areas be necessary during a period of full employment when there is a great demand for goods and services on the part of consumers, government, and business in general?
8. "The higher the expected earning power of new investment, the more investment there should be. The marginal efficiency of capital, therefore, should be shown as a rising, not a falling, line." Critically evaluate.
9. Briefly explain why you would or would not expect the following to affect the marginal efficiency of capital:
   a. An increase in the quantity of capital
   b. A drop in interest rates
   c. A reduction in taxes, with government spending unchanged
   d. An increase in government spending, with taxes unchanged
   e. Development of an inexpensive, practical steam engine for automobiles
10. Investment is more a function of nonincome factors and is more volatile than is consumption. Explain.
11. The letter T in national income analysis refers to the total tax receipts of the government. True or false and explain.
12. In what sense are all economists Keynesians? In what sense are they not?

Chapter 18   The Process and Mechanics of Inflation and Deflation

In the last two chapters we defined our terms and outlined the framework of income analysis. Now with the help of this useful analytical apparatus, we can begin to come to grips with the vital questions concerned with money. Why have short-term interest rates recently been 20 times as high as they were 30 years ago? Why is it that during some periods, as since 1940, nearly all prices rise? Why did prices fall in the early 1930s? Even more important, why is unemployment so high some years? What can monetary and fiscal policies do to achieve full employment and a substantial growth rate for the economy? Can we have, at the same time, a stable price level?

All these questions are complexly interrelated. In general, the value of money is most likely to fall (prices to rise) during a period of full employment and rapid growth. A rising value of money is usually accompanied by increasing unemployment. Moreover, we cannot make simple and arbitrary statements about cause and effect. Falling prices may well be a *result* of unemployment and recession. At the same time, the decline in prices may very well be the *cause* of further unemployment if, as is likely to happen, they cause the consumption function and the schedule of marginal efficiency of capital to fall.

FULL EMPLOYMENT

What happens to the value of money depends to a large extent upon whether or not the economy is operating at full employment. What do we mean by full employment? Certainly not that every able-bodied man and woman between 16 and 65 is working 60 hours a week. Nor do we mean that everyone who would like to be paid $20 an hour will find work. Full employment does not mean that no one will be looking for work. Inevitably there will be an irreducible minimum of unemployment at all times. With a civilian labor force of about 92 million in the United States, there will be four or five million who are looking for jobs even when business is booming.

Part of this unemployment is temporary, resulting from the seasonal nature of some work. There is still no way to get the fruit off the trees in the fall except by hiring laborers. When the harvest is finished, the pickers are unemployed until they can find other employment. Others of the temporarily unemployed may have quit their jobs to look for better ones. Still others are workers whose qualifications are so poor that they are unemployable. To a considerable extent this minimum amount of unemployment represents frictions in the labor market. It is quite possible that at the same time two million are looking for work, employers would like to hire three million. The unemployment exists because the jobs offered are not suited to the qualifications of the job hunters, or the jobs are in another part of the country or for other reasons are not known to or attractive to those looking for work. (We might say that at such times employment is really more than full, for if we were to subtract from the number of unemployed the number of workers that industry would like to add, we might find "net" unemployment to be less than zero.)

Except for this inescapable minimum of unemployment, however, full employment is a situation in which everyone who wants work has a job. Likewise, the other factors of production are being fully utilized. At such times the nation is producing to capacity. From one year to the next its output might rise by 3 or 4 percent as a result of the gradual increase in productivity and the labor force.[1] Real income cannot increase much more than this. If the money measure of national income rises by 10 or 15 percent in a year when the economy is already at full employment, a rise in the price level must be at least a partial cause of the increase.

THE VALUE OF MONEY AT FULL EMPLOYMENT

It is possible for the value of money to rise, fall, or remain unchanged when we are at full employment. Of these, the most likely is that it will fall. When jobs are easy to find, workers will more readily quit their present jobs if their demands for higher wages are not met. When the demand for goods is high, employers will more willingly grant wage increases, hoping to pass the increased costs along through higher prices.

Constant Prices

A fall in the value of money is not a necessary consequence of full employment. If average wage increases are only in proportion to average increased productivity, unit costs will be no higher than before. However, contrary to popular belief, this does not mean that we will avoid inflation if in individual industries wages are increased only in proportion to the increase in productivity. Rather, they must be raised by less than this amount in those industries where increases in productivity are greatest. Why? So that prices of these goods may be reduced, permitting an increase of prices and wages in other industries where increases in productivity have been less or perhaps nonexistent.

The higher wages, made possible by increases in productivity in the most rapidly progressing industries, will have to be shared. This is not an abstract principle of ethics. Competition in the labor market will prevent the higher wages from accruing entirely to the benefit of the fortunate workers in those

---

[1]Conceivably, also, output might rise from an increase in the number of hours worked per week. Again, if most housewives should decide to work outside their homes, the large expansion of the labor force would permit a rise in national income. These reservations, however, merely recognize that full employment is a relative term. We could go from "full" employment to "fuller" employment.

industries. If the more stagnant industries are to continue hiring labor, they must raise their wages too; and, if they must raise their wages when there has been little or no increase in productivity in their operations, they must raise their prices.[2] Hence, if we are to have a stable price level and if the less progressive industries must raise their prices to continue in operation, there must be price decreases in other areas.

Falling Prices

If wage increases were somewhat less than proportionate to average increased productivity, costs would be lowered and prices might also be reduced. Money income of labor would rise less rapidly than in the last quarter-century, but each dollar would buy more. Also, those on fixed incomes would find their purchasing power rising too, so that they, too, would derive some benefit from the increase in productivity. As far as equity is concerned, this would be highly desirable. It is hardly fair that those on fixed incomes—including nearly all retired workers—should be forced to accept a constant or a steadily falling standard of living while others are enjoying a rapidly rising living standard. However, the maintenance of a gently falling price level may be an impractical goal. It would probably increase the problems associated with the maintenance of full employment.

Rising Prices

In any case, monopolistic pressures by labor unions and business will most likely be in the direction of pushing prices up during a period of full employment, as we have seen in the last three decades. Conditions of full employment make it easier for these organizations to secure for themselves a larger share of total production. Rising prices are no hardship as long as one's own money income is rising faster than prices. Obviously it would be impossible at full employment for the money income of the total population to rise much faster than prices, but it is quite possible for the income of some people to rise considerably faster than prices as long as there are some on fixed incomes or incomes that rise less rapidly than the price level. Groups with strong bargaining power can obtain large increases in their real income by wresting a larger share of national income at the expense of those whose money incomes rise less rapidly than prices.

The Value of Money at Less than Full Employment

If the economy is operating only briefly at less than full employment and the volume of unemployed resources is moderate, the value of money may

---

[2]Your grandfather could get a shave and a haircut for 75 cents. Barbers today, working with about the same equipment as they did then and with, therefore, about the same productivity, must get wages several times as high as they did 50 years ago—or we would have no barbers. So, the price of a shave and a haircut has to be higher, because there has been little increase in productivity in the trade during a period when there have been great increases in productivity in other areas.

remain constant or even decline a little. Corporations may prefer to maintain their prices when sales slacken, especially if they are afraid that price reductions may cause sales to drop because the public will expect further reductions. They may also prefer stable prices to flexible prices because they fear heavy government pressures if, in prosperity, the industry attempts to raise prices. Since 1961, the steel, aluminum, and copper industries were forced to rescind price increases that the administration felt to be contrary to the public interest. If it is going to be difficult to raise prices, it is inadvisable to lower them. Likewise, union leaders may feel that to maintain their organization and discipline it is better to raise wage rates, even if all the increase in pay must be turned over as higher dues to help support unemployed members. Certainly they will oppose any wage reduction, knowing that they will have to fight later to get wages back up to the earlier level. Partially as a result of these cost-push or sellers' forces, our economy has been, since 1968, on the horns of a dilemma known as "stagflation," or unemployment and inflation at the same time.

EQUILIBRIA, FULL EMPLOYMENT AND OTHERWISE

A generation ago economists generally assumed that an economy was in equilibrium only at full employment. Whenever unemployment existed, natural forces would, they believed, draw the economy back to full employment. Modern income analysis sharply challenges this view.

Figure 18-1 is similar to Figure 17-3. The only difference is that we are now adding to consumption both investment and government expenditures. On the basis of the consumption function assumed earlier,[3] and assuming that

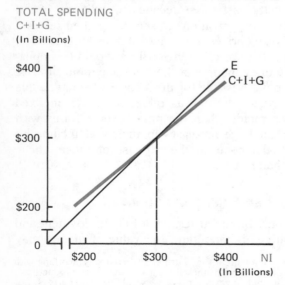

TOTAL SPENDING
C+I+G
(In Billions)

Figure 18-1   Income Equilibrium

---
[3] $C = \$10$ billion $+ \frac{3}{4}$ (NI).

the total of planned investment plus government expenditures is $65 billion, the equilibrium level of income is $300 billion. Only at that point is the total of $C + I + G$ equal to NI, as shown by its intersection of the guideline OE. So the equilibrium level of income is $300 billion under the above assumptions. As long as the consumption function remains unchanged and the total of planned investment plus government expenditures continues to be $65 billion, national income will continue to be $300 billion.

This income level tells us nothing about the amount of unemployment. Perhaps there is full employment when national income is $300 billion, so the economy is fortunate enough to be operating at a full employment equilibrium. Perhaps, however, full employment would prevail at some lower level. In this case money income, but not real income, will be rising steadily, and income will not be at an equilibrium level. Or it may be that there is widespread unemployment at the level of $300 billion—which, however, will now be an equilibrium level, with no forces acting automatically to pull production up to the full employment level.

Income Determination and Realization of Plans

The sum of realized expenditures for consumption, investment, and government at any level of income is, of course, exactly equal to income by definition. If, however, this level of income does not correspond to what the economy plans or wishes to spend, income must change. This is exactly the point of our whole analysis. Whether income is at an equilibrium level depends solely and entirely on whether plans are being realized. When income is at an equilibrium level, there may be changes in plans affecting any or all of the three components. Income then must rise or fall, trying to attain a new equilibrium.

Assume that planned $C + I + G$ is represented by BB in Figure 18-2 (page 440) so income is at OM, where planned $C + I + G = OM'' = OM$. Income is at an equilibrium level because there are no forces tending to drive it either higher or lower.

Now suppose plans are revised in such a way that people plan to spend only ON'' ($=MN$). ON'' is less than MM', and income must fall. Assuming there has been no change in the slope of the consumption function, the new expenditure line may be represented by the line $B'B'$ drawn through N, parallel to BB. $B'B'$ represents the new planned expenditures for C, I, and G, at various income levels. This new expenditure line crosses the guideline, where it is equal to income at R', which is below NN''.

Constrictive and Expansionary Gulfs

In this kind of analysis where we are looking at the difference between actual expenditures (BB) and planned expenditures ($B'B'$) at the existing income level, we might call $M'N$ a *constrictive gulf*. It will force income down to OR, where it again will be in equilibrium (if there meanwhile has been no change in $B'B'$).

We can also speak of an *expansionary gulf* which would force income to a higher level. If we assume income has been *OR*, with planned *C + I + G* represented by *B'B'*, and that plans are revised so that total planned expenditures are now represented by *BB*, *R'S* would be an expansionary gulf, forcing income to increase. If there is no further change in *BB*, income will be at an equilibrium level of *OM*.

Ordinarily when economists speak of *gaps* they are referring to something entirely different from what we have just analyzed. The expansionary and constrictive gulfs are to be distinguished sharply from the gaps discussed in the paragraphs following. They are not the same at all. An important reason for this brief discussion of expansionary and constrictive gulfs is, in fact, to emphasize that gulfs, at the existing income level and resulting from shifts in the *C + I + G* schedule, must not be confused with inflationary and deflationary gaps.

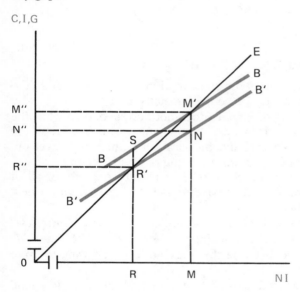

Figure 18-2   Gaps and Gulfs

INFLATIONARY AND DEFLATIONARY GAPS

Gaps, as economists ordinarily use the term in income analysis, do not refer to the distance between *OE* and planned *C + I + G* at the current level of income, which we have labeled gulfs. Gaps involve an additional variable. They are the gap between *OE* and planned *C + I + G* at the full employment level of income. They specifically direct our attention to the fact that only by fortunate chance will the equilibrium level of income happen to be at full employment. Income may be at full employment and not in equilibrium. It may be at equilibrium but not at full employment. That it will be at both full employment and an equilibrium level is, generally, unlikely.

Inflationary Gaps

Refer again to Figure 18-2. This time assume that *BB* represents planned expenditures for consumption, investment, and government, but that the economy would be at full employment, with a constant price level, at *OR*. (Disregard *B'B'*.) *R'S* is then an *inflationary gap*, driving up prices and driving up the money value of income. As will be explained shortly, *OM* is not an equilibrium level of income, and no equilibrium level of income can possibly be reached unless the inflationary gap is closed by a downward shift of *BB*. Income rises indefinitely. Such a gap occurs when, with the economy at full employment, the flow of money income is increased more rapidly than is the output of goods and services. This might result from the public's desire to spend large amounts of past savings, adding to expenditures and, therefore, adding to money incomes but adding nothing to the output of goods and services. Or it might be due to an expansion of bank credit. Whatever the cause, when expenditures are rising faster than the output of goods and services, prices must rise.

We define the *inflationary gap*, then, as the amount by which total planned spending at full employment exceeds the value of current output at existing prices. Alternatively, we may define the *inflationary gap* as the excess of investment plus government spending (*I* + *G*) over planned private saving plus the government's disposable income (*S* + *T*) at the full employment level. In Figure 18-3, if *OR* represents the full employment level of income, the inflationary gap will be *VW*, for at *OR* total leakages (*S* + *T*) are *RV*, but total injections (*I* + *G*) are *RW*. Money income must be rising, and since at *OR* the economy is, by definition, already at full employment, there must be a rise in prices.

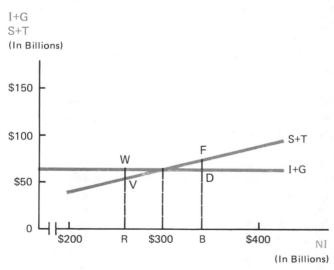

Figure 18-3   Income Equilibrium

Deflationary Gaps

Now assume that planned $C + I + G$ is represented by $B'B'$ in Figure 18-2. (Disregard *BB*.) The full employment level of income we shall assume would be at *OM*, but at that level of income planned spending would be less than income. The *deflationary gap (M'N)* requires that income be at a level below full employment.

Note particularly that even if income is at an equilibrium level, as at *OR* (Figure 18-2), the deflationary gap *M'N* still exists. Because of this gap, the equilibrium level of income is less, by *RM*, than the full employment level. If the gap were closed, the equilibrium level of income would be at *OM*, that is, at full employment.

The Price Level and the Consumption Function

Earlier we noted a number of qualifications to the proposition that consumption depends upon income, but concentrating on the principal relationships, we have not been taking into account these limitations. In analyzing the results of gaps we must first settle a very important question: What effect will a change in the value of money have on the consumption function?

Inextricably tied up with the question of a changing price level is the quite separate question of possible changing expectations of future price levels. A rise in prices might be interpreted as an indication that prices would continue to rise, or might be regarded as temporary, to be followed by a fall or perhaps by no further change. The effect upon consumption will be different in each case. We shall handle this as simply as possible by concentrating upon the effect of the change in the price level itself, assuming that expectations of future prices are unaffected or (which comes to the same thing) that, for the economy as a whole, they cancel out.[4]

Suppose our consumption function indicates that the economy will consume all of a \$40 billion income (after taxes) and save \$5 billion of a \$60 billion income. This corresponds to $C = \$10$ billion $+ \frac{3}{4}\,(NI)$. It states that the probable outcome of an increase in income is that part of the increase will be saved but most will be spent for consumption. However, if this outcome really is the logical and probable one, we surely are thinking in terms of changes in real income, that is, in terms of money income measured in constant dollars.

It is reasonable enough to assume that the proportions of any increases in the output of goods and services that will be consumed are fairly predictable from the records of past production-consumption combinations. From past experience we might expect that, for example, three fourths of any increase in real output will be consumed, as in the preceding consumption function.

Now for the sake of the argument, assume that in the second year the same amount of goods and services is produced but that because prices have

---

[4]The same thing is done in microeconomics, or otherwise demand functions would be shifting around with changing expectations.

risen 50 percent, this product now sells for $60 billion instead of $40 billion. Is there still the same probability that part will be saved?

Recall that in the first case saving was generated by the increase in income, but that consumption was also increased. Thirty-seven and a half percent more goods and services were consumed than when income was $40 billion and saving was zero.[5]

In the second year, only prices have changed. If the public consumes the entire $60 billion of income, it is consuming no more goods and services than it did before. If it were to save $5 billion of the $20 billion extra money income, not only would there be no simultaneous (and greater) increase in its consumption of goods and services, there would be an actual decrease.

Again, suppose prices had fallen by 50 percent between the two periods, and that in both years national income amounted to $40 billion, with zero saving the first year. In the second year the public is producing twice as many goods and services as in the first. Should we suppose that, because national income is $40 billion both years, saving will again be zero, so that in the second year the public will be consuming twice as many goods and services as before and saving nothing? Or does it seem more reasonable to assume that part will be saved, even if the dollar total of income is the same as before?

Surely it is clear that the logic of the consumption function relates to the effect of change in real income rather than in money income. We have thus far ignored the effect of changing price levels because it is only one of a number of qualifications, none of which materially affected the analysis up to this point. But now that we are about to study specifically the effects of inflation and deflation, changes in the value of money are necessarily a key factor.

Significance of Inflationary Gaps

The importance of inflationary and deflationary gaps lies in their effect upon national income. If an inflationary gap exists, such as the gap $R'S$ at a full employment level OR (Figure 18-2), the money value of national income must be driven up. More money is entering the income stream in the form of investment and government expenditures than is being withdrawn as disposable income of the government and savings planned by the public. Total employment cannot increase, since full employment already exists at OR. All that is happening is that prices are rising so that the same volume of goods and services is being produced but is being sold for more dollars.

Thus, the only possible consequence of an inflationary gap is an indeterminate rise in prices. It is a special case of an expansionary gap, for which no equilibrium is possible. The public receives steadily rising money incomes and spends more and more dollars. However, real income is unchanged, since the economy has been operating at capacity the whole time. There would be no reason for people to begin saving more, in real terms, simply because their

---

[5]$15/$40 = \frac{3}{8} = 37.5\%$.

money incomes were higher than before. Conceivably the expansion might continue until money became worthless.[6] There is no certainty that an equilibrium level of income would ever be reached.

However, the consumption function might eventually shift downward as people realized the shrinkage in the value of their liquid assets and began to save more in real terms even though their real income was the same as before.[7] Perhaps the inflation would cause a shift in income distribution, with wealthy individuals, who tend to consume a lower than average percentage of their total income, receiving a larger share of the national income.[8] High prices might lead to a buyers' strike. Or the public might fear that the inflation would turn into a depression and for this reason decide to save more. Thus, somewhere an equilibrium level of income might be attained. But there is evidently no way of knowing where that equilibrium might be, for equilibrium would depend on a new consumption function which could not be estimated in advance.

Specifically, we cannot assume that equilibrium would be attained when, with higher prices, we reached the *OM* income level. True, it is at *OM'* that *BB* of Figure 18-2 intersects *OE*, but that is on the basis of today's prices. When we are pushed from *OR* to *OM* by an inflationary gap, our real income is the same as it was at the outset. If at *OR* we were trying to buy, for example, 10 percent more goods and services than we were producing, presumably we shall still be making the same futile effort when, with exactly the same real income, our income rises in terms of dollars.

Unless the consumption function changes (or planned investment or government spending change), the successive levels of planned spending will lie along path *SX* in Figure 18-4. *SX* can never cross *OE* to indicate equilibrium.[9]

The attempt to overspend income is related to a percentage rather than a dollar amount. If full employment (*OR*) corresponds to an income level of 300 and the inflationary gap (*R'S*) is 30, we should expect the gap to be 40 by the time money value of income (still at the full employment level) has been pushed up to 400. Therefore, the inflationary gap steadily increases; the higher income rises, the larger the gap. The inflationary gap leaves real income unchanged but must force up prices and the money value of income by

---

[6]Of course, unless the Treasury and the banking system had lost control, there would certainly be a reduction enforced in any or all the components of planned expenditure: consumption, investment, and government. Such action, however, would simply close the gap, avoiding the issue of what the effect of such a gap would be. Only as we understand what the outcome would be can we realize the importance of closing the gap to avoid the consequences.

[7]This has come to be called the "real-balances," "net-claims," "wealth," or "Pigou" effect. While as a practical matter its effect is minimal, it has been employed as a theoretical device to refute the Keynesian claim that the economy could be in equilibrium at less than full employment. The pre-Keynesian classical economists emphasized that deflation would eventually increase the value of net assets until people felt sufficiently wealthy to expand consumption to the level required to achieve full employment. See Chapter 19.

[8]See "Average Propensity to Consume," page 447.

[9]When prices are unchanged, the expenditures line will intersect *OE* somewhere. *SX*, however, must always lie above *OE*. In preceding chapters the expenditures line has reflected the decreasing percentage of increasing total real income that will be consumed. *SX* represents a fixed percentage of a given real income at various price levels.

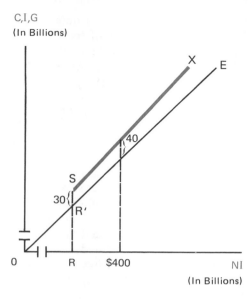

Figure 18-4   Inflationary Gap

an indeterminate amount.[10] The inflationary gap will disappear only with a shift in planned expenditures for consumption, investment, and government; that is, only when the sum of planned expenditures has decreased.

Significance of Deflationary Gaps

A deflationary gap may appear when the economy is at full employment, either because of a drop in planned spending (as illustrated in our analysis of constrictive gulfs) or because planned spending is standing still or growing less rapidly than the nation's capacity to produce. At full employment we can turn out many more goods and services today than we could have at full employment 10 years ago. If planned expenditures were no greater today than the equivalent of our full employment production a decade ago, we would have a deflationary gap and unemployment.

If the effect of the deflationary gap were merely to depress prices, with real income remaining at the full employment level, there would be the same indeterminacy we observed with the inflationary gap. It is highly improbable, however, that the economy would remain at full employment if prices dropped rapidly. Although the economy cannot operate above full employment, it can certainly operate below the full employment level.

---

[10]It has been frequently argued since World War II that a small, controlled inflationary gap will lead to a small, controlled rise in prices, which in turn will encourage a high employment level and, therefore, a more rapid income growth than if the value of money were constant or rising. The thesis is plausible but debatable. We shall not attempt to evaluate it here. See Chapter 24.

Real income can and probably will fall in consequence of a deflationary gap. According to our consumption function, the percentage of total income consumed gradually rises as real income falls. In contrast to the results of an inflationary gap, there is a limit to the change in money income. An equilibrium is finally reached at less than full employment. The gap remains, of course, unless planned expenditures rise to cross *OE* at the full employment level. Then, with the economy in equilibrium at the full employment level, the deflationary gap disappears.

Size of Income Changes Resulting from Gaps

Because the price level must change in the adjustment process, we cannot say how great will be the change in income as the result of an inflationary gap. With deflationary gaps, constrictive gulfs in general, and noninflationary expansionary gulfs, we can legitimately assume that the adjustment process resulting from a change in planned expenditure can be accomplished, ordinarily, with relatively little change in the value of money. We are then justified in using the existing consumption function, for we are assuming that it is primarily real income that is changing rather than only the money value of the existing level of production.

The visual evidence of Figure 18-2 suggests that the change in income from *OR* to *OM* is greater than *R'S* (or *M'N*). Equilibrium is reached, apparently, only after income has changed by several times the amount of the original increase or decrease in planned expenditure. Moreover, if we disregarded the implications of the figures and simply assumed that an increase (or decrease) in planned spending would cause income to rise (or fall) by the same amount, we would find quickly enough that our assumption was incorrect. Through all this analysis we have been assuming that C = \$10 billion + ¾ (*NI*), so that an expenditure of \$65 billion for investment and government will result in an equilibrium at \$300 billion. Why does this consumption function require that the increase from *OR* to \$300 billion be greater than the initial increase in spending (*VW*) in Figure 18-5?

Assume *VW* represents a \$10 billion increase in planned investment spending, raising the total of $I + G$ to \$65 billion and establishing the \$300 billion equilibrium of income as shown by line *B* in Figure 18-5. The former equilibrium, at *OR* income, is indicated by the same consumption function plus the smaller expenditure for investment and by government (line *A*). If the eventual change in income is equal to the initial change in expenditure, the income level at *OR* should be \$300 billion − \$10 billion, or \$290 billion.

But what would really be the income level at *OR*? With $I + G$ = \$55 billion and the same consumption function as before, NI = \$10 billion + ¾ (*NI*) + \$55 billion, or \$260 billion. Evidently the increase of $I + G$ to \$65 billion from \$55 billion changed the equilibrium level of income to \$300 billion from \$260 billion. Similarly, we can ascertain that a drop in expenditures will cause a drop in income several times as large as the original reduction in the expenditures.

C,I,G
(In Billions)

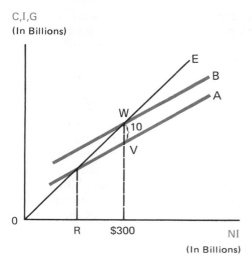

Figure 18-5   Change in Spending

If it is not completely obvious by now, it should at least be suspected that the relationships above must be somehow related to the fact that as income increases, consumption increases by a smaller amount, as stated by the consumption function. We can work this out much more neatly with supplementary analytical tools.

AVERAGE PROPENSITY TO CONSUME

The consumption function is a schedule. It relates the amounts of consumption at various income levels and can be expressed in the form of a line on a graph depicting the amount of consumption to be expected at any income level. Or it can be expressed as the equation of that line. The line and its equation are, of course, just two ways of stating the same thing.

The *average propensity to consume (APC)* is defined as the percentage of income consumed at a particular level of income. If, for example, national income is $40 billion and consumption is at $40 billion, the *APC* at that income level is 100 percent. If at the $80 billion income level consumption is $70 billion, the *APC* is 87.5 percent at that income level. It is 106.25 percent when income is $32 billion if consumption at that income level is $34 billion.

From the consumption function we can state the *APC* at various income levels. We can either read from our regression line the amount of consumption that should accompany a given income, or we can work it out from the equation. The line may be thought of as tracing a series of *APC*s over a range of incomes. Since we drew the consumption function as a straight line,[11] the

---

[11]Starting above the origin (0) with a positive y-intercept indicating some amount of autonomous consumption which is independent of income.

APC must fall continuously as income increases.[12] As income increases, consumption rises also but by a smaller amount. Therefore, the percentage of total income consumed falls as income rises, and the percentage of total income saved, or average propensity to save (*APS*), rises.

THE INDIVIDUAL'S AVERAGE PROPENSITY TO CONSUME

Although we ordinarily relate the *APC* to national income, we often find it useful to relate it to the disposition of an individual's income. If you are earning $3,000 and spending $3,600, your *APC* at $3,000 is 120 percent. But if your income rises to $20,000, your *APC* will decline unless you are a hopeless spendthrift. At the higher level you will probably be saving something instead of spending more than your income. If your *APC* at $30,000 is 80 percent, you will be saving $6,000. Your average propensity to save (*APS*) at that income level will be 20 percent.[13]

In comparing different income groups we may assume that the *APC* is likely to be highest in the lowest income groups. Consequently, we shall be interested in any income redistribution that changes the proportions of total income going to the various income groups. In the last quarter century incomes have become somewhat more equally distributed. As a smaller proportion of total income goes to those in top income brackets, with a low *APC*, and a larger proportion to those in the lower income brackets, where the *APC* is higher, the *APC* for the group as a whole is raised.

MARGINAL PROPENSITY TO CONSUME

A relationship that we often find more useful than the average propensity to consume is the *marginal propensity to consume (MPC)*. The *MPC* refers to the percentage of any additional income that will be consumed. Where the $APC = C/Y$, the $MPC = \Delta C/\Delta Y$ (where Δ refers to a small change). The mirror-twin of the *MPC* is the *marginal propensity to save (MPS)*, expressed as $\Delta S/\Delta Y$. Because extra income that is not consumed is necessarily saved, $MPC + MPS = 1.00$ and therefore $MPS = 1.00 - MPC$. (Using algebra, $\Delta Y = \Delta C + \Delta S$, and therefore dividing by ΔY, we get $\Delta Y/\Delta Y = \Delta C/\Delta Y + \Delta S/\Delta Y$; $\therefore 1 = MPC + MPS$.)

MPC Lower than *APC*

Above we suggested that at $3,000 your *APC* might be 120 percent. However, if your income increased to $3,100, it is unlikely that you would increase your spending by $120. If you increased your consumption by $100, your

---

[12]However, since in fact consumption is only $4.8 billion more than (approximately) three fourths of income, neither the *APC* nor the *APS* will change much as the economy moves from high to still higher income levels. With a national income of $600 billion consumption would be $4.8 billion plus .76 ($600 billion), or $460.8 billion. Thus, the *APC* would be $460.8/$600, or 76.8 percent; with national income of $1,000 billion the *APC* would be $764.8/$1,000, or 76.5 percent. At very low income levels the *APC* would be much higher, as noted above.

[13]The sum of the *APC* and the *APS* at any income level will necessarily be 1.00 (*NI*).

marginal propensity to consume, at an income of $3,000, would be 100 percent, even though at that same income level your average propensity to consume was 120 percent. Quite possibly your *MPC* at $3,000 would be less than 100 percent, as you tried to bring your consumption expenditures more into line with your income.

Similarly, although the *APC* may be 100 percent when national income is $40 billion, the *MPC* will be somewhat less. Common sense suggests that we are likely, not only as individuals but also as a group, to consume a smaller proportion of any addition to income than of total income. Also, from the general shape of the consumption function the *MPC* must be less than the *APC* at all income levels. Unless at every income level the *MPC* was lower than the *APC*, the *APC* would not decline as income increases. The reason that we may consume 110 percent of a low income but only 80 percent of a higher income is that we consume a smaller percentage of an addition to income than of total income. As income rises, the *APC* will draw constantly closer to the *MPC*, although never equaling it.

Technically, the *MPC* is the slope of the line representing the consumption function. The slope of a line is determined by the ratio between the increase in the *y* value and the accompanying increase in the *x* value. This is exactly what we are studying here, with consumption measured on the *y* axis and national income on the *x* axis. More specifically, since we are assuming that the consumption function is $C = \$10$ billion $+ \frac{3}{4} (NI)$, the slope of the line is ¾ and therefore the *MPC* is ¾ (and thus *MPS* = ¼), at least over the range of incomes studied. Whenever income increases by $4, consumption increases by $3, by our assumption. Likewise, a $4 decrease in income will call forth a $3 decrease in consumption.[14]

The Multiplier

If ¾ of any addition to income will be consumed, we see that any initial increase in income will set in motion a train of respending effects, each in turn creating additional income but in ever decreasing amounts. A $100 increase in income will result in $75 of additional consumption and $25 of additional saving. Since the saving represents funds withdrawn from the income stream, the $25 has no further effect in increasing income. But since income is created by consumption (or investment or government) expenditures, income has been increased by $75 in addition to the original $100 increase. When ¾ of this subsequent increase in income is consumed, income is increased still further by ¾ ($75), or $56.25. The respending continues, since each act of induced consumption creates additional income which induces further respending amounting to ¾ of the last increase in income. The first 10 additions to consumption to result from the $100 initial increase in income would be: $75.00; $56.25; $42.19; $31.64; $23.73; $17.80; $13.35; $10.01; $7.51; $5.63.

So far $283.11 of induced consumption has resulted from the original increase of $100 in income. Thus, there has been, to this point, a total addition

---

[14]For a discussion of a declining *MPC*, see the Appendix at the end of this chapter.

of $383.11 to income. From this point on, any further additions will obviously be very small. If we continue the arithmetic far enough, we find the total increase in income resulting from an initial increase of $100 and an *MPC* of ¾ would approach $400 as a limit.

Naturally the greater the proportion of income respent, the greater the total increase in income. If the *MPC* is 90 percent and we carry far enough the series beginning $100, $90, $81, $72.90, and so on, we find the total increase approaches $1,000, including $900 of induced consumption. If the *MPC* is ½, the series beginning $100, $50, $25, $12.50, etc., would approach $200.

The *multiplier* is the numerical coefficient expressing how much total income will increase as a result of the additional spending induced by any initial increase in income. Put differently, the multiplier relates the ultimate change in income for given changes in autonomous expenditures. (You will recall that an autonomous change represents a shift in an entire schedule, whereas an induced change represents a movement along a given schedule.) Since the multiplier works in either direction, it also tells us the total decrease in income resulting from an initial decrease. The total change in income will be the sum of the changes in investment, consumption, and governmental spending.

THE MULTIPLIER AND MARGINAL PROPENSITY TO CONSUME

In the simplest case where the only induced spending is consumption, we only need to know the *MPC* and we can easily find the value of the "simple" multiplier (K). Let ΔI represent the autonomous change in spending, here taken to be investment, and ΔY the resulting ultimate change in income. The "simple" multiplier can then be expressed as $K = \Delta Y/\Delta I$. But since $\Delta Y = \Delta C + \Delta I$ and therefore $\Delta I = \Delta Y - \Delta C$, we may substitute for ΔI, obtaining $K = \frac{\Delta Y}{\Delta Y - \Delta C}$. If we divide the numerator and the denominator by ΔY, we obtain $K = \frac{1}{1 - \Delta C/\Delta Y} = \frac{1}{1 - MPC} = \frac{1}{MPS}$. Thus, the "simple" multiplier is equal to $\frac{1}{1 - MPC} = \frac{1}{MPS}$.[15] When we assume that the *MPC* = ¾, we are also assuming that the multiplier is 4. If the *MPC* were ½, the multiplier would be 2, and if the *MPC* were 9/10, the multiplier would be 10.

This is, to be sure, merely arithmetic. We should not make the mistake of supposing that because we have set up a formula for the multiplier we really know what its value is. We can only say what its value is on the basis of what we assume to be the *MPC*. We still are working with estimates, averages, and approximations. Even if our regression line passed exactly through every

[15]More generally, the "complete" multiplier is equal to $\frac{1}{1 - MPX}$, where *MPX* is the marginal propensity to spend, whether *C, I,* or *G,* that is induced by a prior change in income. Since as a practical matter consumption is the only type of spending thought to be induced inexorably by any initial increase in income, all analysis in this book, unless otherwise specified, will assume that the "simple" multiplier $\frac{1}{1 - MPC} = \frac{1}{MPS}$ holds.

point in our scatter diagram, we would still be making an assumption (although a reasonable one) if we decided that the slope of that line represented the current *MPC*. We would not have proven the current value of either the multiplier or the *MPC* from which it is derived. Conditions could possibly have changed.

Algebraic Derivation of Simple and Complex Multipliers

The multipliers can be derived by examining the algebra of income determination. We have three equations (remember "autonomous" merely means independent of income in this context):

1. $Y = C + I$ The income equilibrium condition.
2. $C = a + bY$ The consumption function, where a = autonomous consumption and $b = MPC$.
3. $I = I_0$ Investment is an autonomous constant.

Solving simultaneously we get,

4. $Y = \dfrac{(I_0 + a)}{(1 - b)}$,

where the multiplier $K = 1/(1 - b)$ and the autonomous spending is represented by $(I_0 + a)$. If we introduce taxes (T) and government expenditure (G), where the former is mainly income taxes and G is autonomously determined, we get five equations:

5. $Y = C + I + G$ The income equilibrium condition.
6. $C = a + b\,(Y - T)$ The consumption function, where a = autonomous consumption, $b = MPC$, and $(Y - T)$ = disposable after-tax income.
7. $I = I_0$ Investment is an autonomous constant.
8. $G = G_0$ Governmental expenditure is an autonomous constant.
9. $T = t + mY$ The tax collection function, where t = autonomous taxes and m = marginal rate of taxation.

Substituting for the terms in equation 5 gives:

10. $Y = a + b\,(Y - T) + I_0 + G_0$

Substituting from 9 into 10 gives:

11. $Y = a + b\,(Y - t - mY) + I_0 + G_0$

Solving 11 for Y yields:

12. $Y = \dfrac{I_0 + G_0 + a - bt}{(1 - b + bm)}$

The more complex multiplier $(K') = 1/(1 - b + bm)$ can be used to predict the ultimate change in income resulting from any change in autonomous spending I_0, G_0, or a. The multiplier $(K'') = -b/(1 - b + bm)$ can be used in the case of a change in t.

The Multiplier and a Single Increase in Income

One important feature of the multiplier must be clearly understood. A single increase of $100 and a multiplier of 4 will not raise income to a $400 higher level. The combination will result eventually in $400 more income than there would otherwise have been. The increase, however, will have been in the form of a series of increments beginning with $100 and constantly decreasing. Suppose Y is the income level at the outset. When the first increase occurs, income in that period will be Y plus $100. In the following income period the income received in the first period is available for consumption. As ¾ of the initial increase is consumed, income becomes Y plus $75. In the next income period income is Y plus $56.25, as ¾ of the added $75 is consumed. Eventually the effects wear off. Income tapers off to approximately Y again insofar as the results of the $100 increase and the multiplier are concerned. The $400 is the sum of the increments in all the periods.[16] This figure includes the original increase of $100 and the $300 of additional consumption induced by the rise in income.

The Multiplier and a Permanent Increase in Income

The above result must be distinguished from what will occur if there is a permanent addition to income. In the latter case, a multiplier of 4 and a permanent addition of $100 to income will eventually raise the income level by $400. Incomes at the start will run Y plus $100, Y plus $175, Y plus $231.25, and Y plus $273.44, and will eventually be Y plus $400.

Significance of the Multiplier and *MPC*

As long as we do not attach an imaginary accuracy to the values that we assume for them, the *MPC* and the multiplier can be useful in income analysis. They clarify the process by which small initial changes in income generate much larger ones. Perhaps a new invention raises the marginal efficiency of capital and stimulates $5 or $10 billion more investment.

1. If the economy was at full employment before the increase in investment, an inflationary gap is created; we cannot say how far income will rise before reaching a new equilibrium or indeed whether an equilibrium will ever be attained.
2. If at the outset there were sufficient unemployed resources, the additional consumption that results from the increase in real income causes the total rise in income to be $20 or $25 billion.

Likewise, decreases in investment (or in government expenditures) cause greater changes in income because of the progressive drop in consumption initiated by the reduction in investment. The important thing, of course, is not pinpointing a change of exactly $20 billion or $25 billion. We should understand clearly that any such figure is only an approximation, depending upon the value that we assume for the *MPC*. What is important is to understand why and how the final change will be greater than the initiating change. The

---

[16]Keynes presented the matter differently, explaining the multiplier as a timeless process. His analysis is a little more abstract and assumes a temporary change in the *MPC*. The fundamental logic is unaffected. See J. M. Keynes, *The General Theory of Employment, Interest, and Money* (New York: Harcourt Brace & World, 1935), pp. 122–123.

multiplier is valuable in that it emphasizes secondary changes in income resulting from changes in induced spending, especially consumption, and it spotlights the importance of the *MPC* as a factor determining how large those secondary changes will be and, therefore, how large the total increase in income will be.

THE ACCELERATOR

The multiplier will not always measure the full extent of the change in income resulting from an initial change in autonomous spending. At times developments are more complex. The increasing consumption may require greater plant capacity, especially if productive facilities are already operating near capacity. Investment increases. The increases in investment will push income still higher. Then further consumption is induced, which may stimulate another increase in investment.

Not only investment in plant, but investment in inventories may be affected by changes in the consumption level. Normally a business relates inventory to sales; it may try to carry a stock that represents a typical month's sales, or more or less depending on the nature of the business. If consumers who have been taking $10,000 of the business's products every month now begin to take $12,000, it will need to keep more goods on hand. The building up of inventories that is likely to result from a higher consumption level is an important form of induced investment, raising income and encouraging further increases in consumption. A drop in consumption, on the other hand, is likely to lead businesses to carry smaller inventories. The decline in inventory investment then reinforces the drop in income caused by the decline in consumption and leads probably to a further decline in consumption and income.

Such an interaction between consumption and investment will raise income by more than would the multiplier alone. The combination may also force a decline in income, for the accelerator, like the multiplier, can work in a downward as well as an upward direction. The combined effect resulting from the interaction of the multiplier and the accelerator is called the *leverage effect*.

The accelerator measures the change in investment resulting from a change in consumption.[17] If a $30 billion change in consumption causes investment to rise by $36 billion, the accelerator is 1.20. We saw earlier that, with a marginal propensity to consume of ¾, an initial and one-time increase in income would set in motion a series of responding effects, continually diminishing. But now we shall see how different the results will be if each added dollar of consumption requires, in the following period, an increase of (for example) $1 in investment.

Without the accelerator we saw earlier that, on the fourth round of respending (period 5, counting the initial increase), income was increased by only $31.64. In Table 18-1, aided by the accelerator, it is $101.96. Also, the

---

[17]Note that the accelerator relates investment to changes in *consumption*; the multiplier is based on the response of consumption to changes in *income*.

Table 18-1   Income Changes with Leverage Effect:
Multiplier-Accelerator Interaction

Period	Column 1 Induced Consumption (¾ of col. 3 in previous period)	Column 2 Induced Investment (change in col. 1 between preced- ing period and previous period)	Column 3 Increase in Income (col. 1 + col. 2)
1	0	0	$100.00*
2	$75.00	0	75.00
3	56.25	$75.00	131.25
4	98.44†	−18.75‡	79.69
5	59.77	42.19§	101.96

*This is the initial increase in income, from whatever cause.
†Induced consumption is now ¾ of $131.25 instead of, as in the earlier example with the multiplier alone, ¾ of $56.25.
‡Induced investment is here negative because the induced consumption in period 3 was less than in period 2. (Negative investment does not require that plant and equipment be dismantled. More likely, plant and equipment wearing out during the year are not replaced, and inventories are reduced.)
§Induced consumption increased by this amount in period 4 over that in period 3.

total additions to income by period 5 are here $487.90 (counting the initial $100), as against $305.08 when only the multiplier was working.

Although we can neatly illustrate the interaction between increases in consumption and investment by assuming values for the multiplier and accelerator and therefore the leverage effect, as in Table 18-1, we must understand that we are only illustrating. Income will be increased by increases in either consumption or investment. The two may at times be interrelated in some such manner as in the example. But we must clearly realize the limitations and the tentative, approximate nature of both measures. We cannot be sure of the value of the multiplier. The value of the accelerator is even more unpredictable. It will vary widely from year to year.[18]

Factors Affecting the Accelerator

Whether an increase in consumption will cause a corresponding increase in investment depends, in general, upon whether additional plant capacity is actually required and upon expectations and the state of business confidence.

1. Obviously the accelerator will be zero when there is a great deal of excess capacity in all lines of production. An increase in consumption will not

---

[18]There are at least two strong criticisms of the strict accelerator theory: (1) it assumes that the firm's decision maker believes both that future demand is always exactly equal to current demand and that the optimal capital-output ratio is technologically fixed at the present level; and (2) it ignores limits on the rate of production of capital goods so that the optimal capital stock and the actual capital stock always coincide.

encourage management to expand its plant simply because it is now operating at 65 percent of capacity instead of at 60 percent.

2. Also, even if all industries are operating at full employment, the value of the accelerator will depend upon conditions in the particular areas of production where consumption increases. Some industries use relatively little capital in proportion to output. An increase in the consumption of food, for example, will probably provide less stimulus to investment than will an increase in the purchase of cars or television sets, assuming that all these industries are operating at full employment.

3. It is often possible to utilize existing equipment more intensively by running extra shifts rather than by adding capital equipment.

4. Since investment is determined largely by the marginal efficiency of capital, expectations and public psychology will cause the value of the accelerator to vary even in otherwise identical situations.

The Accelerator and Durability of Capital Goods

Even if we cannot in practice set a precise figure for the accelerator, we must recognize that the relation involved is an important one. The durable nature of most producer goods will cause the value of the accelerator at times to be high and hence of great importance in income determination.

Suppose that with $20 million of capital equipment a company annually produces $5 million of shoes; that is, it requires $4 of capital for every $1 of sales. (See Table 18-2.) Because this capital is durable, an increase in the sale of shoes will cause a much greater increase in the sale of shoe manufacturing equipment. Suppose that the life of this equipment is 20 years and that the company is annually replacing $1 million of machinery while its sales of shoes continue at $5 million. Now if the demand for shoes should increase by $2 million and if the company requires proportionately more equipment to meet this increase in demand, it will be ordering an additional $8 million of machinery in addition to the normal replacements. For the company to operate on the same capital-output ratio as before, the accelerator here requires four

Table 18-2   **Acceleration Principle:**
Effect of Increased Consumption on Investment

Demand for Shoes	Shoe Machinery Required	Orders for Shoe Machinery		
		Replacements	Additional	Total
$5,000,000	$20,000,000	. . . .	. . . .	. . . .
5,000,000	20,000,000	$1,000,000	0	$1,000,000
5,000,000	20,000,000	1,000,000	0	1,000,000
7,000,000	28,000,000	1,000,000	$8,000,000	9,000,000
8,000,000	32,000,000	1,000,000*	4,000,000	5,000,000
8,000,000	32,000,000	1,000,000*	0	1,000,000

*The increased stock of machinery may eventually cause replacement requirements to rise, but this need not concern us here.

times as great an increase in investment as the increase in consumption. (Note that there will be no such acceleration in the sales of leather. Since the leather, unlike the durable equipment, is consumed simultaneously with the production of shoes and in direct proportion, an increase in the demand for shoes causes the increase in the demand for leather to be only proportionate, not, as might first be assumed, several times as great.)

The Accelerator and the Rate of Increase in Consumption

Will investment continue to increase as long as consumption increases and by four times as much? Definitely not. Here is a principle of great significance to income determination. Suppose that in the next period the demand for shoes increases again but by only $1 million. The demand for new machines drops from $9 million to $5 million. Consumption need not actually decline for investment to decrease. The accelerator reminds us that investment may fall while consumption is still growing, if consumption is increasing at a slower rate than before. It shows us a possible reason for a decline in investment in prosperity, as it becomes more and more difficult for consumption to continue expanding as fast as ever. Because of income and respending effects, the drop in investment may result in a considerably greater further decline in income. The accelerator and multiplier together—i.e., the leverage effect—offer an explanation for at least some of the fluctuations in the income level.

SUMMARY AND CONCLUSION

The average propensity to consume (*APC*) is the percentage of total income that is consumed. It decreases as income increases. The marginal propensity to consume (*MPC*) is the percentage of additional income that is consumed. The marginal propensity to save (*MPS*) is the percentage of additional income that is saved. $MPC + MPS = 1.00$. *MPC* appears to be relatively constant over the range of national income.

The multiplier is the relationship between the final change in national income and an initial change in autonomous spending. It tells us by how much income will increase as a result of increased spending induced by the initial rise in income. The "complete" multiplier is $1/(1 - MPX)$ or one divided by all marginally induced leakages from the income stream (where *MPX* is the marginal propensity to spend on additional *C, I,* or *G*; put differently, *MPX* is the sum of all marginally induced injections).[19] If, as is usually the case, consumption is the only form of induced spending resulting from a change in income, the multiplier is determined by the *MPC*. The "simple" multiplier can be expressed as $1/(1 - MPC) = 1/MPS$.

---

[19]The classic derivation of the "complete" multiplier is found in Paul A. Samuelson, "The Simple Mathematics of Income Determination," *Macroeconomics: Selected Readings,* edited by Walter L. Johnson and David R. Kamerschen (Boston: Houghton Mifflin Co., 1970), pp. 39–49.

The accelerator relates changes in capital goods spending to changes in consumption. More particularly, the accelerator refers to the process whereby a shift in the consumption function causes a temporary disorder in the investment function with a still larger variation in the resultant income. The multiplier and accelerator interact to form the leverage effect.

An inflationary gap is the excess of planned spending ($C + I + G$) over the full employment level of income at existing prices. It is also the excess of investment plus government expenditures over the government's disposable income plus saving planned at full employment.

A deflationary gap represents the opposite relationship; that is, it measures the amount by which the full employment level of income at existing prices exceeds total planned spending. This will be equal to the excess of the government's disposable income plus saving planned at full employment over investment plus government expenditures.

At any time there may be an increase (or decrease) in any or all of the three components of expenditure. Consumption may change spontaneously as a result of a shift of the consumption function, but this is unlikely. The relationship between income and consumption is stable, and until real income changes, the percentages of income consumed and of income saved will probably not change.

The government, on the other hand, may abruptly decide to spend more (or less) for goods and services, and investment fluctuates widely as a result of changes in the marginal efficiency of capital. Neither is dependent primarily on the income level, so, unlike consumption, either may change without a prior change in income.

The effect of these initial changes in spending will be magnified by the leverage effect. If there is little or no effect on prices, the economy will move to a new equilibrium determined by the existing consumption function and the total of government and investment expenditure. If the effect is entirely or largely on prices with little change in real income, we can say only that money income will change by some indeterminate amount.

Except when there is an inflationary gap, the income level is always moving toward an equilibrium and, if the level of investment and government spending remains constant, income will settle at the appropriate equilibrium. There would then be no tendency for it to either rise or fall. This is convenient as long as the equilibrium level happens to be also the full employment level. Unfortunately full employment is often not an equilibrium level, and the economy is either operating at an underemployment equilibrium or is in the grip of a continuing inflation. In the latter case the value of money must fall; in the former case it will probably rise.[20] The inflation or recession will continue as long as the inflationary or deflationary gap remains. Changes in private investment or in consumption (or in saving, which is equivalent to a

---

[20]We say "probably" because since 1968 the United States economy has, mainly because of cost-push forces, been victimized by the perplexing dilemma of "stagflation"—unemployment and inflation simultaneously.

change in consumption) may close the gap; but if the economy is left to fend for itself, it may be years, if ever, before the necessary changes occur, and only after prolonged inflation or recession.

Sometimes monetary policy can help to close the gap. Changes in the level of interest rates, together with changes in the quantity of money, will affect not only the cost of borrowing, but also the general availability of credit. It will be easier or more difficult to borrow; the purposes of the loan, the security offered, the maturity—these and other borrowing considerations will be affected. The result may be a change in investment and also a change in at least some areas of consumption expenditures, especially for cars and other durable goods. If monetary policy can succeed in shifting the total of consumption and investment enough to close the gap, no more action is necessary.

If, however, monetary policy is unsuccessful, changes in government expenditures or taxes can close the gap. If the government takes appropriate action, there is no need to endure years of recession or inflation.

When either type of gap appears, income will change by more than the amount of the gap. If income has been at a full employment and equilibrium level but then there is a "permanent" (at least for several years) drop of $10 billion in C, I, or G, income will fall by more than $10 billion as a result of secondary changes in consumption and therefore in income. The initial decline in income induces the secondary changes in consumption.

Since a gap is smaller than the change in income it creates, the change in income is larger than the amount required to close the gap. In recession an increase of $10 billion in government expenditures may raise income by $30 or $40 billion to the full employment level. A decrease of $10 billion in taxes would be likely to have a somewhat smaller effect, for some of the tax reduction would almost certainly result in increased saving. The reduction of taxes might lead to an initial increase of perhaps $7 or $8 billion in consumption and, therefore, in income, with ultimate effects depending again upon the multiplier. Conceivably, however, there might be psychological effects. If the reduction in taxes were to raise the schedules of the marginal efficiency of capital or the propensity to consume, when an increase in government expenditures would have no effect or an adverse effect on expectations, the total income effect of the tax reduction might be greater.

Discussion Questions

1. Briefly explain what effect, if any, the following would have on the consumption function:
   a. an increase in income
   b. an increase in the marginal efficiency of capital
   c. an increase in the saving function
   d. expectation of a recession
   e. recovery from recession to full employment
2. According to income theory, what is the relation between full employment and the equilibrium level of national income? Explain.

3. If a government is trying to close an inflationary gap by operating with a surplus instead of the usual deficit, does it make any difference so far as closing the gap is concerned whether the government increases taxes by $10 billion, with no change in *G*, or reduces its spending by $10 billion, with no change in *T*? Explain why or why not.

4. If the economy is operating at a full employment equilibrium and a large gap appears, which is more likely to lead to a new equilibrium—a deflationary or an inflationary gap? Explain.

5. The rising price level accompanying an inflationary gap may lead to a downward shift of the consumption function. Explain. Might this lead to a new equilibrium? Why or why not?

6. The rising price level accompanying an inflationary gap may lead to an increase in the consumption function. Explain. Might this change lead to a new equilibrium? Why or why not?

7. Explain the phenomenon which writers have come to call by all of the following names: "real-balances," "net-claims," "wealth," or "Pigou" effect.

8. Can a movement along the existing consumption function close a deflationary gap? Explain.

9. If the average propensity to consume is constant, would the consumption function still be represented by a straight line? Why would it be drawn differently from the consumption functions in our illustrations? Why would such a consumption function appear wildly improbable?

10. What do you think the consumption function of an individual probably looks like, covering an income range of $1,000 to $100,000? Why?

11. Letting $K = \Delta Y/\Delta I$ be the "simple" multiplier, where ΔY is the resulting ultimate change in income and ΔI is the autonomous change in (investment) spending, show that $K = 1/(1 - MPC) = 1/MPS$.

12. "In equilibrium, $MPC + MPS = 1$." True or false and explain.

13. "A shift in autonomous spending (whether consumption, investment, or government) can induce a change in equilibrium income that is a multiple of the initiating change in autonomous spending. The ratio of the ultimate resulting change in income to the autonomous change in spending is called the leverage effect." Evaluate.

14. Disregarding the effect of new inventions and considering only the investment generated by the accelerator, we realize that, if investment is to continue increasing, consumption must increase by greater amounts every year. Why?

APPENDIX: CURVILINEAR CONSUMPTION FUNCTION FOR SOCIETY

Some of the discussion of income analysis assumes too freely that the marginal propensity to consume falls as income rises. It has seemed plausible to suppose that as income continues to rise, progressively less will be spent out of any additions to income.[21] This may well be true of individual incomes. Income differences here are very great. Quite possibly the marginal propensity to consume for most people might be around 100 percent at an income of $4,000 but as

---

[21]See also Chapter 19.

low as 3 or 4 percent at $100,000. Such a consumption function would be represented by a curve, becoming at very high income levels nearly parallel to the horizontal axis.

We saw, however, when we plotted the scatter diagram of national income and national consumption in Figure 16-4 that the points seemed to lie along a straight line. Possibly the line would be curved if our statistics covered a much wider range of income. We have some modest evidence to that effect.[22] Nevertheless, we are hardly justified in assuming, with some other available evidence to the contrary, that the consumption function should really be a curved line; that is, that the marginal propensity to consume falls as income rises.

Perhaps this appears a mere technicality. However, it is of real importance. Appropriate fiscal and monetary policies can hardly be based on misconceptions of the behavior of the economic system.

---

[22]See, for example, Che S. Tsao, "The Linearity Property in the Consumption Function: Estimation, Tests and Some Related Results," *Review of Economics and Statistics* (May, 1975), pp. 214–220.

Chapter 19   Interest Theories and Evaluation of the Income Approach

We have referred from time to time to the level of interest rates, where interest rates are the prices—usually stated as a percentage per year—paid by borrowers for use of the lender's money. It is an oversimplification to speak of the interest rate, as though only one rate prevails. Rather than one rate, there is a structure or complex of rates. These different interest rates, which are in effect simultaneously, range from the relatively low rates charged the federal government on its borrowings (often 6 to 9 percent) to the relatively high rates charged those who borrow from consumer finance companies (often 25 to 35 percent). Table 19-1 depicts some representative bond yields and interest rates on private and public debt from 1929 to 1974.

DIFFERENCES IN INTEREST RATES

The differences that exist among interest rates at a given time reflect the following factors:

1. *Differences in risk.* Government obligations are ordinarily the safest securities available and, accordingly, carry the lowest interest yield. Large corporations can usually borrow at lower rates than can smaller companies with a more uncertain credit rating.
2. *Differences in the administrative cost of handling the loan.* Since the administrative costs of processing and collecting large and small loans are about the same on an absolute basis, the administrative costs of large loans are relatively less expensive to handle per dollar of loan. The cost of analyzing the soundness of a small loan may be as great as the cost of analyzing a much larger one. As much bookkeeping is required to enter a $10 repayment on a term loan as to enter a $10,000 repayment.
3. *Differences in maturity.* Other things being equal, long-term rates are usually higher than short-term rates. One factor determining the relationship between long-term and short-term rates is the expected future level of interest rates. If nearly everyone expects rates to be higher in a year or two than currently, lenders will prefer not to tie up their money in long-term loans unless they are offered a higher return than on short-term. If rates are expected to fall, long-term loans will be made even when they do not offer as high a yield as do short-term. A second factor is the strong preference of some lenders, in particular the commercial banks, for the liquidity of short-term securities, which tends to hold down short-term interest rates.

Table 19-1   Bond Yields and Interest Rates, 1929–1974
(Percent per annum)

Year	U.S. government securities				Corporate bonds (Moody's)		High-grade municipal bonds (Standard & Poor's)	Average rate on short-term bank loans to business— selected cities	Prime commercial paper, 4-6 months	Federal Reserve Bank discount rate	FHA new home mortgage yields	Federal funds rate
	3-month Treasury bills	9–12 month issues	3–5 year issues	Taxable bonds	Aaa	Baa						
1929					4.73	5.90	4.27		5.85	5.16		
1930					4.55	5.90	4.07		3.59	3.04		
1931	1.402				4.58	7.62	4.01		2.64	2.11		
1932	.879				5.01	9.30	4.65		2.73	2.82		
1933	.515		2.66		4.49	7.76	4.71		1.73	2.56		
1934	.256		2.12		4.00	6.32	4.03		1.02	1.54		
1935	.137		1.29		3.60	5.75	3.41		.75	1.50		
1936	.143		1.11		3.24	4.77	3.07		.75	1.50		
1937	.447		1.40		3.26	5.03	3.10		.94	1.33		
1938	.053		.83		3.19	5.80	2.91		.81	1.00		
1939	.023		.59		3.01	4.96	2.76	2.1	.59	1.00		
1940	.014		.50		2.84	4.75	2.50	2.1	.56	1.00		
1941	.103		.73		2.77	4.33	2.10	2.0	.53	1.00		
1942	.326		1.46	2.46	2.83	4.28	2.36	2.2	.66	1.00		
1943	.373	0.75	1.34	2.47	2.73	3.91	2.06	2.6	.69	1.00		
1944	.375	.79	1.33	2.48	2.72	3.61	1.86	2.4	.73	1.00		
1945	.375	.81	1.18	2.37	2.62	3.29	1.67	2.2	.75	1.00		
1946	.375	.82	1.16	2.19	2.53	3.05	1.64	2.1	.81	1.00		
1947	.594	.88	1.32	2.25	2.61	3.24	2.01	2.1	1.03	1.00		
1948	1.040	1.14	1.62	2.44	2.82	3.47	2.40	2.5	1.44	1.34		
1949	1.102	1.14	1.43	2.31	2.66	3.42	2.21	2.68	1.49	1.50	4.34	
1950	1.218	1.26	1.50	2.32	2.62	3.24	1.98	2.69	1.45	1.59	4.17	
1951	1.552	1.73	1.93	2.57	2.86	3.41	2.00	3.11	2.16	1.75	4.21	
1952	1.766	1.81	2.13	2.68	2.96	3.52	2.19	3.49	2.33	1.75	4.29	
1953	1.931	2.07	2.56	2.94	3.20	3.74	2.72	3.69	2.52	1.99	4.61	
1954	.953	.92	1.82	2.55	2.90	3.51	2.37	3.61	1.58	1.60	4.62	
1955	1.753	1.89	2.50	2.84	3.06	3.53	2.53	3.70	2.18	1.89	4.64	1.78
1956	2.658	2.83	3.12	3.08	3.36	3.88	2.93	4.20	3.31	2.77	4.79	2.73
1957	3.267	3.53	3.62	3.47	3.89	4.71	3.60	4.62	3.81	3.12	5.42	3.11
1958	1.839	2.09	2.90	3.43	3.79	4.73	3.56	4.34	2.46	2.16	5.49	1.57
1959	3.405	4.11	4.33	4.08	4.38	5.05	3.95	5.00	3.97	3.36	5.71	3.30
1960	2.928	3.55	3.99	4.02	4.41	5.19	3.73	5.16	3.85	3.53	6.18	3.22
1961	2.378	2.91	3.60	3.90	4.35	5.08	3.46	4.97	2.97	3.00	5.80	1.96
1962	2.778	3.02	3.57	3.95	4.33	5.02	3.18	5.00	3.26	3.00	5.61	2.68
1963	3.157	3.28	3.72	4.00	4.26	4.86	3.23	5.01	3.55	3.23	5.47	3.18
1964	3.549	3.76	4.06	4.15	4.40	4.83	3.22	4.99	3.97	3.55	5.45	3.50
1965	3.954	4.09	4.22	4.21	4.49	4.87	3.27	5.06	4.38	4.04	5.46	4.07
1966	4.881	5.17	5.16	4.65	5.13	5.67	3.82	6.00	5.55	4.50	6.29	5.11
1967	4.321	4.84	5.07	4.85	5.51	6.23	3.96	6.00	5.10	4.19	6.55	4.22
1968	5.339	5.62	5.59	5.26	6.18	6.94	4.51	6.68	5.90	5.17	7.13	5.66
1969	6.677	7.06	6.85	6.12	7.03	7.81	5.81	8.21	7.83	5.87	8.19	8.21
1970	6.458	6.90	7.37	6.59	8.04	9.11	6.51	8.48	7.72	5.95	9.05	7.17
1971	4.348	4.75	5.77	5.74	7.39	8.56	5.70	6.32	5.11	4.88	7.78	4.67
1972	4.071	4.86	5.85	5.63	7.21	8.16	5.27	5.82	4.69	4.50	7.53	4.44
1973	7.041	7.30	6.92	6.30	7.44	8.24	5.18	8.30	8.15	6.44	8.08	8.74
1974	7.886	8.25	7.81	6.99	8.57	9.50	6.09	11.28	9.87	7.83	9.47	10.51

Source: *Economic Report of the President,* 1975 (Washington: U.S. Government Printing Office, February, 1975), Table C-58, p. 317.

4. *Differences in taxability.* A person whose marginal income is subject to a federal income tax of 50 or 60 percent will buy a nontaxable state or municipal bond yielding 5 percent rather than a taxable corporate or federal government bond of equal safety yielding 6 or 7 percent, since the net yield will be higher.

5. *Differences in market imperfections.* If the credit market were perfectly competitive, the above four characteristics would completely describe the differences in interest rates. But credit markets are seldom perfectly competitive. The mobility of funds is often inhibited by a number of factors—but the most important of these are a lack of information for borrowers and lenders and the legal limitations placed on various financial institutions on the kind of loans permitted.

TRENDS IN INTEREST RATES

Table 19-1 also points out that historically interest rates have fluctuated. While all interest rates usually move together in the same direction, they do not move by precisely the same *magnitude*. For the most part these fluctuations have been associated with swings in the rate of economic activity, the rate of money creation, and the rate of inflation.

The interesting and difficult question that has confronted economists for a long time is this: What is the rationale for interest itself, and what causes the general level of interest rates to vary? While we have already alluded to this question, we shall take it up in a more systematic fashion in the succeeding sections, examining not only the modern liquidity preference and loanable funds theories but the classical approach as well. Before attempting to examine the classical interest theory, we will first review briefly the complete classical model.

THE CLASSICAL MODEL

Until the time of the Great Depression, classical economists felt that a free enterprise economy was capable of providing virtually continuous full employment. This self-adjusting, full-employment mechanism envisaged by the classical economists was based on two tenuous assumptions: (1) that "Say's Law of the Conservation of Purchasing Power"—which stated that general overproduction was impossible because supply creates its own demand—was valid; and (2) that wages, prices, and interest rates were flexible.

Even though "Say's Law" guaranteed that the act of producing goods would perforce generate an amount of money income exactly equal to the dollar value of the goods produced, some of the recipients of the income would decide to save a portion of their incomes, thereby constituting a "leakage" in the income-expenditure flow. This is why the wage-price-interest rate flexibility was also needed to insure full employment in the classical model. Thus, even when difficulties arose from a change in the propensity to save or a change in investment opportunities, classical economists envisaged a double line of defense: If flexible interest rates should fail, flexible wages and prices would not.

That is, classical economists contended that any "leakage" in the income-expenditures flow caused by household savings would be exactly compensated by an "injection" in the form of business investment. And it was the interest rate that would guarantee the equality of these saving and investment flows at the full employment level. But the flexible interest rate might fail, for example, because banks might not allow the interest rate to fall to the level necessary to achieve full employment. This could occur if, as securities prices began to rise and interest rates began to fall, banks became net sellers of securities, thereby reducing the supply of money held by the public. But should the flexible interest rate fail, there was another defense. The resulting loss in employment, real output, and real income from the reduced investment and consumption spending could be compensated for by sufficient declines in wages and prices. In short, interest rate and/or wage-price flexibility assured full employment in the classical model. Interest rate and/or wage-price rigidity was the only possible cause of unemployment in the classical system, and the classics did not recognize its existence.

INTEREST—CLASSICAL EXPLANATION

Let us examine more closely how the classical interest rate operated. The classics tried to explain the interest rate as the price at which the supply of savings offered equalled investors' demand for these savings. Interest, they said, is the reward for thriftiness. The higher the interest rate, the more will be saved. This saving schedule is represented by SS. Suppose the demand for investment funds is represented in Figure 19-1 by I_1. At an interest rate of i_1 the amount saved will be OA, as will also be the amount invested. But now

INTEREST RATE

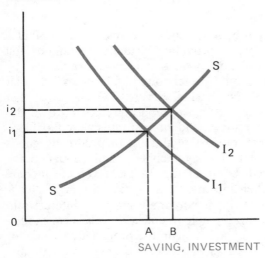

SAVING, INVESTMENT

Figure 19-1   Classical Explanation of
                     Determination of Interest Rate

assume there is an increase in the demand for investment funds, represented by a shift of the demand schedule to I_2. There is no reason for the saving schedule to shift simultaneously. But at the i_1 level of interest rates, the quantity of savings demanded exceeds the quantity supplied. The borrowers' competition for funds drives up interest rates. The higher interest rates induce people to save more. Saving and investment become equal again, now at OB. Similarly, if the investment demand should fall, the supply of savings at the existing interest rate would exceed the quantity demanded; price (the interest rate) would fall; and the quantities of savings demanded and supplied would again be equal.

Modern macroeconomics discredits the classical belief that the interest rate equates household saving and business investment by questioning the linkage between savers and investors. It is argued that savers and investors are for the most part distinct groups who formulate their saving and investment decisions for reasons which are largely unrelated to the interest rate. Moreover, modern analysis questions the theoretical and empirical foundation of the second line of defense, price-wage flexibility.

The conclusions of classical economists were based upon tenuous assumptions, namely:

1. The amount of saving increases with an increase in interest rates.
2. All money income saved is available to borrowers.
3. The only funds available to borrowers are those supplied by savers.

Let us examine each of these assumptions.

Interest Rates and the Amount of Saving

Modern analysis emphasizes that the amount which households desire to save is governed primarily by the level of national income, not the interest rate. In addition, it is argued that the household's saving (and consumption) schedules are influenced by such factors as their holdings of liquid assets; stocks of durable goods on hand; expectations as to future income, prices, and product availability; level of indebtedness; taxation; and general attitudes toward thrift. Even if the interest rate does significantly affect the propensity to save, the direction of the effect is not clear. Perhaps a high interest rate encourages people to reduce their consumption. If your money will not earn more than 3 percent, you may feel that you should spend it all; but if the interest rate rises to 5 or 6 percent, you may become more thrifty. Yet things might work out just the other way. If your saving's goal is retirement income, you may try to increase your savings as the interest rate falls. A retirement income of $3,000 will require you to save $100,000 if you can get no more than 3 percent. If you can get 6 percent, you will need to save only $50,000. The higher interest rate will not only give you the same income with a smaller principal, it will also give you more help in creating that principal if you are putting money aside over a number of years. If the interest rate is 8 percent rather than 4 percent, you will need to save out of your noninterest income much less than half as much to have a given income 20 or 30 years from now.

One of the advantages of the income approach is that it clarified our thinking on this point. It forced us to distinguish between "saving" and what we do with money that we do not wish to spend for consumption goods. The act of saving does not in itself yield interest. It consists of the nonconsumption of income. The level of interest rates does perhaps have some connection with the amount of income that we choose not to consume, but a far more direct and important factor is the one stressed in these chapters—the level of income. Whether you save $50 or $50,000 next year depends primarily upon your income, not upon the level of interest rates.

Disposition of Saving

Income saved is simply income that one does not wish to consume currently. More than that we cannot safely say. Even though saved income may be made available to borrowers, this is not necessarily the case. Classical economists erred in assuming that the sole reason for saving was to receive an income by lending the savings (or by investing them directly). They overlooked the possibility that the saver might choose to hold his savings in the form of money, surrendering the possible income to be more liquid. The person might feel that the money could be spent or lent later to greater advantage. These earlier economists also overlooked the possibility that the money income saved might be used to repay loans, reducing the money supply as loans and deposits are canceled out. This possibility was less important a century ago when deposits were not the major part of our money supply. However, it can hardly be ignored in today's world.

Funds Available to Borrowers

It was once true that the only funds available to borrowers were those provided voluntarily and directly by savers. The funds were not necessarily saved out of current income, but they were sums held by consumers which could be used for consumption purchases. The development of modern financial institutions changed all that. It became possible for the banks to lend, either by issuing notes or by creating more credit. Henceforth, the funds taken by borrowers might bear little relation to the amount of idle funds offered directly by savers.

Concept of Saving

The fundamental weakness of the saving-investment explanation of interest lay in the looseness of its concepts and definitions. No distinction was made between planned and realized saving or between planned and realized investment. Looking at saving only from the viewpoint of the individual rather than of society, these economists failed to see that the more fixed the public's resolve to save, the less the saving that might result as income fell.

More specifically, relevant to the classical interest theory, classical economists did not realize the important distinction between money saving and real saving. It did not occur to them that if, at a time of full employment, financial institutions created more money and other forms of credit, forced saving could result, with savers spending all their money incomes but, because of the rising price level, not consuming the full amount of their real income. In this situation consumers would find themselves with no money savings, but would nevertheless have "saved" in real terms, for the value of what they were consuming would be less than the value of what they had produced at the original price level. What happens to the nonconsumed production? Business or government takes it, not by borrowing the public's money savings, but by bidding up prices with the additional credit it obtains from financial institutions.

These economists looked at savings as the result of personal decisions concerning consumption and nonconsumption of a given money income. The urge to satisfy current desires discouraged saving. By modern standards, such a concept of saving is seen as superficial, and the classical interest theory is unsatisfactory.

INTEREST—LIQUIDITY PREFERENCE EXPLANATION

The writings of Keynes and other modern authors focused attention on the unreality of the classical theory's assumptions. The income approach developed by these economists required a new theory of interest. According to this new theory of income, realized saving and realized investment (using both terms in the broad sense) are equal by definition, and the equating of planned investment and planned saving determines not the level of interest rates but the level of income. The question of what determines the level of interest rates remained to be answered.

Keynes' own explanation struck out along an original line. Interest, he said, is a reward for giving up liquidity, not at all a reward for thriftiness. Liquidity, to Keynes, was the capability to resell a good or asset quickly at its original purchase price.

Part of income will be unconsumed, the amount depending upon the level of income. The question then arises: In what form shall this saving be held? Other things being equal, people usually prefer to hold money rather than less liquid assets. Money represents the ultimate in liquidity; and although its purchasing power may rise or fall, $10,000 is always $10,000. That is, money has 100 percent liquidity. Any other asset for which one may exchange $10,000 will have an uncertain money value, determinable only when the owner actually converts the asset back into money.

Interest is paid to persuade people to exchange their money for less liquid assets. According to Keynes, there are three motives behind the general preference for holding highly liquid cash: balances required for normal operating *transactions*, balances that reflect a *precautionary* disposition, and balances that are frankly *speculative*.

The Transactions Motive

A stock of money must necessarily be held to permit regular and more or less continuous expenditures out of income received at intervals. The person paid weekly or monthly and the professional person receiving fees at irregular intervals must at all times maintain a stock of cash to make daily purchases. Likewise, a business must maintain adequate cash reserves to permit continuous operations. Payrolls must be met, raw materials purchased, and other necessary expenditures made, even if the firm has had no receipts for some weeks or months. This is the transactions motive for demanding money.

The Precautionary Motive

A stock of money may be desired for emergency use to take care of misfortune, such as illness, accident, or loss of employment. Although other assets may at such times be converted into money, to sell these assets quickly may result in a loss. Ready cash is important as a first line of defense, for it is the most liquid of all assets. This is the basis of the precautionary motive.

The Speculative Motive

Many people will hold money because they hope to outguess the market. One can never be certain of the level of interest rates in the future. If interest rates never changed, then anyone who held sufficient funds to take care of the two requirements listed above would have no other reason to hold cash. It would be better to lend additional funds as long as any interest could be earned for riskless loans. Any return received would be more than could be secured by holding cash. However, even if there is no risk of default on the loan, there is always the possibility that interest rates may rise; and if rates do rise, then bonds bought (or loans made) at earlier, lower rates will decline in value.[1] In such a case, a loss is incurred. If the bonds are sold prior to maturity, then the loss amounts to the decrease in the selling price of the bonds. But even if the bonds are held to maturity, there is a loss to the bondholder because of the lower than current market yield on the original investment. Hence, many will hold some cash for this speculative motive (hoping for better returns from future investment) rather than purchase earning assets.

During the 1930s, the great inflow of gold into the United States caused an increase in the public's money holdings. Since people were then holding more money (mostly in the form of demand deposits) than they wished to hold at their existing wealth and income levels and at the existing level of interest rates, they bought bonds, driving up the prices of bonds and consequently driving down the interest rates. Finally, interest rates fell so low that the public was willing to hold the larger quantity of money. The public's buying

[1] Long-term Treasury bonds that had sold for $970 in January, 1967, were selling at less than $770 by the end of the year as the result of just such a rise in market rates. Two years later they had dropped another $100. By 1975 these bonds were still lower as the market rates of interest on some government obligations reached an all time high.

and selling of bonds did nothing to affect the quantity of money, which merely changed hands.[2] But by bidding up the price of bonds, the public brought about a level of interest rates at which it was willing to hold the increased stock of money resulting from the gold inflow.

To the extent that banks also bought bonds, the stock of money was further increased. But the decline in interest rates finally brought about an equilibrium in which there was no further attempt to exchange cash for bonds, hence no further creation of new money by the banks. During this period commercial banks allowed their excess reserves to accumulate to the unprecedented height of $7 billion. They preferred to hold these enormous idle balances at the Federal Reserve rather than hold government bonds yielding $200 or $300 million a year, for they knew the bonds would decline in value if the low interest rates current at that time were replaced by higher yields. They could not be sure when or whether rates would rise; they could be sure that if rates did rise, bond prices would necessarily fall.

In summary, there were two crucial differences between the classical and Keynesian interest analyses.[3] First, Keynes assumed that saving (and hence consumption) depends on income rather than the interest rate. Second, he added the asset (i.e., speculative-precautionary) demand for money to the classical transactions demand.

DETERMINATION OF INTEREST RATES

It may aid in understanding these relationships if we set them down diagrammatically. We may think of the total demand for money (L) as being composed of two parts, $L = L_1 + L_2$. One part is available for transactions (L_1), while the other part is available to satisfy the asset, store-of-value, or precautionary and speculative demands for money (L_2). The more required for transactions purposes, the less will be left to serve as asset balances.

Transactions Demand and Income Level

The transactions demand for money will be governed primarily by the income level. At higher income levels, more money will be demanded for transactions purposes. Unless interest rates are very high, the transactions demand will not be affected by the interest rate. Thus, in Figure 19-2, corresponding to income levels of Y_1, Y_2, and Y_3, we find the amount of money desired for transactions to be OD, OE, and OF. The horizontal axis of Figure 19-2 measures not the actual quantity of money, but rather the desired quantity, or transactions liquidity preference.

---

[2]Unless the public bought from or sold to the banks.

[3]In the complete Keynesian model, as opposed to his interest analysis, there is one additional crucial change. He suppressed the classical labor supply function which postulated that the labor supplied was a function of the real wage, $N = N\left(\dfrac{W}{P}\right)$, and replaced it with an automatically determined money wage, $W = W_0$.

NATIONAL INCOME

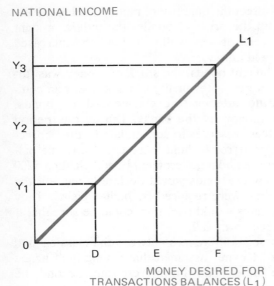

Figure 19-2   Transactions Demand
              for Money

Asset Demand and Interest Rates

The asset demand for money, unlike the transactions demand, is closely related to the level of interest rates. As interest rates rise, the amount of cash willingly held by the public will decline for, in the first place, the higher the interest rate, the greater the sacrifice one incurs by holding cash rather than an earning asset. The cost of holding a million dollars in the form of cash must be reckoned at $100 a day at a time when it might safely be lent at 3.65 percent. If the interest rate drops to 1.83 percent, the cost of holding the million dollars of cash is only $50 a day. In the second place, the higher the interest rate, the less likely it appears that rates will rise still further. Hence, it becomes more desirable to lend now, while rates are still high.

We may summarize these attitudes by a schedule, similar to the ordinary demand schedule. Instead of showing the amounts of a commodity that will be taken at various prices, this new curve will show the amounts of asset money that people will be content to hold at different levels of interest rates. As in Figure 19-2, the horizontal axis measures the amounts of money desired (L_2), but this time related to interest rates instead of income levels. If we know the demand schedule for money and the amount of money available for asset balances, we know from their intersection what the level of interest rates must be. Some holders must, of course, possess the stock of money at all times. The question is: At what level of interest rates will a particular stock be held?

If the available stock for asset balances is $20 billion, the interest rate, according to Figure 19-3, would be 9 percent.[4] If the stock were decreased to $7 billion, interest rates would rise to 12 percent as those most anxious to hold such balances sold bonds at lower prices to get cash. Finally, when bond prices are depressed to a level where bonds yield 12 percent, their price is stabilized. The $7 billion would then be held by those who are so determined to hold money that they are willing to forego a 12 percent return. Others less eager to hold money would hold other less liquid assets—in particular, bonds. If the stock were increased to $37 billion, the interest rate, or cost of holding money balances, would fall. The increased amount of money to be held as asset balances would be accompanied by a rise in the price of bonds and other securities. People would exchange their money for earning assets when they

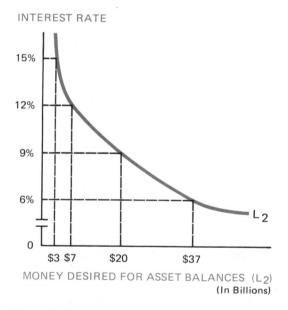

Figure 19-3 Asset Demand for Money or Liquidity Preference Function

---

[4]The stock of money is analagous to the supply function in ordinary demand-and-supply analysis. But in the case of money, the supply function can be thought of as a vertical line at the corresponding stock of money. For example, if the stock of money is 20 billion, supply and demand intersect to produce an equilibrium price (interest rate) of 9 percent. As discussed in this chapter, such a formulation of the supply of money is a bit of a simplification. In truth, the supply of money, as is the case for most supply functions, is not vertical but upward sloping. The amount of demand deposits supplied a commercial bank is positively related to the interest rate available for loans to private bond owners and to the available excess reserves. However, the basic mechanics employed in our diagrams would remain the same whether the supply function is vertical (i.e., perfectly inelastic) or upward sloping.

found themselves holding more money than they wished to hold at, for example, 9 percent. Eventually the price of bonds would rise (and the interest yield, therefore, fall) to the point where there would be no further general attempt to exchange money for less liquid assets. At a 6 percent interest rate the public would be willing to hold $37 billion in the form of asset balances.

Like any demand schedule, this one, which we may call an asset demand or a liquidity-preference function, may shift at any time.[5] At a time when the public generally becomes convinced that the value of money will rise, almost everyone wishes to hold more money, with the result that the curve shifts to the right.[6]

We shall draw it "tailing off" to the right to reflect the fact that at low interest rates the public appears willing to absorb unlimited amounts of cash. This area is called the *liquidity trap*. When long-term rates are down around 2 percent, the public generally decides that the risk of loss from a rise in rates about offsets the scanty yield on loans and is content to hold almost any added amount of cash. As would be true of any demand schedule so drawn, the elasticity in this right-hand section of the curve approaches infinity; we may say the demand for money becomes infinitely elastic at low interest rates. Under such conditions an increase in the money supply will do little to stimulate the economy by encouraging investment, for it no longer causes the interest rate to fall.[7] If business prospects are bleak, it may be impossible to reduce the interest rate below the marginal efficiency of capital. At such times the interest rate, although low absolutely, may be high relative to the marginal efficiency of capital. Then the low level of interest rates provides no stimulus to investment. Further additions to the money stock will accomplish nothing except to increase the stock of money held in asset balances. Classic economists, you will recall, were never faced with this problem, for they assumed that all prices, including interest rates, were flexible and could fall to whatever level was required to achieve full employment.

In contrast to the infinite elasticity of the liquidity preference function at low interest rates, at high rates it appears to be highly inelastic. By the time interest rates have climbed to 12 to 15 percent, total asset balances have been reduced nearly to zero. Further increases in interest rates cannot possibly reduce these balances much more. Under these conditions, if the demand for money increases with no change in the quantity of money, the only result will be a steep increase in interest rates.

---

[5] We are showing that the amount of liquidity demanded depends upon, or is a function of, interest rates. Of course we can call the transactions demand also a liquidity function (even though it is a function of income rather than interest rates), but this designation would be confusing rather than helpful. Whenever we speak of the "liquidity preference function," we shall be referring only to the relationship between interest rates and the desired amount of money.

[6] In itself this would tend to cause a rise in interest rates. However, transactions are likely to fall at the same time. The money released from the transactions sphere is available for satisfying the asset demand; the interest rate might rise, fall, or remain constant as a result of the twofold change. As noted earlier, a desire to hold more cash does not increase loans, however, for one does not increase one's liquidity by borrowing. Rather, the same motives that lead to an attempt to build up cash balances will lead to the attempt to pay off any indebtedness before money becomes more valuable.

[7] Because demand deposits are created by lending against private debts (rather than purchasing nondebt assets, say, Picasso paintings), the creation of demand deposits directly affects the interest rate (rather than affecting only the relative price of paintings).

Income Changes and Interest Rates

We shall now put these two figures together in Figures 19-4 and 19-5.[8] First, assume that the quantity of money is fixed. Part is in transactions balances, the remainder in asset balances. The horizontal axes now measure actual M as well as desired L.

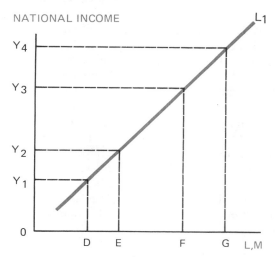

Figure 19-4 Transactions Balances

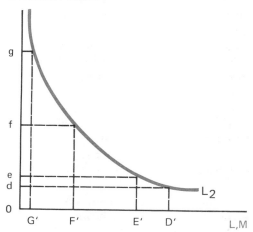

Figure 19-5 Asset Balances

[8]Although we have already established that L is positively related to real income (O), the price level (P), and national income (Y), and negatively related to the interest rate (i), we have not emphasized what the factors are that determine exactly the ratios involved. Some of the most important determinants are: the nature and variety of substitute assets, the society's wealth, the ease and certainty of obtaining credit, the system and regularity of payments in the society, interest rates, and expectations as to future income, future interest rates, and future prices.

An increase in income will increase the amount of money desired for transactions balances. Since we are assuming no change in the total stock of money, the added money for transactions must come from money previously held as idle funds in asset balances. Thus, the higher the income level, the larger the amount of money required for transactions, the smaller the amount available for "liquidity preference proper," and the higher the level of interest rates.

Referring to Figures 19-4 and 19-5, when income is Y_1 and OD is required for transactions, OD' is available for asset balances and the interest rate is d. As income rises to Y_2 and Y_3, OE and OF become necessary for transactions, reducing to OE' and OF' the amount for satisfying speculative desires, and consequently the interest rate is pushed up to e and f. By the time interest rates have increased to g as a result of continued income growth, the high yields have persuaded most holders of asset balances to exchange them for income-yielding bonds issued by corporations trying to increase their transactions balances. This is where the liquidity preference function becomes highly inelastic, since little more can be transferred from asset to transactions balances, no matter how high interest rates may go. Similarly, a decline in income will tend to be accompanied by a decline in interest rates as money is released from transactions and becomes available to meet the demand for asset balances.

Changes in Quantity of Money and Interest Rates

The effect upon interest rates of changes in the quantity of money also can be illustrated by Figures 19-4 and 19-5. In the preceding paragraphs we studied the effect of changes in income, all other things, including money, assumed unchanged. Now we look at the consequences of changes in the quantity of money, all other things, including income, assumed unchanged.

Suppose the economy is operating at Y_2, with OE in transactions balances, OE' in asset balances, and interest rates at e. At this point the total stock of money is increased. What happens?

No more money will be held for transactions purposes, for we are assuming that income continues at Y_2. The additional funds must be held in asset balances, and interest rates will be forced down, since at e we are not yet in the area where the demand for money becomes infinitely elastic. If the increase in money is equal to $E'D'$, asset balances must now be OD', and the interest rate falls to d.

The decline in interest rates may stimulate investment and, with the help of the multiplier, lead to an increase in income. Clearly, however, the increase in the quantity of money will not necessarily cause income to change, for the increased money supply will have little effect on interest rates if they are already very low; also, the marginal efficiency of capital schedule may be so inelastic that there will be little more investment, even if interest rates were to drop considerably.

Some modern analysis goes even further than the Keynesian analysis and emphasizes that the quantity of money demanded is positively related to the physical stock of goods, the price level (the product of which is wealth), and the current level of income, while negatively related to the interest rate. However, the addition of wealth as a factor influencing the demand for money does not change the general tenor of our results. For instance, it is still true that if a person holds an excessive amount of money—given his or her wealth, income, and interest rates—expenditures will be increased until just the quantity of money demanded is held.

Interdependence of Investment and Interest Rates

In presenting his liquidity preference theory of interest, Keynes denied, as we have said, that either investment or saving was a determinant of interest rates. He asserted that his explanation was in terms of a purely monetary analysis, concerned only with the stock of money and the public's desire to hold money. These were the sole determinants of the level of interest rates.

In fact, however, the liquidity preference explanation does not entirely eliminate investment as a determinant of interest rates, as it appears at first glance to do. The reasoning is somewhat circular. As we have seen, Keynes reasoned that:

1. The amount of investment is determined by the level of interest rates (and the marginal efficiency of capital).
2. The level of interest rates is determined, not by investment (or saving), but by:
   a. The public's desire to hold money balances; and
   b. The amount of money available for the public to hold.

However, as shown in the preceding pages, the public wishes to hold two types of balances—asset and transactions balances. Moreover, given the total stock of money:

1. Less money will be available for asset balances, and interest rates will therefore be higher as more money is required for transactions balances.
2. More money will be required for transactions balances when income increases.
3. Income will increase when investment increases.

Suppose that, with no initial change in interest rates or in the quantity of money, there is an increase in the marginal efficiency of capital (*MEC*). The resulting increase in investment will tend to raise income. The rise in income will tend to cause the public to hold more funds in transactions balances. With the total quantity of money unchanged, the additional money in transactions balances will have to be drawn from asset balances. The reduction in asset balances will tend to cause a rise in interest rates, the chain-reaction consequence of the increased investment. Hence, not only is the interest rate a determinant of investment; to some extent, investment is also a determinant of interest rates.

To bring this nexus out even more generally, consider the flowchart in Figure 19-6, illustrating how antidepressionary policy is supposed to work in

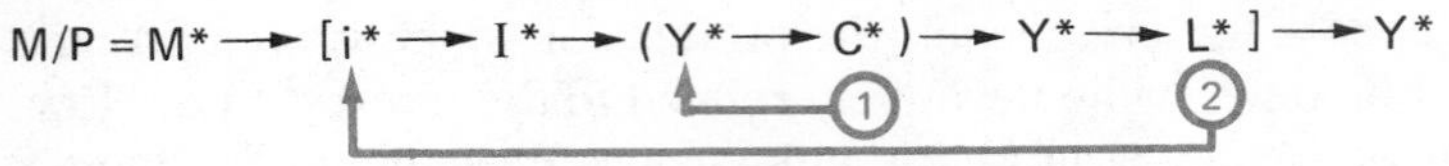

$$M/P = M^* \longrightarrow [\,i^* \longrightarrow I^* \longrightarrow (\,Y^* \longrightarrow C^*\,) \longrightarrow Y^* \longrightarrow L^*\,] \longrightarrow Y^*$$

(*Indicates *real* measures; ① and ② are feedbacks.)

Figure 19-6   Linkages and Feedbacks in the Keynesian System

the Keynesian system.[9] To cure a depression requires reducing money wages, prices, and incomes relative to the money supply; i.e., increasing $M/P = M^*$, the stock of money in real terms (or money relative to prices). This can be done by either reducing P, prices, (by reducing wages, prices, and incomes) or increasing M, the money supply. In either case we get an increase in the real quantity of money (M^*), and people find themselves more liquid, which results in a reduction in the interest rate (i^*).[10] The decline in the interest rate results in more investment (I^*). The new investment will result in more income (Y^*), which in turn will be spent in part on consumption (C^*). We then get feedback 1: the increased consumption (C^*) again creates more income (Y^*), which in turn creates more consumption and so on, cumulating in a magnified effect on income (Y^*) through the multiplier. By this long series of steps the increase in the real quantity of money $(M/P$ or $M^*)$ cures the depression by increasing income, spending, and employment.

But it is feedback 2 that we wish to emphasize. Increases in income caused by greater investment outlays (from either increases in *MEC* or M or declines in i or L_1) tend to increase the transactions demand for money. This has a feedback on the rate of interest.[11] Thus, once again we see that the interest rate influences and is influenced by the rate of investment spending.

This qualification is important to a clear understanding of the liquidity preference theory. It does not invalidate that approach, but does emphasize that it is not quite as revolutionary as first appeared. Keynes stressed money more than did earlier economists, but his interest theory does not, in fact, entirely rule out investment as a cause and determinant of interest.

Interest—Loanable Funds Explanation

Rather than concentrating on liquidity preference, some economists explain interest in terms of the demand for and supply of loanable funds in the financial sense. This is sometimes called the "common-sense explanation." Involving less break with tradition, it substitutes "loanable funds" for the "savings" of the classical explanation. The objections to the classical explanation do not apply, nor is there any fundamental conflict with the propositions of income analysis concerning saving and investment. The loanable

---

[9]This illustration of the Keynesian set of equations is from Abba P. Lerner, "A Program for Monetary Stability: Part Two," *Macroeconomics: Selected Readings,* edited by Walter L. Johnson and David R. Kamerschen (Boston: Houghton Mifflin Co., 1970), pp. 316–324.

[10]Note that all variables with the * superscript are in real terms, deflated by the price level.

[11]Of course only in the case in which M, P, and i are initially constant and *MEC* increases are we sure that the interest rate will later increase from its initial level. Nonetheless, feedback 2 will still operate in all these situations, although it is not certain whether the final i will be higher, lower, or equal to the initial i except in the case of a shift of the *MEC* schedule.

funds formulation does break with Keynes' interest analysis which used stock concepts—the demand and supply of money—by substituting the flow concepts of saving, investment, and money creation.[12]

Demand. The demand for loanable funds will be the sum of what businesses, households, and governments demand for investment and consumption in excess of current income. At any time there will always be some investment opportunities promising an unusually high rate of return and some demanders willing to pay an exceptionally high premium. Some funds will be demanded even at high interest rates. At lower rates more will be demanded. The demand curve, therefore, falls from left to right and is probably interest inelastic. A change in the marginal efficiency of capital will, of course, cause the whole curve to shift (unless simultaneously there should happen to be an offsetting change in consumers' demands for credit).

Supply. The supply of loanable funds will depend partly upon current saving, partly upon funds saved from past income, and partly upon the net change in bank credit.[13] Also, to the extent the public is willing to exchange idle money for savings and loan shares, insurance protection, or similar assets created by other financial intermediaries, the amount of loanable funds will be increased.[14] The principal determinants of the supply of loanable funds will include the amount of excess reserves held by the banks and the income level. At higher interest rates, more lonable funds will be available. Loanable funds theorists do not insist, in contradiction to Keynes, that the supply of savings is interest elastic; that is, that at higher interest rates more will be saved. They say only that a higher interest rate will probably increase the amount of loanable funds available; i.e., the supply of loanable funds is upsloping. The increase, however, might result from an increase in the amount of loans by banks and other financial intermediaries. Planned savings might be unaffected by the higher interest rate, as argued by Keynes.

Elasticity of Demand and Supply. Even if the supply of loanable funds were perfectly interest inelastic, interest rates would rise in response to an increase in demand unless demand also were perfectly interest inelastic. This appears unlikely. As long as either curve is elastic with respect to interest rates, a change in either demand or supply will require a change in interest rates. It seems reasonable to assume that both curves are at least somewhat interest inelastic, especially at the higher end of the rate spectrum.

---

[12]A flow variable has a time dimension, while stocks do not. Therefore, a flow must be expressed per unit of time. The weight of an automobile, money, wealth, savings, and capital are stocks, whereas the speed of an automobile, income, saving, and investment are flows. These concepts may also be used in combination or as ratio variables. The ratio between two stocks (flows) would be, for example, "liquidity" or liquid assets divided by total assets (saving divided by income). The notion of velocity involves a ratio between a flow and a stock; i.e., the flow of income on money transactions divided by a stock of money. The distinction between stocks and flows is one of the most important and one of the most commonly confused in all economics.

[13]The current and past savings of both households and businesses are a potential source of loanable funds.

[14]This is called *dishoarding*. The reverse process, *hoarding*, involves the desire to hold idle cash instead of income-yielding assets.

Comparison with Liquidity Preference Theory. The two explanations look at first quite different. The first states that interest is the price equating the demand for and the supply of the stock of money. The second states that interest equates the demand for and supply of the flow of credit, or loanable funds. Yet they come to about the same thing in the end. Whether we use the one analytical framework or the other, we shall arrive at the same conclusions regarding the effects of changes in the quantity of money or the marginal efficiency of capital or in saving. At one time this was denied. But as the novelty of the liquidity preference approach wore off and it was more thoroughly investigated, various writers made it clear that apparent contradictions between the two explanations were based on differences in implicit assumptions rather than on basic differences in the analyses themselves.[15]

Why then bother to present both theories? Partly because both explanations are used today and neither can be said to be the only correct one. The subject of interest is one on which there has been a good deal of disagreement among economists for a long time. It is not entirely resolved yet, although the differences appear to be narrowing and for practical purposes there is little choice between these two explanations. Their emphasis is different—the liquidity preference approach emphasizing the stock of money, the loanable funds approach emphasizing the flow of saving, investment, and new money creation. They do give us the chance to study interest from two points of view. As a result we should better understand the role of interest and some of its implications for monetary policy.

Carelessly formulated, both the liquidity preference and the loanable funds theories of interest may take in too small an area, implying that the only choice of financial assets is money or bonds. Financial institutions offer other alternatives, including savings deposits, savings and loan shares, insurance, and shares in investment trusts. To the extent that the public holds more of these near-moneys, its demand for money itself will be less, and interest rates will therefore be lower given the quantity of money and bonds. The various forms of credit supplied by financial intermediaries must be taken into account along with money and bonds when we are analyzing causes of changes in interest rates. In this respect the loanable funds explanation seems more easily adapted to the broader coverage than is the liquidity preference analysis, unless one uses a much less restricted definition of money than most economists currently employ.

---

[15]See Gottfried Haberler, *Prosperity and Depression* (3d ed.; League of Nations, 1941), pp. 183–221, for an extended discussion of the basic equivalence of the two analyses. See also S. C. Tsiang, "Liquidity Preference and Loanable Funds Theories, Multiplier and Velocity Analyses: A Synthesis," *American Economic Review* (September, 1956), pp. 539–564; and Paul Davidson, *Money and the Real World* (New York: John Wiley & Sons, 1972). Several economists have tried to reconcile Keynes' innovation—the asset demand for money—with the loanable funds theory by incorporating the flows of speculative hoarding and dishoarding with the flows of saving, investment, and money creation. While this transition often appears simple, there are many problems in this method of formulation. An excellent discussion of these points, as well as interest theories in general, can be found in Gardner Ackley, *Macroeconomic Theory* (New York: Macmillan Co., 1961), Chapter 9, pp. 171–207, especially the "Appendix," pp. 201–207; and *The Theory of Interest Rates*, edited by F. H. Hahn and F. P. R. Brechling (London: Macmillan & Co., 1965).

EVALUATION OF THE INCOME APPROACH

Seldom in the history of economic thought has a new economic theory had so sudden and sweeping an acceptance or so great an effect upon government policies as the income theory, which appeared during the Great Depression. It was partly a matter of timing. Most of the world was struggling with unemployment, excess capacity, and falling prices. A few unorthodox writers had long asserted, without any clear proof, that the traditional policy of cutting prices and costs was an uncertain as well as quite unnecessarily painful way to end depression. The traditional academic answer was that it was the only way. "What goes up must come down." Only after the price level had fallen to its "proper" level could business recover. An increase in the money supply might cushion the necessary fall in prices (quantity theory), although as long as the automatic gold standard was maintained there were limits to the possible scope of monetary policy. No other positive governmental policies were recognized.

Worse yet, the government was expected to take the lead in squeezing the inflation out of the price structure. It was to sternly trim off all but the most essential activities, raise tax rates if necessary, and make every effort to balance the budget. Thus, within the first two weeks of Roosevelt's first administration the Economy Act was passed, providing for, among other things, a cut in war veterans' pensions.

Before the Depression ended the emphasis had changed entirely. The straitjacket of gold had been removed, and efforts to raise the price level were no longer dismissed as reckless inflation. Economists realized that a fall in prices and costs necessarily required also a fall in incomes and therefore a decreased demand. It could not be safely assumed that lower prices would mean more sales, for the public would have less money with which to buy. With respect to repeated government deficits, the President was to say, "We planned it that way." A balanced budget or a budget surplus was no longer regarded as desirable at all times. Economists, businesspeople, legislators, and voters began more generally to accept the idea that in recession or depression the government should use deficit-financed expenditures as a powerful lever to restore prosperity.

Part of the enormous popularity with which the new theory was received in government circles and part of the reason for the speed with which it was assimilated lay in the fact that it offered a magnificently reasoned justification by one of the world's foremost economists for what political leaders wanted to do anyway. It is difficult to balance budgets in depression. It also is difficult to be reelected when millions are out of work, people are losing their homes, and corporations are going into receivership. If taxes can be cut and at the same time the government can spend more money, everyone should be happy. Previously such policies in depression were denounced as irresponsible and probably disastrous. Then, just when it was needed, appeared an imposing theory that claimed the deficits were exactly what the government should insist upon in depression, and the bigger the better. It was enormously popular. To be sure, however, it was not until the Conservative administration of Harold Macmillan in Great Britain and the Democratic administration of John F. Kennedy in the United States that the tools of the Keynesian "New Economics" were accepted wholeheartedly and intentional budget deficits were made an integral part of any program for economic recovery. The Johnson administration went even farther and was the first to employ extensively from the outset the tools and techniques of Keynesian economics. This indeed was the "Age of the Economist."

By showing more clearly the role of modern money, the income theory led to a better understanding of the potentialities—and the limitations—of monetary policy. We began to see why, to overcome deep depressions, we might find increases in the quantity of money, reductions in interest rates, even a devaluation of the dollar, to be hopelessly inadequate. Monetary policy might be helpful in restraining inflation and adequate to counter minor recessions. But when, as in depression, the marginal efficiency of capital is very low and public confidence is shattered, there may be no (positive) interest rate low enough to stimulate additional investment or additional borrowing to buy consumer durables on the scale required for full employment. If the increased quantity of money fails to affect interest rates, investment, and consumption, it is simply hoarded, and income is unchanged.

During World War II and the postwar years the new approach continued to be useful as a guide to the relationships between government expenditures, taxes, and the price level. Much less was said about the quantity of money than during and after World War I. More attention was paid to inflationary gaps and the necessity of increased saving and taxes. Income analysis is as appropriate to the study of inflation as deflation.

Yet no theory has a monopoly on truth. None is a complete, perfect explanation. The income theory has important advantages, but it also has its limitations.

Advantages

The most important advantage of the income theory is that it is not based on assumptions that restrict it to a special case. In the introduction to the chapter on the quantity theory we noted that the commodity theory is a special case of the quantity theory. We may observe here that the quantity theory, in turn, describes a special case. The fundamental weakness of the quantity theorists lay less in their reasoning itself than in their failure to recognize that they were implicitly making several assumptions, with the result that they were describing, not the general situation, but a very special one. As we have seen, where O = real income or output, P = the price level, M = the quantity of money in circulation, and V = velocity = $(P \cdot O)/M$, the quantity theorists assumed:

1. little change in O, and that O was unaffected by changes in M; and
2. little change in V, and that V was unaffected by changes in M.

Necessarily the quantity theorists concluded that an increase in the quantity of money would result in a proportionate decline in its value. In other words the equation used by the quantity theorists summarized the price and output effects of changes in the supply of money, assuming that there was no offsetting change in the demand for money. (Changes in the demand function for money are expressed by means of changes in velocity in this equation.)

The conditions under which the above assumptions would tend to be valid can be seen more clearly if we use the terminology of income analysis. Quantity theorists:

1. assumed a state of full employment;
2. ignored the demand for asset balances, so assumed that any additional money would automatically appear in transactions balances; and
3. assumed a fixed proportion between transactions balances and the level of income, adjusted for changes in income.

Consequently, an addition to the money supply would result in a proportionate increase in money income to maintain the usual ratio between transactions and income; that is, the new money would promptly be spent, and spending would continue to increase until income had been forced up in proportion to the increase in the stock of money. Also, since the economy was at full employment to begin with, the increase in income would be in the price level, not in real output. Therefore, the increase in the price level would be in proportion to the increase in the quantity of money.

Income theorists emphasized the restrictive assumptions of quantity theorists and classical economics generally, and went on to develop a general theory, applicable not only to the special case of full employment, but also to depression and inflation. By concentrating on income formation, they avoided some oversights of traditional economic theory.

Economic analysis was greatly helped by the attention focused on the circular flow of income. Clear recognition of the fact that costs are at the same time income threw a new light on the true significance of changes in costs and prices. It spotlighted the basic fallacy of classical economics—it recommended wage and price reductions to spur recovery from depression and ignored the effect of price and cost changes on total effective demand.

The analysis provided a useful breakdown of the components of income. We could see more easily the causes of changes in income and understand better how depressions could be fought and inflation brought under control. The clear distinctions between the nature and effects of saving and investment were important in helping us understand when and why these components should be encouraged and when they should be held in check.

The average and the marginal propensities to consume were helpful in tracing the effects of both shifts in income and changes in income. They showed how income might rise as a result of a transfer of income from those with a low to those with a high propensity to consume, reducing total saving and increasing total consumption. The marginal propensity to consume explained the cumulative change in income resulting from an initial change.

The average propensity to consume together with the accelerator underscored the possible difficulty of maintaining full employment indefinitely without government intervention. The income theorists clarified the process by which, as income rises to the full employment level, gradually increasing each year from increases in productivity, the average propensity to consume might decline and the percentage of income saved increase. The analysis showed that unless the amount of savings planned at the full employment level was equalled by investment, income would change. And it called attention to the probability that investment might decline while consumption was still increasing, if consumption was increasing more slowly than before. The increase in planned saving and the decrease in investment would result in a deflationary gap, forcing income below the full employment level. And income might remain indefinitely at the unemployment but equilibrium level unless the government took steps to close the gap.

In one sense the Keynesian general approach differs only in method from the classical approach. Recalling Figure 19-6, both schools recognize that to fight a depression calls for increasing the real money supply (M^*); i.e., increasing the ratio of money to prices (M/P). The classical approach calls for reducing the denominator P to achieve that end, whereas the Keynesian (and later the Friedman) approach opts for increasing M. The Keynesian position was based principally on pragmatic grounds. There are numerous institutional rigidities and viscosities that would cause numerous difficulties and lengthy delays before P could ever fall enough to restore full employment. Keynes emphasized that the same increase in M/P can be accomplished more quickly and efficiently by increasing the nominal stock of money.

Of course, in the special Keynesian case discussed above, monetary policy may not work to cure the depression. That is, increasing the stock of money does not work if there is a liquidity trap preventing a reduction in the interest rate beyond some level or if a collapse of confidence causes no further investment in response to a fall in the interest rate. In this case, only fiscal policy will work.

In the extreme opposite case, only monetary policy works and fiscal policy is helpless. This is the classical special case in which, instead of a mild response of the interest rate to the quantity of money or of investment to the interest rate, there are very significant responses of interest to money and of investment to interest. The Keynesian general theory includes both of these extremes and shows that it is a matter of discretion and convenience whether monetary or fiscal policy will, in fact, be used, as each will work.

Limitations

As it has been refined since its introduction 40 years ago, the income theory is not quite as tidy an analysis as it at first appeared. Among the many variables there are interdependencies that at first were unrecognized. Investment and interest rates are partly determined by, partly determinants of, each other. So are investment and income. The income theory originally treated changes in interest rates and in the marginal efficiency of capital as being independent of income, implying that investment was independent of income. We realize now that the interest rate is affected by changes in income as they affect the transactions demand for money, and that the marginal efficiency of capital may also be affected by the income level through the accelerator relation. In short, the investment level, as set by interest rates and the marginal efficiency of capital, may well be affected by changes in income as well as helping determine the level of income. What once appeared to be independent determinants of income have turned out to be determined in part by income.[16]

There has been some tendency to accept the propositions of the income theory as equivalent to eternal law. The theory fits together so well that writers have sometimes forgotten it is based on certain assumptions that may not always correspond to facts. The plausibility of the assumption that the average propensity to consume falls as income increases should not mislead us into supposing that this statement is necessarily true. Admittedly, it sounds reasonable. Also, it is to some extent verified by the statistics. The percentage of income consumed was certainly highest in those years when income was lowest.

However, comprehensive studies suggest that other factors besides current income are important determinants of consumption.[17] The Keynesian simplification may well have been an oversimplification, due in part to the lack of data. Probably more weight should be given to the factors of uncertainty and expectations, as well as to the stock of assets held, liquid or otherwise, and to the rate of change in income. Also, we should bring in incomes of the period immediately preceding. When incomes fall, it is painful to reduce consumption proportionately. This, together with some hope of a return to "normal," may perhaps better explain the increase in the average propensity to consume during depression than the simple statement that we will inevitably consume a higher percentage of a lower income.

Furthermore, living standards rise. There is little change from one year to the next, but over a period of years consumers tend to buy more goods and better goods than they would once have bought with the same income. This behavior may in part reflect the success of modern advertising in creating demand. Probably it is reinforced by the fact that, rightly or wrongly, today many seem to rely on the government to see them through. Confident that the government can prevent a general depression and that in any case it will provide somehow for those who are unemployed, some feel little pressure to

---

[16]It is noteworthy that while some of Keynes' earliest and most sophisticated critics recognized these linkages—e.g., John R. Hicks, "Mr. Keynes and the Classics: A Suggested Interpretation," *Econometrica*, Vol. 5 (April, 1937), pp. 147–159, who developed the *IS-LM* analysis employed in Chapter 20—the overwhelming majority of the beginning textbooks have failed to emphasize them.

[17]See Milton Friedman, *A Theory of the Consumption Function,* a study by the National Bureau of Economic Research (Princeton: Princeton University Press, 1957); Daniel B. Suits, "The Determinants of Consumer Expenditure: A Review of Present Knowledge," *Macroeconomics: Selected Readings,* edited by Walter L. Johnson and David R. Kamerschen (Boston: Houghton Mifflin Co., 1970), Chapter 8, pp. 59–92; and Robert Ferber, "Consumer Economics: A Survey," *Journal of Economic Literature* (December, 1973), pp. 1303–1342. In addition to the factors considered above, Ferber and Suits emphasize the following additional variables thought to influence consumption: stock of wealth, consumer credit, distribution of income, relative prices, previous maximum income, and lagged consumption.

save. The record indicates that our grandparents were more thrifty than we when measured by the percentage of real income saved. The saving function was shifted to the right over the last 50 years, so that to generate a given amount of savings a higher national income is necessary.[18]

These complications interfere with the convenience of the analysis and make it a great deal more complex. They probably, however, are necessary if our answers are to be realistic. The necessity of including them does not destroy the usefulness of the original theory but does warn us against claiming an unwarranted accuracy for it. Its assumptions are far from being self-evident truths.

The error of the assumption that consumption depends only on income was often compounded by the further error of assuming that changes in the consumption function were so slight that they could be disregarded. This led to an exaggeration of the importance of investment (and government purchases) as the sole cause of income change. Events demonstrated that sizable changes in income would result from small shifts in the consumption function, and that we could not safely consider it as an unchanging and purely mechanical relation. The introduction of some new consumer good such as home air conditioning or the sudden growth in popularity of boats or color television sets may cause the public to buy these items, still spending as much as before for other consumption goods. This would cause an increase in the consumption function.

Although the percentage of income consumed depends primarily upon the income level, it is no doubt affected to some extent by the amount of money or value of other assets held. If a market boom doubles (or a bear market sharply reduces) the dollar value of real estate or securities, consumption is likely to change even if income has not yet changed. Also, it is surely conceivable that the consumption function might shift a little as a result of changes in the quantity of money. At a given income level, people might consume a higher than normal percentage of that income if, as at the end of World War II, they were holding unusually large amounts of money. Even if the interest effects are often the most important, it is a mistake to suppose that the income approach proves that monetary policy can be effective only through changes in investment induced by changes in interest rates.

There were other oversimplifications. In their eagerness to show the originality and superiority of their approach, income analysts overemphasized some relationships and underemphasized others. Keynes insisted, for example, that the level of interest rates had no effect whatever on saving, since interest was entirely a reward for parting with liquidity. Various objections were raised to the exclusiveness of this article of the new faith, the point of the British economist Dennis Robertson being especially clearly made. Suppose a boy is promised a reward for winning a race, he suggested. Having won, the boy is offered his choice between an apple and an orange. Should we

---

[18]Raymond W. Goldsmith *et al.*, *A Study of Saving in the United States* (Princeton: Princeton University Press, 1955), pp. 13–19; Suits, *loc. cit;* and Ferber, *loc. cit*.

say that he is given the orange only for giving up the apple or for two things—winning the race and giving up the apple?

At one time income theorists saw changes in interest rates as affecting only the borrower and neglected possible effects on the availability of credit. At the same time they exaggerated the importance of the interest rate to the borrower.

It is an unrealistic oversimplification to suppose that, given the demand for credit, the interest rate is the only determinant of how much will be borrowed. Since interest is the price paid for the use of the funds, it is, of course, an obvious consideration. But there are other factors, some of which may be more important. It may be that borrowers, for both investment and consumption purposes, are generally not very responsive to changes in the interest rate as such. They may feel, however, the effect of other changes that accompany shifts in the interest rate.

Suppose a tight money policy is adopted. Consumers planning to buy cars or household appliances may be little deterred by the higher interest rates. On a $1,000 loan, a rise of two percentage points in the interest rate will make a very slight difference in the monthly payment. But along with the higher rate may come an increase in the required down payment and a shortening of the repayment period which will much more effectively restrain the demand for consumption credit. Likewise, the corporation may find that it must borrow for shorter periods. Tighter money policies may require it to mortgage its property rather than obtain unsecured loans. Perhaps it will have to arrange for regular sinking fund payments to repay the debt. It may be required to give the lender a seat on the board of directors, to pay no dividends to stockholders until the loan is repaid, to extend less credit to its customers, or in other ways to restrict its freedom of action.

There is also an important institutional factor to be considered. Many concerns depend specifically upon commercial banks for their credit. If these banks have no excess reserves, the only way they can increase their loans is by contracting their investments, that is, by selling some of their bonds to either the public or the Federal Reserve Banks. But the banks must take a loss when bonds that they originally bought to show an 8 percent yield are now sold at a price to give the new purchaser a 10 percent yield. The capital loss necessary if the loan is to be made must be weighed against the extra income possible from making new loans. It may make the lending so unattractive that banks will be unwilling to increase their loans. Thus, even if borrowers pay little attention to the level of interest rates as such, they probably find it more difficult to obtain funds at a time when interest rates are high.

There was also the plausible but unsupported assumption that as income rises the marginal propensity to consume falls.[19] In view of the importance of the *MPC* and the multiplier, this unwarranted assumption involved serious error in its implications for fiscal policy.

---

[19]See the Appendix to Chapter 18.

The importance of the "liquidity trap" assumption as an empirical matter is also dubious. Because little support for it has been found in the many empirical studies of the demand for money made in recent years, the liquidity trap is rejected by many economists today.[20] However, there were certain time periods, such as 1940 when the Treasury bill rate at times was 0.014 percent per annum, when few people would sacrifice the liquidity of cash for a very low yield on a noncash substitute. (Actually, because of personal property tax exemptions and subscription rights, these yields on Treasury bills on occasion became zero or even negative).

On a theoretical level some of the more sophisticated defenders of the classical school have pointed out a shortcoming of the Keynesian analysis. They have demonstrated that even if there are rigidities—a liquidity trap and/or collapse of investor confidence—it is still possible to show that wage and price deflation will work via the "real-wealth effect" (also called the "real-balance effect," "net-claims effect," or "Pigou effect").[21]

Put simply, the real-wealth effect states that if prices and wages keep falling, ultimately this will cure the depression. The reason is that although people's land and physical capital assets will fall in value, the purchasing power of their hard money holdings will go up. This increase in real wealth will eventually lead to greater consumption and full employment. As Professor Lerner put it: "If prices fall enough, everybody who has a dollar will become a millionaire, and before that happens he will decide to buy a yacht, as befits his new situation."[22]

The proponents of the real-wealth effect developed this theoretical curiosity because they wanted to round out an ideal abstract system—the classical model—not to offer a practical policy. It does show there is no internal theoretical contradiction in the classical system in that if money, wages, and prices were perfectly flexible and in the case of a depression they could be deflated sufficiently, full employment would be achieved. However, even Professor Pigou—the father of the real-wealth effect and Keynes' most ardent antagonist—took a rather dim view of using hyperdeflation to cure unemployment when the simple expedient of increasing the money supply existed.

It is true that Keynes was careless at times in suggesting that a depression does not depend on price inflexibility. In this sense his theoretical analysis was faulty. But as a practical matter, neglecting the real-wealth effect is not a serious limitation to his income approach, for as even its promulgators were careful to point out, the real-wealth effect is of "no practical significance as

---

[20]See Ronald L. Teigen, "A Critical Look at Monetarist Economics," *Review* of the Federal Reserve Bank of St. Louis (January, 1972), pp. 10–23, especially p. 15, footnote 26.

[21]This theoretical, albeit impractical, suggestion is principally due to the late Professor Arthur C. Pigou (1877–1959) and Professor Don Patinkin.

[22]Abba P. Lerner, "A Program for Monetary Stability: Part Two," *Macroeconomics: Selected Readings*, edited by Walter L. Johnson and David R. Kamerschen (Boston: Houghton Mifflin Co., 1970), p. 319. In technical terms what happens is that the consumption (saving) function shifts up (down), in real, not money, terms, as a result of society's enhanced real wealth and eventually will intersect aggregate supply (investment) at the full employment level.

an automatic cure for depression because it calls for a degree of pure flexibility which does not exist and which could not possibly exist."[23]

Perhaps the most serious objections are really not to the income theory itself but to the misuse of it to justify questionable policies. The theory itself is neutral. Pressure groups find it effective to support their arguments by an appeal to income theory. This is very natural, but it has sometimes led people to believe that the theory itself is unsound.

Union officials, for example, may point to the necessity of maintaining purchasing power as a justification for higher wages. Certainly higher wages for union workers raise their purchasing power, but the increase will probably be at the expense of some other group—at the expense of profits if prices are not raised and at the expense of those on fixed incomes if prices do rise. The net effects are far more complicated than they are made to appear when the amount of investment and the amount of consumption by all others are conveniently assumed to be unaffected. "The interest of those who gain is hardly to be identified with the whole, if the whole includes also those who lose."[24]

Similarly, highly progressive income taxes are often justified on the grounds that they make possible a redistribution of income from those with a low *MPC* to those with a higher *MPC*, hence raising total income. Again the answer is not a necessary, inescapable conclusion from the logic of income analysis. It results from the emphasis upon the *MPC* and the omission of reference to the effects of high taxes upon the amount of investment. Perhaps the highly progressive taxes tend to cause economic stagnation. Also, this argument must be recognized as greatly oversimplified. Granting that the thousand dollars taxed away from a rich person may reduce his consumption by only $100 and increase by $980 the spending of the poor person to whom it is transferred, we can say only that initial consumption spending has been increased by $880. We have no right to assume that the ultimate effect of the transfer will be to cause the entire total of subsequent consumption spending to be 9.8 times as great as it would have been without the transfer. It might be greater and it might be less. It depends upon the marginal propensity to consume of those who would receive the $100 and the $980 respectively and all those who would subsequently be affected.

We should not consider it a fault of income analysis that it is sometimes misused as a means of rationalizing actions that groups have already decided would be in their interest. For that matter, they might also quote the scriptures to support their argument. A more thorough analysis, still in income terms, may show why such policies would be undesirable.

There is one serious limitation. Although income analysis, honestly applied, will indicate just as clearly the appropriate policies to counter inflation as to fight depression, the policies are far more difficult to effect in inflation.

---

[23]*Ibid.*

[24]Edward H. Chamberlin *et al.*, "The Economic Analysis of Labor Union Power," *Labor Unions and Public Policy* (Washington: American Enterprise Association, 1958), p. 9.

The remedies are less palatable than the prescriptions for depression. Increases in government spending and reductions in taxes are always popular, their opposites practically always unpopular. Government deficits cannot be turned on and off like an electric light. It is easy to expand government spending and to multiply government agencies. It is nearly impossible to contract them. For practical, not theoretical, reasons the income approach tends to create an inflationary bias and an erosion of the value of money. The weakness lies not in the theory itself but in the requirements of politics.

SUMMARY AND CONCLUSION

At any time there is no single interest rate but a complex or structure of market rates which can and often do differ widely. There are a number of reasons for these differences—differences in liquidity and safety, administrative costs, term structure, taxability, and market imperfections. Over time these various interest rates usually move together in the same direction, but not by precisely the same magnitude.

"Say's Law of the Conservation of Purchasing Power" encapsulates the classical economists' views on macroeconomics. Put simply, Say's Law stated that since supply creates its own demand, general overproduction was impossible. Even if there were a temporary deficiency in total spending, there would necessarily and automatically be, according to the classics, compensating price-wage adjustments that would ensure that real output, employment, and real income would remain at the full employment level. The fact that saving occurs would not destroy this conclusion for the interest rate was thought automatically to adjust to synchronize the saving decisions by savers and the investment plans of investors. As a result of the Great Depression, classical macroeconomics ended not with a whimper, but with a bang. Lord Keynes in his celebrated *General Theory* (1936) provided an alternative macroeconomic model in which he rejected the classical theory that price-wage-interest rate adjustments will automatically maintain full employment.

The most profound and lasting impact of the Keynesian revolution has been to emphasize demand over supply conditions. Say's long-run law that supply creates its own demand has been supplemented and even supplanted in some circles by Keynes' short-run law that demand creates its own supply.

The classical interest theory, which explained the interest rate as the price at which the supply of savings offered equalled the investment demand for these savings, was found to rest upon three shaky assumptions: (1) saving was positively related to the interest rate; (2) borrowers had access to all savings; and (3) savings were the only source of funds available to borrowers.

Keynes' liquidity preference theory explained the interest rate as a payment for foregoing liquidity and not as a reward for saving. He argued that people demand liquid balances for three principal reasons—transactions, speculation, and precaution. The first of these motives depends largely on the income level, whereas the latter two—known collectively as the asset demand—are influenced largely by the interest rate. Thus, the two crucial differences between the classical and the Keynesian interest analyses are that Keynes assumed first that the rate of saving depends on income rather than upon the rate of interest, and second, that the asset demand for money should be added to the transactions demand. Whereas Keynes' theory stressed the role of money much more than did the classical theory, his interest theory does not completely rule out investment as both a cause and a result of interest rates.

The loanable funds theory of interest employs the flow concepts of saving, investment, and money creation to explain interest rather than the stock variables of the liquidity preference theory. When carefully formulated, these two approaches come to practically the same thing.

While the income approach has both its advantages and its limitations, its sudden and widespread acceptance is unparalleled in the history of economic doctrines. The architect of this powerful movement known as the "Keynesian Revolution" or the "New Economics" was the British economist John Maynard Keynes (1883–1946). His powerful remedy for massive unemployment represented more than a breath or even a gust of fresh air; it grew to a full-blown gale. The dispute between Keynesian and classical economists has now lost most of its acerbity and seems to have been virtually abandoned. In a very real sense, in part, we are all Keynesians now.

Discussion Questions

1. What are some of the factors that cause the existence of a structure, complex, or cluster of interest rates instead of a single interest rate?
2. What two tenuous assumptions undermined the classical economists' model which emphasized that full employment was inevitable?
3. Modern theory states that saving and investment will be equal (if government expenditures are equal to government's disposable income). Classical theory also stated that saving and investment would be equal. The difference between the theories is in their explanation of the cause of the equality. Explain fully.
4. One can save without receiving interest, and one can receive interest without saving. Explain.
5. List the principal determinants of the following, according to income theory. (Disregard the effects of G and T.)
   a. The amount of investment
   b. The income level
   c. The amount of consumption
   d. The level of interest rates
   e. The amount of saving

6. Assuming the stock of money is fixed and that interest rates are above the range of the liquidity trap, how would an increase in income affect interest rates?

7. Briefly explain the probable effect of each of the following on the level of interest rates.
   a. An increase in the quantity of money, with no simultaneous change in the income level
   b. An increase in income, with no change in the quantity of money
   c. An increase in the asset demand for money due to an expectation of higher interest rates, with no change in the income level or the quantity of money

8. Which of the following variables are stocks and which are flows: capital, money, savings, wealth, investment, income, saving, liquidity, consumption function, and velocity?

9. If both the transactions demand and the asset demand for money were completely inelastic with respect to interest, what, if anything, would be the probable result of an increase in the quantity of money, given the following two conditions? (Disregard the possibility of speculation in stocks, real estate, etc.)
   a. At less than full employment
   b. At full employment

10. Keynes asserted that interest rates were independent of investment. What did he mean and what did he overlook?

11. "A decline in interest rates tends to be both a result of and a cause of an increase in the quantity of money." Explain.

12. Briefly contrast the loanable funds explanation of interest rates with:
    a. The classical explanation
    b. The liquidity preference explanation

13. Discuss briefly the factors which are likely to influence the transactions and asset demands for money.

Chapter 20   *IS–LM* General Equilibrium Analysis: A Synthesis

The limitations of income theory and quantity theory can to some extent be overcome if we combine the two approaches. Rather than study the effect of monetary changes alone or changes in investment and consumption alone, we shall analyze the combined effect of changes in all these factors.

Earlier we examined the role of the government and financial institutions in generating a supply of money function. Next, we merged monetary economics with macroeconomics to derive the demand for money function. Together these two forces gave us equilibrium in the monetary sphere. In this chapter we wish to immerse the monetary equilibrium into a general equilibrium sphere in which there is an equilibrium solution in both the money *(LM)* and the commodity *(IS)* markets. The *IS–LM* model is the vehicle we use for showing this broad general equilibrium solution.[1]

With the help of a simple diagram we can summarize the relationships among most of the important general equilibrium variables we have been studying in previous chapters, bringing everything together with just two curves.[2] These curves will summarize the interrelationships between income, interest rates, and:

1. The *real* factors: investment *(I)*, saving *(S)*, and the consumption function; and
2. The *monetary* factors: the quantity of money *(M)* and the demand for money *(L)*.

The analysis emphasizes that for income in the private sector of the economy to be at an equilibrium level:

---

[1]The original presentation of the *IS–LM* model was in John R. Hicks, "Mr. Keynes and the 'Classics': A Suggested Interpretation," *Econometrica* (April, 1937), pp. 147–159. However, it was popularized by Keynes' disciple Alvin H. Hansen, *Monetary Theory and Fiscal Policy* (New York: McGraw-Hill Book Co., 1949), especially Chapter 5. In fact, some writers refer to *IS–LM* analysis as Hicks-Hansen analysis. Although most macroeconomic textbooks utilize this framework in part, an advanced treatment of classical and Keynesian macroeconomics can be found in Don Patinkin, *Money, Interest, and Prices* (2d ed.; New York: Harper & Row, Publishers, 1965), especially Chapters 9–14; Gardner Ackley, *Macroeconomic Theory* (New York: Macmillan Co., 1961), especially Chapters 5–15, pp. 105–418; Martin J. Bailey, *National Income and the Price Level* (2d ed.; New York: McGraw-Hill Book Co., 1971); Richard J. Sweeney, *A Macro Theory with Micro Foundations* (Cincinnati: South-Western Publishing Co., 1974); Axel Leijonhufvud, *On Keynesian Economics and the Economics of Keynes: A Study in Monetary Theory* (London: Oxford University Press, 1968); and Warren L. Smith, *Macroeconomics* (Homewood: Richard D. Irwin, 1970).

[2]In the Appendix to this chapter an algebraic summary of the key relationships underlying this general equilibrium model is presented.

1. Planned investment must be equal to planned saving, at existing levels of
   income and interest rates; and
2. The existing quantity of money must be equal to the quantity desired at the
   existing levels of income and interest rates.

As was explained in Chapter 17, the government can offset an imbalance between planned saving and planned investment to maintain income at what would otherwise be a disequilibrium level. If in the private sector planned investment exceeds planned saving at full employment, the government can close the inflationary gap by decreasing its expenditures, increasing taxes, or both. Similarly, an excess of planned saving over planned investment in the private sector, forcing income to fall, can be offset by increasing expenditures, decreasing taxes, or both in the public sector. We shall return to this topic later in the present chapter.

Now, however, we shall be investigating the behavior of only the private components of income. The reason is this. Private income, investment, saving, and consumption, together with interest rates and the demand for money, are all closely interrelated. Each to some extent determines and to some extent is determined by one or more of the others. In the public sector, however, the disposable income (T) and the expenditures (G) of government are primarily the result of government decisions, not market forces. True, if tax rates are unchanged, an increase in national income will cause an increase in the government's income.[3] The point is, however, the government must decide every year whether to raise tax rates, lower them, or leave them unchanged. Government's expenditures are even less automatically responsive to market forces. They result from deliberate budget decisions. Finally, one of the most important considerations in the decisions made with respect to the levels of government expenditures and taxes is the condition of the private sector of the economy. Government officials must try to decide how possible inflationary or deflationary gaps can best be closed. This requires an understanding of the forces that determine the components of the private sector of national income, the subject to which we now turn.

THE *IS* CURVE

In Chapter 17 we discussed the marginal efficiency of capital schedule, drawn to illustrate that, other things being equal, the lower the interest rate, the more investment there will be. The *IS* curve at first glance looks like the same diagram. (See Figures 20-1 and 20-2.) As before, the vertical axis relates to interest rates and the curve slopes downward from the left. The horizontal

---

[3]Some writers use the term *fiscal drag* to refer to the possible restrictive effect on the economy of this automatic increase in federal tax revenues arising out of an increase in national income, where such revenue is not matched by corresponding expenditure increases and/or tax reductions. To get a better measure of such influences, economists look not only at the actual budget surplus or deficit but also at the hypothetical "full- (or high-) employment budget surplus or deficit," which measures what the size of the surplus (or deficit) would be with the existing tax and spending structure if the economy's national income were at the full (or high) employment level.

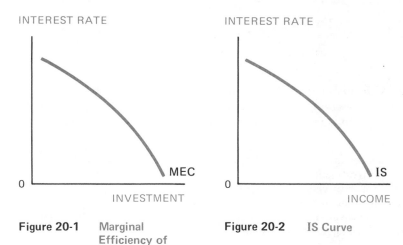

INTEREST RATE

INTEREST RATE

0   MEC

INVESTMENT

0   IS

INCOME

Figure 20-1   Marginal Efficiency of Capital Schedule

Figure 20-2   IS Curve

axis, however, now measures income, not investment. This is the key to the significance of this curve. It traces the path of possible interest rate-income combinations at which income in the private sector will be at an equilibrium level, with planned saving equal to planned investment.

Certainly this curve gives us no direct indication of the amount of saving or investment. Nor can we tell, from just this one curve, what the level of income or interest rates will be; we shall get around to that shortly. All we are now saying is that, other things being equal, the lower the interest rate, the higher the income level—because, as explained in previous chapters:

1. Lower interest rates (usually) cause more investment.
2. The increase in investment causes income to increase (by a multiple amount) to the point that planned saving will be equal to planned investment. Only then can income be at an equilibrium level.

Construction of *IS*

Mechanically, the *IS* curve is derived from the marginal efficiency of capital schedule (relating investment and interest rates) and the consumption function (relating income to consumption and saving). Suppose we have drawn the *MEC* schedule to show investment of:

$10 billion when the interest rate is 6%
$40 billion when the interest rate is 4%
$45 billion when the interest rate is 2%

Suppose we have also found the consumption function to be $C = \$70$ billion $+ \frac{3}{4}(Y)$.

On the basis of these assumptions we would expect the following investment-income combinations:

Investment	Income
$10 billion	$320 billion
$40 billion	$440 billion
$45 billion	$460 billion

More broadly, with this consumption function (or any other linear consumption function) we know that income will always be increased by a fixed multiple (here, 4) of the change in investment.[4] Thus, to convert an *MEC* schedule to an *IS* curve:

1. With the help of the consumption function, work out the income level at one level of investment.
2. For every dollar of change in investment, change the income level by a multiple of that amount, the multiple being determined by the multiplier.
3. Change the horizontal axis to "income" instead of "investment," and enter the income figures you have just worked out.

In summary, as illustrated by Figure 20-3, if the interest rate is 6 percent, the equilibrium level of income (according to the *MEC* schedule and consumption function we assumed above) will be $320 billion. At 4 percent or 2 percent the equilibrium levels of income will be $440 or $460 billion, respectively. At all three points planned *I* and planned *S* are equal, permitting income to be at an equilibrium level. Any change in interest rates will force income to change as a result of the change in investment and the multiplier effects. This would be shown as a movement along *IS*.

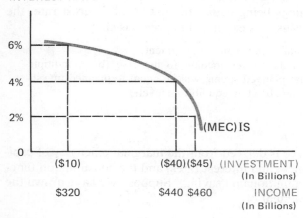

Figure 20-3   (MEC Schedule)
                    IS Curve

---

[4]If it were possible to work out reliable values for all the variables involved, we might find that the consumption function is affected by the level of interest rates, with the marginal propensity to consume higher (or conceivably lower) and therefore the multiplier higher (or lower) at low rates of interest than at high. If so, *IS* would be more (or less) interest elastic than if the multiplier is constant, since changes in interest rates would affect both investment and the multiplier. This possibility is of more theoretical than practical significance.

The *IS* curve is, therefore, downward-sloping. The equation for flow equilibrium in the commodity market is generally presented in the linear form $i = a - bNI$, where a is the constant term or y-intercept, b is the slope of the *IS* schedule, i is the rate of interest, and NI is the level of national income.

Changes in *IS*

Changes in either the marginal efficiency of capital or the consumption function will shift the *IS* curve. If there is an increase in the marginal efficiency of capital, as shown by a shift of the *MEC* schedule to the right, and if there is no offsetting decrease in the consumption function, *IS* must also shift to the right. All we are saying is that if at every level of interest rates there will be more investment than before and the consumption function is no less than before, then at every level of interest rates income will necessarily be higher than before to generate the required increase in planned saving. Put differently, the position of the *IS* curve is shifted by any change in autonomous spending—i.e., any consumption (investment) that is independent of income (the rate of interest).[5]

Alternatively (and less probably), if there is no decrease in the marginal efficiency of capital but there is an increase in the consumption function, *IS* must, again, shift to the right.

1. If the consumption function changed from $C = \$70$ billion $+ \ ^3/_4 \ (Y)$ to $C = \$80$ billion $+ \ ^3/_4 \ (Y)$, then when the interest rate is 6% and investment is $10 billion, income will be $360 billion, $40 billion more than in our earlier example. As the interest rate drops and investment increases, income will, as seen before, increase by $4 billion for every $1 billion increase in investment.
2. If the consumption function changed from $C = \$70$ billion $+ \ ^3/_4 \ (Y)$ to $C = \$70$ billion $+ \ ^4/_5 \ (Y)$, the multiplier has increased from 4 to 5. With $10 billion of investment, income will be $400 billion. Each added $1 billion of investment will cause income to increase by $5 billion rather than by $4 billion as previously.

It should be clear that the *IS* curve will be shifted to the left by any decrease in either the marginal efficiency of capital or the consumption function.[6]

Of course, the marginal efficiency of capital and the consumption function might change simultaneously, the one change perhaps offsetting, perhaps increasing, the effect of the other. But until the public sector is taken into account, only changes in the consumption function and/or the marginal efficiency of capital can change *IS*.

In summary, any *IS* curve illustrates possible equilibrium combinations of interest rates and income, given the consumption function and the marginal efficiency of capital. The consumption function appears to be fairly stable but, as emphasized earlier, the marginal efficiency of capital is far from stable. Like the *MEC* schedule, the *IS* curve may shift abruptly in either direction.

---

[5]As discussed below, any government spending or taxation via fiscal policy will also alter the entire *IS* function.

[6]Or as shown below, by any decline in G or increase in T via fiscal policy.

We must always bear in mind that the best we can expect to do with an *IS* curve is to represent correctly the state of affairs at the moment. We are saying, "Given the existing marginal efficiency of capital and the existing consumption function, we find the following combinations of income and interest rates that will equate planned saving with planned investment. Any of these combinations will permit income to be at an equilibrium level."

The slope of the *IS* function is determined by the slopes of the investment and consumption functions. The *IS* function is flatter (steeper), the higher (lower) the interest elasticity of the *MEC* or investment function and the higher (lower) the *MPC* and hence the higher (lower) the value of the "simple" multiplier.

THE *LM* CURVE

Earlier we developed the liquidity preference or asset demand function, such as shown in Figure 20-4, sloping downward to indicate that the lower the interest rates, the more money people would rather hold than exchange for earning assets. At that time we were investigating the relationships between the interest rate and the desired quantity of money given the *income* level. We showed the demand for money to be highly inelastic at high interest rates and almost infinitely elastic at low rates.

Now we are going to turn this around and look at the relationships between the interest rate and equilibrium levels of income given the supply of and demand for *money*. Even if planned investment and planned saving are equal, income will not be at an equilibrium level if interest rates are rising or falling. Interest rates will be stable and income in equilibrium only when the

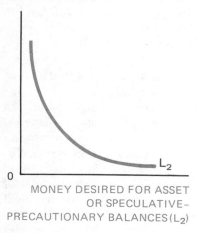

INTEREST RATE

L_2

0

MONEY DESIRED FOR ASSET
OR SPECULATIVE–
PRECAUTIONARY BALANCES(L_2)

Figure 20-4   Liquidity Preference
or Asset Demand
Function

existing money stock *(M)* is equal to the amount of money the public wants to hold *(L)*.

From our new curve we do not know or have any way of measuring the quantity of money, for our axes will be labeled "interest" and "income" as with the *IS* curve. Nor can we with this curve directly measure the demand for money. Changes in either the quantity of money or the demand for money will create a new *LM* curve. But given *M* and *L*, we decide (as explained in Chapter 19) that the higher the income level, the higher the level of interest rates; for the higher the income, the greater the amount of money required for transactions purposes. Therefore, the less remains (of a given quantity of money) to meet the interest-elastic asset demand for money. Rising interest rates ration the money stock, drawing it out of asset balances and into transactions balances. The total quantity of money is unchanged; but when an equilibrium has been attained, the total amount of money desired for both purposes (transactions and asset balances) will be equal to the total money stock.

LM is, therefore, upward-sloping. For the moment we shall not go beyond that and shall represent it simply by a straight line, indicating that as income increases, higher interest rates are necessary to equate the quantity of money desired with the quantity of money available. (See Figure 20-5.) The equation for stock equilibrium in the money market is generally presented in the linear form $i = a + bNI$, where *a* is the constant term or *y*-intercept, *b* is the slope of the *LM* function, *i* is the interest rate, and *NI* is the level of national income.

How would we show an increase in the quantity of money available? By drawing a new *LM* curve to the right of the first. On *LM'*, at any level of interest rates the equilibrium level of income will be higher than before; at any

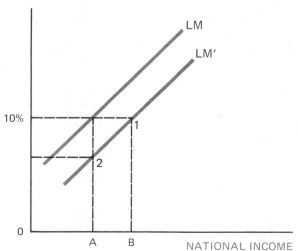

Figure 20-5   LM Curve

equilibrium level of income, interest rates will be lower than before due to the assumed increase in the quantity of money.

Thus, on *LM* the equilibrium level of income was *OA*, assuming a 10 percent interest rate. After the increase in the quantity of money, the new equilibrium level of income is *OB* if the interest rate remains at 10 percent (point 1 on *LM'*). The additional money has all gone into transactions balances. Asset balances are unchanged, so there is no reason for interest rates to change.

On the other hand if, after the increase in the quantity of money, income remains at *OA*, transactions balances are unchanged. The additional money this time settles in asset balances, driving interest rates down to the level at which the public is willing to hold the large balances (point 2 on *LM'*).

Points 1 and 2 are limiting cases of the possible changes resulting from increasing the quantity of money with income initially at *OA*. The actual change would probably be somewhere between them, with some increase in income and some decline in interest rates. A decrease in the quantity of money would, of course, shift *LM* to the left.

Finally, an increase in the demand for money would cause a shift to the left, from *LM'* to *LM*. The increased desire for liquidity, with the quantity of money unchanged, would cause interest rates at every income level to be higher than before. Or if we assume no change in interest rates, we are necessarily assuming a decrease in income. Less money will then be required for transactions balances and more will be available to meet the interest-elastic asset demand; and in spite of the increased demand (schedule) for money, interest rates can remain unchanged. If the demand for money falls (perhaps because more near-money is created), *LM* shifts to the right.

Thus, the *LM* curve includes both the money stock and its velocity and is therefore amenable to both Keynesian and classical macroeconomics. Since any particular *LM* function is drawn for a given money stock, a movement up along an *LM* function necessarily means that income velocity is going up.

Turning to the slope of the *LM* curve, the following generalization applies: The slope of the *LM* curve is flatter (steeper) the lower (higher) the income elasticity of the demand for money and the higher (lower) the interest elasticity of the demand for money.

Does the *LM* curve show what the level of income (and of interest rates) will be? Certainly not. Like the *IS* curve, by itself it merely sets out a series of possible equilibrium combinations of interest rates and income, with no indication of which combination will prevail.

GENERAL EQUILIBRIUM SOLUTION WITH *IS–LM* APPARATUS

Placing the *IS* and *LM* curves on the same graph, we find the level of income and the level of interest rates uniquely determined by their intersection. Only at this point can both the real and the monetary requirements of equilibrium be satisfied:

1. Planned saving and planned investment are equal.
2. The quantity of money held is the quantity desired.

Given:

1. The quantity of money,
2. The demand for money,
3. The consumption function, and
4. The marginal efficiency of capital,

and summarizing their relationships as shown in Figure 20-6, we conclude that interest rates must be at *OA* and the equilibrium income level must be at *OB*. The *IS* curve represents flow equilibrium in the commodity market and the *LM* curve represents stock equilibrium in the money (or financial-assets) market.

INTEREST RATE

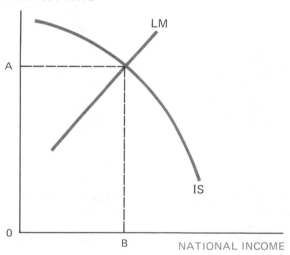

Figure 20-6   General Equilibrium Solution with
IS-LM Apparatus

LM PROBABLY CURVILINEAR

As a first approximation, we have to this point shown the *LM* curve as a straight line. More likely it is some kind of curve. Earlier discussion of the liquidity trap explored the possibility that at very low rates the public may be willing to add indefinitely to their asset holdings. At such times an increase in the quantity of money would not drive interest rates down further. This is another way of saying that if interest rates are very low, they may be affected very little by an increase in income. The added money required for transactions balances may be easily available from the asset balances, which for the time being are almost infinitely interest elastic. If income continues to rise, however, higher interest rates will probably be required, sooner or later, to persuade the public to continue reducing their asset balances. (We shall not repeat here the detailed explanation of the liquidity theory of interest. Review the discussion of the liquidity preference function, Chapter 19, if this paragraph is not entirely clear.)

The above reasoning suggests that *LM* curves probably look somewhat like one or another of the curves shown in Figure 20-7, depending on their interest elasticity.

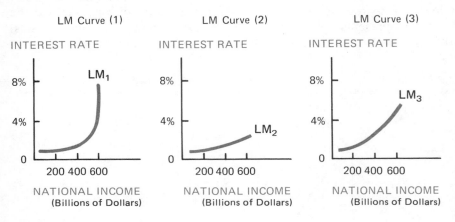

Figure 20-7   Three Alternative LM Curves

We are assuming in all three cases that when interest rates are at very low levels, an increase in income will not immediately cause interest rates to rise. If income continues to rise, the result may be as shown in Curve 1: interest rates rise steeply, with the curve becoming almost perfectly inelastic by the time income has risen to 600. At that point, presumably, nearly all the funds formerly held in asset balances have been transferred to transactions balances. Little more will be available no matter how high interest rates rise. (This level of interest rates relates to the highly inelastic area of the liquidity preference function at high interest rates.) The vertical segment represents the extreme pole envisaged by the classical economists in which fiscal policy is helpless as velocity has reached its limit and only doses of additional money from the central bank will help.

Curve 2 presents the other extreme. If *LM* is highly interest elastic, small increases in interest rates will continue to supply plenty of funds for the transactions requirements of the economy as income rises to 600. If income continued to increase with no increase in the quantity of money, Curve 2 would eventually rise steeply like Curve 1, but over the range of income up to 600 it is much more elastic than Curve 1. The nearly horizontal segment represents the Keynesian liquidity-trap pole, such as occurred with the low interest rates that prevailed during the Depression. No matter how far prices fall or how much the money supply is increased, the interest rate won't fall, investment spending will stay the same, and thus so will aggregate output and employment. Curve 3 is more elastic than Curve 1 and less elastic than Curve 2.

We may also suggest three general possibilities for the shape of the *IS* curves in Figure 20-8. As is true also of the *LM* curves, the different *IS* curves

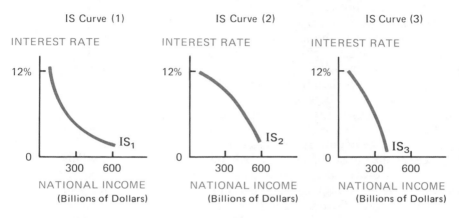

Figure 20-8   Three Alternative IS Curves

might exist simultaneously but in different countries, or they might exist at different times in the same country. In Curve 1 we assume *IS* is highly inelastic at high interest rates and almost infinitely elastic at low rates. The opposite (and more likely) conditions are shown in Curve 2. Curve 3 illustrates a situation in which, by comparison, *IS* is relatively interest inelastic at all levels of interest rates. This last extreme case was also suggested by Keynes. Under such conditions falling prices or an increasing money supply will reduce the interest rate, but this will not stimulate sufficient investment to provide full employment.

CHANGES IN THE PUBLIC SECTOR

Now we are ready to bring the public sector of income into our analysis. In earlier chapters it was convenient to list government expenditures and disposable income separately from private investment and saving. By this terminology, $S + T$ was necessarily equal to $I + G$. It was easy to see how an excess of planned saving over planned investment in the private sector could be offset by an equal excess of public "investment" (government expenditures) over public "saving" (government's disposable income).

At this point, however, it will be more convenient to define I to include G and define S to include T. Investment and saving, thus defined to include both the private and the public sector, will necessarily be equal at all times. Income equilibrium will still require that planned (total) investment be equal to planned (total) saving.

As we saw earlier, an increase in the *MEC* schedule shifts the *IS* curve to the right. Naturally we force a similar shift of *IS* to the right when we add public investment *(G)* to private investment. Total investment at every level of interest rates will be greater than private investment by the amount of government expenditures, so at every level of interest rates income will also be higher than before to generate the necessary increase in saving.

At the same time, the inclusion of government disposable income *(T)* in total saving has the same effect as would a decrease in the consumption function. At every income level total saving will be greater than private saving by the amount of *T*. *IS* is therefore shifted to the left.

It is unlikely that the shift to the right, from the inclusion of *G*, will be exactly offset by the shift to the left, from the inclusion of *T*.[7] This is not important to the analysis. What is important is that, in the first place, the shape of *IS* will be about the same as before and, in the second place, we can easily see the effects of changes in taxes and in government spending.

Let *IS* represent the combinations of interest rates and incomes that, at a given time, will equate total saving and total investment. What could the government do to cause *IS* to move to *IS'*? (See Figure 20-9.) It could increase its spending and/or lower taxes. (Alternatively, it might increase both *G* and *T*, but with a smaller increase in *T* than in *G*, or it might decrease both, but with a smaller reduction in *G* than in *T*.) The increase in *G* would cause total

INTEREST RATE

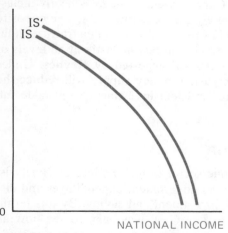

Figure 20-9   **Effects of Fiscal Policy**

---

[7]One consideration would be the amounts of *G* and *T* respectively. Moreover, a billion dollar increase in government expenditures is probably more stimulating to the economy than a billion dollar reduction in taxes.

investment to increase. The tax reduction would reduce total saving, thus increasing the consumption function. Either action would shift *IS* to the right. Moreover, the so-called *balanced budget multiplier* tells us that an equal increase in government taxes and government spending increases the equilibrium level of national income, whereas equal decreases lower it. This occurs because a change in government taxes affects aggregate saving less than a change in government spending affects aggregate spending. Thus, these are the fiscal policies by which a government can frequently counter recession or depression.

Now suppose that the existing state of affairs is represented by *IS'*. Evidently by cutting its spending and/or raising taxes (or by increasing *T* more than it increases *G* or by reducing *G* more than it reduces *T*), the government could force *IS'* to *IS*. These are the fiscal policies by which a government can often counter an inflationary spiral.

SIGNIFICANCE OF THE SHAPE OF *IS* AND *LM*

Under some circumstances national income can be effectively increased or braked by changes in government spending or taxes. At other times these fiscal policies may have little effect, and changes in monetary policy are required. The shape of the *IS* and *LM* curves will determine which approach is likely to be more helpful. Graphically, an expansionary monetary policy is represented by a rightward shift of the *LM* function and an expansionary fiscal policy is represented by a rightward shift of the *IS* function.

Suppose the authorities in country A and country B are trying to raise income. Suppose also that income in country A is at *OA*, as represented in Figure 20-10, page 504, and in country B it is at *OB*, Figure 20-11. Clearly monetary policy, by itself, is more likely to be effective in country B than in country A. In country A, increasing government expenditures or decreasing taxes can increase income by shifting *IS* to *IS'*. But if an increase in the quantity of money has no effect other than to shift *LM* to the right (as our analysis assumes), by itself it will accomplish almost nothing. At the existing income level, interest rates will be lowered little, if at all. Even if they were substantially reduced, there would be little increase in investment, saving, and income because the *IS* curve is highly inelastic at the point where it intersects *LM*. Note too that if the quantity of money is increased and simultaneously the government increases its spending or reduces taxes, most of the change in income will result from the change in *IS* rather than the change in *LM*. Thus, country A represents two extreme cases suggested by Keynes. In the first a portion of the liquidity preference function and hence the *LM* function is horizontal. This means that monetary policy is powerless to influence interest rates. In the second the *IS* schedule is very steep (i.e., very interest inelastic) and perhaps even vertical in places. In this case the lower prices and lower interest rates resulting from the monetary authorities' increasing the quantity of money will be unable to increase investment to the level required for full employment.

INTEREST RATE

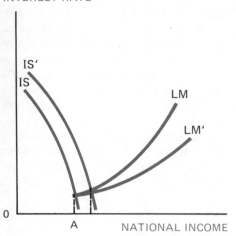

Figure 20-10   Country A
                     Effective Fiscal Policy

INTEREST RATE

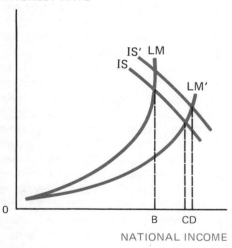

Figure 20-11   Country B
                     Effective Monetary Policy

   In country B we assume that (with the fixed quantity of money) income and interest rates have increased to the area where *LM* becomes highly inelastic. (See *LM* Curve 1, Figure 20-7.) Very little remains in asset balances, and interest rates can rise steeply without drawing much more into transactions balances. Under these conditions changes in taxes and/or government spending can have little effect by themselves. An increase in government spending (or a tax reduction) can move *IS* to *IS'*, but income will remain about the same. The additional government spending (or additional consumption spending if taxes are reduced) is offset by the drop in private investment, choked off by the steep rise in interest rates. In this situation there can be no significant increase in income unless there is an increase in the quantity of money—with (as at *D*) or without (as at *C*) a more expansionary policy of government expenditures and taxation. The situation in which the *LM* curve turns vertical is the classical pole. No shift in the *IS* curve can increase national income since money's velocity has reached its limit. At this classical pole, fiscal policy is impotent without the concomitant use of monetary policy.

Finally, Figure 20-12 illustrates the case in which both governmental fiscal and monetary policy will be effective, individually or in combination. By itself, the increase in the quantity of money would force income to rise to *OD*. Reducing taxes (or increasing government expenditures) alone would here force income to *OE*, and the effect of the two policies together would raise income still higher, to *OF*.

Although we have not shown this graphically, the shape of the *IS* curve is also crucial. In general, monetary policy is more effective the flatter the *IS* curve, and fiscal policy is more effective the steeper the *IS* curve. This is because the investment multiplier is larger in the first instance and the government expenditure multiplier is larger in the second instance. Can you demonstrate this?

To summarize: Monetary policy is more effective the flatter and therefore the more interest elastic is the *IS* curve[8] and the steeper and less interest

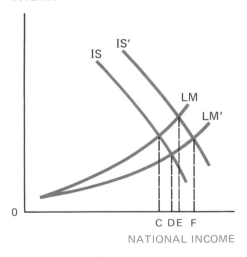

INTEREST RATE

NATIONAL INCOME

Figure 20-12 Effective Fiscal and
Monetary Policy

[8]Which, of course, reflects the curvature of the investment (*MEC* curve) and the consumption function.

elastic is the *LM* curve.[9] Fiscal policy is more effective the steeper and therefore less interest elastic is the *IS* curve and the flatter and more interest elastic is the *LM* curve.[10] More precisely, monetary (fiscal) policy is more effective when the *IS* schedule has a small (large) absolute slope and/or the *LM* schedule has a large (small) absolute slope. (Test yourself by first shifting the *LM* curve with flat and steep *IS* curves and then shifting the *IS* curve with flat and steep *LM* curves, in all cases using linear curves for convenience.)

CONTROLLING INFLATION

Figures 20-10, 20-11, and 20-12 suggest the extent to which an inflationary gap may be closed by tighter monetary policy and by tax increases or spending cuts by government. We now assume that *IS'* and *LM'* are the existing curves which may be shifted to *IS* and *LM* by restrictive policies. Not surprisingly, we find that in country A monetary policy is much less effective than in country B, just as it was less effective in promoting expansion. In country B, changes in taxes and government spending will accomplish less than in country A; the gap here must be closed primarily by monetary policy. In Figure 20-12, both types of action will help control the inflation.

FISCALISTS (KEYNESIANS) VS. MONETARISTS (FRIEDMANITES)

In the period after Keynes' *General Theory* but before the Korean War, the study of monetary economics was largely abandoned. However, since 1950, largely through the efforts of Professor Milton Friedman of the University of Chicago—building upon the older quantity theory of the classical economists—there has been what some have called "the rediscovery of money." Most aggregate analysis conducted today is a synthesis of the classical-Friedman and Keynesian ideas. These models espouse the moderate position that "money does matter" (perhaps even the stronger maxim that "money matters much") in place of the two extreme philosophies that "money does not matter" or "money alone matters."

Policy Differences

Nonetheless, these two camps continue to differ in the relative importance they attach to the means to achieve a given result. In particular, the

---

[9]Which, in turn, reflects the shape of the asset demand for money (liquidity preference schedule) and the supply of money function. Most presentations assume, for convenience, that the latter is given and fixed rather than interest rate sensitive as is, in fact, the case.

[10]The introduction of Pigou's "real-wealth" effect makes the *IS* curve flatter and therefore makes monetary policy more effective by enhancing the impact on *NI* of changes in the money supply. The *IS* curve is flatter with the real-wealth effect since lower interest rates not only increase investment but also increase wealth and therefore induce consumers to spend more. Hence, both investment and consumption spending increase and work to expand *NI* when interest rates fall as wealth effects are introduced.

fiscalists believe that fiscal policy is the most important means available to the government for affecting the level of economic activity, whereas the monetarists believe that monetary policy is more important.[11] The differences on policy as viewed by the monetarists are these: (1) The long-run effects of monetary policy are entirely on nominal variables—nominal *NI*, the general price level, and nominal interest rates—with little, if any, influence on real economic variables such as output and employment. In the short run, monetary policy can affect both real and nominal variables. (2) The long-run effects of fiscal policy on nominal *NI* are insignificant since government outlays financed by taxes or borrowing from the public tend to "crowd out" an equal amount of private expenditures. In the short run, fiscal policy can affect movements in output and employment.

As will be discussed in Chapter 22, most economists today favor a judicious blend of both monetary and fiscal policy. To them, the real question is whether the response of economic activity is larger, more predictable, and faster with monetary or fiscal actions.

Analytical Differences

Because the "monetarist revolution" (or "counterrevolution" as you wish) has spawned such as enormous outpouring of writings on the pros and cons of Keynesian and neo-Keynesian and quantity and neo-quantity theories, it is impossible within the space limitations to review all the nuances and subtleties here. The Appendix to this chapter does show the differences within an algebraic framework, and footnotes 11 and 19 in Chapter 15 give several references for the interested reader to peruse. However, it is useful to review some of the major points surrounding this interesting controversy.

1. The classical school, built upon the two major pillars of Say's Law and the quantity theory of money, emphasized that money did not influence the interest rate. Real things, such as the interest rate, were thought to be determined only by real forces.
2. Keynes stressed that the interest rate is a monetary phenomenon determined by the demand and supply for money and not by saving and investment as believed by the classical writers.
3. Keynesians emphasize the asset demand for money and the monetarists (and the quantity theorists) the transactions demand. The Keynesians feel that changing the money supply influences aggregate spending and *NI* only if it changes the interest rate and only if spending functions are interest elastic.
4. While the classical writers were most interested in and their model was most valid in the long run, modern monetarists apply the analytical framework of the quantity theory to the short run. Unlike the earlier quantity theorists, the new monetarists maintain that: (a) while income velocity is not a fundamental constant of nature, it is predictable, thus providing a

---

[11]An engaging dialogue, meant for popular consumption, by two celebrated economists representing the two opposing camps can be found in Milton Friedman and Walter W. Heller, *Monetary Vs. Fiscal Policy: A Dialogue* (New York: W. W. Norton & Co., 1969).

direct and reliable link between the money supply and NI;[12] and (b) changes in the money stock not only change the price level, but in periods of unemployment they also affect real output.

SUMMARY AND CONCLUSION

The IS and LM curves are a refinement of income theory, taking into account the interdependence of investment and interest rates overlooked by Keynes. If interest rates were in fact independent of the amount of investment, we could agree that, other things being equal, the one requirement for income equilibrium is that planned saving and planned investment are equal. But if, as income adjusts to an increase in investment, interest rates are forced higher (by the need for larger transactions balances), then investment must change again, this time downward. Then income falls, causing interest rates to drop and investment to increase again. Other things equal, there would be a diminishing series of oscillations, approaching an equilibrium level of income. Equilibrium will be reached only when planned saving is equal to planned investment and, in addition, there is no further incentive to increase or reduce asset balances. In other words, total cash balances held must be equal to total cash balances desired at that income level and that level of interest rates.

At the intersection of the LM and IS curves both requirements are satisfied. At that point there is no incentive for further change in interest rates, spending, or income—until, of course, a change occurs in public saving or investment or in the determinants of private saving and investment (the marginal efficiency of capital, the consumption function, the quantity of money, and the demand for money).

Subject to its own qualifications then, the IS-LM analysis is a useful analytical tool.[13] With it, as with any theoretical abstraction, we must always remember the basic assumptions. Bemused by the details and the elegance of the analysis, we may be tempted to declare, for example, that monetary policy cannot possibly be effective if circumstances are as shown in Figure 20-10. This is nonsense. We can safely say that, under the circumstances, monetary policy can do nothing to stimulate investment by lowering interest rates. This the figure does faithfully represent. But note we are assuming that the increase in money will have no effect at any time except that it may lower

---

[12]Sophisticated quantity theorists are not surprised that NI has climbed about twice as fast as the money stock since 1939. After declining for a long time before 1945, velocity started rising gradually. This has been the result of several factors: (1) high (nominal) interest rates, (2) inflation, (3) greater usage of credit cards and computers, and (4) better methods for scheduling inventories of money.

[13]The qualifications of the consumption function were discussed in Chapter 16. In addition, in a famous extension of the Hicks-Hansen analysis, Warren L. Smith, in "A Graphical Exposition of the Complete Keynesian System," *Southern Economic Journal* (October, 1956), pp. 115–125, added prices, wages, and employment. Later Robert A. Mundell, "An Exposition of Some Subtleties in the Keynesian System," *Weltwirtschaftliches Archiv* (December, 1964), pp. 301–312, extended the IS-LM analysis still further by incorporating economic growth into the model. These two articles are reprinted in *Macroeconomics: Selected Readings*, edited by Walter L. Johnson and David R. Kamerschen (Boston: Houghton Mifflin Co., 1970), Chapters 3 and 5, pp. 19–26 and 32–38.

interest rates. That is, we are assuming that the only effect of an increase in the quantity of money will be that *LM* shifts to the right. This the figure does not prove or even suggest.

Purely to simplify the analysis and permit us to deal with one thing at a time, we assume, in constructing *IS*, that it will not be shifted by changes in the quantity of money. Often this assumption will correspond with the facts. [14] At other times it may not. There are surely times when an increase in the quantity of money might be interpreted, rightly or wrongly, as an indication of inflation ahead or at least of better times ahead. The marginal efficiency of capital is based, you recall, on expectations. The increase in the quantity of money, by affecting expectations, could conceivably lead to an increase in the marginal efficiency of capital and at the same time to an increase in the marginal propensity to consume. (Suppose people have been postponing purchases but that the increase in money restores confidence and encourages more spending—not a necessary consequence of an increase in the money supply, but surely not an impossible consequence, especially if interest rates are falling and the prices of bonds and stocks are rising.) For either or both reasons, the *IS* curve would shift to the right. Even country A may not need tax reductions or increased government spending.

The analytical apparatus of the *IS* and *LM* curves is no better and no worse with its assumptions than are most other economic abstractions. Like them, it is useful in analyzing economic processes but is only an aid to, never a substitute for, thought. [15] It cannot possibly be used to grind out automatic solutions to problems of policy, as is sometimes carelessly implied.

The two central themes of the "new monetarists," according to Professor Friedman's restatement of the quantity theory, are: (1) the quantity theory is a theory of the demand for real money balances rather than a theory of the price level; and (2) the quantity theory is based on the empirical generalization that the demand for money is relatively stable over time.

In summary, despite the limitations of the *IS-LM* apparatus described above, it is very useful, not only in synthesizing the interdependencies of money, interest, and income on the one hand and monetary and fiscal policy on the other, but in synthesizing the viewpoints of the monetarists and the fiscalists. It combines these viewpoints by providing a theory of velocity in which velocity is a direct function of the interest rate. Two of the leading proponents on each side admit, in slightly different ways, that the theoretical

---

[14]The *IS-LM* framework is also considered deficient by some because it treats bonds and real capital as a single asset. Thus, money substitutes only for bonds, not for existing assets or output. See Keith M. Carlson, "Monetary and Fiscal Actions in Macroeconomic Models," *Review* of the Federal Reserve Bank of St. Louis (January, 1974), pp. 8–18.

[15]In 1930, as the Depression began, President Hoover urged business to refrain from wage cuts; he emphasized the importance of maintaining purchasing power. This was a common sense policy which later would be rationalized by income theory. At the time, however, too many economists argued that wage reductions were inevitable and proper; they implied that only an economic illiterate would attempt to prevent them. Recovery required, they claimed, a fall in wages and other costs. Then prices would fall, and, as everyone knows, the quantity demanded usually increases when price falls. They overlooked the key assumption which is a necessary condition of the law of demand—"other things remaining equal." Specifically, incomes fell as costs and prices fell; less was demanded than before. What was proven was not an error in the law of demand but the folly of overlooking its qualifications.

differences between the moderates in the two camps is quite small. Nobel laureate and celebrated fiscalist Paul A. Samuelson puts it this way: ". . . the monetarist counterrevolution reduces to debate about the shapes of *LM* and *IS*."[16] The noted monetarist Milton Friedman states that ". . . the basic differences among economists are empirical, not theoretical."[17]

Discussion Questions

1. In view of the size of government expenditures today and government's disposable income, why do we ignore *S* and *T* when we are studying the nature and shape of the *IS* curve?
2. In preceding chapters we saw that, according to Keynes, income would be in equilibrium at the point where planned saving was equal to investment. The *IS* curve traces a series of such points. Is every point on the curve an equilibrium position? Why did Keynes assume there would be only a single point where they would be equal?
3. Given one other relationship, we can easily convert a marginal efficiency of capital schedule to an *IS* curve. Explain.
4. The analysis presented in this chapter adds a second condition required for income equilibrium. Briefly explain.
5. With the liquidity preference function, what are the two variables we are relating and what variable, included in the *LM* curve, is held constant? What are the two variables in the *LM* curve, and what variable, included in the liquidity preference function, is held constant? Why do the two curves consequently look quite dissimilar?
6. In terms of the simple liquidity preference function of Chapter 19, how would you graphically represent an increase in the demand for money? Would you expect an increase in the demand for money if interest rates fell? Briefly explain your answer.
7. In terms of the *LM* curve, how would you show the effect of an increase in the demand for money?
8. If income is in equilibrium, and ignoring the possibility of changes in taxes or government expenditures, could either interest rates or income change unless there is a change in at least one of the following: the marginal efficiency of capital schedule, the consumption function, the quantity of money, or the demand for money? Briefly explain.
9. All five of the factors that we are relating to income and interest rates are expressed in terms of money. Which, if any, of these five factors were emphasized by the traditional income analysis as first stated by Keynes? Which three are called "real" factors? Why?
10. The *IS-LM* analysis includes the stock of money but not its velocity. True or False? Explain.

---

[16]Paul A. Samuelson, *Economics* (9th ed., New York: McGraw-Hill Book Co., 1973), p. 352.
[17]Milton Friedman, "A Theoretical Framework for Monetary Analysis," *Journal of Political Economy* (March, 1970), p. 234.

11. Show what would happen, within the *IS-LM* framework, if: (a) the Keynesian liquidity trap was operative; (b) there was a Keynesian collapse of the investment function's sensitivity to changes in the interest rate; and (c) there was an occurrence of the Classical pole where fiscal policy is almost powerless.

12. With the *IS–LM* curves, how can we show the effect of changes in taxes, government spending, and monetary policy?

13. In terms of the *IS–LM* analysis, under what conditions will changes in government spending or taxes be more effective than changes in the quantity of money in closing inflationary or deflationary gaps?

14. What are the conditions, in terms of the slopes of the *IS–LM* functions, under which monetary policy is most effective? What about fiscal policy?

15. How in general does the introduction of "Pigou" or "real-wealth" effects affect the relationships in an *IS–LM* model?

APPENDIX: ALGEBRAIC COMPARISON OF CLASSICAL AND KEYNESIAN MODELS[18]

RELATIONS

Relationship	Classical	Keynesian
1. Demand for Money	$M = \ell Py$	$M = \ell Py + L(r)$
2. Production Function	$y = y(N)$	$y = y(N)$
3. Demand for Labor	$\dfrac{dy}{dN} = \dfrac{W}{P}$	$\dfrac{dy}{dN} = \dfrac{W}{P}$
4. Supply of Labor	$N = N\left(\dfrac{W}{P}\right)$	$W = W_0$
5. Saving Function	$s = s(r)$	$s = s(y)$
6. Investment Function	$i = i(r)$	$i = i(r)$
7. Equilibrium in Capital Market	$s = i$	$s = i$

DEFINITIONS

Where M = quantity of money in circulation

ℓ = transactions demand expressed as a fraction of money income

L = asset (speculative-precautionary) demand for money

P = price level

r = interest rate

y = output

N = employment

W = money wage rate

W_0 = autonomously determined money wages

s = saving

i = investment

---

[18]Gardner Ackley, *Macroeconomic Theory* (New York: Macmillan Co., 1961), Chapter 15, pp. 399–418. Although most of the equations should be obvious, equation 3 perhaps should be commented on. It merely states that, following standard microeconomics, to maximize its profits any firm should demand labor up to the point where each worker's real wage rate *(W/P)* is equal to his or her marginal productivity *(dy/dN)*.

   This algebraic comparison reveals three obvious differences between the classical and the Keynesian models: Keynes included the asset (speculative-pre-cautionary) demand for money in equation 1 along with the classical transactions demand in his total demand for money function. He used rigid money wages in equation 4 in the place of the flexible wages in the classical supply of labor function. And finally, in equation 5 Keynes assumed that saving and therefore consumption depended on income rather than on the interest rate. While it is debatable as to which of these three changes is the most important, one respected scholar argues, with some validity, that the consumption function is the "kingpin" of the Keynesian system.[19]

---

[19]*Ibid*., p. 406.

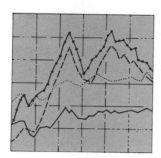

PART 6

Business Cycles and Monetary and Fiscal Policy

Chapter 21   Cyclical Fluctuations

To this point we have been building our foundation. We have outlined the development and present structure of our banking system, and discovered how the banking system can expand or contract the money supply and force interest rates lower or higher with the assistance of and subject to the direction of the Federal Reserve Banks. We have considered the special circumstances under which a change in the commodity content of money or in the total quantity of money may sometimes lead to a change in the value of money or the level of national income. We have analyzed the process of income determination and explored the complex interrelations between the income level, the value of money, the level of interest rates, and monetary and fiscal policies.

Now we are ready to apply this knowledge. We have arrived at the most stimulating and challenging area of our subject. Our knowledge of how the financial mechanism operates, together with our grasp of analytical tools such as the multiplier and accelerator, the propensity to consume, and the relation between saving and investment, will help us to understand how the nation can encourage an expansion of output and how it can successfully fight both recession and inflation.

To some extent the level of economic activity is affected by monetary policy, that is, by changes in interest rates and in the quantity of money. To some extent it is controlled by the government's fiscal policy, that is, by taxes, borrowing, and expenditures by the government. By qualitative as well as by quantitative changes in its fiscal policy, the government can exert a powerful and at times dominating influence upon the economy. Together, monetary and fiscal policy offer great promise that major depressions will not occur again and that the business cycle may be largely eliminated.

During the 1930s the business cycle was a topic in which interest was particularly keen. People wanted to learn why the economic system had ground to a halt and how it might be set in motion once more. It seemed evident that there were connections of some kind between the stock and flow of money and the level of economic activity. The problem was to discover those relationships. Some way should be found to put idle workers and idle machines back to work. Somehow the problem of excess capacity (or insufficient demand) should be solved.

With our entry into World War II, our problem quickly changed. By 1943 we were at full employment. While the war continued, there was no longer the question of how to absorb unemployed factors of production, but rather the question of how to allocate the suddenly scarce resources. We found ourselves facing not generally excess capacity and depression, but generally excess demand and inflation. Since 1943 we have had no prolonged periods of widespread unemployment. There have been recessions, but the economy has quickly recovered and output has climbed to new levels.

Certainly we have not arrived at the millenium. Today we are still trying to solve the problem of persistent unemployment in particular areas of production. It is not easy, for example, to put coal miners back to work when the cause of their unemployment is not a general business stagnation but the joint result of the substitution of other fuels for coal and the mechanization of coal mining. The energy crisis has alleviated this group's problem somewhat. Not so fortunate are theater organists and telegraph operators who were in great demand 40 or 50 years ago when the structure of our economy was different. Monetary and fiscal policies can do little to overcome this so-called structural unemployment. Since World War II we have also been frequently concerned about our slackening growth rate, caused by inadequate additions to capital. The difference between a 3 percent and a 4 percent yearly increase may appear inconsequential. Yet with a 4 percent growth rate the national product would double in about 18 years, compared to 24 years with a 3 percent rate. We are trying to stimulate growth and at the same time maintain a reasonable stability. Sometimes we find ourselves trying to cope with areas of structural unemployment and insufficient investment to provide for a high growth rate and at the same time attempting to check an excess of spending in all areas, which is causing spiraling price inflation. Since 1965 the war in Viet Nam, increasing government expenditures in many other areas, and a high level of both consumption and investment spending have created an inflationary gap, which has become even more severe in the mid-1970s.

At least, however, we have not experienced another depression. Today's college students, having never known a major depression, are likely to take prosperity for granted. The Depression they know only as ancient history, occurring somewhere between two world wars. It has been, they may suspect, exaggerated by the old folks, and, anyway, it could never happen again.

It would be hard to exaggerate the effects of the Depression. We have already touched on some of them, particularly as they related to the banks, and we know that by early 1933 the banking system had broken down completely. We should remember, too, that in 1932 and 1933 there were between 12 and 16 million people continuously out of work. The total employed labor force at the time was less than 39 million. At least one out of four was unable to find work. As a group, young people represented a large share of this unemployment, for employers were not adding new employees and anyone who did not already have a job found it almost impossible to secure one. On the other hand, older people with families and financial responsibilities were in even more desperate circumstances when they lost their jobs. Even under the best of circumstances it is harder for them to find new employment. In either case there was heartbreaking discouragement when for months and years it seemed that society simply had no use for the millions who were looking for work. As a result of the decrease in employment and the fall in prices, national income dropped from $87 billion to $40 billion. Billions of dollars of goods and services that might have been produced and consumed if employment had remained at the level of 1929 were never created. Moreover, the population was steadily growing, so that by 1940, when there were again as many employed as in 1929, there were still more than 8 million unemployed as compared to 1.5 million unemployed in 1929. Not until 1943, when 12 million people were in the Armed Forces, did unemployment again fall to the level of 1929.

While it would be comfortably reassuring, it would also be dangerously complacent to suppose we shall never have another depression. True, the experience of the 1930s should help us to prevent, or at least to overcome, a repetition of that disaster. Also, there have been a number of fundamental changes in the operation of our economy since 1930, most important being the enormously increased role of government. Depressions are much less likely today.

However, the notion that depressions are a thing of the past is not at all new. Many in the 1920s felt that the banking and credit improvements effected by the Federal Reserve would keep us at a continuously high income level, and that such depressions as might occur would become progressively shorter and milder. It is always tempting to assume that existing conditions will never change. Three decades ago many economists espoused a "secular stagnation" thesis and were afraid that in the years ahead we would find ourselves in a chronic state of depression. We did not, and some then assured us that prosperity could never end. Others less hopeful have been insisting for years that the nation, if not the world, is on the edge of economic collapse. In the mid-1970s, with both the pound and the dollar under heavy pressure internationally, with interest rates in Great Britain and the United States at their highest levels in a generation, with the value of money continuously falling, and with the sharp decline in the securities markets, some of these writers were convinced that a major depression was imminent and inevitable. Earlier, in 1953 and 1966, there also had been frightening forecasts of disaster.

Most careful students of monetary economics take a more hopeful view. They are not so naive as to believe that the fires of economic activity, left to themselves, will burn tidily with a constant glow. At times the flames may flare up, at times subside. The important fact is that we have learned how to do something about it. Rather than allow a conflagration to develop and wait until it finally burns itself out, we should expect to check the flames. Conversely, we can add more fuel if the fire begins to burn too low. There is no reason that we should endure the economic ills of inflation and recession as something beyond our control. We can control our economic destiny, especially with the powerful tools of monetary and fiscal policy. But we must know how to use these controls. If we adopt the wrong policies, we may encourage minor recessions to grow into major catastrophes. Or we may create inflationary pressures that eventually we find hard to control and which themselves may lead to an economic breakdown.

To better understand what can be done through monetary and fiscal policies to overcome or prevent depressions and to control prosperities, we need, first of all, to know something about the causes of the business cycle. Why, when we are enjoying a reasonably comfortable prosperity, do we not continue indefinitely at a high income level? What causes the downturn? Alternatively, when income is falling, why does it finally cease to fall and presently begin to rise? What is the business cycle?

RECOGNITION OF THE BUSINESS CYCLE

Study of the business cycle is comparatively recent, for until modern times people were not aware that business cycles existed. In fact, cycles were probably much less important before the Industrial Revolution. There were occasional panics—the tulip craze in 17th century Holland, Law's speculations in France, and the activities of the South Sea Company in England in the 18th century—all due primarily to financial excesses and easily apparent. They were considered, however, isolated events. It was not clear that business passed through good times to bad and back to good again with some degree of regularity. There were almost no statistics available and the tools of statistical research had not been developed. By the 20th century, and particularly since World War I, governments and central banks have been collecting and publishing many statistics and scholars have been studying them, supplementing them with such figures as might be obtainable for earlier years. An index of business activity in the United States since 1790 has been computed.[1] Although for recent years the index is based on a large number of measurements, for the early part of the period it is computed from 10 series, including imports, exports, commodity prices, and a few other available figures. The rhythmic nature of the business cycle over this entire period is clearly visible, even though since World War II we have been spared the painful depressions of earlier cycles.

Forty years ago a depression was, by definition, a phase of every business cycle. By that definition, there has been no business cycle for 40 years. In the discussion that follows, "cycle" will be used in a broader context, referring to an alternate expansion and contraction of activity regardless of whether the contraction is allowed to develop into a depression.

In studying any time series of business activity, one usually finds four types of movement, all occurring simultaneously. There is often a *seasonal* movement: there is less building in the winter than in the summer; department store sales are heavier before Christmas than at any other time. There is often

[1]The Cleveland Trust Company index.

a *trend*: an industry may be gradually growing or declining. There are also *random* movements and *cyclical* movements about the trend. We find, in charting these fluctuations, that it is difficult to eliminate the effects of the random movements, but we may largely eliminate the effects of trend and seasonal movements, leaving the cyclical and the random movements as a remainder.[2]

With the elimination of seasonal and trend factors, a surprisingly regular pattern of business fluctuations results, whether one is studying the fluctuations in a single industry or the movements of a composite index of business activity. The movement is not completely periodic, nor should we expect it to be, especially since there appear to be a number of rather well-defined cycles which jointly determine the cyclical behavior of business as a whole. There is a 3-year cycle and another cycle of 8 to 11 years, besides, perhaps, yet another cycle of 40 to 50 years. In addition, there is a special cycle of about 18 years in the construction industry, as well as some other individual cycles. Even if each of these cycles were perfectly regular, the pattern resulting from their joint effect would be far from simple. When some are rising while others are falling, the general level of business may be little changed. When a number of these cycles are simultaneously in a trough or at a peak, their combined effect will be pronounced.

EXPLANATIONS OF THE CYCLE

The most clearly marked cycle of general business activity ordinarily runs from 8 to 11 years and is the one ordinarily referred to in discussions of the business cycle. Many explanations have been put forward, which may be broadly differentiated as external and internal theories.

External theories explain the cyclical fluctuations in business as the responses to cyclical forces originating outside the field of business itself. Some writers have noted that there are cycles of approximately the same length in sunspot activity, suggesting that the business cycle is thus the result of extraterrestrial forces. Others, moving close to astrology, have attempted to show a connection between planetary movements and the level of business. According to some of those who explain the cycle as due to sunspots or other cosmic causes, there is no way the government can control or prevent the cycle, although it may be able to alleviate somewhat the misery of the depression. Wars are considered part of the same great pattern of rhythms and as inescapable as the business cycle. No matter what financial controls are instituted and no matter what policies the government adopts concerning taxing and spending, we cannot possibly escape the depression that is in store. We are sure to experience it, no matter what changes we may make in our financial institutions.

Theories of this kind are not taken very seriously by most economists today. While emphasizing the error of supposing the business cycle to be

---

[2]Many statisticians today prefer not to eliminate the trend. The considerations involved are technical and do not concern us here. The cyclical fluctuations stand out more clearly with the trend removed but are quite evident even if the trend is retained.

eliminated, most analysts avoid the mechanical prediction that is likely to result from an excessive emphasis on the periodicity of the cycle. They prefer to take into account the institutional changes that have been and are being made and to consider the overall state of business rather than to argue, for example, that because it has now been eight years since a depression, we must certainly have one within the next three years no matter what we do.

Concerning *internal theories*, a number of writers have offered explanations emphasizing some particular factor—the expansion of bank credit, new inventions, overinvestment, and the like. All internal theories have this in common: they attempt to explain the cycle in terms of the operation of the economic system itself and to show that our economy is organized in such a way that it must alternately expand and contract around what is usually called normal.

This is not the place to detail and evaluate these various theories.[3] We shall concentrate on certain aspects of cyclical fluctuations that are most closely related to our economic institutions. Consideration of appropriate fiscal and monetary policies follows in subsequent chapters.

THE UPSWING

As we have said, the business cycle consists of the alternate rise and fall of business activity. Since it is easier to explain why a movement, once under way, gains momentum than it is to explain why it reverses its direction, we shall first discuss the cumulative forces which operate to drive business further along in the direction in which it is already moving. Modern income analysis is particularly helpful here with its emphasis on the roles played by consumption, saving, investment, and fiscal policy.

Confidence and Investment

When business is on the upswing, there is a general optimism which frequently becomes stronger the longer the boom lasts. The confidence in the boom has been likened to the confidence of skaters in the safety of the ice. At the outset only a few brave individuals will take the risk. Seeing that they are safe, others follow in increasing numbers. The larger the party becomes, the greater becomes public confidence, and at the same time the more dangerous the situation becomes.[4]

Earlier, in explaining the concept of the marginal efficiency of capital, we emphasized the importance of expectations. The physical productivity of proposed capital additions is often easily ascertained and its cost is usually known with tolerable accuracy. The important question determining whether the investment will be made is the price at which the business believes it can

---

[3]For a more comprehensive discussion of business cycle theory, see Carl A. Dauten and Lloyd M. Valentine, *Business Cycles and Forecasting* (4th ed.; Cincinnati: South-Western Publishing Co., 1974).

[4]The analogy is imperfect. To a point the increase in business activity strengthens the economy and justifies the increased confidence. But as the economy moves from prosperity into inflation, the ice becomes precarious as confidence continues to increase and the crowd grows larger than ever.

sell the product. As the general level of business activity rises and employment increases, businesses are encouraged to go ahead with programs of plant expansion. Prices may not as yet have started to rise, but it becomes more probable that a high level of sales will insure the profitability of the investment. Later, of course, the increasing bottlenecks that appear as full employment is neared encourage a rise in prices which adds further impetus to the movement. Entrepreneurs realize not only that the chances of profitable investment are made better than ever by the rising prices, but also that any delay on their part is likely to result in their paying more for the equipment they want. For these reasons a high and probably rising level of investment is characteristic of the upswing, directly increasing national income.

Increase in Consumption

At the same time, consumption is rapidly increasing for two reasons. Confidence affects consumption as well as investment; also, consumption is increased as a result of the investment.

As long as people are uncertain of the future, they attempt to postpone any but the most necessary expenditures. If possible, they will spend less than their income and set something aside as a reserve against emergencies. With the improvement of business conditions they begin to spend more freely. The propensity to consume shifts so that of any given income more will be spent.[5] Many will draw on their savings to spend more than their income. Also, they make large purchases on credit; for example, they pay $500 down on a $4,000 car. At first the increased consumption may largely reflect the fact that the public is glad to increase its purchases when business conditions inspire confidence. Later, the expectation of rising prices may encourage further purchases, especially of durable goods.

Also, the increased investment causes increased consumption because of the multiplier. Part of the additional income from the investment will be spent by those who receive it and part will be spent by each who in turn receives any part of these funds. If the marginal propensity to consume is one half, an increase in investment will lead eventually to an equal increase in consumption. If people are consuming three fourths of any addition to their incomes, a $10 billion increase in investment will lead to an eventual increase of $30 billion in consumption.

Moreover, the increase in consumption may lead to an increase in investment via the accelerator. If the economy is operating at full employment, modest increases in the demand for consumer goods may lead to very large increases in the demand for producer goods. If such increases in investment (and income) do appear, there will be a stimulus for still more consumption.

---

[5] A shift of the propensity to consume (consumption function) is a movement of the entire schedule or line by which we represent it. At all levels of income more (or less) will then be consumed than before. Do not confuse this with an increase in the average propensity to consume. The latter is a movement along the line, not of the line. As we saw earlier, a fall in income tends to increase the average propensity to consume, so that at low income levels the average propensity to consume may rise to 100 percent or higher. The consumption function, however, does not automatically rise when income falls.

Money and Banking During the Upswing

The banking system plays an important role in the business cycle. In fact, one theory of the business cycle makes the banking system the sole cause of the cycle. Most students of the subject today do not go that far. The nature of the cycle appears to be too complex to be summed up under a single cause. In particular, as we have just seen, it is important to study the fluctuations in durable goods and to realize the interactions between consumption and investment and their effect on the overall level of business, a type of analysis to which the income approach is especially well suited. However, most of the changes that occur in consumption and investment would be impossible under a barter system and much less marked in an economy making no use of credit money. If not causal factors, money and banking are certainly essential conditioning factors.

Typically, the quantity of money increases during the expansionary phase of the cycle. Businesses borrow from the banks to increase their working capital and sometimes, through sales of bonds to the banks, to raise long-term capital for plant expansion. Consumer credit also increases when times are good. To some it may appear a little surprising that consumers borrow more in good times than in bad, for they suppose the average consumer is more likely to borrow from the banks when he or she is out of work and cannot pay the bills. It must be remembered, however, that the more desperately the individual needs a personal loan, the less likely it is that he or she will be able to obtain it from the bank. Distress loans, if made at all, will be for small amounts, and they will ordinarily be obtained from relatives and friends or from pawnshops or personal loan companies. But in prosperity, the public is willing to go into debt for new cars, new houses, new furniture, major repairs, and improvements. The banks supply most of the credit for such purchases, sometimes by granting a loan directly to the consumer, often by lending to businesses so that they may extend more credit, or by lending to agencies such as commercial credit companies and sales finance companies which pass the credit along to consumers. Whenever the banks make any of these loans directly or indirectly, new deposits are created and the supply of money is increased. For the economy as a whole, the expansion of loans and deposits is inflationary, but the individual bank is concerned primarily with the characteristics of its own loan applications. Prosperity converts risky loans to sound ones, and the bank feels its lending policy is justified.

The velocity of money increases simultaneously. This support to the boom could occur even without credit money since it involves only the spending of money already held. Both businesses and consumers spend more freely, as already noted, with part of this spending being financed out of cash balances. Also, nonbank lenders supply funds previously idle. When nearly everyone decides to hold less cash, the result will simply be that the turnover of money increases. As soon as one person spends money, someone else receives it. In prosperity there is no less money to be held than formerly and, as we have just seen, there is probably more. With the rise in both the quantity and the velocity of money, the effective money supply is doubly increased.

THE DOWNSWING

When national income is falling, the cumulative forces that tend to cause it to continue spiraling downward are similar in nature to the reinforcing factors of the upswing. Pessimism replaces optimism. The uncertain business outlook causes the postponement of investment. There appears to be little point in expanding plant capacity when existing facilities are excessive. As a result of the multiplier effect, the drop in income will be greater than the decline in investment. Consumption declines, not only because less income is being received as a result of the drop in investment, but also because the pessimism causes a shift of the consumption function, so that at all income levels less will be consumed than normally. In the real estate field vacancies mount as people move to smaller quarters or double up with relatives, so new residential construction declines and rents and real estate prices fall. The demand for consumer durable goods declines drastically, since the purchase of such goods can ordinarily be postponed for a few years if necessary. Unemployment figures rise as workers are laid off in the construction industry and in industries producing durable goods, whether for producer or consumer. Prices and wages fall, further reducing income. The greater the rise in unemployment and fall in prices and income, the darker the picture appears and the more frantically those who are still employed attempt to reduce their expenditures. Income must continue to fall as long as planned saving is greater than investment. If the contraction is not somehow arrested, it may continue until both net investment and saving are negative. Not only is there then no expansion of capacity, but existing plant is not being maintained and depreciated equipment is not being replaced as it wears out since plant capacity still exceeds demand. Matching this disinvestment is the dissaving that occurs as more is withdrawn from past savings than is currently being saved.

LOWER TURNING POINT

We come now to the question of why eventually the direction of the income movement changes. Common sense assures us that the downward spiral of income cannot continue until there is no income, no production, and no employment. Even in the depths of depression there continues to be at least a limited demand. Although people may be buying few fur coats and television sets and cars, they must at least buy food. The money may come from their own earnings if they are fortunate enough to be still employed, or it may come from earnings of those from whom they borrow, or it may come from past savings. Charity or relief organizations may provide some of it, but ultimately, unless new money is created, the source must be from earnings, current or past.

The money spent to purchase these basic requirements—food, shelter, utilities, bus fare, a little gasoline perhaps, especially for those whose work requires it—becomes income to those engaged in the production of these goods and services. Few, to be sure, are making large incomes. The very fact that there continues to be a demand for agricultural products encourages a movement from the cities onto the farms, and an increased supply of farm products appears at the very time when consumption is being curtailed, so that the price of farm products drops and farmers, too, find it difficult to make money. But even if most farmers are losing money, still income is being created, of course, as they hire labor and buy seed, spray, fertilizer, and other necessities. Someone receives it.

Reduction in Costs and Prices

At one time business cycle theory stressed heavily the reduction in costs and prices that accompanies depression.[6] A cut in wages was supposed to make it possible to reduce prices, sell more goods, and employ more workers. According to this argument, the fall in prices caused an increase in sales, so that when the depression had gone on long enough to reduce costs to their proper level, business and employment would tend to pick up and income would once more begin to rise.

Although a fall in prices may sometimes cause an increase in sales revenue,[7] it is altogether too naive to suppose that it will necessarily do so. In the first place, the fall in prices entails at the same time a fall in income. If all incomes remained the same while all prices were falling, the likelihood of an increase in sales would be greater, but the results to be expected from a simultaneous fall in the price level and in income are not easily predictable. The fall in income causes the demand curve to shift to the left, and the amount taken at the new lower price may be unchanged, greater, or less than before. In the second place, a decline in prices, even if incomes were unchanged, would not necessarily stimulate sales and might reduce them. If the public felt that falling prices were an indication of further declines in the future, they would postpone many purchases in the hope of buying at still lower prices later. In other words, the expectation of additional price reductions causes a leftward shift of the demand curve, just as does the fall in income. The exact results cannot be known in advance. Consequently, economists no longer place so much reliance on the curative effect of price and cost reductions in depression. In certain areas where there is a highly elastic demand for the product, such action may prove helpful. Conceivably, the construction industry, for example, might be stimulated if construction costs all along the line were reduced, and the resulting increase in income might be multiplied through respending so as to provide a real aid to recovery. The results would depend entirely upon how effective the reduction in housing costs was in stimulating new building or, more generally, upon the responsiveness of sales in any industry to price reductions.

---

[6]Other factors were also mentioned, such as the accumulation of excess reserves by the banking system, increased efficiency of production, the eventual necessity to replace durable goods, and so on.

[7]If demand is elastic.

Impetus to Recovery

More promising is the possibility that income may rise as a result of some event not directly connected with the cycle. For various reasons such an increase may occur. Important inventions may be made that will so raise the marginal efficiency of capital as to cause large-scale investment. From about 1830 to 1930 the building of the railroads, the development of public utilities, and the growth of the automobile industry caused billions of dollars of investment and were of tremendous importance in maintaining the generally high income through this period. From 1945 to the present there has been tremendous investment in such growth industries as airplanes, chemicals, electronics, energy, and recreation.

A war that begins when a nation is still in a depression will certainly raise income as every effort is made to maximize production. This is hardly a desirable way to end a depression, but it is unquestionably effective.

The opening of new markets may cause an expansion of investment if productive facilities must be increased. Through the 19th century this, too, was an important support of our national income as the frontier was pushed westward and new cities and states came into existence.

Population growth may aid the economy to round the lower turning point, though its direct effect is likely to be gradual, giving support to any recovery impetus rather than being the immediate cause of an upturn. An increasing population represents an increasing potential market but, as the Asiatic nations evidence, does not guarantee a high income level.

A somewhat similar cause, likely to be more effective in the short run, is an increase in the number of households. The uncertainty of depression may cause many young people to postpone marrying. If eventually they decide to wait no longer and marriages increase, the demand for houses, furniture, household equipment, cars, and so forth will also increase. Whether these things are bought out of savings or on credit, income must rise from the increase in spending.

Also, the longer the downswing continues, the more equipment that is finally worn out. The purchase of consumer and producer durable goods cannot be postponed forever. Replacements must finally be made, perhaps giving enough momentum to the economy that it begins to move upward.

Yet it must be admitted as altogether possible that none of these causes may be effective and a depression may drag on indefinitely. That was one of the most disturbing features of the last serious depression, from which we did not fully emerge until we entered World War II. No really big inventions appeared and the investment opportunities offered by improved zipper designs and the like were insufficient. The chapter of geographical frontier expansion had been closed decades before. Population was still growing but at the slowest rate in our history. We could not seem to establish the basis for a firm recovery. Indeed, the question was raised during these years—by the "secular stagnationists," most notably Harvard's Alvin H. Hansen—

whether this nation could expect in the future to recover automatically from depression and enjoy prosperities such as it had known in the past. It appeared that of the three most important supports of our earlier high levels of national income, two had disappeared. With no more frontier and with a more slowly growing population, inventions would have to provide a lift formerly supplied by all three factors. (As things worked out, the government's vast expenditures soon created a new and powerful support.)

At any rate, if the system does appear to be on dead center, as we can see may well be the case, the most practical expedient appears to be a massive public works program to generate additional income. There is no reason that, to raise national income, a government's expenditures must be for war. Hitler eliminated unemployment in Germany principally by building up a war machine. The effect on national income would be no less if money were spent on roads, parks, airports, and public buildings rather than on fighter planes, ships, and guns.

UPPER TURNING POINT

Earlier we left unanswered the question of why the forces causing income to expand did not continue indefinitely, driving income to levels ever higher. By now the answer should be apparent, at least in part.

Some economists have ingeniously explained the upper turning point as being due to the nature of the banking system, or to the fact that the expansion of bank money was providing credit too cheaply, or to various other causes. Some of these explanations assume the maintenance of the automatic gold standard and hence are inapplicable today. Others rest on doubtful or perhaps unrealistic assumptions, difficult to prove at best. Most economists today feel that such explanations do not offer a helpful general theory of cycles or turning points, although they may help to describe the course of events in some particular cycle.

For a general explanation of the upper turning point of business, the most helpful approach seems to be the same kind of analysis of the creation and disposition of income that we have followed to this point. One of the most basic concepts of this analysis is the identity of realized savings and investment[8] and the effect of this identity upon income. As long as planned investment exceeds planned saving, income will increase, and vice versa.

Interrelations Between Consumption and Investment

We saw that during the upswing the respending of income resulting from investment induces a high consumption level. In turn, high profits and, via the accelerator, increasing consumption encourage investment. We saw also that to maintain a high level of induced investment, consumption must increase continuously. A constant consumption level, no matter how high, will not require continuous net investment expenditures. Depreciated machinery will

---

[8]Disregarding taxes and government spending.

be replaced, of course, but this is really a special form of consumption rather than an increase in our stock of goods.

If there is a serious shortage of producer goods, some time may be required to complete the necessary investment induced by higher consumption. It is difficult to see, however, how the investment can continue indefinitely. When the rate of increase of consumption declines, investment may decline absolutely even though consumption is still increasing absolutely. From there the course of events is familiar. The decline in investment causes a decline in income, consumption is curtailed, income falls further, and the downward spiral is in progress.

The fundamental point in this analysis is the assumption that consumption will presently begin to level off or at least will increase at a slower pace than before. This is certainly an assumption, not some eternal truth. It is still occasionally challenged, and Say's Law, which states that supply creates its own demand, is again cited to remind us that the nation has the purchasing power to buy all the goods it produces.

Say's Law is acceptable as a general description of a long-run tendency, but we cannot escape the problem of the business cycle simply by declaring that it does not exist. If purchasing power and the desire to spend were synonymous, the business cycle would probably be indiscernible. But as was brought out in an earlier chapter, the money and credit institutions make it very easy to defer the exercise of one's purchasing power until a later date. It is the very essence of the business cycle that purchasing power is exerted at an uneven rate. Sometimes the spending of past savings and the expansion of credit increase it; at other times additions to savings and the contraction of credit decrease it.

Our basic assumption of an eventually declining rate of increase in consumption appears to be a reasonable one. This decline gives trouble for two reasons:

1. It causes planned saving to increase more rapidly. Now we know that realized saving must equal investment and that if planned saving exceeds investment, income must fall. A drop in income causes realized saving to be less than planned saving and permits the equating of realized saving and investment. Hence, when planned saving increases, investment must increase to offset the increase in planned saving if income is not to drop.
2. Unfortunately the slowing down of the increase in consumption is more likely to encourage a decline in investment than an increase. As shown by the acceleration principle, for induced investment to increase, consumption must increase by a constantly increasing amount. An increase of a billion dollars in consumption this year requires an increase of more than a billion dollars in consumption next year and still more the following year if investment is to increase next year and the year after. Consequently, as consumption begins to level off in the prosperity phase of the cycle, investment rapidly declines. The period of expansion ends and recession begins.

We can say much the same thing, although a little less precisely, without making specific reference to the multiplier and accelerator. During the course of the boom the opportunities for profitable investment gradually disappear. Businesses cannot go on indefinitely building more hotels and office buildings, adding to steel plant capacity, installing additional generating equipment, and so forth. As more and more of these goods are completed, it becomes apparent that at existing prices supply has mostly caught up with demand. The new offices are rented, not to people who until then have been unable to find offices, but to tenants of older buildings. Faced with mounting vacancies, the owners of older buildings reduce their rents. As rents begin to fall, the attractiveness of further building diminishes. Similarly, in other fields the steadily rising capacity makes it difficult to utilize the capacity fully without reducing prices, and the probability of further investment in producer durable goods becomes progressively more questionable.

Effect on Consumption of an Increase in Consumer Debt

The expansion of consumption in prosperity is ultimately checked by the mounting total of consumer debt. During the upswing installment sales and other credit purchases stimulate the increase in consumption. By the time several million people have gone into debt for new homes, furniture, cars, and other items, they are temporarily out of the market, both because they have the goods and because for several years they will be paying off debt. For this reason, too, excess plant capacity begins to appear.

Saving-Investment Relationships

At the same time that the outlets for investment are drying up, planned saving is likely to be increasing at a record pace. Toward the end of the boom incomes are high and individuals refrain from consuming all their income. If these funds were supplied to business, either directly or through banks and other financial institutions, they would reenter the income stream. But since business is no longer expanding, the saving is not only unutilized, it is actually never realized. At the same time, as bank loans are paid off, deposits are contracted. The resultant increase in excess reserves gives banks the power to lend but does not directly cause new loans to be made. The lack of profitable investment opportunities will defeat the general attempt to save. The principal investment that does take place may be unintended and undesired, manifesting itself in increased inventories resulting from unexpected sales declines. This kind of investment is apt to be quickly followed by reductions and cancellations of orders, and the recession has begun. All that has been accomplished by the attempted saving is a reduction in income which will continue until planned saving is equal to investment. Also, with business prospects becoming more gloomy month by month, net investment may drop to zero or below and income may be forced down to so low a level that planned saving will also be zero or negative.[9]

---

[9]Net investment will be zero if inventories are being restocked as they are sold, and capital equipment is being replaced as it wears out. Capital is then being maintained at a constant level. But if businesses are shortening their inventories and are not replacing worn out equipment, the capital stock is shrinking and net investment is negative.

One of the points that particularly disturbed the stagnationists before World War II was the possibility that a wealthy nation might find it almost impossible to maintain full employment without continuous large government deficits to counteract the large saving possible at full employment. A poor nation is not faced with this problem. Its income is so low, even in prosperity, that planned saving will never be large. Also, one reason for its low income is its lack of capital goods. Such saving as is planned can readily be used for the expansion of industry, as the opportunities for profitable investment are abundant. The wealthy nation, however, is likely to have already built up its industrial capacity. It is faced with the dilemma of somehow offsetting the large saving that will be possible at full employment and which, if not offset, must force the economy into a recession. As a result of the long-sustained boom beginning with World War II, continuing into the postwar period, and supported by the Korean War and our activity in Viet Nam as well as by our programs of international aid, the possibility of secular stagnation has faded into the background. It would be rash to conclude that it has permanently disappeared from view, even if our most recent policies have centered on the directly opposite problem of checking excessive investment and encouraging insufficient saving.

THE PHILLIPS CURVE TRADEOFF: EMPLOYMENT VS. INFLATION

Professor A. W. Phillips was the first to quantify an important tradeoff relationship brought about by cyclical fluctuations.[10] The so-called Phillips Curve, shown in Figure 21-1, pictures the tradeoff between price-wage inflation and unemployment in the economy by its position in the short run and by its induced shifts in the longer run.

Short Run

Because the typical Phillips Curve is drawn downward sloping, with the unemployment rate measured on the horizontal axis and the inflation rate on the vertical axis, the cost of reducing the rate of unemployment (inflation) is a higher rate of inflation (unemployment). In the hypothetical figures given in

---

[10]A. W. Phillips, "The Relation Between Unemployment and the Rate of Change in Money Wage Rates in the United Kingdom, 1861–1957," *Economica* (November, 1958), pp. 283–299. The literature since that time is voluminous. However, it has been surveyed in Paul A. Samuelson and Robert M. Solow, "Problem of Achieving and Maintaining a Stable Price Level: Analytical Aspects of Anti-Inflation Policy," *American Economic Review* (May, 1960), pp. 177–194; Roger W. Spencer, "The Relation Between Prices and Employment: Two Views," *Review* of the Federal Reserve Bank of St. Louis (March, 1969), pp. 15–21; and Milton Friedman, "The Role of Monetary Policy," *American Economic Review* (March, 1968), pp. 1–17. These three articles are reprinted in *Macroeconomics: Selected Readings*, edited by Walter L. Johnson and David R. Kamerschen (Boston: Houghton Mifflin Co., 1970), Chapters 23, 24, and 35, pp. 243–263 and 371–381. Of course, it would be possible to draw a curve relating other key macroeconomic variables. For instance, one could depict a Klise curve showing the tradeoff between economic stagnation and inflation or a Kamerschen curve illustrating the tradeoff between economic stagnation and income inequality. However, to this date there has been no great call for such diagrams! One might then ask: "Why the popularity of the Phillips Curve?" If there is an answer, it must be "blowing in the wind."

Figure 21-1, to eliminate inflation entirely (i.e., achieve a zero rate of inflation), point *A*, would require an unemployment rate of approximately 11 percent. To get something close to full employment, say, 6 percent unemployment, would involve, as point *B* indicates, an inflation rate of about 9 percent.

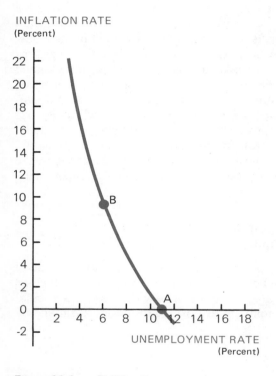

INFLATION RATE
(Percent)

UNEMPLOYMENT RATE
(Percent)

Figure 21-1   Phillips Curve

Thus, the Phillips Curve depicts graphically the tradeoff between unemployment and inflation in the short run and therefore the dilemma facing macroeconomic policymakers. How much inflation (unemployment) should the economy be willing to endure to reduce unemployment (inflation)?

This problem has become especially acute in the difficult period since 1965 when the economy has suffered "stagflation"—rising prices coupled with a stagnation of employment and growth rates. One reason for this is the greater presence in our economy of cost-push (or sellers') inflation which begins to push up wages and prices before full employment is reached. Our economy typically has suffered from a greater mixture of what is called demand-pull (or demanders') inflation which apparently is a bit more controllable by the old-fashioned medicine of monetary and fiscal policy. The more

modern cost-push inflation has to date successfully evaded any such easy solution.[11] In graphical terms, the Phillips Curve has been pushed rightward and
outward from its position in the late 1950s and early 1960s. The cost of reducing unemployment or arresting inflation has gone up.

Long Run

Some economists have challenged whether there is a clear-cut tradeoff
between inflation and unemployment in the long run as there is in the short
run with the simple Phillips Curve. According to the "accelerationist" hypothesis, once expectations are considered, the tradeoff, if any, is between
unemployment and the speed and direction—call it the "acceleration"—of the
change in inflation and not inflation itself. Put graphically, the critics argue
that the vertical axis should correspond not to any particular inflation rate
(e.g., 5 percent), but to a particular rate of change of inflation (e.g., 5 percent
per annum). They maintain that there is a "natural" unemployment rate in the
long run, dependent on a host of basic economic and demographic factors, for
which all the monetary and fiscal policy in the world is helpless to change. All
the macroeconomic managers can do, they claim, is twist the short-term Phillips Curve. Thus less inflation (unemployment) now means more inflation (unemployment) later. In their view the simple Phillips Curve is based on the
illusion that people do not correctly anticipate inflation. It provides no role for
a lagged inflation effect—i.e., for the rate of inflationary expectations—in determining the present inflation rate.[12]

In short, the critics of the simple Phillips Curve formulation emphasize
that there is a difference between the short run, in which the labor force does
not take inflation into account, and the longer run, in which all anticipate
possible shrinkages in the purchasing power of the monetary unit. At this
point policymakers continue to use monetary, fiscal, and a sprinkle of "incomes" policy (the latter referring to governmental guideposts, controls, collective bargaining, etc.) to get a "better" Phillips Curve. Ideally, they want to
shift it permanently leftward and inward so as to reduce the tradeoff costs of
less inflation or more employment. Critics feel that some basic reforms—such
as reducing tariffs and quotas, moderating or eliminating job market discrimination which would render the labor market more efficient by reducing the
search time and costs for workers between jobs, and increasing the training of
more skilled workers—are urgently needed before we can achieve a "better"

---

[11]Graphically, the "pure" sellers' (demanders') inflation can be represented by a completely
horizontal (vertical) Phillips Curve. In either extreme case, no tradeoff is possible. With "pure"
cost-push inflation the economy suffers a certain inflation rate irrespective of the unemployment
rate, and with "pure" demand-pull inflation it suffers a certain unemployment rate no matter
what the inflation rate.

[12]There is still another group which feels that the Phillips Curve framework is correct, but
that there has been a rightward and outward shift in it over the past decade, partly because of the
influx into the labor market of teenagers and women, who tend to have relatively high unemployment rates. To date, the evidence is much more substantial for the acceleration theory based
upon expectations than the labor market hypothesis.

Phillips Curve. They argue that shorter run palliatives such as price controls, while perhaps being temporarily successful in cooling inflationary expectations, tend to misallocate resources. (The inefficiencies associated with artificial prices are discussed in the Introduction).[13]

SUMMARY AND CONCLUSION

Some businesspeople, newspaper columnists, and other writers are quite disturbed by the income approach analysis of the business cycle. They find particularly objectionable the argument that the attempt to save may be the cause of depression. The idea that saving may be harmful contradicts all the copybook maxims. It is not hard to write emotionally about the savings of the past which made possible our magnificent heritage of industrial equipment, the greatest in the world, which makes possible a standard of living that is the envy of every other nation. However, it is rather pointless. No one will dispute it. There are times when saving is beneficial. War is one example, and no one would claim that at such a time saving should be discouraged. A period of industrial development is another time when saving is indispensable. But the question is: What will be the effect of attempted saving after the nation has become industrialized and if opportunities for profitable investment are becoming more scarce?[14] We simply cannot assume that no matter how much is withdrawn from the income stream as saving, it will necessarily all reappear as funds supplied to business for expansion, even if at times that will be the case. At other times the withdrawals may pile up as idle hoards of cash or be used to pay off debt owed to the banks, thereby contracting the circulating medium. At such times all that the saving accomplishes is a reduction in total income. From the point of view of the individual concerned, saving may always be a virtue; but from the point of view of society, it is not a virtue when it contributes to recession and depression. Saving, as such, is a leakage from the income stream.

In any event, no matter how objectionable the logic of the savings argument is, even the most conservative businessperson is ordinarily quite ready to agree that in recession the public should be induced to save less. At least at such times it becomes clear that the public must spend more freely if business is to prosper.

Finally, people in responsible positions in government and in finance, whose work requires them to study the operations of the economic system as a whole, have been quick to realize the usefulness of income-determination

---

[13]Strict Friedmanites argue that the real long-run Phillips Curve is vertical at the "natural" rate of unemployment. Less unemployment now necessarily means more unemployment in the future. The only way the actual unemployment rate can be brought temporarily under the "natural" unemployment rate is by continuously increasing the inflation rate. Such a state of affairs cannot continue indefinitely.

[14]It is not inevitable that opportunities for investment will disappear when a nation reaches a high level of industrialization. If the population is growing rapidly or if the standard of living is rising fast, the increase in consumption may make continued large-scale investment necessary. So, also, may improved techniques and new inventions. The possibilities do not warrant our assuming that there necessarily will always be sufficient investment outlets to offset the savings possible at a high income level.

theory. It is safe to say that, faced with the threat of a severe depression, no administration, Republican or Democratic, would again set as its primary goals the immediate trimming of government expenditures and balancing of the budget. There would be debate over the most suitable policy implements and about the respective advantages and disadvantages of tax reductions, increases in government spending, and other measures to reduce planned saving and increase expenditures, both public and private. About the policy itself, the raising of income, there would be little question. Understanding their causes, we can control both recessions and inflations, not eliminating their every trace, but checking their amplitude and shortening their duration.

The Phillips Curve shows that it is necessary to trade off between reducing unemployment and holding the price level stable. There is some controversy as to whether the simple short-run Phillips Curve is valid in the long run.

Discussion Questions

1. Why were business cycles not only unrecognized but probably of little importance before the 18th century?
2. Differentiate broadly between internal and external theories of the business cycle.
3. Is the business cycle a cause or a result of changes in the marginal efficiency of capital?
4. During the upswing of the business cycle, would you expect investment to increase as a result of a movement along the investment function, as a result of a movement of the investment function itself, or both? Explain.
5. During the upswing of the business cycle, would you expect consumption to increase as a result of a movement along the consumption function, as a result of a movement of the consumption function itself, or both? Explain.
6. "An increase in income will increase the consumption function." True or false and explain.
7. How would you expect the multiplier and accelerator to contribute to reinforcing and reversal forces in the private sector of the economy?
8. Which of the following would you expect to be the hardest hit and which the least affected by depression? Why?
   a. A chain grocery store
   b. A steel mill
   c. A cigarette manufacturer
   d. A manufacturer of jet planes for the airlines
9. During the 19th century the United States recovered from depressions without the aid of either fiscal policy or any centrally directed monetary policy. Why do we feel today that the government should take action to facilitate recovery?
10. What is the relationship between planned saving and investment when the business cycle is moving from prosperity to recession?
11. Discuss what the Phillips Curve emphasizes about the short run.
12. Is the Phillips Curve valid in the long run? Explain.

Chapter 22   Monetary and Fiscal Policy

Through its spending, taxing, and borrowing activities, which we call fiscal policy, the government holds powerful controls. During the last 35 years it has begun to learn how to use these controls to stabilize the economy. To a lesser extent the Federal Reserve, by its monetary policies, can also help to promote prosperity and prevent both inflation and recession. By open market operations and by changes in reserve requirements, margin requirements, and the discount rate, the Federal Reserve can encourage monetary expansion and low interest rates or discourage borrowing by tight money policies. In addition to its anticyclical objectives, the Fed has tried to accommodate the government's sale of bonds and to promote long-term economic growth. Its least disputed success has been in its efforts to accommodate the Treasury in its sale of bonds.

There are other possible means of coping with the problems of recession, inflation, and growth. Neither monetary nor fiscal policy is a sovereign remedy to cure all ills. It may be necessary to regulate monopolies more closely, whether on the part of management or labor. Legislation may be required concerning working hours, overtime, minimum wages, and working conditions, all of which may have some bearing on cyclical problems. In singling out monetary and fiscal policies, we are simply remaining within the confines of the text. Applying what we have learned of the forces governing the value of money and the generation of income, we should be able to analyze the effect upon the economy of the monetary policies of the Federal Reserve and the fiscal (and possibly monetary) policies of the federal government.

In contrast to some other types of action, both monetary and fiscal policy are controls of extremely broad scope. To that extent they are more consistent with economic liberalism than were the detailed regulations of, for example, a code of the National Recovery Administration specifying minimum wages and prices for each industry, or of a bulletin of the Office of Price Administration setting forth maximum prices to be charged for each commodity. Through monetary and fiscal policies a common framework is set up within which each individual is free to operate as desired, subject to the same general controls as everyone else.

For centuries governments have regulated their money. They have changed their standards, devalued, issued paper money, refused to redeem it, and so forth. All such activities are in a sense examples of monetary policy. However, the term monetary policy usually refers today to steps taken by the banking system to accomplish, through the monetary mechanism, a specific purpose believed to be in the general public interest.

Thousands of individual banks, guided, like other firms, by self-interest, cannot develop and carry out an effective monetary policy. There must be a centralized monetary authority, such as our Federal Reserve Banks, to which profits are purely incidental. Whether or not its decisions are always correct, at least they will not be biased by self-interest.

A few years before the Federal Reserve System was established, the Secretary of the Treasury at times shifted Treasury balances back and forth from the Treasury to the national banks to reduce monetary strains. This was the nation's first monetary policy as we are using the term here — our first experience with monetary operations undertaken deliberately for a public purpose. In this instance the purpose was limited and negative. The purpose was to minimize the effects of the Treasury's taxing and spending activities upon the money market.

With the establishment of the Federal Reserve System the possibility of broader monetary policies appeared. At the outset, however, policy was simple and narrow, guided by the amount of gold held by the Federal Reserve Banks. Not until 1920 did the Federal Reserve begin to determine monetary policy by the requirements of the economy.

Broadly, monetary policy may involve changes in either or both the quantity of money or the cost of money (level of interest rates). Also broadly, the philosophy of monetary policy may be either discretionary or automatic. According to discretionary policy, the traditional approach, maladjustments should be corrected and stability promoted by changes in the cost of money and in its growth rate. The philosophy of the automatic policy is that stability will result (and maladjustments be prevented) by providing a stable and predictable money supply. Discretionary changes should not be allowed, for they increase, rather than check, maladjustments in the economy.

DISCRETIONARY MONETARY POLICY

Why should we expect monetary policies to have important effects on the economy as a whole? How can changes in the quantity of money or in the level of interest rates affect output and prices? The answers to such questions depend upon our monetary theories.

Monetary Policy and Quantity Theory

According to traditional quantity theory, the relation between monetary policy and the control of the business cycle was simple and direct. An increase in the quantity of money resulted in a fall in the value of money. In prosperity the rise in prices could be halted by reducing the quantity of money or checking its increase; and if prices fell in depression, the price level could be restored by increasing the money supply.

Such changes required, of course, some amount of monetary management. This management might be required to operate within the framework of the gold standard, but it would certainly not be the same thing as the automatic gold standard. The automatic gold standard, it was assumed, might eventually come out with the same result, but a longer period of adjustment would be required since it would be necessary to wait for gold movements to determine the quantity of money.

During the decade from 1919 to 1929 faith in monetary controls was at its height. In this country we had discovered the great power that the Federal Reserve could exert over bank credit expansion, and there was a general feeling that such progress in credit control would prevent depressions such as we had known in the past. To be sure, few responsible bankers or economists were quantity theorists to the extent that they supposed that the price level was determined solely by the quantity of money. Accepting the formulation $MV = PT$, they recognized the interrelations between the price level, the quantity of money, the velocity of circulation of money, and the level of total transactions. But in spite of the careful qualifications with which writers of the day might surround their statements concerning the effect of changes in the quantity of money, they generally concluded that a strong degree of control over the level of prices and of business activity was possible through varying the quantity of money.

Perhaps the limitations of monetary policy in depression would have been more apparent in advance if in previous years we had been using the cash-balance type of quantity equation rather than the transactions type. The former, in emphasizing the general desire for liquidity characteristic of depression, might have indicated the probability that extra money created at such a time would to a large extent be used to increase cash balances and that, with nearly everyone attempting to increase cash balances, little of the additional money would be spent. At any rate, there was widespread disappointment as, in spite of the increase in deposits and gold certificates resulting from devaluation and gold imports, in spite of the silver purchases increasing deposits, and in spite of increases in bank reserves and deposits resulting from unparalleled open market purchases of Treasury obligations by the Federal Reserve, the price level stubbornly refused to recover to the level of the 1920s.

Monetary Policy and Income Theory

During the 1930s the usefulness of the income approach became widely appreciated. As stressed earlier, this line of analysis does not dispute the quantity equations but sets them aside in favor of other factors that appear more useful and less subject to qualification. Instead of being concerned with the quantity and velocity of circulation of money, it goes into the interactions among income components, the propensity to consume, the inducements to invest, and similar considerations.

In light of this analysis, the issue of additional Treasury currency or the increase of Treasury borrowing from the banks is seen to have one advantage in depression over an equal increase in private borrowing from the banks. In all three instances the quantity of money will increase. But only in the first two will there be no offsetting reduction, at the time, in the propensity to consume. When individuals (and corporations) borrow from banks, the money increases, but at the same time the borrowers are aware that since they are in debt they must henceforth restrict their consumption (and their dividend policies) so that they can repay the loan. If, however, the government borrows from the banks or issues more currency, the public is not under the same compulsion to check its own spending simultaneously. Later, if taxes are levied on the public to pay off government securities held by the banks or to retire Treasury currency, the taxes will reduce the public's consumption.[1] Since the government debt, like the money stock, if reduced at any time should be reduced in periods of inflation, this check on public spending at such times will again help restore stability.

But the income approach also indicates that merely increasing the quantity of money is likely to be of quite limited effectiveness in combating a depression. If the added money can be made to circulate by placing it in the hands of those who are likely to spend it, favorable results may be expected. These results are from the increase in spending, however, not from the simple fact that the quantity of money has been increased. About all that is accomplished by merely increasing the monetary stock, according to the income approach, is that the public is enabled to hold more money. This increase in liquidity permits a fall in the interest rate. If this fall is sufficient to bring the level of interest rates below the marginal efficiency of capital, investment will be stimulated and a recovery will develop. Otherwise the increase in the quantity of money will be of little aid.

Furthermore, as advocates of the income school point out, it is the change in the level of interest rates rather than in the quantity of money that is the stimulating factor; and if the monetary authorities can bring down interest rates without changing the quantity of money, the chances of success would be about the same. By either method it is doubtful that much can be accomplished, however, since in depression the marginal efficiency of capital is likely to be so very low that investment will not be stimulated by any (positive) interest rate, however low.

Income analysts call attention also to the difficulty that at low interest rates lenders may be unwilling to part with liquidity, preferring to hold idle funds rather than tie up their money at such a time. The expectation that interest rates would eventually be higher encouraged the banks to accumulate billions of dollars of idle reserves during the Depression. To overcome this obstacle and discourage this speculative liquidity, some writers suggested the possibility of a perpetually low level of interest rates, in good times as well as in bad. If it were generally believed that rates would never rise again, there would, of course, be no point in holding cash uninvested, waiting for higher rates. This argument for continuously low interest rates was especially stressed by those who feared the likelihood of secular stagnation and felt that our major problem in the years ahead would be to avoid chronic depression.

Also, a few years ago some felt that commercial loans would never again constitute an important determinant of the money supply and that other types

---

[1]No exact formulation can be made. A billion dollars of taxes will probably reduce consumption by less than a billion, to the extent that the taxes take funds otherwise saved. Much depends, however, on whose taxes are increased.

of loans were little restrained by high interest rates in prosperity. They pointed out the difficulties experienced in the past in working interest rates down in
depression and argued that the economy would run more smoothly if we
abandoned flexible interest rates in favor of a permanently low level of rates
and depended upon fiscal policy and selective monetary controls to check any
excessive expansion.

The steady inflationary pressures of the last 35 years have weakened the
appeal of these arguments. Logically, fiscal policy can check inflation. But
unfortunately, there are practical and political considerations that, in turn,
check fiscal policy. An anti-inflationary fiscal policy — higher taxes or reduced government spending — is almost invariably unpopular. We find that
monetary policy is still important.

One of the most effective implements of monetary policy in fighting inflation is the ability to raise interest rates. So, although we had a long period of
easy money, that era is temporarily ended. The discount rate of the Federal
Reserve Banks in the 1920s sometimes reached 7 percent. Between 1934 and
1950 the discount rate was never higher than 1½ percent and most of the time
was even lower. In 1957 it was raised to 3½ percent for the first time since
1933. The 4½ percent rate imposed in 1965 was the highest discount rate in 35
years. In 1969 the discount rate was 6 percent. By 1974 the rate had climbed
to 8 percent, presumably to the confusion of those who, 30 years earlier,
anticipated that interest rates would never rise again. Yet even these rates
were low as compared with those of some other countries at the time. Since
1957, rates of 4 to 10 percent have been in effect in many other countries, and
a few central banks set rates of 15 and 20 percent and even higher.

The additional powers the Federal Reserve received during the 1930s
made it less necessary for the Federal Reserve Banks to rely on the discount
rate than when the discount rate was almost their only means of control. But
the Banks are evidently by no means ready to throw out the discount rate as a
control device.

Methods of Regulating the Money Supply

The logic of discretionary monetary policy requires that the growth of the
money supply be checked in prosperity to avoid inflation and encouraged in
recession or depression to promote recovery.[2] We know that the Treasury
and the banks create money. We also know that the banks may increase the
money supply when they hold excess reserves and can make loans and investments. The principal means by which the money supply may be varied accordingly are as follows.

Banking System Operations. Without any government action, the banks
and the Federal Reserve may cause changes in the quantity of money. First,
the commercial banks may increase or decrease their loans to business and

---

[2]The solution is considerably more complicated when, as in the 1970s, there was "stagflation" — recession coupled with inflation.

consumers. This is, however, the very factor that requires regulation or counteraction, as the case may be. The growth of bank loans may need to be restrained in prosperity. In depression new loans are not being made as fast as old loans are being paid off.

In the second place, the banks may purchase securities formerly held by nonbank investors. In this case it is less likely that the banks are providing money that the borrower will spend to purchase plant and equipment, but deposits are nonetheless increased. The banks are holding fewer excess reserves and more earning assets; the public is holding fewer earning assets and more bank deposits. If the public elects to spend these additional deposits, the increase in the money supply will effect the economy. If the public is simply attempting to increase its liquidity by building up larger cash balances, as in a depression, the new deposits have little direct effect. Similarly, the banks may contract deposits by selling securities from their portfolios to the public.

In the third place, the Federal Reserve may engage in open market operations. If its holdings are sufficiently large at the outset, its sales can force so large a contraction in member reserves that the member banks must reduce their loans and investments. If, as in a depression, the Federal Reserve Banks wish to increase member reserves, they buy Treasury securities. Remember that, no longer required to maintain reserves against either their notes or their deposits, the Federal Reserve Banks can buy any amount of securities. The only limit is the size of the Treasury's total marketable debt. The Federal Reserve Banks can sell, of course, only that portion of the Treasury's total debt that they are holding. This would seem to suggest that the Fed's power to expand credit is greater than its power to contract it. In a way, it is. However, purchases, which increase member reserves, tend to be less effective as a control mechanism than sales, which contract them. Banks must reduce their loans if their reserves are deficient, but they are not compelled to expand their loans when they hold excess reserves. As during the 1930s, they may prefer to hold reserves greatly in excess of requirements.

Government — Currency Operations. The Treasury has the right to issue currency. Besides coins, it issues gold certificates (and formerly silver certificates) and is sometimes given the right to issue pure credit money, such as the greenbacks of the Civil War period. Anyone ignorant of the nature and importance of demand deposits might suppose that, with this right of currency issue, the Treasury would have great influence over the money supply. The fact is that, except for the currency that the public never sees, that is, the gold certificates, the Treasury's currency operations normally have little effect, directly or indirectly, on the amount of money in the hands of the public. Our most important money is in the form of deposits. If a currency expansion is to result in an expansion of the total quantity of money, it must cause a deposit expansion or at least not be offset by an equal decrease in deposits.

Gold Certificates. When the Federal Reserve Banks were required to maintain reserves against their liabilities, changes in gold certificates outstanding exerted a powerful leverage because of the changes they created in legal and excess reserves of the Fed. This is no longer true. However, changes in gold certificates outstanding continue to affect the reserve position of member banks.

An increase in gold certificates automatically increases deposits and assets of the Federal Reserve Banks. At the same time member bank deposits and legal and excess reserves increase. Whether this is the full extent of the change in the quantity of money depends upon the consequences of the excess reserves; these, in turn, depend upon circumstances. If there is little demand for loans and the member banks were already holding substantial excess reserves, they may now simply hold larger excess reserves. If member banks have been rejecting loan applications because they were loaned up and if the Federal Reserve Banks do not, through open market sales or by raising reserve requirements, wipe out the Treasury-created excess reserves, banking system deposits will probably rise by several times the amount of the increase in gold certificates.

Other Treasury Currency. Changes in other Treasury currency would be a weak and uncertain mechanism with which to attempt to implement monetary policy. If Congress were to authorize the Treasury to expand the greenback issue or raise its buying price and purchase more silver by issuing more silver certificates, what would be the principal consequence? At any time the public is already holding all the currency it wants. Otherwise more Federal Reserve notes would have been supplied. The new Treasury currency would simply replace Federal Reserve notes in circulation. Total currency in the hands of the public would be the same as before, since the public would take the surplus currency to the banks, which would return it to the Federal Reserve Banks. Member banks' required reserves would increase by a percentage of the public's increased deposits. At the same time, member banks' legal reserves would increase by the full amount of the currency they deposited in the Federal Reserve Banks, so their excess reserves would also increase. However, all these consequences could be offset by higher reserve requirements and open market sales if the Federal Reserve chose.

Government — Borrowing Operations. The Treasury can change the amount of money in circulation by another method which is somewhat less obvious and considerably more easily handled than varying the quantity of Treasury currency. That method is its borrowing operations. The Treasury can increase the volume of deposits by borrowing from the banks to pay off maturing securities held by nonbank investors and can decrease deposits by the opposite procedure. Likewise, the government can reduce taxes and borrow from the banks, increasing deposits, or it can decrease deposits by taxing more and retiring bank-held securities. Or, leaving the level of taxes unchanged, the government may vary its expenditures by borrowing more or less from the banks and the rest from nonbank sources.

Quantity of Money Needed

We should be able to get some idea of how much money may be needed in the years directly ahead by looking at the relation between the money supply and the gross national product. However, it can be only a general approximation. As Table 22-1 indicates, since World War II there has been a fairly steady (but not monotonic) fall in the ratio (*K*) of money to *GNP*.[3] People are finding they can hold less money in proportion to income than they customarily held 20 or 30 years ago.

Money, you recall, is not the only indirect liability issued today. The commercial banks have long held a preeminent position as financial intermediaries. The indirect debt that they issue to the public in exchange for the public's direct debt (including the customers' promissory notes and corporate and government bonds that their customers wish to exchange for deposits) constitutes our most important money. But there are other financial intermediaries besides the commercial banks. These, too, issue their indirect obligations for the public's direct obligations. True, their obligations are not money, but they compete with money. They are alternative assets for the public. The more savings deposits and savings and loan accounts a person holds and the greater the value of a person's paid-up life insurance, the less that person's demand for money.

Some of these nonbank financial institutions have grown more rapidly since 1900 than have the banks. Their liabilities have to some extent replaced banks' liabilities. So, too, have savings bonds and other highly liquid obligations of the Treasury and other large borrowers. When interest rates are high, businesses and consumers alike are especially eager to substitute earning assets for their temporarily idle cash. For an educated guess, suppose we assume that:

1. *GNP* continues to grow at about the same rate as during the last 10 years;
2. The price level continues to rise at about the same rate as over the last 10 years; and
3. The ratio of money to income continues to run approximately 20 percent, as currently.

On this basis, by 1980 *GNP* will be nearly $2.0 trillion; total money to handle this rate of production will be about $400 billion.[4]

No doubt the actual figure will be something a little different. If, however, it is a great deal lower, it is likely that prices and/or output will be falling; if it is a great deal higher than $400 billion, prices will probably be rising more rapidly than since 1965.

---

[3]This of course is equivalent to a rise in the income velocity of money.
[4]We could alternatively estimate the money supply by extrapolating its growth rate over some earlier period. The results should be similar.

**Table 22-1   Money Supply, Gross National Product,
Income Velocity, and K, 1929–1974**
(In billions of dollars)

Calendar Year	(1) GNP at Current Prices	(2) Money Supply (M_1, currency plus demand deposits)*	(3) Income Velocity of Money (1)/(2)	(4) Money Supply ÷ GNP (K) [(2)/(1)]
1929	103.1	26.5	3.9	25.7%
1930	90.4	25.4	3.6	28.1%
1931	75.8	23.6	3.2	31.1%
1932	58.0	20.7	2.8	35.7%
1933	55.6	19.5	2.9	35.1%
1934	65.1	21.5	3.0	33.0%
1935	72.2	25.6	2.8	35.5%
1936	82.5	29.1	2.8	35.3%
1937	90.4	30.3	3.0	33.5%
1938	84.7	30.1	2.8	35.5%
1939	90.5	33.6	2.7	37.1%
1940	99.7	39.0	2.6	39.1%
1941	124.5	45.4	2.7	36.5%
1942	157.9	55.2	2.9	35.0%
1943	191.6	72.3	2.7	37.7%
1944	210.1	86.0	2.4	40.9%
1945	211.9	99.2	2.1	46.8%
1946	208.5	106.0	2.0	50.8%
1947	231.3	113.1	2.1	48.9%
1948	257.6	111.5	2.3	43.3%
1949	256.5	111.2	2.3	43.4%
1950	284.8	116.2	2.5	40.8%
1951	328.4	122.7	2.7	37.4%
1952	345.5	127.4	2.7	36.9%
1953	364.6	128.8	2.8	35.3%
1954	364.8	132.3	2.8	36.3%
1955	398.0	135.2	2.9	34.0%
1956	419.2	136.9	3.1	32.7%
1957	441.1	135.9	3.3	30.8%
1958	447.3	141.1	3.2	31.5%
1959	483.7	143.4	3.4	29.7%
1960	503.7	144.2	3.5	28.6%
1961	520.1	148.7	3.5	28.6%
1962	560.3	150.9	3.7	26.9%
1963	590.5	156.5	3.8	26.5%
1964	632.4	163.7	3.9	25.9%
1965	684.9	171.3	4.0	25.0%
1966	749.9	175.4	4.3	23.4%
1967	793.9	186.9	4.3	23.5%
1968	864.2	201.7	4.3	23.3%
1969	930.3	208.7	4.5	22.4%
1970	977.1	221.4	4.4	22.7%
1971	1,054.9	235.3	4.5	22.3%
1972	1,158.0	255.8	4.5	22.1%
1973	1,294.9	271.5	4.8	21.0%
1974	1,397.4	284.4	4.9	20.4%

Source: *Economic Report of the President*, 1975, and *Federal Reserve Bulletins*, various issues.
*As of December of each year.

Variation Required in Interest Rates

When economists began to write in terms of income analysis instead of the quantity of money, they found it more difficult to make a good case for the use of monetary policy. The trouble was that they wanted to emphasize that the effectiveness of monetary policy lay in changes in the interest rate rather than simply and directly in changes of the quantity of money. Yet it was not easy to show that a variation in interest rates would ordinarily make much difference to the borrower. In depression, few wanted to borrow money, even if interest rates were nearly zero. In prosperity, the marginal efficiency of capital was high and borrowers were not deterred by high interest rates.

It might be argued that if the monetary authorities simply continued raising interest rates long enough, a level would finally be reached that would discourage investment. If a rate of 9 or 10 percent did not effectively put on the brakes, a rate of 15 or 20 percent might. According to this view, the reason monetary policy seems ineffective in fighting inflation is that it has been inadequately employed.

There are several objections to pushing interest rates to a very high level:

1. It would make monetary policy more ineffective than ever in depression, for it would make the public more eager to hold idle balances as interest rates fell. No matter how much additional money they created, the monetary authorities might find it impossible to push interest rates below, perhaps, 5 or 6 percent. In other words, the liquidity trap would be strengthened in depression by the public's expectation of much higher rates later.
2. The impact of interest rate changes varies from one business to the next. A rate high enough to check overall investment adequately would have disastrous effects on some individual industries, especially construction. A desirable monetary policy should contribute to business stability, not create large areas of extreme instability.
3. Very wide swings in interest rates would encourage wide swings in the value of securities. As interest rates rise, the price of existing bonds (other than savings bonds) necessarily falls. Bonds then become more attractive than stocks, and stock prices also fall, as in 1968–1974. The crushing pressures of a 15 to 20 percent interest rate on the securities market would lead to thousands of bankruptcies as individuals, corporations, and especially banks and other financial institutions found the value of their assets shrinking by perhaps 50 percent or more.

It is probably not only undesirable but usually unnecessary to resort to extremely high interest rates to implement an effective monetary policy. Early income theorists oversimplified the analysis, concentrating almost entirely on the borrower's responses to changes in interest rates. They overlooked the possible effects on the lender.

1. Borrowers, though not responsive to changes in the interest rate, may be affected by the availability of credit. There cannot be a borrower without a lender.

2. Lenders may be responsive to changes in the interest rate, so that the availability of credit is increased when interest rates fall and is decreased when interest rates rise.

When interest rates drop a little, institutional lenders may decide to sell their government bonds to realize the capital gains. They would then have more funds to lend to other borrowers. When rates rise, the drop in bond prices may discourage these lenders from selling bonds. Instead they are more likely to try to buy some of the bonds held by the general public. When commercial banks buy bonds from the public, deposits are expanded and excess reserves decreased. Funds will at such times be less available to current borrowers, even if interest rates have changed only moderately.[5]

Other Implications of Monetary Policy

Besides the matter of the availability of credit, there are other implications of monetary policy largely overlooked by early income theorists.[6] It is much too sweeping to say that monetary policy cannot possibly be effective except to the extent that by lowering interest rates it may cause more investment. This conclusion results from the simplifying assumption that both the consumption function and the investment function are completely unaffected by monetary policy. Granted this assumption, the logic of the analysis leads inescapably to the conclusion that, unless monetary policy affects interest rates and unless the investment function is interest elastic, monetary policy cannot possibly affect income. How realistic is this assumption?

The consumption function, it was emphasized earlier, may be affected by various factors. The amount of income consumed at a particular income level may be changed because of future income or future prices. It may also depend to some extent on the amount of assets, liquid or otherwise, currently held.

The investment function is, we know, to a very large extent determined by expectations, and it is highly unstable. It appears possible that if the money supply were substantially increased in recession, both businesses and consumers would be encouraged to spend more — that is, both the consumption function and the investment function would increase.

Unless we are quantity theorists, we cannot claim that these functions must be increased by an increase in the quantity of money or decreased by a reduction in the quantity of money. We should admit the possibility, however, which would allow a much greater potential for monetary policy than is often implied.

Perhaps it is partly a matter of timing. If a recession is allowed to spiral rapidly into a deep and long depression, ushered in by a sensational stock market collapse and accompanied by a deluge of bank failures, confidence may be so severely battered that monetary policy can have little effect. Under

---

[5]Deposits will be increased by a billion dollars whether the banks buy that amount of bonds from the public or lend that amount to the public. The new deposits are much more likely to be promptly spent, however, in the case of the loans.

[6]See the discussion of the monetarists in Chapter 20.

less drastic conditions, however, monetary policy would appear to have a greater potential than just lowering interest rates to possibly stimulate more investment.

AUTOMATIC MONETARY POLICY

Although most bankers and economists today feel that the advantages of a centrally determined, discretionary monetary policy are self-evident, there are a few competent economists who remain unconvinced.[7] The record indicates, they believe, that the monetary authorities, if they have not done the wrong thing, have done too little too late. Misunderstandings and mistakes of the Board of Governors and the Federal Reserve Banks in 1930 turned what might well have been only an ordinary recession into the Great Depression. Also, due to the inherent lags of monetary policy, by the time changes become effective they may be entirely inappropriate. Discretionary policy necessarily means, they say, uncertainty and confusion. Instead of constantly adding new techniques of monetary management, we should be streamlining and simplifying monetary policy. Reserve requirements should remain constant, and Federal Reserve Banks should no longer be authorized to lend to member banks nor discount for them. The Banks' control over margin requirements should be repealed, as should their control over interest rates paid by member banks on their deposit liabilities. Since the automatic gold standard no longer seems a practical guide to a nondiscretionary monetary policy, the System might be instructed to use its open market powers to insure a 4 percent annual increase in total currency and demand deposits. Small maladjustments would then tend to correct themselves rather than be magnified by the mistakes of the money managers. In short, critics argue that the record gives evidence that the Fed misunderstands its powers and purposes and has difficulty deciding on the most efficacious action, even when it has a firm goal in mind.

Most bankers and financial writers feel that these charges and recommendations are unwarranted. Mistakes have been made and no doubt will always be made. But we are constantly learning more about how money and banking affect the economy. We should be able to improve the quality of our management. Specifically, the authorities should have enough discretionary power to counter changes in the public's desire to hold money, which could affect velocity of circulation even if the quantity of money were increased according to some fixed formula. Moreover, even if demand deposits and currency are increased yearly by a constant amount, there could be complications from changes in the stock of near monies, especially time deposits. Some discretionary changes may be necessary. It seems unnecessarily pessimistic to

---

[7]For a well-stated presentation of this argument, see Milton Friedman, *A Program for Monetary Stability* (New York: Fordham University Press, 1959); and Milton Friedman, "A Program for Monetary Stability," *1962 Proceedings of the Conference on Residential Financing*; further references to his more recent works are contained in footnote 11 of Chapter 15; also, Henry Simons, "A Positive Program for Laissez Faire," in his *Economic Policy for a Free Society* (Chicago: University of Chicago Press, 1948).

argue that because Federal Reserve authorities a generation ago lacked central banking experience, they will never be able to take the proper actions.[8]

FISCAL POLICY

Every government that collects taxes, spends the proceeds, and occasionally borrows or reduces its debt has some kind of fiscal policy, if this term is used very narrowly. Someone must decide who to tax, and how much to tax, and how to spend the revenues. Since the Depression we have realized the much broader importance of fiscal policy as an implement of control, permitting the government to prop up a sagging economy or close an inflationary gap.

Years ago, on the theory that the restoration of public confidence required, above all else, that the government balance its budget and, even more important, avoid "inflationary" monetary issues, the federal government tried hard to avoid borrowing in depression from the banks or from the public. Instead of increasing government expenditures, creating income and employment, the government cut its spending and trimmed its payroll. Both President Hoover and, in his first term, President Roosevelt attempted to balance the budget as national income fell, and each criticized the other for failing to accomplish it. Today there are few who would advocate a balanced government budget in depression, no matter how important they might consider it to be at other times. Also, there is less conviction today that an increase in the money supply during the depression (whether brought about by the Federal Reserve or the Treasury) will necessarily result in a price inflation.

Tools of Fiscal Policy

In various ways a government can exert pressure upon the economy by the way it handles its fiscal powers. It can tax differently, spend differently, or borrow differently. Each of these can be of some effect.

Tax Redistribution. Respecting the effects of tax redistribution, it is impossible to make objective decisions. The average propensity to consume appears to be lower for those in the high income groups than for those with lower incomes. It is accordingly argued that if, in depression, income tax rates are made more progressive, then the same total of taxes will involve less of a leakage from the income stream. If people in lower income brackets are taxed a billion dollars less, chances are that their spending will increase by nearly a billion dollars. If wealthy people are taxed a billion dollars more, presumably they will save less but will continue to spend almost as much as before.

This is a proposition that cannot be easily verified. Also, it pertains to only one round of spending and does not take into account the area in which that spending occurs. We can hardly assume that, as long as income is spent

---

[8]Remember that initially they did not even grasp the significance of open market operations.

one time, it makes no difference who gets it. In depression the field of consumer durables is hit especially hard. It is at least conceivable that total respending effects might be greater if an extra half billion were spent, presumably by the well-to-do, for cars, air-conditioning, and new homes than if an extra billion or more were spent, presumably by lower income groups, for more food. We are not saying that it is more important, more equitable, or even more desirable to satisfy the demand for durable goods at the expense of other demands. The point is that if the demand for consumer durables is stimulated, the further respending may possibly be greater than if the money went originally for groceries. If so, we may find the country spending more for both durable goods and groceries. At any rate, it is a little naive to look only at the initial spending by different income groups and jump to conclusions on that basis.

In addition, there are two other weaknesses in the argument. In the first place it ignores the policy's effect on the incentive to invest, and in the second place the policy does not seem to be reversible.

We have already seen that investment is one of the components of income and that it is determined largely by the marginal efficiency of capital. To the extent that individuals are investing, they will normally be individuals with higher than average incomes, subject to the rapidly rising surtaxes on income. It seems quite possible that taxes of 70, 80, and 90 percent on any additional income may chill the enthusiasm of individuals considering an investment opportunity that involves much uncertainty.[9] If the marginal efficiency of capital is only 30 or 40 percent, they may receive only 3 or 4 percent net after paying taxes on the extra income — if the investment turns out successfully. If they feel they should have a potential net yield of 10 or 20 percent to offset the risk involved, they may have to see the likelihood of an annual return of 100 percent or more, before taxes, to induce them to invest. Otherwise they are more likely to shop around in the bond market for tax-exempt municipal bonds already outstanding, purchase of which is not investment in the economic sense. A reasonably safe 6 percent municipal bond may yield them, after tax, as much as the successful investment can yield, and with the bond they will be more sure of receiving the income.[10]

There is, besides, another way in which high tax rates on high incomes tend to lessen investment. The high taxes decrease the amount of private savings that will be made. In the long run the volume of savings in the economy will set a limit to the possibilities of private investment.

---

[9] The depressing effects of high tax rates upon investment are slightly offset by the possibility of deducting some losses when computing one's taxable income. Against the fact that they will get only a part of the gain, if it materializes, investors can weigh the fact that if the investment results in a loss, their net income, after tax, will be reduced by part of the amount of the loss. Thus, people subject to 70 percent tax on any additional income may reason that if the venture succeeds they will take 30 percent of the profits and if it fails they will bear about 30 percent of the loss. The rest of the loss will be borne by the government, which will collect less taxes from them.

However, the extent to which losses may be used to offset other income (and reduce tax liability) is restricted in various ways. Restricted offsets are better than no offsets, but they do not completely cancel the effect of high income taxes. As a result, risky venture capital is heavily penalized.

[10] In 1975 the maximum rate of 70 percent applied to income in excess of $200,000 for a married couple (and to income in excess of $100,000 for a single person).

Thus, even if we could accurately measure the increase in consumption that would follow the shift of a billion dollars of taxes from low income groups to high, we would not know the net effect of the policy upon income. We would need to know also the change in investment that resulted. Conceivably, the net result would be negative. There is no assurance that we might not find consumption increased by $.7 billion, investment decreased by $.8 billion (or more), and income down by $.1 billion (or more) as a result of this attempt at an expansionary policy.

Note, too, that there is no necessary reason that, as a result of an increase of $1 billion in taxes paid by the wealthy, the decrease in investment would be less than $1 billion. Possibly the higher taxes on high incomes would be construed as an antibusiness policy or a turn toward socialism, and, rightly or wrongly, the marginal efficiency of capital would fall. Investment might drop by several billion dollars as the result of the shift of a billion dollars more of taxes to the shoulders of the wealthy. It certainly is an oversimplification to assert as a truism, needing no proof, that a redistribution of taxes from lower income groups to higher will automatically raise national income.

The other objection to tax redistribution as a device to help control the business cycle is that it appears to be mainly a rationalization for income redistribution rather than an honest and sincere attempt to develop a workable fiscal policy. In depression the alleged advantages of increasing the progressiveness of income tax rates are explained. But if the logic is sound, then in inflation the policy should be reversed. That is another story altogether. Of course there are political ramifications. It is hard to imagine any Senator, at least one hoping for reelection, standing up to tell the Senate and the nation that an effective way to fight inflation would be to raise tax rates on small incomes and at the same time lower the rates on the top brackets.

If, then, the redistribution of the tax load is destined to move always in one direction, we cannot expect it to be a useful device for fiscal policy. We already have taxpayers turning over 70 percent of their "last" dollars to the government. Already taxpayers filing separate returns and with incomes of no more than about $22,000 are turning over to the government almost 50 percent of their "last" dollars. If these are the rates that we maintain in prosperity, it is difficult to see how we can greatly increase the progressiveness of the rates in depression.[11]

Expenditure Redistribution. The possibility of varying the types of government expenditures is of some theoretical but limited practical importance. Some government purchases, especially of certain types of goods, may be

---

[11]The subject of taxation is an intricate one that we cannot attempt to cover thoroughly in a few pages or even chapters. There is much dissatisfaction with the present system of rates that are nominally very high but that in effect are lower — often much lower — due to loopholes the law permits in defining taxable income. If all loopholes were to be closed, all rates could be lowered. Perhaps then it would be possible to increase the progressiveness of tax rates in depression, if they were at the outset not higher than perhaps 40 or 50 percent. There still remains the basic question, however, of whether, with the return of prosperity, the rate structure would be amended to impose less progressive rates again. If not, this device would be useless as a tool of countercyclical fiscal policy.

more stimulating to the economy than other purchases, particularly of services. Typically heavy industry is more seriously hit in depression than are most other lines of production. If the government were to spend a billion dollars more in highway construction or housing projects and spend a billion dollars less on education and postal service, its total expenditures, although no larger than before, would probably be more stimulating to the economy. The obvious difficulty is that it is often impractical to reduce or eliminate individual expenditures, and it is simpler to increase some and leave the others unchanged than to try to keep total expenditures constant. Still, we may profitably remember that the effectiveness of a government's fiscal policy is not to be measured entirely and simply by the amount of its deficit or surplus. The quality of the spending and taxes also has something to do with it.

Debt Redistribution. Also, there are implications for the economy in the way in which the Treasury handles a deficit or surplus. If the government must borrow during inflation, it can appropriately push the sale of savings bonds and appeal to lower and middle income groups. Chances are good that if people in this income range are going to lend much to the government, they are going to have to reduce their consumption. If in inflation the government cannot avoid operating at a deficit, it can at least minimize the deficit's inflationary consequences by encouraging an offsetting decline in consumption.

During depression, a deficit will more effectively raise national income if not offset by reduced consumption. The Treasury at such a time is most likely to borrow from the banks or from the well-to-do, whose purchases of government securities presumably will not affect their consumption.

If the government's income is greater than its expenditures, the Treasury may use the surplus to redeem bank-held securities or repay other obligations.[12] In addition to the monetary repercussions, there are also income effects. Taxes, we know, are a leakage out of the income stream. There is no net leakage if the money drained out as taxes reappears in the income stream. It does reappear if the government spends it for goods and services. In the case of a surplus, however, the government is not spending it. It is only turning the money over to someone else in exchange for maturing securities. The question then is: Will the money be spent, either for consumption or for investment, by the one who receives it? If you have to reduce your consumption this year by $1,000 because of the taxes you are paying, but your neighbor, repaid $1,000 by the government, feels he now has $1,000 more to spend, the Treasury surplus has had no net contractive effect. If, however, your neighbor holds the money idle or exchanges it for existing assets, there has been a leakage from the income stream. There has likewise been a leakage if your neighbor repays a bank loan with the income the government transferred from you to him. The funds received by the bank are not income to the bank. You surrendered income when you paid your taxes, and no other factors of

---

[12]The effects on the quantity of money should by now be obvious. When taxes collected from the public are used to repay money borrowed from the banks, the quantity of money shrinks. If, instead, nonbank lenders are repaid, the quantity of money is unaffected.

production received it. In this instance there is not only a leakage from income but also a contraction in the quantity of money.

Balanced, Surplus, and Deficit Budgets. The most important implement of fiscal policy is the relation between the government's total expenditures and its total disposable income. Should there be a deficit, a surplus, or a balanced budget?

Vary Tax Total. A budget surplus can be turned into a deficit without necessarily increasing government expenditures by a penny. Instead of spending more, the government can tax less. This is a fairly recent development. When Hoover was trying to fight the Depression in 1931 and 1932, there was little that Congress might have accomplished by cutting taxes even if it had tried. The total tax bill was too small to be of much effect.[13] Today, with the federal government regularly taking more than $275 billion, it could, simply by lowering taxes and continuing its present level of expenditures, bring about bigger deficits than we have ever had — even in World War II.[14]

We should not suppose that the way in which the deficit is created is a matter of no consequence whatever. As usual with economic questions, there are arguments on both sides. The advantages of decreasing taxes rather than increasing expenditures in depression are briefly:

1. The tax reduction can be put into effect almost immediately. Public works programs, other than leaf-raking projects, are likely to be slower in starting. It takes time to plan them and time to put them into operation.
2. By either a reduction in taxes or an increase in government expenditures the government can allow the public to have more goods and services. The reduction in taxes lets the public itself select the extra goods that it will consume. The public can spend the additional after-tax income as it chooses. By contrast, the increase in government expenditures requires the government to decide what extra goods the public shall have. The government may decide that more roads are what is most needed, or more housing, more post offices, or more hospitals. No doubt the public will be glad to have any of these added goods and services selected by the government. For instance, the public will unquestionably enjoy a billion dollars worth of superhighways. The question is: Would they perhaps enjoy even more an additional billion dollars worth of cars, television sets, clothes, or whatever else they might have bought if their tax bill had been cut a billion dollars? Except for dedicated socialists, most people would rather see consumption decisions made, whenever possible, by the individual rather than the state. "Big Brother" may know what is best for us, but we would like to have the freedom to make our choices, even if they are not always completely rational.
3. Tax reduction in depression, instead of the expansion of government spending, offers less encouragement to the proliferation of government

---

[13]Total receipts of the federal government in 1932 were $2 billion.
[14]From 1942 to 1946 our deficits ranged from $21 to $55 billion annually. The largest deficit during the Depression was less than $4.5 billion.

bureaus and agencies. The government's role in production is not inflated, and there is less interference with private enterprise. Other than roadbuilding, there are few activities in which the government can engage that will not conflict with private business. We are not concerned here with any vested interests of private producers, but with the simple fact that if the country is struggling to recover from depression, investment must rise if there is to be a strong and lasting recovery. If business feels that government is offering unfair competition — in housing, electric power production, or elsewhere — the increase in government spending may be more than offset by a decline in investment or by its failure to rise. The technique of tax reduction is thus, in general, more encouraging to business since it offers no threat of competition. It can be still more encouraging if it includes a specific lightening of business taxes.

4. A tax program is more easily reversed in prosperity than is a spending program. An increase in taxes will win no popularity contests, it's true. But it is not resisted with the dogged determination that meets most proposed cuts in government spending. It appears sometimes that one of the most strongly entrenched interests in the country is represented by the public payrolls. People whose jobs are not affected tend to be generally indifferent to the importance of regulating public expenditures. People have a hard time realizing that they cannot get something for nothing. They are reluctant to see any reduction in the "free" goods and services provided by government. The role of government tends to become steadily greater when expenditures (and activities) are increased in every depression and almost never decreased in prosperity.

5. Possibly the tax reduction would be interpreted as evidence of a more favorable attitude toward business. If so, it might raise the marginal efficiency of capital, thereby stimulating more private investment.

Vary Expenditure Total. Those who believe that the budget should be changed from the side of expenditures rather than receipts point out:

1. A program of public works puts money in the hands of the unemployed, who really need it. Tax reduction leaves more money in the hands of those who already have enough income to tax.

2. The stimulus to the economy from a given deficit will be greater if it is brought about by increased expenditures. Respending effects will be less with the tax cut because:
   a. The average tax cut is likely to be small. A billion-dollar tax reduction might involve $100 less in taxes from each of ten million taxpayers. By the time this takes the form of $2 less withheld from the weekly paycheck, it is unlikely to cause consumption to skyrocket. Five thousand dollars more income to each of 200,000 unemployed would be a billion dollar initial and direct increase in expenditure. Besides, 1 person receiving $100 more a week will spend more of the increase than will 50 people receiving $2 more a week.
   b. Also, the marginal propensity to consume is probably higher for the unemployed person, whose income is much less, than for the taxpayer. Accordingly, the multiplier effects will be greater, at least for the first round of respending.

3. There need be little delay in putting a public works program promptly into effect if the government will plan ahead for suitable and worthwhile projects to undertake in recession. Before the economy has had a chance to spiral downward into depression, the support of the government employment program could be mobilized to maintain purchasing power, confidence, and consumption.

4. In depression some industries are hit especially hard. Machine tools, for example, and steel are likely to fare worse than consumer goods industries. If Pittsburgh steel mills are running at 60 percent of capacity and St. Louis shoe factories are operating at 80 percent, a sound program for recovery should recognize the far more desperate situation in Pittsburgh. Public works programs are much more flexibly adapted to meeting local needs than are tax reductions, for they can be set up where the need is greatest.

5. There are some very desirable goods and services that private enterprise is ill-suited to provide. Highways are the obvious example. Conservation programs, urban public transportation systems, and parks and recreational facilities are other areas where government may be able to operate more effectively than private enterprise. During depression the government can broadly expand its activities in these fields without forcing any reduction in production elsewhere, since it is using factors that would otherwise be producing nothing at all. Jobs are created, incomes are raised, and the public is provided with valuable goods and services that it might otherwise never have.

Types of Budget Policy

The range of possible budget policies is greater than simply the choice between a balanced and an unbalanced budget. There are differences in the extent to which and the recommended means by which deficits and surpluses may be attained.

Traditional. The traditional policy is to balance the government budget whenever that can possibly be done. Deficits can be expected in war and may be necessary in serious depressions. But in normal times the budget should be balanced with at least a small surplus to be used to retire debt outstanding. Ideally, the government should have no debt or only a small one. The government's credit will be maintained and its affairs will be financially sound if, like any prudent individual or corporation, it regularly lives within its income. In prosperity, when tax receipts rise even if tax rates are unchanged, the government can afford to expand its services and buy more goods. In depression the government, like any other business, must economize. Its revenues are going to be less since incomes are falling. Perhaps by raising tax rates it may be able to gain more disposable income. It should cut out all but the most necessary expenditures, for if it fails to balance the budget it proves itself to be grossly irresponsible.

Few students of money and banking can be found today to support the traditional policy. It is now generally agreed that the nation is not just another business firm or individual. It is all-inclusive. If it goes into debt, it usually borrows within its own borders. It is in debt to its own citizens. If they are eventually to be repaid, they will be the ones who will pay the debt, and vice versa. The credit of a nation depends in the long run on its ability to tax. The more prosperous the nation, the greater the taxes that can be collected. The important thing for the government to do in depression is not to reduce expenditures to the point that they can be covered by current income. Rather, it should take the initiative, when private enterprise lags, to restore full employment and a high income level.

A positive government program to fight depression will probably require a substantial deficit, along one or the other or perhaps both of the lines discussed earlier. Depression is exactly the time when government expenditures should be greatest. The social cost of public works is the goods and services that the private sector of the economy must sacrifice to permit the public works. There is no social cost of public works when they are utilizing only productive factors that would otherwise be unemployed. The economy is losing no goods that would otherwise be produced by these same factors, employed by private enterprise. From the cost point of view, we only owe ourselves more money if the expenditures are deficit financed.

Conversely, in prosperity the government should be reducing, not expanding, its operations. The particular mechanism of finance chosen — taxes or loans — is not the basic issue. The crucial point is that, at a time when productive resources are fully employed, the only way the government can employ more factors of production is by having the private sector employ fewer productive factors. We cannot, as in depression, count the government production as pure gain. Private enterprise must sacrifice goods and services to permit the government to use factors of production for its own projects.

One final point should be noted. Occasionally and quite correctly it is argued that there is a multiplier effect even with a balanced budget. Whenever the government is spending exactly what it receives in taxes, total spending is greater than it would be without the taxes and expenditures. This is because at least part of what the government receives in taxes would otherwise have been saved — that is, not spent for consumption. But if the budget is balanced, the government is spending the entire amount, by definition. This net addition to spending is, of course, an addition to income and will launch the usual respending effects as people spend part of any increase in their incomes.

So it is sometimes asked: Why should we not counter depressions and inflations by increases and decreases in government spending but with taxes equally changed so that the budget is always balanced? Conceivably, we could do this, but it appears impractical. The difficulty is that variations in expenditure would have to be much larger than when deficits and surpluses are involved. Five billion dollars of government expenditures financed in depression by borrowing that amount from the commercial banks results in an initial income creation of $5 billion of income. If financed by taxes, of which perhaps $2 billion are otherwise saved, the net income creation from the government's taxing and spending is only $2 billion. If the public would have spent as much as $4 billion of the $5 billion they were taxed, net income creation is only $1 billion. Depending upon the extent to which taxes reduced private spending, it might require $15 or $20 billion of tax-financed expenditures to raise income by as much as $5 billion of expenditures financed by borrowing from the banks. It would not be easy to be forever adjusting the level of expenditures and taxes on the vast scale that would be necessary. To find, on the massive scale required, really worthwhile and desirable programs that could be turned on and off would probably be impossible.

Pump Priming. At one time, especially in the early days of Roosevelt's "New Deal," there was much talk of the pump-priming policy. The idea was that the government should incur a deficit for a year or two to promote a recovery and that the economy would then continue to improve without further assistance. The deficit, it was believed, need not be very large. The main thing was to get money circulating again and restore public confidence.

A few years later the tools of income analysis had been forged. With these concepts to aid them, the theorists found the weaknesses of the pump-priming philosophy. The marginal propensity to consume and the multiplier, derived from it, showed that the respending effects from a temporary government deficit would not be very large and would quickly be dampened. Unless something else happened, the income level would soon settle back where it had been. Certainly if investment moved sharply upward, triggered by the increase in consumption, then there could be an interaction between the multiplier and the accelerator that would cause income to rise rapidly to the level of full employment. But investment was not likely to increase when almost every business was plagued with excess capacity. One might, it appeared, continue indefinitely to prime the pump with annual deficits of $3 or $4 billion without ever ending the Depression. Possibly a much larger deficit, such as that incurred during World War II, might have effectively primed the pump. No one suggested it. Indeed, many were deeply distressed by the comparatively small deficits during the Depression.

Compensatory Spending. Then compensatory spending was proposed. According to this philosophy, the budget might be balanced over the cycle, although if on balance there were a small deficit, we should not be concerned. No one has ever suggested that the budget should balance every month, or every day or hour. There is no more reason that it should balance every 12 months. In periods of depression the government should increase its expenditures. Tax rates in depression should be unchanged or perhaps reduced. In either case tax revenues will fall and deficits will be incurred. In a period of prosperity and accompanying inflation, a reduction of government expenditures and an increase of taxes will yield surpluses to reduce the debt built up in hard times.

Most economists today favor some form of compensatory government spending. There are two possible ways to effect such a policy, one essentially automatic, the other discretionary, as explained below.

Automatic Budget. Some[15] propose that ordinarily the government's total expenditures and tax rates should be left alone. The rates should be set at such a level that the budget will be balanced at times of full employment. If a surplus persists, taxes should be lowered. Otherwise rates should be left unchanged. When national income falls, the government will receive less in taxes since the unchanged rates will bring in less revenue when applied to the lower incomes. A deficit will automatically appear. No one will need to decide how large the deficit should be. There will be no arguments about how to reduce taxes and whose taxes should be reduced the most. There will be no decisions about what and where public works should be undertaken and no time needed to implement the program. The evils associated with an ever-expanding sphere of governmental activity are avoided. The thorny problem of reversing depression policies in prosperity is eliminated altogether. When depression yields to recovery and prosperity, the unchanged expenditures and tax rates automatically bring the budget back into balance.

This approach is basically a conservative one by modern standards. It recognizes the importance of some kind of compensatory government spending to offset the uneven rate of spending by the rest of the economy and attempts to keep it within clear and fixed bounds. It avoids forecasting as well as policy decisions. It minimizes the role of the managers.

Functional Finance. The general heading "functional finance" includes proposals for discretionary management of the government's taxing and spending activities.[16] The fundamental point stressed by these economists is that neither a deficit nor a surplus can be judged by itself. We cannot say that one is "bad," the other "good." Prevailing conditions determine whether there should be a deficit or a surplus. A deficit is "bad" at a time of full employment, but a surplus is just as "bad" in depression. The aim of the government should be not to balance the budget at all costs, but to give maximum support to recovery and to check inflation — in short, to stabilize the economy. There is no necessary reason for the budget to be balanced, even over the cycle.[17] We should unhesitatingly borrow in depression, regardless of how large the current deficit or the total debt. Even if the debt becomes so large that we have to borrow to pay the interest, there is nothing to worry about. As long as prices are not rising, the borrowing can continue, whether from the public or from the banks. If prices do begin to rise, then the policy can be reversed. Higher taxes, lower expenditures, and government surpluses will reduce the income stream and remove the inflationary pressures.

The difference between these economists and those who favor an automatic policy is more quantitative than qualitative. Advocates of functional

---

[15]Notably the Committee for Economic Development.

[16]The term "functional finance" was coined by Abba Lerner. See "Functional Finance and the Public Debt," *Social Research* (February, 1943), pp. 38–51.

[17]The appropriate concept for this philosophy is not the actual budget surplus or deficit, but the full employment budget surplus or deficit which measures what the budget situation would be at full employment at the existing tax and spending structure. For example, over the period 1969 through 1972 the actual budget showed a deficit, whereas the full employment budget recorded a surplus.

finance believe that the automatic adjustments are likely not to be large enough to be effective. They have confidence in the ability and discretion of the managers who are to decide what shall be done. They seem to be confident also — in spite of the record, one might add — that the government can operate its fiscal policy in a scientific way, nicely adjusting its deficits and surpluses to the needs of the economy as precisely as a thermostat alternately turns the furnace and the air conditioner off and on in response to the changing temperature. Although the automatic policy school is much less sanguine than this group about the ability of the experts, it does concede that in an emergency it may be necessary to go beyond the bounds of automatic policy and deliberately increase government spending or reduce taxes.

SUMMARY AND CONCLUSION

In the decade following World War I, monetary policy was unchallenged. No one talked about fiscal policy, for there was little to say other than that the government should live within its income. By monetary policy the authorities could control the price level, the volume of loans, and the level of business activity — or so it appeared. We had finally organized a central bank. Our loosely constructed, unintegrated banking structure was operating more smoothly, or at least less badly, than it ever had. The Board of Governors had discovered how to use open market operations to increase or decrease the reserves of the member banks. The business cycle was now controlled; there would be no more depressions; this was the new era.

The disillusionment with monetary policies during the 1930s caused a swing in the opposite direction. The newly developed income theory emphasized the importance of income creation rather than money creation. It provided a framework for analysis of the ways in which the government might contribute to recovery through its taxing and spending programs. For several years monetary policy went into almost total eclipse.

Today a better balance has emerged. We can see that both monetary and fiscal policies are useful. We need not decide which of the two we shall use when we can very well use both.

It does seem probable that monetary policy is more likely to be useful during the boom than during depression. By one means or another an inflation can be reined in by monetary policy, at least in part.[18] In depression there appears to be much less that purely monetary measures can do. If the quantity of money is increased, individuals and corporations simply hold more idle money. Total spending is little affected, and income and employment remain depressed.

If we are successful in holding production generally at full employment levels, we should, therefore, be able to work with both monetary and fiscal policy. One consequence is that the Treasury and the Board of Governors will

---

[18]The "stagflation" of the 1970s is perhaps the outstanding exception to this proposition.

share the responsibility for controlling the economy. Another consequence is that we shall have the advantages of both types of policy.

One of the greatest advantages of monetary policy is its impersonality. The rules are laid down and everyone is to abide by them. At least as far as the quantitative controls are concerned, there is no differentiation, no special treatment.(Qualitative controls are seldom employed, other than the control over stock market credit.) Also, monetary policy can be changed rapidly. Administrative lag is minimal.[19]

Fiscal policy tends to be more concerned with special interests. It considers whether to tax this group more, this group less; whether to spend more money in this area or that one; and whether to help this industry or that one through government purchases. It magnifies the role of government. Also, fiscal policy is slow if it is used as a discretionary rather than automatic tool. It takes time to decide what to do, for many people must make the decisions with due regard to political considerations.

At the same time, fiscal policy has a more direct influence on the income stream than does monetary policy. Its administrative lag may be longer than that of monetary policy, but its operational lag may be much less. It goes to work directly on the process of income creation, increasing or decreasing the flow by its expenditures and taxes.

Together with monetary policy, fiscal policy can be a powerful stabilizer of the economy. In this second half of the 20th century our large and rising national debt and our large and rising government budget lend themselves to the effective implementation of both types of policies.

Discussion Questions

1. Distinguish between fiscal policy and monetary policy. How can their effects be conveniently illustrated with the *IS* and *LM* curves?
2. Might an increase in the quantity of money close a deflationary gap through its effect on consumption? Explain. Can you suggest why income theory tends to emphasize only the effect on interest rates?
3. Suppose the Treasury sells $1 million of defense bonds and uses the proceeds to repay $1 million of a maturing bond issue held mainly by the commercial banks.
   a. Is the Treasury engaged in fiscal or monetary policy?
   b. What results would you expect the action to have on the quantity of money? On the velocity of money?
4. What has been the trend of income velocity since World War II? Why?
5. In what way has the rapid growth of nonbank financial institutions tended to change the ratio between money and national income?

---

[19]There is another lag — operational lag — which is of increasing concern to economists. By the time monetary policy is effective, the economic situation may have changed sufficiently to make its effects procyclical rather than anticyclical.

6. Quantity theorists often erred in overestimating the importance of changes in the quantity of money, but income theorists have also often erred in underestimating it. Explain.

7. Why do some prominent monetary economists recommend that the Federal Reserve Banks no longer be permitted to lend to the member banks, control their reserve requirements, dictate the maximum interest rates they may pay, or control margin requirements?

8. Briefly explain three reasons why the proposal to increase total consumption in depression by raising the taxes on upper income groups while lowering taxes on lower income groups is hardly promising.

9. Quite apart from the question of how a government finances a deficit, there are two ways in which it may create a deficit. Explain briefly which way you would probably prefer:
   a. If you were a prosperous professional.
   b. If you were unemployed and without income.
   c. If you were a carpenter or plumber.
   d. If you were a conservative.
   e. If you were a liberal.

10. Since the public works of the ancient and the medieval world (pyramids, triumphal arches, colosseums, and cathedrals) were not related to the marginal efficiency of capital, this type of investment tended to be more stable than today's industrial investment, which sometimes needs something of this kind to supplement it. Explain.

11. What does the philosophy of "functional finance" espouse?

12. The principal weakness of the compensatory spending philosophy of fiscal policy is not in its theoretical implications but rather in its political implications. Briefly explain.

13. Discuss what type of lags might be present in the implementation of monetary and fiscal policy.

Chapter 23   Monetary and Fiscal Policy, 1914–1945

The United States' experience with monetary and fiscal policies over the years 1914 to 1945 was not a good one. These policies were sometimes incorrectly applied and at other times correctly but too weakly applied. It was not until the post-World War II period that the purpose and power of monetary and fiscal policy truly began to be understood.

MONETARY POLICY

In its early years the Federal Reserve took little responsibility for the determination of monetary policy. Reserve officials, like the founders of the Federal Reserve System, thought of the Federal Reserve Banks as being primarily the lenders of last resort rather than as the institutions to control bank credit. Most bankers and monetary experts still held to the commercial loan theory of banking. Also, they supposed that the type of lending a bank could do could be controlled by permitting the bank to borrow only under narrowly specified conditions. They concluded that as long as the Reserve Banks would discount only eligible commercial and agricultural paper, the member banks would confine the bulk of their lending to this area. Therefore, the amount of credit would automatically be correctly proportioned to the needs of the economy. The Reserve Banks might have to vary discount rates from time to time to protect against a gold outflow which would strip them of their reserves or to guard against the inflationary consequences of a prolonged gold inflow. Aside from this, no policy seemed necessary and no decisions appeared to be required as long as the commercial loan principle of banking was upheld. Unaware of the need for a centrally determined monetary policy, Reserve authorities did not press for the powers that would let them exercise a monetary policy. The Federal Reserve could change the discount rate. That was about it. The nature of open market operations was not realized. Changes in reserve requirements and other discretionary controls were not to be given to the Board for 20 years.

World War I

The Federal Reserve System had not been long in operation when its responsibilities were vastly increased by the entry of the United States into the First World War. It was clearly the task of the Federal Reserve to mobilize the nation's financial resources and to help the Treasury borrow the funds it needed.

The banking system played a less direct role in financing World War I than it was to take a generation later. About $3.6 billion, or about one sixth of the total increase in the public debt, was taken by the commercial banks. In the next war the banks were to take about $70 billion, over a fourth of the total increase.

The traditional concept that banking was concerned primarily with short-term commercial and agricultural loans discouraged the banks in 1917 from investing heavily in securities. Many felt that only the existence of the war justified such investment and that when the war ended, the banks should dispose of most of their bonds. Also, banks were increasing their loans in World War I, partly to finance industry, partly to cooperate with the "borrow and buy" program. Individuals were encouraged to borrow money from their banks to buy goverment bonds. The effect was much the same as though the bonds had been sold to the banks in the first place, since deposits were increased. However, it was somewhat less inflationary to the extent that borrowers gradually repaid their loans. To encourage individuals to borrow and buy, the banks ordinarily charged the same interest rate on the loans that the borrowers were receiving on the bonds.

During World War I the Federal Reserve Banks seldom held more than $200 or $300 million of Treasury securities. Member banks needed more reserves, both to permit them to expand their loans and to replace the reserves they lost as a result of the public's demand for more currency. Instead of using open market operations, as during World War II, to provide additional reserves for the banking system, the Federal Reserve Banks created reserves by making advances, usually against government obligations. By the end of the war the total of discounts and advances exceeded the total of member bank reserves. In other words, the member banks were operating entirely on borrowed funds. Bank credit expansion was discouraged by this procedure, since both the Federal Reserve Banks and most of the member banks felt that banks should not remain permanently in debt to the Federal Reserve. If the Federal Reserve, rather than waiting until a bank needed to borrow and then lending to it on the security of government bonds, had instead purchased securities in the open market, as it did during the Second World War, the member banks might have had the same amount of reserves without going into debt.

There were several reasons why the Federal Reserve did not engage in open market operations in 1917. As mentioned above, it was not considered desirable that the member banks should invest heavily. The Federal Reserve Banks were newly organized and had not acquired their present strength. They were required to redeem their liabilities in gold or gold certificates upon demand. They did not have a large volume of excess reserves. Most important, Reserve authorities did not at that time fully realize the nature of open market operations, feeling that the primary purpose of open market purchases was to permit the Reserve Banks to increase their income when business was slack and member banks were not borrowing.

Postwar Inflation and Depression

The Treasury wanted the easy money policy continued after the war. Inflation, however, had already set in. In the spring of 1919 the Federal Reserve began to raise the discount rate, pushing it finally to 7 percent.

The rise in interest rates which resulted from the hike in the discount rate naturally caused a steep decline in the price of outstanding bonds, carrying lower rates. Government bonds sold during the war dropped to around $.80 on the dollar in the postwar period. Especially in view of the fact that many of these bonds had been sold to individuals entirely without investment experience, the Treasury and Federal Reserve were criticized for irresponsibility. The program was one, however, for which neither the Federal Reserve nor the Treasury was qualified by experience.

Another consequence of the high discount rate and the insistence of the Federal Reserve Banks upon credit contraction was that member banks began a massive liquidation of their debts at the Reserve Banks. This was the important consequence of the "borrow and buy" technique, whereby the contribution of the Federal Reserve Banks was limited to a readiness to make temporary advances in the form of loans with government securities as collateral. Since the Reserve Banks had not themselves bought securities, the member banks' reserves were increased only to the extent of their own indebtedness to the Federal Reserve Banks. They were now encouraged to get out of debt. As they repaid their loans at the Federal Reserve, member banks reduced their reserve balances. With less reserves they had to trim their deposits by reducing the volume of loans to their customers. Money in circulation contracted. Prices collapsed in the United States and abroad. In the short but sharp depression which began in 1920, the index of industrial production declined 25 percent.

Inflation of the Late 1920s

The economy, except for agriculture, quickly recovered and remained at satisfactory levels until 1930. Federal Reserve authorities began in this period to comprehend the nature of open market operations and to realize that such operations were an unexpected and powerful tool for credit control. At the same time, the Board of Governors began also to recognize the importance of exercising a national credit policy rather than 12 separate regional credit policies. Machinery for coordination of open market operations was organized, and the Board declared that such operations would be governed by the requirements of commerce and with an eye to prevailing credit conditions. In their annual reports the Board began to discuss the policies they had enforced to stabilize the economy.

The most important single monetary development during the period was England's return to the gold standard in 1924 at the prewar parity of $4.86+. This action was severely criticized later; but to the monetary conservatives and traditionalists, it seemed obvious at the time that a return to the prewar gold standard, at the prewar exchange rate, would lay the soundest foundation for a return to the prewar prosperity.

At any rate, London wanted to see easy money in the United States when it returned to gold. Low interest rates here would have three advantages for England. England could borrow easily in New York and probably would be needing to borrow gold, at least temporarily, to maintain a free gold standard. Also, a low New York rate would encourage other foreign banks in search of loans to borrow in this country rather than in England and would thus reduce the pressure on the London money market. Finally, the lower the rate here in comparison to the London rate, the more short-term balances would flow to London rather than to New York.

An easy money policy was, therefore, followed in this country to accommodate England. There is some question whether the easy money policy was in our best interests. However, the price level was remarkably constant at the time, and the easy money policy was later reaffirmed and continued. Not until 1928 did the Federal Reserve begin applying the brakes. By this time we were clearly in a speculative boom.

Although Reserve authorities can exercise some control over the quantity of money, they cannot do a great deal to control the velocity of money, which was being increased by nonbank loans to finance stock purchases. Corporations and individuals with temporarily idle money were lending it on call in the stock market since call money rates were rising and from the viewpoint of the individual lender such loans were very safe. These loans did not, like bank loans, increase the quantity of money, but they did increase its turnover.

A confusing situation confronted the Board in the first part of 1929. The general price level was steady. The level of business activity was moderate. Construction was declining. At the same time prices in the stock market were still whirling upward. It had not taken remarkable skill to make money in stocks since 1927. In fact, it had been almost impossible not to make money. In the two and a half years leading up to the autumn of 1929, the Dow-Jones industrial average had skyrocketed from 150 to almost 400 (a level it was not to reach again for a quarter of a century). Volume increased enormously as more and more people found how easy it was to get money without working for it. They saw Godchaux Sugar go from 3 to 36 in two years, while Saco Lowell went from 3¼ to 44 and Checker Cab from 3 to 80. With stocks such as these, a $10,000 investment could in two years yield a profit of as much as a quarter of a million dollars. Even better, the buyer needed to put up only $2,000 margin. Plenty of lenders were happy to make loans of up to 80 percent on stock collateral.

At that time the Federal Reserve had not yet been given the power to raise margin requirements. It could make credit tighter generally but could not tighten credit in particular areas. The question was, then, whether to raise discount rates drastically in the hope of checking the excessive speculation or to leave rates unchanged so that a tight money policy would not restrain legitimate business activity. The Federal Reserve Banks, emphasizing the speculation, favored tight money. The Board stressed the importance of encouraging business and refused to allow an increase in discount rates.

The Great Depression

The consequences of the Depression ushered in by the stock market collapse in October, 1929, have been reviewed elsewhere.[1] Here we shall note only the role played by the Federal Reserve.

During the Depression the Federal Reserve's most important action to increase the money supply was taken in 1932 when the Glass-Steagall Act permitted it to use government securities as collateral for Federal Reserve notes and freed the gold that had been tied up as note security over and above the 40 percent minimum then required. At that time the Federal Reserve purchased a billion dollars of Treasury obligations, more than doubling its holdings. In 1933 it added about $600 million more to its portfolio of government securities, thereafter holding its securities at a constant level until 1940, when it slightly reduced its investment.

This activity in the investment market had less effect on the total money supply than one might suppose. Although the $2,430 million of government securities held in 1934 was more than 10 times the amount held in 1928, the volume of bills discounted or bought in the open market had declined during the same period from $1,544 million to $7 million. To a considerable extent the securities merely replaced the bills, preventing a decline of the Federal Reserve's assets but not greatly increasing them.

Thus, there were modest changes in member reserves despite the Federal Reserve's purchase of $1.9 billion of Treasury obligations between 1929 and 1933. The Federal Reserve did restore reserves from the low level of 1931, but not until 1933 were reserves higher than in 1927. On the basis of these figures it appears doubtful that much attempt was really made at the outset to overcome the Depression by monetary policy.

Also, although Reserve authorities did inaugurate an easy money policy, they were unnecessarily deliberate about putting it into effect. Ordinarily the discount rate had been kept below the rates commercial banks charged. Between 1929 and 1931, however, market rates dropped faster than the discount rate. This was hardly designed to encourage borrowing by the member banks, since they would pay more for the use of borrowed funds than they could earn with those funds. In this respect Federal Reserve policy seems to have encouraged further deflation and credit contraction.

Eventually, however, discount rates leveled off at 1 to 1½ percent, not to rise until after World War II. Admittedly no one was able to finance a home at 1 percent because the Federal Reserve was discounting at that rate. The public could not borrow as cheaply, and on some types of loans it was difficult to provide funds at really low rates. In some fields, however, rates were below even this 1 percent rate and were far less than they had been previously.

After 1933, member reserves increased rapidly, although the Federal Reserve played a passive role. They jumped abruptly to $4 billion by the end of 1934 and thereafter increased by more than a billion dollars a year, principally as a result of the gold inflow into the United States. By 1940 they amounted to $14 billion, of which more than $6 billion was excess reserves. As early as

---

[1]See Chapter 3.

1936, excess reserves were greater than total reserves had been in any of the pre-Depression years. The magnitude of these billions of dollars of excess reserves can be appreciated only if we realize that for the system as a whole excess reserves had been almost nonexistent in earlier years. The excess reserves of some banks would be offset by the reserve deficiencies of others. In the years 1929–1931, when figures were first tabulated on excess reserves, they averaged less than $100 million, well under 1 percent of excess reserves a decade later.

The Board of Governors uneasily studied the rapidly massing excess reserves and the general economic situation. Prices had begun to rise, there was a mild revival of interest in the stock market, and business was improving. Commercial banks held excess reserves by the end of 1935 sufficient to have permitted them to create upwards of $30 billion of deposits. Their new control over reserve requirements of member banks provided the Board with a means of reducing these excess reserves. In 1936 and again in 1937 they raised reserve requirements. The second increase took requirements to the maximum levels the law allowed. Thereafter there was little the Reserve authorities could do to control excess reserves, which continued to grow until we entered World War II. Nor was there any attempt to reverse the easy money policy, although admittedly it was accomplishing very little.

World War II

When the United States entered the war in 1941, the Board of Governors accepted as the principal goal of monetary policy the accommodation of the Treasury. Inflation, said the Board, was to be prevented by taxation and direct controls. From their list of tools to combat inflation they omitted monetary controls altogether.

Provisions for Continued Easy Money. Among the steps the Board took to ensure easy money, we may specifically note the level of rates established and the freezing of interest rates for the duration of the war. To encourage banks to borrow freely, Reserve authorities established a rate on discounts and advances (secured by eligible collateral other than Treasury obligations) close to the absolute minimum. This rate was 1 percent. In addition, the Federal Reserve established a preferential rate, which was to be more important. It could be safely assumed that most banks obtaining advances would present short-term government securities as collateral. Advances thus secured were made at a special rate of ½ percent per annum. Besides these two rates on discounts and advances, a discount rate of three eights of 1 percent was established on Treasury bills, and the Open Market Committee instructed the 12 Banks to purchase at that rate all Treasury bills offered. This rate, maintained throughout the war and for two years thereafter, was intended to prevent any rise in the bill rate. It was impossible for the market price of bills to fall below the level at which the Federal Reserve stood ready to take all that were offered. The authorities hoped also that the unqualified marketability and liquidity of bills would result in their wider distribution. In this they were to be disappointed, as will shortly be explained.

Most important of all, Treasury and Federal Reserve authorities stated, upon our entry into the war, that the existing level of interest rates would be maintained. This freezing of interest rates for the duration of the war was something new. It had two important results. It made lenders more willing to lend at current rates, since they could not expect that by waiting they could later lend at higher rates. Also, it assured, at least temporarily, the liquidity of all government securities, no matter what the maturity.

Also, since the Reserve Banks could hold interest rates down only by holding security prices up, the policy of freezing interest rates tended to cause an increase in the Federal Reserve portfolio and in member bank reserves and to decrease the need for member bank borrowing. This was in strong contrast to the credit arrangements provided during World War I, when member banks went into debt to get additional reserves. In World War II, the total discounts, advances, and "Other Reserve Bank credit" outstanding at any one time reached $1.2 billion at its wartime peak in May, 1943,[2] and for most of the time during the war did not exceed $.5 billion. In contrast, holdings of government securities bought by the Federal Reserve in the open market increased from $2.2 billion in November, 1941, to $23.3 billion in September, 1945. Primarily, the banks were not borrowing, even at the exceedingly favorable rate of ½ percent. They were selling bills and certificates to the Federal Reserve Banks; or what amounted to much the same thing, they were supplied with reserves when nonbank investors sold securities to the Federal Reserve. Such sales were the direct consequence of the Federal Reserve's support of the securities market.

Paradox of the Fixed Pattern of Interest Rates. The joint determination of the Treasury and the Federal Reserve to freeze the existing pattern of interest rates may seem a rather routine affair. Actually, the policy was most paradoxical. The pattern that was fixed was a pattern based upon the expectation of change. The policy was most successful while some doubt remained as to whether it would succeed. When the determination and ability of the monetary authorities to maintain the pattern were evident, the failure of the program was assured.

The rates maintained varied from three eights of 1 percent per annum on 91-day Treasury bills and seven eights of 1 percent per annum on 1-year certificates on up to 2½ percent on bonds running 25 years or longer. The investor could receive over twice as high a rate of return from 1-year obligations as from 91-day securities and could receive over six times as high a rate on long-term bonds as on bills. Why was the short-term rate so far below the long-term rate?

Because since 1933 short-term rates have generally been below long-term rates, many people today assume that such a pattern results from some natural law of finance. The fact is that such a relationship is by no means inevitable. From 1920 to 1932 short-term rates were higher than long-term rates about half the time, and in the 20 years from 1900 to 1920 short-term rates were higher than long-term rates most of the time. (Sometimes they were

---

[2]About half the level reached in World War I.

considerably higher.) Since 1966 short-term rates have occasionally edged above long-term rates.

The reason that from 1933 to 1941 short-term rates had been far below long-term rates was simple and logical. In a period when all interest rates are low and rates are generally expected to rise eventually, the short-term rates will naturally be the lowest. Only for the additional compensation of a higher rate will lenders consent to accept the greater risk inherent in long-term securities of loss due to a rise in rates. The long-depressed rate structure in effect in December, 1941, reflected this expectation of higher rates. The eager bidding for short-term securities had reduced their yield almost to zero. If a pattern of rates was to be fixed, the simplest procedure seemed to be to freeze the existing pattern—hence, the first paradox of a fixed pattern based on the expectation of change.

As long as investors entertained any doubt as to the maintenance of this pattern, they continued to demand some short-term securities as insurance against a possible rise in rates. The Treasury was able to place publicly all its maturities. When it became clear, however, that rates would not change and that, due to the Federal Reserve's readiness to buy all maturities at par or above, all securities were equally liquid, investors realized the advantage of buying the more profitable longer term securities. Thereafter, there was little public market for short-terms, especially for Treasury bills, most of which gravitated to the Federal Reserve.

For most of the war years Treasury bills amounted to little more than a rather elaborate subterfuge permitting the Treasury to borrow directly from the Federal Reserve while apparently securing the funds from the open market. Congress had authorized the Treasury to obtain temporary, emergency loans from the Federal Reserve, not at any time to exceed $5 billion. Occasionally it utilized this provision, although at no time did the total of such borrowings exceed $1.3 billion. However, by June, 1947, the Federal Reserve held over $14 billion of bills, or about 90 percent of the total amount outstanding. For several years the Federal Reserve had been the chief purchaser of such securities, to which the market was little attracted.

Repeatedly, the Open Market Committee attempted to make arrangements whereby they could replace maturing bills directly through the Treasury without going through the motions involved in having the market first acquire the unwanted bills and then turn them over to the Federal Reserve. As early as 1943 Reserve authorities pointed out that the Reserve Banks were taking as much as half the Treasury's weekly offerings. The Treasury insisted, however, that the bills continue to be sold on the open market and recommended that the Federal Reserve Bank of New York manage affairs in such a way that the market would absorb whatever amount of bills the Treasury should issue. By arranging with the brokers and dealers in government securities to take all the bills offered (and sell them immediately to the Federal Reserve), Reserve authorities were able to maintain the fiction of an effective market rate of three eights of 1 percent on Treasury bills. The unreality of the three eighths of 1 percent rate on bills by the end of the war is illustrated also by the fact that, when in 1947 the rate was finally permitted to find its own level in a free market, it quickly rose to about 1⅙ percent, about three times as high as the rate that for years had been artificially maintained.

Speculation in Bonds. One inevitable result of the fixed pattern of interest rates was the development of considerable speculation in Treasury bonds. This speculation was also encouraged to some extent by the Treasury's policy of making only limited amounts of bonds available to the commercial banks, which consequently bid up the price to obtain bonds that the public had purchased from the Treasury during the War Loan drives.

Some evidence of this speculation appears in the statistics concerning debt ownership. Total holdings of savings banks and insurance companies increased by considerably less than the amounts that they subscribed for in the various Loans, clearly indicating their offsetting sales between the Loan drives. (Many of these sales were to the commercial banks, which wanted more bonds than the Treasury had alloted them.)

The term *speculation* is really an inaccurate characterization of the "free rides" that were available to investors who purchased Treasury securities for quick resale at a certain profit. Although the amount of premium was reduced as the longer term bonds were made ineligible for bank ownership, there continued for the duration of the war to be the same assurance of some profit and the same guarantee that there could be no loss, with the Federal Reserve supporting the market. For the duration of the war, no issues of Treasury bonds dropped below par. On all a premium developed.

This rise in the price (or decline in yield) of long-term obligations was a natural consequence of the freezing of a pattern of rates based on an expectation of changing rates. Market support was designed to keep rates from rising, not to cause or prevent their decline. No provision had been made to prevent bonds from selling above issue prices but, as we have seen, the price of short-term securities was supported to the extent that finally the Federal Reserve held 90 percent of all Treasury bills outstanding. The logic of a fixed pattern of rates requires that the rates should be close together. If there is to be no change in the general level of interest rates, there is no particular reason that long-term securities should carry nearly seven times as high a rate as short-terms. With a floor but no ceiling on security prices, the long and short rates could move closer only through a decline in the former.

Bank Credit Expansion. Banks, as well as other corporations, found it advantageous to dispose of some of their short-term securities and acquire the more profitable long-term issues. The important difference was that when the banks took such action, the quantity of money almost inevitably increased. The principal purchaser the banks found for their bills and certificates was the Federal Reserve, so new reserves were created as the banks disposed of such securities. If the banks had then purchased the same amount of long-term securities from the Federal Reserve, the new reserves would have been cancelled. The Federal Reserve, however, held few long-terms. The banks, therefore, purchased such securities from the Treasury or from the general public. To the individual bank concerned, there appeared to be nothing objectionable in its decision to exchange a million dollars worth of short-term securities for the same amount of longer maturities. For the system as a whole, however, the policy resulted in credit expansion, since securities were being sold to the Federal Reserve for new reserves and were being purchased with new deposits, several dollars of which might be created by the banking system against each dollar of the new reserves. During the war this bank credit expansion was not particularly troublesome. By 1945 the total of currency and demand deposits was three times its 1939 level.[3]

FISCAL POLICY

Except in wartime, little attention was paid to fiscal policy until about 40 years ago. The unswerving rule was, "Balance the budget whenever possible." A little over a century ago, in 1857, the national debt per capita amounted to $1. Ten years later it had rocketed up to $75 as a result of the Civil War. A long series of small but comfortable surpluses together with an increase of nearly 200 percent in the population brought the per capita debt down to $12 by 1914. From there it shot up to $230 by 1920. Regular annual surpluses in the neighborhood of a billion dollars whittled away nearly half of this increase during the following decade, and by June 30, 1930, the per capita national debt was a trifle over $130.

Since then things have been very different. Even before war broke out in Europe in 1939, our per capita debt had more than doubled. After we went to war ourselves, the really impressive deficits began. Thus, today we find ourselves with a per capita national debt of well over $2,500.

World War I

We might say a word about Treasury policy during World War I to clarify policies followed during World War II. Before 1917 the Treasury had had little experience in selling securities to investors other than commercial banks, which wanted the bonds as collateral for their own note issues. During the war the Treasury wanted to encourage nonbank bond purchases to hold down the inflationary consequences of a great expansion of bank credit. A tremendous campaign was organized to sell bonds. Also, the Treasury offered fairly attractive terms. Income from bonds was made tax exempt, and interest rates were 4 percent and higher.

Results were quite disappointing. Because of the complaint that the Treasury was offering too low a rate, the Treasury raised the rate on subsequent issues. Sales thereafter were hampered by the anticipation that there might be further increases in the interest rate, which would necessarily cause a fall in the price of outstanding issues. Also, the Treasury was freely criticized in the postwar period for its irresponsibility in allowing the price of government bonds to decline so sharply. This first experience with handling a really large public debt was to prove extremely useful to the Treasury a few years later when a much greater war required borrowing on an immensely larger scale.

---

[3]Exclusive of interbank and United States government holdings and less cash items reported as in process of collection.

Depression

During the early years of the Depression and in both Hoover's administration and Roosevelt's first administration, the government was still trying to balance the budget. On the plea of the Secretary of the Treasury that the credit of the Treasury be protected, Congress reduced government spending and increased taxes in 1932. Also, the Roosevelt administration the following year vetoed a veterans' bonus and reduced government salaries as further economy moves. During most of Roosevelt's first term the emphasis was on monetary measures and price-fixing rather than on fiscal policy. It was from 1932 to 1934 that the dollar was devalued, the silver buying program begun, the issuance of greenbacks authorized, and the character of the Federal Reserve note altered by the Glass-Steagall Act. It was also during this period that the National Recovery Administration (NRA) briefly flourished until declared unconstitutional.[4]

In spite of the attempts to balance the budget, a succession of government deficits appeared (and, except for 1969 and a few other years since World War II, has continued). Tax receipts continued low because incomes were low. Government expenditures were rising because something had to be done both to keep people from starving and to give people some kind of employment. A host of government agencies appeared which we cannot review here, but which were generally concerned with increasing income and liquidity. With lower receipts and higher expenditures the government naturally operated at a deficit. A few years later these deficits were to be justified and praised by economists using the new income approach to economic analysis, and the administration was to announce, "We planned it that way." But in the early years of Roosevelt's administration deficits were a source of apology, not pride.

The original grim determination to balance the budget somehow was at least partly responsible for the Robin Hood philosophy of fiscal policy which appeared during the Depression—take from the rich and give to the poor. The government found, as had Robin Hood, that it is much more expedient to take from the rich than to take from the poor, for the rich make up a minority that is not generally popular. Some politicians favored such policies anyway on humanitarian or equalitarian grounds. Others felt that the reduction of income inequality was an important step in controlling the business cycle. The income approach suggested that this type of income redistribution might cause income to rise by increasing total spending, since the marginal propensity to consume would probably be higher for those who received it than for those who gave it up as taxes. But all these arguments tended to be rationalizations, for, to repeat, until the late 1930s the government felt that it should balance the budget and was trying to find, somehow, the extra taxes to meet its regular expenses as well as the special expenditures required by the Depression. Otherwise it might have given to the poor without taking from the rich, borrowing instead of taxing. The expansionary effect came from the spending,

---

[4]In effect, the NRA was an attempt to raise prices by permitting producers to get together in determining prices, a kind of legalized collusion.

not from the taxes, no matter how the taxes were imposed. If the government had depended more upon deficit finance from the start, it might have avoided the discouragement to investment that was involved in its ''soak the rich'' and ''soak business'' tax programs, and perhaps the economy could have staged a recovery on its own without requiring the help of a world war.

On the other hand, larger deficits might have so shaken public confidence that recovery would have been difficult.[5] If the effect of government deficits had been better understood, the government's attempts to promote recovery would have been more successful. Between 1933 and 1940 the national debt was doubled. Yet we were still in a serious depression as late as 1940. Through part of this period the government had been apologizing for the deficits, and politicians out of office had been attacking the financial irresponsibility of the administration for overspending its income. The public, with this kind of leadership, can hardly be blamed for its distrust of the steadily rising national debt. In terms of income analysis, government expenditures increased, but a general lack of confidence held down the amount of the respending. Consumption was, therefore, increased little, and the value of the multiplier was low.[6] There was little investment, for there was much idle capacity. Unless consumption increased (or new inventions or new markets appeared), there was little reason for any plant expansion or inventory increases. Also, the antibusiness atmosphere of much of this period's legislation was not designed to stimulate investment.

Under these conditions the pump-priming policy first attempted was doomed to failure. There was nothing that would cause an initial modest rise in income to be magnified into a large and permanent increase. All that could be hoped for was that the multiplier would cause income to rise by somewhat more than the amount of the deficit and that maybe someday conditions would change and a deficit would no longer be necessary. Meanwhile, the Depression continued, the only difference being that in some years it was worse than others. Economists began to question whether we could reasonably expect to again have an old-fashioned prosperity and whether we might not have to expect the government to operate at a deficit most of the time if we were to have full employment.

World War II

The dizzying deficits of the war years showed how inadequate had been the deficits with which the New Deal had tried to fight the Depression and showed, too, how quickly depression could be overcome by really large-scale government spending. Just the increase in the national debt between 1943 and

---

[5]Deficits were far greater during the war years, it's true, with no shattering of public confidence. There is, however, a difference between a peacetime deficit and a wartime deficit. Curiously enough the former, which would give us more goods and services to enjoy, tends to worry us while the latter, representing goods that will to a considerable extent be exploded, blown up, or shot down, is taken in stride. In wartime we have other things to worry about besides the size of the government debt.

[6]True, the *MPC* of the unemployed person put to work on a government project is probably high, and the person may spend 100 percent of the increase in income. The question is, what is the *MPC* of those who next receive this income? Unless they, too, increase their consumption, the respending effects very quickly taper off.

1944 was one and a half times as great as the entire debt in 1940, even after 10 years of deficits and with most of the debt from World War I still unpaid. But with annual deficits of over $45 billion, the unemployment that had persisted for a decade melted away and the problem quickly became not depression but inflation.

A major war tends to promote inflation no matter how it is financed. The government employs millions. Some carry carbines, some wash dishes, some pilot planes or ships, and still others are indirectly employed by the government to manufacture munitions. One thing they all have in common. Their services do not increase by a nickel's worth the supply of goods and services available to consumers. Thus, the demand for consumption goods is greatly increased (by the incomes the government pays), but the supply of consumption goods is unchanged. The only way in which inflationary pressures can be avoided is by somehow draining away this additional purchasing power, either by taxation or borrowing.

Necessity for Wartime Borrowing. There are some advantages to borrowing, and the Treasury did borrow about 60 percent of its expenditures during World War II. The point is not that the borrowed money gives the Treasury purchasing power it could not otherwise have. Still less does it permit the economy to postpone paying for the war by, somehow, acquiring goods from the future. The essential point to understand is that a war is fought with goods and services produced at the time or accumulated previously. In this year's battles the generals can no more use planes and tanks of the future than they can use soldiers of a future generation. The limits to the supply of war materiel that can be provided are set, not by financial considerations, but largely by the physical productivity of the economy. The civilian economy and the military must depend primarily upon the goods and services making up current national income, supplementing these to some extent by using goods created in earlier years, that is, by capital consumption.

This being the case, the question may well be raised why the Treasury should borrow at all during a war. Certainly the reason can hardly be that the war period is one in which deficit finance is required to combat persistent unemployment, for the nation will find use for all available resources. There is a certain maximum of steel, petroleum, aluminum, and copper, and of fabrications of these and other products, that can be produced. This flow of goods along with services currently produced is the national income, to be divided between the government and the rest of the economy. Since at full employment the national income cannot increase, the only way that the government's share can increase is by reducing the share available to the public. Taxes are the obvious means to this end.

Loans and Taxation Compared. It is, of course clear enough that every dollar borrowed from an individual is a dollar that could instead be taxed away from him. Perhaps less apparent is the fact that during a period of full employment government expenditures financed by the banks also take away from the public (real) income which it might otherwise enjoy. The results are altogether different from what may be expected from bank-financed deficits during depression, when the spending power of the public increases simultaneously with an increase in the total output of goods and services. During at least the later years of a war the nation is operating at full employment. The Treasury spends the newly created money to acquire goods and services that otherwise the civilian economy might have taken. In the absence of price controls and rationing, an inflationary price rise sets in. The public may spend for consumption its entire money income, but the rise in prices causes "forced" saving; the public is unable to consume its entire real income. If price controls and rationing are enforced, individuals simply cannot spend all their money income on the limited volume of goods and services available to them. In short, whether the Treasury relies on taxation or whether it borrows from the public or from the banks, during a period of full employment the public must at the time go without those goods and services that the government requires. There is no way to postpone the cost of the war. Taxation permits a rational and fairly equitable allocation of that cost. Inflation causes the cost to be allocated irrationally and indiscriminately.

Advantage of Borrowing. Nevertheless, there is a compelling reason for borrowing part of the funds required for the war and for borrowing part of them by inflationary methods.[7] The point is this: the single consideration of a nation at war is to win the war. Everything else is secondary, including the desirability of maintaining a stable price level, avoiding monetary inflation, and following conservative financial policies. A violent, uncontrolled price inflation would be a handicap to the war effort. But a moderate inflation of the money supply may facilitate the expansion of output and the conversion to a war economy, tasks that must be accomplished as swiftly as humanly possible. To a large extent this depends upon public morale. Certainly borrowing cannot take away from a given national income a larger amount than can taxation. But because of its effect on the public, borrowing is likely to make possible a larger national income than would result if the government were to depend entirely upon taxation for its revenue. The important fact to be realized is that heavy taxes are a deterrent to production. Despite all the official appeal to "stand behind the man behind the gun," both labor and management are unlikely to put forth their greatest efforts without the familiar stimulus of additional income.

Although public sentiment opposes the war profiteer, and there is widespread agreement that no one should profit from war, as a matter of practical expediency some additional money income is necessary in war. To this extent monetary inflation is desirable at such a time, whether the government issues paper money or whether it borrows from the banking system. Every nation engaged in the war resorted to inflation to defray a part of the costs, and rightly so. Of course, this is not at all the same as saying that the quantity of money was increased by exactly the right amount, but there had to be some inflationary borrowing. Within four years the money *GNP* increased by 70

---

[7]Strictly speaking, it is not the borrowing but the spending of the borrowed money that may be inflationary.

percent. Simultaneously, there was a tremendous change in the composition of that output.

The spending of the proceeds of these inflationary loans resulted in higher incomes. It was important that the public retain some part of this additional income as a stimulus to production. Moreover, from the standpoint of equity, borrowing has the advantage that it is on a voluntary basis. One has no choice in the matter of paying taxes, and one gains only a tax receipt. People may choose to lend or not, and they would naturally prefer to buy a $1,000 bond than to pay the same amount in taxes. When incomes are being so steeply increased and there are so many changes in the economy, it is impossible to devise a satisfactory tax system that will absorb all the public's purchasing power except that amount which the public can be allowed to spend. Inevitably, such a program would involve individual inequities and injustices. Results will be better if part of the public's excess purchasing power is taxed away and part is borrowed. This procedure, besides stimulating production, permits individuals to decide for themselves the total amount that they will place at the disposal of the government, rather than arbitrarily establishing that amount by impersonal tax legislation. It permits flexibility.

Also, borrowing is frequently necessary to provide the Treasury with immediate funds. Bills must be paid even if taxes have not yet been collected. Also, if, as is usually the case, estimates of the government's financial requirements prove to be too low, recourse must be had to borrowing.

Borrowing is more appropriate in the initial stages of the war effort than in the later stages. If the nation is not at full employment at the outset, the borrowing will facilitate the expansion of output. Also, the temporary borrowing avoids the need for immediate drastic tax increases and permits an equitable tax program to be developed. Finally, as eventual victory appears in sight, people will be more willing to bear large tax burdens.

Methods of Borrowing. Above we noted that part of the borrowing will have to be by inflationary methods. It is incorrect to assume that the spending of borrowed money is necessarily inflationary. Much depends upon how the money was borrowed.

Borrowing from Central Banks. If a government borrows from the central bank and spends the money, deposits and reserves of the commercial banks are increased by equal amounts, and the excess reserves of the commercial banks are increased. The more the government borrows and spends, the greater becomes the lending capacity of the commercial banks. Inflation is almost inevitable, especially after the nation's economy reaches the full employment level.

This case is of little practical importance in the United States, however, for the Treasury does not regularly borrow directly from the Federal Reserve Banks. By law the Treasury may not borrow more than $5 billion at any time from the Federal Reserve Banks. The Treasury ordinarily and rightly considers its right to borrow this limited amount as an overdraft privilege. Occasionally it borrows for a day or two when its balances are temporarily inadequate. Otherwise it obtains its money on the market.

Borrowing from Commercial Banks. When the Treasury borrows from commercial banks, new deposits are created. As the Treasury pays its bills, these deposits are transferred to the public, which must hold the additional money. Even if at a later date the Treasury regains the money in taxes, as soon as the Treasury spends it the new money is again in the hands of the public.

There may be times when the banks would be lending anyway, if not to the government, then to industry. The more the government borrows, the lower are excess reserves of the banking system, until presently the banks can expand credit no further. At such times the government's borrowing may cause no more monetary inflation than would have taken place anyway.

But in wartime the Federal Reserve Banks impose no credit restrictions and stand ready to supply additional reserves to permit a credit expansion limited only by the Treasury's demands for more money. Then bank loans to the Treasury become highly inflationary. The effect is the same as though the Treasury printed additional money, as it did during the Revolutionary and the Civil Wars. Its inflationary tendency is, however, offset to the extent that an increase in production accompanies the increase in the money supply.

It should be clear that borrowing from the banks is not in itself inflationary. Even the spending of the additional money would not necessarily be inflationary if the public did not attempt to respend the money after it was transferred to the public by Treasury expenditures, and if the public were not also spending money already in its possession. The government will require, perhaps, about one half of the national income to carry on the war. This amount is decided, not by financial considerations, but entirely on the basis of the productive capacity of the economy. By one means or another the government will purchase this volume of goods and services to further the war effort. Suppose that in constant dollars this amounted to $1,000 billion. If (real) national income were to increase by $400 billion and the public were voluntarily to reduce its consumption by $600 billion, there would be no inflationary consequences from bank loans of $1,000 billion to the government. The trouble is, of course, that in practice the public and the government are both spending freely. The increase in the money flow is greater than the increase in (real) national income. The cause of inflation at such a time is not the borrowing nor, in itself, government spending. It is the competitive spending by the government and the public.

A moderate reliance on inflation to finance a war has the real advantage discussed earlier. But it has some other apparent advantages that are more obvious as well as more dubious. It is the easiest way for the Treasury to secure funds, the interest cost is least, and it is more popular than are high taxes. When, as formerly, the government printed the additional money it needed, there was no interest cost whatever. When, today, the government borrows from the banks, it can obtain large amounts readily with a minimum of sales work and accounting and at very low interest rates. As the Federal Reserve supplies the banks with additional reserves and supports the price of Treasury obligations, the banks find their choice to be whether they will hold additional excess reserves, yielding no returns, or additional securities, as liquid as reserves but providing some income. Under such circumstances, they will lend at rates of less than 1 percent.

If, influenced by these considerations, the Treasury depends largely on the banks to finance the war, the total cost of the war, in dollars, will greatly increase because of the price rise which will accompany the inflation of the money supply. The postwar economy will be faced with the problems created by this swollen stock of money. If price controls are removed at that time, the pressure of higher incomes and an increased money supply will tend to cause an abrupt fall in the value of money, redistributing wealth in favor of debtors and bearing heavily upon creditors, including those who lent to the Treasury. If price ceilings are not removed after the war, enforcement becomes more difficult, shortages and black markets develop, and an expanded bureaucracy is required to attempt to make the ceilings effective.

Also, the national debt will be larger if inflationary borrowing techniques are used. Because prices are rising, the government must borrow increasingly larger amounts. True, in the case of an internally held public debt, the nation owes it to itself. The size of the debt is less important than in the case of a debt owed to citizens of another country. In the latter case the nation, to repay the debt, must create goods and services and turn them over to the foreign creditors. An internally held debt is less troublesome, since the group that is being repaid is also the group that is being taxed to provide the funds for repayment. Still there are frictions. Within this group it is not necessarily the same individuals who are taxed and who are repaid. In particular, there is the difficulty that a large part of the postwar taxes for debt service and retirement will probably be paid by people who during the war were in uniform and unable to invest heavily in government bonds.

Borrowing of Past Savings. A third source of funds for the Treasury is from past savings of the public. The spending of these sums will also be inflationary, although less so than the spending of bank loans discussed above. The borrowing of past savings does not increase the money supply, but it tends to increase the velocity of money, which just as effectively increases the money flow as does an addition to the money stock. In some instances the owner would otherwise have held this money idle. The Treasury's spending of such sums is as inflationary as spending new deposits. In other instances the owner of the savings who had not bought government bonds would otherwise have spent the money for goods and services. In such cases total spending will be less as a result of the loan. The government would have spent that amount anyway, whether or not this individual had provided the funds through purchases of government securities, but the individual's expenditures for goods and services were in this case reduced by the purchases of government bonds.

Borrowing of Current Savings. The fourth source of funds is from current savings. The noninflationary character of such borrowing arises from the fact that it requires the public to restrict its consumption. In this it is similar to taxation. Under utopian conditions where the incentives provided by inflation would not be required and where all war costs would be met out of taxes and loans of current savings, there would be little need for rationing and price controls. The public would not attempt to increase its consumption, and if necessary would reduce it in order that the government might take as much as it needed of the national income. After paying taxes and lending current savings, the public would be left with only enough money to purchase the fraction of the national product that it was supposed to receive.

In such a case it would be particularly easy to realize the fact that the "cost" of the war must be paid at the time. Either by taxes or by voluntary loans the public would surrender its claims to, perhaps, one half the national product. It must be realized that whatever the methods of finance the public can obtain only that portion of national income that the government decides shall be made available to the public. Inflation accomplishes the same result, either by price increases which reduce the public's purchasing power or by requiring price controls and rationing. Except to the extent that inflation facilitates the expansion of output, noninflationary borrowing (and taxation) are preferable financial methods.

This restraint upon public consumption was the principal reason the Treasury borrowed from the general public during the war. It was not that the Treasury needed those dollars. It could have obtained them elsewhere more easily and at a lower interest cost. The Treasury wanted to restrain private consumption to reduce inflationary pressures. It wanted to persuade people to increase their saving. Otherwise the appeal to the public would have been pointless. If bonds were bought only with funds that would have been saved anyway, the bond sales did little to check inflation. But bond sales, through appeals to patriotism, provided the opportunity to appeal for more saving. The real reasons for selling securities to the public were well understood by the Treasury. Besides restraining inflation, bond sales to nonbank investors would create a large pool of fairly liquid savings that would aid in overcoming a possible postwar slump and would aid industry in reconverting to a peacetime economy.

Special Borrowing Techniques. Two techniques of borrowing in World War II were the result of lessons learned in the First World War. In the first place, interest rates were prevented from rising. The monetary experts in the Treasury and the Federal Reserve knew that if rates were once raised, they would have to be raised repeatedly. The only way to prevent a substantial rise was to prevent any rise.

In the second place, the savings bonds introduced a few years earlier were extraordinarily suitable securities to sell to the general public. Admittedly they were not perfect. They offered the buyer no protection against rising prices. Also, since they were a demand obligation, they were later to make the control of inflation more difficult, as millions were cashed after the war. But during the war and to a lesser extent after the war they did help the Treasury to reach out for the savings of the masses and to appeal for a great increase in those savings. No one could lose by a fall in the market price of these bonds, for they never would be sold on the market. They were safe for the most naive investor. Also, since they were sold in denominations as low as $25, people could buy them regularly out of current income, the least inflationary type of borrowing the government could do.

The Inflationary Gap—Rationing and Price Controls. With so much of the war financed by borrowing and with around 40 percent of the loans being made by the commercial banks, an inflationary gap soon appeared. The amount of money entering the income stream as investment (including government spending) was larger than the amount of intended savings (including taxes) at the full employment level of income. Higher taxes and high pressure campaigns to persuade the public to buy bonds helped to raise the level of intended saving but did not bring it up to the level of the government's expenditures in an all-out war. Disposable money income rose rapidly without a corresponding increase in the output of consumer goods and services. Worse yet, there was a decrease and in some cases a complete cessation of production of the very kinds of consumer goods on which Americans ordinarily are especially eager to spend any additional income—that is, durable goods, including cars, houses, washing machines, and the like.

The large inflationary gap required the imposition of price controls and rationing. In peacetime, prices are generally the rationing machinery. Goods go to those who will pay the most for them. Those goods will be produced that yield the highest profits to their producers. In wartime, prices have little to do with it. The government decides what shall be produced, how much, and by whom. If no price ceilings were imposed, the public could bid up prices for the limited supply of consumer goods, eventually spending all its income for these goods. When prices are held down, the quantity demanded—at existing prices—exceeds the quantity supplied. People must stand in line, and the people who are able to secure goods are those who can afford to spend their time waiting in line. To increase efficiency by cutting down on shopping time and at the same time to share the output of goods fairly, rationing must be imposed. During the war Americans had to have ration coupons as well as money if they were to buy shoes, meat, sugar, gasoline, or many other items.

Did rationing and price controls do anything to reduce the inflationary gap? Or did they merely reduce the price rise that otherwise the gap would have caused? They did both. Obviously the price ceilings checked price increases. The rationing, however, reduced consumption. No matter how much money a person had, he or she could legally buy only the limited amount of goods authorized by the ration book. This forced reduction of consumption was simultaneously an increase in saving, reducing the gap between investment and saving.

SUMMARY AND CONCLUSION

A philosophy of credit control by the Federal Reserve was gradually evolved rather than being implicit in the original legislation. In the Federal Reserve's early years the commercial loan theory of bank credit was as widely accepted as the theory of the gold-coin standard. Both were supposed to provide a framework within which business might operate with a minimum of discretionary, authoritarian control. They were thoroughly laissez-faire in their implications. All the Reserve authorities were required to do was to see that the banks made short-term commercial and agricultural loans and that the gold standard was maintained.

The first responsibility involved no discretionary policy whatever. Reserve Banks were authorized to discount only short-term commercial and agricultural paper. The presumption was that banks that presented such paper for discount were lending principally in this area and that businesses that obtained short-term loans would use them only as sources of working capital. The second responsibility merely required that the Banks and the Board raise the discount rate whenever gold reserves were too low and lower the rate when gold reserves were unnecessarily high.

Only later did Reserve authorities begin to comprehend their much wider responsibilities to business and the economy generally. They had only the briefest experience with monetary controls when they were forced to cope with contradictory and disturbing conditions preceding the crash in 1929. If their leadership was less than inspired during the ensuing years, the inadequacy of their background may have been largely responsible.

Also, admitting that the Federal Reserve played a passive role during most of the Depression, we also may agree that there is probably not a great deal that monetary policy could accomplish at such a time. Fiscal policy is more direct and more effective in increasing income. Had there been a better and earlier understanding of the appropriate fiscal policy to support and reverse a falling national income, it is likely that the Depression would have been both shorter and more shallow. Unfortunately for a number of years the government's fiscal policy made things worse instead of better.

Finally, we might consider the monetary and fiscal policies in effect during World War II. The Treasury borrowed most of the money it spent during the war. Together with the Federal Reserve, the Treasury froze interest rates until the war was over. By holding down interest rates and by placing a larger part of the debt in short-term securities, where interest rates were lowest, the Treasury succeeded in reducing the computed average rate of interest on the debt from 2.5 percent in 1940 to 1.9 percent in 1945 at the same time that it increased the debt by nearly $200 billion. This was no mean accomplishment. It is in striking contrast to the near doubling of rates during the First World War, when the debt was increased by only $24 billion. At the same time, this fiscal policy inextricably involved also monetary policy. These two were interdependent.

We must realize that the Treasury's determination to hold down interest rates necessarily determined the type of securities that would be sold and the distribution of the debt. It required that a large part of the debt be taken by the banking system. It required a monetary inflation and encouraged a fall in the value of money. The soaring price level of the postwar years, after the removal of price ceilings, must be recognized as one of the harmful consequences of the cheap money policy.

Treasury officials did not emphasize this point when they pointed to their success in holding down interest rates. Frequently they stated that they arranged their borrowing in such a way that the banks took only what was left of the various issues after nonbank investors had completed their purchases. What is overlooked by this claim is that the amount taken by nonbank investors depended in part upon the terms offered by the Treasury, in other words, upon the level of interest rates. The supply of funds that nonbank lenders were willing to lend was a curve, not a point. Like any supply curve, the supply of funds offered by nonbank investors is the schedule of the amounts they are willing to offer at various prices—the "prices" in this instance being interest rates. Higher rates may not really have encouraged a great deal more nonbank lending to the Treasury, but presumably they would have had some effect, reducing the Treasury's reliance upon the banks. There does not appear to have been any inescapable reason that the commercial banks should have taken 40 percent of the securities issued by the Treasury during the war. We have earlier noted the reasons that some degree of inflation appeared necessary. There is no evidence that so much inflation was required, and it is misleading to imply that the Treasury was completely passive in the matter of bank credit expansion.

One fact must be frankly recognized. A towering public debt tends to encourage policies of easy money and to lead to a gradually rising price level. The Treasury wishes to borrow at low rates to obtain the billions of dollars required each month for the refunding of maturing issues. Also, the Treasury and the administration are well aware of the increased difficulties that the Treasury would face if there were to be a fall in the price level and in the level of national income. Like any other debtor the Treasury finds it easier to pay the interest on the debt, and perhaps occasionally even to retire some of the debt, when the value of money is low. Unlike other debtors the government is in a position to force a decline in the value of money. It is much more likely to take prompt, effective action against a fall in prices than against a rise, the more so since the former action would be more politically popular, regardless of the national debt. The debt furnishes a strong additional bias for inflation. If, then, prices in the future are to be free to move in one direction only, it is clear that a gradually falling value of money is an altogether likely consequence of the debt.

If this inflationary bias can be checked and if the Federal Reserve, rather than the Treasury, is to have the principal responsibility for controlling bank credit, the greatly increased public debt will permit some variations in the techniques of credit control. Certainly there will have to be cooperation between the two agencies. On that basis, at a time when the Federal Reserve is attempting to restrain credit expansion, the Treasury can be of great assistance in its management of the debt. By retiring bank-held securities with the proceeds of loans from nonbank investors, it could force a decrease in deposits. A reversal of this procedure would help the Federal Reserve stimulate credit expansion when that appears necessary. Possibly a technique might be evolved for changing the classification of bank-eligible and bank-restricted bonds in line with changing credit conditions. Through the administration of its Tax and Loan Accounts the Treasury can cause changes in deposits and reserves of the banks.

The Federal Reserve may also be able to exert considerable influence upon bank reserves by its policy with respect to government obligations. With the banks holding around $60 billion of government securities, relatively slight changes and moderate uncertainties regarding Federal Reserve policy may prove quite effective. Also, the almost $90 billion of securities held by the Federal Reserve give it a tremendously powerful instrument of control if it is free to utilize it.

Discussion Questions

1. "In its early years the Federal Reserve took little responsibility for the determination of monetary policy." True or false and explain.
2. Why did the Federal Reserve Banks purchase almost no Treasury bonds during World War I?
3. Since Reserve authorities can exercise control over the quantity of money, why could they not control the speculative stock market boom of the 1920s?
4. "Monetary policy was unable to overcome the Depression." Briefly summarize the justification for this statement.
5. "Perhaps monetary policy was ineffective in the Depression because proper monetary policies were put into effect too late." Briefly summarize the justification for this statement.
6. "When the United States entered the war in 1941, the Board of Governors accepted as the principal goal of monetary policy the prevention of inflation." True or false and explain.
7. What were the unfavorable consequences of the Treasury's borrowing operations during World War I which led to the imposition of a ceiling on interest rates during World War II?
8. Compare the Federal Reserve's purchases of Treasury securities during World War II with their purchases during World War I. What were some of the reasons for the difference?
9. What happened to the prices of long-term Treasury securities as a result of the ceiling on interest rates during the years 1941 through 1945? Why?
10. What is the difference between pump priming and the theory of the multiplier? Under what conditions might a pump-priming operation be successful?
11. What are the principal advantages and disadvantages of borrowing $30 billion from the public in wartime rather than increasing taxes by that amount? What is the most common fallacy concerning this policy?
12. Which of the following methods of financing a war will require the public to save?
    a. Taxation
    b. Borrowing from the public by the Treasury
    c. Borrowing from the banks by the Treasury
13. Disregarding enforcement difficulties, is government rationing better suited to a wartime or a peacetime economy? Why?
14. How is inflation related to saving?
15. Compare the utility of savings bonds during inflation and during depression.
16. "A large national debt furnishes a strong bias for inflation." Explain.

Chapter 24 Monetary and Fiscal Policy, 1946–1971

The United States, like other industrial nations, found itself after World War II in an economic climate basically different from what it had known before the war. An almost uninterrupted prosperity prevailed. Every three or four years a moderate recession or readjustment appeared, but there was no tendency for these temporary slowdowns to generate further declines in income, turning recession into depression. Prosperity quickly returned. Some felt it returned almost too quickly and that in our anxiety to avoid depression we unnecessarily encouraged a persistent inflation. Others argued that only by creating constant inflationary pressures could we maintain full employment. But about the time the latter view had become widely accepted, there began to be increasing evidence of the difficulties of managing a controlled inflation and of corresponding efforts by monetary authorities and government to halt the rise in prices.

POSTWAR FEARS OF DEPRESSION AND INFLATION

Although the entire postwar period has been one of relative prosperity, our economic outlook has gradually changed. During the early years, to about 1958, there was widespread gratification that no postwar depression had materialized such as we had experienced after the Civil War and World War I. Even with the stimulus of war production removed and millions of demobilized people looking for work, there was no sign of a return of the massive unemployment of the 1930s that many had feared. Instead, the national income forged steadily higher in real terms as well as in inflated dollars. At first the heretical view of a few advance guard economists, the proposition that a perpetual but controlled inflation would guarantee prosperity, became more and more widely accepted as almost self-evident. The depressing thesis of chronic depression and stagnation, never universally accepted but at one time widely supported, disappeared from sight.

About the time of the recession of 1958, government officials, business leaders, and economists began gradually to find our position and our policies less satisfactory and much in need of reappraisal. We had avoided a depression, it is true. We were steadily growing, and that was to our credit. The trouble was that we were not growing fast enough. The annual increase in our output was insufficient to absorb the annual increase in our labor force. Some months we found that although employment had increased, perhaps to a new high, unemployment had also increased. We found that our recovery periods were becoming shorter and weaker. At the peak of the recovery we were not experiencing full employment; 4 or 5 percent of the labor force was unemployed instead of the practical minimum of 2 or 3 percent. We found that, after making allowance for changes in the price level, the rate of increase of our output was less than that of most other industrialized nations. Our national income determines not only the level of employment but also our standard of living (consumption); our future growth, as affected by our additions to capital (investment); and our national security, as well as our output of important public goods and services such as roads, hospitals, and education (government), not to mention the extent to which we are able to help the less developed countries raise their own productivity. It is vital that we spur a lagging economy.

With this dissatisfaction with our growth rate came a growing doubt that continuous inflation and cheap money were practical means to implement prosperity. However appealing the lure of these techniques, the hard realities of our gold drain and the world's increasing distrust of the dollar forced us, if not to lay them aside entirely, at least to try to supplement them by more orthodox policies.

Euphoria of 1945–1958

Looking back, we may feel it is almost incredible that in the months immediately following the war there was a real fear, especially in Washington, that the nation might quickly find itself again in deep depression. What were the principal factors that encouraged, instead, a national income soon much higher than even during the war?

In the first place, we know the money supply increased greatly between 1942 and 1945. The total of demand deposits and currency outside banks doubled during the war. In addition, there was a great increase in time deposits and savings bonds. In fact, their total increase was even greater than the increase in the money supply. Although we do not classify either of these as money, their holders often considered them as the equivalent of money. Together with money, this near-money supported a tremendous demand for goods and services in the postwar market.

Certainly we need not be quantity theorists to see the inflationary potential of this vastly augmented supply of money and near-money. The additional money had permitted a rising level of money income during the war. The higher money income, along with price controls that keep prices from rising, would have permitted more consumption and more investment. However, rationing temporarily prevented much change in consumption and investment since the government needed so much. The extra money income was received and often held idle. But when rationing ended, the income was spent. Had we had serious unemployment at the time, the upsurge in consumption would have been welcomed as putting people to work. Since in fact we were already at full employment, inflation was almost inevitable. As the money was spent and time deposits and savings bonds were converted to money and also spent, the money income resulting from this consumption and investment increased faster than could the output of real goods and services. This is inflation.

The public was all the more encouraged to spend freely after the war because it found itself out of debt to an extraordinary degree. Since people had not been able during the war to buy the things they wanted, they had used some of their additional income to pay off prewar debts. This liquidation was further stimulated by the Federal Reserve's regulation of consumer credit during the war.[1] At any rate, consumer credit dropped from $9 billion in 1941 to $6 billion in 1945. From there it was to increase spectacularly to $22 billion by 1950, to $56 billion by 1960, and to approximately $190 billion by 1975. Similarly, real estate credit declined a little during the war, from $38 to $36 billion. It doubled in the first five postwar years, and by 1975 was approximately $700 billion or roughly 20 times the level of 1945. The public lost no time in getting back into debt as fast as it possibly could.

True, the increase in debt was not quite so drastic as the above figures would suggest. Part of the doubling of consumer credit and real estate credit merely reflected the rise in prices. Very roughly, around a fourth of the increase might be attributed to this factor. Except for a slight drop in 1949, the indexes of both consumer prices and wholesale prices rose steadily from 1939 to 1952. They leveled off between 1953 and 1955, and then resumed their briefly interrupted climb. Wholesale prices leveled off for seven years (1958–1964) and then began to rise again. Consumer prices rose every year. The rise in prices was in part a result, in part a cause, of the increase in debt, just as it was also partly a cause, partly a result, of the high level of employment and income. Also, since incomes were simultaneously rising, the ratio of debt to income did not rise nearly as much as did the debt itself.

Redirection in 1958

Reappraisal and redirection of economic policies is seldom sudden or complete. It would be misleading to imply that in 1958 we abruptly altered our analysis and unanimously agreed upon a new economic course. Some had never favored the prescription of perpetual inflation; some favor it still. It was in 1958, however, that the course of events enforced a new respect for the old concept of stable prices. Our monetary and fiscal policies could no longer be oriented to purely domestic considerations. They had to recognize the limitations imposed by our obligations abroad.

As the strongest and richest free nation in the world, we had certain international commitments. We had to shoulder a large part of the enormous cost of the common defense of ourselves and our allies. We had to help the underdeveloped nations raise their living standards by increasing their productivity—not merely for charity, but for our own self-interest of holding them in the society of free nations. To fulfill these commitments we needed to export far more than we imported.

As far back as 1950 there began to be indications that our almost morbid concern with the possibility of depression was leading us to continue policies no longer suited to the times. As Europe replaced war-shattered factories with

---

[1]See Chapter 11.

the newest, most efficient equipment, the United States began to find it progressively more difficult to export. We had taken for granted that our goods would always be in demand, no matter how fast our prices rose. We had argued that our rapidly rising wage rates were immaterial in view of the unsurpassed productivity of American labor. But with the new plant and equipment, the productivity of European labor began often to equal and sometimes to surpass that of American labor. Wages in Europe were increasing as well as in America, but the rate of increase in the productivity of labor was much greater in Europe. Although our exports exceeded our imports, the margin was rapidly shrinking. It became too small to cover our foreign aid programs, military expenditures abroad, and overseas investments. A so-called balance of payments deficit appeared for the United States.[2] To permit our prices to continue their steady rise appeared, rather suddenly, disastrous.

Some economists were reluctant to contemplate the abandonment of the easy money policies. They argued that, although prices certainly had risen in the United States, they had risen even more in most other countries, proving, they asserted, that our inflation could not be a causal factor of our balance of payments deficit. This kind of comparison of international price levels is really meaningless. As was emphasized earlier, all that any price index can possibly show is the percentage of change in the prices of a given collection of goods over a certain period of time. With a little juggling of the years chosen for comparison, one can prove almost anything. In the second place, some prices will be much more important than others. The American steel industry, for example, has found it increasingly difficult to meet foreign competition, regardless of whether prices in general have been rising more or less rapidly than in foreign countries. Finally, the crux of the matter is this. Whether our price inflation was more rapid or less rapid than inflations in other countries is irrelevant. Our inflation was excessive in light of our balance of payments problems. To export more and import less, we had to halt, or at least slow down, the continuous rise in our prices.

Continuation of easy money and rising prices was also rationalized on the grounds that the stimulus these policies would give to domestic production and employment was far more important than their effect on our transactions with the rest of the world. Yearly deficits in our international balance of payments were of no real consequence, it was argued. There was no reason to be disturbed by our steadily increasing debt to foreigners, for everyone knew the dollar was sound; everyone knew it was as good as gold; everyone knew foreign banks wanted all the dollars they could get to use as reserves for their own currencies.

For a time these arguments prevailed. A slow but persistent gold drain beginning in 1950 reduced the Treasury's stock by about $2.7 billion. The gold flow was briefly reversed in 1956 and 1957, when the Suez crisis reduced the exports of some of our competitors. But in 1958 United States gold losses suddenly became alarmingly high. In the first six months we lost $1.5 billion. By the end of the year we had lost $2.3 billion, nearly as much as in the six

---

[2]See Chapter 26.

years from 1950 to 1955. Federal Reserve and Treasury officials were shocked at how far and how fast international confidence in the dollar had fallen.

The trouble was, foreigners did not seem to realize that they wanted an unlimited stock of dollars. They did not seem even to understand that the dollar was always going to be as good as gold and that the United States Treasury would always be able and willing to sell them unlimited amounts of gold at $35 an ounce. They were increasingly uneasy about their continually mounting stock of dollars. Bankers abroad were openly concerned by the apparent unwillingness or inability of the United States to halt inflation. They saw that, in spite of our repeated gold losses, our government continued to operate at a deficit. They concluded that our inflation, our domestic and international deficits, and our gold losses would all continue. Naturally they feared that our international accounts would become increasingly disorganized, our gold losses would accelerate, and we would eventually be forced to devalue the dollar. As everyone knows, the mere fear of devaluation can force devaluation if it leads to a run on the dollar. If the United States was to restore confidence in the dollar, it was necessary to provide not assurances and guarantees, but concrete evidence that we could and would continue to sell gold freely at $35 an ounce. The most positive proof of our intentions would be to stabilize our price level.

The United States found itself suddenly in a position it had not known for more than 40 years. Traditionally, central banks had regulated their discount rates not by domestic considerations, but in accordance with their gold position. The Bank of England during the 19th century and until World War I and the Federal Reserve Banks in the first few years of their operations had raised the discount rate whenever their gold stocks were too low. As the tighter credit led to higher interest rates in the market, gold flowed in from abroad to take advantage of the high return. Also, (although not fully understood at the time) the higher interest rates checked investment. Income fell; consumption fell; employment dropped, as did wages, costs, and prices. The fall in domestic prices stimulated exports while discouraging the import of foreign goods. All this tended to convert a gold outflow to an inflow. If the inflow became excessive, discount rates were lowered, interest rates fell, and the inflow decreased or disappeared.

Since World War I, however, the Federal Reserve Banks seldom had any occasion to be concerned about protecting their gold (or gold certificates) then required as reserves. Our gold stocks were more than ample. They were even more sufficient as gold poured in during the 1930s. As a result, the Federal Reserve had been able to disregard our gold position and set discount rates solely with reference to our domestic requirements. Whenever the industrial tempo slowed, interest rates could be lowered. Any gold loss that resulted due to short-term capital movements or other factors could safely be ignored. Suddenly it could be ignored no longer. Our shrinking gold stock could easily become inadequate. Under the circumstances we could not afford the luxury of very low short-term interest rates and rising prices, no matter how much unemployment appeared. If we were to maintain confidence in the dollar, we had to stop the gold outflow.

Not only the Federal Reserve but also the Treasury had to reexamine its policy. Short-term capital movements were not the principal cause of our difficulties, although they could aggravate them. The fundamental problem was that we had to buy less from and sell more to foreign countries. This was the hard fact with which the inflationists had to contend. The argument that, regardless of what other countries were doing, we could go on forcing a continuous decline in the value of the dollar suddenly lost much of its force. Monetary and fiscal policies were changed in an attempt to reduce inflationary pressures.

MONETARY POLICY

The postwar monetary policy of the Board of Governors has often been criticized. In particular, some have argued that Federal Reserve authorities did not move promptly and with vigor to prevent the rise in prices that drove the index of wholesale prices up by 40 percent in the first two years after the war.

Continuance of Rate Pattern, 1945–1947

Actually the hands of Reserve authorities were tied by the requirement that the wartime level of interest rates be continued.[3] Tight money was the obvious monetary policy to restrain inflation. But a tight money policy was impossible if Federal Reserve Banks were to continue the wartime interest rate pattern, that is, to continue supporting the price of government bonds, because:

1. If the yields on government securities were not permitted to rise, interest rates elsewhere were unlikely to rise.
2. Increases in the discount rate would do nothing to tighten bank credit. Banks had no reason to borrow from the Federal Reserve when they held a tremendous volume of securities that the Reserve Banks were committed to purchase at par.
3. Open market operations were simply out of the question. The Federal Reserve Banks were supporting the price level of government securities by freely buying them. If the Banks had tried to tighten credit by open market operations, they would have had to sell government securities. Such sales would have tended to push down the prices of the securities and push up their yields, which of course was in flat contradiction to the Federal Reserve's responsibility to keep the prices up and yields down.

It should be noted, incidentally, that the difficulties with credit control were not a result of the particular pattern of rates that was frozen but are inherent in any program of rate stabilization. No matter what rates might be maintained, the Federal Reserve would still need to take, without limit, all

---

[3]More than a year after the war had ended, the only change in interest rates was that the Federal Reserve had discontinued the preferential rate of one half of 1 percent on loans with short-term government securities as collateral. (See Chapter 23.) The endsheet contains historical statistics from 1929 to 1974 on the interest rates on U.S. government three-month Treasury bills, on the interest rates on high-grade (Aaa) Moody's corporate bonds, and on the Federal Reserve's discount rate.

securities offered. Credit control and stabilization of interest rates are diametrically opposed.

The trouble generally encountered with any program of price supports is that, once adopted, it is difficult to abandon. For three reasons there was opposition in the postwar years to discontinuing the price support of government securities that was holding down interest rates.

First, there was the possibility that the price of long-term securities might drop considerably. Some feared that a panic might be touched off in the bond market if rates were allowed to rise. A sharp decline in bond prices might prove highly embarrassing to banks and other financial institutions holding large bond portfolios and conceivably could be highly damaging to public confidence.

In the second place, the Treasury wished a continuance of low rates to hold down the cost of servicing the debt. It must be remembered that, due to the huge floating debt, the Treasury by necessity must borrow tens of billions of dollars every year, even when the government is not operating at a deficit. Merely to refund the bills already then outstanding that matured yearly required each year nearly a hundred billion dollars of current borrowing. In addition to these amounts, billions of dollars of notes and bonds mature each year, and the Treasury redeems billions of nonmarketable securities at the holder's request. Although a small part of the debt has been retired through tax surpluses, almost all the maturing securities are either directly exchanged for new securities or repaid with the proceeds of new borrowing. When interest rates are rising in the market, the Treasury must offer higher interest rates on its new securities than it was paying on the old ones. With a debt of the present size, an increase of even one half of 1 percent in the average interest rate adds more than one and a half billion dollars a year to the Treasury's interest cost.

In the third place, some recommended that interest rates be kept permanently low. Rate increases in booms, they said, did little to check credit expansion. Rate reductions in recession might easily prove futile, being unappealing to the borrower and highly discouraging to the lender.

During the Depression many lenders had held their money idle rather than lend it at the very low rates prevailing. People expected interest rates to rise sooner or later and knew that a rise in interest rates would mean a fall in the price of bonds and other long-term obligations bearing a fixed interest rate.[4] If, on the contrary, they had been sure that there was no possible chance that interest rates would presently be higher, then there would have been no point in their preferring to hold money rather than government bonds or other high-grade obligations.

Hence, it was argued by some after the war that the Federal Reserve should use its other powers to control credit—powers that, for the most part, Reserve authorities originally did not hold or did not know how to use when the discount rate appeared to be their only implement. Interest rates should cease to be a control device, and the level of interest rates should be held

---

[4]See the discussion of the speculative demand for money in Chapter 19.

constant. Such a policy would make less likely the kind of credit deadlock that appeared in the 1930s.

None of the arguments justified the continuance of the rigid price supports. Bond prices sagged when interest rates eventually were allowed to rise, but there was no panic in the bond market. The greatest increase was in short-term rates, which were at unrealistic levels by the end of the war. Since the short-term securities were soon maturing, their market value was not greatly affected by the higher rates on new short-term offerings. Conceivably long-term rates might have risen more than they did, especially if the general level of rates had been steeply advanced. But they were not to be greatly affected by the moderately higher interest rates that came into effect in 1951.

The Treasury's interest costs increased, but income taxes partly recaptured this additional interest. To maintain low interest rates for the perpetual accommodation and encouragement of Treasury borrowing appeared unwise when the government showed so little ability or inclination to balance its budget even in inflation. It seemed wiser to permit rising interest rates as at least a mild restraint on a continuous expansion of the national debt.

Finally, a policy of continuously low interest rates would involve a movement away from the broadest type of monetary control and an increasing reliance on direct and specific, qualitative controls. There are times when a greater emphasis on qualitative credit controls may be helpful, but it seems unnecessarily arbitrary to abdicate the control over interest rates. This philosophy of perpetually low interest rates was one that grew out of the Depression. By 1950 it had lost much of its appeal.

Return to Free Interest Rates, 1947–1951

Repeatedly, Reserve authorities pointed out the conflict between supporting the bond market for the Treasury and regulating bank credit in accord with the needs of the economy. When recession occurred in 1948, it became clear that market stabilization continued to result in credit conditions that were inappropriate to the needs of the economy in general. At this time interest rates were falling and the prices of government securities were rising. To stabilize the market, the Federal Reserve Banks began selling securities on the open market. This kept their price from rising, which was the purpose of the sales. However, at the same time it decreased member bank reserves and raised interest rates. A reduction in member bank reserves and the increase in interest rates were the exact opposite of what was appropriate in a period of contraction and falling income. They tended to cause further contraction.

Federal Reserve Begins Return to Independent Policy. Finally, the Federal Reserve Open Market Committee served notice in 1949 that there was to be a return to traditional credit control. Promising that they would continue to maintain orderly conditions in the bond market, the Open Market Committee said that their policy would hereafter be determined primarily by the needs of commerce, business, and agriculture.

The next year the pendulum was swinging the other way. Even in the first half of the year employment had been increasing, loans rising, and prices inching upward. Then war broke out in Korea, setting off a wave of speculative and precautionary buying by both industrialists and consumers, remembering the many shortages during World War II. The price level rose faster than ever.

During all this time the Treasury had been adamant in its demand for continued easy money. All that the Federal Reserve had been able to do to move toward free interest rates had been to thaw the rate on 91-day Treasury bills, in 1947,[5] and to encourage a slight rise in the rate on 1-year certificates. The Federal Reserve Banks had raised the discount rate in 1948 and again in 1950. The move was an empty gesture as long as member banks could get all the reserves they wanted by selling intermediate and long-term government securities at pegged prices to the Reserve Banks. It was impossible to exercise any control over their loan expansion, at least until such time as they might have disposed of their total government securities to the Reserve Banks, a possibility that dismayed Reserve authorities since member bank bond portfolios were about five times as large as existing member reserves.

The continued insistence of the Treasury for a continuation of the cheap money policy culminated in head-on conflict in the fall of 1950. Disregarding the arguments of the Federal Reserve and in spite of the new 1¾ percent discount rate, the Treasury went ahead in August with the announcement that it would refund nearly $14 billion of bonds and certificates with another issue of 1¼ percent 13-month notes. This was a direct challenge to the Federal Reserve and amounted to a declaration by the Treasury that the Treasury, not the Federal Reserve, would determine the level of interest rates.

The Federal Reserve accepted the challenge and caused the Treasury's offering to be unsuccessful. At the same time it took care that the refunding operation of the Treasury should not be a total failure. The problem was to show who was to be master of credit control and at the same time to avoid placing the Treasury in any real difficulty that might have undesirable repercussions on banking and credit. More than that, the Federal Reserve by its actions was asserting its independence to state that it felt the interests of the Treasury were contrary to the general public interest. It was, in short, issuing a reprimand to the Treasury.

The actual operation was simple enough, but it was on a massive scale. The Federal Reserve proceeded to bring about a rate of about 1⅓ percent on short-term government securities by selling billions of dollars of such securities from its portfolio. Yields on bills and certificates were pushed higher than at any time since 1933. Therefore, nobody wanted the 1¼ percent notes that the Treasury was preparing to issue in exchange for maturing obligations. If the Federal Reserve had stopped at that point, the Treasury might have been seriously embarrassed by the sudden necessity to raise billions in cash almost overnight, for the holders of the maturing securities were to be given their

---

[5] See Chapter 23.

choice of cash or the new securities, and the majority of holders would probably have demanded cash.

To avoid precipitating a crisis for the Treasury, the Federal Reserve itself bought on the open market most of the maturing obligations that were about to be refunded. It then accepted the 1¼ percent notes the Treasury was offering in exchange, sparing the Treasury the need to raise the cash. Of course, Federal Reserve earnings were adversely affected by the operation. The irony of the situation, however, lay in the fact that since the Federal Reserve was already turning over to the Treasury most of its profits, ultimately the Treasury would bear the cost of the disciplinary action taken by the Federal Reserve, because its receipts from Federal Reserve profits would be reduced by that amount.

"Treasury-Federal Reserve Accord." In the bitter political row described above, only the short-term rate was in question. The Federal Reserve was still pegging the bond market, and the 2½ percent bonds were selling above par. After the Federal Reserve had forced the increase in short-term rates, there was lively and caustic discussion of the proper level for long-term rates and a political fight over the roles of the Fed and the Treasury. Officials of the Federal Reserve and the Treasury, bankers, members of Congress, and even the President took part in the argument. At one stage it appeared possible that the Federal Reserve was to be subordinated to the Treasury and made into little more than a marketing agency for Treasury securities. However, an agreement was reached on March 4, 1951, and the announcement was made jointly by the Secretary of the Treasury and the chairman of the Board of Governors:

> The Treasury and the Federal Reserve System had reached full accord with respect to debt-management and monetary policies to be pursued in furthering their common purpose to assure the successful financing of the Government's requirements and, at the same time, to minimize monetization of the public debt.

The results were not very startling, and certainly did not measure up to the frightening possibilities that had sometimes been suggested as consequences of such a move. The average yield on long-term Treasury obligations rose gradually after the "Treasury-Federal Reserve Accord."

Other Aspects of Monetary Policy, 1945–1956

The problem of regaining control over interest rates so dominated the Federal Reserve's monetary policy in the postwar years that other monetary controls were of little importance. The Board of Governors received the power to raise reserve requirements above the usual legal maximums temporarily. Margin requirements were varied occasionally, on the average about once a year. The Board's authority to regulate consumer credit, first granted during World War II, had expired in 1947. The consequent ballooning of consumer credit was somewhat disturbing under the best of circumstances and definitely undesirable when the nation found itself again at war. Control over consumer credit was reimposed by the Defense Production Act of 1950, which also authorized the Board for the first time to regulate real estate credit.[6] Both controls were by law ended two years later, somewhat prematurely as events were to show in 1953.

There was another innovation in the monetary policy of this period in the program of Voluntary Credit Restraint, undertaken in 1951. Under the leadership of the Board of Governors, committees were organized to represent principal lending institutions—commercial banks, savings banks, savings and loan companies, life insurance companies, and investment banks. Their responsibility was to discourage the making of loans other than those essential to the war effort. It was a voluntary program, and it was one of restraint rather than control. Borrowers applied to the usual lending agencies, but the agencies made their decisions by considering the general desirability of the loan rather than simply whether it would be safe. When in doubt, the lender could refer to the regional VCR committee.

VCR covered a wide range of loans, including real estate credit, foreign investment, and commercial and agricultural credit. It even controlled government lending as high as the state level.

The program of Voluntary Credit Restraint is another of those areas where we find economics and politics closely intertwined. The possible infringement of states' rights began to disturb President Truman. In (the election year of) 1952 he asked that henceforth any borrowing programs voted by local groups should be free from the control and standards of the VCR. Later that year the entire program was dropped.

In 1953 a Republican president was in the White House for the first time in 20 years. There had been much talk of "sound money" in the campaign. Some conservatives wistfully hoped that this might mean a speedy return to the automatic gold standard. They did not get their wish, but they did find an administration that appeared much more conscious of the evils of a steadily depreciating dollar and much more anxious to try to halt the upward spiral of prices.

Federal Reserve authorities were heartily in sympathy. The discount rate was raised to 2 percent in early 1953. This was its highest level in 20 years. Although the 2 percent rate was still low in comparison with rates in the 1920s, it served notice that the Federal Reserve expected to tighten up on money and credit.

Perhaps, as some of its critics claim, the Board of Governors stepped on the brakes too hard in 1953. Instead of rising, as usual, the gross national product flattened out. The discount rate was lowered in 1954, and reserve requirements were reduced. Open market purchases increased the Reserve Banks' holdings of government securities to the highest point in history.

Later, with the return of prosperity, the Federal Reserve pushed up the discount rate by successive steps to 3 percent. This was a level with which the younger generation of bankers had had no previous experience.

---

[6] See Chapter 11.

Recession and Recovery, 1957–1958

The Republicans had emphasized the issue of halting inflation. They had had some success in this attempt. Between 1953 and 1955 the index of consumer prices and the index of wholesale commodity prices varied by only a fraction of 1 percent. The recession of 1953–1954 had certainly helped to keep prices from rising, but there appeared to be some grounds for cheers as the price line was held the next year.

Discount Rate. As prices once more began to climb in 1957, the Board of Governors announced that by a tight money policy they would do everything in their power to check further inflation. It was clear that they considered inflation to be the nation's principal monetary problem. The portfolio of the Federal Reserve Banks was already at the lowest level since 1953. In August of 1957 the discount rate was raised to 3½ percent, the highest level in almost 30 years. Critics of Federal Reserve policies were quick to claim that this action was taken at a time when the economy was poised between recession and further prosperity, and that it was largely responsible for the recession that began in 1957, almost immediately after the increase in the discount rate.

In spite of the decline in employment,[7] production, and income, prices stubbornly refused to retreat and in fact were fractionally higher by December than they had been in August. The Federal Reserve, still concentrating on the evils of inflation rather than on the dangers of recession, refused to be stampeded into reversing its policy. Not until November did it take any action, and then only to reduce the discount rate by one half of 1 percent, a step characterized by financial writers at the time as "too little and too late."

The criticism was not entirely justified. The reduction might well have been made sooner. It does appear that the Board was slow in recognizing the need to reverse its policy. But there was little reason for the financial community to conclude so gloomily that the Federal Reserve would take no further action. Previous experience should have demonstrated that changes in the discount rate are ordinarily made by fractional steps and that large changes are made by a series of such changes rather than by a single large reduction. By April, 1958, the Board and Banks brought the rate down to 1¾ percent, the lowest level since 1955.

Those who felt that the Board should be taking more positive action still insisted that lowering the discount rate did little more than indicate the Board's approval of credit expansion. It did nothing directly to make credit easier. Banks could borrow more cheaply. But the banks did not need to borrow, for their customers were doing little borrowing. Hence, the lower discount rate was scarcely more than an ineffective gesture.

---

[7]Employment figures must be used with caution. The total number employed in 1958 was much greater than in 1941 and higher than in any year except 1956 and 1957. Yet there were nearly three times as many unemployed in 1958 as in 1952 or 1953. Also, the percentage of the labor force unemployed was much lower in 1958 than in 1941. Because of the growth in the labor force it is possible sometimes to see a simultaneous increase in the number of employed and the number of unemployed. Historical data on the unemployment rate from 1929 to 1974 is shown on the endsheet.

Other Controls. Early in 1958 the Board resorted to the much more powerful tool of reserve requirements. They lowered requirements repeatedly between February and April. The reductions automatically increased excess reserves of member banks. They stimulated credit expansion and improved business psychology. The evidence that the Federal Reserve was going to enforce monetary ease and the realization that there was at least a possibility that prices might begin to rise again encouraged businesses to think in terms of expanding their inventories instead of continuing to contract them.

Monetary Restraint, Beginning in 1958. A rapid outflow of gold necessitated a sharp reversal of monetary policy by mid-1958. Margin requirements were raised twice before the end of the year. Beginning in September, discount rates were raised to 2 percent, and by successive increases they were taken within 12 months to 4 percent, a level not seen since early 1930. On the other hand, reserve requirements, which for all banks had been substantially lowered earlier in the year, were not raised. Nor did the Federal Reserve reduce reserves by open market sales.

It is not hard to understand why the Federal Reserve did not make use of open market sales and increases in reserve requirements to make more effective its tight money policy. The Federal Reserve was walking a tightrope. Experience in years past had shown all too clearly the danger of applying restraints with too heavy a hand. The goal was not to throw the economy into a state of shock by enforcing a massive contraction of credit, but to serve clear notice that the easy money policy had been set aside. For this purpose increases in margin requirements and the discount rate were admirably suited. They discouraged credit expansion but did not force a great and immmediate contraction.

After much discussion, the Federal Reserve abandoned the so-called "bills only" policy.[8] Remembering the difficulties they faced after World War II, when they held large amounts of long-term securities, the Federal Reserve Banks had been for a number of years purchasing very few securities with a maturity of more than a year. Unquestionably the Federal Reserve's freedom of action is greatest when it holds only short-term securities. By selling short-term securities the Open Market Committee can simultaneously decrease bank reserves and raise short-term interest rates. If, instead, the Committee must sell long-term securities, they must move very circumspectly if they are not to cause an excessive fall in bond prices by their selling operations.

However, the international weakness of the dollar appeared to call for the change in policy. By selling some of its short-term securities the Federal Reserve depressed the price of such securities, thus raising their yield. This rise in short-term interest rates was essential to discourage an outflow of foreign capital to other countries, where short-term rates were higher than in the United States. At the same time the purchase of longer term securities tended

---

[8]A misnomer. It was not 91-day bills as such but short maturities which had been emphasized. The Open Market Committee was just as ready to purchase bonds with, for example, a 30-year maturity—provided that by the time they bought them the bonds were within a few months of maturity.

to hold down interest rates other than short term. It allowed, in short, a general structure of interest rates low enough to encourage expansion of domestic production and at the same time a short-term rate high enough to discourage the exchange of foreign dollar balances for gold.

The Money Squeeze, 1965–1966

For several years following 1960, the Federal Reserve's policy was one of gentle restraint.

1. Reserve requirements against demand deposits were unchanged.
2. Ceilings on interest rates the banks might pay on time deposits were gradually raised.
3. Margin requirements were reduced to 50 percent during the stock market slide of 1962, then restored the next year to 70 percent.
4. The discount rate was gradually returned to the 4 percent level that had been briefly in effect in 1959 and 1960.
5. Most important, by 1965 the Federal Reserve had added $13 billion to its portfolio of government securities. Since, however, currency in circulation had increased during the five years and the nation's gold stock had continued to fall, member bank reserves were increased by only $3.5 billion. With the nation at substantially full employment all through this period and with gross national product (in constant dollars) increasing about 6 percent a year, the increase in the banks' reserves was modest. From 1960 to 1965 gross national product had increased by one third, while bank reserves had increased by one sixth. In relation to income, the quantity of money was somewhat reduced.

Suddenly it became obvious that much more restrictive measures must be employed. The cost of the war in Viet Nam was rapidly growing as also was the government's domestic spending. Net private investment had doubled since 1960, and consumers were spending a third more than in 1960. Consumer prices had risen steadily, and in 1965 wholesale prices, after nearly 10 years of stability, also began to climb again. Meanwhile, our gold reserves had in 5 years dropped nearly 25 percent, to less than $14 billion. Clearly the government was still unwilling to apply fiscal brakes. The stage was set for the most drastic exercise of American monetary policy in a generation.

Discount Rate. In December, 1965, the discount rate was raised to 4½ percent. This made headlines. Even in the early years, from 1915 to 1930, before the Federal Reserve had acquired its later controls over bank credit, the discount rate was generally below 4½ percent. Not for 35 years had it been so high, and for 20 of those years it had not risen above 2 percent. Unmistakably the Federal Reserve was announcing a major shift in policy.

Net Borrowed Reserves. Borrowing from the Federal Reserve Banks became not only more expensive but also more necessary. Since 1960, indebtedness of the member banks to the Federal Reserve Banks had been less than member banks' total excess reserves; the difference was net free reserves.

Beginning in 1965, free reserves disappeared, as member banks' total borrowings from the Federal Reserve became greater than excess reserves. Net borrowed reserves increased rapidly in 1966, and by fall exceeded $500 million.

Continued Inflationary Pressures. As Reserve authorities had anticipated, the inflationary pressures of the economy became still greater in 1966, in spite of the Federal Reserve's application of the brakes. As we were soon to discover, these pressures were to become even greater a few years later.

Disintermediation. Commercial banks, mutual savings banks, and savings and loan associations vigorously competed for savings. What hurt them most, however, was not that they were losing funds to each other. They were, collectively, losing funds to the open market. This so-called disintermediation, as the financial intermediaries were bypassed, did not decrease the total quantity of money (currency plus demand deposits) but did reduce the lending power of the intermediaries. If a million dollar demand deposit, subject to a 16½ percent reserve requirement, is exchanged for a time deposit, against which a 4 percent reserve is required, the banking system's excess reserves are increased by $125,000, and it can increase loans (and demand deposits) by about $500,000 (after allowance for currency drain). In this instance, demand deposits are somewhat less than before, but the total of demand deposits plus time deposits is increased.

Again, suppose someone turns over $1,000 to a savings and loan association. For the banking system as a whole, lending power is unaffected. The transfer of the demand deposit from the original owner to the savings and loan changed the ownership, not the total, of demand deposits. The lending power of the savings and loan is, of course, increased as also is the total of demand deposits plus savings and loan accounts.

With distintermediation, individuals themselves make loans or purchase securities rather than turn over their money to a financial intermediary. When they buy securities, their deposit is transferred to the seller; total demand deposits of the banks are the same as before, their required reserves are the same as before, and they are unable to increase their loans. (Similarly, when individuals invest directly rather than through the mediation of a savings and loan or savings bank, these institutions do not get the increase in lending power that additional savings and loan accounts or savings deposits would provide.)

Consequences. The rise in bond yields coupled with the correctly anticipated fall in corporate profits set off a major decline in the stock market. More directly concerning the lives of millions, housing starts declined precipitously and in the fall of 1966 were at a 20-year low. Residential construction is probably more sensitive than any other major industry to changes in interest rates and the availability of funds. Typically, it involves long-term financing, often with very little owner equity. Individuals were reluctant to enter 25- or 30-year contracts at what were then regarded as high interest rates. Speculative builders, trying to finance apartment houses and subdivisions of homes, often could not find at any price the millions of dollars they needed that were ordinarily supplied by financial intermediaries.

It was unfortunate that housing had to bear the brunt of the credit squeeze. The purpose of a tight money policy is, however, to reduce demand. Something has to give. It can be taken for granted that the demands that will be most affected will be those to which interest rates and the availability of money are most important. If we feel that this kind of check on excess demand is unsatisfactory because of its automatically discriminatory impact on construction, we should turn instead, or simultaneously, to fiscal policy, which can be administered somewhat more selectively.

The administration deplored the tight money policy. One Congressman impassionedly demanded to know whether President Johnson or the Board of Governors was running the country. Finally, however, Washington admitted that the restraints imposed by the Federal Reserve had been a major factor in preventing even greater inflationary pressures from developing, and indicated that (with another election now over) the government would cooperate by a more restrictive fiscal policy.

Apparently monetary policy could now gradually be relaxed. Net free reserves appeared again early in 1967, the discount rate was lowered, market rates softened, and money became less scarce. Even though we had not reverted to easy money, we no longer were experiencing the drastically tight money of 1966.

The Second Money Squeeze, 1967–1970

Fiscal policy turned out to be more expansionary than ever. The government's good intentions did not prevent a deficit in fiscal 1968, a deficit double the total deficit over the three previous years. International problems continued also. Prices, rising steadily but slowly since 1966, began climbing faster.

The Federal Reserve repeatedly raised the discount rate until by 1969 it stood at 6 percent for the first time in 40 years. Margin requirements were raised in 1968. Also, for the first time since 1953, reserve requirements of the reserve city banks were slightly increased. They were, however, still well below the requirements prior to 1958.

The Federal Reserve Banks continued to add several billion dollars of Treasury securities to their portfolios every year, an amount that some analysts felt was undesirably large during a period of inflation. Primarily, however, these purchases did not increase member reserves but merely restored the reserves the banks were losing as the public continued to increase its holdings of currency. Since reserve requirements had been increased and also since, except in one year, our output of goods and services, measured in constant dollars, was increasing, the addition to reserves was modest. These relatively small increases did not permit the banks to satisfy the demand for loans; net borrowed reserves rose as they were forced to borrow from the Federal Reserve Banks. Banks and other lenders rationed the relatively scarce loanable funds by raising interest rates. In the market, interest rates rose to the highest levels in more than 100 years.

More broadly, although other components of national income, measured in current dollars, continued to rise, profits fell in 1969 and 1970. In constant dollars, gross national product, after increasing by $32 billion in 1968, grew by only $19 billion the following year; in 1970 it fell $3 billion; and in 1971 it rose by $22 billion. (The endsheet shows real *GNP* in 1958 constant dollars from 1929 to 1974.)

The monetary restraints were criticized by some as excessive, by others as inadequate. Certainly they did not halt the rise in prices. One of the greatest problems in halting a price inflation, however, is that the longer it has continued, the harder it is to stop. This one had been going on for 30 years.

Perhaps monetary policy should have been even tighter, with a smaller increase or even a reduction in the money supply. If we had been willing to accept whatever increase in unemployment and fall in national income that might have been necessary to check inflation, a tighter monetary policy, continued indefinitely, might finally have been completely successful in ending, or at least slowing down, the rise in prices. There was growing dissatisfaction, however, with the fact that prices continued to rise more rapidly than ever even as real income dropped and unemployment increased to 6 percent. Also, investors and financial institutions were under pressure as prices of both stocks and bonds declined sharply. There was mounting criticism of the Federal Reserve's policies, especially from Washington. A government can have little chance of reelection if both capital and labor as well as consumers are against it, angered by the continued inflation. Political realities required that monetary policy be eased and other controls employed.

In 1970 the Federal Reserve began to relax the constraints. The discount rate was reduced. The money supply began to grow more rapidly. By 1971, market rates of interest, although still high, were well below the peak levels of 1969 and 1970. It appeared clear that if inflation was really to be checked, the Federal Reserve could not do the job alone. The government would have to cooperate with a strong and effective program.

FISCAL POLICY

Until Lord Keynes wrote his classic *General Theory* in 1936, economists did not have a systematic analytical foundation for conducting anticyclical fiscal policy. Our ability to use fiscal policy successfully improved in each decade from the 1940s through the 1960s. The economic problems of the 1970s proved less amenable to fiscal policy. However, fiscal policy remains a potentially useful instrument for moderating cyclical fluctuations under certain circumstances.

Fanning the Flames of Inflation

The most important single characteristic of our fiscal policy since the end of World War II has been its persistent contribution to inflation. This was partly deliberate and partly unavoidable. Certainly the mechanics of income formation and the results of fiscal policy were well enough understood by

1945. There could be little doubt of what would happen if, with full employment prevailing, there was to be a substantial increase in the total spending for consumption, investment, and government. It was obvious that if such an increase should begin to develop, it should be checked, since its principal result would be an increase in prices rather than an increase in production, which was already straining at the seams. Consumption and investment might be checked by higher taxes; government spending could be checked by lower appropriations. In general, however, taxes were reduced and government expenditures increased, the exact opposite of what should have been done.

Depression Psychosis. Many economists and government officials were still deeply concerned in 1945 that the United States might fall back into depression. In 1945 it was very easy to remember that except for the last three years of the war the United States had had continuous and massive unemployment ever since 1930 and that nothing the government or the banking system could do seemed to do any good. It was easy to remember, also, that competent American economists were debating, only a few years earlier, whether our economy might not have developed to the point that, in the future, depression would be a chronic condition and prosperity (unless implemented by government spending programs) the exception, not the rule. Also, it was less than a dozen years since some distinguished economists had charged that American industry had mistakenly created a great amount of excess capacity in the 1920s. Industry, they said, should not be allowed to figure overhead costs on the basis of all this idle equipment for which there was no economic justification. During the war, however, industry had been urged to expand plant and equipment. By 1945, its capacity to produce was far greater than in 1940.

These considerations weighted the decisions and colored the thinking of economists and government officials, particularly in 1945 and 1946. The possibility that, after having helped win the war, the United States might now stumble back into unemployment and depression was a political and economic nightmare.

In addition, the economic forecasts immediately following the war were, with few exceptions, very poor. In almost every instance they were too low. These forecasts were frequently based on the relationships discussed in Chapter 17. Forecasters found the new short-cut forecasting technique irresistible. The level of investment and government expenditures was estimated without too much difficulty. On the basis of this spending and the prewar consumption function, total income was computed.

As we saw earlier, there is nothing wrong with the logic of this type of forecast. Granted that we have a close estimate of the total amount of investment (private investment plus government expenditures), we can derive a close estimate of total income provided we are assuming the correct relationship between consumption and income. The errors in these forecasts were caused by the fact that the consumption function had shifted. Most economists assumed too readily that the consumption function was constant. As things turned out, the public was willing, at all levels of income, to consume a higher percentage of income in 1945 and 1946 than in the prewar period.[9]

We can simply, if inaccurately, illustrate by supposing that the consumption function increased from $C = \$50 + .6(Y)$ to $C = \$50 + .7(Y)$. If the total of investment (private and government) is estimated as about \$60 billion, then income should be, according to the first consumption function, about \$275 billion.[10] By the second function we would estimate income at \$367 billion. Evidently, an apparently minor shift of a decimal from .6 to .7 can cause a forecast not only to miss the bull's-eye, but to miss the target entirely.

In this atmosphere of caution and doubt the administration shaped its policy during the transition from war to peace. The backlog of deferred consumer demand was recognized but minimized. Much more attention was paid to the cancellation of war contracts, the closing down of defense plants, and the demobilization of millions of servicemen. Some predicted that the number of unemployed would probably be eight million or more. In an attempt to maintain prosperity, the administration urged that industry grant wage increases wherever that could be done without raising prices. Government spokesmen called attention to increases in productivity that had appeared during the war and indicated that government controls over wages would not now be used to prevent substantial wage increases to maintain the purchasing power of labor. Labor leaders needed no further encouragement to demand higher wages, and there were strikes in steel, coal, the automobile industry, and many other fields. The dreaded postwar depression turned out to be a very minor recession, and although production dropped somewhat in 1945, by early 1946 production was increasing. Shortly we faced the classic inflation situation. The flow of money income was being increased more rapidly than the flow of goods. Rising prices, instead of checking demand, increased demand by leading the public to expect further price increases. Consumers and businesses hurried to spend idle balances and borrow additional sums to spend before prices rose higher. Naturally prices continued to rise.

Tax Reductions. Besides the errors in judgment and the mistakenly pessimistic outlook, there were political considerations. An important one was taxes. Personal income taxes had never been so high in this country, nor had business carried such a heavy tax load. Though high taxes were needed to check consumption and investment and hold down the yearly increase in money income, the public clamored for tax relief, especially when, for the first time in 17 years, the government had a small surplus in 1947 and a large one in 1948. Government surpluses appeared to have gone out of fashion, and

---

[9]Remember, it was not simply because incomes were higher that people were consuming a higher percentage of income. That would have indicated only a higher average propensity to consume. It would have been a movement along the curve, but not a shift of the curve. Instead, because of their greater confidence, their large volume of liquid assets, the long scarcity of goods, and for other reasons, people were willing to spend a higher percentage of income at all levels of income. The consumption function itself had changed.

[10]$Y = C + I$. $Y = \$50 + .6Y + \$60$. $.4Y = \$110$. $Y = \$275$. See Chapter 17.

tax rates were lowered in 1949 to permit a reassuring, familiar little deficit again. The outbreak of the Korean War led to higher rates temporarily, but they were again reduced in 1953.

Need for Increased Government Expenditures. Finally, there was no way to avoid the enormously increased government expenditures. Just as we had found ourselves in a new world after the First World War, we now found ourselves even more closely involved with the rest of the world. We might have wished to turn back the clock to a quieter era where, wrapped in the cloak of the Monroe Doctrine, we could ignore the quarrels in Europe and Asia, but we were not to have the chance. We began by making loans and often gifts to other parts of the world. Sometimes these were to relieve starvation and crisis. Sometimes they were to help rebuild war-destroyed industrial plants. Sometimes they were to increase the capital of a backward nation and to help it to a greater prosperity. Often these programs were attacked as pointless giveaways to foreigners. Perhaps some were unnecessary. But we must remember that poverty and misery are the breeding ground for communism and that if we can help other nations raise their living standards, we may be at the same time strengthening our alliances.[11]

Later we found ourselves again at war. After hostilities ended in Korea, we still had greatly increased defense appropriations. It was argued that these expenditures simply could not be avoided. Nor could the cost of rocket research and the development of intercontinental ballistic missiles be avoided, particularly after Russia placed in orbit the world's first artificial satellite. Before long we were spending billions in Viet Nam. Of course, these tremendous government expenditures, made at a time when there was full employment, were inflationary. That could not be helped as long as we were unwilling to pay more taxes.

Inflationary Bias of Government. Centuries ago, Roman emperors repeatedly debased the currency. This was a primitive kind of inflation, but it did supply money for the troops, public works, and social security of the day, and other imperial programs. Hundreds of years later, British and European rulers followed the Roman example.

Today the debasement of currency is only incidental—a result, rather than cause, of inflation. With easily created paper money—bank notes and especially demand deposits—governments today have enormous power to inflate the money supply and drive up prices. Unfortunately they also have a strong incentive.

If we must have one or the other, most people would prefer inflation to depression. The condition begs the question, however. If we were in a depression, the government would reduce taxes and increase government spending until the depression disappeared. As we have learned over the last 40 years,

---

[11]Of course, this is far too large a question to treat thoroughly here. Admittedly we cannot buy allies. Granted, too, that some nations we have helped have been singularly adroit in concealing any friendly feelings they may have for us. It still seems better to do what we can by such programs of foreign aid than to let other nations feel that their only hope lies in turning to the Soviet Union.

inflations are not so easily halted. The appropriate fiscal measures are clear enough, but tax increases and reductions in government spending are politically dangerous. For this reason, and because the public does not always understand what is going on, governments often allow inflations to continue.

For governments, inflation has a special advantage. It would be reckless to assert that it is because of this advantage that our inflation has gone so long unchecked. On the other hand, it appears reasonable to assume that nearly every member of Congress must be aware of it and that most of the public is not. The advantage is simply this. Most of the revenue of the federal government (and also of many states) comes from income tax. Income tax rates are progressive, and exemptions and deductions are fixed except when, after 10 or 20 years, Congress changes them. Therefore, if prices rise and people's incomes rise by the same percentage, their taxes rise by a higher percentage; the government increases its share of the real national income.

Only if the tax rate were the same at all income levels, and there were no exemptions or deductions (or if these two items were a fixed percentage of income rather than a fixed amount), could we assume that people's total income taxes would increase by only 50 percent if their incomes increased by 50 percent. With the far more desirable progressive income tax, people may have been paying no taxes at all until their incomes increased. Or if they were already paying taxes, the taxes reflected the exemptions and deductions to which they were entitled. The assumed 50 percent increase in money income not only increases their taxable incomes by more than 50 percent (since their exemptions and deductions are not simultaneously increased); in addition, their taxes on the increase in their incomes is at a higher rate than the tax rates they were paying on their previous incomes. Necessarily, with a progressive tax the marginal rate (on the highest increment of income) is higher than the average rate (on total income). The average rate must rise as income increases.

Although the progressive income tax is generally conceded to be the most equitable tax from the standpoint of the taxpayers' ability to pay, its effects are distorted by inflation, which results in a concealed increase in taxes. When prices are rising, the taxpayers' real incomes, after tax, are reduced, even if their money incomes, before tax, are rising as fast as prices.

In short, government finds that if it permits (or encourages) prices to rise, its own revenues rise more than proportionately. It is no secret that persistent deficits at full employment will almost necessarily lead to rising prices. The public, which generally opposes an increase in taxes, is either unaware or irrationally unconcerned when the government increases its share of the national income by means of inflation. If our government is unaware of it, we must be sending the wrong people to Congress.

Combating Recession

Since in the immediate post-World War II period the government's fiscal policy tended almost always to be expansionary, and since, also, the recessions were modest, there were few major reversals of policy during these years. Not counting the slump in 1945 to early 1946, resulting from the reconversion to peacetime production, we had five recessions prior to 1972, all mild.

1948–1949. Prices, which had been steadily rising for years, leveled off and slightly declined between 1948 and 1949. Consumers had been rapidly going into debt since the end of the war, and they had bought a lot of goods, especially consumer durable goods. They were somewhat less ready to continue buying on credit, especially since prices had been rising rapidly. Besides, the Board of Governors had reinstated its control over consumer credit late in 1948.

The falling price level caused inventory disinvestment which in turn caused income to decline. As long as businesses expected prices to continue rising, they tried to increase their inventories. Falling prices and the expectation of further price declines encouraged businesses to use up their inventories and postpone restocking as long as possible. Where in 1948 inventories had been increased by $4 billion, in 1949 they were reduced by almost $3 billion, a net change of about $7 billion in investment. This change in inventory was the principal cause of the recession. By itself, it was greater than the total decline in national income.

A number of factors contributed to recovery. Construction continued strong, only slightly below the level of 1948, which had been at a record level. The decline in income automatically reduced tax payments, which the cut in income tax rates further reduced. Government expenditures, at the same time, increased about 20 percent, partly because of more spending by state and local units. Government transfer payments were larger due to the unemployment benefits it began to pay. So, since its gross revenues were smaller and its disposable income (T) was further reduced by the transfer payments, and since at the same time its expenditures (G) for goods and services were larger, the government's fiscal policy increased disposable personal income and encouraged personal consumption, which actually increased to new highs in 1949 in spite of the decline in national income.

1953–1954. In the fall of 1953 the second postwar recession began. It was generally similar to the previous one. Government expenditures had dropped sharply with the ending of hostilities in Korea. Investment in inventories again dropped sharply. Together these two components were responsible for a $10 billion drop in expenditures. Some competent authorities felt the situation had become alarming and warned that unless the administration promptly undertook a massive program of public works the United States would shortly find itself in a worse depression than that of the 1930s.

Here was a real problem for the new administration. The Republicans had not been in office a year when business turned down with the threatening possibility that things might quickly become much worse. For political as well as economic reasons it was crucially important that prosperity be restored. At the same time, the administration had pledged itself to fight inflation. It wanted to avoid taking action that would later encourage a further rise in prices. In spite of some forecasters' predictions of disaster, the government decided to go slow.

Already, as it happened, Congress had voted (in 1953) that personal income taxes be reduced. As in the previous recession, the reduction in tax rates together with the effect of lower incomes upon tax payments reduced the total amount of taxes paid by the public. The reduction in the tax load encouraged personal consumption. Disposable personal income and also personal consumption were again at all-time highs, as they had been in the earlier recession. Construction was likewise at an all-time high. Orders for producers' durable equipment, although a little below the level of the preceding three years, were still comfortably high. Under these circumstances the decline proved to be quite modest and short-lived.

1957–1958. The third postwar decline dipped deeper than had the two previous ones. This time, in addition to an unusually large reduction in inventories, there was a $6 billion drop in investment in producers' durable equipment. The latter decline was ominous. Usually a fairly short period of readjustment suffices if the principal trouble is that inventories must be trimmed. After a few months, current sales have reduced the merchants' inventories and they resume their orders to the manufacturers. But when the difficulty appears to be excessive plant capacity, years rather than months may be required for the readjustment. The economy has to grow up to the level of its productive capacity. It was also disturbing to see the annual rate of residential construction dipping $2 billion in the first half of 1958. The total of personal consumption expenditures held up astonishingly well, partly because of the operation of automatic stabilizers such as increased unemployment benefits and, with lower incomes, lower taxes. However, the relatively unchanged total of personal consumption expenditures concealed an important shift in consumer spending. Consumers were spending more on services and nondurable consumer goods in 1958 than in 1957. On consumer durable goods they spent billions of dollars less. The sale of new automobiles was especially disappointing. Steel production dropped sharply with the public buying fewer cars, refrigerators, furnaces, and other durable goods. In some industries and in some areas, unemployment rose disastrously.

Once more the administration had the unenviable duty of deciding what to do. Some insisted that a large public works program would be the only effective way to raise national income immediately and appreciably, and that it should be undertaken at once, before a deflationary spiral set in. Others argued that a tax reduction would also result in more spending, but with individuals rather than Congress doing the spending. They claimed, too, that a tax reduction could be put into effect much more quickly than could a spending program and that, anyway, it was high time for a general revision and reduction of taxes.

The administration took the position that unless the situation clearly became worse there should be neither a tax reduction nor a great increase in public works. Considering that 1958 was an election year, the decision was courageous. (It was also suicidal politically.) The public clamored for more spending and lower taxes. The administration stated its belief that the decline would end by the summer of 1958 and that income would rise without any more prodding from fiscal policy than what was already planned. As in 1953 to 1954, the administration felt that recession was the temporary and less important problem and that the long-run and critical problem continued to be inflation. It was unwilling to take actions that might, perhaps, shorten the recession by a month or two but at the cost of laying the foundation for still more inflation later.

Subsequent events showed the correctness of the administration's diagnosis and prescription. By the end of the summer there was clear evidence that recovery had set in. And as the stock market in the fall of 1958 made one new high after another, it seemed clear that investors took for granted that inflationary pressure would be renewed.

1960. The economy had not established a strong recovery from the previous recession when it turned down again in 1960. The long steel strike (July 15–November 7, 1959) contributed by halting the upward momentum of the economy. Consumption spending and construction were especially hard hit during the strike and for some months thereafter.

The most important cause of the downturn, however, was the violent turnaround in fiscal policy. During the first quarter of 1959, the Treasury's deficit was running at an annual rate of $15 billion. Fifteen months later its surplus was at an annual rate of $6 billion. The government's rate of annual contribution to the income stream had been reduced by $21 billion, for the administration was making a desperate attempt to stem our gold losses by checking our domestic inflation.

Deficits Resumed, 1961. With a return of Democratic control of the administrative as well as the legislative branch, much less emphasis was placed on the restraint of inflation by fiscal policy while much more emphasis was placed on the importance of increasing our *GNP*. Knowing the importance of checking inflation to strengthen the international position of the dollar, the President by a memorable show of force obliged the steel industry to rescind its price increases in 1962. But the government incurred substantial deficits in fiscal 1962 and 1963 as the administration attempted to raise the level of *GNP* and reduce the unemployment level.

In early 1963 the President asked Congress to reduce taxes. The significant and novel distinction between the justification for this cut and previous arguments for tax reductions since 1930 was that this cut was not proposed to close a deflationary gap by creating a temporary deficit. Rather, the President argued that a deficit was more likely, over the years ahead, without the cut than with it. A reduction of corporate and individual tax rates would stimulate greater production. Lower rates, applied to the larger base, would yield a larger total revenue and an eventual balance or surplus. The economy was to be stimulated, not only by the deficit, but also by the incentive of less punitive taxes. Conservatives had presented this argument for years with increasing defiance and despair. Now, labeled as "new economics," it prevailed.

There is no way to measure the effectiveness of the tax cut in reducing potential deficits, for there are too many variables. In spite of the lower rates (or because of them) total tax receipts were higher than ever before in our history. Not only that, but from one year to the next they increased more rapidly from 1964 to 1967 than they had increased from 1961 to 1964. All this was in accord with the administration's argument. However, part of the increase in tax receipts resulted from the effect of rising prices upon income, that is, from inflation. Also, government expenditures increased by almost the same amount, so that the deficits were nearly the same as before.

Accelerated Inflation, 1965–1968. The government's fiscal policy as inflationary pressures built up in 1965 was uninspired to say the least. There were clear indications from every quarter that dangerous pressures were rapidly developing. Unmistakably, there was an inflationary gap, and there was no doubt that it was widening.

Anyone with an introductory course in economics knows that an inflationary gap is closed by a reduction in total spending and that total spending is the sum of what is spent by consumers, business (for investment), and government. An increase in taxes will reduce spending for consumption and investment. A cutback in government expenditures will also reduce total spending. What did the government do? It increased its own spending, both in Viet Nam and at home, and refused to raise taxes. In short, its fiscal policy was exactly what would help close a *deflationary* gap.

One uncertain step was taken in the direction of reducing aggregate demand. In 1962 business had been permitted to take an accelerated depreciation on new construction, thereby reducing its taxable income, and also to reduce its tax liabilities by 7 percent of the cost of any new machinery and equipment acquired. In effect, business could buy equipment at a 7 percent discount. The purpose of this legislation, as explained at the time of its passage, was to stimulate investment and increase the rate of growth of national output. The accelerated depreciation and the investment tax credit were suspended at the end of 1966.[12]

Perhaps the best thing that can be said for this measure is that it showed political acumen. Instead of seeing income taxes raised or seeing some domestic expenditures of the government reduced, the average individual could see that his benevolent government was still looking out for him by turning to business for additional revenue.

On economic grounds it is more difficult to make as good a case for the policy. The investment tax credit (and provision for accelerated depreciation) were never intended as on again, off again measures. They are unsuitable for such operation because of their inherent lag. Investment decisions are made months in advance and, once initiated, often take months to complete. If Delta Airlines orders a fleet of new planes in June for delivery the following

---

[12]By the end of May, 1967, the government had changed its mind and reinstated the credit, retroactive to March 9. Businesspeople who had gone ahead with their investment programs in January and February were understandably unhappy. So were those who between mid-March and the end of May had canceled their programs.

year, it cannot cancel the order a few months later because the investment tax credit has been suspended. Neither can investment programs be expected to respond immediately when the tax credit is restored.

There is another, more fundamental difficulty. Granted, at least one of the three components of national output must be reduced if aggregate demand is excessive and inflation is to be avoided. Granted, too, voters will be unhappy if government expenditures are reduced or if higher taxes force a reduction in consumption. Generally, however, the long-run interests of the nation are likely to be better served by reducing either consumption or government expenditures in periods of inflation than by reducing investment. The reduction in installation of new plant and equipment will adversely affect output in subsequent years, and total real income will grow more slowly.[13] Giving a smaller slice of the national pie to investment permits larger slices of the existing pie to go to government and consumption, but it means the pie as a whole will fail to grow as rapidly as it might. It also means that the output per manhour, commonly although inaccurately referred to as the productivity of labor, will grow more slowly. If workers must use machinery that is 10 or 15 years old, they will probably produce no more than they were producing 10 or 15 years earlier. They can then hardly justify demands for higher wages on the basis of their increased productivity. Still more important, if in other countries obsolete equipment is being replaced with more efficient machinery, but in this country investment is lagging, unemployment of American workers rises as we begin to import more and export less. This simple truth should be obvious, but it never prevents demagogic attacks on any governmental efforts to check consumption or government expenditures rather than investment. Probably we are fortunate that the industrialization of the United States began in the 19th century rather than today.

No moves were made, however, to check consumption until January, 1967, when the President announced that he would ask Congress to raise taxes temporarily to reduce inflationary pressures. The timing was perfect politically. Economically it left something to be desired. The economic outlook was much less dazzling than it had been a year earlier. It appeared quite possible that the tax increase, if it materialized, might come just as the economy was entering a recession.[14]

Congress was reluctant to raise taxes, however, and insisted that there should first be a reduction in government expenditures. Finally, after a pledge (unfortunately, never fulfilled) that expenditures would be trimmed by $6 billion, Congress agreed to a temporary surtax, adding 10 percent to the amount of the regular income tax on all income from April, 1968, to June, 1969. Meanwhile, the international pressure on the dollar intensified, especially after the British devaluation[15] and the increase in the bank rate in London.

---

[13]Probably the most quoted of all the post-World War II growth models which emphasize capital-output ratios is the Harrod-Domar growth model. See Roy F. Harrod, *Towards A Dynamic Economics* (London: Macmillan & Co., 1948); and Evsey D. Domar, *Essays in the Theory of Economic Growth* (Fair Lawn: Oxford University Press, 1957).

[14]Perhaps if fiscal policy is to operate satisfactorily, recessions should come only in election years, inflations only in the odd years. In any event, a year later there had still been no increase in taxes.

[15]In November, 1967. See also Chapter 27.

1969–1971. A modest surplus and a small deficit marked the first two years of this period. By 1971, however, one of the largest peacetime deficits in our history to that time, accompanied by rising prices, rising unemployment, and disturbing business failures, convinced the administration of the need for price controls.

At the outset the government had attempted by traditional controls to halt inflation. The surtax was extended for a year by the Tax Reform Act of 1969. At the same time the investment tax credit was again suspended to discourage expenditures for plant and equipment. Also, a number of loopholes were closed to force the very wealthy to pay more taxes. (There was some indignation when it was reported that the year before there had been 301 persons who received tax-free incomes of $200,000 or more—56 of them receiving incomes of $1 million or more.)

At the same time, however, Congress decided it was necessary to woo the voters again. Having established that business and millionaires were to be taxed more heavily and that the surtax was only temporary, the government slightly increased the personal exemption. The political value of this package is apparent, especially since the increase in the personal exemption is most important to people in the lower income brackets, particularly if they have large families. Economic conditions at the time, however, hardly justified any tax reductions.[16]

Partly as a result of the surtax the government's receipts slightly exceeded its expenditures between June, 1968, and June, 1970, with a surplus of $3.2 billion the first fiscal year, a deficit of $2.8 billion the second. The administration at first expected a small surplus by June, 1971. (The endsheet shows the federal government's budget surpluses and deficits from 1929 to 1974.)

By December, 1970, however, it appeared necessary to change priorities, policies, and goals. Business was sluggish. We were in a recession. The unemployment rate had nearly doubled during the year. Giant corporations such as Penn Central and Lockheed were in or on the brink of bankruptcy. A number of the largest cities were skirting financial disaster. Consumers, lacking confidence, were not spending freely.

The administration had originally hoped that monetary policy would spur the lagging economy. The Federal Reserve had permitted an increase of a little over 5 percent in the money supply but rejected suggestions of greater increases. Moreover, it became constantly more evident that we were in a situation that monetary policy could do little to correct. Even if larger additions were made to the money supply, they would not necessarily lead to more spending. For a prompt increase in national income it appeared the government would have to assume the direct responsibility by increasing its expenditures. Since an increase in taxes would weaken the stimulus of the government's additional spending, the government would borrow the money. It was decided there would be substantial deficits in both fiscal 1971 and 1972,

---

[16]It must be admitted that, although the timing was bad, the personal exemption probably should have been increased. The increased 1971 exemption was, in terms of real income, little more than 50 percent of the original exemption provided 30 years earlier. To be sure, perhaps the government was overly generous when it decided, in 1942, that a man with a wife and two children to support should not be subject to tax on the first $2,000 of his income.

and the deficits exceeded $23 billion in each year. To make matters more difficult, in spite of the recession in 1970, prices were rising more rapidly than ever. The index of consumer prices had risen to 116.3 from the 109.8 level of a year earlier. By the end of 1971 the index reached 121.3, and by 1972 it stood at 125.3 (see the endsheet).

Strongly opposed to price controls at the outset, the administration had hoped to accomplish its objectives within the framework of a free market. By 1971, however, it was apparent that if government deficits and easy money were to be employed to restore prosperity, prices would rise faster than ever—unless they were directly controlled.

The first move suggesting the possibility of eventual resort to controls was taken in February, 1971. For months the President had been trying unsuccessfully to persuade building trades unions and contractors to create a voluntary wage-price stabilization plan for the industry. In this area prices and wages had been moving up steeply, due partly to the strong demand for housing and other construction and partly to the fact that construction results in a joint product. Carpenters, painters, electricians, and plumbers all know that there will be just as many houses built even if the cost of their individual contributions is increased by a few hundred dollars. Each union had been demanding, and gaining, substantial wage increases. The index of the cost of homeownership had risen from 96 in 1966 to 133 by 1970, double the increase in the overall index of consumer prices, which rose from 97 to 116.[17]

In February the President suspended the Davis-Bacon Act of 1931. The result was that contractors on federally aided projects were no longer required to match the highest wages on similar construction work in the area. The President was not yet ready to impose controls, but was determined that the unions and contractors should agree to some form of voluntary control.

A few weeks later the suspension of the Davis-Bacon Act was revoked when contractors and labor leaders agreed to cooperate with the newly organized Construction Industry Stabilization Committee. Labor-management boards were to pass upon collective bargaining agreements, with their decisions to be reviewed by a committee representing labor, management, and the public. To this point the administration was still refusing to institute direct controls or even establish guidelines for acceptable settlements.

Finally, in August, 1971, the President announced a 90-day freeze on wages, prices, and rents, pending the establishment of a more permanent policy. At the same time he ruled that the Treasury would no longer, except under special circumstances, sell gold to foreign governments. (Discussion of this development will be postponed to Chapter 27.) He also asked Congress to restore once more the investment tax credit, to remove the 7 percent excise tax on automobiles, and to advance to January, 1972, the tax reductions (in the form of increases in the amounts of exemptions and standard deductions) scheduled for January, 1973. These measures were designed to encourage more spending by business and consumers. Without some kind of price controls such increases in spending could increase the pressure on prices rather than create more jobs and increase the flow of goods and services.

[17]*Federal Reserve Bulletin*, August, 1971.

In addition, the President placed a 10 percent surcharge on imports and asked Congress to reduce the government's budget for fiscal 1972 by about $5 billion. The surcharge was related primarily to our international monetary problems, discussed in Chapters 26 and 27. The reduction in the budget was slightly more than the reduction in tax revenues from other parts of the program. It did not result in a surplus but rather prevented the large deficit anticipated for 1972 from becoming even larger.[18] The logic of this reduction in government spending, at a time when business and consumers were being encouraged to spend more freely, was this. Most of the reduction in government spending was to be accomplished by postponing increases in transfer payments and increases in wages to federal employees. The government was to continue to consume about the same amount of goods and services as before. It was hoped that unemployment would decline as investment and consumption expenditures increased. If, however, the government was also to be spending more than ever but creating few new jobs in the process, inflationary pressures might be intensified. Instead of more spending for more goods we might be spending more for the same goods. We would then still have high unemployment, and we would also continue to have serious international monetary problems. Unfortunately the economy soon began to suffer "stagflation"—high unemployment and rising prices. The unemployment rate was 4.9, 5.9, 5.6, 4.9, and 5.6 percent from 1970 through 1974 at the same time that all price indices were inexorably rising. We shall examine this development more closely in the next chapter.

SUMMARY AND CONCLUSION

The combination of high interest rates and the ceiling imposed by Congress 50 years ago on the rate that the Treasury might offer on bonds effectively shut the Treasury out of the long-term market from 1965 through 1972. The average maturity of the debt steadily shortened as one maturing bond issue after another was refunded with notes (of up to 5 years) or bills. By 1969 more than half the national debt was due to mature within a year. The Treasury was required to borrow, every year, an amount equal to half the total national debt.

As one consequence, the rate ceiling impeded monetary policy, for the Federal Reserve had to expand the money supply at an inflationary rate to support the Treasury's security issues. Another consequence was the creation of the enormous floating debt, often considered by its holders as nearly equivalent to money.

The Treasury was finally given permission to issue notes of up to seven years' maturity, and it brought out its first seven-year issue in 1970. Also, the Treasury was authorized to issue up to $10 billion of bonds without regard to the interest ceiling; e.g., in 1971 it issued some ten-year bonds with a 7 percent coupon. These bonds and seven-year notes slightly lengthened the average maturity of the debt. There was little hope for real improvement in this area, however, until either market rates of interest became much lower

---

[18]The deficit was $2.8, $23.0, $23.2, $14.3, and $3.5 billion in 1970, 1971, 1972, 1973, and 1974, respectively.

(the imminence of which appeared unlikely) or the restraint of the interest rate ceiling was removed.

By far the most important development in the area of fiscal and monetary policy during this time was the attempt to raise the national income by a combination of fiscal and monetary policy and at the same time prevent further increases in wages and prices by some kind of direct controls.

Some economists have been urging for years that wages and prices be controlled. Time may prove them right. Their argument, as persuasively advanced by John Kenneth Galbraith, is that both labor and management have become so powerful that they can force up wages and prices regardless of current monetary and fiscal policies. Workers strike for higher pay. Management resists for awhile to assert its own strength, but eventually accedes to most of the demands. Then it raises prices. As this goes on in one industry after another, the price level and the general level of wage rates rise even if the monetary authorities and the government are trying to stabilize prices. For monetary or fiscal policy to be effective in controlling prices, it is claimed, both labor and management should be a great deal more competitive than, in fact, they are.

One possible remedy, which few would support, would be to reduce the power of labor and management by breaking up the giant unions and giant corporations. If American automobiles were produced by one hundred or more separate firms rather than almost entirely by four and if in each firm there was a separate union, it would be much more difficult for firms to raise their prices when they raised wages. If they approved excessive wage demands, they would probably be forced out of business. Realizing this fact, union members would moderate their demands rather than risk losing their jobs. This approach, however, appears unpromising.

The other remedy would be for government to control the increases in individual wages and prices. The controls might be direct, as during World War II. They might take the form of guidelines from Washington, but this approach in the past has had little success. Union leaders have flatly declared that no one in Washington is going to tell them how much they are to earn, and management's reaction has sometimes been similar. Again, the controls might result from some kind of enforced "voluntary" cooperation, as in the construction industry in early 1971. Somehow, however, the interests of the general public as well as of management and labor would be considered.

One's attitude toward wage and price controls reflects a general economic philosophy. When Adam Smith, 200 years ago, argued that the government should reduce its controls, he was a liberal, opposing conservative businesspeople and politicians. Today, those who urge more government control are called liberals. The conservatives would prefer to rely more heavily on market forces.

Perhaps our modern liberals are right, and today's society will have to depend permanently and to an increasing extent upon government controls. If so, it is unfortunate. There are serious disadvantages to such a policy. For one thing, there is the simple matter of enforcement. In wartime there is more cooperation from the public than can be expected at other times. Even during

World War II, however, there were many evasions, although 65,000 paid employees and 325,000 price control volunteers were attempting to police the program. There is some question as to whether many volunteer workers would be available, year after year, in peacetime. We probably should realistically expect a vastly expanded bureaucracy, which would still be ineffective in enforcing the controls.

Again, there is the same sort of political problem to which we have repeatedly referred with reference to fiscal policy. Labor has many times the votes of management. It is perhaps more idealistic than realistic to hope the controls would apply with equal force to both sides. The President can order the steel mills to lower their prices; the public is happy to see the greedy corporations brought into line. If, however, he were to order that wages in the steel mills be reduced, he would surely be attacked as an enemy of labor and the people and a friend of big business. This consideration would be unimportant to a strong dictator but can hardly be overlooked in a democracy.

Any program of controls is almost necessarily bitterly attacked on all sides as each segment of the economy feels that it is being discriminated against. No matter how foolish the objection, many will take it seriously. (Perhaps the most temperate comment of one of the nationally known labor leaders, after he realized that his initial invective against the wage-price freeze was not receiving the support he expected, was to the effect that he would have no objection to a fair system of controls, applying equally to all. If this seems to you to be a reasonable position, perhaps you should devise a system that all groups will agree is fair to everyone.)

The most fundamental objection to any system of wage and price controls is that it distorts the structure of production, often resulting in the production of less of the goods and services that people want. Sometimes other goods, not especially desired, are produced instead; sometimes nothing is substituted. For example, some months after the end of World War II price controls were still in effect. Even in New York City it was nearly impossible, except in the black market, to find an ordinary white shirt, at that time an indispensable item of the businessman's wardrobe. On the other hand, one could find any number of white shirts with long sport collars, for, since the manufacturers had not been making them before the war, these shirts were not subject to as low a ceiling price. As soon as the price controls were removed, the standard shirts again appeared on the shelves. As an example of more serious consequences, there has been little relaxation of the rent controls imposed in New York City during World War II. Thousands of homes and apartments have been boarded up or pulled down when, with today's higher maintenance costs, they could no longer be profitably rented. The rent controls are not the sole cause of New York's housing problems, but they are an important contributory factor.

It is also a great mistake if, as a result of political pressures, profits are frozen. There is, admittedly, a fine opportunity for demagogues to protest that wage-price controls are unfair, oppressing labor while allowing businesses to make more money than ever. The issue is hardly that simple. Take the case of our economy from 1965 to 1971 when wages were rising while profits were falling. The total of wages and salaries in 1971 was 160 percent of the 1965 figure. Profits in 1971 were 96% of the 1965 figure (and less than 90% of 1966 profits). It would have been rather simplistic to conclude that, in fairness to labor, we should have prevented any increase in profits, which were already depressed. In the second place profits are indirectly controlled anyway by the control of prices. Also, profits of most corporations are already taxed at 50% (and taxed again as personal income when paid out in dividends).

Most importantly, profits are the guide to what, how much, by whom, and for whom goods and services will be produced. If we discard this guide, we have little choice other than to abandon free enterprise entirely and turn over to the government the direction of the entire economic process. Certainly there are some who would favor such a development. The rest of us, however, should not walk blindly down that path with no idea of where it leads.

Discussion Questions

1. By the logic of income analysis, economists have been pointing out for the last 30 years that it is possible for a government to arrive at a balanced budget by a series of government deficits.
   a. Briefly summarize the argument.
   b. Does it make any difference whether the deficits are incurred during a depression or at full employment? Why or why not?
2. Until 1945, in this country and abroad depressions developed after major wars. Why did a depression not occur after the greatest war in history?
3. At times the Federal Reserve has tried to force short-term interest rates up and at the same time hold long-term rates down. Why? What difficulty does this create for the Federal Reserve?
4. Briefly explain how governments can cause inflation and give three ways in which governments benefit from inflation.
5. For a time it appeared that the great increase in the national debt during World War II would make it difficult to exercise an effective independent monetary policy. Explain.
6. What was the so-called "Treasury-Federal Reserve Accord" of March 4, 1951?
7. The Federal Reserve's ceilings on interest rates payable by financial institutions led to disintermediation, which reduced the lending power of these institutions. Explain both parts of this statement.
8. Disintermediation does not reduce the quantity of money but it does reduce the lending power of banks. Explain.
9. "An advantage of monetary policy is that it is a broad control, affecting all business activity impartially and equally." True or false? Explain.
10. Why were, with few exceptions, the economic forecasts immediately following World War II so very poor?
11. "Today the debasement of currency is only incidental, a result rather than a cause of inflation." True or false and explain.
12. What are some of the built-in stabilizers that have helped prevent recessions from developing into major depressions since World War II?
13. "If fiscal policy is to operate successfully, recessions should come only in election years, inflations only in odd years." Comment.
14. Are wage and price controls consistent with free enterprise? Explain.

Chapter 25　Monetary and Fiscal Policy Since 1971

The U.S. economy since 1971 has been disturbing for most people, but especially for believers in traditional monetary and fiscal policy. It has exhibited a period of prolonged and deep economic recession combined with intensive inflation. From 1945 to 1971 most debate centered on whether monetary and fiscal policy was being implemented properly. Since 1971 economists have increasingly questioned whether monetary and fiscal policy can be effective in combating certain kinds of cyclical fluctuations even if applied optimally. Alternative methods of fighting business cycles have been discussed and actually applied since 1971.

INITIATION OF DIRECT CONTROLS[1]

The year 1971 represents a watershed in American business cycle history. Instead of trying to attack the inflationary problem by monetary and fiscal restraints as in 1966–1967 and 1969–1970, beginning in August, 1971, another approach was attempted. Direct controls on prices and wages were initiated in hopes of restraining inflation without the adverse effects of lost production or employment. Acting under the authority of the Economic Stabilization Act of 1970, the President announced on August 15, 1971, an immediate 90-day freeze on prices, rents, wages, and salaries, and announced the creation of a Cabinet-level Cost of Living Council (CLC) to administer the freeze and advise on further stabilization actions and policies.[2]

The inflation of the early 1970s began in the mid-1960s in response to increased governmental outlays for the Viet Nam War and accelerated implementation of social welfare programs, and was fanned by the inflationary methods of financing these activities. In addition to inflation, the U.S. economy in the summer of 1971 was facing a growth rate that was insufficient to reduce unemployment to the desired level and our international balance of payments was rapidly deteriorating. Although the administration had taken limited steps to influence wage and price behavior directly in 1969 and 1970—especially in the construction industry (see Chapter 24)—there was still some question as to whether the administration should intervene directly in holding down wages and prices by adopting what is called an "incomes policy," and

---

[1]This section draws heavily on the excellent *Economic Report of the President* for various years.
　[2]While the CLC made the principal policy decisions, policy was implemented through an organizational system headed by the Director of the Office of Economic Preparedness, which was delegated the authority to administer, monitor, and enforce the freeze.

if so, on what scale and in what way.[3] However, on August 15, 1971, the administration inaugurated a powerful, but temporary, price-wage control system. In total it consisted of a three-part, integrated package: (1) international measures aimed at the balance of payments;[4] (2) controls concerned with checking inflation; and (3) fiscal measures directed, in combination with the international measures and controls, at accelerating economic growth and reducing unemployment. The freeze was followed by a comprehensive, mandatory, and more flexible system of controls known as Phase II.

The basic premise of the wage-price control system was that it was needed to break the expectations, fixations, and patterns of inflationary behavior built up since 1965. This was the continual theme echoed in the *Annual Reports* of the Council of Economic Advisors in the early 1970s.

There were a number of different stages or phases of the incomes policy since its inception in 1971. Table 25-1 gives the names and dates of these various stages or phases.

Table 25-1   Incomes Policy under the Economic Stabilization Act

Freeze I	August 15, 1971, to November 14, 1971
Phase II	November 14, 1971, to January 11, 1973
Phase III	January 11 to June 13, 1973
Freeze II	June 13 to August 12, 1973
Phase IV	August 12, 1973, to April 30, 1974

Incomes Policy Scenario

Without going into the numerous details, the incomes policy scenario under the Economic Stabilization Act went like this: Economic programs were initiated in August, 1971, with a 90-day wage-price freeze (Freeze I), and then Phase II stabilization controls were put into effect November 15, 1971, which lasted until January, 1973. The President's Council of Economic Advisers in January, 1973, concluded that progress had been made in abating inflation and viewed the future with "a strong sense of optimism." A year later many people considered the program a disaster. Phase III, which succeeded Phase II on January 11, 1973, was on a largely self-administered basis. It was terminated abruptly on June 13, 1973, by a 60-day price freeze (Freeze II). This in turn led to Phase IV on August 12, 1973, which provided for the removal of controls on a sector-by-sector basis and culminated in a congressional refusal to extend the Economic Stabilization Act when it expired on April 30, 1974. The country was so disillusioned with controls at this date that

---

[3]The pros and cons of an "incomes policy" are taken up in the "Summary and Conclusion" of Chapter 24. Four of the most serious shortcomings are (1) the direct costs of enforcement; (2) the indirect costs, including political logrolling; (3) the loss of allocative efficiency by distorting production; and (4) its ephemeral nature—it has never worked successfully anywhere for an extended period of time.

[4]Most notably, the U.S. suspended the convertibility of dollars into gold or other international reserve assets and imposed a temporary surcharge on imports, usually at a 10 percent rate.

the Congress rejected the idea of standby authority for possible reimposition of controls or of a monitoring system on wage-price developments in key sectors of the economy.

Thumbnail Sketch of the Various Programs[5]

The basic principle of the initial Freeze I as applied to wages, prices, and rents was that the rate of payment during the freeze period—August 16 to November 13, 1971—could not exceed the rate in effect during the base period—July 16 through August 14, 1971. The CLC's policy decision was to allow only a minimum of exceptions to get the most emphatic possible halt to inflation.

On October 7, 1971, the President announced the outline of the Phase II program which was to be mandatory, comprehensive, flexible, and durable in the interest of equity and effectiveness.[6] Although the Economic Stabilization Act of 1970—the legal basis for the Freeze I and Phase II control programs— was scheduled to expire at the end of April, 1972, Congress, in response to a Presidential request, extended it to April, 1973. The announced goal of the Price Commission was to hold the rate of average price increases throughout the economy to "no more than 2½ percent per year" to conform to the CLC's goal of reducing inflation to no more than 2 to 3 percent by the end of 1972. The Price Commission also articulated the general rule that no price might be increased beyond the ceiling price established for the freeze period, except in accordance with its regulations. The Pay Board guidelines stated that permissible annual pay increases would be those normally considered supportable by productivity increases and cost-of-living trends with the initial general standard set at 5½ percent.

As 1973 began, the administration felt that the economic conditions seemed good for a substantial modification in the Phase II system of controls. The reduced inflation rate and a reduction in excess capacity led the administration to move to a new regimen of controls, known as Phase III, which attempted to reduce the mounting delays and costs entailed in submitting requests for price increases, having them reviewed, and finding detailed interpretations of the increasingly complex rules, by making the basic principles of regulation developed during Phase II self-administered. The need for greater flexibility was an important reason for the change to a self-administered program of wage and price behavior.

The disappointingly high inflation rate in the first half of 1973 led the administration to seek a more stringent controls system than Phase III, but one flexible enough to respond to changing economic developments. On June 13, 1973, the President declared a 60-day freeze on prices (Freeze II), to be followed by a new set of Phase IV controls. More instances of price increases

---

[5]Details of the different phases and freezes can be found in various issues of the annual *Economic Report of the President*.

[6]The primary body created to develop standards and make decisions on all changes in prices (including rents) was the Price Commission, composed of 7 public members. The body created for all changes in compensation (wages, salaries, and fringe benefits) was the Pay Board of 15 members, composed of an equal division among business, labor, and public representatives.

occurred during the 1973 Freeze II program than the 1971 Freeze I program partly because of the extreme upward pressures on farm prices. The final regulations for Phase IV were announced on August 6–10 and were put into effect on August 12, 1973, for the wholesale, retail, manufacturing, and service industries.[7]

The Phase IV system was stricter than that of Phase II.[8] While the main objective of Phase IV was to slow inflation, plans for eventual decontrol were also implemented. Lumber, copper scrap, public utilities, and coal sold to public utilities were decontrolled at the outset. Later the prices of fertilizer, nonferrous metals, lumber, autos, cement, and rents were decontrolled.

EFFECTIVENESS OF INFLATION CONTROL UNDER THE ECONOMIC STABILIZATION ACT

Over the nine-year period from the end of 1965 to the end of 1974, consumer prices rose by 53 percent, or at an average of 5.9 percent a year.[9] While there were fluctuations (twice during the period the inflation rate declined significantly), the inflation rate was substantially higher at the end of the nine-year period than in any of the other years. Over the five-year period 1965–1969 the CPI rose at an annual rate of 3.4 percent, whereas over the five-year period 1970–1974 the CPI increased at a rate of 6.1 percent. On this basis many people concluded that the incomes policy program initiated under the Economic Stabilization Act was a failure.

However, the President's Council of Economic Advisers on January 1, 1974, was not so sure. For example, they said: "The effect of the controls program on the rate of inflation in 1973 cannot be known with certainty either today or ever." They felt that the inflation rate in 1973 might possibly have been even greater without controls. Moreover, they felt that:

> The effectiveness of controls obviously cannot be judged by 1973 alone. The operation of the controls during 1971 and 1972, bringing about a good balance in the structure of wages, may have helped to avoid a repetition in 1973 of the kind of wage spiral the country was experiencing before August, 1971. On the other hand, if controls did hold down prices during 1973, the possibility remains that these prices will catch up in 1974 or later.

At a minimum this statement certainly contained considerable truth as 1974 and 1975 prices skyrocketed.

Some Price Comparisons

One way to examine the effectiveness of the incomes policy is to look at the changes in prices and wages during the control period. The evidence in

---

[7]Earlier regulations were put into effect for the food (July 18) and health (July 19) industries, as it was felt especially quick action was required in these areas.

[8]In particular, cost-justified price increases which had been built up in earlier control periods were eliminated, add-ons to maintain percentage markups were not permitted, and some new base prices were set below those of Phase II.

[9]The inflation from 1965 to 1969 was commonly considered to be the result of demand-pull factors, whereas the spiral from 1970 to 1974 also contained cost-push factors such as monopolistic price and wage setting by domestic and foreign (especially oil-producing) business firms and labor unions. The *GNP* price deflator rose at a rate of 1.5 percent from 1959 to 1965, at a rate of 4 percent from 1965 to 1972, and at a rate of 5.9 percent from 1972 to 1974.

Table 25-2 shows that while Freeze I and Phase II did moderate inflation, the shift from Phase II to Phase III coincided closely with the acceleration of inflation from its moderate 1972 pace. Apparently Phase III was perceived by many as a signal that controls had ended since it was self-administered.[10] Moreover, the inflation rate climbed in 1974. Table 25-3 shows that both consumer and wholesale prices inflated substantially in 1973 and 1974. Also, in 1974 consumer prices increased every month from the preceding month. Moreover, the unemployment rate in the 1970s was significantly higher than it had been for some time.

Some Major Factors in the Collapse[11]

Why did the wage-price controls, which seemed to be doing the job in 1971 and 1972, collapse in 1973? While there is no clear explanation, at least five factors have been identified which offer partial explanations.

1. *International forces.* International factors erupted that were beyond the control of the U.S. economy: (a) the world's lagging food supplies coupled with rising food demand; (b) the October, 1973, Arab oil embargo which resulted in an unprecedented fourfold increase in the price of oil flowing from the cartel of oil-producing countries; and (c) the worldwide phenomenon of inflation—e.g., consumer prices in the year ending March, 1974, rose 7 percent in Germany, 13 percent in France, 15 percent in Britain, 16 percent in Italy, and 24 percent in Japan.
2. *Short-term value of direct controls.* Direct controls are thought to be inherently incapable of long-term effectiveness in a market economy, producing allocative distortions, slowing economic growth, and becoming increasingly unenforceable. Wage and price controls are like penicillin shots—if you keep receiving them, they lose their effectiveness. The 90-day freeze of 1971 and the 14-month stabilization effort of Phase II were probably stabilizing because they were short-term, and inflationary expectations had not been sufficiently crystalized.
3. *Demand-pull forces.* Direct wage-price controls are much more ineffectual in coping with the traditional demand-pull type of inflation, such as occurred in 1965–1969, than with the cost-push variety that largely prevailed from 1970 to 1974. In 1971, wage pushes were coming especially from the construction, health service, railroad, and steel industries.
4. *Monetary and fiscal policies.* These traditional countercyclical, fine-tuning devices were not fused in the subtle and complex manner necessary to choke off stagflation. Both monetary and fiscal policy were expansive from 1970 to 1974. The nation's money stock was increased at an average annual rate of 7 percent from early 1970 (a period marked by recession) to the end of 1973. By comparison, from 1964 (the last year of relatively stable prices) to 1970 the money stock rose at a 5 percent annual rate; in the previous decade money increased at a 2 percent average annual rate. Government expenditures, using the national income accounts budget, rose at about a 9 percent annual rate from early 1970 to the end of 1973. This was about the same as the rapid pace of the 1964 to 1970 period which included

[10] Surprisingly there is little evidence that consumer prices rose exceptionally fast in the areas in which the administration of controls were relaxed in Phase III. See the *Joint Economic Report of the President*, 1974, pp. 103–104.

[11] Our discussion is indebted to Milton Derber, "The Collapse of Wage-Price Controls," *Illinois Business Review* (July, 1974), pp. 6–8.

the sizable military build-up for Viet Nam. From 1955 to 1964, government outlays increased at a 6.3 percent rate. Average tax rates had been reduced through tax reform, cuts in excise taxes, increases in personal tax exemptions, and the restoration of an investment tax credit. The combined effect of these fiscal actions was to shift the national income accounts budget from an $8 billion surplus in 1969 to four consecutive deficits in the period from 1970 through 1973, averaging over $14 billion per year.

Table 25-2   **Measures of Price and Wage Change during the Economic Stabilization Program**
(Percentage change; seasonally adjusted annual rates)

Price or Wage Measure	Freeze and Phase II Aug., 1971 to Jan., 1973	Phase III Jan., 1973 to June, 1973	Second Freeze and Phase IV June, 1973 to Dec., 1973	Calendar Year during which Controls were in Effect Throughout	
				Dec., 1971 to Dec., 1972	Dec., 1972 to Dec., 1973
PRICES					
Consumer price index:					
All items	3.3	8.3	9.6	3.4	8.8
Food	5.6	20.3	18.6	4.7	20.1
All items less food	2.7	5.0	6.9	3.0	5.6
Commodities less food	2.0	5.2	5.2	2.5	5.0
Services	3.5	4.3	8.4	3.6	6.2
Personal consumption expenditures deflator	2.4	6.7	8.1	2.7	7.4
Wholesale price index:					
All commodities	5.7	24.4	14.3	6.5	18.2
Farm products and processed foods and feeds	13.3	49.8	8.8	14.4	26.7
Industrial commodities	2.9	14.4	17.2	3.6	14.8
Finished goods, consumer and producer	1.8	11.7	21.4	2.2	15.6
Crude and intermediate materials	3.7	16.2	14.1	4.5	14.1
WAGES					
Average hourly earnings, private nonfarm economy	6.1	6.3	7.6	6.3	6.7
Average hourly compensation:					
Total private economy	6.3	8.4	7.6	6.8	8.0
Nonfarm	6.5	8.2	7.9	6.9	8.1
Average hourly earnings, private nonfarm economy	6.2	5.8	7.5	6.5	6.7

Source: Department of Labor (Bureau of Labor Statistics) and Council of Economic Advisers. Cited in the *Economic Report of the President*, 1974 (Washington: U.S. Government Printing Office, February, 1974).

Table 25-3   **Yearly Consumer and Wholesale Prices and the Unemployment Rate Before, During, and After the Economic Stabilization Program**
(1967 = 100)

	1965	1966	1967	1968	1969	1970	1971	1972	1973	1974
Consumer Price Index	94.5	97.2	100.0	104.2	109.8	116.3	121.3	125.3	133.1	147.7
Compounded Annual Rate of Change (Year to Year)	1.7	2.9	2.9	4.2	5.4	5.9	4.3	3.3	6.2	11.0
Wholesale Price Index	96.6	99.8	100.0	102.5	106.5	110.4	113.9	119.1	134.7	160.1
Compounded Annual Rate of Change (Year to Year)	2.0	3.3	0.2	2.5	3.9	3.7	3.2	4.6	13.1	18.9
Unemployment Rate	4.5	3.8	3.8	3.6	3.5	4.9	5.9	5.6	4.9	5.6

Source: *Economic Report of the President*, 1975 (Washington: U.S. Government Printing Office, February, 1975).

5. *Psychological forces*. If the administrative controllers have a fundamental disbelief in wage-price controls, as President Nixon's chief economic policymaker, George Schultz, was known to have, the people controlled will also be unenthusiastic, and the effectiveness of the controls will flag. There are also equity considerations. For example, some critics felt that the control program favored big business, especially banking, by not restricting high profits or interest rates, and favored big pressure groups.

THE 1974–1975 RECESSION[12]

As this section is written, it appears that the recession of 1974–1975 will be substantially moderated by 1976. The 1974–1975 recession featured a greater contraction of output and was of longer duration than any of the four previous recessions since 1950. The 1974–1975 recession also differed from the earlier recessions in terms of causal forces. All the other previous recessions since 1950 were preceded by, and accompanied for a time by, periods of pronounced monetary restraint (relative to the trend rate of money growth). By contrast, the 1974–1975 downturn was preceded, and accompanied for a time, by stimulative monetary and fiscal actions.[13]

Some of the confusion and complexity of the 1974–1975 recession could be eliminated if the period from 1973 to 1975 is divided into two stages. The first stage of the recession, which began in the late fall of 1973, was largely a response to constraints placed on aggregate supply. In particular, our economy's ability to produce was diminished by unfavorable weather, increased

---

[12]This section draws heavily on Arthur F. Burns, "The Current Recession in Perspective," *Monthly Review*, Federal Reserve Bank of Atlanta (June, 1975), pp. 94–99, and Norman N. Bowsher, "Two Stages to the Current Recession," *Review*, Federal Reserve Bank of St. Louis (June, 1975), pp. 2–8.

[13]Fear of continuing "double-digit" inflation led the Fed to raise its discount rate in 1974 and 1975 to about 7½ percent from the 4½–5½ percent level which prevailed from 1971 to 1973 and led it to slow markedly the growth rate of the money supply beginning in the second quarter of 1974.

energy costs, increased environmental and safety costs, devaluation of the dollar, and price and wage controls. The second stage of the recession, which began in the early fall of 1974, reflected in addition a reduction in aggregate demand. In a very real sense, the deep and prolonged 1973–1975 contraction was, in effect, two recessions. Improvements in both the supply and the demand side were instrumental in our recovery. Elimination of wage and price controls and the existence of more normal weather were important factors in reducing our supply constraints. Sizable federal deficits, and the money creation incurred in financing them, along with a decided upturn in consumer confidence, were significant in perking up aggregate demand.

The 1974–1975 recession can also be viewed as a culmination of a long economic cycle. There have been numerous long economic cycles combining two or more ordinary business cycles. There were such long waves from 1879 to 1894, 1894 to 1908, 1908 to 1921, and 1921 to 1933. While these long cycles differ in a number of ways, they have one important common factor—each culminated in an economic decline of more than average intensity.

The long cycle that, as this is written, appears to be approaching its natural end may be dated somewhere from 1958 to 1961. The upward movement was checked briefly in 1967 and interrupted more severely in 1970. However, the sustained upward trend of the economy every year from 1961 to 1971—measured in terms of annual total employment, disposable personal income, or personal consumption expenditures—ended in 1974. Thus, the unemployment rate of 5.2 percent in January, 1974, became 9.2 percent by May, 1975.

THE FUTURE

Where do we go from here? The immediate outlook for the mid-1970s is bleak. It is ironic that the controls were eliminated at the very time when the inflation rate had reached a new peak in 1974. And through all of 1974 prices continued to increase. The best guesstimate of economists as this is written is that, short of some Draconian austerity measures by the administration, it will be 1976 to 1980 before we have any reasonable hope of truly getting both inflation and unemployment under control, although we should have some modest increases in real output (real *GNP*) before then.

A number of specific actions have been proposed, some of which may be implemented by the time you are reading this, to improve our economy. They include lower taxes for the poor, higher taxes for the rich, public monitoring of wage-price behavior in key sectors of the economy, adoption of a Brazilian-style program of indexation in which all components of income are tied to a price index,[14] stricter control over the money supply by the Fed, elimination

[14]As a comprehensive measure, indexing, which is not a solution to inflation but a palliative, is not as practical in a democracy as in a dictatorship. There are already 60 million people who are indexed through future payments from Social Security. There are some 5½ million people who have a collective bargaining contract which has an indexing clause in it. Variable interest rates are being sold presently. For an interesting analysis of the costs and benefits of indexing, as well as some positive proposals, see *Essays on Inflation and Indexation*, Domestic Affairs Study 24 (Washington: American Enterprise Institute, October, 1974), especially Ch. 2 by Milton Friedman and Ch. 3 by William Fellner. Note that the widespread use of an indexation, escalator, or "tabular standard" clause is not new or untried, going back to at least 1707.

of restrictive and anticompetitive practices in agriculture and other industries, an overhaul of tax and expenditure procedures and fiscal programs, attempts to increase productivity and efficiency, attempts to increase capacity and remove bottlenecks, stimulation of market competition, attempts to increase government efficiency and economy, attempts to break world-wide supply bottlenecks, a governmental role as an "employer of last resort," etc. It is unlikely that any of the radical proposals involving fundamental change will be introduced for some time. President Ford's earliest economic proposals were quite moderate in posture. What he proposed in October, 1974, was a mild placebo for the economy's inflation and unemployment pains which included: a tax surcharge of 5 percent for one year on corporate taxes and on a portion of personal income taxes paid by taxpayers whose income was above a certain level; an increase of the investment tax credit from 7 to 10 percent and permission for corporations to deduct the dividend paid on preferred stock; a two-pronged program to extend unemployment insurance benefits by 13 weeks and create additional public service jobs whenever unemployment exceeded 6 percent nationally; the provision of $3 billion for mortgage purchases to finance about 100,000 houses; more vigorous enforcement of the prevailing antitrust laws; an attempt to balance the budget by cutting out or delaying programs; removal of all remaining acreage limitations on rice, peanuts, and cotton and allocation of all fertilizer supplies to enable farmers "to produce to full capacity"; and a number of voluntary suggestions mainly aimed at reducing our energy consumption and expanding our energy production. In addition to his proposals to Congress, President Ford appealed to every American to "grow more, waste less" and "drive less, heat less" to help increase food supplies, lower prices, and save scarce fuel supplies.

Unless the American zeitgeist has changed radically since the early 1970s, such exhortations are unlikely to have a substantial impact. Moreover, before they became law, Congress or President Ford vetoed some of these proposals and offered still other bland alternatives. For instance, by early 1975 President Ford wanted a modest tax decrease (tax rebate) instead of an increase and an energy program aimed at inhibiting demand and eliciting the supply of domestic energy.

This much is clear: Given the new problem of cost-push inflation and stagflation, an incomes policy is needed to supplement monetary and fiscal policy to give our economy a better Phillips Curve.[15] But the unsolved problem of modern economics is to get an agreement as to just what form an incomes policy should take.

SUMMARY AND CONCLUSION

The year 1971 started and the year 1974 ended a great new experiment—peacetime direct controls on prices and wages. While the various phases and

---

[15]You will recall that the Phillips Curve depicts the tradeoff between inflation and unemployment by its position in the short run and by its induced shiftings in the long run. Unfortunately, cost-push inflation has led to stagflation in which traditional anti-inflation measures only result in unemployment and stagnation.

freezes programs may have had some short-run success, their long-run value in stopping stagflation is in doubt. Some extreme monetarists, such as Professor Milton Friedman, feel this result was inevitable since they believe the long-run Phillips Curve is vertical. This means that any reduction in unemployment below the structurally given "natural" rate of unemployment which is achieved now is inexorably at the expense of more unemployment in the long-run future. They believe that in the short run policymakers can temporarily achieve below-natural unemployment rates only by continually stepping up the inflation rate. Eventually they feel the piper has to be paid. Most economists do not share these monetarists' strong, pessimistic view of the Phillips Curve relationship.

A number of economists besides the extreme monetarists question the efficacy of direct controls. In 1973, the last full year of direct controls, the U.S. economy was characterized by the following: inflation was acute; skilled labor markets were tightened; physical capacity was strained; foreign oil was embargoed; productivity growth slowed; food prices rose sharply (the "kitchen crunch"); fiscal and monetary policies were less expansive; money markets were squeezed; exchange-market turmoil required central bank cooperation and intervention; etc. Although most direct controls went off in April of 1974, the stagflation problem worsened in 1974. By 1975 the U.S. economy was in a recession more severe than any since 1950. This recession was brought on by both flagging aggregate supply and aggregate demand. The administration was confronted with three problems: unemployment, inflation, and the economy's vulnerability to oil embargoes.

At this time there is no general concensus as to which incomes policy, along with the old time religion of monetary and fiscal policy, will give our economy a better Phillips Curve. However, there is concensus that inflation has to be curbed, for it is, in the words of news broadcaster Eric Sevareid, ". . . an acid bath against the cement that holds the economy together."

Discussion Questions

1. Give a brief historical sketch of the five different incomes policies utilized under the Economic Stabilization Act from August, 1971, to April, 1974.
2. How did Phase III differ from Phase II?
3. Do you agree with the 1974 President's Council of Economic Advisers that "the effect of the control's program on the rate of inflation . . . cannot be known with certainty either today or ever"? Explain.
4. Discuss the five major factors in the collapse of wage-price controls in 1974.
5. What type of programs can you suggest for abating stagflation?

PART 7
International
Banking

Chapter 26   Balance of International Payments

In this chapter we shall focus on the transactions that occur between countries as a result of international economic relations. International economic relations involve the movement of goods and services, people, and capital across national political boundaries. To understand these economic and financial transactions, one must first understand the economic basis for international trade, which represents the heart and fundamental content of international economic relations.

ECONOMIC BASIS OF INTERNATIONAL TRADE

Geographic specialization increases efficiency and output just as occupational specialization does. Geographic specialization, based on differences in productive capacities, leads to differences in comparative costs. These cost differences provide the basis for mutually advantageous international (or interregional) trade. Thus, the basis of trade among regions within the same country and among different countries is the same—the comparative economic advantages which each region and country has in the production of particular goods and services.

A region or country will have a comparative advantage in the production of those particular goods and services which its soil, climate, topography, natural resources, labor supply, and capital supply are relatively best suited to produce. For example, within the U.S., Florida and California have a comparative advantage in citrus fruits, the Plains states in grain and pork, and the North Central and North Eastern states in heavy manufactures. Internationally, the U.S. at one time had a comparative advantage in some heavy manufactured goods; Canada in wheat and wood pulp; Japan in textiles, steel, and toys; Australia in wool; and France in wines and perfumes.

More generally, a country will tend to have a comparative advantage in those goods and services which require in their production a large proportion of those productive factors which are relatively abundant in that country, for the greater the relative abundance of any productive factor, the cheaper will be its price (cost to firms) and therefore the cheaper will be the products using large amounts of that factor. Thus, since the U.S. is a capital-abundant and labor-scarce country, manufactured goods are relatively cheaper than hand-made goods (such as toys, lace, and pottery). Argentina is a land-abundant and capital-scarce country and therefore has a comparative advantage in beef and wheat.

Under free and competitive international economic relations, each country tends to specialize in and export those goods and services in which it has comparative advantages and to import those goods and services in which it has comparative disadvantages (i.e., in which other countries have comparative advantages). This is called the *law of comparative advantage*.

By engaging in international trade according to the law of comparative advantage, a country gains a reduction in its social opportunity cost. This occurs for the following reason. The social opportunity cost of imports is the exports required to pay for the imports. If the resources used to produce exports are less than the resources that would be required to produce at home the goods and services imported, there is a net social economic gain.

If countries specialize and trade in accordance with the law of comparative advantage, goods and services that are imported will be less costly to society than if they were produced at home. However, the fact that trade reduces the social opportunity costs does not mean that each country necessarily has more of all goods. Each country may have a smaller physical volume for domestic consumption of the commodities in which it has a comparative advantage. Canada, for example, may have less wheat but more cloth after trade than compared to its no-trade, autarky position. But it can be demonstrated that the gain from more cloth more than compensates Canada for the loss of wheat. Moreover, the combined amount of all goods consumed can possibly be greater for each country from the employment of a given amount of resources with trade than without it. Whether it will depends upon the country's preference pattern (i.e., on its social indifference curve).[1]

Another benefit of international trade is the greater variety and wider choice of products made available. Trade also has the related benefit of offering greater (foreign) competition to producers operating in monopolistic domestic markets. Stated broadly, the gains from international trade result from allocating resources in the economically most efficient manner. No region or country can achieve an optimal allocation of its scarce resources in economic isolation from other regions or countries.

UNITED STATES BALANCE OF PAYMENTS

Exports and imports are ordinarily the most important types of business requiring international settlement. There are, however, many other such

---

[1]While the source of the gain from trade is a lowering of the social opportunity cost, the share of the gain accruing to any one country is a function of the terms of trade which, in turn, depends upon the rate of exchange. The more favorable a country's terms of trade and therefore its exchange rate, the more is its share of the gains from trade.

transactions. Instead of buying French exports we may travel to France and buy goods there. Payment is the same, however—currency and bank balances must be exchanged at some point. Likewise, our hotel bills abroad, rail fare, guide hire, and other services will ordinarily have to be paid in the foreign currency rather than in dollars. Any interest or dividends we owe to foreigners, if not paid in their currency, will have to be converted by them into their currency before they can use the funds in their own country.

We may conveniently set down a summary list of all the economic and financial transactions during a period that give foreigners claims upon us and those that give us claims upon them. Such a table showing international payments and receipts is called the *balance of international payments of the United States*. The two sets of claims will necessarily and always be equal. In this respect the balance of payments is like any balance sheet in that debits must equal credits. At the same time it somewhat resembles a profit and loss statement, for it is a record of what has happened over a period of time.

It is useful to define precisely what is meant by a "debit" or a "credit" since balance of payments accounting does differ somewhat from other types of accounting. As good a rule of thumb as any is that debits (credits), if settled by cash, would create a cash outflow (inflow). Put differently, a balance of payments debit (credit) is any international transaction which gives rise to a claim for payment (receipt) against (for) a resident of a country. Thus, for example, imports, gifts made, assets acquired, or liabilities reduced create cash outflows if settled by cash, whereas exports, gifts received, assets given up, and liabilities incurred create cash inflows if handled by cash. Whether an item may or may not in fact be handled through an actual cash payment or receipt is immaterial. Our test refers to an imaginary thought process—viz., if settled by cash—and not to an actual exchange of money. Thus, there is nothing paradoxical about the acquisition of a short-term asset (a cash outflow) being counted as a debit.

Suppose an American receives wine from France. It may have been a gift, but that does not matter. Using the above test, it is clear that wine or any commodity coming into a country gives rise to a claim for payment, so it is a debit in the U.S. balance of payments. (The actual cash payment, if the wine is an import, is not the debit, for that is a different transaction.) Any commodity or service coming into a country is a debit, whether payment is made or not. Similarly, a capital outflow, such as an American resident purchasing stocks and bonds from a nonresident, would be a debit in the U.S. balance of payments since the imaginary cash payment would go out of the U.S. (The nonresident need not be selling foreign securities. If a person from France sold some American Telephone and Telegraph stock to an American, that would still be a debit.) In general, all capital outflows out of the U.S. are debit transactions in our balance of payments.

Viewed in this sense, a country's balance of payments can be thought of as a sources (receipts) and uses (payments) of funds statement. There are three sources of funds for a country: (1) its current receipts; (2) any increase in its liabilities (borrowing); or (3) any decrease in its assets (sales of assets, or dishoarding). Similarly, there are three uses of funds for a country: (1) its current payments; (2) any decrease in its liabilities (debt repayment); or (3) any increase in its assets, whether in the form of larger financial assets (lending), real assets (investment), or money (hoarding). Clearly the sum of a country's sources of funds must equal the sum of its uses of funds. As discussed below, the existence of disequilibrium depends on whether it is defined in terms of the trade balance (merchandise exports relative to imports), the basic balance (current account plus long-run securities transactions), the official reserves transactions balance (basic balance plus private purchases of short-run securities), the net liquidity balance (official reserve transactions balance minus foreign private net purchases of short-run U.S. securities), etc.

It is important to distinguish the balance of payments from the balance of trade, which relates only to exports and imports of merchandise. The balance of payments includes these items—which usually do not balance out—and, in addition, all the other receipts and expenditures that, together with merchandise transactions, must necessarily balance. In other words, the balance of payments includes flows of goods and services and evidences of debts and ownership.

The five major items in any balance of payments are: (1) goods and services, which include commodity and service imports and exports; (2) net remittances and pensions, that is, private gifts, grants, and pensions; (3) net government transactions, which include loans, grants, etc.; (4) net capital movements; and (5) accommodating, balancing, compensating, or financing transactions, that is, gold and international reserves, including the "paper gold" or Special Drawing Rights created in 1969 and first issued in 1970 and allocated by the International Monetary Fund to be used only by central banks and governments in settling international debts. Whenever the total credits for the autonomous items in (1) through (4) are not sufficient to cover the total debits, as has been the case in the United States for the last 20 years, the United States can sell gold (or whatever foreign monies it possesses), give up its SDRs, or convince foreign countries to hold dollar balances (i.e., make "accommodating" capital inflows) which represent credits to the United States. Disequilibrium in a balance of payments is often defined as existing when a nation's autonomous receipts are not sufficient to meet its autonomous payments. (Balance of payments disequilibrium is discussed in more detail below.)

We shall divide the United States balance of payments statements into two major categories, listed in Table 26-1 as Section I and Section II.[2] All these transactions either gave us claims on the rest of the world or gave the rest of the world claims on us. We shall show in the left hand column the

[2]The official statements no longer show this division. There may be some advantages to running everything together, but it provides a poor basis for an introductory explanation. We have omitted some of the detail and some of the balances and have attempted to clarify the statement by using more than one column to record credit items, debit items, and balances. Otherwise, Table 26-1 shows the balance of payments in the same sequence and terminology as it was officially reported in 1974. Since the format is repeatedly modified, this table will probably not correspond exactly with later statements.

Table 26-1   United States Balance of Payments, 1974
(In millions of dollars)

	Credit Items	Debit Items	Balances
Section I			
Goods and services			
Exports..	97,081		
Imports...		102,962	
Military transactions (net).......................		2,099	
Travel and transportation (net)..............		2,435	
Investment income (net)..........................	9,679		
From U.S. direct investment abroad........	18,240		
From other U.S. investment abroad........	7,703		
From foreign investment in U.S.		16,263	
Other services (net)................................	3,926		
	(126,950)	(123,759)	
1. Net on goods and services (= sum of preceding)	3,191		
2. Remittances, pensions, and other transfers (net).........		1,775	
3. U.S. government grants (excluding military).................		5,441	
A. Balance on Current Account................			− 4,025
(= sum of 1 + 2 + 3)			
Long-term U.S. government capital flow (net)..............	1,043		
Long-term private capital flow (net)............................		7,598	
4. Total, long-term capital (net)		6,555	
B. Balance on Current Account and Long Term			
Capital (= sum of A + 4)..			−10,580
5. Nonliquid short-term private capital flow (net)		12,955	
6. Allocations of Special Drawing Rights (SDRs)..............	0*		
7. Errors and omissions (net)...	5,197		
C. NET LIQUIDITY BALANCE...			−18,338
(= sum of B + 5 + 6 + 7)			
Section II			
Liquid private claims of U.S...		5,464	
Liquid U.S. private liabilities..	15,732		
8. Net liquid private capital flow.......................................	10,268		
D. OFFICIAL RESERVE			
TRANSACTIONS BALANCE...............................			− 8,070
(= sum of C + 8)			
Financed by changes in:			
9. Nonliquid liabilities to foreign official agencies,			
reported by U.S. government and U.S. commer-			
cial banks (net)	655		
10. Liquid liabilities to foreign official agencies**	8,849		
U.S. official reserve assets (net):			
11. Gold	0		
12. Special Drawing Rights at IMF.....................................		172	
13. Convertible currencies...	3		
14. Gold tranche positions in IMF		1,265	
	(9,507)	(1,437)	
NET..			+ 8,070

Source: Adapted from *Federal Reserve Bulletin* (June, 1975), p. A58. This statement was termed "preliminary." Details may not add to totals because of rounding.
*There was no SDR allocation for 1973 or 1974.
**This is "liquid liabilities to foreign official agencies," 8,253, and "other readily marketable liabilities to foreign official agencies," 596.

claims of the United States, or credit items. The second column shows claims on the United States acquired by foreigners, or debit items.

Goods and Services (Item 1)

The largest and most obvious items under this heading are exports and imports of goods and services. Our exports gave us a credit balance of almost $97.1 billion. This was more than offset by our imports of nearly $103.0 billion. The U.S. trade balance (i.e., exports minus imports) has been positive throughout this century (up to 1974) except for 1971, 1972, and 1974.

In addition to these transactions, several others are reported here. Military transactions overseas, like our imports, resulted in the consumption of $2,099 million of foreign goods and services by Americans. The only difference was that consumption was on the spot rather than in this country. American tourists were also consuming foreign goods and services, and many American shippers were using foreign shipping lines. On balance, foreigners supplied more goods and services for American tourists and shippers than we provided for them, so we owed them the difference, $2,435 million. On the other hand, the dividends and interest we received from past American investment abroad were more than 50 percent larger than the dividends and interest we owed foreigners for their investments in this country.[3]

After the credit entry for other services that we provided for foreigners, we find the net effect of all these transactions left us with a claim of $3,191 million on the rest of the world (Item 1). To this point, we had supplied foreigners with more than we received from them.

Remittances and Pensions (Item 2)

If someone living in one country sends money to relatives or friends in another country, this remittance must be included for a complete reckoning of international claims. So must pensions paid by individuals or firms in one country to residents of another. The net difference between such claims of and those upon the country is entered in the balance of payments statement.

For the United States this entry always appears as a debit item, because most of these payments are made by residents of this country. One reason is that we have more immigrants. These people, with families and friends left behind, are especially likely to send remittances abroad. Also, incomes are higher in this country. It is easier here to set aside money for others elsewhere; besides, extra funds are generally more urgently needed in other countries than they are in the United States. Consequently, on balance these payments always result in an increase in the claims *against* the United States.

---

[3]"Direct investment" is investment in the national income terminology, such as factories built abroad by American firms. "Other" investment refers to American-held securities of foreign corporations.

United States Government Grants (Item 3)

Government grants exclude military transactions, accounted for earlier in the statement. Government foreign aid grants are included. These, like private gifts, result in debits in our balance of payments statement.

On first thought, some are surprised to find that our gifts are debit items. It seems, somehow, as though we should be credited for our generosity rather than owe for it. But think about this a moment. Suppose you send a $50 draft to a relative or friend overseas. Possibly that person would hold it, unspent. In this case the draft becomes a $50 claim on the United States economy. More likely, the recipient either buys $50 of American goods or sells the draft to someone else who wants American goods or services. In either case, $50 of our exports (which are credit items) will be financed by your gift. The point is, something must offset all our credit items, for somehow foreigners must have received the purchasing power to buy our goods and services. Their ability to buy from us is created by their sales to us (which also includes their sales of gold) and by our loans to them. It also results from our gifts to them. After all, what is a gift but a loan that is not repaid?

The relationship is perhaps even more clear in the case of government aid programs. Suppose the United States government provides $5 billion of foreign aid. That $5 billion is a part of the goods and services we are supplying to foreign countries. It might include, among other things, a million bushels of wheat, a thousand tractors, and five thousand generators. We have not "sent them money," although we may have placed money at their disposal with which they purchased the goods they required. We include these government grants not to increase the total but to complete the record. If the figure were omitted, the statement would not balance. We would have supplied them with $5 billion of goods and services for which they neither paid us with their own goods and services nor owed us. We are merely acknowledging that state of affairs in our listing of the foreign aid grant.

By now we have taken into account all international transactions other than capital movements and transfers of reserves. The net total of all these, called the "balance on current account" (Item A), gave the rest of the world claims of $4,025 million on us in 1974.

Long-Term Capital (Item 4)

The principle involved in the recording of capital movements is simple enough. We know that anything that gives foreigners a money claim on us appears as a debit item in our balance of payments. In the case of our merchandise imports, this is quite obvious. In the case of capital movements, our purchase of foreign securities (or import of securities) similarly results in a debit item. Any of their own securities that we return (export) to foreigners adds to our credit items. By the same logic, their purchase (our export) of American securities is a credit entry in our balance of payments, and if we later repurchase (import) some of these securities, our balance of payments is debited accordingly.[4] Also, foreigners invest directly in this country by building branch factories here, and we similarly invest directly abroad.

The official balance of payments statements present this information in some detail. Here we show only the net total of these movements of private capital, a debit of $7,598 million. Also included in the $6,555 million total of long-term capital movements is a credit of $1,043 million, the result of the United States government capital flow.[5]

Nonliquid Short-Term Private Capital (Item 5)

Short-term private capital movements are divided into two categories (Items 5 and 8). The first group pertains to short-term capital that is unlikely to change hands. The present holder will continue to hold it and probably will renew it upon maturity. This nonliquid short-term capital is recorded here in Section 1, next to the movements of long-term capital. We imported $12,955 million more of such claims than we exported.

Allocations of Special Drawing Rights (Item 6)

The International Monetary Fund (see Chapter 27) in 1974 allocated no Special Drawing Rights to the United States. SDRs are created by the IMF on agreed occasions and are allocated to members in accordance with an accepted formula—but without any payment by them—to serve as a supplement to their international monetary reserves. These SDRs may be transferred somewhat like gold from one national monetary authority to another. (In truth, SDRs have limitations in their usage that give them a bit less general acceptability than gold.) In 1970, 1971, and 1972 the IMF allocated the United States $867 million, $717 million, and $710 million of SDRs respectively, which helped us finance our deficits in those years. These SDRs were equivalent to the line of credit a bank creates for a customer. In those years, SDRs were shown as credit items since they gave us a claim on the rest of the world. In 1973 as well as 1974 the U.S. received no allocation of SDRs. (See also Item 12.)

---

[4]The import of securities is called *capital export*. Although this terminology may at first glance appear confusing, it is really logical. (Study again the discussion of gifts.) When the United States imports securities, these items are normally offset by part of our exports, in the first heading; or perhaps by part of foreigners' nonliquid short-term claims against us (in Item 5); or by part of the change in our liquid liabilities to foreigners (in Section II). These are the capital which is being exported. The imported securities are simply what we receive in payment for our capital exports.

[5]At this point, as a result of repeated refinement and redefinition of terms by statisticians, the original clarity and basic simplicity of the statement begins to suffer. The individual items (not shown in Table 26-1) include government purchases of foreign long-term securities, repurchases of United States long-term securities from foreign holders, and international repayments of long-term loans. They also include a portion of the Treasury's short-term liabilities, but only to firms other than official reserve agencies. (See Item 9 for nonliquid short-term liabilities to official agencies.) Moreover, although short-term, they will presumably be renewed, rather than repaid, at maturity. They are therefore classified as "nonliquid" and included with the long-term capital movements. The justification claimed is that, although nominally short-term obligations, they are essentially long-term items, and the statement will be more meaningful if they are listed with the long-term capital movements.

Errors and Omissions (Item 7)

An entry for errors and omissions is necessary due to imperfections in the data and lack of complete information respecting prices. Also, some transactions are not officially recorded.

Net Liquidity Balance (Item C)

The sum of everything we have set down in Section I is a net increase of $18,338 million in our liabilities to the rest of the world. It will necessarily be offset, of course, by subsequent entries, but since these are of a basically different nature, we include them in a separate section.

In Section II we record the changes in our liquid liabilities to overseas creditors (Items 8 and 10), changes in our nonliquid short-term liabilities to foreign official agencies (Item 9), and changes in our official reserve assets (Items 11–14). Since the total of all transactions listed in Section I resulted in a United States deficit of $18,338 million, we must have had either an equal credit as a result of these short-term capital movements or a change in our official reserves.

Liquid Private Capital Flows (Item 8)

For years foreign banks and other private holders were increasing their short-term claims against American firms. This credit item for the United States, resulting from our export of short-term securities and bank deposits, was then offsetting part of the deficit shown in the liquidity balance, reducing the amount to be settled by official reserve transactions. It was at about this time that the government statisticians revised the format of the balance of payments statement. They pointed out that *private* holdings of dollars were not really a meaningful claim on United States reserve assets but were acquired to facilitate international trade and finance. Only the *official* holdings of liquid claims were a real claim on United States reserves and therefore the measure to watch. Accordingly, the statisticians subtracted the credit on short-term capital movements from the liquidity balance and came forward with a balance (Item D) that they called the "official reserve transactions balance." In 1968, when our liquid private debt increased by $3.2 billion, the deficit of $1.6 billion on the net liquidity balance was converted into a surplus of $1.6 billion on the official reserve transactions balance.[6] In 1969 a net liquidity deficit of $6.1 billion was transformed into a $2.7 billion surplus on official reserve transactions. Apologists for our repeated balance of payments deficits on the customary basis of the liquidity balance could argue that these deficits were not especially important and that the significant (and much more favorable) item was the balance on official reserve transactions.

---

[6]The net liquidity balance was introduced in 1971. The difference between it and the former liquidity balance is in the treatment of private liquid assets, changes in which formerly appeared in Section I rather than in Section II. Balance of payments statements for years prior to 1971 have now been restated to show the net liquidity balance.

Unfortunately this window dressing eventually was confronted with a much greater deficit on the official reserve balance than on the older liquidity basis. In 1970 the liquid capital flow reversed abruptly, with a reduction of over $6 billion in liquid liabilities of American firms to private foreign banks and other foreign firms. The resulting debit added to the deficit of $3.85 billion shown in the net liquidity balance and pushed the deficit on the official reserve balance to nearly $10 billion. In 1974, as shown in Table 26-1, there was another abrupt change in magnitude, and the resulting net liquid private capital flow credit of approximately $10.3 billion (Item 8), when added to the deficit of approximately $18.3 billion shown in the net liquidity balance (Item C), reduced the deficit on the official reserve transactions balance (Item D) to only $8.1 billion.

Financing the Deficit (Items 9–14)

The first two of the last six entries show the changes in our liabilities to foreign official agencies (governments, central banks, and the International Monetary Fund). We increased slightly our nonliquid liabilities but increased substantially our liquid liabilities by over $8.8 billion. At the same time we turned over a minuscule amount of our reserves held in convertible currencies (Item 13), had no change in our gold reserves (Item 11), and actually gained some gold or foreign currency in our IMF position (Item 14). However, as opposed to 1973 but similar to 1970, 1971, and 1972, our loss of reserves was (temporarily) reduced by using $172 million (Item 12) of the SDRs allocated to us in previous years (Item 6). By this combination of an increase of $9.5 billion in our liabilities to foreign official agencies (Items 9 and 10) and a net increase of $1.4 billion in our official reserves of gold and convertible currencies (Items 11–14), we obtained a credit of $8.1 billion, offsetting the deficit on the official reserve transactions balance (Item D).

1973–1974 Summary

The U.S. trade balance (as is shown in Table 27-1 in the next chapter) had deficits in 1971 (− $2.7 billion), 1972 (− $7.0 billion), and 1974 (− $5.9 billion), and a slight surplus in 1973 (+ $0.5). What major events transpired during 1973 and 1974 that influenced our schedule? In 1973 there were massive short-run capital outflows in January and February, a dollar devaluation on February 12, a floating of major currencies against the dollar followed by continued dollar depreciation until early July, a strengthening in the international price of the dollar, and a substantial increase in foreign direct investment in the United States. During 1973 the rates of increase of agricultural commodity exports and petroleum product imports significantly exceeded the rates of increase of total exports and imports respectively. In 1974 U.S. international transactions were affected by the higher oil prices resulting from the operation of a foreign oil cartel (OPEC); a slight reduction in the inflow of foreign capital for direct investment in the U.S.; the depreciation of the U.S.

dollar against most major currencies; high, though differing, rates of inflation here and abroad; cyclical downturns in many countries; and the removal of controls on capital flows. Excluding petroleum imports from the general merchandise exports to the OPEC, U.S. exports exceeded imports by $5 billion in 1974. Certainly the major factor explaining the 1973 trade surplus was the considerably improved price competition for U.S. products in world markets, which was aided by the reduction in the international price of the dollar through the 1971 and 1973 devaluations. However, the most significant international development during the 1973–1974 period was the decision of many nations to institute flexible exchange rates for reasons of national self-interest. The details of all these events are taken up in the next chapter. In addition, Table 27-1 in the next chapter shows the numerical values for several alternative measures of equilibrium from 1960 to 1974.

Except for the modest trade balance surplus in 1973 there were deficits in the trade balance, the basic balance, the net liquidity balance, and the official reserve transactions (settlements) balance every year from 1971 to 1974. These deficits were significantly smaller in 1973 than in 1971 and 1972, but returned to high levels once again in 1974.

PURPOSE OF BALANCE OF PAYMENTS STATEMENTS

Total credits in the balance of payments statement equal total debits. This definitional identity is, in itself, as meaningless as similar tautologies we have studied earlier—for example, $MV = PO$ or $S = I$. With any such statement the significant thing is how the quantities are equated. If two products or two sums are always and inevitably equal to each other, then necessarily some quantity or quantities must be dependent variables, adjusting to changes elsewhere in such a way as to preserve the equality. Also, some quantity or quantities must be independent, or the two totals would never change. Which are the independent (autonomous), which are the dependent (accommodating or compensating) variables?

Balance of payments statements are not mere pieces of bookkeeping, tidy arrangements of figures to prove, every year, that total debits again equal total credits. Rather they are useful in showing at a glance the results of a nation's international transactions. Often they indicate the need for a change in policies. The United States, for example, could hardly dismiss its heavy and almost continuous gold losses from 1956 to 1971 with the airy generalization that they didn't matter since, after all, total debits equaled total credits. Unless we were eventually to lose all our gold, we had either to place an embargo on gold or remove the causes of the drain, which are elsewhere in the balance of payments. In 1971 the United States announced it was suspending the convertibility of the dollar into primary reserves, though the dollar remained convertible into other currencies in the foreign exchange market. In 1973 the U.S. averred that it would no longer sell its gold holdings to foreign nations, meaning that gold no longer could play an important part in settling balance of payments accounts (see Item 11 in Table 26-1).

On any part of the balance of payments statement, debits will probably not equal credits. But a credit balance in one area must be offset by a debit balance elsewhere. Since the credit balances must be exactly offset by debit balances so that their algebraic sum is zero, we see again that some part of the statement must refer to residuals, or dependent variables. Essentially, this part is Section II in Table 26-1.

Alternative Measures of Equilibrium

While our discussion of balance of payments equilibrium will focus on liquidity and reserves, alternative measures of equilibrium are useful for some purposes. It is always critical to determine what is aimed for in a definition of balance of payments before deciding which of the alternative measures is most useful. Since the balance of payments always must balance, a particular way of measuring a deficit constitutes a definition. Any definition, such as a deficit, must be judged on its usefulness and its link with theory to the relevant problem. For instance, a definition of equilibrium that is appropriate for most countries may not be right for a key-currency country (perhaps also serving as a reserve or financial center) such as the United States. Thus, for example, years of U.S. "deficits" did not necessarily indicate an excess supply of dollars on the foreign exchange market.[7] Similarly, in view of current international monetary practices, a deficit doesn't have the same significance in a world of floating exchange rates (even "dirty" floats when some official intervention prevails) as with fixed rates. The Council of Economic Advisers put it this way:

> In a world characterized by the managed floating of exchange rates, measurement of the overall balance of payments has become less important. In a fixed exchange rate world, one of the major functions of overall measures of the balance of payments was to signal to policy makers when a given exchange rate had become untenable. To the extent that exchange rates are allowed to adjust automatically in response to payments imbalances, it is no longer necessary to communicate the desirability of an exchange rate adjustment to the policy maker. Of course, to the extent that exchange rates remain constrained by official intervention in the foreign exchange market, the balance of payments numbers will continue to indicate when such intervention may need to be relaxed.[8]

In a nutshell, equilibrium in the balance of payments is an elusive concept. What else might one consider besides reserves and liquidity in defining equilibrium? There are several factors. Is there unemployment? What is the

---

[7]Charles P. Kindleberger, "Measuring Equilibrium in the Balance of Payments," *Journal of Political Economy* (November–December, 1969), pp. 873–891. Also see John Pipenger, "Balance of Payments Deficits: Measurement and Interpretation," *Review* of the Federal Reserve Bank of St. Louis (November, 1973), pp. 6–14; Donald S. Kemp, "Balance of Payments Concepts—What Do They Really Mean?" *Review* of the Federal Reserve Bank of St. Louis (July, 1975), pp. 14–23; and Patricia Hagan Kuwayawa, "Measuring the United States Balance of Payments," *Monthly Review* of the Federal Reserve Bank of New York (August, 1975), pp. 183–194.

[8]*Economic Report of the President*, 1974 (Washington: U.S. Government Printing Office, February, 1974), p. 193.

relevant time period (i.e., is the equilibrium static or dynamic)? Is the economy open or does it impose import restrictions, exchange controls, and tariffs? Is the economy continually taking care of seeds of change such as inventories, lack of confidence in the government, and excess liquidity? Certainly an economy which achieved equilibrium in terms of reserves by suffering substantial unemployment or imposing restrictive quotas would have attained a costly victory. Thus, for example, Charles P. Kindleberger, in attempting to account for many of these factors, defines equilibrium as "that state of the balance of payments over the relevant time period which makes it possible to sustain an open economy without severe unemployment on a continuing basis."[9] Moreover, it has been further suggested that, on a wider view of the social sciences, equilibrium in the balance of payments should be combined with political stability into a more generalized equilibrium. While this is an interesting proposal, it is not yet possible. Indeed, our present balance of payments techniques are not sophisticated enough to handle even the additional economic considerations described above. For this reason we shall continue to emphasize traditional reserve and liquidity approaches to equilibrium.

Balance of Payments Deficits and Surpluses

The net liquidity balance in Section I of Table 26-1 is what is often referred to as the balance of payments deficit or surplus. Obviously it is a deficit (or surplus) on only part of the balance of payments, but it is the part that presumably includes the independent variables. It is the amount that must be offset by changes in one or another or all the remaining components—short-term private capital movements, short-term credit transactions between the government and foreign official agencies, and reserves.

As already indicated, we may, if we choose, concentrate our attention on the deficit (or surplus) in what the statisticians have labeled the official reserve transactions balance. The two balances will not be the same, of course. In fact, one may show a deficit, the other a surplus. They pertain to different things, and there is no reason to suppose that one is more correct or even more significant than the other. Both are useful. The point to understand is that, whether we are studying the net liquidity balance or the official reserve transactions balance, we are recognizing that it will be exactly equal to the sum of the individual items following it. Because the net liquidity balance showed a deficit of $18.3 billion, and there was a net credit of $10.3 billion on liquid private capital flows (for a total deficit of roughly $8.1 billion), there was necessarily a credit of approximately $8.1 billion as a result of the changes in short-term liabilities and official reserves as shown in the last six entries.

It is true, of course, that we can make the same statements with respect to the balance on current account and the balance on current account and

---

[9]Charles P. Kindleberger, *International Economics* (rev. ed.; Homewood: Richard D. Irwin, 1958), pp. 469–485. In his fifth edition (Irwin, 1973), Chapters 18 and 23, he discusses the problems of defining balance of payments equilibrium in a considerably less detailed manner.

long-term capital. Moreover, for some purposes these balances are more suitable than the other balances. The balance on current account reflects current trade patterns and the normal net flow of gifts and grants from the United States. The balance on current account and long-term capital is often referred to as the "basic" balance. Except for the government items, it is responsive to long-run market forces and differentials. It attempts to measure the extent to which the "long-run" or "underlying" demand for foreign exchange has exceeded the "long-run" or "underlying" supply of foreign exchange during the period.[10] Neither of these balances, however, has quite the significance as the two we have previously discussed. The difference is this. All the transactions listed in Section I and totaled in the net liquidity balance may be considered independent variables. The transactions listed in Section II are mostly the dependent variables, bringing the statement as a whole into balance. Usually the deficit in the net liquidity balance is offset partly by an increase in United States private liquid liabilities and partly by a loss of reserves.

Significance of Surplus or Deficit

The usefulness of this segregation of changes in liquid foreign capital, special government transfers, and changes in monetary reserves is unquestionable. All other items in the balance of payments tend to be autonomously determined. The items in Section II, by contrast, are for the most part residuals, or dependent variables.

The distinction is this. We do not export *because* we have received or shipped gold. We do not insure foreign cargoes *because* foreigners have larger or smaller bank deposits in New York. We do not build factories abroad *because* a foreign government is paying off a loan it received from the United States government. Rather, our exports depend upon the quality and price of our goods; the demand for our services depends upon our ability to perform those services and our charges for them; and our direct investment overseas depends upon the outlook for profits. Likewise, gifts, private or public, are not determined by the amount of gold or short-term balances held, nor are purchases of foreign securities or real estate ordinarily governed by such considerations. All these transactions are autonomous, primarily the result of market forces.

On the other hand, unless the sum of all the preceding transactions does, purely by chance, balance out, the result has to be a change in the items in Section II. A deficit in Section I may be offset by gold sales, by borrowing

---

[10]Deficits and surpluses in the basic balance do not necessarily imply a disequilibrium which requires corrective action by the government. The *Economic Report of the President*, 1974 (Washington: U.S. Government Printing Office, February, 1974), pp. 194–195, explains why: "To the extent that changes in net private holdings of short-term foreign assets are voluntary, the existence of a surplus or deficit need not imply that it is either undesirable or unsustainable. When such changes are quite large in any one year, however, there is a strong possibility that the change is a temporary response to unusual circumstances, such as differences in interest rates. In these cases, some governments might be inclined to intervene to moderate the exchange rate fluctuations which could result from large shifts in short-term foreign assets."

from the International Monetary Fund, or by drawing against foreign deposits held by the Treasury. To the extent that it is offset by none of these types of payments, it must appear as an increase in the short-term debt owed to foreigners. These categories in Section II are the dependent (accommodating or compensating) variables, bringing the statement into balance.

It would be not only an oversimplification but a serious error to suppose that every item in Section II must always be a dependent variable. Specifically, there will sometimes be large movements of short-term liquid private capital that increase the deficit on the net liquidity balance rather than offset part of it. Foreign businesses may ordinarily accept dollar balances in settlement of part of their claims, resulting in a credit for Item 8. At other times they may have less confidence in the dollar and withdraw their dollar balances. At such times the change in liquid private capital is clearly an independent item. It might be due perhaps to speculation, perhaps to changes in bank regulations, or perhaps to something else. In any case, it certainly is then not primarily a direct result of changes in Section I.

Disequilibrium of Balance of Payments—Deficits and Surpluses

For the few countries that are major gold producers, gold is as normal an export item as are cotton, oil, and wheat for other nations. These gold producers may be able to maintain or increase their own gold reserves at the same time that they exchange millions of dollars of gold for the goods and services of other countries.

With the exception of gold-producing nations, no nation can sustain large balance of payments deficits indefinitely.[11] We can rule out special government transactions, for although they are helpful in an emergency, they could hardly be a permanent component of a nation's balance of payments; the government could not indefinitely borrow money abroad. If the deficits are settled by gold sales, the nation's gold stock will eventually be exhausted.[12] If they are settled by increases in the short-term debt owed to foreigners, the constantly increasing mass of current liabilities must eventually lead to a loss of confidence in the nation's currency and to a run on its gold, if gold is available. In whatever way these persistent deficits might be settled from one year to the next, sooner or later there would have to be changes to remove the causes of the deficits.

Continuous balance of payments surpluses are equally impossible. For one thing, surpluses for some nations are impossible unless there are deficits for others; we have just seen that, with insignificant exception, nations cannot

---

[11]This again points out the usefulness for separate definitions for different countries, since transactions that are autonomous for one country might be accommodating for another. But in using the same definition for all countries, with a growing volume of international transactions, key currency countries should be added to the gold producers as countries that can sustain "deficits" more or less indefinitely, as long as the deficits are not too large.

[12]While the role of gold has so diminished in importance in international trade since 1971 that it has even dropped out of all of the accounts, it is used here for convenience. The term "paper gold" or SDRs could be used instead in the interest of realism.

have permanent deficits. Besides, even if the surplus of one country were the result of temporary but consecutive deficits of many other countries, the constant surplus would not be an equilibrium position. If the surplus was settled in gold, the nation would eventually hold all the monetary gold of the world; if settled in short-term claims on other countries, the nation would find, sooner or later, that these assets were excessive in relation to any use to which they could be put. Even if it were possible, the constant surplus could be undesirable.[13] The country's productive capital and therefore its productive capacity would be greater or alternatively its domestic consumption would be greater and therefore its living standard higher—if the country were not exchanging so much of its production for gold and claims on foreigners. Thus, either a continuous deficit or continuous surplus is an indication of a disequilibrium in a nation's balance of payments.

Disequilibrium—Unilateral Transfers

However, there may also be a disequilibrium even though there is no deficit or surplus. The deficit (or surplus) may have been avoided because of foreign aid or excessive long-term loans from (or to) other countries.

Consider the case of the underdeveloped and famine-ridden little country, Povertania. Povertania has no gold to sell, no SDRs, no reserves held in convertible currencies, no gold tranche position at the IMF to draw on, and there is no foreign demand for Povertania's bank deposits and short-term securities, since it would be difficult to convert them into other currencies and there is little for which to exchange them in Povertania. A balance of payments deficit is, therefore, impossible. However, to help Povertania raise its standard of living, the United States government is providing $100 million of aid every year. Because of these gifts from the United States, Povertania is importing more than it exports. But Povertania cannot go on forever receiving aid from the United States or any other country.[14] To the extent that the gifts are a significant item, Povertania's balance of payments is in disequilibrium.

Disequilibrium—Abnormal Long-Term Capital Movements

Perhaps, instead of giving Povertania free goods, Americans are making long-term investments in that country. These imports of long-term capital do not necessarily indicate a disequilibrium situation. Povertania might continue for 50 years or more to borrow on long term. If the borrowing is not excessive and if it leads to industrialization, Povertania's productivity will rise and eventually it can begin to retire the debt. But if the borrowing is regularly abnormally large, then there is a disequilibrium in the balance of payments.

---

[13]A constant surplus is not always undesirable, provided "constant" doesn't mean "forever." Consider the Arab oil-producing countries for example. The petrodollars can't be spent currently and shouldn't be, since a flow of income will be needed when the oil runs out. And there may be good reasons why they (now) favor short-term to long-term investment.

[14]While Povertania may be unjustified in counting on U.S. aid until doomsday, the aid may be no more transitory than, say, the market for its major export.

Unlike deficits, surpluses, and gifts, the concept of abnormal capital movements is relative rather than absolute. What constitutes a normal flow will depend upon the country concerned. Wealthy and highly developed countries will tend to invest considerable sums abroad, where the marginal efficiency of capital is likely to be higher. Also, the investment makes it easier for them to continue to have temporarily a favorable balance of trade. Eventually such a country may be in the position of England before World War II, receiving a great deal of income from overseas investments. The less highly industrialized nations will tend, on balance, to be importers of long-term capital (exporters of securities), as was the United States during the 19th century. They exchange securities in their companies for goods supplied by the investing nations. But (assuming no balance of payments deficits or surpluses) in all such cases we may properly speak of a balance of payments equilibrium, for the capital movements are normal.

If, however, the long-term capital movements are clearly larger than are warranted by long-run economic considerations, they must finally decline as the rate of return on capital is brought into line with that elsewhere. Then, unless the disequilibrium in the balance of payments has been corrected, it will show up in a different form—either as a deficit (or surplus) or as gifts.

In summary, a nation's balance of payments is said to be in disequilibrium if there are persistently (1) substantial deficits (or, alternatively, surpluses); (2) large gifts; or (3) abnormally large long-term capital movements. These entries are not the causes but merely the symptoms of the disequilibrium.

Balance of Payments and Foreign Exchange

Finally, in discussing the components of the balance of payments, we have mentioned the transactions that give rise to the supply of and demand for foreign exchange. The billions of dollars of goods and services that we export and all our other claims on foreigners must be paid for either in foreign currencies or in dollars. Also, we must pay them for the goods, services, securities, and so forth that they send to us. We may pay them in dollars or in their own currencies, using bills of exchange (drafts) for this purpose.

When we pay someone in this country, there is no problem. The individual finds it as convenient to receive dollar drafts as we find it convenient to use dollars for payment. But foreigners have, ordinarily, as little direct use for our dollars as we have for their currencies.[15] If the terms of the particular contract permit us to make payment in dollar drafts, the creditor abroad will convert the dollars into francs, pesos, or pounds by selling the dollars to a countryman who needs them to pay a creditor in this country. Also, if we are committed to make payment with drafts in terms of the foreign currency, then we must buy those drafts from someone in this country who has foreign bank balances to sell.

---

[15]As is pointed out in Chapter 27, this condition is subject to change as the result of two conflicting factors. The Eurodollar market has (over)expanded quite a bit in the last few years. On the other hand, with floating exchange rates, monetary authorities have less use for dollars.

Just as there is a cluster of interest rates determined by the demand and supply for money, there is also a cluster of exchange rates determined by the demand and supply for foreign exchange. Foreign exchange rates are prices of national monetary units expressed in terms of other national monetary units. In the next chapter the determinants of these exchange rates are taken up.

TECHNIQUE OF MAKING INTERNATIONAL PAYMENTS

The details of the mechanics of international payments are a little complex sometimes. The basic principle is simple.[16] Countries are able to settle what they owe (the debit items) by using the amounts that they are owed (the credits). Total debits always equal total credits.

When a business in New York purchases goods from a shipper in London, arrangements must somehow be made for the buyer to make payment in dollars, the seller to receive payment in pounds. One of the parties to the transaction must be concerned with foreign exchange. It may be either. The contract will naturally have to specify a price in terms of some currency, but there is no more reason that it be in dollars than in pounds. (In fact, it might be in still a third currency, although such an arrangement is more common in the case of transactions between countries neither of whose currencies is widely used internationally.) Both buyer and seller would prefer payment to be in their own currency. Hence, the currency specified will depend to some extent upon the relative bargaining power of the parties as well as by the acceptability of the two currencies. In the old gold standard days it made little difference which currency was used. By contrast, for a number of years after World War II most American businesses selling abroad insisted on being paid in dollars. They avoided payment in currencies that were more subject to devaluation. Also, foreign nations were having trouble exporting to us, so the demand for their currencies was weak. Americans who accepted such currencies had trouble finding buyers for them. Importers abroad were often unable to secure dollars, so regardless of how much money they held in terms of their own currencies, they could not buy American goods. Because of the strength of the dollar, foreign exporters would have been glad to receive dollar drafts in payment; but in many cases it really made little difference to them whether we paid them in dollars or in their own currency because they ordinarily were required to sell to their government part or all of the dollar exchange they received.

In the case of an American import, if payment is made in dollars, the English exporter sells the dollars to an English bank for pounds. If payment is made in pounds, the American buys pounds from an American bank. The banks are in a position to purchase and supply foreign exchange through their branches abroad and their relations with foreign correspondent banks as well as by the fact that they are selling to one customer the foreign balances they have bought from another customer.

---

[16]In the examples that follow we shall ignore governmental restrictions on foreign exchange, taking them up in Chapter 27.

SUMMARY AND CONCLUSION

Geographic specialization based on differences in productive capabilities leads to differences in comparative costs. These cost differences provide the basis for mutually beneficial trade. The law of comparative advantage emphasizes that each trade area tends to specialize in and export the commodities in which it has a relative or comparative advantage—based on its relative factor endowments—and to import those commodities in which it has a comparative disadvantage. The gains from trade include a reduction in the social opportunity costs, a greater variety of products, and greater competition in domestic markets.

The balance of payments is a record of a country's international economic relations over a given period, usually one year. It includes the value of all transactions between domestic and foreign residents over that year. Following double-entry bookkeeping procedures, the total payments and total receipts must necessarily be equal since the monetary value of every transaction is recorded both as a debit and a credit. Since it is impossible for the entire balance of payments to show either a deficit or a surplus, equilibrium analysis compares selected items. Where the line is drawn depends on how useful this procedure is in analyzing some relevant problem through economic theory. Probably the three most commonly used measurements are: (1) the "basic" balance (current account plus long-term capital transactions), (2) the net liquidity balance, and (3) the official reserve transactions balance. In general, a deficit disequilibrium in the balance of payments may be arrested or eliminated entirely by exchange rate depreciation, price and income deflation, exchange rate controls, or structural adjustments in the allocation of resources.

Exchange rates are prices of foreign currencies expressed in units of the domestic currency. In free and open competition, exchange rates are determined by the aggregate quantity of foreign exchange demanded and the quantity supplied.

Discussion Questions

1. What is "comparative advantage"?
2. What can a region or country hope to gain by engaging in trade according to the law of comparative advantage?
3. What are the three sources (receipts) and three uses (payments) found in a country's balance of payments?
4. Which 2 of the 14 numbered entries in the United States balance of payments would you expect to be affected by our purchase of Volkswagens from Germany? Briefly explain.
5. Since the money is a claim, regardless of who holds it, does it make any difference to the United States balance of payments whether you return from a weekend in Nassau with a $100 bill still in your pocket or instead spend it in Nassau?

6. In the balance of payments statement we show both exports and imports in Section I. Does this imply that there is no interdependence between them, since items in Section I are supposed to be the independent variables and items in Section II the resultant and balancing variables? Explain.

7. Which of the following transactions will result in a credit on the U.S. balance of payments? Briefly explain why or why not in each case.
   a. Gold sales by the U.S. Treasury
   b. Dividends paid on foreign securities owned by Americans
   c. Foreign grants by the U.S. govenment
   d. Remittances sent by people in this country to friends or relatives abroad

8. Classify each of the following as a debit or credit in the United States balance of payments:
   a. United States Army expenditures for local services in Viet Nam
   b. American purchases of British sports cars
   c. Loans to Europe made by United States investors
   d. The construction of factories abroad by American firms
   e. Dividends on foreign securities owned by Americans

9. Item 8 in the balance of payments, net liquid private capital flow, might, as a dependent variable, be changed by an increase in our exports (other items in Section I remaining unchanged). Or, as an independent variable, it might be changed as a result of foreigners' distrust of the dollar. Explain.

10. Discuss what additional factors might be considered in analyzing balance of payments equilibrium besides the liquidity and reserve balances.

11. Is it possible:
    a. To have a deficit in the balance of payments?
    b. For the balance of payments to be in disequilibrium? Explain.

Chapter 27   International Monetary Problems and Attempted Solutions

Foreign trade, like other economic activity, is dynamic. We would hardly expect international trade relationships to be constant from one decade to another. Some degree of change would be natural as new products appear, the demand for other products disappears, tariffs and other controls are tightened or relaxed, markets are expanded or contracted, and the patterns of international trade are constantly being adapted to changing conditions.

Since 1914 international trade has been disrupted by a succession of tremendous forces. World War I caused violent dislocations. During the 1920s the world attempted to rebuild its international trade, but progress was interrupted by the worldwide Depression. World War II followed before international trade had recovered from the effects of the Depression.

If these changes had come slowly and gradually, adjustment to them would not have been so difficult. They came so fast that it was impossible to adjust fully to one before new problems had been created by the next.

THE INTERNATIONAL FINANCIAL ROLE OF THE UNITED STATES

An underdeveloped but rapidly expanding nation, rich in natural resources, is likely to become a debtor nation to build up more quickly its stock of capital. If this program is successful, the nation will eventually no longer need to borrow from foreign countries and can begin to reduce its debts. It may finally become a creditor nation, lending to other nations to help them increase their capital or for other purposes.

The United States as a Borrowing Nation

Until the last quarter of the 19th century, the United States had ordinarily an unfavorable balance of trade. This excess of our imports over our exports indicated that, attracted by high yields, Europeans were lending and investing in this country. The goods we received and for which we gave no goods in exchange aided our industrial development. We were a debtor nation; England, Germany, France, and other European nations were our creditors.

The United States as a Mature Debtor Nation

After 1873 we usually had a favorable trade balance. We no longer needed to borrow heavily abroad, and the favorable balance of trade permitted us to pay interest and dividends to the foreigners who had earlier supplied us with capital. According to the logic of the balance of international payments, discussed in Chapter 26, the interest and dividends to foreigners for which the paying nation is debited must be offset by credits of equal amounts; merchandise exports are an important source of credits.

The United States as a Creditor Nation

As a result of World War I we found our international role suddenly reversed. From being a great debtor nation we became, almost overnight, one of the world's greatest creditor nations. Most of our own securities had been repatriated. The warring nations of Europe had required their citizens to sell to the respective governments American Securities, dollar balances, and other claims on Americans. The governments then sold the securities in this country to obtain dollars with which to purchase munitions. At the same time they borrowed heavily in this country to buy still more of our goods.

As a creditor nation, the United States might have accepted during the 1920s a surplus of imports of goods and services to permit other nations to service and perhaps reduce their debts to us. Instead, we raised our tariff rates. At the same time we illogically complained because the European nations were asking that the war debts be forgotten. We tended to emphasize ethics and moral responsibility and to ignore the elementary fact that there was not enough gold in the world to permit foreigners to pay us by shipping gold. We forgot also that the debt had been incurred by our shipping not gold but goods. The simplest, most obvious way for them to have paid us would have been by shipping us more goods than we shipped them. The dollar balances they might thus have acquired would have been available to meet interest charges and repay the principal.

We continued to stress, however, the alleged desirability of a favorable balance of trade for the United States. Despite our creditor position such a balance was possible as long as we continued our new peacetime policy of lending abroad. The credit resulting from our favorable trade balance was offset by the debits from the new foreign loans and investments that we were making. As a result of our imports of their securities (and of some other transactions, including expenditures of American tourists), we were able to continue shipping foreigners more goods than they shipped to us. We were lending them money to buy our goods and service debts they already owed us. If this was not financial perpetual motion, it was at least pretty fancy juggling. It certainly did nothing to solve the dilemma of how we could expect to continue indefinitely selling to foreign nations more goods than we bought from them, increasing their indebtedness to us, and at the same time expect them to repay their debts.

In 1930 the Depression temporarily ended most of our foreign lending,[1] so that foreigners were unable to continue buying as much of our goods as before. Nor could they maintain their previous level of imports by increasing their own exports, for in 1930 we raised our tariff barriers still higher for the admitted purpose not of increasing revenues but of shutting out many imports. In 1932 and 1933 the dollar volume of our foreign trade had declined to one third the average level of the 1925–1929 period.

DETERMINATION OF EXCHANGE RATES OF PAPER CURRENCIES

When nations are on the gold standard, the rates at which their currencies are exchangeable are basically determined by the gold contents of the respective currencies. The gold standard was generally abandoned during the 1930s. When nations are no longer on the gold standard, what determines the rates of foreign exchange? In the absence of government regulation, what decides whether 5, 30, or some other number of units of a nation's currency shall be required to purchase one unit of the currency of some other country? Basically it is a question of demand and supply. We shall explore this a little more critically.

Purchasing Power Parity Theory

The most generally accepted explanation of the supply and demand relationship between currencies is that currencies will tend to be exchanged on the basis of their comparative purchasing power. If $1 will buy about 5 times as much as a franc, the price of the franc should be around $.20, the price of the dollar around 5 francs. If the franc is selling for much less than $.20 when the franc will buy about one fifth as much as the dollar, American imports from France will tend to increase (and American exports to France decrease). This trade situation will increase the demand for francs in the United States (and decrease the American supply of francs). Consequently, in a free market the price of francs, in dollars, will tend to rise.

There are admittedly difficulties with this concept, the most important being that it is impossible to measure accurately the comparative purchasing power of two or more currencies in the way in which we need to measure it. In each country there may be an excellently constructed index of wholesale prices. But these indexes will include commodities that do not affect the country's international trade. There may be a great increase in the price of certain commodities that a nation produces for domestic use only and that are not produced elsewhere. Such price increases might cause marked changes in the nation's index of wholesale prices but at the same time have little or no effect on foreign exchange rates.

---

[1]Not until 1958 did foreign nations again sell as many bonds in this country as they did in the 1920s.

We cannot solve the problem by computing indexes of the prices of only those goods that do enter international trade, for the question of what goods will be exported and imported is in part decided by the level of exchange rates, the very thing we are trying to explain. We know that as the value of a nation's currency falls in terms of foreign currencies the country will be able to export some goods which previously it could not profitably sell abroad, and it will no longer import some types of goods. Comparison of cost indexes based on only the commodities that are internationally traded would show that, whatever the existing level of exchange rates might be, it would be an equilibrium rate.

Balance of Payments Theory

As we know, merchandise is not the only item which involves foreign exchange. A nation may be borrowing or lending abroad; services, tourist expenditures, interest and dividends, and other items create a supply of and demand for foreign exchange. Consequently, some suggest that exchange rates can better be explained by considering the entire balance of payments rather than by purchasing power parity. Within limits this position appears logical. Not just our merchandise exports, but all the credit items in our balance of international payments add to our supply of foreign exchange; all the debit items, not imports alone, constitute our demand for foreign exchange.

There is some danger that the balance of payments theory of exchange rates may be used to justify tariffs, exchange controls, and other restrictive policies. Some nations have claimed their international situation to be such that a permanent balance of payments deficit would be unavoidable without government intervention. They may be correct in deciding that such intervention is preferable to permitting a deflation of the domestic cost-price structure or to reconciling themselves to a smaller volume of imports and a lower standard of living. But it is doubtful that a nation will find it impossible to have its balance of payments deficit corrected, no matter what adjustments are made by free market forces.

We may agree that the balance of payments theory offers a more complete explanation of the level of foreign exchange rates at any particular time than does the purchasing power parity theory. Still, the magnitude of some of the items in the balance of payments depends upon the respective purchasing powers of the two currencies. Fundamentally, exchange rates depend upon the comparative purchasing power of the currencies in question.

Fluctuations in Exchange Rates

When nations are on paper standards, exchange rates may fluctuate over a wide range. Although the general value of a nation's currency in terms of other currencies might be determined, as shown above, by its comparative purchasing power or by the nature of its balance of international payments, foreign exchange rates at any particular moment might be much above or much below the normal level.

Suppose most of a nation's exports were made at one season of the year. Its supply of foreign exchange would at that time be large, and foreign exchange would tend to sell at a low price. If, later in the year, most of its imports were brought in, foreign exchange would then tend to rise in price due to the increased demand.

Seasonal variations of this kind would, however, tend to be minimized simply because they were regular and predictable. Suppose the franc regularly tended to rise in the summer. If everyone recognized that this was a purely seasonal phenomenon, this rise would be checked by sales of spot exchange, offset by purchases of forward exchange; that is, New York bankers would sell francs for immediate delivery, borrowing abroad the necessary francs to cover these sales or liquidating short-term investments they held abroad. They would simultaneously contract to buy francs to be available in three or four months. Their purpose in this arbitrage transaction would be to sell francs at a higher price than they paid.

Note that forward exchange is paid for, not when the contract is made, but at the later date, when the buyers actually receive the foreign exchange. They are not paying for it months ahead of time, so they are not making a short-term investment; they are not buying it at a discount. Consequently, the price for forward exchange normally will be the same as spot exchange, or it may be a little higher or a little lower, depending on supply and demand conditions and upon interest rates in both countries.

In the particular case above, the summer price of spot exchange would tend to be somewhat higher than the summer price of forward exchange, since we are assuming that the market recognizes that the demand for francs will be less by fall. But the bankers' arbitrage operation will minimize the price differential. They do have an interest cost, explicit or implicit, in Paris. However, the spot sales of francs simultaneously increase their lending power in New York. If interest rates are the same in Paris and New York, the arbitrage has no net interest cost, and as long as there remains any difference between the prices of spot and forward exchange, the bankers can continue making their risk-free profit. But as their operations increase the demand for October francs and simultaneously increase the supply of July francs, the two prices would tend to come together.[2]

On the other hand, speculation often intensifies fluctuations due to uncertainties. If speculators believe a foreign currency is likely to fall in value, they sell it short, temporarily borrowing abroad and hoping to buy it at a lower price later. Such speculation tends to drive the price of the currency below what it would otherwise be. Likewise, speculators' purchases of foreign exchange may at other times tend to cause sudden and sharp increases in the price of foreign exchange. Impossible under the automatic gold standard, such gyrations of exchange rates can be highly unsettling.

---

[2]When francs are strong in New York, the dollar is weak in Paris. French bankers would simultaneously be buying dollars in the spot market and selling dollars in the forward market.

Need for Comparative Stability

Foreign trade would be almost impossible if rates were allowed to vary considerably from month to month and even from day to day, depending on speculative activity. If in 1936 you were placing a £ 10,000 order with a British exporter, you might possibly have been willing to take the risk that you would be required to pay somewhere between $39,800 and $40,200. You would probably not have cared to assume the risk that you might have to pay as much as $45,000 for your £ 10,000 order. Of course, you could have avoided the exchange risk by specifying that you would pay a certain number of dollars, but this would merely have transferred the risk to the Englishman. The exporter, similarly, might have been ready to accept the risk of receiving dollars that might be worth some amount between £ 9,950 and £ 10,050, but would probably have been unwilling to contract to receive a dollar sum that might be worth anywhere from £ 9,000 to £ 11,000, or perhaps still more or even less.

Stabilization Funds

Since the day-to-day stability of exchange rates once guaranteed by the general use of some form of the gold standard no longer existed after 1931, governments attempted by various means to stabilize rates by administrative action. The simplest, least arbitrary device of this kind is the stabilization fund, used by the Treasury or perhaps the central bank for the purchase and sale of foreign exchange. The function of such a fund is to help commercial banks even out seasonal and other temporary fluctuations. At a time of year, for example, when imports greatly exceed exports, the Treasury may offer foreign exchange, increasing the effective supply and preventing a rise in its price (a fall in the exchange value of domestic currency). When exports exceed imports, the Treasury may prevent a fall in the price of foreign exchange by buying foreign exchange temporarily in oversupply. Most governments have been operating stabilization funds for more than 35 years.

It must be emphasized that the purpose of such funds is, as the name indicates, merely to stabilize, not determine, exchange rates. They are in strong contrast to the policies considered below.

INTERNATIONAL MONETARY POLICIES DURING THE DEPRESSION

Almost every nation attempted during the 1930s to relieve the problem of unemployment by shutting out the import of goods from abroad. Most nations were trying, at the same time, to increase their exports, hoping to increase their gold reserves and employment. A single nation might successfully carry out such a policy, but at a time when almost every country wants an export surplus, there can be little trade.

As one nation after another rapidly abandoned the old, more or less automatic, gold standard and the gold exchange standard, two principal types of monetary policies evolved. Some nations devalued their currencies, either by formally redefining the gold content of their currency, as in the case of the United States, or by allowing their currency, no longer redeemed in gold, to fall to a lower level in terms of currencies still tied to gold. Other nations instituted systems of exchange control. Eventually many nations were to use both techniques.

Devaluation

A nation can usually expect to increase its exports by lowering the price of its goods to foreigners. One way to accomplish this is by lowering its whole domestic cost-price structure. Such a reduction in costs is slow, difficult, and painful; it is likely to be accompanied by unemployment and bankruptcies. The other alternative is more inviting. By devaluing its currency a nation may make its goods immediately cheaper to foreigners without depressing the domestic price level. After the devaluation of the dollar in 1934, for example, the franc, formerly worth about $.04, was suddenly worth nearly $.07. The French importer who might wish to buy dollars to pay for American goods had been paying about 25 francs for a dollar. After our devaluation, the importer could buy a dollar for about 15 francs. Until France devalued again (in 1936), the French importer found the United States an excellent market in which to buy. At the same time that we were encouraging exports, we were discouraging imports. An order for goods worth 100,000 francs that previously would have cost an American importer about $4,000 cost about $7,000 after the dollar was devalued.

Although many nations found it necessary to devalue their currencies during the 1930s, devaluation is not a reliable device for overcoming depression.

1. It can be effective only if other nations with which the devaluing nation trades do not devalue their currencies in turn.
2. It tends to force the burden of adjustment onto other countries. As has occasionally been remarked, in a period of worldwide depression it is a device for exporting unemployment. For exactly this reason devaluation by one important country to help increase employment is apt frequently to be offset by a wave of devaluations by other nations.
3. It weakens public confidence in the currency devalued.

Exchange Controls

Germany was the principal nation that did not devalue its currency during the Depression. Only a decade earlier Germany had experienced a disastrous inflation. There was some fear that currency devaluation might lead to another such inflation. Also, the German government wanted to be able to import cheaply to aid its program of industrial and military development. As long as the mark was not devalued, devaluations elsewhere would reduce the cost, in German marks, of imports.

At the same time, since Germany would be able to export only with difficulty to countries that had devalued, its supply of foreign exchange would be limited. Anyone in Germany who owned dollars, pounds, or other devalued currencies, or who had claims payable in any such currencies, might have used the foreign exchange to buy foreign goods that could have been sold in Germany at a high profit. The German government nationalized foreign exchange, however. It purchased all foreign exchange held by German concerns and individuals and was thereafter the only official buyer or seller of foreign exchange. Some other nations followed similar policies but regulated exchange transactions less elaborately.

Simultaneously, Germany blocked sums due to foreigners. The debts were still outstanding, but there was no easy way to get the funds out of Germany. If, as a result of previous exports to Germany or investment in German securities, you were owed RM10,000 ($4,000 at the official exchange rate), there would have been, before Germany blocked such accounts, a number of ways by which you might have received payment. Possibly, although not usually, you might have received gold. Ordinarily you would have received a check drawn on an American bank and payable in dollars. Your German debtor would have bought the dollars from a bank. Or again, you might have received payment in Reichsmarks, which you could have sold to your bank. Or you might possibly have taken RM10,000 of German exports and sold them in this country for dollars.

None of these possibilities existed after foreign balances in Germany were blocked. To whatever extent Germany might be able to sell goods abroad, the German government was determined that such sales should be used to finance current imports, not the repayment of old debts.[3]

With its monopoly of foreign exchange, the German government worked out an elaborate system of exchange rates, adapted to its domestic and international policies. Marks were sold at various prices, depending upon the uses to which they were to be put. Since Germany was undertaking a rearmament program, it wanted, as far as possible, to utilize domestic production to supply the armed forces rather than increase exports. Therefore, anyone who wished to buy marks to purchase German goods ordinarily paid a high rate for them. On the other hand, people could travel cheaply in Germany since they could buy special travel-marks at a little over half the price of the official mark. Germany regarded tourist expenditures as a particularly desirable source of foreign exchange, since a large part of such expenditures would be for services that could be provided without reducing German production in other areas. The hotel accommodations, railroad seats, and river boats on the Rhine would be available anyway, whether or not tourists occupied them.

Germany also developed a system of so-called *Aski marks*. German importers paid marks into special Aski accounts. The marks in these accounts

---

[3]Also, as a result of blocking the sums owed to foreigners, Germany was in a good position to bargain. Payments might be made if the creditors agreed to a scaling down of the interest and principal, or the creditors might be allowed to use their marks to purchase long-term securities. Furthermore, as the market value of these blocked claims fell abroad, the German government was able to buy some of them at a discount in foreign countries and present them at home for payment in full. Foreign creditors often preferred partial payment to no payment, and part of German's foreign debt was wiped out.

were then available for the purchase, by foreigners, of goods to be exported to the same countries from which the imports had come. By making the Aski marks available at an attractively low price, Germany could arrange to export to those particular countries from which it was most anxious to import. Also, it could later use the same device to exploit countries that had come under its political control. They were required to purchase their marks at a high price, receiving few German imports in return for the exports they were obliged to provide for Germany.

In no other nation was there the same elaborate classification of foreign exchange rates. Some nations did, however, maintain two exchange rates— one official, the other free. At the official rate of exchange, the nation's exports would be expensive to foreigners. That rate was applicable to exports that were in great demand abroad. The foreign exchange that the government thus obtained at a low price was made available for imports that the government specially favored. Many concerns could not export if foreigners were paying the official rate for the nation's currency. They were allowed to sell in the free market their receipts of foreign exchange, and they received a higher price than they would have received from the government, buying at the official rate. This higher priced foreign exchange was purchased by importers who could not obtain foreign exchange from the government.

DEVALUATION AND EXCHANGE CONTROL AFTER WORLD WAR II TO COUNTER A BALANCE OF PAYMENTS DEFICIT

The stresses imposed by World War II resulted for a number of years in a continued dependence upon policies of devaluation and exchange controls, used for different reasons and purposes than during the 1930s. Most nations emerged from the war with their economies dislocated and in some cases with their industries largely destroyed. They were in a poor competitive situation, particularly with respect to the United States. At the same time they were heavily in debt abroad, especially to the United States.

To finance current imports, foreign governments were obliged to monopolize and ration foreign exchange. England, which had relied principally on the relatively mild device of a stabilization fund during the 1930s, was forced to block sterling, just as Germany had earlier blocked marks. Otherwise England's exports might have been used to reduce debts rather than pay for current imports urgently needed for the reconstruction of England's economy and for the maintenance of its living standard. England wanted to pay its debts eventually, but could not possibly pay them immediately.

Disequilibrium at the Existing Level of Exchange Rates

England found, as did many other countries, that there was a substantial disequilibrium in its balance of payments as a result of World War II. It had lost most of its overseas investments, which it sold during the war to buy munitions abroad. It was no longer receiving much interest and dividends from overseas with which it had formerly financed much of its imports, and, as noted above, its manufacturers were unable to compete aggressively in international markets due to the war-ravaged condition of British industry. As long as England attempted to maintain the existing level of exchange rates, it found that unusually large British exports of gold and securities would be required, as well as gifts from other nations, principally the United States.

To correct a disequilibrium in its balance of payments, a nation does not necessarily have to turn an unfavorable trade balance into a favorable balance. Imports and exports are only two of the current items in the balance of payments. However, they are usually the most important items. To correct the disequilibrium, it will almost certainly be necessary to reduce imports, increase exports, or both. Equilibrium will be restored when, without unilateral government transfers, any imbalance on total current transactions is offset by normal long-term capital movements. At least four possible roads are open to a country that is losing its gold or must depend on gifts or excessive loans from other countries.

Fall in Prices

The traditional course, and a generation ago the only course, was to permit a fall in the nation's price level. Under the 19th century type of gold standard, this tended to result automatically. Since today we recognize other alternatives, we question the need or wisdom of deflating prices. A fall in the price level is likely to be accompanied by large-scale unemployment, bankruptcies, and crises. In the face of such disturbances nations naturally attempt to avoid a drop in the price level and income and to reestablish and maintain an equilibrium by one of the alternative techniques introduced during the Depression—exchange controls and devaluation.

Exchange Controls

The government may establish a partial or complete monopoly of foreign exchange. However, disequilibrating factors may still be present. At the official rate the demand for foreign exchange usually exceeds the supply, since the purpose of the government's monopoly is to establish a lower price of foreign exchange (that is, a higher value for its own currency) than the price that would result in a free market. The government can do little about increasing the supply, although attempts have sometimes been made to stimulate exports by subsidies. Usually, however, the government attempts to reduce the demand for foreign exchange.

This may be done by outright rationing. Importers may be limited to some percentage of the amount of foreign exchange that they have had in earlier years. Or the rationing may be used as an instrument of political control, foreign exchange being supplied to those industries or even to those individuals in favor with the administration, other firms going without foreign exchange even if they are thereby forced into bankruptcy.

As either an alternative or a supplementary control, the government may also directly restrict imports. Tariffs are one means. Or import quotas may be set. Likewise, the government may require that licenses be obtained for all imports. By any of these means the government attempts to insure that the scarce foreign exchange will be used in ways that are of greatest benefit to the country rather than in ways that are of greatest profit to the importer. For example, licenses might be denied for the import of cosmetics and jewelry to conserve foreign exchange for the purchase of food, machinery, and essential raw materials.

Certainly such government management, or interference, is directly opposed to laissez-faire. We must look beyond the controls, however, and remember the basic reason the government imposes them. It is attempting to avoid the fall in income that is required to reduce the domestic price level to a point where the existing exchange rate can be maintained. The disequilibrium in its balance of payments can be overcome if the price level abroad rises, as may eventually happen; or if the domestic price level falls, which the nation is determined to avoid but which would normally occur under laissez-faire; or by a fall in the price of its currency in terms of other currencies. Also, possibly the nation may presently be able to increase its exports as a result of the introduction of new products or improved manufacturing and selling techniques, or the nation may be able to increase its credits from other items in the balance of payments. But if, while waiting for the disequilibrium to be corrected, the government is going to maintain both the domestic price level and the exchange rate, then there simply will not be enough foreign exchange. At the artificial level of exchange rates, the demand for foreign exchange will exceed the supply. This calls for rationing. If the shortage of foreign exchange is acute and if certain imports are urgently needed, the government will have to see to it that the scarce foreign exchange is used for purposes that are of greatest advantage to the nation.

Devaluation

Another principal remedy available to a nation faced with a persistent balance of payments deficit is to devalue its currency. By so doing it can, without immediately affecting its domestic price level, make its goods cheaper to foreigners and make imports more expensive. By this stimulus to exports and restriction on imports, the government may hope to increase the available amount of foreign exchange at the same time that it reduces the attractiveness of foreign exchange.

This solution may appear much simpler than the exchange controls just considered. After World War II a number of nations devalued, but for quite different reasons than 20 years or so earlier. After the war they had little unemployment, and prices were rising rather than falling. They devalued in an effort to obtain more foreign exchange, particularly dollars, by increasing their exports. They hoped to maintain or increase their imports, not reduce them.

Devaluation tends to improve the balance of trade and worsen the terms of trade of the country that devalues. In every instance, however, the results depend upon a complex interrelation of factors. It is at least theoretically possible that the terms of trade, as well as the balance of trade, might be improved. Or conceivably both might be worsened or possibly unaffected.

With Physical Volume of Trade Unchanged (Inelastic Demand for Exports and Imports). There would be no doubt about the effects if we could assume that after devaluation the physical volume of a country's imports and exports would remain just as they were before devaluation and that domestic prices would also remain unchanged. These assumptions are unrealistic in the extreme, but represent a limiting case that will help us understand the issues involved. For simplicity we shall assume a 50 percent devaluation.

Suppose that when the British devalued in 1967 they had reduced the value of the pound from $2.80 to $1.40. And suppose also that before devaluation the United States had been shipping to England 11,000 typewriters at $280 each and England had been shipping to us 1,000 sports cars at £1,000 each, and these were the only goods exchanged. England's exports would have been bringing in $2,800,000, but it would have been paying $3,080,000 for the typewriters. England would have an unfavorable balance of trade amounting to $280,000, or £100,000. After a 50 percent devaluation England's 1,000 cars, still selling at £1,000, would earn only $1,400,000. The 11,000 typewriters would still cost $3,080,000. Its unfavorable balance of trade would now have increased to $1,680,000, or £1,200,000 in terms of the devalued pound. Besides finding that its unfavorable balance of trade had multiplied alarmingly, England would find also that on the basis of the devalued pound it now received only 5 typewriters for each car exported, although formerly it received 10. As a result of devaluation, each car exported would bring in only half as many dollars, but the American goods would cost just as many dollars as before. (Or we may say, in terms of sterling, Great Britain's exports would be the same as they were before, but the imported typewriters would now cost twice as much in sterling as they did before devaluation.) However we look at it, we see that the terms of trade as well as the balance of trade would certainly have deteriorated for Great Britain.

With Dollar Value of Trade Unchanged (Unitary Elasticity of Dollar Demand). But now consider another conceivable extreme. Suppose that instead of the physical volume of trade remaining unchanged, it is the value of trade in terms of dollars that remains unchanged. We shall still suppose that in both countries the manufacturers do not change prices in terms of their own currencies. The United States continues to sell $3,080,000 of typewriters, represented as before by 11,000 machines. England continues to sell $2,800,000 of cars, but (still assuming a 50 percent devaluation) to earn that many dollars, it would now be shipping 2,000 cars instead of the earlier 1,000. As before, the terms of trade have shifted to England's disadvantage, but in this case the unfavorable balance remains at $280,000, as it was before devaluation. (In terms of sterling, the unfavorable balance would be twice as large as before.)

With Elastic Demand for Exports. It is most improbable that in practice either the physical volume or the money value of exports and imports would be the same after devaluation. As economists describe it, the first case would represent a perfectly inelastic demand, the second a demand curve of unitary elasticity. The value of Great Britain's automobile exports will increase if the demand for those cars is elastic, for by definition demand is elastic if total receipts rise as price falls.

After a 50 percent devaluation, if the British car is selling for the same price in pounds, it is selling for half its former dollar price. If the demand for British sports cars is elastic, so that dollar receipts increase as a result of the lower price in dollars, we may suppose that total sales rise to perhaps 3,000 units, selling for £3,000,000. If, at the same time, the British demand for typewriters is also elastic, imports of American typewriters will be reduced, since typewriters now cost twice as much in pounds as before devaluation. Where earlier England was buying 11,000 typewriters at £100, it will buy less than 5,500 at £200—if, to repeat, its demand for typewriters is elastic. Suppose it buys 4,000. It is spending £800,000 for them instead of the £1,100,000 it was willing to spend when it could buy them at £100. In short, with £3,000,000 of exports and £800,000 of imports, England now has a favorable trade balance of £2,200,000. In terms of dollars, it is now importing $1,120,000 and exporting $4,200,000, giving it $3,080,000 to use for other purposes, including debt service. However, it is still true, as in both the previous cases, that the terms of trade have moved against England. Regardless of the trade balance, it receives only 5 typewriters for each car it exports instead of 10, as before devaluation.

With Inelastic Supply of Exports. Let's consider another general possibility. So far we have assumed in each instance that the domestic manufacturer did not change the price. Technically, we have been assuming a supply that is perfectly elastic. Now to see the principle involved, we shall suppose that the British manufacturers decide to mark up the price of cars. This they will do if supply is inelastic. Perhaps nearly all their output is already being exported. If they are already operating near capacity, they may decide to raise their price by, perhaps, 50 percent. The car will still cost, in the United States, less than before devaluation. In spite of the increase in its London price (in sterling), it now sells in the United States for $2,100[4] instead of $2,800.[5] England might now sell around 1,400 cars at the new price of £1,500, a total of £2,100,000. If England is spending £800,000 to buy 4,000 typewriters, as we assumed in the previous paragraph, we find again that its balance of trade has improved since devaluation, although by a smaller amount. We note also that this time the devaluation has not resulted in so much damage to its terms of trade. England now receives 7½ typewriters for each car it exports.

With a Fall in the Price of Imports. Finally, what would be the result if the typewriter companies were so upset at losing their overseas market that they

---

[4]$1.40 × 1,500.
[5]$2.80 × 1,000.

drastically cut prices? Suppose manufacturers reduced the price to $210 in the attempt to maintain their sales volume. At $210, the typewriter will cost the British importer $210/$1.40, or £150. This is still much higher than the old price of $280/$2.80, or £100. In spite of the cut in the dollar price tag, we cannot expect to export 11,000 typewriters as in predevaluation, pre-price-cut days. Assume, however, that England does take 8,000 at the new price. These will cost £1,200,000. If at the same time it is selling us 1,400 cars for a total of £2,100,000, it has a favorable trade balance of £900,000, giving it $1,260,000 of dollar exchange that can be used for other purchases or purposes. This is quite an improvement over its original unfavorable balance of £100,000. How about the terms of trade? England is still receiving 10 typewriters for each car, as before devaluation. If it can raise the price of cars a little more without reducing its American sales—and remember, in spite of their having been marked up from £1,000 to £1,500, these cars are selling in the American market for $700 less than before devaluation—or if the dollar price of typewriters should be further reduced, the terms of trade as well as the balance of trade would be improved for England by its devaluation. This, of course, would be the ideal, if unlikely, result for a devaluing nation.

Summary. To sum up, we have seen that devaluation's effect upon a nation's balance of trade and terms of trade will depend upon, among other things, the elasticities of supply and demand of the country's imports and exports. Unfortunately these concepts are easier to define than measure. The analysis is useful in describing a simple price-quantity relationship when we are holding constant all other variables, including money income. But in real life there will be many imports and exports rather than only one of each. Also, a country will be trading with many countries rather than with only one. To make things still more confused, there will be complications from the reshuffling of factors of production; more factors will be demanded both by the producers whose exports are expanded and also by industries that begin to produce goods formerly imported. These changes will affect the whole cost-price structure, the flow of money income, and finally demand itself. Thus, nothing really remains constant. A scientific, precise measurement of elasticity is impossible. Although the final results of a devaluation demand upon these elasticities, they certainly cannot be predicted in advance. There are too many variables, uncertainties, and unknowns. Devaluation, when it appears inevitable, must be undertaken more hopefully than confidently.[6]

---

[6]By a different analysis, unrelated to elasticities, E. V. Morgan finds that devaluation is most likely to be successful when there is a high level of employment but no inflation in both the devaluing country and those nations with which it trades. At such times devaluation may be helpful in correcting price differentials or offsetting a decline in the demand for a nation's products. It is an acceptable means of combating a balance of payments deficit due to these causes, although it is generally discredited as a device for countering depression. (See "The Theory of Flexible Exchange Rates," *American Economic Review* [June, 1955], pp. 279–295).

In the trade literature, the Marshall-Lerner conditions state that depreciation will improve the balance of payments and appreciation worsen it if the sum of the elasticities of demand for a country's exports and of its demand for imports is greater than one. However, this condition is broadly correct only if the supply elasticities are relatively large and if the balance of payments is in equilibrium at the outset. See, e.g., Charles P. Kindleberger, *International Economics* (5th ed.; Homewood: Richard D. Irwin, 1973), pp. 328–336 and 493–500; and Franklin R. Root, *International Trade and Investment* (3d ed.; Cincinnati: South-Western Publishing Co., 1973), p. 244.

Devaluation is likely to be a temporary palliative rather than a fundamental cure, especially if the nation concerned is unwilling to halt inflation. In this respect it appears to offer no advantage over the various expedients of exchange control. By either line of action or by both, the government is attempting to keep prices from falling. Price rises are more easily tolerated, although they renew or intensify the problem. Prices are quite likely in the end to rise after devaluation, both in consequence of the stimulus given to income by the increase in exports and as a result of the higher price of imported goods. The latter is particularly important for countries that import much of their food and raw materials. The cost of living rises, wages go up, prices are marked higher, and the country finally may find that again it is confronted with a balance of payments deficit, and perhaps it again devalues its currency.

Structural Adjustments

Sometimes the sources of disequilibrium are structural maladjustments resulting from a shift in a country's comparative advantage, owing to a change in relative factor supplies, technological developments, changes in the pattern of international demand, etc. For instance, in the late 1950s and early 1960s part of the U.S. deficit disequilibrium was due to Western European countries' and Japan's rapid advances in manufacturing production, such as steel. In the early 1970s the U.S. and other oil-importing countries were finding their deficits mounting under the pressure of quadrupled petroleum prices from the Arab and other oil-producing countries. Unfortunately there is no simple and straightforward means for quickly correcting a structural disequilibrium. In general, it takes an adaptive and flexible economy with mobile and responsive factors of production to make the needed adjustments.

ATTEMPTS SINCE WORLD WAR II TO FACILITATE RECOVERY OF INTERNATIONAL TRADE

We have already mentioned the gifts and loans that the United States government made to foreign countries after World War II to aid in their reconstruction. In addition, various agencies have been organized for the purpose of promoting trade recovery and international long-term capital movements. The two most important are the International Monetary Fund and the International Bank for Reconstruction and Development.

International Monetary Fund

The International Monetary Fund (IMF) was organized by 30 original signatory nations at the Bretton Woods Conference in 1944. Its specific purpose is to aid members in securing foreign exchange for current account transactions. Each of the current 126 member nations has subscribed to the capital of the Fund, the quota of each country depending upon its resources, the normal volume of its foreign exchange transactions, and other considerations. Payment is made partly in gold or United States dollars, partly in the members' own currencies. When, because of temporary disequilibria in the exchange markets, nations are unable to obtain foreign exchange from other sources, they may purchase it from the Fund. In effect, the nation puts more of its own currency into the Fund and withdraws the currency desired. Thus, the Fund holds, as a result, the original quota of the borrowing country plus the additional currency that the country pays for the foreign exchange required. At the same time the Fund holds less of the currency that it has provided, so that its total assets are unchanged.

However, even though the total of its assets is unchanged, the Fund cannot continue its operations if its assets are presently in the form of currencies for which there is little demand. Accordingly, the purchases referred to above are considered loans of foreign exchange, to be repaid. A nation is not permitted to continue borrowing (that is, purchasing exchange) when the amount of its currency held by the Fund amounts to twice the amount of its original quota. Also, as a nation's indebtedness to the Fund increases, the interest rate on its borrowings from the Fund is raised. Furthermore, the Fund may declare a particular currency to be scarce and, thereafter, ration it among the members. These restrictions have been unpopular with some nations, but they have been necessary if the Fund's usefulness is to continue.

Besides providing foreign exchange when necessary, the Fund attempts to promote stable exchange rates and the removal of restrictions on foreign exchange. Members have agreed not to change the par value of their currencies without first notifying the Fund. Changes of 10 percent or less may be made whether or not the Fund approves. Changes of more than 10 percent are to be made only to correct a fundamental disequilibrium. Even though the Fund disapproves such a change, the nation may still proceed with it, but it may then find itself unable to purchase exchange from the Fund.

International Bank for Reconstruction and Development

Also organized at Bretton Woods, New Hampshire, was the International Bank for Reconstruction and Development. Its purpose, in contrast to that of the Fund, is to provide long-term funds. Its capital was originally contributed by the same nations that formed the International Monetary Fund. The greatest individual share contributed was and is that of the United States. There were over 110 member nations by 1974.

The Bank may lend directly when loans are not otherwise obtainable on reasonable terms, raising the required funds through the sale of its own bonds. It may also either participate in or guarantee loans made by others. Its loans, if not made directly to governments, must be guaranteed by the governments where the loans are made.

The function of the Bank is to make loans, not subsidies or gifts. Projects for sound business loans to underdeveloped countries require careful investigation and planning. There are many questions to be answered, quite apart from the routine considerations that would be taken into account in lending to industrialized nations. One is the availability of technologically qualified native labor; great capital installations are useless if there is no one to supervise and maintain them. Also, there must be a reasonable assurance that political instability, unreasonable tax and labor laws, or hostility toward foreign capital will not make the projects unprofitable or the loans uncollectible.

In its first seven years the Bank lent only about $200 million a year. Its loans have gradually increased in recent years, facilitated by the organization of the International Finance Corporation (IFC) and the International Development Association (IDA).[7] These affiliates can make some commitments that would not be suitable for the Bank. Unlike the Bank, the IFC does not require government guarantees. Also, it now has the right, not only to lend to foreign corporations, but also to buy their stock. It has assisted in underwriting, an important aid where financial markets are almost nonexistent. Loans made by the IDA are interest free, but carry a service charge of three fourths of 1 percent on the balance outstanding. With nothing due on the loan for the first 10 years and with 40 years thereafter in which to repay it, less developed countries can often borrow from the IDA when they would be unable to borrow from the Bank.

CONTROLLED FOREIGN EXCHANGE— ADOPTION AND RELAXATION

Between 1900 and 1930 most nations were on some form of the gold standard, except during World War I and for a few years thereafter. Foreign exchange rates ordinarily could fluctuate only within the narrow limits imposed by the gold-shipping points. This was a great convenience to those engaged in foreign trade, but it required that any disequilibrium in the nation's balance of payments be corrected through changes in the domestic price level, with resultant effects on income and employment.

The onset of depression caused a general moving away from the international gold standard and the substitution of various nationalistic policies designed to improve domestic conditions. The conviction grew that, since price levels and exchange rates could not both be kept constant, it would be better to stabilize the price level and vary exchange rates when necessary or to control foreign exchange in such a way that the economy would be better insulated from depression in other countries.

World War II caused great new changes and dislocations in the world's trading patterns. In many countries the government took the position after the war that one of its principal concerns must be the maintenance of full employment. Partly for this reason strong efforts were made to prevent any fall in the price level—hence the persistence of controlled foreign exchange, permitting governments to maintain expansionary domestic policies.

Most governments had to ration their sales of foreign exchange, as noted earlier. For a number of years United States dollars were in especially great demand. Since foreign countries were pegging their own currencies at unrealistically high levels, the price of dollars was artificially low and the demand far exceeded the supply.

---

[7]In 1956 and 1960 respectively.

By 1959, however, the world had successfully weathered the Depression, World War II, the Korean War, and the great postwar reconstruction and readjustments. Europe no longer depended on the United States. Having rebuilt and modernized its productive equipment, Europe was competing successfully in the international markets with American producers. Also, development of the European Common Market reduced old tariff barriers that once restricted trade between European nations. Still further, many other countries began to control inflationary pressures with more determination than did the United States. As foreign nations bought less from us and exported more to us and to other nations, their reserves of gold and dollars increased. Rationing and restrictions were no longer necessary, and the world's principal currencies became once more freely convertible.

The International Role of the Dollar

Because the dollar was so greatly in demand after World War II, it came to be the currency most widely used to supplement gold as reserves of central banks. At that time there could be no danger of the dollar being devalued, when already it appeared too low in terms of other currencies. The heads of central banks abroad could rely even more confidently on the stability of the dollar in terms of gold than on the stability of the British pound, once the great international currency. Dollars, then, became an important supplement to gold as an international monetary reserve.

As other currencies strengthened, however, the dollar weakened. The added gold reserves held by other nations came to a large extent from the United States, whose stock declined from $23 billion in 1957 to $13 billion by 1967. Simultaneously foreigners increased their net dollar balances from $11.4 billion to $18.9 billion.[8] Because they held more gold and more dollars, central banks abroad were stronger and their currencies were more in demand. But the dollar was weakening alarmingly. Most of our gold was tied up as backing for the gold certificates required at that time as legal reserves against the notes of the Federal Reserve Banks. Our free gold, that which was available for export, was only $3 billion.

Before World War I a gold reserve of 15 percent against short-term liabilities would have been considered more than adequate. According to the rules of the automatic gold standard, the nation would unquestionably redeem in gold upon demand and at a fixed price. But in light of the gold embargoes, exchange restrictions, and especially devaluations of more recent years, international bankers might easily be stampeded, as they saw gold reserves continuing to decline and dollar liabilities continuing to climb. They might, reasonably enough, have concluded that sooner or later the United States would be forced to devalue or refuse to sell gold—or have no gold left. The prudent policy, then, for every central bank would seem to have been to exchange all

---

[8]Short-term liabilities to foreigners reported by banks in the United States less short-term claims on foreigners reported by banks in the United States.

its dollars immediately for gold while it was still available at $35 an ounce. Such a run on the dollar would, of course, have forced the United States to devalue or place an embargo on gold—exactly as feared.

Meanwhile the second most important international currency, the pound, was also very weak. By oppressively deflationary domestic policies Great Britain was struggling to improve its own balance of payments position and reduce the pressure on sterling. Here, too, a run on gold could have forced a devaluation or a suspension of gold sales.

The significant point is that the bankers realized all this very well. They knew they must work together or most would suffer heavy losses. They did not permit a flight from the dollar or the pound to develop. Although they took some gold, they also allowed their short-term balances in London and New York to continue to accumulate. They cooperated with the United States Treasury, the Bank of England, and the IMF in working out arrangements to relieve temporarily the pressure on these currencies, giving Great Britain and the United States time to try to work out ways of correcting the cause of that pressure—their balance of payments deficits. There was none of the precipitate and irresponsible raiding that forced the breakdown of gold standards and gold exchange standards a generation earlier.

Like Great Britain, the United States, at the insistence of the Federal Reserve Banks, tried by a tighter monetary policy to reduce domestic demand and halt or at least slow down the rapid rise in prices. In addition, the amount of purchases that American tourists might bring back, duty free, was reduced from $500 to $100. More important, by the so-called interest-equalization bill the income on foreign securities held by Americans was taxed to reduce the yield by about one percentage point, and long-term loans made by American firms to foreigners were similarly taxed. By a program of voluntary (foreign) credit restraint, the government urged American business to refrain temporarily from making investments abroad, either in securities or in plant and equipment, and asked American banks and other lenders to limit their loans to foreigners. The government also attempted to provide services and information to help American firms increase their exports.

Unfortunately balance of payments deficits are stubborn and not quickly corrected. The gold drains were slackening but not yet reversed. Great Britain, once banker for the world, held less than $2 billion of gold by 1967 — less than Italy or Switzerland and less than half that of France or Germany.

Devaluation of the Pound, 1967

Finally, the inevitable could no longer be postponed. The pound was devalued by 14 percent in November, 1967. Instead of being worth $2.80, the pound was then valued at $2.40. This was a trifle less than half of its traditional value of $4.86 in the 19th and early 20th centuries. The devaluation was necessary, however, not so much as a result of speculative pressures as of Great Britain's inability to correct its persistent balance of payments deficits, which had continued in spite of the strenuous efforts to eliminate them.

Naturally the greater the number of currencies devalued, the greater the pressure on nondevalued currencies. Nations that do not join in the devaluation must expect to see a fall in their exports, an increase in their imports, and a worsening of their balance of payments position.

About 20 less important currencies were immediately devalued proportionately. In these currencies the price of sterling remained the same as before, so the British devaluation would not affect the trade of these nations with Great Britain.

There was widespread speculation that the dollar would be next, and for several days following the devaluation of the pound investors feverishly bought gold and the stocks of gold companies. The speculative stampede was quickly halted, at least temporarily, by the announcement that six other nations were joining the United States in a gold pool to support the dollar. The United States would not alone bear the responsibility of supplying gold. Too much was at stake. These governments (Great Britain, West Germany, Italy, Belgium, the Netherlands, and Switzerland) feared that if the dollar were devalued, a collapse of international commerce and finance might follow, probably leading to massive unemployment and worldwide depression.[9]

Two Prices for Gold

Finally, the long-averted run on gold began. The soothing syrup of official assurances that the price of gold would remain constant could no longer check the fever of speculation. The public began buying hundreds of tons of gold, supplied by the international gold pool centered in London.

Great Britain's balance of payments had worsened, despite the devaluation of the pound. This led to speculation that a second, larger British devaluation might be unavoidable and imminent.

Also, with every passing day the dollar appeared more vulnerable. The Treasury's gold stock by February had fallen to less than $12 billion, of which less than $2 billion could be paid out as long as Federal Reserve notes were subject to a reserve requirement. Far more important, there were no indications whatever that the United States was prepared to take any important steps to reduce its balance of payments deficit; on the contrary, it appeared likely that it would be larger than ever. Speculators became convinced that in months or perhaps weeks the United States would be forced to abandon the gold price of $35 an ounce, which it had been maintaining by selling gold freely at that price to foreign central banks and, through them, to the public. The new price, they believed, would probably be at least twice as high.

In the first two weeks of March, 1968, the public bought about half a billion dollars of gold in London. This rapid flight of monetary reserves into private hoards made it all the more certain that gold sales at $35 an ounce

---

[9]Much of the speculation appears to have been by the ill-informed. The fact is the international gold pool had been in existence for years. The only important change—and that had occurred five months earlier—was that France had quietly withdrawn from the pool.

could not possibly continue much longer, for reserves would soon be exhausted. In the stampede on Thursday, March 14, another half billion dollars of gold was sold.

Now excluding about $10 billion in private hands, the total known monetary gold stocks of the world was then only about $40 billion.[10] With the scramble for gold developing, the entire amount could disappear into private hoards within a few weeks. Action could be postponed no longer.

The London gold market and most other gold markets, with the exception of Paris, were closed Friday. The representatives of the gold pool met in Washington over the weekend with representatives of the IMF. To halt the drain of reserves, they agreed to sell no more gold, except to central banks, and to refuse to sell to any central banks that continued to sell gold to the public. Individuals buying gold would have to buy it from other individuals, presumably at a price above $35. Moreover, individuals could no longer assume that they could always sell gold to their governments, for the gold pool agreed also to end the free purchase of gold. Suddenly gold became a less attractive asset for speculators. (Two years later when the price of gold in the private sector of the market threatened to drop below $35, the United States Treasury announced that it would buy limited amounts of privately held gold when necessary to maintain the official price—and the value of its own gold stocks.)

Finally, Congress removed the reserve requirement against Federal Reserve notes. Most of the gold sold in London had been supplied by the United States Treasury, which lost $1.4 billion during March. By the end of March the Treasury's free gold was down to about half a billion dollars. The legislation increased it to more than $10 billion.

By no stretch of the imagination could one suppose that these gold measures were going to correct in any way the basic weakness of the dollar (and the pound). The balance of payments deficits of the United States were unaffected. As long as they continued, distrust of the dollar would not only continue, but increase. It was perfectly clear that all these policies could accomplish was to buy a little time. During this period of grace we could perhaps, by other measures, wipe out the balance of payments deficits. Otherwise the ultimate result would necessarily be either devaluation or an embargo on gold.

Comparisons between financial policies of governments and private firms are often misleading, especially when we are discussing domestic policies. A long series of domestic budget deficits may often be properly justified on the grounds that they will cause national income to rise, thereby increasing tax revenues. Also, the government always has the power to borrow from the banks or even print more money, which its citizens must accept.

When it is a question of sustained deficits in our dealings with the rest of the world, however, the government may indeed find itself in virtual bankruptcy when it is selling gold to foreign governments at a fixed price whenever they demand it. Like a person on the verge of bankruptcy, the government

---

[10]In 1975 it was still only about $50 billion.

may make every effort to persuade its creditors to refrain from demanding payment and to accept instead more I.O.U.s. If the creditors still insist on taking gold, as is their right, either the Treasury's vaults are eventually bare or, more likely, the government finally either refuses to sell gold or sells it at a higher price. This is equivalent to the action of the firm that, as a result of bankruptcy, finally settles its claims, scaled down to the point that it can cover them.

Technically the nation is not bankrupt, for as a sovereign state it can, without going through receivership or the courts, decide at any time whether it is going to continue to honor its obligations. The fact remains, however, that the position of the bankrupt firm and the position of the government that devalues its currency or stops selling gold are disturbingly similar.

In any case, the deficits on our net liquidity balance continued, and the pressure on the dollar continued. An intensifying factor in 1970 was short-term capital movements. The more basic difficulty was the world's continuous demand for more liquidity.

WORLD PROBLEM—INSUFFICIENT LIQUIDITY

For the same basic reason that the choice of domestic monetary policy is often difficult, the world is finding it hard to solve the problem of providing sufficient reserves to permit adequate international liquidity. Again there are political as well as economic considerations, further complicated by the fact that many nations are concerned rather than one alone. There are basically two questions: Why does the world need more liquidity? How can that liquidity best be provided?

Need for Liquidity

Respecting the first question, there is little disagreement. The need for greater liquidity today is a consequence of the large balance of payments deficits and surpluses today. Note that the liquid assets, such as gold, held by governments are not used directly to buy goods from foreigners, nor are they received directly for a nation's exports. They are used only for settling differences. Disregarding other international transactions, we can say that, no matter how great a nation's international trade, no reserves at all would be lost or gained as long as its exports were exactly equal to its imports. In all probability, however, they will not be exactly equal. As trade expands, it is only natural that the difference between exports and imports will usually increase also.[11] By the same logic, as foreign aid programs, military expenditures overseas, tourist expenditures, and international capital movements also increase, balance of payments deficits and surpluses must be expected to increase also. International reserves must be large enough to permit deficit

---

[11]The post-World War II growth in the gold stock has fallen far short of the growth in international trade. For instance, in 1948 (1958) the gold stock was 64.6 (40.8) percent of world trade. In 1974 it was only 13.2 percent.

countries to settle with their creditors without running out of funds. Otherwise the world might find itself in a poker game where a few players hold all the chips.

Providing Liquidity—Gold at $42.22 an Ounce

It is around the question of how liquidity is to be provided that the debate swirls. A conceivable possibility, that at the moment appears very unlikely, would be for nations to use only gold as reserves against their money, for international purposes at least, and for each nation to continue permanently its present price of gold, never resorting to devaluation. Foreign exchange rates could vary only within the narrow range of the gold shipping points, that is, by not more than about 1 percent, since every nation would freely buy and sell gold. This corresponds to the type of gold standard in effect in most industrialized nations 60 years ago. Why, then, is there almost no support today for this particular solution?

In earlier chapters we reviewed the difficulties that the automatic gold standard occasionally created, tending to create inflations and depressions and also to transmit them from one country to another. We saw that it imposed rigid limits on the possible scope of monetary and fiscal policy, and for that reason is today in general disrepute. Today we believe that recessions should be overcome and long depressions prevented by prompt and effective application of monetary and fiscal policies rather than, as in the old days, dragging on for years until prices, incomes, and costs were gradually forced to a lower level by thousands of bankruptcies and massive unemployment. For this reason alone, few governments today want to return to the automatic gold standard or feel that it would be a practical and permanent solution.

Besides this major objection, there would be two other difficulties with this solution with gold at $42.22 an ounce.[12] In the first place, for decades the world has been using gold plus some currencies, especially dollars and pounds, as reserves. If we now reverted to gold alone, at the existing price for gold, there would be a desperately difficult deflationary transition as the world adjusted to the smaller reserve base. A steep, worldwide collapse in prices and incomes, similar to that of the 1930s, would almost inevitably result.

Also, gold production is not easily increased. About 70 percent of the world's production of 50 million ounces annually comes from South Africa, a little over 10 percent from the Soviet Union, and about 5 percent from Canada.[13] To make matters worse, not all the gold mined in a year goes into monetary reserves. The nonmonetary demands of dentists, jewelers, hoarders, and manufacturers often exceed the annual increments of gold production. For the first time in history, no gold was added to the free world's

---

[12]The official price of gold was raised from $35 per ounce to $38 per ounce by the Smithsonian Agreement in December, 1971. It rose from $38 to $42.22 an ounce in conjunction with the announcement in early 1973 that the dollar would be devalued in terms of SDRs.

[13]The data available concerning gold production or use by Communist countries is much less reliable than that of the free world.

monetary stocks in 1966. The gold reserves of the free world did not exceed the 1966 level until 1972–1974, when they were slightly higher. Even today for the world as a whole there is only about 2¼ billion ounces of gold in existence, or approximately 5.6 million 400-ounce brick-size bars. Clearly we cannot possibly count on gold production alone, at today's price for gold, to provide the continuous increase in international liquidity that is required.

Gold Only, at a Higher Price

To overcome the difficulties discussed in the preceding paragraphs, some propose that the price of gold be raised substantially, possibly to about five times its present level.[14] There would be no effect on foreign exchange rates, since all nations would simultaneously raise their gold prices. The result would be that the money value of the world's gold would be, for example, five times as great as before. With this great increase in gold reserves, foreign countries would not need to hold part of their reserves in the form of dollars or pounds. Also, the increase in the price of gold would presumably provide a stimulus to gold mining, increasing production in terms of ounces as well as in terms of money. In addition, it is suggested, gold would be relased from hoards to be sold at 400 percent profit. Thus, at a higher price, gold alone could provide all the liquidity needed.

Conceivably this solution may some day be adopted. In contrast to the one discussed previously, it is not obviously impossible. It is subject, however, to serious criticism.

Consider again the basic objection to an automatic gold standard. Unless a nation's gold reserves far exceed its needs (as for the United States in 1940), its monetary and fiscal policies must be tailored to the requirements of its balance of payments position rather than to its domestic needs. High interest rates and a reduction in spending must be enforced to check gold outflows, even if these policies lead to unemployment rates of 20 or 25 percent. It is difficult to believe that governments today will tolerate such constraint or would long remain in power if they did. A higher price for gold today would temporarily provide the needed liquidity, it is true. How will additional reserves again be provided, however, if continued expansionary policies around the world lead in 20 or 30 years to new liquidity problems?

One possibility is that the world price for gold would then increase again. If this were to be the generally expected result, it is hard to imagine that the gold standard would operate satisfactorily. Remember that the secret of the gold standard's success 60 years ago was the absolute confidence that the price of gold would not be raised, ever. In those days, even if Great Britain's gold reserves were only a very small percentage of its liabilities abroad, everyone took it for granted that, somehow, Britain would continue to pay out gold upon demand at the existing price. With this kind of trust, there was no

---

[14]Since March, 1968, there have been two gold prices: the official gold price (now $42.22) for governmental and IMF settlements and the free market price which fluctuates with supply and demand. The price of gold in the private bullion market in London was $65, $112, and $175–$200 at the end of 1972, 1973, and 1974 respectively.

reason for runs to develop. If, however, it becomes eventually taken for granted that every now and then the price of gold will be raised, then the individual citizen or individual government has every reason to hoard gold. Runs also have every reason to develop against any treasury that begins to lose a little gold. Banking, whether national or international, must be based on confidence. Recurrent increases in the price of gold would surely destroy that confidence, and gold would be a far less satisfactory reserve money than in the past.

A second possibility is that all governments should solemnly agree that, after raising the price of gold now, no one would ever raise it again. Although this has actually been suggested from time to time, it does not merit serious consideration as a practical program. It assumes, obviously, that governments will do nothing to fight depression and unemployment unless they have plenty of gold in their vaults. The automatic gold standard would be restored, and the United States, for example, would at times permit a drop of $50 or $100 billion in the gross national product rather than allow gold to leave the country or devalue the dollar. This is fantastically unrealistic.

The third possibility is that when reserves again become insufficient we find some better way to increase them than by raising the price of gold. Of course, if there is some better way we should be adopting it now.

The French government has strongly urged raising the price of gold, taking the position that gold is the only real money. Great Britain and the United States have vigorously opposed it. The logic of the argument must be the same, whether expressed in French or English. Why, then, the disagreement?

One economic aspect, which it is hard to imagine could be overlooked by the logical and thrifty French, is that in recent years France has been steadily converting its dollar balances into gold. If the price of gold were raised to $211.10 (5 × $42.22) an ounce, they could sell the gold back to us for at least five times what they paid us for it. This alone would encourage them to support this proposal and us to oppose it.

It can scarcely be doubted, however, that the primary considerations are political rather than purely economic. It seems unlikely that France insisted on taking gold (as certainly was its right) merely because it wanted to force an increase in gold prices and profit from it. More probably, France demanded gold for the express purpose of putting pressure on Great Britain and the United States, hoping to force us, along with other countries, to devalue. Why? To lessen world confidence in these currencies. Nations that, unlike France, have been willing to hold pounds and dollars instead of gold would discover what a mistake they had made in trusting the stability of these currencies, which after devaluation would be worth less than before in terms of gold. In the future these countries, like France, could be expected to use only gold as reserves.

With their currencies then in much less demand, Great Britain and the United States would be forced to contract their international role. We could not afford to carry on military operations abroad, maintain large military installations in other parts of the world, or continue investing billions of dollars in Europe, which many Europeans regard as dollar imperialism. Just as Great

Britain has already been forced out of its once dominant international position, so too could the influence, political and commercial, of the United States be seriously weakened.

We cannot expect any simple solution of this dispute, reconciling interests that are diametrically opposed. Washington repeatedly and forcefully declared that the dollar would not be devalued. However, as discussed below, in late 1971 and again in early 1973 the dollar was devalued. There were similar declarations concerning sterling. France was gratified by the British devaluation, though disappointed that it was not larger. France waited hopefully for a substantial devaluation of the dollar and the emergence of the franc as the leading international currency.

Gold Plus Strong Currencies

As previously observed, most nations provide for their international liquidity by holding both gold and other currencies that are convertible into gold.[15] The trouble with this arrangement is that it places an excessive burden on the nations whose currencies are used as reserves by other nations. If other nations are, on the whole, to increase their reserves of pounds and dollars, the short-term liabilities of Great Britain and the United States must increase. The larger our short-term liabilities become, however, the more distrustful foreign bankers become of the dollar, and the more of their dollars they exchange for gold, still further weakening the dollar. The stronger then becomes foreign insistence on retrenchment and deflation in the United States.

Earlier we noted that, if the price of gold is not raised materially, a decline in gold production is not unlikely. If, over 20 or 30 years, the world's monetary gold reserves were to increase by perhaps 15 percent, foreign governments might have no objection to holding 15 or 20 percent more dollar reserves than they had held earlier. If, however, this turned out to be too slow a growth in reserves, there would be a demand for more currency reserves. Unfortunately the larger the currency reserves became, the less confidence there would be in those currencies, and the greater would be the pressure to drain gold from Great Britain and the United States. Unless they were willing to accept serious depressions, these "key-currency" countries could be repeatedly forced to declare a gold embargo or perhaps to devalue. Either course would have serious implications for the future acceptability of these currencies internationally.

Paper Gold

Evidently, neither gold alone at a constant price, nor gold alone at an increasing price, nor gold plus strong currencies appears to be a practical solution to the problem of providing international liquidity. There is,

---

[15]For example, in 1974 the world's total reserve assets were held in the following proportions: 23 percent gold stock; 6 percent SDRs; 4 percent reserve position in the IMF; and 67 percent foreign exchange.

fortunately, another possibility that is subject to none of the limitations of the preceding reserves.

Additional liquidity could be provided by the creation of international money by the International Monetary Fund. Just as, domestically, our Federal Reserve Banks can create additional reserves for member banks, so the IMF could create additional reserves for treasuries by purchasing securities. This credit money would not be in the form of dollars, pounds, or any other national currency. Thus, it would avoid the difficulties, referred to above, encountered by nations whose currency is used as reserves by other nations. Like gold, it would not be used for domestic transactions. Its sole function would be to serve as international reserves, providing the needed additional liquidity. Because this new credit money would be used for the same purposes as gold, it has sometimes been characterized as paper gold.

The idea is not entirely new. At the end of World War II there was some discussion of the advisability of creating an international currency. Then, however, the world's stock of monetary gold was less obviously inadequate than it is today. The principal difficulty at that time lay in the fact that it was so unevenly distributed, with most of it in the United States. Partly for that reason also, monetary officials in this country distrusted the possible consequences of providing enormous credit facilities and placing them at the disposal of war-impoverished nations.

Since then, as we have seen, most of those nations have made strong recoveries. Their currencies were made fully convertible, thanks to the increase in their holdings of gold, pounds, and dollars. Today the new international currency is urged, not to provide purchasing power for battered nations, but to supply more liquidity for the world in general.

It goes without saying that sometimes monetary conservatives throw up their hands at the very suggestion that governments should agree to treat some kind of new paper money as gold. Outright inflation! One might call it inflation, depending on how one defines that word. But regardless of what it is called and granting that almost certainly it would have been an impractical and unnecessary policy a century ago or even 50 years ago, what can we say about its possible usefulness today? This is an excellent question to consider in these final pages, for much that has been explained at length in earlier chapters can now be summarized in a few short paragraphs.

Consider for a moment the operation of a local bank and its relations with its community. Bridges and highways are built to serve the community. Through bond issues the money is borrowed so that the area may immediately begin to benefit from the improvements in transportation. The bank buys some of the bonds. Therefore, the quantity of money is increased.

Factories, apartment houses, and homes are built, to a large extent with borrowed money. The bank supplies some of this money and, as always when it makes loans, it creates money. Employment in the community increases so that payrolls grow. So, too, do merchants' inventories. To carry their inventories and meet their payrolls, the merchants borrow at the bank. The quantity of money is increased. Consumers buy cars, television sets, and other durable goods, often on credit supplied by the banks. Again the quantity of money is increased.

We have seen that the great advantage of credit money is that it does permit a nation's stock of money to increase in step with increases in output rather than in step with changes in the mining or importing of gold. Regulating authorities insist, to be sure, that the individual bank cannot lend without limit; it must have adequate reserves. But where do those reserves come from? Bank reserves in this country, we know, are also credit money. Part of the reserves are vault cash, which is credit money created either by the Treasury or the Federal Reserve Banks. The other, larger part is manufactured by the Federal Reserve Banks as they buy Treasury securities, crediting the deposits maintained at the Federal Reserve Banks by the member banks. (At one time we required that a fractional reserve in gold be held against these deposits, but like almost every other nation we have now dropped the reserve requirement.)

Is there really any reason that the same thing cannot be done on an international scale? As the world's stock of goods and current output of goods and services increase, additional reserves can be created by an international monetary authority such as the International Monetary Fund, just as reserves are created by the Federal Reserve Banks to meet domestic credit needs. If everyone at the poker table is given more chips, the game can go on. Of course, if losers keep losing, they will eventually be more in debt than ever. Simply increasing the supply of chips is not going to turn poor players into good ones. If all players are of about the same skill, however, the increase in the chips will allow time for a change in the cards to help those who have been losing.

Like the other solutions proposed, this policy would give the world more time to eliminate balance of payments disequilibria and for deficits to be changed to surpluses and vice versa. Unlike them, it does not simultaneously weaken international confidence by changing the price or the availability of gold. It does not make present currencies less acceptable in the future, intensifying the need for liquidity later. It avoids the dislocations and stresses that would probably be encouraged by any other policies proposed.

Special Drawing Rights

The advantages of paper gold are, understandably, much more apparent to the United States today than they were 30 years ago. They are much less clear today to some of the nations that supported the proposal then. The IMF has not as yet created a new international money. However, member nations have always had the automatic right to borrow from the IMF up to the amount of their original gold contribution to the Fund. (Larger amounts could be borrowed, but they had to be negotiated with the IMF and carried a higher rate of interest.) After the monetary crisis of 1967 the IMF began lending more freely by creating Special Drawing Rights (SDRs), which increased the amount that could be borrowed automatically by member nations. About $9.5

billion in total SDRs were distributed by the IMF according to a rigid formula—based on a nation's contribution to the IMF—in 1970, 1971, and 1972. None were distributed in 1973 and 1974. The U.S. had $0.9, $1.1, $2.0, $2.2, and $2.4 billion in SDRs in 1970, 1971, 1972, 1973, and 1974 respectively.

Often the press refers to the SDRs as ''paper gold.'' There are two important differences between the SDRs and the paper gold discussed in the preceding section. In the first place, they are not a new international money. The SDRs are no stronger than the currencies underlying them. In the second place, a treasury that utilizes SDRs is borrowing from the Fund. Eventually it must repay the loan, just as a commercial bank must repay a loan that it receives from a Federal Reserve Bank. There is no permanent creation of additional reserves, such as results domestically from Federal Reserve open market operations.

The SDRs are comparable to discount operations of the Federal Reserve Banks. They provide temporary credit, but do not permanently increase the reserves of the individual members. There have been strong objections raised (a generation ago by the United States, today by other countries) to any development (such as paper gold) that would permit individual countries to continue indefinitely to incur balance of payments deficits. Thus, although SDRs provide temporary credit, international reserves are still basically either gold or strong currencies. The problem of insufficient liquidity has not been overcome. Since the United States continued to incur balance of payments deficits after the crisis of 1967, another crisis was inevitable.

In mid-1974 the value of an SDR was $1.20 in U.S. dollars. It originally was worth $1.00, but the two official dollar devaluations changed it. Before 1971 the value of the SDR was based on the U.S. dollar, the value of which was in turn based on gold. In 1974 the new value of the SDR was based on a package of several currencies.

Short-Term Capital Movements

The dollar was subjected to additional pressures in 1970 as a result of a rapid outflow of short-term capital. One cause of the capital outflow was that interest rates had fallen sharply in the United States. In general, short-term rates were lower in the United States than in any of the other important money centers. A second cause was that speculators were becoming increasingly convinced that the dollar would be devalued. They sold their dollar claims for other currencies, knowing they would have a sure profit if they could later switch back to the devalued dollars.

As a result of the new gold policy, foreign firms and individuals could no longer directly drain gold from the United States. They could, however, exchange dollars for other currencies. An Italian banker, for example, holding $50 million of United States Treasury bills, could sell them and then sell the dollar proceeds for deutsche marks (or other currencies). In a completely free market, such operations on a large scale would cause the price of the dollar,

in terms of deutsche marks, to fall. Both the American and German governments were attempting, however, to keep the ratio of the dollar and the mark
fixed within a very narrow range. This required that the Treasury and the
Federal Reserve support the price of the dollar by buying dollars with marks,
and that the Bundesbank (the German central bank corresponding to our Federal Reserve Banks) hold down the value of the mark by selling marks for
dollars. The result from both operations was a rapid increase in our short-
term liabilities to the Bundesbank. These liabilities, unlike those held by private firms, were redeemable in gold upon demand.

True, the German government fully cooperated with the United States
Treasury. Not since 1964 has Germany purchased gold from the United
States, nor have most other European nations. To avoid, if possible, precipitating another international financial crisis, they allowed their dollar balances
to increase, year after year. In spite of their cooperation, however, the dollar
was becoming steadily more unstable internationally. The growing mass of
foreign short-term claims was an important factor leading to the speculation
against the dollar in 1971.

Eurodollars

One more comparatively recent development further increased the
world's stock of dollars and encouraged speculation against the dollar. The
Russians, wanting dollars but remembering that their dollar balances in the
United States had been impounded during World War II, began in 1960 to
deposit their dollars with European and British banks. This was the first substantial use of what are called Eurodollars, now widely used in Europe. Probably because Eurodollars are relatively new, few Americans understand exactly what they are, and tend to confuse them with the results of balance of
payments deficits.

A Eurodollar is simply a deposit liability, payable in dollars, of a bank
outside the United States. The bank may be a branch of one of the big American banks, or it may be a foreign bank. It stands ready to accept dollar deposits from anyone, foreign or American, individual, bank, business firm, or government. It also stands ready—note this well!—to make dollar loans to
anyone.

Suppose that British Motors receives a draft for a million dollars, drawn
on the Chase Manhattan Bank in New York. Is it holding Eurodollars? Certainly not. It may return the check to New York to be credited to the account
it keeps with some bank in Manhattan. However, British Motors might decide
instead to deposit the check with one of the Eurodollar banks in London. It
does not convert the dollars into sterling. It holds a million dollar deposit in
London. These are Eurodollars, and one way in which they might (but not
necessarily will) originate is as a result of American imports. By far the more
important source of Eurodollars, however, has nothing to do with imports or
exports. The key appears at the end of the paragraph above.

Most Eurodollars originate in exactly the same way most American dollars originate. They are created as the banks make loans and investments. Foreign banks, like American banks, operate on fractional reserves. The reserves of the Eurodollar banks are their dollar deposits in United States banks and in other Eurodollar banks.[16]

The Eurodollar bank that receives British Motor's $1,000,000 draft on the Chase Manhattan Bank now owes British Motors $1,000,000 and at the same time increases its reserves by $1,000,000 by depositing the check in a New York bank with which it has an account. The new Eurodollar deposit in London is, for the moment, backed 100 percent by the added dollar deposit in New York.

Assuming that the London bank previously had neither deficient nor excess reserves and that it tries to maintain a reserve of 10 percent against its deposits, it now has $900,000 of excess reserves. This amount it lends to someone, somewhere, who wants to borrow dollars. (Note, it might even lend them to a New York bank or, of course, to some other borrower in America, Europe, or elsewhere.) Suppose it lends $900,000 to the Cunard Line, which it uses to pay for fuel oil. It does not, of course, draw $900,000 of currency from New York and turn it over to Cunard. It simply credits Cunard's account with $900,000, which Cunard turns over to the oil company. The oil company deposits the $900,000 with another Eurodollar bank. This second bank now has $900,000 of new deposits and $900,000 of new reserves. It lends $810,000, creating another $810,000 of Eurodollars.

We are simply looking at the familiar process of bank credit expansion. If we ignore the possibility of a currency drain (which is far less likely than in the case of a domestic credit expansion), we realize that, maintaining 10 percent reserves, the Eurodollar banks as a group can create nine Eurodollars for every Eurodollar they receive. Most Eurodollars are thus created by the banking system.

The growth of Eurodollars was stimulated by the interest rate ceilings imposed on American banks by the Federal Reserve. By 1969 these ceilings encouraged many large depositors to withdraw their deposits from banks in the United States and redeposit the proceeds abroad, as Eurodollars, at a higher interest rate. Then the United States banks, short of funds, borrowed Eurodollars abroad, causing the supply of Eurodollars to increase. For this and other reasons the stock of Eurodollars expanded rapidly in 1970, doubling to about $60 billion.[17] This was about four times the level of 1968.

Fixed Exchange Rates Begin to Crumble

In June, 1970, the Canadian government stopped buying United States dollars. Canada's overall official reserves, including gold, SDRs, United

---

[16]The reserves in Eurodollars cancel out, however, for the Eurodollar banks, so that their only net reserves are their dollar deposits (or other highly liquid dollar assets) in the United States.

[17]*Review* of the Federal Reserve Bank of St. Louis (July, 1971).

States dollars, and other currencies were more than adequate. In buying still more American dollars to help maintain the official parity between the Canadian dollar and the American dollar, the Canadian government's cash balances had dropped 70 percent in the preceding three months.[18] Consequently, the Canadian dollar was allowed to float, that is, to find its own level in a free market.

During the fiscal year ending June 30, 1971, the United States Treasury lost $1.5 billion of gold, bringing its stock down to $10.5 billion, the lowest level since 1936 and, under the circumstances, clearly inadequate. The $9.8 billion deficit in our official reserve transactions balance during 1970 was followed by one of $29.8 billion, $10.4 billion, $5.3 billion, and $8.1 billion in 1971, 1972, 1973, and 1974 respectively.

In May, 1971, a panic flight from dollars to marks developed. On May 4 the Bundesbank was obliged to absorb $1.2 billion to maintain the dollar's official value of 3.66 marks. In the first hour the following day it acquired another $1 billion. Then it stopped buying dollars, allowing the mark to float. There was really nothing else for Germany to do. As long as the Bundesbank continued to create additional marks to exchange for dollars, it was inflating the German money supply. In the 12 months ending March, 1971, it had been forced to increase the quantity of money by 22.5%—entirely due to the dollar inflow, according to the Bundesbank—and this was at least twice as great an increase as was desirable for the German economy. As a Bundesbank officer observed, they found themselves in a rather desperate situation, with their monetary policy being dictated primarily by Washington.[19] Other nations too were complaining about the inflationary consequences of our deficits for their economies.

The Gold Embargo

Finally, the U.S. government took a dramatic step. On August 15, 1971, at the same time that he imposed a 90-day freeze on wages and prices, President Nixon announced that the United States was suspending the sale of gold and would impose a 10 percent surcharge on most imported goods other than raw materials and foodstuffs. Now the dollar was floating, as also, at least to some degree, were many other currencies.

For years foreign bankers and statesmen had been highly critical of our balance of payments deficits. They had, however, shown little interest in our repeated requests that they contribute more to the costs of mutual defense and that they remove subsidies, quotas, and preferential tariffs discriminating against American goods. The gold embargo and the surcharge, however, drew their immediate and concerned attention. Apparently they had, more optimistically than realistically, expected us to correct our balance of payments deficits and at the same time continue to buy as much from them and sell as little to them as before.

---

[18]*Wall Street Journal* (June 1, 1970).
[19]*Wall Street Journal* (May 6, 1971).

They protested that we were now forcing recessions abroad instead of properly correcting our deficits by restrictive measures at home that would force our costs and prices down until we could compete more effectively in international markets. It was hardly that simple. In the first place, even if we undertook such a domestic policy, the final result would still be that foreigners would export less and import more, encouraging recession abroad. In the second place, for the United States, international trade is much too small to determine our monetary policy. In contrast to foreign economies, for which international trade may amount to as much as 25 percent of the gross national product, foreign trade creates only about 6 percent of our gross national product. We are naturally unwilling to enforce a long recession or depression to improve this small part of our national production. For this reason some American economists have for several years urged that the dollar be allowed to float permanently, so that our foreign trade would have no effect on our monetary policies.

Permanently Floating Rates

Permanently floating exchange rates offer a possible solution to the persistent problem. They would put an end to balance of payments deficits and surpluses, for there would no longer be any attempt to fix the values of currencies in terms of gold or in terms of each other. If a nation was spending more abroad than it was receiving from abroad, the supply of its currency, at the prevailing price, would be greater than the demand. The price of its currency in the international financial markets would fall. Then the nation would begin to sell more and buy less abroad. Its balance of payments would always be approximately in equilibrium.

The problem of insufficient liquidity would also disappear. Since governments would no longer be trying to stabilize foreign exchange rates, there would be little need for treasuries to hold reserves of gold, dollars, or other foreign currencies. Thus, a nation's monetary policy could be governed solely by its domestic requirements without creating international monetary crises from time to time.

There has been some objection to floating exchange rates on the grounds that they would hinder foreign trade by the uncertainty they would create for firms engaged in foreign trade.[20] An importer, agreeing to pay a fixed sum of foreign currency at a later date, would not know exactly what the price of the foreign currency would then be. This is a rather superficial objection, for at the time of signing the contract to buy the goods, the importer could make a forward cover purchase of foreign currency to have it available when needed. However, forward markets are very thin beyond one year. On the other hand, under pegged exchange rate systems, one cannot count on indefinite exchange rate stability.

---

[20]After President Nixon's August 15 edict, the dangers of a free or "clean" float, in which supply and demand alone determine exchange rates, prompted many nations to resort to "dirty" floats, in which there is official intervention.

Speculative pressures would probably be less if exchange rates were floating permanently rather than fixed. Stabilization funds do conveniently iron out the little fluctuations, holding foreign exchange rates in the market to within one or two percent of the official rates. They prevent for years, however, the gradual rise or fall that market conditions might require in the value of a currency. The exchange rates, fixed 20 or 30 years earlier, become steadily and progressively more unrealistic. Finally, speculators become convinced that a major currency realignment is imminent. They sell the overvalued currency for other currencies. The flight of short-term capital begins, and the pressure is on; another crisis is at hand. Instead of being accomplished gradually over the years, the long-postponed readjustment is made all at once. This, of course, richly rewards the speculators.

While models can be constructed in which speculation is destabilizing, if speculators buy low and sell high, their influence is normally stabilizing.[21] Furthermore, under flexible exchange rates, countries are less tempted to impose controls on trade and capital movements that interfere with efficient resource allocation.

Devaluations and Revaluations

As negotiations on realignment began, the French renewed their demands that any settlement must include a steep increase in the price of gold, that is, a substantial devaluation of the dollar. Spokesmen for the United States, hoping to prevent or at least to minimize the dishonor of devaluation, declared the dollar would not be devalued. Any realignment of exchange rates would have to result from upward revaluations of other currencies.

A compromise was hammered out in December, 1971. The dollar would be devalued by 8.6 percent by increasing the price of gold to $38.[22] Belgium, Holland, West Germany, and Japan would simultaneously revalue their currencies a little higher, so that they would be worth from 11.5 percent to 17 percent more than before in terms of dollars. Italy and Sweden would devalue by 1 percent, to make their currencies worth 7.6 percent more in comparison to the dollar. France and Great Britain would not redefine their currencies, which would therefore be 8.6 percent higher in terms of dollars.

It was also agreed to allow currencies to fluctuate a little more freely than before. Stabilization operations would hold the market price of currencies within 2¼ percent of their official price rather than within 1 percent, as formerly. There was also a promise that European and Japanese tariffs and quotas would be reduced.

While past negotiations have reduced tariffs somewhat, they remain a significant obstacle to trade.[23] In the major industrial countries approximately 60

---

[21]The classic source is Milton Friedman, "The Case for Flexible Exchange Rates," *Essays in Positive Economics* (Chicago: University of Chicago Press, 1953), pp. 157–203.

[22]Since no provision was made for lifting the gold embargo, the result was that instead of not selling gold at $35 an ounce, the United States would not sell it at $38.

[23]See *Economic Report of the President,* 1974 (Washington: U.S. Government Printing Office, February, 1974), pp. 212–220.

percent of all trade in industrial products remains subject to tariffs, and the average rate of such tariffs is about 10 percent. Furthermore, while tariffs in the aggregate have been substantially reduced, some very high tariffs remain on, for example, a few important consumer goods. About 4 percent of all trade is still subject to tariffs of 20 percent or more.

Although the U.S. government in late 1971 and early 1972 was confident that the combination of a cheaper dollar, trading concessions, and an increase in SDRs would permit a fairly rapid correction of its balance of payments malady, it was to be proven wrong.

Trade Balance

Why was the 1971 devaluation necessary? Perhaps Table 27-1, which shows four alternative measures of balance of payments disequilibrium, provides the quickest answer. From 1960 to 1971 the U.S. had a deficit every year in its balance of payments using the basic balance or net liquidity measure (with the exception of 1961 in the basic balance measure) and had a deficit in 9 of the 12 years in its official reserve transactions balances. Even the traditionally large U.S. trade surplus began to erode after 1967 and even showed a deficit in 1971 and 1972 before returning to a modest surplus in

Table 27-1   Alternative Measures of Disequilibrium, 1960–1974
(In billions of dollars)

Year	Merchandise or Trade Balance (exports minus imports)	Basic Balance (current account plus long-term capital)	Net Liquidity Balance	Official Reserve Transactions Balance
1960	4.89	−1.19	−3.68	−3.40
1961	5.57	0.01	−2.25	−1.35
1962	4.52	−1.03	−2.86	−2.65
1963	5.22	−1.33	−2.71	−1.93
1964	6.80	−0.08	−2.70	−1.53
1965	4.95	−1.83	−2.48	−1.29
1966	3.82	−2.11	−2.15	0.22
1967	3.80	−3.72	−4.68	−3.42
1968	0.64	−1.94	−1.61	1.64
1969	0.61	−3.64	−6.08	2.74
1970	2.16	−3.78	−3.85	−9.84
1971	−2.72	−10.56	−21.97	−29.75
1972	−6.99	−11.24	−13.86	−10.35
1973	0.47	−1.03	−7.61	−5.30
1974^p	−5.88	−10.58	−18.34	−8.07

Source: *Economic Report of the President,* 1975 (Washington: U.S. Government Printing Office, February, 1975), Table C-89, p. 351; and *Federal Reserve Bulletin* (June, 1975), p. A58.
^{p}preliminary

1973, only to become negative again in 1974. The 1971 negative balance of trade was the first since 1893. Nearly 25 years of balance of payments deficits indicated that too many of our goods were noncompetitive in the world market.[24]

From 1960 to 1971 the U.S. dollar changed from the world's premier and strongest currency to one which was vulnerable to mass speculation. The two most important reasons for this evolution were the increasingly rapid diffusion of the sophisticated technology that the U.S. had previously dominated and the persistent domestic inflation. Under the then-prevailing regime of fixed exchange rates, the dollar was overvalued. This meant that imports were more attractive and exports less attractive.

While the U.S. basic balance had been persistently in deficit from 1960 to 1971, demand for dollar balances was sufficiently high to cause an accumulation of foreign-held dollar balances. However, the sharp increase in the deficit in both the net liquidity and official reserve transactions balances in the spring of 1971 precipitated an international monetary crisis. This culminated in the December, 1971, Smithsonian agreement to realign world exchange rates, including devaluation of the dollar against major currencies.

As expected, the U.S. situation did not improve immediately. While import prices rose, a booming domestic economy kept the quantities of imports up in 1972, resulting in even larger trade and basic balance deficits but substantially reduced net liquidity and official reserves balances.

Another U.S. Devaluation

The continued exchange market pessimism about the dollar lead to another formal devaluation by the United States on February 12, 1973, by an additional 10 percent with respect to gold (SDRs). After the devaluation, the average exchange rate of the dollar against the currencies of its major trading partners was down 16 percent from the April, 1970, benchmark of the floating of the Canadian dollar or the end of the old fixed exchange rate system. The 1973 attempt to establish realistic exchange rates was superceded by generally floating rates.

The devaluation did result in a modest trade balance surplus of $0.5 billion in 1973. Although the basic, net liquidity, and official reserve transactions balances remained negative, they improved substantially over 1972. However, as indicated earlier, the managed floating of exchange rates makes the measurement of the overall balance of payments less important.[25] Two factors dominated the merchandise trade account. Poor harvests abroad resulted in large increases in the price and quantity sold of U.S. agricultural exports. At the same time, the world price of oil increased dramatically during the year

---

[24]It is estimated that in 1950 the U.S. produced 39 percent of the world's output. By 1970 we were producing 30 percent. Over the same period our production of automobiles dropped from 76 percent to 31 percent, and steel declined from 46 percent to 20 percent. *Time* (January 24, 1972).

[25]In particular, the managed floating of exchange rates changes the analytical meaning of the official reserve transactions balance, which measures the net direction and magnitude of official intervention in the foreign exchange market. Since exchange rates were both fixed in early 1973 and floated later, the official reserve transactions balance would not be terribly meaningful.

following the decision of the major Arab oil producers to embargo oil shipments to the United States in October. The relatively slow growth of total imports during 1973 despite the rapid increase in imports of crude and refined petroleum products suggests that the dollar depreciation had a significant effect on U.S. trade. All in all, "international trade and investment grew at a near record level during 1973, despite the strains placed on the international economy by massive capital flows, large fluctuations in exchange rates, and strong price pressures due to crop failures, capacity limitations, and cutbacks in oil production by the major producers."[26]

In 1974 all four alternative measures of disequilibrium showed a deficit. During 1974 U.S. international transactions were affected mainly by four forces: (1) the sharply increased petroleum prices in world markets; (2) the adjustments to exchange rate changes which occurred since 1971; (3) the cyclical downturn in many industrial countries; and (4) the high, though differential, rates of monetary growth and inflation throughout the world. While these factors are discussed in more detail below, it should be noted that these factors are interrelated and exerted both favorable and unfavorable pressures on the U.S. international accounts. The 1974 trade deficit can in large part be attributed to the sharp increase in oil prices. In fact, when the influence of higher oil prices is removed, the 1974 U.S. trade balance shows an improvement as compared to 1973.

Five Major Developments in the Early 1970s

In writing a scenario to describe what major international developments occurred in the early 1970s, five events stand out.

1. The first was the decision of many governments to institute flexible or floating exchange rates. While following widely differing practices in managing their currencies, most countries continued to intervene in the foreign exchange market to varying degrees. In short, the international monetary system evolved away from a fixed exchange rate to a new, not yet fully determined, payments mechanism.
2. The second was the Arab and other oil-producing countries' cartel power to extract increased revenues, called petrodollars, for their oil exports. For instance, our oil-import bill skyrocketed from $8.3 billion in 1973 to about $25 billion in 1974 after the cartel of major oil-exporting countries, led by Iran and Venezuela, jumped the price from about $2.50 a barrel in October, 1973, to more than $10 a barrel by January, 1974. While eventually these revenues will have to be used to either import more goods and services or be invested in foreign assets, the short-run adverse impact on many countries' balance of payments will be pronounced. Moreover, there is another danger. The World Bank estimated that if oil purchases continued at their 1974 pace, the Organization of Petroleum Exporting Countries (OPEC) would by 1980 have amassed currency reserves totaling $653 billion. This would be three times the total of existing official currency reserves of all the nations of the world. While such long-run predictions

---

[26]*Economic Report of the President,* 1974 (Washington: U.S. Government Printing Office, February, 1974), p. 181.

usually turn out to be singularly inaccurate, it is clear that certain Arab
leaders will have enormous political clout in the years ahead.

3. A third development was the adoption of new measures for controlling
capital movements. While many major industrial countries tightened capital controls—previous common restrictions included discriminatory reserve requirements and penalty rates or prohibition of interest on nonresident deposits—the U.S. on January 23, 1974, suspended three kinds of
restraints it had maintained since the 1960s: an interest equalization tax on
purchases of foreign securities, restrictions on foreign direct investments
by U.S. corporations, and limitations on foreign lending by U.S. financial
institutions. Thus, in the future, while the dollar depreciation and emerging
oil problems are likely to increase the quantity of dollars demanded in
international markets, the relaxation of U.S. capital controls, as well as
differences in interest rates and inflation rates, is likely to increase the
quantity of dollars supplied in international markets.

4. The apparent end of gold as a significant means of settling international
payments imbalances was a fourth important development. We previously
discussed the important announcements in 1971 and 1973 that signaled
most sharply this development. After this, gold was no longer much used
as the basis for international transactions between the central banks of the
world. Two further aspects of this development merit further consideration—the use of SDRs discussed below and the change in policy that
allows Americans to legally hold gold once again.[27] Since 1933 private citizens were not legally allowed to buy or hold gold; only public authorities—
the Treasury and the Fed—could. One interesting question is: what will
this new policy do to the price of gold?[28] A usual first response is that gold
bugs will drive up the price of gold. Given the supply curve of gold (reflecting the cost of mining and propensities to hoard), the American demand does add to the world demand and, therefore, the price should rise.
But this conclusion is not inevitable. For one thing it ignores risk and the
estimated future demand. If inflation abates or if alternative investments—
bonds, commodities, land, stocks, etc.—become more attractive, the demand for gold may drop. Moreover, non-Americans may have bid up the
price in anticipation of the gold-hungry Americans' demand after the law
was changed. Finally, the supply may not be static but may shift rightward
as central banks owning large quantities of gold that they no longer need
for official business offer gold for sale. Taking into account risk, expectations, and possible government action, it is not absolutely certain that allowing Americans to buy gold must increase the price of gold. Moreover,
sales taxes, retail markups, and the lack of a dividend from the sterile
investment in gold must be considered in calibrating an overall yield.

5. A final major development was the greater reliance on the SDR and the
movement toward making the SDR the formal numeraire of the future

[27]The government allows commercial banks but not federally-insured savings and loans associations to deal in gold. There are numerous other rules which apply to the lifting of the 41-
year-old ban on the private ownership of gold in 1974. Incidentally, the troy ounce used in gold
trading is a strange unit of measure which was invented in Troyes, France. It equals 1.097 common ounces.
[28]An interesting discussion of this is contained in Robert L. Heilbroner, *The Economic
Problem Newsletter* (Fall, 1974), pp. 2–4.

international monetary system.[29] A *numeraire* is the common unit of account in terms of which all other relative values are measured. Under the Bretton Woods agreement, gold was the de jure or formal numeraire, although the dollar became the de facto numeraire since it was officially tied to gold. When the tie was broken between the dollar and gold and therefore between the dollar and the SDR, there was no widely accepted numeraire. There was wide agreement that the SDR should eventually become the de jure and de facto numeraire. But to do so, it was necessary to establish an agreed-upon procedure for calculating the value of the SDR in terms of individual currencies. Since the SDR is not traded in the market against currencies, there is no one obvious relationship. The most widely suggested idea was to value the SDR in terms of an average of the major currencies. In June, 1974, the IMF's Committee of 20—a group of the world finance ministers which included the U.S. Treasury Secretary—agreed to base the SDRs' value on a package value of 16 world currencies. The U.S. dollar was to contribute about 33 percent of the value. By mixing together a basket of currencies, the value of the SDR will not be dependent on the fortunes of a single currency. At this point the only role for gold agreed to was to let countries with financial problems use their gold as collateral for interest and borrowing.

SUMMARY AND CONCLUSION

One fact at least must now be clear. Although 30 years ago the dollar was the strongest currency in the world, it has lost much of its luster. We can no longer delude ourselves that it is so intrinsically sound and so universally desired that foreigners will want to accumulate it forever. That was quite evident by the severe capital outflows that occurred in the early 1970s. Since then its acceptability has not been improved by two devaluations nor by the fact that even foreign governments can no longer demand gold for their dollars. We can hardly assume that we are in a position to dictate to the rest of the world concerning gold prices, foreign exchange rates, international reserves, or other international monetary problems.

The United States had almost continuous deficits in its balance of payments from the late 1940s to the mid-1970s. A deficit disequilibrium may be remedied by any one or a combination of the following methods: exchange rate depreciation, price and income deflation, devaluation, or structural adjustments in the allocation of resources.

The U.S. in the early 1970s tried price and wage controls domestically and devaluation internationally in an attempt to solve both its internal and external problems. While the cheaper dollars through devaluation did at least temporarily improve our trade picture, continuing inflation in this country made our trading advantage short-lived. It appears that inflation of varying degrees of severity will continue to be a problem throughout the 1970s.

---

[29]Our discussion of the SDR is indebted to the *Economic Report of the President*, 1974, pp. 208–209. Also see the more detailed treatment in Dhruba Gupta, "The First Four Years of SDRs," *Finance and Development* (June, 1974), pp. 6–9 and 31.

In the early 1970s five major developments occurred which greatly affected the entire international economy: (1) Many countries adopted flexible exchange rates; (2) the foreign oil-producing countries' cartel extracted considerable petrodollars from oil-consuming countries; (3) capital movement controls were relaxed by some and tightened by other countries; (4) gold apparently ended its long reign as the principal means of settling international debts; and (5) SDRs were pushed forward as the new de facto and de jure international numeraire.

Most of the short-term capital sent out of this country in the early 1970s has not yet returned. If there were a general conviction that there would be no further international monetary crises and readjustments in the foreseeable future, we could reasonably expect a large inflow of short-term capital as foreign balances were converted back into dollars. It appears, however, that bankers and investors are waiting to see whether the United States has truly solved its problems. If there is any indication that we are making no real improvement, and especially if interest rates are lower in the United States than in Europe, it is highly probable that we shall soon experience another, perhaps greater, capital outflow and that eventually we shall have to adopt even more drastic measures.

Discussion Questions

1. Briefly explain the circumstances under which a nation requires: (a) a favorable balance of trade, and (b) an unfavorable balance of trade. To simplify this question, consider only exports, imports, and capital movements.
2. What is meant by the purchasing power parity of foreign exchange rates and how was it approximated when the automatic gold standard was operating?
3. Even without any intervention by governments or central banks it is unlikely that regularly occurring and anticipated seasonal fluctuations in foreign exchange rates would be very large. Explain.
4. List and briefly explain the principal ways by which a nation may attempt to overcome a deficit in its balance of payments.
5. Under what conditions might a nation find both its balance of trade and its terms of trade improved after it devalued its currency? Under what conditions would devaluation lead to a deterioration of both its balance of trade and its terms of trade?
6. What are the Marshall-Lerner conditions?
7. Suppose that Germany has been exporting 100,000 Volkswagens a year to the United States, and that Germany now devalues its currency by 50 percent. The United States does not devalue.
   a. What positive statement can you make about the terms of trade, assuming no changes in domestic prices in either country?
   b. Why would the devaluation be likely to encourage a rise in prices in Germany?
   c. What effect would the rise in prices have on the terms of trade?

8. Assuming no change in domestic prices in either country, what effect would the devaluation cited in question 7 have on United States imports of Volkswagens, assuming that the demand for these cars is:
   a. Completely inelastic? c. Of unitary elasticity?
   b. Somewhat inelastic? d. Somewhat elastic?

9. Discuss briefly the basic differences between the specific purposes of the International Monetary Fund and the International Bank for Reconstruction and Development.

10. List five ways in which international liquidity might be provided, indicating the principal weakness of each.

11. What are the advantages and disadvantages of floating or flexible exchange rates?

12. Discuss five major developments which occurred in the early 1970s which affected the entire world economy.

13. State whether the United States generally had a favorable or an unfavorable balance of trade in each of the following periods, and in a line or two explain the circumstances in each case.
    a. 1800–1875 d. 1919–1929
    b. 1876–1913 e. 1940–1970
    c. 1914–1918 f. 1971–1974

Index

	PRICES			MONEY SUPPLY, CREDIT,						
	Consumer price index	Wholesale price index	Implicit price index (*GNP* deflator)	M_1 (currency plus demand deposits)	M_2 (M_1 plus time deposits at commercial banks other than large CDs)	M_3 (M_2 plus deposits at nonbank thrift institutions)	Currency	Demand deposits	Time and savings deposits	
Year	1967 = 100		1958 = 100	Billions of dollars						
1929	51.3	49.1	50.6	26.5	——	——	3.9	22.6	——	
1930	50.0	44.6	49.3	25.4	——	——	3.7	21.7	——	
1931	45.6	37.6	44.8	23.6	——	——	4.1	19.5	——	
1932	40.9	33.6	40.2	20.7	——	——	4.9	15.8	——	
1933	38.8	34.0	39.3	19.5	——	——	5.1	14.4	——	
1934	40.1	38.6	42.2	21.5	——	——	4.6	16.9	——	
1935	41.1	41.3	42.6	25.6	——	——	4.8	20.8	——	
1936	41.5	41.7	42.7	29.1	——	——	5.1	24.0	——	
1937	43.0	44.5	44.5	30.3	——	——	5.5	24.8	——	
1938	42.2	40.5	43.9	30.1	——	——	5.5	24.6	——	
1939	41.6	39.8	43.2	33.6	——	——	6.0	27.6	——	
1940	42.0	40.5	43.9	39.0	——	——	6.7	32.3	——	
1941	44.1	45.1	47.2	45.4	——	——	7.9	37.5	——	
1942	48.8	50.9	53.0	55.2	——	——	11.5	43.7	——	
1943	51.8	53.3	56.8	72.3	——	——	16.3	56.0	——	
1944	52.7	53.6	58.2	86.0	——	——	21.9	64.1	——	
1945	53.9	54.6	59.7	99.2	——	——	25.3	73.9	——	
1946	58.5	62.3	66.7	106.0	——	——	26.4	79.6	——	
1947	66.9	76.5	74.6	113.1	——	——	26.4	86.7	35.4	
1948	72.1	82.8	79.6	111.5	——	——	25.8	85.8	36.0	
1949	71.4	78.7	79.1	111.2	——	——	25.1	86.0	36.4	
1950	72.1	81.8	80.2	116.2	——	——	25.0	91.2	36.7	
1951	77.8	91.1	85.6	122.7	——	——	26.1	96.5	38.2	
1952	79.5	88.6	87.5	127.4	——	——	27.3	100.1	41.1	
1953	80.1	87.4	88.3	128.8	——	——	27.7	101.1	44.5	
1954	80.5	87.6	89.6	132.3	——	——	27.4	104.9	48.3	
1955	80.2	87.8	90.9	135.2	——	——	27.8	107.4	50.0	
1956	81.4	90.7	94.0	136.9	——	——	28.2	108.7	51.9	
1957	84.3	93.3	97.5	135.9	——	——	28.3	107.6	57.4	
1958	86.6	94.6	100.0	141.1	——	——	28.6	112.6	65.4	
1959	87.3	94.8	101.7	143.4	210.9	299.4	28.9	114.5	67.4	
1960	88.7	94.9	103.3	144.2	217.1	314.4	29.0	115.2	72.9	
1961	89.6	94.5	104.6	148.7	228.6	336.5	29.6	119.1	82.7	
1962	90.6	94.8	105.8	150.9	242.8	362.9	30.6	120.3	97.6	
1963	91.7	94.5	107.2	156.5	258.9	393.2	32.5	124.1	112.0	
1964	92.9	94.7	108.9	163.7	277.1	426.3	34.3	129.5	126.2	
1965	94.5	96.6	110.9	171.3	301.3	462.6	36.3	134.9	146.3	
1966	97.2	99.8	113.9	175.4	317.8	485.2	38.3	137.0	157.9	
1967	100.0	100.0	117.6	186.9	349.6	532.6	40.4	146.5	183.1	
1968	104.2	102.5	122.3	201.7	382.3	576.8	43.4	158.2	204.1	
1969	109.8	106.5	128.2	208.7	392.2	593.5	46.1	162.7	194.5	
1970	116.3	110.4	135.2	221.4	425.3	642.8	49.1	172.3	229.3	
1971	121.3	113.9	141.4	235.3	473.1	727.9	52.6	182.7	271.2	
1972	125.3	119.1	146.1	255.8	525.7	844.9	56.9	198.9	313.8	
1973	133.1	134.7	154.3	271.5	572.2	919.6	61.6	209.9	364.5	
1974	147.7	160.1	170.1	284.4	613.5	981.7	67.9	216.5	419.4	

Source: *Economic Report of the President* (Washington: U.S. Government Printing Office, February, 1975).